GUERRILLA ☆ PRINCE

BOOKS BY GEORGIE ANNE GEYER

The New Latins

The New 100 Years' War

The Young Russians

*Buying the Night Flight: The Autobiography of a
Woman Foreign Correspondent*

Guerrilla Prince: The Untold Story of Fidel Castro

Waiting for Winter to End

Americans No More

GUERRILLA ☆ PRINCE

THE UNTOLD STORY OF

FIDEL CASTRO

GEORGIE ANNE GEYER

Andrews McMeel
Publishing

Kansas City

Guerrilla Prince: The Untold Story of Fidel Castro
copyright © 1991, 1993, 2001 by Georgie Anne Geyer.
All rights reserved. Printed in the United States of America. No part of this
book may be used or reproduced in any manner whatsoever
without written permission except in the case of reprints in the context
of reviews. For information, write Andrews McMeel Publishing,
an Andrews McMeel Universal company,
4520 Main Street, Kansas City, Missouri 64111.

First published by Little, Brown and Company, 1991
Second revised edition, 1993
Third revised edition, 2001

Library of Congress Cataloging-in-Publication Data:
Geyer, Georgie Anne, 1935–
  Guerrilla prince : the untold story of Fidel Castro / Georgie Anne Geyer.—
3rd rev. ed.
    p. cm.
  ISBN 0-7407-2064-3
    1. Castro, Fidel, 1927-—Psychology. 2. Cuba—History—1933–1959. 3.
Cuba—History—1959- 4. Heads of state—Cuba—Biography. I. Title.

F1788.22.C3 G48 2001
972.9106'4'092—dc21
[B]   2001053523

CONTENTS

CONTENTS

PART III: *"EL"*

PREFACE

WHEN THE SOVIET UNION officially collapsed, in 1991, after six full years in which its new leaders struggled unsuccessfully in a desperate last move of the empire to liberalize the vast and rigid Marxist state from within, it seemed clear to most of the world that the dominant system of the future would be forms of representative government and forms of economic freedom. Intellectuals in Washington gave arcane little talks about the world having reached the "End of History"—that was supposed to mean that liberal democracy, with its backup components of free markets and the civic order, had triumphed so totally that no one would ever again even dare to suggest another road to development.

Occasionally, someone versed in history would recall Alexis de Tocqueville, the great French writer and social philosopher who had toured early America in the 1830s and emerged out of his voyage with the classic work about American political and civic culture, *Democracy in America*. He had predicted at the end of the first book of *Democracy in America* how America and Russia seemed inevitably to be the two countries of the future. "There are at the present time two great nations in the world, which started from different points, but seem to tend towards the same end," he wrote. "I allude to the Russians and the Americans. Both of them have grown up unnoticed; and while the attention of mankind was directed elsewhere, they have suddenly placed themselves in the front rank among the nations, and the world learned their existence and their greatness at almost the same time."

PREFACE

De Tocqueville surely saw with utter clarity how different the two emerging egalitarian "empires" of the world were; nor did he harbor any romantic illusions about the stark duality of their starting points. "The conquests of the American are gained by the plowshare; those of the Russian by the sword," he wrote. "The Anglo-American relies upon personal interest to accomplish his ends and gives free scope to the unguided strength and common sense of the people; the Russian centers all the authority of society in a single arm. The principal instrument of the former is freedom; of the latter, servitude."

Yet he ended the first book of *Democracy in America* by saying, "Their starting-point is different and their courses are not the same; *yet each of them seems marked out by the will of Heaven to sway the destinies of half the globe.*" (Italics added for emphasis.)

Throughout the twentieth century, the world witnessed that drama being played out. Both egalitarian systems easily replaced and subsumed within themselves the world's tired old histories of didactic royal courts, exploitive colonialism, and autocratic monarchies. Between 1917 and 1991, these two worlds and their two ideologies literally dueled for the soul of the world.

It seemed to many that, by the time de Tocqueville's insightful prophecy had played itself out and by the time the great confrontation had ended, the world finally had its answer.

Indeed, the drawing rooms and the corridors of power in the West were by then so filled with such total assurance that it was now simply assumed that the democratization of the world—and the capitalization of all of its economies—would occur both inevitably and spontaneously.

As a result, billions of dollars were poured into Russia from the West, with no thought of what Russia's historically closed, isolated, and xenophobic culture and mind-set could bear—or how any Russian regime would be forced to transform them on their own cultural and psychological terms. When these moneys only helped the new quasi-criminal "oligarchs" to ruthlessly seize most of the economy of Russia—buying out or forcing out the Communist authorities of the big state enterprises and creating a new autocracy in Russia that would soon be almost as bad as the old—Western officials were first amazed and finally deeply disappointed.

Still imprisoned within its own autocratic and paranoid historic mind-set, and now indirectly influenced by the Western multiculturalism that claimed there were essentially no differences between peoples, the Russian reality only sunk deeper and deeper into post-Communist hopelessness.

But after the official disintegration of the Soviet Union in December of 1991, other leaders who had followed its ideological example, whether out of ambition, faith, or the need for total power, also fell by the wayside, most of them dramatically. None was now more expected to fall into irrelevance, if not oblivion, than Cuba's longevous President Fidel Castro.

To many, he was still the Cuban revolutionary who had inspired the twentieth century with his derring-do against the United States; but now his Soviet state benefactors were gone, dissolved into the mists of history. That meant that his Soviet subsidies were gone as well and, since he had never created any kind of a real economy, it also meant that any real vestiges of an independent civil society had disappeared. But it also meant for the West that there were no more Cuban-sponsored guerrillas fighting across the Third World; no more Soviet missiles, tanks, and intelligence training for Havana; and essentially no more political "place" for Fidel Castro in the world.

Surely everyone thought that the man that three generations had known, with an only assumed intimacy, as "Fidel" had become no more than a curiosity and no more than a fossilized memory of "revolution" and glory. Oh, he was still admired, but more as a symbol of the past than as a working, operational leader. Shorn of his guerrilla columns and economically impoverished—and even now at least temporarily abandoned by younger generations in the West who shamelessly reneged on revolution as they fell in love with material wealth—Fidel Castro Ruz surely seemed no longer someone to be taken seriously.

But this analysis did not turn out to be true.

In fact, it is the judgment behind this new publication of *Guerrilla Prince* that, as the twenty-first century already weaves its way, the reality and the example of Fidel Castro as "the" modern example of the charismatic leader giving life, through his person, to a devastated people at a certain time of weakness and vulnerability in its history is becoming more, instead of less, important.

Today one sees more and more countries facing the same realities all across the world—in fact, even worse realities—than those which Fidel Castro's Cuba faced in the sixty years leading up to his 1959 *triunfo*.

Atimia is a special Cuban word which describes an "unfinished society" or a "dependent society." It was widely used in Cuba in the first sixty years of the twentieth century to characterize the weakened and indecisive

Cuban society that Castro was so uniquely able to mold to his ambitions and to his passions. This was supposedly an atmosphere within countries that would pass as people developed. Yet today, in supposedly totally different parts of the world, one finds again that same, hopeless old *atimia* atmosphere.

Indeed, one finds whole peoples and whole regions fighting, not for development and not even in actual wars against specific enemies, but against the disintegration of their core being as societies, in much the same way that Cuba had fought against exactly that same erosion.

Think about the increasingly dominant trends in the world.

The disintegrative trend began in the last half of the twentieth century with the internal collapse of Lebanon in the 1970s, when the balance of power between Muslims and Christians that had held the country together for more than a decade fell apart over Muslim population gains. A variation of the process of national disintegration moved to Iran in the late '70s, when that historically rich country turned in upon itself in religious warfare largely caused by the Shah's too rapid forcing of change upon his people. By the late '80s and early '90s, the national-disintegration geopolitical "gene" had overtaken first the Soviet Union, then Yugoslavia; and every year since then has seen a creeping dissolution in varying and supposedly very different parts of the world. Whether in Central Africa, Central Asia, Indonesia, the South Sea Islands, or the Andes, countries like the Congo, Afghanistan, Indonesia, and Colombia were becoming poisoned centers from which disintegration spread over more and more of the countries and regions around them.

By 2001, for instance, it looked very much as though Indonesia, once one of the most promising countries in the postcolonial and nonaligned world of the 1950s and '60s, might collapse into its many component parts. In fact, many analysts saw Indonesia as the "new Yugoslavia," only now the names were not Bosnia, Croatia, or Kosovo, but the Moluccas, Fiji, the Solomon Islands, Mindanao in the Philippines, and Irian Jaya in New Guinea.

Even some of Castro's old "friends"—also men whom the respectable corridors of power had disdained—were back in the picture. While no one was looking in the 1970s and '80s, Libyan President Muammar Qaddafi was training his own revolutionaries in his camps in the desert. By the turn of the century, they would be the most sanguinary dictators in West Africa, men like Charles Taylor of Liberia and Foday Sankoh of Sierra Leone.

It had also been assumed during the '90s that Latin America was inexorably and inevitably going the democracy–free market–civic society route, whose patterns and parameters were essentially laid down by the American and European examples. Latin America, after all, it was often recalled in development circles, was the only Western and predominantly Christian part of the Third World, and so, even culturally, it would be expected for Latin America to develop in tandem with Western principles. And yet by the turn of the century, it was clear that the "End of History" certainty was hardly applicable even there.

Across Latin America, but particularly in the Andes, the pat Western formula for development was not working. Argentina, Ecuador, and Brazil were in grave danger of financial collapse. Central America had come out of the terrible civil wars of the '70s and '80s, with the Left defeated and with the Right having moved to the center, but they were still only little countries with bare-bones economies, too many people, and diminishing opportunities. In Nicaragua, the Marxist Sandinistas, who had seemed so solidly beaten by democratic elections in 1990, almost made a comeback in 2001 but were beaten by democratic forces.

In the Andes observers saw, initially with astonishment, a kind of replaying of the Castro model and even the Castro mystique.

On his seventy-fifth birthday, in August of 2001, for instance, where did Castro go? Not to his home region of Santiago de Cuba and not even to the sacred old revolutionary eyries of the Sierra Maestra, but to the jungles of Venezuela! There, the man who would be the "next Castro," if he could, and the leader who praised Fidel as the "great revolutionary leader of the Americas," the Venezuelan President Hugo Chávez, feted and feasted Castro at a birthday party out in the jungles of Santa Elena de Uairen.

It was surely a scene worthy of Fidel's own historic sense of melodrama! There, where a four-hundred-mile-long power line to Brazil was being inaugurated, the handsome, hawk-nosed Chávez, a former military man who was by then completely patterning himself after Fidel, dramatically sang "Happy Birthday" to Castro while a four-piece local band played the music! Even Castro was struck momentarily speechless.

But Venezuela was important for Fidel Castro on the occasion of his third quarter century of life and his forty-second year of rule for far more than birthday parties. Hugo Chávez had been a young Venezuelan military officer when he attempted a coup against the government and was then imprisoned in the early '90s; the world was amazed when he was over-whelmingly elected president in 1998 as a result of twenty years of the corruption of the only formally "democratic" governance by the two official parties. It was all disturbingly similar to Cuba's experience and pattern in the first half of the twentieth century.

By the time of Castro's birthday party, Chávez had become a Fidel "groupie," following his model in every possible way. To symbolize this amazing new relationship, this new-style populist, Leftist but not Communist, had tied the two countries' intelligence systems together and was giving Cuba oil in exchange for human beings, as in medieval times. Along with doctors, Cuba was sending three thousand physical-education teachers and sports coaches to pay for the oil. Chávez was also changing the education system to the Cuban model. The fact that Chávez was not breaking with the United States and was still selling oil to it was a new factor in Castroite revolution, but it did not really dilute the charismatic qualities of the approach.

There was also a curious new fact at work here: like so many of the magic-realism sagas that have characterized Latin American art and literature, this stream-of-political-consciousness story doesn't end there. For the unpalatable truth for those unregenerate or would-be "revolutionaries" in the world was that this (by now) dour and authoritarian and aging Fidel Castro met his adoring Venezuelan "brother" with empty hands. Fidel's ideology was dead—his people did not even have rice and beans to eat and Cuba was sinking back to the preindustrial age. He was now simply ignored by the United States but, infinitely worse, totally abandoned by the Russians as Russian president Vladimir Putin even went so far as to close the Lourdes listening post in Cuba, underlining the island's unimportance to Moscow.

Still, such practical realities were not to hold back those who were still in love with revolution in place of everything else. That same week, it was discovered that the Irish Republican Army, or IRA, was working in Colombia with the Marxist guerrillas who were direly threatening the Colombian state on behalf of the drug mafias—Castro's old "network" was still far from dead.

What's more, Castro had still another group to inspire and to use, one that sprang upon the world in the late 1990s from Seattle to Quebec City to Genoa. In many ways, it was that antiglobalization movement—that complex and varied movement of violent anarchists, serious environmentalists, little old ladies with well-meaning intentions, Old Left capitalism haters, and ardent activists who feared that the globalized companies and mentality were taking over the identity given men and women by nation-states—that was carrying through and fulfilling many of Castro's original intentions. His movement against capitalism and the "multinationals" of the 1960s had now, in many respects, provided the organizational structure for the movement against globalization and the international companies of 2000.

In all of these respects, far from disappearing, he had simply become the elder statesman of continuing chaos.

In all of these cases, you could find weakened peoples and polities needing to meld themselves with a great leader and to lose themselves in his charismatic embrace. Fidel Castro, the leader, would pass from the scene, but the need for his kind of leader was only increasing. Fidel Castro's story will not be over for a long time.

But far more important than any of those historic factors—and the element of character that ties Fidel Castro inexorably to the coming world—was what happened in New York and in Washington, D.C., on September 11, 2001. When radical anti-American terrorists bombed and destroyed the two World Trade Center skyscrapers and then hit the American Pentagon, they were acting out in full psychopolitical dress exactly the same obsessively fanatical anti-American hatred that Fidel Castro has so nurtured and embodied across the world for almost the entire twentieth century.

While there is no evidence, at least as of this writing, that the Cuban leader was in any way involved in the horrific and world-shaking events of September 11, there is also no question that (1) in his early days, he pioneered virtually all of the early terrorist techniques (as outlined in this book) and that (2) he even frightened the Russians during the 1962 Missile Crisis because he was so avid to hit the United States with missiles. There is too much evidence that he has thought with deadly seriousness about bombing American nuclear plants and that he has advanced biological and chemical production facilities not to be very sober about his intentions, as former CIA director R. James Woolsey warns on the cover of this book.

GEORGIE ANNE GEYER
Washington, D.C.
October 1, 2001

ACKNOWLEDGMENTS

I N THIS NEW and updated edition, I am delighted and honored to acknowledge the many new men and women who have helped make possible this book, the third English-language edition of *Guerrilla Prince*.

I want above all to thank my wonderful colleagues at the unique and indeed singular syndicate where I have happily hung my hat for more than twenty years, Universal Press Syndicate in Kansas City. The first paperback edition, in 1993, was the idea of our then vice president, Kathy Andrews, backed by our president, John McMeel. My immediate editors at the syndicate, Elizabeth Andersen and Alan McDermott, have consistently provided me, through our work on the columns we have produced three times a week since 1980, with invaluable insights into the character of the many charismatic leaders I have interviewed over the years. Many others in our syndicate—our president, Bob Duffy, as well as Lee Salem, Tom Thornton, Hugh Andrews, Julie Roberts, and Christi Clemons Hoffman, plus others in our book division, Andrews McMeel Publishing, have carried through this new edition with the grace and style that characterizes all of our operations. I thank them for their work and encouragement.

In Washington, my special thanks also to my enormously able assistant, Rita Tiwari, for her cheerful efficiency and for relieving me of many tasks so that I could continue to update and upgrade this work. Earlier assistants, including Rebecca Coder, Ariane de Vogue, and Cynthia Gallagher, will always have my thanks for their enthusiastic work on the original book.

ACKNOWLEDGMENTS

At the same time, a full ten years after the controversy over the first work, it has been particularly gratifying to see the popular cable TV network Showtime producing a three-hour film on Castro based on this book. Here, I want to acknowledge and thank the film's director, David Attwood; the producers Jose Ludlow and David Anderson; the stars; and, especially, Gloria Salas, our charming Showtime impresario during the filming.

Indeed, in December of 2000, I visited the set in Mexico City for several days with one of my early assistants on the book, Rebecca Coder. We were received graciously by the stars, directors, and producers and treated to a spectacular lobster lunch in one of those enchanting and sophisticated cafés in the very same city where Fidel planned his revolution and where, despite Mexico's modernization, Fidel's spirit seems at times still to live.

When I asked the film's British director what the "interpretation" of Fidel would be, he answered, "We want this to be the *real* Castro. We want to say, This is honest, this is the way he is!" And standing on the set of the elegant old Spanish mansion that day, the young Mexican actor Victor Huggo Martin, who plays the young Fidel (and looks and acts stunningly like him) told me, "Don't worry, we understand him."

I also had a very special experience as a writer. During lunch that first day, the group began to ask me about Castro—to query me, actually very seriously, for I had to remember that while they had the serious work of defining him dramatically without knowing him, I had known him but defined him only in print. What was he really like? How did he talk? What was he like at dinner? How did I first meet him? For the first time, I could see how my original work—the interviews with Castro himself, the years of research in Latin America that gave me the historic background for this work, and the final, patient splicing together of the whole saga—was now emerging on the entirely new level of drama. It was the kind of "moment" writers rarely encounter in their lives.

The material had gone from my original absorbing of it, to the pages of the book, to the minds of the producer and director, and, finally, to the dramatic formation of it by the actors. The mysterious circle of creation.

But in terms of the film, there is one person I must thank more than anyone: Hollywood and New York producer Richard Maynard. It was he who came to me shortly after the original book was published in 1991 with the idea of doing a TV film, he who carried the idea through for ten long years, and he who was a bottomless source of innovative ideas and encouragement. We both had many moments when we thought there would never be a film at all; those fears, gratefully, were not realized.

My gratitude also goes to William Ratliff and the Hoover Institution library at Stanford University for their generous and welcome housing of all my research work, including all of the original interviews that my staff and I did for this book. The Geyer Collection at Hoover is something I am particularly proud of, since my training at Northwestern University, as well as during my Fulbright year at the University of Vienna (1956–57), was in history. All of the materials are there, carefully filed, annotated, and preserved for the use of others who seek information on Castro or on his type of charismatic leader.

After this definitive decade—for it was in this decade that the Soviet Union collapsed and Fidel's world changed completely—the original interpretations of *Guerrilla Prince* still hold up. I like to think that is because his innate personal and political secrecy compelled that this work be done largely through oral history.

Five hundred interviews were conducted specifically for this book, in twenty-eight countries—these ranged from Cuba to the Soviet Union, from India to Cyprus, from Finland to Nicaragua, Panama, and El Salvador. In addition to those, I drew upon at least four hundred interviews that I had conducted in the twenty-six years that I had worked as a foreign correspondent and as a syndicated columnist.

Before I began this book, well-intentioned people told me that it would be difficult to "trust" most of those I wanted to interview; virtually anyone involved in the saga of Fidel Castro would have such fixedly impassioned opinions that most responses would be skewed to one extreme or another. This did not happen. People seemed to pause, put their well-understood personal feelings aside, and then talk with remarkable frankness and veracity. While the personal interviews and oral histories were crucial in this book about a man who so fiercely husbands his secrecy, the approximately six hundred books and the seven hundred pieces of periodical literature were invaluable in filling in the historical mysteries and in completing the picture of this man.

Cuban-American thinkers, historians, and biographers whose imaginations seemed to be caught by this unorthodox project were so open, so helpful, and so gracious that it would be impossible for me ever to repay them, much less note all of them here. Ernesto Betancourt, an early close

ACKNOWLEDGMENTS

associate of Castro's in the Revolution and later the director of Radio Martí, is to be thanked first, not only for his informed critiques of the book at every corner but indeed for helping to inspire the book and dispassionately always illuminating the shadowy corners of Castro's mind. Lord Hugh Thomas offered the historian's priceless mind to guide the journalist's more practical quest. Rafael Díaz-Balart put his mind and memory generously to work on remembering, Enrique Trueba led me untiringly to sources I never dreamed of, and Carlos Alberto Montaner offered always that special sensitivity of the poetic writer. Justo Carrillo gave unstintingly of his time and thoughtfulness of his vast historical knowledge of Cuba. Luis E. Aguilar and Irving Louis Horowitz read and masterfully critiqued parts of the book. Jack Skelly put his expert knowledge of Cuba to work and helped in too many ways to mention. Historians Richard Leopold and Michael Beschloss gave me invaluable encouragement and practical advice, while Alexander George encouraged me not to fear biography, by noting that "journalists have the great advantage over historians of being able to know their subject."

Since this book was intensely psychological, I was blessed to find psychiatrists like Dr. Facundo Lima, Dr. Marcelino Feal, Dr. Jerrold Post, Dr. Ruben Dario Rumbaut, and others to interpret the particularist psychology of Fidel Castro. In particular, I wish also to thank my late and brilliant mentor on the charismatic authority, Dr. Heinz Kohut, who patiently formed and endlessly "taught" this novice journalist in Chicago in the 1960s and '70s.

Finally, my deepest thanks go to my original publisher, Little, Brown and Company, who brought out the first edition of this book in 1991. The book would never have been published at all without my dauntless editor, Frederica Friedman, who from the beginning had faith in the book. I am particularly grateful to her for her intelligence and for her sheer professional good sense at every juncture of the publication.

INTRODUCTION

FIDEL CASTRO'S life and mine have paralleled and intersected in strangely prophetic ways.

In 1950, I traveled to Cuba for the first time, with my parents. I was fifteen, and my enchantment with the exquisite, sensuous, languid Cuba of that era laid the basis for my later enchantment with all of Latin America. That year, a young and unknown Fidel was violently making his way through the political jungles of the University of Havana. In 1955, I studied in Mexico City at Mexico City College. The budding young revolutionary Fidel was also in Mexico City that year, organizing his new movement. Finally, in the 1960s, I spent months in Havana and interviewed Castro four times, I lived in the Guatemalan mountains with one of the guerrilla movements he inspired, and from that point on my professional life seemed to revolve around following the wake of Fidel Castro across the world. Whether in Guatemala, Angola, Nicaragua, El Salvador, Vietnam, Panama, Portugal, Laos, Poland, Syria, Mozambique, Uruguay, Chile, Jamaica, Grenada, or the Soviet Union, Castro's tactical and strategic hand and genius could be traced everywhere—and always it was poised like a dagger against the United States. Indeed, Castro's Cuba was already becoming the prototype for guerrilla and irregular activism across the Third World.

Still, why was I driven—for that is the only word—to write this unlikely book and to uncover as many facts as humanly possible about a man whose entire being demanded his not being known? Looking back, I think it all really started on July 26, 1966, when for ten hours I stood in the Plaza de la Revolución in Havana and watched Castro "speak" to the Cuban people on the anniversary of his Moncada attack. As the hours passed and as he ceaselessly cajoled, hectored, and commanded the crowd, I simply could not grasp what it was that I was seeing. Tidal sweeps of emotional waves moved inexorably from the caudillo to the masses and back again. An American-trained Cuban psychiatrist, Dr. Claudios Palacios, told me days afterward what he thought was going on: "In the square, there is a kind of dialogue between him and the people. Oh, the people do not speak, but from time to time, they applaud. And they find that he is saying exactly what they are thinking." If this was not strange enough for me, a woman of the "rational" North, it seemed even more jarring to me that, while every other man and woman I knew seemed to be in the thrall of Castro, I was not. In the initial hours I spent with him, I neither liked nor disliked him, but he enticingly puzzled me. So it was that I began to question the very nature of his tie to and his control over so many people.

Meanwhile, from those years of the 1960s until this moment, my scope of inquiry enormously enlarged, and almost always it focused around these kinds of leaders: Third World dictators, modern caudillos, "Marxist" revolutionaries, countryside guerrillas, and charismatic leaders, Muammar Qaddafi, Juan Perón, Salvador Allende, Omar Torrijos, the Ayatollah Khomeini, Saddam Hussein, Daniel Ortega, Cesar Montes, Manuel Noriega. . . . Soon enough, I began to realize that, as Max Weber could have told me, these types of leaders remain unknown because they *need* to remain unknown. It is the distance, the unknowability, the mystery, and the remoteness of the charismatic leader that underlies his emotional control.

More and more, then, from the late 1970s on, the idea of a definitive Castro biography—politically definitive, historically definitive, but above all psychologically definitive—gripped me. Through my work in Latin America from 1964 onward, I knew many sources who had known Castro, often intimately, at various stages of his life. I kept hearing incredible stories about him, most of them even having the benefit of being true. As I traveled constantly around the world, I became more impressed and amazed at the scope of his power. The realization gradually grew in me that virtually everywhere the United States had had major foreign policy crises in these years (in at least one of which, the Missile Crisis, the denouement could have been fatal), the hand of Fidel Castro could be found.

I began the book by posing questions that his presence in the world, in effect, posed to me: What exactly was going on there in the plaza? What was the nature of the spell that Castro wove over his "masses"? How was it possible that a man from a small and powerless island should have been able to garner so much power that he could effectively challenge the American superpower itself?

I began this strange Odyssean intellectual and political adventure into the soul and psyche of this unknown leader in a systematic journalistic manner. What did I find? First I found that the most tiresomely popular and even obsessive questions about him are almost totally irrelevant. When did he become a Communist? When did he cease being a democrat? Did the United States and Dwight Eisenhower drive him to Marxism? Were the Russians wooing him before the Revolution? I found that most of the accepted "truths" about him were either wholly or largely untrue. For the real Fidel Castro, a fascinatingly and ostensibly "public" person, is really a meticulously secretive and secreted person, a tactical and strategic genius wholly without human principle who guilefully knows how to weave useful myths and spin historic tales—and, much of the time, even he himself believes them. To the United States, but also to an amazing degree to his own people, he remains as unknown today as he was in the Cuba of 1959, which he proceeded to transform with a wave of his "princely" Machiavellian hand in a manner never before seen in Latin America—or, for that matter, most of the world.

Because of his masterful hold over them, few Cubans have paused since 1959 (or have dared so to pause) to question who "Fidel" really is. They have accepted the distance, in great part to protect themselves from breaking the spell that gives their life form and meaning; above all, they have needed the distance and its concomitant control. But those questions are inside them, too. One day in 1985, for instance, I was taking Cuban diplomatic officials in Washington to lunch, hoping to convince them to aid me in returning to Cuba. At first, the diplomats insisted properly that, while a personal book about Castro was fine for the United States, "Of course, no one in Cuba is interested in Fidel's personal life, in his private life. . . ." By the end of the lunch, however, they were beseeching me, their eyes glistening and their voice intense, "Was he ever married? Does he have children? Where does he live? You said his father came from Galicia?" A chill passed over me that moment, for Castro was the man who controlled every waking moment of their lives and they did not have the faintest idea who he really was!

Spurred on by scenes like this one, my staff and I traveled everywhere I felt there could be something important to learn or know about this phantasmagoric man. I went twice to the northwest of Spain, to his father Angel Castro's Galicia, found his uncle and other relatives and even found the pitifully poor stone house of Angel's impoverished boyhood. Bogotá, Miami, New York, Los Angeles, Houston, Lexington, Daytona Beach, Austin, Fort Lauderdale, Stanford, San Francisco, Madrid, Warsaw, Tegucigalpa, Managua, Paris, Munich, Vancouver, New Delhi, Cairo, Nicosia, Kingston, London, Cali, Caracas, Santo Domingo, Manila, San Juan, Panama City, San Salvador, San José, Mexico City, Moscow, and Helsinki: all became ports of investigation.

It used to be that to know what went on in the power centers of the world, we could depend on classic or traditional history and historians, upon documents in archives, and upon the memoirs of responsible people. But while the larger and more traditional world is still blessed by the great works of our historians, there also remains and often predominates in the twentieth century a new "irregular" world of lurking guerrillas, of nameless militiamen, of documentless states where historic archives rest in the heads and hands of natural dictators. Indeed, the world I have covered since 1964 is more and more the irregular world. I watched countries we thought permanent simply close down, not only to historians but to journalists as well. Through all this, I came to realize that we must create new methods of investigation, if we were not ironically to leave tens of millions of people in the ambiguous "Information Age" imprisoned without any knowledge from outside and without any acknowledgement of their suffering.

How, finally, did I make decisions on "what is true" about such a deliberately elusive and deceptive man as Castro? I simply approached this type of "history" in the same way one would conduct a deeper kind of journalism. Having gathered all my facts, information, and interpretation, I carefully compared versions of history and applied common sense and probability.

At times, I felt I knew him very, very well. I found "Fidel" in many leaders in the world. He was the metaphoric Western Hemisphere Hispanic "brother" of the sanguinary "dear leader" of Ethiopia, Mengistu. He was the "cousin" of the charismatic Archbishop Makarios of Cyprus, whose

INTRODUCTION

Socratic "conversations" with the masses almost exactly paralleled "Fidel's." In the end, he was frighteningly close to Mao Tse-tung, striking out at the fading light with executions and with even a Cuban form of Cultural Revolution. But along the way, he was above all that ancient/modern political creature, the leader who takes over a country and transforms it by first making himself and the people one and then positing everybody else as outside, alien, destroyable. He was always the existential motor, not of Communism, and certainly not of democracy, but of the classic human aggression of the naturally born dictator of men.

In the end, I knew that my early instincts about him had been right. Everything people thought they knew about Fidel, they did not know. Everything they did not know was what was important. I think that is why Cuban intelligence wanted and plotted for at least two years to steal, copy, or "get" the book.

That is why Castro told an interviewer in 1986, "No, I will never talk about my personal life, but soon, without my collaboration, everything will be known."

That is why I wrote this book: I want everything to be known. I want people to say, after they have read it, "But, of course . . ." And then—"Oh, my God!"

GEORGIE ANNE GEYER
Washington, D.C.
June 27, 1990

PART I

FIDEL

1

DREAMER OF THE DAY

All men dream, but not equally. Those who dream by night in the dusty recesses of their mind, wake in the day to find that it was vanity. But the dreamers of the day are dangerous men for they may act their dreams with open eyes. This I did.

—T. E. Lawrence

AS THE CENTURY came to a close, and as the kaleidoscope that Fidel Castro had created in his Cuba turned and turned, seeming to reflect the opinions of the world, one could see the "truths" about him still changing too; for often they change color as the lights of history fall at geometrical or seasonal angles.

One could argue the case, as the world would from the twentieth to the twenty-first century, that "revolutionary Cuba" was still very much in evidence. Even after the collapse of the Soviet Union, and despite it, the Communist party in Cuba had grown substantially. In fact, it grew faster during the 1990s than during the 1980s. No longer the liberation-movement guerrilla, the new Communist party member was now the "civic soldier"! With 800,000 members in a population of 11 million, it was larger than ever. With most of the generals being friends of Raul Castro's and with 65 percent of them hailing from the Castros' own Oriente province, the majority of them were making high dollar salaries out of tourism, and so there seemed little chance of a civil war within the army or of any direct challenge to Castro.

There had been virtually a complete turnover of the elites. Nobody who had joined the politburo in the 1960s was still there anymore. Except, of course, one man!

Fidel was—still—chief of state, head of the government, first secretary of the Communist party, commander in chief of the armed forces, *líder máximo,* and general inspirer and revolutionary hero of the nation. He allowed no organized faction, and what he could not directly control with force and with the power of his personality, he controlled with his guile; he liked to put two people in charge of the same area, for instance, and then observe the inevitable unraveling of the personalities. He still held to essentially one motto: "The United States is the historic enemy of the Cuban people."

The repression was consistent, too: Freedom House, rating the regime, called it as repressive as Libya's or Syria's and somewhat more repressive than China's. (In general, the world ignored such findings.)

Although support for Castro within Cuba certainly had waned, there was no real challenge to his rule at home, even though, by the 1990s, certain Cuban "technocrats" and scholars were interacting more with the rest of the world and there was some small peasant and worker organization from below. Abroad, his manifold failures seemed almost not to touch him—he was still lionized in most countries as the revolutionary hero of the twentieth century, seemingly no matter what he did.

Yet one could equally argue another case.

There were many who insisted that Cuba was changing entirely, that Fidel had become merely the relic of a bygone age, respected for his early courageous exploits but now merely a kind of iconoclastic national form which loosely defined a country that, within itself, was evolving inexorably to a freer economy, to a freer life, and to freer minds.

These analysts pointed to the fact that, after all, by the turn of the century and despite the U.S. embargo, which Americans easily skirted by going through third countries, Cuba was hosting 1.6 million tourists a year, roughly one-tenth of them Americans and two-thirds of those Cuban-Americans. And they were having themselves quite a time!

Most often, they were doing that in the five-star Spanish hotels along the glorious Cuban coasts (where Cubans, not incidentally, were not allowed to pass). Americans were dining at Xanadu, once the Du Pont family's luxurious beachfront mansion at Varadero, and playing at the new golf courses that were being built across the island. In 2001, Bergdorf Goodman's spring catalog was shot in Cuba. A delegation of Hollywood executives met with Fidel and were, of course, appropriately impressed.

On the other hand, with the extreme poverty facing most Cubans, prostitution had returned to the island with a vengeance, and Edward Wasserman of the *Miami Herald* quoted an avid male Italian visitor as noting approvingly of the Cuban scene, "It's unusual to pay so little for girls so young." The reporter further noted that this new "plunge into tourism," far from being a confirmation of Castro's Cuba's development or opening to the outside world really only "looks very much like the latest chapter in Cuba's chronic, abject reliance on foreign money, a dependency that spans decades and transcends politics. It speaks of an historic failure to develop a measure of self-sufficiency in agriculture and industry. It is an enthusiastic surrender to a foreign domination more subtle, but no less real, than the one Castro claims to have repulsed forty years ago."

He further noted of the changing revolutionary icon, the long-dead Ernesto "Che" Guevara, how "the image of Che now is ripped from its political context, redeployed as a decorative motif on T-shirts, caps, silk-screens. . . . Che is Cuba's most universally recognized mascot, a Mickey Mouse to the emerging network of theme parks."

Americans and other foreigners who went there illustrated a strange sense of déjà vu, sometimes almost as if all those years of estrangement between Cuba and the United States from 1959 onward had never quite happened. "I just had a wonderful time there," a prominent Arab-American who traveled there with a high-level Internet business group remarked upon his return in the spring of 2001. "For three days, we went to nightclubs, bought cigars. Oh, we had to meet Castro, and, sure, everyone wants to meet him." He hesitated. "But he talks too much. Then when we returned to Miami, I admitted to the immigration official that I had two-hundred cigars, illegal because of the American embargo—he just laughed and passed me through."

It was this kind of American dipping into Cuba, and finding the water just fine, that reminded some skeptical observers of the Americans who had come in the pre-Castro period, only to have a good time in a gorgeous tropical paradise, with gin and girls and glamour. But to a young American diplomat who had served in the American Interests Section in Havana, "These Americans go there and they think it's normal. Because they don't see the real Cuba. I was there during the Pan American Games in 1981, and the Americans and the Cubans began chanting to Fidel Castro. Two Cuban kids began jeering. Then they were very silent. Two Cuban agents just closed in upon them and held them there, speechless, until they moved them out."

When a high-level delegation of American intellectuals went to Cuba in 2000, Castro kept showing up at their dinners, and keeping them up till all hours of the morning while he alone (of course) talked, until the last night they made so many excuses that he did not come. One prominent American writer remarked after the trip, "He's not only a ham actor but a very bad ham actor." This . . . was new. Where had the days gone when intellectuals would wait in Havana for days, and sometimes even for weeks, merely to see "*El Caballo*"?

And then, when these visitors walked through Old Havana—or when they traveled across the island—they soon became interested in the one thing that is truly "new" in Cuba, which is the process of historic, artistic, and, particularly, architectural restoration of the old that suddenly began taking place everywhere on the island at the end of the 1990s. Beautiful manors along the Malecón Drive in Havana, which had been physically falling into the sea, literally shedding their skins into piles of rubble, now were being restored. UNESCO had big projects, but they were all projects not to move toward a truly modern future, with representative government or economic alternatives or intellectual freedom, but to return Cuba to its past. It was as if Castro was now determined to present to the world, as his creation, this beautiful world that he had himself nearly destroyed.

To some, seeing this return to the past on this level, it sometimes seemed as if Cuba had, after all, just surrealistically stopped somewhere in those days of old. But where, exactly?

The Havana Libre Hotel, the former Hilton, still used the same exhausted towels they had used in 1959—the "HH" embroidered on them gave them away. Cuban exiles who were permitted to return to Cuba in the late 1970s and early 1980s thirsted for a resurrection of their memories, but they were fearful of finding only changes. To their amazement, they found that, to the contrary, almost nothing had changed. *Todo tal cual, tal como era*, a young Cuban exile journalist in Spain, Emilio García Meras, kept repeating to himself when he returned. "Everything just the same, everything just as it was." García had pictures of his childhood, and he was stunned once again to find the same images. "The same crystal windows there. The baths. The iceboxes were from the time of Humphrey Bogart. . . . It was as if it were a bad dream, as if we had arrived at an enchanted city. *Todo tal cual, tal como era.* Perhaps it would have been better if I had not grown either."

Time, and movement, and memory, too, had become all intertwined and intermingled, all mixed and mottled, in this new/old Cuba—but then, long before Fidel Castro was even born, Cuba always had a flair for the surreal. Political Cuba even before Castro was characterized by an eerie juxtaposition of seemingly unnatural or incongruous images, which one finds usually in art. A new and, to many, unsettling surrealism had simply again set in.

Yet it could also not be denied that, even by the turn of the century, with all of his manifold economic, military, and human failures, Fidel Castro remained a hero in much of the world's minds.

He had taken a beautiful but fragile society and made it into a world power. He had made himself the symbol and arbiter of that power almost everywhere in the world. He represented David against Goliath—yet it must be understood that his was no peaceable, docile, gentle David (no peacenik at all, as some of the peace movements would have it) but a David armed to the teeth; no mere Don Quixote tilting against windmills but a praetorian David of the Old Testament.

Indeed, the incongruity of his life to many observers lies in the fact that nearly all of his accomplishments were not in the much-heralded social world at all but virtually exclusively in the military world. Just like the Spanish caudillos of old—and, indeed, even like those of the twentieth century.

Fidel Castro had, after all, smitten the dread and archaic dictator Fulgencio Batista, cuckholded the great and all-powerful United States of America, and "freed" his Cuban people. He had sent hundreds of thousands of his own officers and soldiers, as well as guerrillas of a dozen nationalities (twenty thousand of them), all trained carefully by him, sweeping Napoleonically from one end of the globe to the other, destroying governments from within, and creating *new* legitimacies without in the manner of no power in history. From Mexico to Moscow to Managua, and from the universities of Minnesota, Mainz, and Minsk, Fidel Castro remained the single modern revolutionary of epicentral consequence.

By the thirtieth anniversary of the Revolution in 1989, Castro had more troops around the world than all the other Communist leaders put together.

His military was the largest in Latin America, larger even than Brazil's. Because of the enormous levels of Soviet arms deliveries and aid, the Cuban army numbered 145,000 men, but these already substantial numbers were backed by 110,000 ready reserves and more than a million men and women in the Territorial Troops Militias. Cuba, with slightly more than 10 million persons, was probably the world's most completely militarized country—57,000 troops in Angola, 5,000 to 7,000 in Ethiopia, and hundreds and thousands from South Yemen to Libya, to Nicaragua, to Mozambique, to Syria, Equatorial Guinea, Tanzania, Guinea-Bissau, North Korea, São Tomé, Algeria, Uganda, Laos, Afghanistan, and Sierra Leone.

But numbers only sketch the form of the unique, odd power of this modern man. To understand its pervasiveness, it is necessary to look at the global consequences of guerrilla warfare in the twentieth century. For although the roots and practice of the "little warfare" of *la guerrilla* reach deep into history, it was Castro who invented, or perfected, or expanded the uses of every single one of the techniques of guerrilla warfare and of terrorism that were then dramatically additionally enlarged upon by the Palestinians, the Iranians, and the Central American guerrillas. Without Fidel Castro's advice and support, there would have been no Nicaraguan Sandinistas, no invasion of Grenada, no guerrilla movements from El Salvador to Uruguay to Chile, no destruction of democracy in the Southern Cone, no Marxist Angola, Mozambique, or Ethiopia. There would have been no new political, ideological, and strategic balance of power in southern Africa, and no supernational "drug state," defended by Leftist guerrillas he had trained, spreading like an evil and consuming Rorschach blot across Latin America, with its own armies and borders. There would have been no extension, for the first time, of Latin America's reach within the United States, no first and no second Marxist-Leninist state in the Western Hemisphere. In short, he devised virtually every twentieth-century technique with which the weak fought the strong. From 1959 on, wherever the United States had a watershed foreign policy crisis, Castro's formative hand could be found.

But he did even more. He transformed legality; he led the way, for example, to a "new logic," which allowed stateless Iranians to "try" American hostages from Teheran to Lebanon. He was an alchemist of the law, the century's doctor of disintegration, and its vicar of breakdown. When the toll was counted, it would be charted on the rolls of history that he was in substantial part responsible for the fall of Nikita Khrushchev, for bringing the world to the brink of nuclear war in the Missile Crisis, for John F. Kennedy's death, for the massive and threatening Central American immigration to the Texas borders, for America's humiliation at the Bay of Pigs (which led America directly into the quagmire of Vietnam), and for the threat of Irangate and thus the Iranian realignment in the Gulf. Hell, he even once overthrew a government in Zanzibar!

His techniques of wooing, of cajoling, of flattering were brilliant. He made people his accomplices, and they thought he was their friend. He established dialogues that went nowhere, but what matter? His late-night visits were designed precisely to keep people waiting and impose his power upon them until, by the time he arrived, they were pathetically grateful, flattered, and relieved. Who could go home without "seeing Fidel"? How kind he had been! How he had wooed them with red-carpet treatment, with the perception of closeness to absolute power! He tiresomely repeated statistics until no one could possibly challenge him. He dealt with himself in conversation with mocking self-deprecation, and people whispered to one another, "See how sincere, how humble he is. He can't continue his errors because he always admits them."

But what did any of them really know? What did they know about Mirta, his only wife? Who knew that she lived reclusively now in Madrid with her conservative, jealous second husband? Who knew that if she ever dared talk about the "great man" she had loved and married, she would never see their son again?

And what did they know about Isabel Custodio, the beauteous Spanish Republican teenager he had wanted to marry in Mexico?

What did they really know about Celia—the irreplaceable Celia Sánchez?

What did they know about the gorgeous, mischievous, voluptuous Naty Revuelta, who helped finance the Revolution and then made the odious mistake of turning down Fidel's proposal of marriage before he came to power? And what did they know of Naty's daughter by him, the infuriating Alina, who had inherited her mother's beauty and her father's temper, and who had once actually shouted at him, "You are a mediocrity!"

What did they know about Gloria Gaitán, the dark rose of Bogotá? Or about Dalia, the "woman from Trinidad," and the five children she had borne Fidel?

9

What, for that matter, did they know about the Tropicana dancer, about the woman who had said he smoked "the whole time," about the ungrateful girl who dared to complain that he never took his boots off, about Marita Lorenz who so awkwardly tried to kill him, about the Cuban actress who confided to Fidel's interpreter, "You can't imagine what a brute he is, what a selfish monster, he just put his pants down, and quick." Then she smiled. "But, of course," she added, "the monster can't control the pleasure I feel knowing that the monster is Fidel Castro."

The same mystery that Fidel so carefully wove about his affairs he also created about his houses. In the early days, Cubans and foreigners knew that he had often stayed at Celia's famous walk-up apartment on Calle Once in the Vedado section of Havana. They knew he had a Spartan room there, with a single bed, a balcony with exercise machinery, and a small study. He made sure that people got the impression that, as one Indian ambassador's wife noted, he was accessible to the Cuban people because Celia's little house had no lawn and so his car would be parked on the road, apparently very "publicly" and casually, just outside the building. "There was this psychological thing that you are not cut off with huge lawns and trappings of a presidential or a prime minister's house," Mrs. Ambika Soni argued. But then she thought for a moment, seeming to puzzle over a contradictory reality. She added, with sudden revelation, "No, he was visible, not accessible."

Most of the Cuban people did not know that their leader, while having no true home, actually had an extraordinary range of houses. There was a mansion in historic Siboney near Santiago, another on 49th Street in Havana. There was an estate in Candelaria, "La Deseada," and about ten kilometers away from there lay his lordly hunting estate, "La Víbora," which remarkably resembled the huge estates that Eastern European leaders had seized from the old aristocrats in the early years of Communism. When Fidel hunted there, he would instruct the Cuban Air Force to send a small plane or a helicopter to skim the mangroves and scare up the ducks so they could be more easily shot, and if his pilots died in such adventures, as they did, it was their privilege. Some of his homes even had bowling alleys made in Japan.

He had a complete island, Cayo Piedra, near Cayo Largo, which was reserved for the *líder máximo*'s most intimate and personal affairs. A sophisticated facility that included every type of game and a heated pool, this "home" served other purposes besides recreation or the ever-constant

wooing of foreign visitors, pilgrims, and supplicants. Fidel's Panama operations—financial dealings that were a kind of "caudillo capitalism"—were
conducted in the most total secrecy in places like Cayo Piedra and the
strange, isolated Orwellian settlement of Barlovento, which opened to the
sea but was wholly closed to Cuba. In these somehow ominous and eerily
depersonalized villas by the sea, shadowy international buccaneers like
Robert Vesco could come and go in a world without immigration laws or
visas, live in surrealistic and clandestine comfort in a stateless world, suspended in time and place, and provide Fidel Castro with virtually everything he needed, from Apple computers to American machine guns.

Tens of millions of dollars flowed through Cuban "corporations" like
CIMEX, a front enabling the Cuban Ministry of the Interior to receive dollars for Cuba in exchange for every sort of "business," from false visas
(142,000 between 1985 and 1989 alone) to the illegal use of dead bodies.
Indeed, Cuba had become a country which talked "Communism" while
privileges spun off from the center for the Castro elite in every direction.

Meanwhile, the many students of Fidel's character and Messianic techniques tried desperately to analyze the man.

"The issue of his legacy is open," Damien Fernandez, the respected
Professor of International Relations at Florida International University, told
me when we discussed "Fidel." "His legacy will be interpreted for us, it will
become one of the areas of discussion. In the end, Fidel will outlive himself in politics, in symbolism and myth—and he will, as always, cause others to rally 'round him. He will aim at 'Fidelismo without Fidel.' Fidel is a
positivist, and he has always believed that society can be engineered, and
so he will leave a country devoid of pragmatism and with no sense of civil-
ity or civic duty, in which people just want to withdraw from politics. For
the Cuban people, it will be how do you define a Cuba without Fidel, but
with Fidelismo—'Fidelismo but without Fidel.'"

Castro's language, others analysts pointed out, was still the language of
war, of conflict, then of war again. Robert E. Quirk ended his book on Castro, Fidel, with the assurance that the "Maximum Leader would see Cuba
destroyed, before he gave up his power and his prerogatives."

The great nineteenth-century German sociologist Max Weber, who had so
brilliantly analyzed the "charismatic authority," as he called this special
kind of power-driven personality, saw the Fidel-style charismatic as "knowing

that it was endowed with the supernatural, superhuman and always exceptional qualities." The charismatic was a mesmerizer and a sorcerer whose spell was welcomed by whole peoples at their times of weakness so that they literally melded with the leaders, supposedly to be brought back to health, as in a return to the womb—but really only giving up their will to the Great Leader.

Structured and institutionalized societies may strive to pass down truths from generation to generation and from century to century and to build civilizations upon them; but the charismatic leader expresses his own truth as revealed passion—his strength lies in testimony and not scientific proof, and his connection with his followers is one of impassioned love and dependence rather than one of rationality or even really of true self-interest. And this is one first reason why the charismatic leader never builds institutions; not only is he psychologically incapable of doing so, but he knows intuitively that such an effort would only serve dangerously to take power away from him.

But what is most often forgotten is the fact that the charismatic authority must also be recognized as such by the masses, just as the masses are dually dependent upon him for fulfillment at dangerous periods of their history. Far from expressing the "will" of his followers, the charismatic authority actually expresses their duty or obligation—to the führer, to the *vozhd,* to the caudillo—and always without the intermediation of the institution.

Dr. Jerrold M. Post, a distinguished professor of psychiatry, political psychology, and international affairs at George Washington University who has produced some of the world's most important work on the psychology of leaders, has made the important point that we must distinguish between "reparative charismatics," like Dr. Martin Luther King, Jr., and Mahatma Gandhi, leaders who represent and bring out the transformational and redemptive qualities of their followers, and those that are "destructive charismatics," who must always find an enemy to attack.

Not surprisingly, he put Castro in that second category, and saw his often-expressed identification with historic figures like Moses and Christ as proof of the narcissistic extremities of his personality. "In his view of himself," Post has said, "Fidel regularly talks about Moses and 'crossing the river.' There is an implicit acknowledgement of not reaching the promised land. He also identifies himself with Christ, and he's said that even the 'King of Kings' would not accept certain acts of the Americans—and neither would I!

"And remember, as a man grows older, he becomes more like him-self—and the gap between dream and reality grows.

"At the extremities of these personalities," Dr. Post went on, "narcis-sism means such an involvement with self that there is no possible involve-ment with others. These people are exquisitely sensitive to any perceived slight. Their thin-skinned anger comes to be narcissistic rage. The charis-matic system is a grandiose façade sitting on a sea of inferiority; and when their dreams are shattered, they tend to strike out, like Saddam, withdraw-ing from Kuwait, burned the oil wells. The most dangerous time for Fidel Castro would be if faced with failure or with public disapproval, with the idea that he is not the grandest leader of them all. That's when he's most dangerous, when he has to repair his image by striking out at others.

"In the early years, there was this chemical exchange between him and the people. When others were dropping of exhaustion, he was gaining power and energy. But how fragile it all is! We tend to think of people mel-lowing with age, but old wishes don't fade away. For leaders consumed with glory, they only grow more obsessed. With aging messianic leaders, there can never be enough to end their heroic life."

With Castro, Post noted, the three major themes in political psychol-ogy about this type of leader all come startlingly together: (1) his narcis-sism, which is of the most dangerous type, the kind of malignant narcissism that Saddam has and that Hitler had—they are so concerned with their own grandiosity, they can't empathize with others' pain; (2) his paranoia, which means he blames everyone else for everything; and (3) his absence of conscience, which leads to unconstrained use of aggression to realize goals.

Damien Fernandez, meanwhile, listed these points as components of *Fidelismo:* "(1) the pursuit of politics as absolute; (2) radical nationalism, accompanied by inflated ideas of Cuban exceptionalism; (3) a concentra-tion of power in the leader which is resonant of fascism; and, (4) the state as the provider of equity." One could be struck by the degree to which these qualities were those not of the "scientific Communism" of the East but of the traditional caudillos or strongmen of Mother Spain.

Then suddenly, in the late 1990s, a new theme began to emerge out of the hours and hours of mental wandering and intellectual obfuscation of Castro's speeches and interviews: the question of his "succession," or, as he interestingly enough put it, "the transition."

13

In 1997, the entire schema of thinking about the succession took on a new importance and all at once demanded attention within Cuba. At the Fifth Communist Party Congress that year, Fidel abruptly brought the entire question out in the open as never before; but he was speaking by then, with an apparent new seriousness, *no longer of his succession but of a transition to* "Fidelismo *without Fidel.*" (Italics mine.) Suddenly, he seemed to be growing concerned about passing on his "ideology," or, as he likes to call it, his "doctrine."

Now he was even dealing with exactly those questions of institutionalization that he had so long evaded—and that, indeed, the charismatic leader must evade because they so threaten his total hold on power.

"What was happening?" asked Professor Jaime Suchlicki, the respected head of the University of Miami's Institute for Cuban and Cuban-American Studies. "Suddenly he was thinking about continuity—in speech after speech since the party congress. He doesn't want the revolution to fade."

In another speech, Castro insisted that there would be no change in Cuba's political system despite all the speculation about his death. "Now they talk about the famous transition," he said in a news conference. "I have read hundreds of articles about that famous transition. 'Who will come after Castro? Will his brother, Raúl, be able to control the situation?'" Then he added sagely, "You cannot cover the sun with your finger!"

And therein, again, one can hear the true words of Fidel Castro: he is the sun and all those poor mortals have only miserable little fingers with which to try—so pitifully, really—to fend off his penetrating rays!

It was no accident that he always met foreign visitors at midnight—or at 1:00 A.M. or even sometimes at 3:00 A.M. Those were his "dinner hours," his "calling times." It was no accident that only he alone talked then, often for eight or nine hours, before his exhausted, but often also enchanted, victims were released to collapse into bed and to think how "lucky" they were to have "talked with" Fidel Castro.

They really should have taken their cue from the fact that he always met with people at night, and that he was always secretive and mysterious when they asked, as they often did, about what he actually did during the day. For Fidel did indeed dream with open eyes. He was always T. E. Lawrence's Dreamer of the Day, and he was always the consummate Actor of the Night.

2

GNARLED ROOTS

The Gallego ... lives from the land and the sea and continues being a dreamer, a lover of secrets, believing that not everything that is buried is dead.

—Galician author Alvaro Conqueiro

O N THE WESTERNMOST arm of Galicia, that secreted and wearied northernmost province of Spain, a mute and mystical regiment of cliffs faces the same sea that led Christopher Columbus to the New World. Here, wild white waves crash in the long, damp winters; but in the summer the land gleams with that same inner emerald light of Ireland or Scotland, whose bagpipes it plays. The cliffs were long ago named Cabo Finisterre. This was the cape where the superstitious Galicians—or, more popularly, Gallegos, as they were always called in Cuba—believe that the "world ends."

Even today, Galicia is a place that seems strangely unfinished, impermanent, a place of farewell and good-bye forever. Many of the houses stand half finished. Many of the more modern ones are on stilts so the animals and the farm machinery can find cover underneath them in the harsh storms. It is a quiet place, lonely and unchanging, where everything is waiting for the Gallego men to return from their self-imposed exiles. But they never did. They were doomed to leave their physical—and their political—seed elsewhere.

In this country and that country
And all, all have gone.
Galicia, without men who have stayed
That they find work.
And, in exchange, orphans and orphans
And meadows of solitude
And those who won't have children
And children that don't have countries
And hearts that suffer long and mortal absences
Scenes of winds and deaths
That will never console.

Rosalía de Castro is no relation to Fidel, but she is equally as famous in her drear land. She is Galicia's tragic and evocative poetess, and she wrote those classic lines about the faithless land that spawned the boy whose name in Spanish loosely meant "faithful."

It was from Spain that Christopher Columbus sailed to the New World. But the Castilians of the southern Spanish province of Castile, who peopled most of Latin America, left of their own volition, and they sailed under the winds of their own passions for gold and for faith. When the Gallegos left their part of Spain, it was for quite different reasons.

The *emigración!* The year, 1853, a time of drought and agricultural crisis. Two million Gallegos left for the New World. They were forced to leave. Dark-coated, dull-eyed, and unsmiling, they went knowing they would never return. *Compañía del Pacífico,* the ships advertised matter-of-factly: "Services via Magallanes . . . then on to Havana, Panama, Ecuador. . . ." The emigrants carried with them the awareness that Galicia is a deceptive—a delusionary—land. It looks all green and fertile, with grazing cows and small plots of soil lovingly staked out, but underneath the land is rocky and barren, spare and skeletal. The Gallegos grew sad not because they were persecuted, like the Jews or the Protestant "heretics." They were not. Not forced away by war or by conquest, Rosalía's brothers were sad because they sent themselves away.

On December 8, 1875, the name of Angel María Bautista Castro Arguiz was inscribed in the birth register of Láncara, a small village in the beautiful but barren mountains of the province of Lugo, in Galicia. The baby boy was born to typically poor Gallego peasants in a gray stone Galician house with dirt floors. Even when new, the house leaned against a small hillock, as though it had been born tired.

Only an hour away, in the small seaside city of Ferro del Caudillo, northeast of the big city of La Coruña, another Gallego boy, who would turn out to have remarkably similar Gallego traits as Angel Castro, was born on December 4, 1892. It was not really as unusual as it might seem that both Angel Castro, father of Fidel, and Francisco Franco came from such a forgotten and uninvolved corner of the world as Galicia. The dictators of the modern world virtually all emerged out of the ignored outskirts of empire: Napoleon, the Corsican; Hitler, the Austrian; Stalin, the Georgian.

Angel Castro grew up among reserved and secretive people who liked to nod unsmilingly and say, "A man is owner of his silences and prisoner of his words." It was a world of exaggerated pride and of the deep sense of shame that lurks like a shadow behind that pride. Politically, the Gallego expressed himself through the traditional political caudillos of Spain, men who despised compromise, men who were brave horsemen and great orators interested in power and honor, men to whom the truth of personal testimony was infinitely more important than scientific proof. But among the men of Galicia there were also those who were called *caciques*. Different from the traditional caudillos, the *caciques* were political operators—local political benefactors not unlike New York or Chicago aldermen—who understood all too well that favorite Gallego proverb, "God save you from a Gallego with power."

As a teenager, Angel Castro worked as a day laborer for a while in the fields near the trout-filled River Neira, and he liked to gamble at cards. The old priest of Láncara, Ramón López Neyra, years later described the young Angel as "sympathetic, a singer, and quick with cards—he never lost." But as he approached manhood, Angel realized more and more that there was no future for him in Galicia. So, at age twenty, he decided to become a "soldier of Spain" in faraway Cuba. Poor but adventuresome, Angel accepted thousands of pesetas in payment from a rich Spanish boy's family to fight in his place against the *americanos*.

Spain had always been religiously and culturally, emotionally and atavistically, anti-Protestant, anti-Reformation, and anticapitalist. Spain was the first child of the Counterreformation and at the same time her most avid lover. To the Spanish in the New World, the Protestants of the North were the purest of heretics, and Spain was the truest child of the Holy Mother Church's Catholic faith. But most important, the Spain from whose roots Angel Castro sprung was, indeed, the first totalitarian system of modern times, imposing by power of arms and the Holy Inquisition a total faith on anyone it came upon. In the sixteenth and seventeenth centuries, as the brilliant writer on Spain V. S. Pritchett has written, Spain was no "normal" country, but "the master-race of the world, the founders of the first great empire to succeed the Roman Empire. . . . They fought to preserve, and for a long time successfully did preserve, the spirit of the Middle Ages. It was their triumph, their distinction, and their tragedy."

Spain was aristocratic, heroic, grand, dignified, courageous, manly, generous. Spaniards excelled in oratory and leisure. The northern Protestant virtues, on the other hand, were the "little virtues" of thrift, diligence, punctuality, prudence, perseverance, honesty, reliability. In the New World of the eighteenth century, Spaniards were still fighting duels in defense of their honor, while the Protestants to the north of them were writing doctrines guaranteeing life, liberty, and the pursuit of happiness and the equality of all men before the law.

All of these extraordinary differences could not but have created jealousy, resentment, and finally the rage of Spain against its increasingly powerful Protestant neighbor to the north; but it was the war of 1898, when an imperial Spain, in its last dying breath, lost its last and most treasured colony, Cuba, to the Yankees of the Americas that anti-Americanism foraged into the Spanish soul like a gnawing cancer. To this day, the Spaniards of Galicia still refer to the Spanish-American War as *el desastre,* or the disaster.

Angel Castro sailed away from the "Cape of the End of the World," as had so many of his brothers, to fight for Spain and its "big virtues." He carried ever with him that special inner sadness and cynicism but also that dogged determination of the historic Gallego to succeed on foreign shores and to educate his children. So once the war was over and Cuba was lost for Spain, Angel returned briefly to Galicia, found it still a hopeless land, and returned to Cuba for good.

In those turbulent days of the turn of the century, the Bay of Nipe on Cuba's rugged northeast coast was one of the most beautiful corners of Cuba. The bay and its shores were a drowsy area of low and very green rolling land, with meandering rivers and mountain ranges that were friendly and gentle, in sharpest contrast to the severity of Galicia. Angel chose the area wisely because this part of Cuba, known as the Oriente or simply the East, was at that very moment on the vertiginous verge of commercial discovery. But when Angel arrived—a poor and penniless laborer—it was an open and savage land, as ignored by the fashionable, fun-loving, impeccably white-suited Cubans of Havana as Galicia had been ignored by Madrid.

After the war, power in Cuba remained perversely with the Spanish, who still dominated the economy, with the *americanos* who now moved to expand their industries everywhere in Cuba, and with the rich Cubans. The poor *campesinos,* the intellectuals, and the blacks, who had come to be called in Cuban slang the *Mambises,* lost out in every aspect.

Once he decided to stay in Cuba for good, Angel started out by working as a simple day laborer for United Fruit, that overweening symbol of American expansionism and Manifest Destiny. But with a seemingly endless capacity for work and his unlimited Gallego ambition, the wiry little man with the set and determined expression of the jaw soon rose to become a sugarcane contractor in charge of fifty to sixty men who did the beastly difficult work of cutting the cane. Angel was the boss—everyone felt it—but the real "boss" of the area was sugar itself, and it would be "King Sugar," the wealth and bane of Cuba, that would inspire, enrage, and finally bedevil Angel's son. It was the dependency spawned, nationally and personally, by the sugar industry that would early set the stage for dictatorship in Cuba, because sugar maintained its labor force in a kind of slavery long after slavery was itself abolished. Indeed, sugar was the major reason why Cuba came so late to nationalism, creating in the Cubans an uncertain nationalistic spirit that was further complicated by the fact that Cuba's point of reference was not Latin America, and not really Spain, but the United States of America.

In every way, Angel Castro was an irregular in Cuban society. He was the eternal outsider. He would remain the "soldier of Spain" in a Cuba heady with new independence. But with rare energy and ruthlessness, Angel soon carved out a place for himself in this strange and hostile land. Like many of his neighbors in the "Wild East" of Cuba, he was far from meticulous about the manner in which he expanded his dominion. He would go out at night with his men on horseback, and in the dark they would "move the fences," thus always expanding his land into unclaimed areas. To do this, he simply paid off and in some ways came to control the all-powerful Rural Guards. Within a few years, his hacienda, "Manacas," grew to ten thousand acres and dominated the area which swept up to the Sierra de Mayarí.

His expansionism also coincided with the sugar boom that followed the First World War. Angel became a wealthy man who soon had hundreds of men working for him. And when the boom collapsed, he remained wealthy; cautious Angel Castro kept his money not in the banks but in his own strongbox. "He was a real *guajiro*," Angel's good friend Don Hodgkins, one of the United Fruit managers, recalled decades later, using the colloquial and affectionate term for the Cuban peasant. These two unlike men, from two utterly unlike societies, liked each other. Angel had a way of "acquiring" one of the United Fruit tractors every once in a while and painting it a different color. Not infrequently, after the two men had drunk a bottle of cognac together, Hodgkins would wander out to Angel's farm, scrape away some of the paint on a tractor, and then tipsily usher it "home" to United Fruit.

Angel's marital life was as self-styled as everything else about him. He first married a respectable schoolteacher named María Louisa Argota and they soon had two children, Pedro Emilio and Lidia. But the marriage began to founder when the family brought into their remote and isolated household a new maid named Lina Ruz, who most probably came from Pinar del Río in the far western region of the island. Lina was probably only about fourteen years old when she came to the Castro house; and when María Louisa found out about the girl's affair with her husband (probably through an anonymous letter), she simply left the house. "To find an old man living with such a young girl," one of the neighbors sniffed, shaking her head at the memory. Some years after the arrival of Lina, Angel and María Louisa were divorced.

Rawboned, with a long nose and her brown hair pulled back, Lina roved around the Castro plantation on horseback, carrying a pistol and a Winchester, shooting off a round to call the family to meals, wearing high boots under her loose and carelessly revealing dresses. She ran the Castros' store, where their workers could buy supplies with a kind of *vale* or promissory note or voucher from Angel.

While everyone seemed to like Lina, no one ever accused her of being a good housekeeper. The Castro house looked much like a Western cowboy version of "home." It was of raw wood, round, and it stood up on stilts, in mimicry of the sad houses in Galicia. There was a rough staircase leading up to the front door for protection against the bandits who hid all over this area. The inside of the house mirrored the chaos that soon became evident in the interworkings of the entire family. Chickens roosted freely on the chairs, without apology, so that before visitors sat down they needed to brush away whatever the chickens or any of the other animals had left there.

Visitors were often astounded because the Castro family liked to eat standing up. (After he became ruler of Cuba, nobody could understand why it was that Fidel Castro so often ate standing up!) But, if the house was filthy, Angel's room was meticulous. The table had a tablecloth on it, and there were often cigars burning somewhere for Angel loved cigars. There was a lookout point on top of the roof, where he would climb to survey his farm. The Gallego would stand there, looking out over his domain and smoking his cigar, in much the same manner that Fidel later would come to survey all of Cuba (and perhaps on a very clear day this younger Castro might even glimpse symbolically his faraway empire—Angola, Ethiopia, and Nicaragua).

While Angel was still officially married to María Louisa, Lina began to bear him a horde of children out of wedlock that would eventually include Raúl, Emma, Juanita, Angelita, Ramón, and on August 13, 1926, Fidel Alejandro Castro Ruz (named for Angel's wealthy business friend, Fidel Pino). He was born, at least in Fidel's later memory, at two in the morning and in the middle of a devastating cyclone. "I was born a guerrilla, because I was born in the night," Fidel told the Brazilian priest Frei Betto, many years later. "It was a little like a conspiracy."

There was something very different about the Castros from other Cubans: despite their colorful life together, they had no sense of family. Their relations were endlessly conflictive and unharmonious. Cubans who watched them over the years, and even studied them, and even liked them, were mystified by this lack of family feeling, which was so intensely strong in most Cubans that it was almost uncapturable in words. When Pedro Emilio, Angel's son by his first marriage, later started a radio soap opera about his family, called *The Castros of Birán,* other Cubans were scandalized by what was at least depicted as their behavior. (And Angel, typically, finally paid him off, probably with about forty thousand dollars, to stop it.) The Castros lived together in the nouveau wilderness of Oriente, a family without a past, without a religion, without a sense of real Cuban identity, like a little savage tribal band; and yet, because of their money, they were in an odd way "privileged." Certainly, Fidel saw it this way when he later told his friend from the Revolution, Carlos Franqui, "I was born into a family of landowners in comfortable circumstances. . . . Everyone lavished attention on me, flattered, and treated me differently from the other boys we played with when we were children. These other children went barefoot while we wore shoes. . . ."

There were, however, many conflicts and influences on him as a boy that Fidel never, ever spoke of, and the main one was surely his illegitimacy. Never—not in any writing or in any interview or in any reference—did Fidel ever refer to the fact that he and his siblings were bastards in a Cuba that, despite a certain understanding of illegitimacy, was Roman Catholic and Spanish Puritan. "The Cubans could make Fidel feel bad just by mentioning his mother," Barbara Gordon, a friend of Fidel's wife in nearby Banes, remarked many years later. "Just to say '*tu madre*' in a certain way was a terrible insult in Cuba." And José "Pepe" Figueres, the president of Costa Rica and an early supporter of Fidel, told me that "In Latin America, and especially in Mexico and Cuba, to insult someone all you have to do is to mention his mother. Even the name of the mother! Maybe Fidel is an extreme case. He could have suffered terribly from being a bastard son."

Fidel suffered even more from the fact that he had been born of a father who had come to Cuba as a "soldier of Spain." By all accounts, this tormented him, for the boys in school mocked him as doubly illegitimate—politically as well as personally. Rafael Díaz-Balart, his wife's brother and at one time Fidel's closest friend, recalled that Fidel frequently spoke almost enviously about the Díaz-Balart aristocratic heritage. "Often he told me, 'Rafael, you have a name; I don't have a name, I have a negative name.' And so, he hated, without reason." And so, too, this man without a name eventually created one: he made the name of Fidel Castro synonymous with a totally different Cuban culture, a politics, and even the religion he never had.

The historic age of modern Cuba that would eventually form Fidel Castro had begun in 1868 with the Ten Years' War of Independence; and if any war was war as prologue, this one was it. Conceptually and militarily, like so much in Cuban life, the war lacked sense and cohesion. It claimed thousands of casualties but there were almost no large battles. The Cubans naturally, and apparently without plan, fell back on what they instinctively knew from Mother Spain, *la guerrilla,* or the "little warfare" that Spain had invented and employed so successfully in response to Napoleon's serried legions. Under the brilliant and innovative Dominican general, Máximo Gómez, who commanded the war from its center in Oriente, Cuban guerrillas taunted and tormented the Spanish regular troops from one end of the island to the other, setting fire to property and destroying everything in the way.

But the Cubans lost the Ten Years' War, and the country was left with more than two hundred thousand dead on both sides and the island destroyed. Still the conflict did not end. By 1895, uprisings were intensifying, particularly after the dramatic arrival by sea of "The Apostle," José Martí. Here, in one small, black-mustachioed, sensitively intellectual man of romance and of thought, was the savior: the leader and the inspiration of Cuban independence. It was José Martí, the restlessly patriotic Cuban thinker, who would give his name to the entire "Martiana" generation of 1895, the first of the great Cuban "generations" that would mark the cycles of Cuban history the way election campaigns mark the cycles of North American history. It was José Martí that Fidel Castro would quote, and use, and misuse, more than any other single person in Cuban history.

Born in Havana in 1853, Martí began speaking out against the Spanish when only sixteen years old. Sent to a Spanish jail, where he was forced to work in the rockpits, he lived a horror he would never forget. After being exiled from Cuba, he roved restlessly from country to country—to Spain to seek out the roots of the oppressor, to turbulently romantic and always revolutionary Mexico, and finally to the United States, with which he had a profoundly confused love-hate relationship. It was ironically in his New York exile that he was most happy. There he proselytized, giving his richly variegated speeches and churning out the immense pile of patriotic writing that would inspire a generation. Eventually, as he formed his Cuban Revolutionary party, a name that later parties would repeat, Martí spoke passionately, in universal terms applied to little Cuba, about freedom, about the human soul, about hope, about *la patria.* And he spoke always about death. He would switch suddenly from inspirational and uplifting verse to darkly rhapsodic invocations to death. He wanted to die with his "face to the sun," he said, and the phrase found its way not only into his movement but into Franco's anthem, *"Cara al sol."* He ended his famous call to arms in the Montecristi Manifesto morbidly with "Victory or the Sepulchre."

But if Martí was a man of vision, he also had a practical, astute side. Before disappearing into Cuba, he had enough common sense to give an interview to George E. Bryson, the noted war correspondent for the *New York Herald,* outlining the movement's aims for Americans.

Martí's landing on the Cuban coast at Maisí Cape, on April 11, 1895, was not unusual. Landings by sea to "free Cuba" were eternal verities in Cuban political life. Indeed, since there was no American-style institutionally mandated way of change in Cuba, revolutionaries and prophets, real and false, always chose as their method of evoking the revolutionary spirit "a landing," which meant a heroic and daring challenge to power, and then a moving in upon and over the old power by the new. Actually, though weak in numbers, Martí's group had by then every possible motivation to tap the will of the Cubans to fight. The Spanish had appointed General Valeriano Weyler as commander in chief in this second war, and he soon became known as "The Butcher," when he herded several hundred thousand men, women, and children into concentration camps where tens of thousands died terrible deaths.

Fidel Castro, Martí's spiritual son, would have used these "excesses" on the part of an enemy to his advantage. "The Apostle," José Martí, ever more the early Cuban, instead chose, in effect, to commit suicide.

It all ended very quickly in a small skirmish, nothing "important," which took place only thirty-nine days after Martí had landed in Cuba. Once again, General Máximo Gómez commanded the Cuban forces. When the fighting broke out, Gómez asked Martí to move to a safer area, but Martí, who had never before been in this Cuban countryside much less in a full-scale guerrilla war, actually headed in the direction of the enemy. He rushed into the midst of the Spaniards, on a white horse, and was not unexpectedly shot dead.

Gradually in those years after the death of Martí, the Cuban people began to reveal the depth of their inner delirium and their lack of psychic walls. The denizens of this "insignificant" little island floating somewhere between dream and daydream were ripe for the grandiosity that would eventually pit them on the side of one superpower and against the other. As Cuban poet Guillermo Cabrera Infante put it, by Martí's choice of a kind of "silver bullet" for his sacrificial death, "he forced the Cuban infant republic to be born with a corpse around its neck, a dead weight that was not merely a hidden suicide but a family disgrace. . . ."

Meanwhile, as Cuban patriots reeled at Martí's untimely death, war fever continued to build up in the States. As the weeks and months passed, the necessary chauvinism was supplied by an inflamed press, with Joseph Pulitzer's *World* and William Randolph Hearst's powerful papers tolling the bells of jingoism. Then, on February 15, 1898, the U.S.S. *Maine,* a great ship anchored in Havana harbor, was mysteriously blown up, and two hundred sixty-six American seamen were killed. "Remember the *Maine!*" the young American nation cried, and America remembered by going to war.

Not far from where José Martí martyred himself, the only real land battle of the brief war that ensued occurred on July 1, 1898. This battle for San Juan Hill, led by Theodore "Teddy" Roosevelt and his "Rough Riders," was so greatly enhanced by the historic imagination of Manifest Destiny as to be almost unrecognizable in fact. History has the *americanos* riding up the hill courageously against Spanish firepower. In truth, many of the U.S. soldiers had lost their horses and had to straggle up the hill on foot. It didn't matter. The Americans were the supermen of the age, and they reveled even in the exuberant chaos of it all. "Yesterday we struck the Spaniards and had a brisk fight for two and a half hours," Teddy Roosevelt wrote later of the great day. "The Spaniards shot well, but they did not stand when we rushed. It was a good fight."

Just over a month later, an armistice was signed which effectively dissolved this last Latin American outpost of the great Spanish empire.

Now, to celebrate "their" victory, American generals rode alone, without their Cuban "allies," into the historic city of Santiago—the city that was the very birthplace of Cuban rebellion and revolt. There, in a scene so humiliating to the fragile Cuban nationalism that Cuban nationalists would dwell on it nearly every waking moment for years to come, the Americans raised their flag—not the Cuban flag—over the governor's palace. Cuban General Calixto García and his men waited in despair and humiliation outside the city while the "anticolonialist" Americans seized not Cuba but Cuban independence.

By the ensuing Treaty of Paris, the Cubans felt themselves even further humiliated, as more American rights over Cuba were stated, enforced, and finally taken for granted. For the Americans, Cuba now really was only prologue. In the next thirty years, well into the twentieth century, the "American Century," the North Americans would move into the Dominican Republic, into Haiti, and into Nicaragua—always with the best intentions of protecting those spendthrift little countries from European creditors and keeping others out of the Western Hemisphere. But these interventions left behind deep wells of resentment that were waiting to spring to the fore in the young nationalist generations of the next fifty years.

By the end of the Spanish-American War, any real break between the United States and Cuba was palpably impossible. The United States was Cuba's most important trading partner, with some thirty million dollars invested in Cuba's economy. Despite the opposition of the U.S. Senate, which voted against American occupation of the island once the hostilities ended, the end of the war was followed by three years of military occupation, with Cuba becoming ostensibly independent only in 1902.

In the meantime, in 1901, the United States forced the Platt Amendment upon the Cuban constitution. Named after Republican Senator Orville Platt of Connecticut, the amendment gave the United States the right to intervene militarily in the island again if civil war erupted or if Cuba was not kept clean and free from dangerous disease (two things eternally threatening to the Americans, the Cubans noted). The amendment further restricted the Cuban government's capacity to incur debts and to enjoin treaties with a third power, and it enabled the United States to establish a naval base at Guantánamo. "These terms," the great British historian Hugh Thomas wrote tellingly, "were as severe on Cuba as were those that the treaties of Versailles and St. Germain imposed on defeated Germany and Austria in 1919—and were as strongly resented." The difference was that Cuba ostensibly had "won" the war.

Three decades later, Fidel Castro grew up in an age of those Martiano heroes always marching through his mind out of the past. He grew to young manhood in a conflicted Cuban world of bitterly won half freedoms and tragic victories, and he yearned always and ever to restore the greatness that he knew must be Cuba's and which his generation never stopped breathlessly speaking of. Above all, his generation of obsessive Cubans "knew" that the fault and the guilt for what they were could not be theirs—that would be too terrible, that would be adding a too monumental burden on top of the Sisyphean ones they already carried. No, the fault must be the Americans' and the guilt must accrue to American officiousness and to the American generals who took Santiago for—and, thus, from—the heroic Cubans.

3

PRAYING TO WIN

I saw him as a boy with many ambitions. He wanted to succeed in everything. They called him, "El Loco, Fidel," but he was
charming. He was a very curious mix. First, he was a boy from
the countryside, but from a rich family. He was a boy both
rough and charming, a mixture of Spain and Cuba. . . .

—Father Armando Llorente, Fidel Castro's mentor
at the Jesuit high school

N THAT REMOTE eastern end of Cuba, in the village of Birán, the
Castro children came to be blown to the ends of Cuban society like
unattached leaves before the onslaught of inexorable winds of
change.

Fidel was from the start an unusually violent child, letting his mind
rove in school, where he invented war games for hour after hour. He loved
sports and reveled in their competitiveness, but what he enjoyed in strength
he lacked in discipline. In baseball, for example, he was a powerful pitcher,
but he had little control. One day, the hitter, Roberto Martínez, told him, as
they played in the hot afternoon of Birán, "Fidel, no more."

"Why?" demanded the angry young Castro.

"Because I'm tired," Roberto said. "When you throw the ball all over,
we need to put two catchers behind you."

One day when Fidel was a teenager, he wanted to use Angel's car.

Angel said no, and Fidel ran furiously from the house. Shortly there-
after an employee raced into the house, crying urgently, "Don Angel, Fidel
is trying to start the car. He says if he can't start it, he will burn it!" Fidel
was stopped in time, but few of the onlookers had any question in their
minds that he would indeed have burned the car.

José Pardo Llada, Fidel's close friend and later political opponent,
related that in those early days in Oriente, one of Fidel's favorite games was
waiting for the train to cross a bridge over the Mayarí River. When the loco-
motive was only a few yards from the bridge, Fidel would jump into the
tiny, cramped space under the groaning tracks. There, with intense excitement, he awaited the passing over of the powerful train. "It made his entire
body vibrate," Pardo Llada wrote. "All the while he was hanging with his
hands to the wood that protected him."

The other children were quite different, especially (and almost symbolically) his younger brother, Raúl. While Fidel was big and brawling and
uncontrolled, Raúl was small, closed, and logical. Even as a child, Raúl represented culture and family, in sharpest contrast to the early deracinated and
basically unsocialized Fidel; and it was Raúl who was concerned with questions of social justice and of ideological organization, while Fidel was the
very embodiment of an action that was always assiduously exploring the
outer limits of personal sovereignty.

While the truth can never be proven, rumors too consistent to be
ignored circulated for years in Birán and elsewhere to the effect that Raúl
had had another father, perhaps a somewhat mysterious officer named Captain Felipe Mirabal, who was head of the Cuban army base in nearby
Banes, the United Fruit town. Other potential "fathers" were also regularly
discussed. Certainly, sexual mores were loose enough in Birán and it is
more than likely that in such an open and unconventional place a woman
like Lina would or could have had other lovers from time to time.

But the only "proof" of any other father besides Angel was the oddly
preferential treatment that Mirabal, an officer of Batista, was given in
prison once Fidel took power. Captured and immediately jailed, Mirabal
was sentenced to death but strangely enough he was never executed, while
all around him were falling like poor hunted animals to Fidel's and Raúl's
deadly execution squads.

Whatever the true story, friends of the family always give some cre-
dence to the question of Raúl's paternal origins and whenever the subject

of Raúl was brought up to Mirabal in prison he became oddly cold and quiet and would not speak.

It is certain that Fidel got his first feelings for social justice (as amorphous as they were) and his first experience with "democratic" politics (as dirty as it was) on Angel Castro's farm. He watched as his father, now the Gallego version of the Cuban *cacique,* paid off the "political captains" who were running for office, each controlling hundreds of votes. "Politics were controlled by money back then," Castro told his friend Carlos Franqui. "I remember people going in and out of the room where the safe was kept at home. . . . Eight or ten thousand pesos were spent on each political campaign. I formed a very poor opinion of all this." Lina, too, constantly railed about the political payoffs — to greedy journalists as well as to the politicians — but that was largely because she was, as Fidel kindly put it, "thrifty."

As a boy, Fidel never really saw any semblance of a working democratic system; he saw a rural spoils system, with everybody in on the take and the winnings going to the strongest; and he made clear all his life that he identified that putative but false and corrupted early "democracy" with the far more real and internalized democracy of the United States of America. The fact that his cold and authoritarian *cacique* father happened to be the strongest man around was both satisfying to him and disgusting to him; but despite these conflicting responses, it was from Angel that he learned. From Angel he absorbed his first contempt for the traditional systems of "law" — and the supremely successful example of how to create one's own law. From Angel he garnered his scorn for the bureaucracies of the world, and from Angel he learned every trick in the trade for preempting, coopting, and utterly destroying such pedestrian restraints on one's appetites.

Left on their own, Angel and Lina might well never have married, but if their children were to be educated in Catholic schools, the couple had to legitimize their union.

Many years later recalling the little school in Birán and then the Colegio La Salle and the Colegio Dolores, Fidel recounted: "I spent most of my time being fresh in school. Maybe because of my family's position, or my age, I remember that whenever I disagreed with something the teacher said to me, or whenever I got mad, I would swear at her and immediately leave school, running as fast as I could. . . . One day, I had just sworn at the teacher, and was racing down the rear corridor. I took a leap and landed on a board from a guava-jelly box with a nail in it. As I fell, the nail stuck in my tongue.

When I got back home, my mother said to me: 'God punished you for swearing at the teacher.' I didn't have the slightest doubt that it was really true."

His manipulative and sometimes violent actions, which seemed to please him a great deal for both their sheer ingenuity and their rather notable effectiveness, soon hardened into patterns. He rebelled and insulted everyone so many times—he was going back to school, he wouldn't study—that, as he later told the priest Frei Betto, with obvious relish: "I was already an expert in those things."

World War I had left ten million men dead on the blood-soaked soil of Europe, but it had scarcely touched faraway Cuba. Indeed, the early 1920s marked a time when the United States' limited colonialism in Cuba stood in all its Puritan glory. Thanks to American and Cuban doctors, yellow fever was wiped out; thanks to American politicians, democratic institutions were supposedly being grafted onto the infirm institutions of the Spanish isle. And all the while, American tourists looking for crocodile shoes, a pretty *mulata,* and a night at a sensuous Cuban nightclub brought American dollars to the island in windfalls. After World War II, sugar prices soared and legendary fortunes were made by both Americans and Cubans, including Angel Castro, in what came to be called the hysterical "Dance of the Millions." It was in these years, just before Fidel's birth in 1926, that the great palaces, clubs, casinos, and country clubs of Havana were built and that the gleaming white city on the blue Caribbean, with the great historic Morro fortress glowering over its harbor like some brooding reminder of unsettled ancient conflicts, became one of the most delectable cities of the hemisphere—and one of the most Americanized.

"Ahh, the twenties," Dr. Rubén Darío Rumbat, a prominent Cuban psychiatrist, reminisced with me one day in Houston, sighing with the poignance of the history he had learned as a child. "That was a time of prosperity for Cuba. The 1920s were described as the years of the 'fat cows.' We had seven good years. Sugar went increasingly high—it was vertiginous. There was wild prosperity. Then General Gerardo Machado took power. He was a popular president at the beginning. Then came the period of the *vacas flacas*—the lean cows. Machado came in on a wave of adulation, it went to his head. He began as a nationalist, an average military man, cunning. He built much of the capital. Then he began to repress the press, he reformed the constitution to remain in power. . . ."

Before the Machado dictatorship, the presidencies of the "New Cuba" had revolved back and forth between the two major parties, the Conservatives and the Liberals, with at least the ostensible and formal leadership of the nation passing finally to a small group of men who had fought prominently in the war of independence. But that budding political democracy, as fragile as it was, died with the Cuban masses' submission to a man the Cuban Communist party leader, Juan Marinello, called a "tropical Mussolini."

As Machado's thugs roamed the country, hundreds of people suspected only of disloyalty to Machado were murdered. The University of Havana became the center of opposition and was permanently closed in 1930, along with all high schools and normal schools. In response to the growing repression, underground organizations of students and professionals were formed, most important the ABC, whose classically nonsensical name has remained a deliberate secret. As an impressionable Fidel Castro was growing up in Cuba, the ABC—a group of students and professional people similar to the later PLO in Lebanon, to the Tupamaros in Uruguay, and to the FMLN in El Salvador—began to use "urban terrorism" all over Cuba. They employed the bomb-in-the-street, they killed policemen, and they thought in politically complex enough terms to use terror to try to induce the United States to intervene in Cuba to overthrow a Machado who could not keep the "order" the North Americans so loved.

To an extraordinary extent, many of the later tactics that Castro would employ began with the ABC. Copied from an early secret society formed in France before the French Revolution, the ABC, like Communism, had as its basic unit "the cell." As in Fidel's later movements, people in the cells did not know one another, and they were backed by actual terrorist squads ready to die for the Revolution. The ABC's philosophy was as broad and as amorphous as Fidel's would be—the former generation had failed, colonialism must be expunged from the Cuban economy, and Cuba must be independent of the United States. Throughout all the Cuban revolutionary "generations," those three simple expositions about told it all.

To Cuban democratic politician and thinker Justo Carrillo, Cuba had emerged from the Spanish-American War as a nation paralyzed by *atimia,* or "restricted sovereignty." He used the unusual Spanish word specifically because *atimia,* meaning "loss or deterioration of status," fit those early years of Cuba so well. "Cuba," he said, "was born *atimia.*" Indeed, a fragile Cuban nationalism had emerged out of the war against the Spanish who had so dominated Cuba for four centuries. "However, once that goal was accomplished," the Cuban writer Carlos Alberto Montaner wrote, carrying Carrillo's ideas further, "Cuban nationalism, like a bow being readied for combat, became menacingly taut at the sight of only one target: the United States. The irony was that, to a considerable degree, Cuba owed her political independence and relative economic prosperity to that same country. Hence the weakness and ambivalence of Cuban nationalism. . . ."

But now the United States did nothing. This was a new period in the never really predictable, cyclical personality swings of the *americanos,* swings that smaller lands could be forgiven for not quite understanding. Sometimes it seemed the Americans were driven by sheer power, sometimes held back by guilt, sometimes driven forward by dreams of saving the world—at any one moment, who could know? At this moment, Franklin D. Roosevelt was president, with his Great Depression at home and his "Good Neighbor Policy" abroad in Latin America. Of the situation in Cuba, FDR in 1933 ordained, now ironically to the disappointment of many Cubans, that there was "no possible question of intervention."

In August of 1933, Machado was finally driven from power by a combination of military and popular power. But the drama of the 1930s was only beginning. With the end of that brief but bitterly definitive dictatorship, a new generation of Cubans, politically and intellectually formed in new ways, took the place of the "Generation of 1895." Appropriately called the "Generation of the '30s," they were to dominate Cuban political life until 1959.

One day when Fidel was a teenager at the Colegio Dolores in Santiago, he sat down and wrote a letter to President Franklin D. Roosevelt. In a style as guileful and as apparently humble as the style he would later employ so successfully with *las masas,* he told the American president: "My good friend Roosevelt: I don't know very English, but I know as much as write to you. I like to hear the radio, and I am very happy, because I heard in it, that you will be president of a new era. I am a boy but I think very much but I do not think that I am writting to the President of the United States. If you like, give me a ten dollars bill green american, in the letter, because never, I have not seen a ten dollars bill green american and I would like to have one of them." He also asked the American president to sign the bill. Soon, a letter from Franklin Roosevelt was posted on the bulletin board at

Dolores. In it, the president of the United States of America thanked Fidel Castro for his "letter of support and congratulations."

One of Fidel's classmates, Luis Aguilar, a bright-eyed and charming young boy from a well-to-do Santiago family, was fascinated by this fellow student who had the nerve to write to Franklin D. Roosevelt. One day while Fidel was playing soccer, Luis approached him. Luis had to know—why would a simple boy at the Colegio Dolores in Santiago do such a thing? Fidel explained simply that he had read about Roosevelt's election in the newspapers and had decided to write to him. But he was disappointed, he told Luis. Roosevelt had sent him only a letter and no money.

At times even then, Fidel posited his person in terms of a kind of raw but intense gladiator doing battle against social injustice and for social "purity." When the boys from La Salle would go with the La Salle fathers on their motor launch, *El Cateto,* to the nearby island of Rente for an outing, they would return in the evening along narrow streets lined with bars and brothels. As they walked in two columns on either side of the street, the prostitutes and their customers would appear at the windows and dare them to come in. In later years, Fidel himself would credit his near-obsessive hatred of red-light districts to this early trauma, although his later obsessions with fighting prostitution were far more profound and complex than simply such an innocent early experience.

In 1941, the darkest year of World War II, the year Adolf Hitler attacked Russia, Francisco Franco was in power in Spain, and the Japanese attacked Pearl Harbor, Fidel Castro entered the most prestigious school in Cuba.

The Colegio de Belén, or the College of Bethlehem, in the wealthy suburbs of Havana stood like a citadel of Spanish culture that could have harkened back to the Inquisition. Built in 1926, to the world it presented a flat, four-storied front, with a powerful baroque façade. In back, the building was rounded, with small wings that extended like social roots into many levels of Cuban society. Sometimes called a "real palace of education," it provided a regal, intellectual showcase for the Jesuits, who were almost all very conservative Spaniards in those years and almost all *Franquistas,* or followers of that same Generalísimo Francisco Franco who had been born so near to Angel Castro in Galicia. They presented the young Fidel, who already had a distinct personal penchant for total order and total control, with what was actually an incongruously comfortable and comforting environment.

At Belén, Fidel seemed to have multiple personalities: different, contradictory, and often warring with each other. At times he appeared to be a normal, mischievous, life-loving boy, clumsily seeking nobility and searching to find himself. But at other times his darker side would emerge like a suddenly gathered storm cloud. Years later, his friends of that time would only shake their heads helplessly in trying to connect the different Fidels.

Father Armando Llorente was his mentor, and to this tough-minded Spanish Jesuit, Fidel showed his first side, that of a boyish lad who loved sports and mountains and adventure and often seemed quite capable of doing valiant things.

"Later, when he was in power, I knew exactly what he was going to say because it was so predictable," Father Llorente told me one morning years later in Miami, looking out across the waters that now separated him from Cuba and from what little was left of Belén (thanks to that same ambitious boy). "He was a good student. . . . He was not deep, he was intuitive. He has a radar! And . . ." Father Llorente paused. ". . . he also had the cruelty of the Gallego. The Cuban is courtly. The Cuban would give up before he made people suffer. The Spaniard of the north is cruel, hard."

But Father Llorente loved the boy then—and he continued, like so many of the people who came under Fidel's spell, to "love" him in some ways always.

Under the guidance of Father Llorente, who had dreams of forming young men who would become the future governors of Cuba, some of the students at Belén formed a club called the Exploradores, or Explorers. Seventy boys and only the best ones could belong to it. Fidel became the group's chief. Father Llorente organized them like the military, for they would often camp in the mountains where there was some danger from wild pigs and who knew what else?

On one of their excursions it rained all day, turning the normally complacent river into a tortuous flood. Fidel and the priest found themselves on one side of the river; the younger boys and all their things were on the other. "*Bueno,* Father," Fidel said, "it is sixty meters and the river is so terrible that even a peasant on horseback couldn't make it." Father Llorente answered, "*Bueno,* Fidel, we have to pass over that river. The younger boys are on the other side. You, Fidel, have to go first."

Fidel got a rope, put it in his mouth, and swam across the dangerous waters, holding the rope fast in his teeth. Once he was safe on the other side,

Father Llorente started across, hanging tightly onto the rope. Suddenly he slipped and fell on the stones and was about to be washed away down the river when Fidel, a strong swimmer, dashed in to save him. Once they arrived safely on the "other side," he gave the priest a big hug and said, "Father, this is a miracle, let us say three Ave Marías to the Virgin." In that magic and spontaneous moment, the two knelt and said the three Ave Marías underneath the night sky.

Despite moments such as these, Fidel did not ever become really religious. Later in life he confided to the Brazilian Leftist priest Frei Betto that "I never came to have a religious faith, because all of my force and attention was consecrated in my life to the acquisition of a political faith, at which I finally arrived through my own convictions."

If his lust for life did not extend to religion or really to any spiritual belief, it did extend to other areas—and always with flair and always with the whiffled suggestion of violence. "He knew everything by heart," his schoolfriend José Ignacio Rasco recalled. "In school, he used to make a joke with us. He would read the page of a book and throw it out. At the end of the book, he was left with the index only. We could ask him, 'Fidel, what does the book of sociology say on page fifty-three?' And Fidel could tell us. He had a really photographic memory."

As for his violent side, his fights would later become legendary. Indeed, his temper seemed to be always on the ready, waiting to explode against anyone who dared to challenge him. One day at Belén, Fidel was chatting with some girls when a fellow student, Ramón Mestre, provoked him by calling him "crazy." Fidel flew into a rage, got into a fistfight with Ramón—and, for one of the few times in his life, lost. "Fidel bit me on my left arm," Ramón Mestre recalled. When the fight was finished, Fidel ran to his room and brought out his pistol, which he brandished crazily until one of the priests separated them. But Fidel never forgot. Later, when he became ruler of all of Cuba, he sent Mestre to prison, if not only because of the early fight, certainly in large part because of it.

Another day, before classes started, Fidel bet a fellow student five dollars that he could run his bike into a wall and not get hurt. He then began riding his bike down a large hall with columns. Before long he crashed head-on into one of the columns, injuring himself so severely that he had to be hospitalized for several days.

That same incessant passion to do and to be, regardless of intent or outcome, was extended to sports. When he first came to Belén, he did not know how to play basketball, but as basketball became a fashionable sport, Fidel determined to become the best at it. He began to practice day and night. Finally, the priests had to put a light on the court because of *"El Loco Fidel."* His desire to win was so extreme that on several occasions he actually forgot which team he was playing for, switching in the middle of the game and making a basket for the other team.

The school coach, Otilio "Capi" Campuzano, liked the determined athlete with the desire to win at all costs but he admitted that the young man tried his patience. "Fidel drove me crazy," he remembered, "always asking me what he had to do to be a leader, what he had to do to make himself known. He said he was a greater orator than even the leaders of Cuba and could do something great."

Fidel tried desperately at Belén to hone his oratorical skill—or, at that time, nonskill. For, despite his braggadocio, this man who was later to move millions with his resounding voice was then a notably poor speaker. He wanted to join the oratory group, the Academia Literaria Avellaneda, named after a prominent Cuban poetess, but in order to join he had to give a ten-minute speech without notes. After failing several times because of nervousness, he was finally accepted.

Some noted that while he was at Belén, Fidel spoke a florid Spanish. Later, when he came to power, he simplified his Spanish, much as Gamal Abdel Nasser gave up classical Arabic and used the street Arabic when he came to power as a revolutionary leader in Egypt. At any rate, "debating" in any form was never desirable to Fidel. He liked even then to state something and have it immediately agreed to, saying repeatedly and with emphasis, *¡Porque lo digo yo!,* "Because I say it!"

When it came to grades, Fidel again showed his ability to get what he wanted in his own way. To graduate from Belén, students needed to pass a state examination plus the school's private exam. In his last year, Fidel was suspended from both his French and logic classes for the good reason that he had barely studied. Fidel considered the situation a bit, then reached an agreement with his teacher: if he earned 100 percent on the state exam, he would be allowed to take the school exam. So, he studied round the clock for three days for the state exam, earned a 100 percent mark in both subjects, and was then allowed to take the school exam, which he also passed.

Raúl Castro was at Belén for a time, but "always in the shadow of his brother and always ready to defend Fidel, because without him he was nothing," as Father Llorente recalled. Raúl was expelled after one year, giving rise to speculation among some pro-Castro as well as anti-Castro Cubans that he was a homosexual. From all accounts, this is untrue, although there remain close friends who insist upon it. To the contrary, Raúl seems to have been the real womanizer among the brothers and Llorente himself says Raúl left "because of his studies only."

During all of this time, there was another Fidel, a Fidel who was seeking out a philosophy, an ideology, a rationale for the restless power he felt so turbulently inside him and which he seemed instinctively to know he would some day exercise. And at this time in history—and in his history—Fidel found what he was seeking among the European Fascists.

Since World War I, the philosophy of Fascism had writ its fiery and fanatical will across Europe and across much of the world. Adolf Hitler had called for the repeal of the humiliating Treaty of Versailles in 1923; he had named himself German chancellor in 1933 while his storm troopers fought bloody battles on the streets of Germany and marched in forbidding torch-light parades; at his height, the *New York Times* said he was more powerful than Genghis Khan as he made himself both legislator and executive of Germany (as Castro would do in Cuba). Benito Mussolini had founded his own party, the *"Fascidi combattimento,"* in 1919; he made himself "Il Duce" in 1921, with a "radicalism of the right"; his forty thousand Black-shirts marched on Rome with bayonets in 1922 and took over the government. And in 1923, General Miguel Primo de Rivera seized power in Spain.

Actually, it is rather easy to understand why a boy like Fidel should scour around among the Fascists for studies in power and for the tactical vehicles for coming to power. For the Fascist state ignored that old and bothersome democracy with its "phony" electoralism, and embodied and enthroned statism, the advocation and justification of that all-powerful, all-intrusive state government that more and more people were coming to see as the only way to transform pure geographical "accidents of history" into modern nation-states. Of it all, what finally most appealed to Fidel was the idea that the Fascist "new men" were soldiers. Even Fascism's literature was filled with military metaphors, starting with the Fascist constitution of Italy which stated that "Fascism is a Militia at the service of the Nation."

With this ideological background of the time, Fidel clearly revealed who his heroes were in his personal life. He walked soberly around the campus with a copy of *Mein Kampf* (*La Lucha*) under his arm; in his room, he had a map on his wall upon which he charted the movements and successes of the Axis armies across Europe; for hours, he would stand before a mirror holding a primitive, early recorder, and mimicking Mussolini's speeches over and over again.

None of this was really surprising either. "All the dictators have the same style," Dr. Marcelino Feal, a prominent Cuban psychiatrist, told me in later years, "and Fidel was often studying the behavior and style of all of them: Mussolini, Hitler, Primo de Rivera, Lenin, Trotsky, Stalin, Perón. Everybody who could give him a feature to imitate and take advantage of."

In Hitler, Fidel studied a leader who was profoundly and comfortingly anti–Anglo Saxon and who created a power base from an alienated and atomized lower middle class not unlike the workers and farmers who were awaiting a similar "Messiah" in unfinished Cuba. But most of all what Fidel saw in Hitler was the degree to which histrionically he was, in C. J. Jung's sensitive and revealing terms, "the mirror of every German's unconscious . . . the loudspeaker which magnifies the inaudible whispers of the German soul until they can be heard by the German's unconscious ear. . . ."

The brash and daring Mussolini offered a still more interesting role model for Fidel, who later taught his people to shout to him, *¡Comandante-en-Jefe, Ordéne!,* words which were uncannily similar to Mussolini's exhortations to his crowds to *Credere, Obbidire, Combattere* ("Believe, Obey, Fight"). Always Mussolini played endlessly on the theme of the rich versus the poor nations, and Mussolini's artistry in wooing (and despising) the people through his speeches was eerily akin to Fidel's. "When the masses are like wax in my hands," Il Duce said once, "when I stir their faith, or when I mingle with them and am almost crushed by them, I feel myself to be part of them. All the same, there persists in me a certain feeling of aversion, like that which the modeler feels for the clay he is molding."

But, by far, Fidel's premiere model and hero—until late into his life— was the Spanish Falangist José Antonio Primo de Rivera, the Spanish caudillo and thinker who founded the Spanish Fascist party, the Falange Española (Spanish Phalanx) in October 1933, and who lived from 1903 to 1936. The ideas of "José Antonio," who like the later Fidel was known by the adoring masses only by his given names, sprang directly out of those of his father, General Miguel Primo de Rivera, who ruled Spain with a strong hand from 1923 to 1930. Primo not only had the same incredible intuition as Castro, his political style was actually called by historians like Raymond Carr "intuitionism." And the elder Primo de Rivera's paternalistic care for his nation bordered on eccentricity. Spaniards ate too much—so they were counseled to take "one large meal once a day between five and seven, with no lunch." How similar to the later Fidel, who would try personally to regulate everything in Cuba from the artificial insemination of cows to the health regulations of the *posadas,* or government-run motels, where apartment-starved Cubans could go to make love on the hour or the half hour.

Primo's curious catchphrase "constant plebiscite of public opinion" was also to become a basic concept of Fidel Castro's political thought and a direct predecessor of Fidel's "direct democracy."

José Antonio never ruled like his father and was indeed only a member of the Cortes, or parliament. But the younger Primo had a tremendous emotional effect, in large part through his hortatory writings. Like his father, he heralded the idea of *Hispanidad,* a movement for the unity of all Spanish-speaking countries. In a course on the history of Latin America at Belén, one priest who greatly influenced Fidel's generation, Father Alberto de Castro, expounded over and over on the idea of *Hispanidad,* giving the young Fidel reasons, philosophies, excuses for Latin America's failure in the face of the Americans' glorious successes. *Hispanidad* offered the young Fidel his most total political rationale for a collective Spanish will to stand up against the Americans. "He had dreams of the great Spanish nation," Father Llorente recalled. "It touched him greatly."

In the end, José Antonio was arrested at the outbreak of the Spanish Civil War, given a summary trial, and executed—but it was General Francisco Franco who would take up his banner and treat José Antonio as a martyr, just as Fidel would later unbeknownst to the world meld himself to Francisco Franco.

When Fidel was graduated from Belén in the spring of 1945, the entire family came to celebrate. "There was such happiness," Father Llorente recalled. "You never heard an applause so great! I was the one who wrote under his photograph in the yearbook." He paused and thought for a moment. "He was different," he added simply. Then he showed me the historic yearbook. There, under the picture of a serious young man with a long Gallego nose and distant eyes, was written: "Fidel distinguished himself always in all subjects related to letters. A top student and member of the congregation, he was also an outstanding athlete, always courageously and proudly defending the school's colors. He has won the admiration and affection of all. We are sure that, after his law studies, he will make a brilliant name for himself. Fidel has what it takes and will make something of his life."

Father Llorente always recalled those magical days when there was still an air of innocence in Cuba. "I said to him many times, 'You are born to do something great, Fidel.' I could see that he liked that very much. With Fidel, you always had to challenge him. He becomes a giant before a challenge. He's not going to fight against Haiti or the Dominican Republic. . . ."

And then Father Llorente recalled the times when, touched, he would see Fidel praying in the chapel. He smiled a canny Jesuit smile and said, "I would see him alone, praying in the chapel. I knew what he was praying for—he was praying to win."

4

THE UNIVERSITY YEARS—
"YOU AND I"

The worst that could have happened was that Fidel would be
converted into a Communist then. First, because he wasn't
one. I knew that very well from his ideas: but it was fatal from
the political point of view for him. . . . The party at that time
had the idea of the fight of the masses, and Fidel had the idea
of the moment and in direct action—that is to say, in popular
insurrection.

—Alfredo Guevara, Communist party member
and friend of Fidel at the university

IDEL WENT HOME to Birán that long and sensuously hot summer of 1945, and both he and his parents realized that it was the last
time it was really to be his home. He roved restlessly across the
always-increasing lands of his father and over the valleys and beaches of
his childhood. The world war that he had studied so impassionedly finally
was over. But the loss of the Axis did not seem to disturb him; being basically nonideological, Fidel was a student of their tactics, not always or necessarily their beliefs. Now he would study their failures.

Ironically, his father and mother had decided to send him to the University of Havana because they were convinced that he would become a
lawyer and would protect their properties. How little they knew their son!

In the turbulent and troubled halls of the university, Fidel would discover an entirely new world of political action—and of political violence.

That summer, Fidel's mother seemed inordinately proud of her son, but it was still another summer of conflict between Angel and Fidel. This was not unexpected. Throughout his life, Fidel retained at best an ambivalent attitude toward his father and at worst one that ranged between cool indifference and angry resentment. Nevertheless, even against a domineering and sometimes angry father, Fidel was usually able to exercise his implacable will. The day before he was to leave for Havana and his new life, Angel gave in to his son's entreaties and, despite his wiser judgment, bought him the new American car he so wanted.

From the outside, Cuba in those "halcyon" years seemed a happy island, particularly to the more sober, puritanical, hardworking *americanos*. Cuba was "respectable" America's most beautiful and desired mistress. The little country was prospering, and to the tourists who poured into the island to enjoy Varadero and the Tropicana (not to speak of the prostitutes of the Calle Trocadero and the lascivious pornographic shows of "Superman," who copulated on stage with woman and beast) Cubans seemed almost to cavort through life, they had such a joyously special capacity for living. And so the less "life-loving," the bill-paying, the world-ordering *americanos* flowed like quicksilver down to Havana to attempt for brief and shining moments to share just a little of that blithe Cuban spirit. Josephine Baker was singing at the Tropicana again, the daiquiris were delicious at Hemingway's favorite Sloppy Joe's Bar, and the war was over; the lights were on again all over the world.

It never occurred to most Americans that the Cubans might not really be so happy as they seemed. After all, while the North Americans thought they "knew" Cuba, in reality there were virtually no outstanding American historians or social scientists who had studied Cuba. To American policymakers, Cuba was not a country to be taken terribly seriously, particularly now that the postwar "American Century" was soaring toward its unquestioned zenith of power and wealth. What in the world, after all, would possibly make the "big" world even remotely dream that "little Cuba" could ever be anything important?

The triumphant Americans, rulers of the world, had not only won the war, they had broken the riddle of atomic fission and loosed mankind's first controlled nuclear chain reaction. Now they were determined to order the entire world in their own image; and so they set about to rebuild Germany, to reform Japan, and to create a United Nations that would bring peace and world order to all. But as they directed plans for the world's future, they continued to think of war and violence on the same grand scale of the fighting in Europe and the Pacific. Once again, they tried to structure the peace so that conflicts between the big countries would never reoccur, even while the very nature of conflict was tilting toward the irregular wars, toward the low-intensity conflicts, toward the guerrillas of Cuba.

The Fidel who went to the University of Havana that October of 1945 both attracted and repelled his fellow "students," some of whom even came to study, for this was a classic Latin American university system that was half devoted to learning and at least half devoted to fomenting political action. Physically, Fidel stood out. He was markedly tall in a country of generally short men. "He didn't look like the typical Cuban," Max Lesnick, his close friend of the time, recalled. "He looked like the perfect Greek, Spaniard, Gallego." But Lesnick recalled too that, while Fidel's physical presence was impressive on some levels, it was also *orangutinesco,* or stooped like an orangutan. Lesnick was amazed in later years to note his friend's erect military bearing.

In his personal habits, it was soon obvious that Fidel was Lina's son. He was so sloppy that he was almost immediately named *Bola de Churre,* "Greaseball." Nevertheless, on some occasions, students would see Fidel meticulously attired in the finest of suits. He seemed to be trying out different versions of himself on the world.

Fidel lived in a boardinghouse in Calle "Ele," on the corner of 17th Street. By all accounts, his room mirrored his disorderly and searching ways, except for his growing and beloved library of José Martí, which he guarded with some care. "There were old newspapers and cigarette butts on the floor and on the table . . . ," recalled another friend, Bernardo Viera. "Five or six pieces of dirty underwear were thrown in a corner. His *guayabera* [white Cuban shirt] couldn't possibly have had more sweat over the dirt." Years later, when Viera was in exile in Venezuela because of that very same friend, he told me, laughing, "Now, every time I hear from some visitor to Cuba that the country is dirty, it seems to me that Fidel has simply extended the dimensions of that room to all of Cuba!"

But, if Fidel was a contradictory person in those days, even more so was the University of Havana a place of contradictions. The two-hundred-year-old university was a complex of elegant tropical buildings that sprawled gracefully over several hills right in the middle of a new commercial and tourist center in the elegant neighborhood of Vedado. Majestic Greek columns guarded the schools of science, philosophy and literature, law, architecture and engineering. A dramatic rise of one hundred and sixty-three steps led to the famous "Escalinata," which provided a background of Greek theater for the many dramas that were taking place there—and, more important, for those that would.

By Latin tradition, universities were autonomous in Cuban society. Police were not permitted to enter the campus, which thus provided a "sanctuary" not only for ideas but also for politicized people of all sorts. Indeed, in the Cuba of that time, the Cubans saw their counterpowers in terms of two centers, which they referred to as "two hills." One hill was the equivalent of the American Pentagon, the major military base called Camp Columbia. The other hill—the intellectual, but also more and more the political hill—was the "sacred" hill of the university. With the government so corrupt, the university became the arena and the stage for the most dramatic and symbolic working out of "politics."

Fidel loved it; he had found his milieu. And, as ever in Cuban history, there was the shining hope that, this time, this generation would find the key to unlocking the answer to Cuba's endless searchings for legitimacy.

As it happened, Fidel came to the university exactly at the end of those cycles of "generational politics" that had marked the trajectory of the Cuban decades from Martí's "Generation of 1895" to the "Generation of the '30s." In 1944, Ramón Grau San Martín, a leader of the democratic party popularly called the *Auténticos,* or the Authentic Ones, won the presidency. The list of his party's promises and intentions was noble and progressive. Once in office, the *Auténticos* actually did begin to carry out much of their program. But then the old curse of corruption raised its ugly head and President Grau, in earlier days the professional idealist around whom the hopeful students flocked, soon became a despised figure, bloated with vice.

In this atmosphere, Fidel soon developed his own "gang" of friends, who, at first, were good boys, boys from middle-class families—in sharp contrast socially and sociologically to the boys he would find, choose, and mold later on in the first phase of revolution. These early friends were boys with names like Justo Fuentes, Alfred "Chino" Esquivel, Raúl "El Flaco" Granados, Rafael del Pino, Baudilio "Bilito" Castellanos, and Alfredo Guevara. Alfredo was already a Communist party member and was the only one to stay with Fidel throughout his many transformations ideologically and politically—most of the others would either leave Cuba or languish in one of Fidel's prisons.

It took, as so often in Latin America, something as plebeian as a rise in the bus fares to bring these students to the streets. Fidel made his debut in Cuban politics by organizing the demonstration against Grau and his supposedly innocent increase in the bus fares. That day, a large bank of students marched down the streets with a huge Cuban flag. At the corner of Infanta and San Lázaro avenues, the police stopped them, beating them with sticks and guns. Fidel was wounded the worst. After having his head wrapped up at the hospital, he and Raúl made the first of many visits to the newspapers and the radio station. Fidel, as always, knew exactly how to exploit the situation.

Three days later, the students announced another demonstration, and this time President Grau grew so alarmed that he agreed to receive their leaders in a delegation. Only at the last minute was it decided that Fidel should also go because he cut such a wonderfully martyred figure with his head still wound up like a mummy's. They went to the palace to meet the old and always cordially smiling president and there Fidel revealed one of his amazing predilections.

Since it was particularly warm that day, President Grau invited them to step out on his balcony to get some fresh air. Meanwhile, his assistants had all left, so the moment witnessed a symbolic emptiness of power. At this point, Fidel suddenly whispered to his coconspirators, "I have the formula to take power and once and for all get rid of this old son-of-a-bitch." His comrades were stupefied as he explained, "Now, when the old guy returns, let's pick him up, the four of us, and throw him off the balcony. Once the president is dead, we'll proclaim the triumph of the student revolution and speak to the people from the radio."

"Vamos, guajiro, tú estás 'chiflado'" ("Listen, redneck, you're nuts"), Chino Esquivel told him. And when Fidel insisted on his astounding plan, Enrique Ovares finally squelched it by saying, "We came here to ask for a lowering of the fares on the buses, not to commit an assassination." It is important to remember that Grau, for all his faults, was not a dictator but one of Cuba's first democratically elected leaders.

It was at this time that Fidel began to speak publicly and also to get rid of the fear that had overwhelmed him at Belén when he had tried to join the oratory club. He planned his first speech for November 27, 1946, and the date was not arbitrary. In the Spanish tradition, Cubans were always looking soulfully at the most tragic moments of their history. For these, not times of victory, represented their "true" moments of glory. Fidel now chose one of the most shining moments of memory. It was on November 27, 1871, that hated Spanish colonial authorities had executed eight University of Havana medical students accused of having desecrated the grave of a Spanish officer. The Spanish had intended the executions to frighten and cow the populace; instead, they had shocked the struggling society to its depths.

Recalling Fidel's speech that day, his friend Rafael Díaz-Balart said in later years: "You must remember that the 'Spanish question' was for us like yesterday's afternoon." In fact, it was Rafael who wrote most of the speech. One early morning (it was about 4 A.M.) when they were studying, Fidel suddenly demanded: "Rafael, write me a speech." His friend, tired but eager for political adventure and for declaration as well, wrote all but the last two paragraphs. The speech was given at what the Cubans call an *acto*—or an act with a dramatic spiritual or patriotic effect—in the Havana cemetery to a small group of students.

Even in those early days, Fidel was remarkably clear about his political ambitions. He told everyone within sight about his intentions. Perhaps it was just that ingenuous quality of his that lulled so many into a sense of unconcern about his motives. "At that time, I loved Fidel Castro," Dr. Mariano Sorí Marín, a Cuban doctor who would help Fidel, recalled. "He was like me—a political agitator. Besides, he was very intelligent. A megalomaniac with a sense of grandiosity! He never could be a democratic president, but he was a man who was personally very attractive and charming. When you were with him, you liked to be with him or liked yourself more."

Fidel began to develop personal mannerisms that even then tied people to him. "He was always inventing something to make himself stand out," Max Lesnick recalled of those days, "to make himself appear to excel. He was trying to conquer everyone and anyone who could help him realize his plans. Then he would say, *'Tú y yo'*—'You and I'—because when Fidel would speak with someone, he would always say, 'No, because you and I are the only ones here.' The 'you' always changed—the 'I' was always he. He would be with me, and say, 'Max, because you and I are here in the university, and we are the only ones who can . . .' Then you would see him on the other corner with Walterio Carbonell, saying, 'Because, Walterio, you and I are the only ones . . .' And then afterwards, we would all see one another and smile and say, 'You and I . . .' "

But if his classmates smiled with amusement while they were away from him, they never made jokes at his expense. He would not tolerate it—and he never pardoned or forgot it. "I believe," Lesnick added, "that Fidel would rather pardon a physical assault against him than someone's ridiculing him."

In those days, Fidel continued to rummage about with the ideas of Primo de Rivera's *Hispanidad*. One day, he and Luis Aguilar, his bright friend from the Colegio Dolores in Santiago, were discussing a popular new book, *Dialogues over Destiny* by Gustavo Pitaluga, a European author who lived in Cuba. The book in a strange way characterized Cuba's grandiose vision of itself as not just another Latin American country, but as a special arm of imperial Spain, going so far as to suggest that Cuba alone had a great destiny, even to be the leader of a confederation of Caribbean states. Aguilar argued with Fidel, saying it was doubtful that English-speaking Jamaica or French-speaking Haiti would want to follow Cuba. But Fidel said no, Pitaluga had posited the correct destiny for Cuba—and when he said this, his face took on the look of the dreamer or the seer.

Nevertheless, this dreamer of *Hispanidad* was an indifferent student when it came to the actual history of the Americas. "I had to flunk him," his professor, Herminio Portell Vilá, recalled. "He was never there. Did he show interest in Hispanic America?" The old man, sitting then in his favorite Cuban restaurant in Miami, the Versailles, chortled as he told me, "He tried to make it, not study it."

Above all, Fidel wanted to be president of the FEU, the Federation of University Students, the antechamber to political power in the country. Fidel, however, was not successful at winning any major electoral office at the university. Even more than at Belén, at the university he was always slightly outside—and thus always forced to devise new strategies to power. At heart, there was an ambivalence about him. He was an interesting fellow, but he was never really one of the crowd. He would never forget that, and one day he would let them know the price of their never having allowed him to be one of them.

Enrique Ovares, who served five years as president of the architecture school and three terms as FEU president, has said the reason for Fidel's unelectability was that he could not work with others. He was too independent. Ovares also said that this was why the Communists, who were small in numbers but well entrenched in the university, if not in Cuba as a whole, did not support Fidel. "Anybody who followed closely Fidel's political process as a student knows that Fidel at no time maintained relations with the Communists," Ovares said. "Fidel was . . . a negative type for the party because he was an individual who would say 'white' today, and 'black' tomorrow, and 'gray' the day after. He was totally independent, he could not be controlled."

When he first met Alfredo Guevara, Fidel joked that he would become a Communist immediately, but on one condition—"If I can become Stalin!"

The simple fact is that Fidel Castro was even then a consummately—a classically—nonideological man. He was a man of action, of tactics, of strategies. He was the son of the Inquisition and the seeker of absolute power; he was never even remotely the son of boring Moscow and of dour collectivism. Interestingly enough, there is not the slightest disagreement about this perception among his friends at the university. For it simply makes no sense that a rebellious, ambitious, sublimely individualistic youth like Fidel would gravitate to the Communist party of old fogies, steeped in their ideological rigidity and absorbed with their incessant organizing of the labor unions at Moscow's demand.

But despite his failure to win elections, Fidel never gave up. He contacted just about everyone he could to get into student politics, and he was tireless in his efforts to succeed. He would walk up and down the Avenida Infanta, stopping on the corner at Vicki's, a favorite student café where they carved their names for posterity on the wooden tables. He would meet with people, discuss, and then meet with more people. One day he got the idea to support his political ambitions by selling *fritas* to the students. *Fritas* were Cuban hamburgers, and this, as far as the records show, represented Fidel's first and only real attempt at "capitalism." Unfortunately, perhaps for the world, he had to close the *frita* stand within a month because there was no profit. "One guy ate all the *fritas*," Chino Esquivel sadly summed up.

Two things did definitely come out of his attempt to win at student electoral politics. When Angel learned that Fidel was involved in politics, he cut off the $500-a-month allowance he had been sending him, thus forcing

Fidel to move to a less expensive boardinghouse. Many times, Fidel appealed for more money to his brother Ramón, who still assisted Angel on the farm, but this only made Angel more angry. The second thing that he gained from his experiment was an even deeper disdain and hatred for electoral politics than he already had from watching his father and his political pals in Birán.

But if Fidel failed to win elections in those full and formative years at the university, he nevertheless took a big leap toward his future. Once he had told Rafael Díaz-Balart that Al Capone was a stupid man because he never formed any ideological *traje,* or form. If he had, Fidel said, he would be famous, and not remembered only as a gangster. In his second year at the University of Havana, at the age of twenty, Fidel became something that to this day very few people will acknowledge and that he has never even remotely spoken of—a classic gangster. Unlike the lamented Al Capone, however, Fidel had his *traje,* and it was sheer Machiavellian power tactics.

5

REDEMPTIVE VIOLENCE

Many of them who died as gangsters, victims of an illusion,
today would be considered heroes.

—Fidel Castro

LATE IN THE AFTERNOON one day in December 1946, Fidel
suddenly appeared at the door of Rafael Díaz-Balart's apartment in
Havana. His clothes were even more disheveled than usual and his
face had the expression of a man reeling at the edge. "Rafael, let me in," he
blurted out, "I just killed Leonel Gómez."

"You what?" Rafael said, stunned. "What are you talking about?"

Only a few weeks before, Rafael recalled, Fidel had told him, as they
engaged in one of their endlessly intense conversations about power and
political position, that Leonel Gómez and Manolo Castro, two recognized
and particularly violent leaders of opposing student gangs, were his
"obstacles." Rafael had shaken his head and disagreed. "No," he told him,
"not Manolo. The obstacle is Leonel Gómez, because he is going to win
the student federation elections." Fidel agreed and insisted suddenly that
an attack had to be prepared on Leonel Gómez, but Rafael never dreamed
he would carry out such a harebrained plan. Macho talk like that was
cheap at the university of the time.

Now, safely inside Rafael's apartment, Fidel insisted that the assassination had not been planned. He had been standing atop a hill at the uni-

versity, he explained nervously to Rafael, with two *hombres de confianza,* or trusted attachés, of Manolo Castro. Suddenly, out of the adjoining streets, they noticed a car down below on Rionda Street. The car belonged to rival gang leader Leonel Gómez and now they watched in pregnant silence, their eyes riveted on the car whose path curled slowly below them like a snake. The car moved as if in a dream along Rionda Street, a cul-de-sac with no outlet. Knowing that Gómez had to return the same way to get out of the circle that now entrapped him, a kind of blood lust passed over the three men who only minutes before had been standing so insouciantly at the top of the hill.

"Let's kill him; he has to return," one of them said.

"Fine," Fidel said, and his eyes turned back to the prey.

When the car turned around, the three started to fire wildly and several persons walking below were wounded. But Fidel's eyes gleamed. He was perfectly calm then, he told Rafael. He took aim and he shot. Within minutes, the assassination of Leonel Gómez was announced agitatedly on the radio and Fidel had fled to Rafael's uneasy sanctuary.

Of all the myriad periods of Fidel's early life, the most mysterious and most open to dispute is that of his gangster years in the university. Not surprisingly, his admirers and apologists ignore the time or angrily reject it, and yet the evidence of persons who knew him then is overwhelming.

First of all, far from being unusual or outside of the norm, violent gangs—also called *bonches,* or bunches, *grupos de acción,* or action groups, or the "Happy Triggermen"—were the leitmotiv of behavior of the times. In the Cuba of the 1940s, there was even the sense, which in some ways was precursor to the kind of self-righteous sacred rage of the Lebanese militias in the 1970s and 1980s, of violence as a sort of redemption, of the notion of the romantic cauterization of an infected society through violence. Of those days, the noted Cuban writer Guillermo Cabrera Infante wrote, "Gangster mobs pillaged the dark and mouldy streets of Old Havana, killing one another for ideologies even more obscure than the streets themselves. . . ." Fidel himself remarked when he took power in 1959 that his five years at the University of Havana studying law, ironically, were "much more dangerous than all the time I fought against Batista from the Sierra Maestra."

For the many sensitive students who neither reveled in nor sought out this violence, it was a time of ceaseless nightmare. "Every day some one or other of our companions was killed," Teresa "Teté" Casuso, the beautiful and self-centered young woman of earlier but similar student days who would later become a close collaborator of Fidel's, wrote with the compelling sorrow of the times. "I remember that one day I got home to study for an examination in biology after a very dear friend, recently married and happy, had been killed not half an hour after we had stood talking on the University steps. I opened the book and read a sentence of Claude Bernard's, 'Death is a phenomenon of perfection.' My eyes filled with the image of my friend's corpse as it had been carried still warm to the University hospital. I threw the book from me, violently."

The roots of the student gangs had really been sown during the Machado dictatorship, but they were richly fertilized in the ensuing disillusionment with "democracy" that followed the strongman. Since the post-Machado administrations controlled by Batista failed to punish those who had abused and killed citizens under the protection of Machado, once Batista left power in 1944 gangs of young men and women arose across the island to do it themselves. These enraged students prided themselves on their courage and excused their violence because they were "revolutionaries." They invented and spoke a formal language of revolution, parts of which only the initiated could know. The sick spirit of this era brought forth surrealistic "heroes" in a society that constantly skirted ever more the bounds of reality. One leader, Jesús González Cartas, was called *El Extraño,* The Strange One, and he received supplicants sitting on a throne with an eerie light illuminating his face.

Meanwhile, Grau, who had entered presidential office in 1944 declaring grandly that it was "the people" who had taken power that day, soon looked away while his appointees formed private armies against the gangs to protect their own areas of graft and special privilege. Grau, who finally left office having allegedly misappropriated more than $174 million, later complained bitterly of the gang members' ingratitude.

From the time of his birth, Fulgencio Batista Zaldivar seemed strangely destined to be the man—his followers called him *El Hombre,* "The Man," denoting his exalted macho—that Fidel Castro would pit himself against. Born near Birán, in that same Oriente where the Castro children had been born and grew up, he had even at one time worked for Angel Castro. But Batista was no Gallego; he was a typical Oriente mix of Indian, black, and

Spanish, a fact that all his life tormented him. His largest accomplishment in early life after joining the new Cuban army was being named a court sergeant-stenographer. But he really came into his own after the successful "Sergeants Revolution" that finally unseated Machado in 1933.

Batista was compellingly handsome in those early days—he had such a sensuous smile that he was nicknamed the "pretty mulatto"—and his dramatic machismo was represented by the dark leather jacket he liked to wear, with of course his handgun in his holster. Formally, Batista was army chief of staff from 1934 to 1940 and, as such, was stronger than any president; then he held the presidency from 1940 to 1944, when he peacefully turned over power. In 1944, Batista's candidate for president lost, and Batista gamely "allowed" Ramón Grau, who had won, to fill the position at the urging of United States ambassador Spruille Braden, who was following FDR's policy of backing democratization in Latin America. Batista then went into comfortable, but temporary, exile in Daytona Beach, Florida.

Occurring as it did against this bitter background of disillusionment and frustrated violence, Fidel's stratagem in shooting Leonel Gómez stands as a case study in the understanding of his abilities for grasping power.

When Fidel entered the university, he began immediately to scrutinize the leaders of the most important gangs—and in their own way they were an impressive lot. Many were men bigger than life and more evil than most. Rolando Masferrer of the MSR, or Movimiento Socialista Revolucionario (Socialist Revolutionary Movement), was to become Batista's worst henchman and most adept killer. He was a natural combatant who had fought, as had so many Cubans, on the Communist side during the Spanish Civil War. A classic figure of dread, he was in the "game" of Cuban violence for power and not for ideology and so he found no problem at all in switching from Spanish republicanism to Batista militarism. Alongside him was the other powerful figure of the MSR, Manolo Castro, who headed the student federation during most of Fidel's time at the university. Manolo Castro obsessed Fidel, who did everything possible to win his favor—but Fidel's idea was to become not his friend but his successor.

The other major gang, the UIR, or Unión Insurreccional Revolucionaria (Insurrectional Revolutionary Union), the gang to which Leonel Gómez belonged, was headed by Emilio Tro, who had fought with the United States forces in the Pacific during World War II. President Grau, knowing he could not control the gangs but wanting to use them for his own pecuniary benefits, often rewarded gang leaders with paid positions for which they did no work. These jobs were called *botellas,* or "little bottles."

But, why did Fidel shoot Leonel Gómez? Fidel shot the UIR leader, in his typical Machiavellian style, in order to get the attention of MSR's Manolo Castro and to ingratiate himself with Manolo in order to enter the MSR and eventually take Manolo's place. But as is usually the case with Fidel, that rather simple reality did not emerge until much later and by that time Fidel's maneuvering had changed and confused the entire picture.

For the truth was that Leonel Gómez did not die. Fidel had shot him in the lung, but he survived after some time in the hospital. Gómez gave Fidel's name, as well as that of Chino Esquivel, to the UIR as those responsible for the attack. Indeed, in a special meeting of the UIR, Fidel was accused of the shooting. But now Fidel's luck, his charisma, his spell, danced once again into play. His original purpose in shooting Gómez was fulfilled, but with an ironic twist. Fidel did not win over Manolo Castro, nor was he invited to join the MSR. He did, however, gain the friendship of Emilio Tro, head of the UIR and (unbelievably) Leonel Gómez's own gang.

"It seemed that Emilio Tro had a certain sympathy for Fidel and, far from acting on the consequences of the aggression suffered by one of his men, Tro was converted into a *padrino* or godfather of Castro," Fidel's friend Max Lesnick summed up. From that moment, Fidel Castro was accepted into the UIR, and he was obviously very pleased with the outcome of his "princely" machinations.

A few days after meeting with Tro, Fidel even showed up at the university in a UIR car to demonstrate his new relationship with the gang. The new pistol that he now carried even more proudly than his old .45 was given to him by Tro. With a little luck and a great deal of savvy, Fidel had graduated from accused "assassin" to close intimate of the "assassinated" man's leader.

But if he had gained a friend in Emilio Tro, he had also alienated the two powerful leaders of the MSR, Rolando Masferrer and Manolo Castro. These two men made no secret of their contempt for Fidel. However, their differences with their hot-tempered, impetuous fellow gangster would be temporarily forgotten in an international episode that would, in effect, be a dress rehearsal for dramas yet to be performed by Fidel Castro.

This time, both Lina and Angel Castro were enraged with their son. They had sent him to all the best schools; they had worked night and day, as Gallego parents do, to educate him; they had given him cars; and they had generously sent him money even while he was playing gangster at the university. But this new development was too much—Fidel, their great hope and their brightest and bravest son, had enlisted in a cockamamy scheme to invade the neighboring Dominican Republic! Most incredibly, the invasion was being organized, on the Cuban side, by Fidel's worst enemies, the hated Rolando Masferrer and Manolo Castro.

The Cayo Confites Expedition, as the invasion came to be known, was headed by Dominican patriot Juan Bosch, an intense and passionate intellectual who had long advocated the overthrow of the despised dictator Rafael Leónidas Trujillo. Now, from his headquarters in a small hotel in Havana, Bosch put together a fascinating and unique political alliance.

Cayo Confites, a *cayo,* or key, much like any of the other sandy and barren spits of land that suddenly spring up from the brilliantly azure waters of this northern part of the Caribbean, was chosen as the spot where a disparate group of men would train for invasion under an unregenerately blazing sun. The expedition marked an historic turning point because never before had Cubans, Dominicans, Venezuelans, and Costa Ricans come together to fight as one Latin American body of fighters. They formed a veritable preview of what Castro himself would create later. Indeed, without knowing it, they were the forerunner of Castro's international revolutionary brigades. But after seeing what happened at Cayo Confites, Fidel would organize his groups with far greater care and caution.

When Angel and Lina got wind of Fidel's planned participation in Cayo Confites, they were beside themselves. They went immediately to Havana and called upon Bosch, who agreed to get in touch with Fidel at Cayo Confites and bring him back for a meeting the next day.

Fidel was in a distinctly defiant mood when he marched into Bosch's hotel room headquarters, and he was already in uniform. Angel showed his disgust immediately at this uncontrollable son, while the observant Bosch carefully watched. Looking suddenly tired, old, and drawn, the usually vigorous Angel stubbornly refused to rise in greeting when Fidel came in, and only looked away. Lina and Fidel's older brother Ramón (colloquially known as "Mongo") both embraced him, but Lina was, as always, clear about her feelings. "It isn't Trujillo who will kill you," she shouted at her son. "It is Masferrer."

But Fidel merely slipped comfortably into that "internationalist" mode that would later serve his ambitions so well, explaining that this was his "duty." At that point, Angel even offered him another automobile—autos seemed to be the stuff of the father-son exchange—and urged him instead to get out and "go to the United States."

But Fidel only drew himself up self-righteously. "You don't seem to realize, Papa," he said solemnly and more than a little pompously, "that Cuba was liberated through the great efforts of a Dominican, General Máximo Gómez. And that we Cubans have a debt of honor with Santo Domingo. I want to pay this debt, and it is because of this that I want to fight against Trujillo. . . ."

When I spoke with José Pardo Llada years later, he told me that Fidel fully believed this. "He is a mystic at times," Pardo said. "And it is certainly true that the idea of 'one Caribbean' with all of the antidictator forces fighting together was a strongly held part of his large passion of global national liberation."

The meeting ended abruptly. Without even saying good-bye, Fidel stalked out and headed back to the remote Cayo Confites, that empty sandy key where twelve hundred men of various nationalities were already in training.

The fact that his enemies from the MSR headed the Cuban force was not really an obstacle. He took care of that problem with his typical instinctive understanding of where to look for sponsorship and how to use power for his own protection. His first action had been to go directly to Juan Bosch, who was particularly won over by the young Cuban's apparently sincere insistence that he wanted "to go to die for the liberty of Santo Domingo." Bosch agreed to talk with the Cuban leaders, Manolo Castro and Rolando Masferrer. With pressure from Bosch, they finally agreed that, yes, Fidel could go to Cayo and moreover that while there, he would be safe, at least from them.

But Fidel, with his incredible sense of where to put pressures and when, took double precautions by also going to Enrique Ovares, the student federation president and a "comandante" of the infant invasion force, to ask him also to speak with Manolo Castro. Ovares relayed to Manolo Fidel's wish for some "guarantee" that he would not be harmed if he joined the expedition. Manolo replied, "Fidel is a shit, but he is right. I am going to speak to all these people and Fidel will go to the camps."

Perhaps Fidel was still not totally convinced, for he now somberly prepared a little "Last Will and Testament."

The gaunt, ethereal, and gentlemanly Bosch had always thought of the traditional Cuban as someone focused "single-mindedly toward the conquest of happiness by the jubilant route of hedonism. The Cuban has a talent for pleasure." But now, on that remote spit of sand, suddenly he saw a wholly new type of Cuban. Many years later, Juan Bosch reminisced with me in Santo Domingo about those days and about the young Fidel Castro he was just then getting to know and whom he would later come to adore.

"One day we were talking and there was a shot. Some began to run around. What had happened was that one man had wounded himself with his gun and his whole stomach was hanging out. We had a medical team who took him immediately. I observed Fidel carefully during all this time. His gaze was fixed on the face of the wounded man. Someone said, 'Put in the stomach,' and there was terror on the face of the man. But Fidel just kept looking, very serious, showing nothing. The man died. It was an accident. But I will always remember that Fidel was very cold and serene. The fact was that he made no demonstration of emotion; and he continues to be that way."

All the leaders of the Caribbean and many of Latin America, populist and new democrat alike, took part in the Cayo Confites expedition: Rómulo Betancourt of Venezuela, Juan José Arévalo of Guatemala, José "Pepe" Figueres of Costa Rica. . . . Despite an underlying violence and mistrust, the disparate group was held together by a rabid hatred for Trujillo; for while the rest of the Caribbean, exemplified by this very expedition, was moving with heady new hope toward forms of representative government, the Dominican Republic under Rafael Leónidas Trujillo stood at that moment as *the* horror of the ancien régime. "Trujillo was no old-fashioned comic-opera Latin caudillo," the American historian John Bartlow Martin wrote. "Except that it lacked an ideology, his was a true modern totalitarian state, complete with racism, espionage apparatus, torture chambers, and murder factories. Trujillo's spies, or informers, were everywhere. And fear was everywhere, a sickness on the land."

In one infamous night, his troops massacred upwards of twelve thousand Haitian workers on the hated and feared Haitian border. He killed people personally at his summer home at Villa Mella and threw their remains into the river. Curiously, he erected a monument to his mulatto mother, a forty-foot-high pole, and when he put his mother's statue on top of it, right over the very spot where he had been born, everyone saw it as the highest symbolic penis on the island of Hispaniola.

But the strength of the Cayo Confites Expedition—that is, the joining together of Cubans, Costa Ricans, Dominicans, and Venezuelans for a single purpose—was also the source of its failure; for everyone in the Caribbean, including most definitely Trujillo himself, knew just about every detail of the well-advertised plan. The situation approached the ludicrous when Trujillo sent a circular note to the governments of the various other South American nations advising them of the entire invasion-in-preparation and calling for "international consultation."

With his uncanny feeling for weaknesses in people and in systems, Fidel early on complained to the others that the expedition was far too public; he was horrified at the lack of secrecy. "He was afraid it would be a total mess," the Dominican Virgilio Mainardi Reyna recalled. Fidel, as usual, was all too right; his fears were almost always his best allies.

Two days before the total collapse and failure of Cayo Confites, the revolutionaries learned that Trujillo's private yacht, the *Angelita,* was traveling slowly and deliberately, like a circling shark, along the north coast of the Oriente. Not unexpectedly, Fidel was one of the first to volunteer for the small group that started out in pursuit in a fast PT boat filled with machine guns and even one light cannon. The little band discovered the luxury yacht fifteen miles from Baracoa, in the extreme east of the island, and leapt aboard it with the flair of seventeenth-century pirates. Though no one really expected to find the Dominican dictator aboard in such an openly vulnerable position, Fidel immediately began shouting, "*¿Dónde está Trujillo? ¿Dónde está Trujillo?*" Where is Trujillo? Where is Trujillo?

Trujillo, of course, was not on board, but that did not for a minute stop Fidel from getting in a parting shot. When the Cayo Confites men left the yacht, he shouted at the Dominican crew in farewell, using Trujillo's nickname, "Chapitas": "And tell Chapitas that he can expect me some day soon to fulfill my promise to kill him." It is noteworthy that within twenty-four days of his triumphant entry into Havana in 1959, Castro was in Venezuela, giving money to still another expedition to overthrow Trujillo. Trujillo eventually was assassinated, but not by Fidel Castro. In another of those ironies of history, it was a group of CIA-backed Dominicans, who hid their guns in the American-owned "Wimpy's" supermarket in Santo Domingo, who finally succeeded in killing Trujillo in 1961.

Sharks—long, gray, slowly circling and encircling sharks. Fidel had nursed a morbid fascination with the sullen and methodically lethal creatures and with their strange and terrible beauty ever since, as a child in Birán, he would travel to the sea, sit with the fishermen, and listen to their tales of hunting sharks. Later the shark came to have a special symbolic importance to Fidel. I once stood with him on the beach near Havana as, surrounded by adoring Cubans, he spoke for hours about the beauty and strength of sharks. But they never had so much reality for him as they did at the end of the Cayo Confites adventure.

Fidel and the other *expedicionarios* were actually en route to Santo Domingo when President Grau ordered them back. The expedition had been called off, even though some of the men were already at sea in a ship they would then cynically call *Fantasma,* or the ghost. Under his agreement with Manolo Castro and with Masferrer, the ending of the expedition meant that the truce was at an end, so Fidel jumped off the ship and swam eight or nine miles through the shark-infested waters of the Bay of Nipe, all the while holding his gun above his head and thus creating an early legend about himself. Others on board ship were taken prisoner by the Cuban military, but not Fidel. To this day, Juan Bosch believes that Fidel jumped ship not only to avoid his gang enemies but to avoid a capture too humiliating for his future ambitions.

Fidel had turned twenty-one on the barren, mosquito-infested Confites Key, with enemies on every side. His first entry into international insurrection had turned into such a farce that his parents were convinced he had "learned" a lesson. The truth was completely the contrary. Cayo Confites was like catnip to an eager tomcat. Cayo Confites showed Fidel how even abject "failures" can be transmogrified into at least partial successes. So, far from being a silly or childish adventure to be discarded when childhood passed, Cayo Confites was Fidel's first step into that "gallant" world of "internationalism" that would rule his life and torment the United States for the next four decades.

There is every indication that Fidel, who all his life showed such little feeling for any individual person, genuinely liked and took to the UIR chief, Emilio Tro. He liked—and mimicked—Tro's control of power. He always quoted Tro, saying in the man's favorite words, "I don't ask any quarter because I don't give any quarter." But even while Fidel was taking bayonet practice under the hot sun of Cayo Confites, Emilio Tro died in the manner in which he, symbolic of that era, chose to live. On September 15, 1947, as he was eating dinner at the home of the chief of police of Marianao, the suburb of Havana where Belén was centered, rival gunmen surrounded the house. After an extraordinary three-hour gun battle comparable to the best—or worst—of Chicago's gangland murder sprees, Tro died with eighteen bullets in his body in what came to be popularly known as not just a normal shooting but a "massacre." When Fidel heard of Tro's murder, he reportedly felt for one of the few times in his life a genuine sense of personal loss.

In the overweaning dialectic of the era, with murder mating with murder to create more murder, Manolo Castro was soon to be next. This quintessential mix of gunman and revolutionary, a mix which Fidel would also study and pattern himself after, died on February 22, 1948, gunned down on the streets of Havana. "Who shot Manolo Castro?" is a question that haunted Fidel's life for many years because there was always the possibility and the suspicion that he took part in the murder. He was, indeed, hanging about the streets that day; and various friends, like Enrique Trueba and Bernardo Viera, saw him and found him unusually nervous and high-strung near the place where Manolo finally died. But research does not indicate that Fidel even shot at Manolo Castro and in fact that question is of importance only because it lived and persisted to become a kind of lightning rod for questions about Fidel's character: Fidel was, in fact, by that time clearly so naturally and so normatively violent that one murder more or less in those days hardly defines his character in any important way.

In the years following Cayo Confites, Fidel began—partly through his supreme intuition and partly through trial and error—to use the power of the newspapers (there were fourteen daily papers in the Cuba of this period!) to manipulate the impressionable people of his troubled country. He was to become, among so many new things, the first truly successful media revolutionary.

Vicente Báez, an activist friend of Fidel's from this period, recalls that when staging a protest, Fidel would wait until the press and the cameras arrived and then get hold of a torch to illuminate his face. When the pictures came out in the newspapers the next day, it would of course be Fidel's face that would command the attention of the reader. On at least one occasion, Fidel faked a police beating to get some of the notice he forever and so insatiably craved. Dr. Richard Martínez Ferrer, who was in residency at the hospital of the University of Havana at the time, recalled: "One night there was a knock on my door, and suddenly Fidel appeared with a huge bandage on his head. It must have been about eight o'clock at night, in 1949 or 1950. He said he needed help. I told him to come in, and he responded immediately, 'About two hours ago, I went to the newspaper office and the police attacked me, and I had to go to the emergency room and a doctor bandaged me. . . .' He asked me if he could stay in the doctors' dorm for the night. . . ." Dr. Martinez was disturbed by the unusual request, but he finally agreed.

When the doctor got up to go to care for a patient, Fidel asked him to bring him back a copy of the *Prensa Libre* newspaper. Dr. Martínez was astounded when he bought the paper, for across the front page a banner headline read: "Student Leader Assaulted by Police." In the upper right-hand corner was a picture of Fidel with the huge bandage encompassing his entire head.

"I returned to the room with the paper," Dr. Martínez told me in Miami in 1984. "I opened the door. Fidel was supposed to be there, waiting for me." He paused and shook his head. "He was there, but without the bandage. I was amazed. 'What happened to you?' I asked him. And he replied that nothing had happened, that he had had to do this to get front page on the paper."

Fidel was not only learning how to use the media, he was soon trying out every possible type of symbolic action in a society that, in the absence of reality, was living more and more drowned in the realms of symbolism and the manipulation of it.

Then, in March of 1949, there occurred an event that was tailor-made for the talents and anger of Fidel Castro. A small group of drunken and rowdy United States Marines clambered boorishly atop the statue of José Martí in the beautiful Central Park of downtown Havana and one of them urinated on it, defaming the sacred memory of Martí, "The Apostle," the inspiration for the great and uncorrupted new Cuba that was being born. The marines barely got out with their lives, and were only gingerly rescued by the Cuban police. The next day, the United States ambassador, Robert Butler, met with the Cuban foreign minister and provided him with a sincere statement of apology. But later, when Butler filmed his apology for the

Cuban people, it was apparent to everyone that he could not even remember Martí's first name.

It was as if Fidel had been waiting for just this sort of event to occur. Immediately, he formed an honor guard, which flanked the statue soberly and angrily all night. The next day, he called for an immediate protest demonstration at the U.S. embassy. The student protesters walked from the university to the American embassy, Fidel's group moving ahead with rocks held taut in their pockets. When they were about half a block away, they began throwing stones at the windows, creating a huge ruckus before running to the Bahia Restaurant in front of Havana Bay, where they watched the police cars rushing to the embassy, their sirens blaring.

In a further gesture of apology, the Americans put a wreath of flowers at the statue, and Ambassador Butler agreed to meet with the students. Indeed, the newspapers covered the meeting and even ran a picture of Butler with some of the young Cubans. This marked the first time that Fidel Castro's name appeared in the Cuban press in a really important way. It was also proof, if any more were needed, that the young leader knew not only how to use events to his advantage but also how to create events of his own. But this was a first—it was the first time Castro used the anti-American sentiment in Cuba to evoke a response from the hated *americanos*.

6

A PARENTHESIS

Con esa muchacha me voy a casar. [This is the girl
I am going to marry.]

—Fidel Castro, when he met Mirta

FIDEL'S COURTING of Mirta Díaz-Balart, the lovely green-eyed girl with the dark blond hair and the wistful smile, from one of Cuba's wealthiest families, marked the period in his life that was closest to a time when he lived like a relatively normal man, one who felt and acted on simple and even pure and uncalculated feelings. The courtship took place at the university, to the staccato of guns and killings. But there were also lazy, drowsy summer days on the languorous Puerto Rico Beach in Mirta's hometown of Banes. There were simple joyous days—and nights—when this girl from a very proper, if also troubled, family was always properly chaperoned. In later years, the idea of "Fidel Castro" being chaperoned could only strike one as the extreme of the unlikely or the ludicrous, but those were different days.

But even then, behind the relative normalcy, there moved always the shadow both of the violence of the time and of the violence of Fidel Castro. Behind the deep love Mirta felt for the vigorous young "god," with his curly brown hair, his broad shoulders, and his aquiline Gallego nose, lurked always the warning of the ruin and tragedy he would bring to her life, as indeed he brought it to nearly all the women who became close to him.

Fidel met the young Mirta one day when her brother, the rightfully ambitious Rafael Díaz-Balart, introduced them at the busy, politicized, unkempt law school cafeteria. Mirta was then an innocently but also sensuously pretty and dedicated student of philosophy and letters. Her professors recall her as being as committed and disciplined a student as Fidel was not. Even the most anti-Castro observers recall the meeting as love at first sight.

Filled with a lusty and indiscriminate sensuality, Fidel was even then extremely attractive to women. But on dates, he bored because he would never stop talking politics, recalled his friend of the time, Emilio Caballero. "I do think he was in love with Mirta," Caballero told me one March afternoon in Miami. "But many times, he had a date but didn't go because of political meetings."

Perhaps what puzzled his friend most was that Fidel—unlike virtually every other Cuban man of that time—never danced. He didn't like flowers, he didn't like animals, and he didn't like singing. But not dancing was the worst—it was a sacrilege in Cuba, not to dance! But dancing was revealing, dancing was humanizing, dancing was equalizing, and Fidel abhorred revealing himself or putting himself ever on the same level as others.

His friend Max Lesnick recalled Fidel's inordinate shyness and awkwardness with women. On one occasion, he and Fidel were in Havana when three "very pretty, very well-dressed young women" walked up to them to ask a question. Lesnick remembered that Castro behaved "with incredible shyness. This man who was capable of discussion with a youth, an old man, a politician, or a student, froze in front of these girls."

There was another side of Fidel with women—a cruel and mocking side that would remain with him all his life. Friends recall that Fidel once dated—cynically pursued, in truth—an extremely ugly, pockfaced woman from the youth group of the progressive Orthodox party. This woman was of interest to Fidel only because she controlled certain key party votes. They had an affair, and he presumably got what he wanted, for once her political use to him was over, he made the most vulgar and ugly remarks to everyone about her.

Throughout his life, Fidel had fiery political ambitions, but his sexuality was cold and calculating. Women were to be used, coolly and most often quickly, qualities which some observers felt came out of the Jesuits' teaching about the consummate "sinfulness" of sex. With Mirta, at least at first, it was different. She had about her that ardent, languorous, romantic dreaminess that seemed to cling to all of her family. Soft-spoken and cultured, she had the startlingly beautiful Díaz-Balart eyes which, in her brothers, reflected a deep and vigorous sensuality. She, Waldo, Frank, and Rafael were a handsome brood—but they were not a happy one, despite the fact and finally because of the fact that their father was the respected mayor of the United Fruit town of Banes, the lawyer of Batista, and a middle-class man of substance.

Nothing could have possibly excited all the ambitions, all the complexes, and all the resentments of Fidel more than this single woman. For in her he found personified not only a valiant family of the war for independence, but also the entire most inner nexus of Batista power and the most egregious extension of American power in Cuba, if not the Caribbean. Only sixty miles away from the rustic and squabbling Birán where he was born, there existed the world of Banes that might as well have been on another planet. Banes was the very "American" world of the sugar industry, of the aggressive and triumphant United Fruit Company, the scion of the "American Century."

"Few places in Cuba were quite so dominated by the North American presence," the historian Hugh Thomas noted. Here, instead of the enveloping dark forests that Angel cut away with so much sweat, were luxurious lawns and impressive tropical homes. Here American and Cuban employees of United Fruit played polo, swam in their pleasant swimming pools, and shopped in boutiques for American goods, which arrived regularly and smartly by ship. Here one found in Mirta's Banes a burgeoning and upward-striving middle class of Cubans who lived like Americans, prayed like Americans (many, including Rafael Díaz-Balart, became Protestants), and expected more out of life like Americans. Banes had more ties to New York than to Havana.

Nor were the Americans modest or apologetic about their claims on Cuban land: it was, after all, Manifest Destiny, it was their civilizing duty.

Banes was actually two towns, divided by a bridge over a small river: "Overtown," which was the Cuban side of town, with its own elected mayors and council, and "Colonia Americana," the American town. (*Colonia* meant only "town" and had no connotations of "colony.") Everybody used the beaches and the golf course, and on the Fourth of July, the Americans and the Cubans held a huge picnic at the American Club. Indeed, life in Banes in those days was remembered by nearly everyone in later and more troubled years as a rare, halcyon existence, a special era caught in time like a moment of Cuban Camelot.

Reflecting still further the divisions and complexities of the Cuba of those times, Mirta's family had a home in each of the two towns of Banes. Her grandmother kept the Cuban house with her uncle and two cousins, and the immediate Díaz-Balart family lived formally in the Colonia Americana house. "We would go back and forth between the two houses," her brother Waldo, who was closest both in age and in feeling to Mirta, described it to me.

Life was fun in Banes, life was positivistic, life was American and therefore the future! Mirta's childhood boyfriend, Jack Skelly, brought back a record for her once of a song then very popular in the States, "Queenie of the Burlesque Show." And when Mirta walked down the aisle at her graduation from the Quaker high school, that was the song they were playing.

The problem for the Díaz-Balart children, and especially for Mirta, was Angélica, the classically "evil" stepmother. "There was that bad situation between Angélica and Mirta," Waldo recalled, with a sadness that remained even after so many years. "Angélica was very neurotic. On Sundays, we went to the Catholic Church and then came home and became spiritists. Angélica practiced spiritism—she talked to the spirits—and it was very frightening to see as a child. She talked to the glasses. . . . Oh, it was terrible," he added.

Angélica's "spiritism" was actually part of the forbidden Santería religion brought to Cuba by the native African slaves. Santería had no real structure of power; in this and in many other respects, its prevalence in Cuba, even among white Cubans, presented a vacuum that a "man of magic" such as Fidel Castro was to become could easily fill. "You need to go into Cuban native religion and see how that psychologically made it possible for the believers to accept Fidel as a total leader," Waldo suggested perceptively one day in Madrid in 1985.

The domineering Angélica, with her piercing black eyes and her hair pulled severely back behind a strong forehead, kept Mirta tied to her every and most fickle call. Friends would shake their heads in sadness and in anger as they saw how Mirta, planning to go out, would be peremptorily called back to care for Angélica when at the last moment the woman predictably would develop "a headache." They talked even then about the possibility that Mirta saw marriage to Fidel as a "way out." But Mirta, always the proper lady, never complained.

A PARENTHESIS

Mirta and Fidel tried to stay out of Angélica's way. They would meet secretly at the house of Mirta's friend Barbara Gordon, which was cater-corner from the Díaz-Balart house. Like the other homes there, Barbara's had a well-kept lawn, bordered with palm trees and flowers. In that long-ago, in those romantic evenings filled with such promise, in that manicured town, Mirta and Fidel would stand in Barbara's garden or sit on a bench and talk about their future life together.

The routine of the young couple now flowed back and forth between the still-savage milieu of the Castros' Birán and Banes. If Mirta actually liked the huge and rustic Castro farm, as she always cheerfully said she did, Fidel by all accounts was in a kind of constant inner—and, often enough, outer—rage about her Banes. The Americanophile town represented everything he hated, which was in part what attracted him to Mirta and carried him in his resentment even into the extraordinarily inappropriate state of matrimony. In Banes lay everything he would smite and destroy—but, in a real sense, also desire to embody.

It can hardly be seen as accidental that all of the women Fidel became deeply involved with were of one precise profile: all were upper class, Americanized, English-speaking, beautiful (most, but not all, were blond), and from "old families" who had fought against the Spaniards. With these women, he could act out on both the most refined and the most primitive levels the drama of his personal politics, his vendetta against the United States, his anger against his domineering father, and his hatred of the "traitorous" Cuban middle class.

Now, as he visited Mirta in Banes, his rage seemed to focus on United Fruit's Puerto Rico Beach. Along this long, white stretch of pristine beach, the Boy Scouts, American Club party-goers, Girl Scouts, volunteers, and money-raisers for good causes à la the American way of Banes came to play. Fidel was in a constant state of fury because there were fences all around the beach, and gates, all maintained and duly overseen by United Fruit. In truth, a key was needed for the first gate (of several) only, and almost anyone could get one from the fruit company. But this tolerant ease of entry, like all the half-colonial measures of United Fruit, seemed only to obsess him the more. Those gates would often drive him to early harangues that presaged his later speeches and at those times Mirta would simply lapse into embarrassed silence or look away. After he came to power, one of the first things he did was to unlock the gates.

Fidel's always lurking violence also began now to surface in strangely dark ways. One day he went hunting and shot an albatross. This in itself was an unusual act, because shooting or harming these "good" birds in any way was considered bad luck. Fidel, however, who often enough spurned common beliefs, chose not to heed the warning of the Ancient Mariner. He not only shot and killed the beautiful bird, he dragged it back to Banes and threw it in the back window of Jack Skelly's kitchen while a group of Mirta's friends were there. The poor dying creature landed on the stove, terrifying everyone.

Indeed, the violent side of Fidel's nature seemed in those days already to be deepening into a cold contempt for even the simplest living creature. One day, in later years, Fidel, Rafael Díaz-Balart, and Rolando Amador, another politically ambitious friend, were driving in Fidel's car to a political meeting, where each was going to speak. "We were on a part of the road of the central highway that was completely deserted," Rolando Amador recalled. "Suddenly Fidel said, 'I'm going to practice my shooting.' He had a .45 caliber pistol." Rafael, too, recalled the bucolic scene that Fidel then assaulted and shattered. "There were these beautiful cows out in the field," Rafael remembered. "He got out of the car and took his gun and began to shoot them. When I asked him why, he said that he was practicing. That was how easily he could later shoot informers."

Fidel and Mirta were married on October 10, 1948, the same day that Carlos Prío Socarrás was inaugurated president of Cuba, succeeding Ramón Grau. The marriage looked splendid on the surface: two handsome young people, both of well-to-do families, both educated, very much in love with each other and filled with idealistic yet realizable hopes. How "right" it all seemed to those who witnessed the wedding. But the shadows were not only closing in on this seemingly blessed couple, they were right there in the church for Fidel was still being threatened by the gangs in Havana. So as Mirta and Fidel spoke their vows, many who watched them were terrified that one of Fidel's ever-lurking enemies would attack. But not Fidel. As they were leaving on their honeymoon, he amusedly opened the valise he was carrying. Inside was a pistol. "I'm not worried," he told his friends. "I have this, and I had it with me at the altar." The wedding was ironically listed in the *haute* upper-class paper, *Diario de la Marina,* and some wags said that thusly Fidel had "finally achieved what he wanted" socially, too.

With the election of Carlos Prío Socarrás, the year 1948 ended on a note of hope for the island of Cuba. And that hope reflected the times. Scores of formerly colonized countries were becoming independent with such speed that mapmakers could barely keep up with their new contours: India, Pakistan, Burma, the Philippines . . . The Allies were trying to rebuild the postwar world with a United Nations, with a Marshall Plan for Europe, with the modernizing of Japan, and with aid to Turkey and Greece to fight Communist influences there.

It was also in these years of the late 1940s that Fidel could watch the Soviet Union in particular and Communism in general move with a ruthless and apocalyptic new certainty across the globe. It was in 1948, the year of the Castros' marriage, that the Communists staged a coup and took over Czechoslovakia. In 1949, East Germany established its own Communist government and George Orwell's *1984* was published. Having withdrawn from most of their other colonies, the French, with stubborn foolhardiness, insisted upon staying in Vietnam.

While the Castros' wedding trip had some of the little eccentric trademarks of Fidel, it also revealed him in a brief and unprecedented fling with bourgeois life, paid for, as everything in his life, by someone else. The senior Rafael Díaz-Balart, Mirta's father, had given the young couple ten thousand dollars for a three-month honeymoon in that most symbolically American of cities, New York. Pocket money in the amount of a thousand dollars had been provided by none other than Fulgencio Batista, who in 1948 was nothing more than a former president in exile in Daytona Beach and a friend of both families.

There was more than one reason, however, for Fidel's going to New York at this time. The wedding offered a perfect excuse for getting him out of the gun sights of the gangs in Havana. Furthermore, going to New York was a kind of sacred pilgrimage for him, a way of confirming his messianic vision of himself. For hadn't "The Apostle" himself, Martí, also left Cuba to engage in his patriotic work in New York?

The newlyweds began their honeymoon in Miami, then moved by train to New York, in December of 1948. "I am not going to deny that I enjoyed some of Miami's magnificent comforts," Fidel later told his friend Carlos Franqui. "For the first time, I knew a T-bone steak, smoked salmon, and those things that I, a youth with a big appetite, appreciated a lot."

In New York, Fidel used part of the ten thousand dollars to buy a white Lincoln Continental whose door opened—sign of the times—at the touch of a button. "He only had the money to buy a new car, like a Pontiac," Rafael Díaz-Balart related years later, "but Fidel fell in love with his enormous Lincoln, it was *grandissimo*, huge. . . ."

Mirta's sloe-eyed and handsome brother, Rafael, had married a lovely, sweet woman, Hilda, only a few months before, and was now living in New York. As one of a small but progressive band of Cuban Protestants, he was attending Princeton Theological Seminary and for a time he was a minister in Lower East Side Manhattan at a church that had three congregations: Puerto Rican, White Russian, and American. But he soon gave up the pastor's life and, like his closest friend Fidel, went passionately into the politics that would make them mortal enemies. But that was then still in the dim future.

Fidel and Mirta asked "Rafa" and Hilda to get them a furnished room in the same building where they lived on 82nd Street. By all accounts, the honeymoon was happy—even rapturously happy—if fleetingly so. Fidel tried during this time to learn better English—indeed, he simply took a dictionary and determined to memorize two hundred words a day—but he never did learn really good English.

Fidel's responses to the United States that he hated so totally on an abstract and political level were curious indeed every time he came face to face with the powerful and exuberant nation. He admired the great cities, and at one point his critical judgments were momentarily stymied when he was able to buy a copy of Karl Marx's *Das Kapital* openly in a New York bookstore. He saw "the contradiction between the furious anti-Communist spirit of the times in the States and the fact that you could buy editions of Marx in a bookstore in New York." But later he resolved his questioning in an appropriately dialectical manner by deciding that imperialism had so much power that "in reality the presence of Marxist books in a bookstore threatened them little."

Rafael and Hilda returned to Cuba from Miami by plane, while Fidel and Mirta took the slower route by ferry from Key West. The young newlyweds watched the coast of the *americanos* fade slowly and definitively out of sight as the boat churned its way toward Cuba across the narrow channel of those mere but symbolic miles that separated the two peoples, before Fidel himself would close it.

Despite the internal social and political problems of the Cuba of this era, these were wonderful days for young politicized Cubans and their dreams. "We were making plans," Rafael Díaz-Balart told me years later. "Who would arrive at power first? Who would be president of Cuba?" He and Fidel were very close in those years. They were friends; they were brothers-in-law. "In 1948, we had this type of relationship." He shook his head. "And then, ten years later, he entered power and I had to go into exile forever because of him. If someone had told us that at this time. . . ."

Fidel and Mirta soon established themselves in a series of small apartments in Havana and Vedado. José Pardo Llada recalled that at one point Fidel deliberately and typically moved into an apartment directly in front of a military camp where the streets Primera and Paseo came together and where there was a permanent guard of up to ten soldiers. "This is the place that offers me the greatest guarantees for my life," Pardo recalled Fidel telling him, smiling broadly from their little balcony. It was typical "young Fidel" instinct and the act incorporated his sardonic "humor"; he was already using the constituted society he so abhorred to protect him, even as he was beginning his campaign to destroy it.

Their friends remember Fidel and Mirta at this time as a very happy couple, and they recall that in the beginning Fidel treated Mirta well, even protectively, in the old macho Cuban sense. "They were in love with each other," Chino Esquivel told me. "Fidel was handsome, and when he wants to be polite . . . he is the best." But those ephemeral days were not to last. Fidel somehow never really got around to getting a paying job and continued to rely on money from Mirta's father and monthly checks from Angel. But the fathers were also beginning to tire of supporting him, and Mirta began desperately to need money. In addition to that, within three months of their marriage, she found herself pregnant.

Mirta's neighbor and old boyfriend Jack Skelly recalled the time he spent with Mirta and Fidel that summer back in Banes. "I hadn't seen Mirta for four years," he reminisced nostalgically of the young woman he had loved so much. "She was about six months pregnant. I went up and gave her a big peck on the cheek, and she was very happy to see me. Every night, practically, we played dominoes—canasta was the rage that year—by hurricane lamp, arguing. . . . We went fishing, and hunting, and Fidel was always with a gun, with a pistol. He shot at me four times with a .22 while I was swimming. . . ."

At the end of that lazy summer in Banes, when events appeared so deceptively calm on the surface, the Castros' first and only son was born. As was Cuban practice, this firstborn was named after his father and immediately nicknamed "Fidelito." The interpretation given to the event by the curious and largely unknown first biography of Fidel Castro is worth noting. The book, *Fidel Castro, Biografía,* was written in the winter of 1959, immediately after Fidel's *triunfo,* and not only was it published in Havana and written by the well-known biographer Gerardo Rodríguez Morejón, it was written with the acknowledged aid of Fidel's mother, Lina Castro, before her disenchantment with her victorious son. As with the illegitimacy of the Castro children, the story of Fidel's marriage and of his devotion to his new son seems out of some Disney-like dreamworld of the kind that Fidel would strive always to keep around his personal self: "New sentimental perspectives were opened for this young man who, despite his impetuosity and his firmness of character, is a young man noble and sentimental. Fatherhood offers the most powerful reasons for his family affection, and the angelical charms of the little newly-born charmed him completely." This idyllic portrait of Fidel as father and family man is stunningly far from the truth.

In reality, as the first enchantment with the new child wore off, relations between Mirta and Fidel became more and more strained. Now there was almost no money at all, for Fidel ever more persistently disdained working. Less and less did he even come home to eat, preferring to have chop suey with his political friends at El Pacífico, a favorite Chinese restaurant. Friends noticed that, when he did come home, he would often bring his most distasteful political pals with him and insist thoughtlessly that Mirta cater to them until the early hours of the morning.

Mirta struggled valiantly and cheerfully to keep things going, but the fact was that she now often had no milk for the chubby Fidelito and that friends often had to lend her money when the electricity was shut off for lack of payment. It was increasingly humiliating to her quiet pride. She knew that even when Fidel did have money, he never spent it on his family, a trait he shared with most of the charismatic leaders of history.

It was in those days of 1949, the year of his son's birth, that Fidel began to exhibit—in ways so strange and obsessive they were almost surrealistic—an amateurish and thus even more dangerous fascination with genetics. It is impossible to pinpoint the exact moment this fascination began, but

Rafael Díaz-Balart remembered an incident from Fidelito's babyhood that clearly foreshadows what was to become a consuming passion that aimed at not merely gaining control over human beings but over nature itself.

Fidelito had been the healthiest of babies when suddenly he became gravely ill. The pediatrician came, and he was deeply alarmed, but at the same time he could find nothing specifically wrong with the child. The family was worried—and bewildered. Then Mirta discovered that Fidel, on his own and quite deliberately, had been feeding the child three times the amount of formula he was supposed to have. When she confronted him with this fact, Fidel simply answered matter-of-factly that he wanted the child to grow "big" faster, that he should be "stronger" than other children. Shocked, she stopped the overfeeding, and when it occurred again several months later, she knew by then what it was.

"Fidel never knew how to love," Jorge Valls, the talented thinker and poet of the Revolutionary Student Directorate, told me years later. "Giving himself was something he didn't know. He was too worried about his theatrical role." Which makes it all the more amazing that Fidel ever married Mirta or anyone at all. Certainly, Mirta was his one and only attempt to love any one person, to place his trust and affection in one human creature. "Fidel tried a respectable marriage, which failed; he tried respectable politics, which failed," Dr. Marcelino Feal, the canny Cuban psychiatrist, analyzed. "Society ignored him, so he became society to form it in his own creation."

On Fidel's ability to love, American writer Gene Vier wrote, "Castro . . . demonstrates another characteristic of the charismatic, that no single person represents an absolute value. They are always seeking the universal, which implies a detachment from the particular, a detachment that pervades Castro's friendships—no particular person has an absolute value for him." The charismatic leader cannot have a wife, cannot be seen to care for another individual or for his children, cannot give himself to another person. The true charismatic leader is a vehicle, a human sieve, a "purifying" agent, through which the soul and spirit of his people passes: there cannot be anyone standing between this sacred exchange and complaining of rent money or milk for the baby. Asked "What if Hitler were to marry?" the great psychoanalyst C. G. Jung once said clearly, "He cannot marry. If he married, it would not be Hitler marrying. He would cease to be Hitler. Hitler was no real *personal* psychology. Hitler cannot give a promise. There is no person there to give the promise! He is the megaphone which voices the mood or the psychology of the eighty million German people."

In his later life, Castro would instinctively understand these imperatives of the myth and spell of the charismatic leader—and always act brilliantly upon them. He would hide his marriage from the Cuban people, and indeed from the world. Fidel's analysts and early biographers not only accepted but connived in guarding the secret, in part because they too were under the spell of the *líder máximo*. "Virtually nothing is known of the circumstances of this marriage, which was fated to be destroyed by politics within five years," Tad Szulc wrote typically in his 1986 biography of Castro.

Yet, that "mystery" of the marriage, like all the "mysteries" about Fidel, was no mystery at all; alert and watchful people were there with him at each and every turning point. The absence of personal information which would make Fidel a man, and not just a myth, made him seem unknowable and therefore omnipotent. That was the idea, of course, and Fidel manipulated it masterfully. Dr. Marcelino Feal explained it: "This is the way he keeps power and strength. Mystery keeps him from losing."

7

THE *BOGOTAZO*

No soy un hombre, soy un pueblo. [I am not a man,
I am a people.]
—Jorge Eliecer Gaitán

A BIG SENSUOUS MAN with hypnotic eyes and a charismatic style of speaking that drew the very soul out of the suffering poor of Colombia, Jorge Eliecer Gaitán was at the heady zenith of his political career on that fateful April 9, 1948. That morning, which was to be his last, the big rugged populist who was considered the political hope of Colombia paused to lean over his desk in his law office in the Edificio Nieto in downtown Bogotá to scrawl on his small calendar pad a reminder about a rushed lunch with the Venezuelan democrat Rómulo Betancourt. Then, curiously enough, underneath, in words that would long bewilder history, he wrote down two other names: "Fidel Castro" and "Rafael del Pino." The two Cuban students would be stopping by to see him that afternoon between two and two-fifteen.

Gaitán stood at that moment as the indisputable leader of the Liberal party of Colombia, the reformist party in a country burdened singularly by all the old ills of Spanish America: Hispanic authoritarianism, rigid landed aristocracy, and a Middle Ages Catholic Church. As Gaitán sat at his desk that April morning, Colombia's historic fight with the antediluvian Conservative party was boiling up to its final bitter battle of wills and of beliefs.

And everyone predicted that Gaitán, the "man of the people," would win the elections that year. Gaitán's mission was to reform and transform a backward and retrogressively rigid society into a progressive, forward-thinking one, and while the populace loved him, the Conservatives were narrowing their eyes and whispering to one another in the alleys and boulevards of Bogotá that this "firebrand must never be permitted to come to power."

Bogotá is a quintessentially dark city, it lies high in the most somber and lumpen parts of the Andes, and it seems always to be covered with a kind of shroud. But this day it was festooned with flags for the hosting of the Ninth International Conference of American States, which was to create the regional organization of the U.N., the Organization of American States. President Truman's secretary of state, George Marshall, was attending, as were all the foreign ministers of the Americas. But underneath the incongruously "gay" atmosphere in this brooding city, other goals were being set and other promises were being made. In Bogotá, where there were twenty to thirty assassinations a day, plots and counterplots multiplied like dark clouds, and political rumors continually wafted through the coffeehouses.

Wearing his suede jacket and big loose pants (dressed up, for him), Fidel Castro had arrived in Bogotá on March 29 with three other Cuban students, Rafael del Pino, FEU president Enrique Ovares, and the Communist Alfredo Guevara. They were there to meet with sympathetic Leftist Colombian students to make final plans for a hemisphere-wide anti-imperialistic and anti-American student congress that was to take place as a kind of counterconference to the "American" meeting that was being held in the dignified capitol building. Indeed, it was the Argentine dictator, Juan Perón, who sponsored their trip, in a show of populist-Leftist solidarity. So when Gaitán learned of the students' plans, he agreed to meet with them and to help them. Years later, I spoke with Gaitán's daughter, Gloria, about her father's attitude toward the students, and she told me simply that "Fidel was part of a group of Colombian students who had the great support of Papa. My father was going to give them a *salón de asamblea* in one of the public buildings for their student congress." This beautiful, raven-haired woman then paused for a moment, remembering. "Fidel also later spoke to me about the meeting," she added, finally. "He told me that my father had impressed him greatly, that he was a man of great force who could touch and stir the people."

Fidel and Rafael del Pino met with Gaitán at 10:30 A.M. on Wednesday, the seventh of April. Fidel, showing clearly his native confidence, did not appear to be in any way disconcerted at being in the presence of one of the great Latin American leaders and he spoke to him grandiloquently about the anticolonial objectives of the student congress. "Gaitán grew very enthused about the idea of the congress," Fidel said later, "and he offered us his support. He conversed with us, and he was totally in agreement with the idea of closing the congress with a great mass demonstration."

Gaitán, who was physically as well as rhetorically compelling, seeming almost to burst out of his tight suits and vests with sheer animal energy, made a second appointment with the two young Cubans for the afternoon of April 9. He gave them copies of some of his speeches with handwritten, personal dedications, and bade them farewell.

Approximately fifty minutes before the Cuban students were to meet again with Gaitán, the popular leader walked out of his office building, late but presumably on his way to meet Venezuelan leader Rómulo Betancourt. But Gaitán never kept that luncheon appointment. A poorly dressed mestizo Colombian named Juan Roa walked up to him and shot him several times.

Guillermo Pérez Sarmiento, director of the United Press office in Colombia, was lunching at the Tivoli Bar, across the street, when he heard the voice of the crowd chanting as one, *"Mataron a Gaitán, mataron a Gaitán."* "They've killed Gaitán, they've killed Gaitán." He ran from the bar to the spot where Gaitán, his friend, lay dying. "I bent over in consternation and cried out, 'My God, what has happened, Jorge?' "Pérez related. "I touched his face, but he did not open his eyes . . . I could see that he was lying in an enormous pool of blood. . . . He opened his eyes and contracted his mouth in a grimace which seemed to me to be a smile. Then he closed them again. I will never be able to forget this glance filled with sorrow and sweetness. . . ."

Pérez then saw the assassin, who was being held by two desperate policemen. He had a greenish face and was gripped by panic. Although Pérez and others tried to keep the assassin alive, if only for "useful" purposes, they were unable to control the hysterical crowd, which moved in and quickly and savagely beat the man to death. At this moment the city exploded in the way that only rigid and authoritarian societies finally explode. All the rage and hopelessness inside a smoldering people was suddenly ignited, and the "fire" spread across Bogotá like a blackened blot of blood across a human body. The *Bogotazo,* or a kind of "frenzy" in Bogotá, as the two days of madness which followed the death of Gaitán came to be called, would come to be synonymous with apocalyptic violence.

It is at this moment, too, that Fidel's behavior, and emotions, and above all analysis of the situation became so revelatory. He and the other Cuban students were sitting in an open-air café around the corner from Gaitán's office. "You've got to realize that the scene was completely chaotic," Enrique Ovares recalled later. "It was utter madness. Guevara and I decided to get off the street and walk back to our boardinghouse. Fidel and Del Pino claimed they were going back to the hotel." Ovares didn't see Fidel again until four that afternoon, when a street mob swept by the boardinghouse, shouting, *"Al palacio, al palacio . . ."* "To the palace, to the palace . . ."

"Fidel, armed with a rifle, was part of the horde," Ovares related. "So was Rafael, but I don't remember seeing any gun on him. Fidel was excited, very excited, and acting like a hysterical demagogue. He tried to persuade us to join them, saying, 'The police have come in with us and are giving us arms. The army will line up with us any moment now.' I didn't want to go. It would have been crazy and just asking to be shot by someone in that drunken mob. . . . Castro rejoined the mob, drunk with the looting, burning and shooting."

Over and over, to describe those incredible scenes Fidel later used hydric symbolism: the Colombian people were an ever-moving "ocean," a "sea" of humans flowing over the city, a "river" raging inexorably through the streets, a "torrent," an "upsurge," a "deluge." One can see and hear clearly here the echoing predecessor of Fidel's later "masses" of "the people," for Fidel already responded to action by the masses; he never understood individual effort and conscience and, indeed, there was nothing in his life to force him to do so. It was at this moment, further, that his actions begin to pattern themselves into a moving revolutionary collage as, moving about Bogotá in this violent "high," he intuitively touched or tried to touch every lever of power.

First he moved with the now-murderous crowd toward the capitol, a big, formal, gray building, its incongruously gay flags frozen in time in this half-light of revolution. There he waited and watched as the multitude thronged past the helpless police, and destroyed almost totally the inside of the historic capitol. From there, Fidel ran with the crowd to the parliament, where he watched an "eruption." "Because it was that," he wrote later, "an eruption of the people. . . ."

Now the cadence of physical movement and symbolic motion picked up, as the crowd headed for the police station, the third center of power Fidel confronted that day. The mob poured into the station, trying to find weapons; all Fidel found was a tear-gas gun and several cartridges. He entered a room filled with men standing around looking demoralized and panicky. Suddenly he realized that they were police officers, and he asked them if they had any weapons or army fatigues. "I was not dressed for a war," he recalled later. So he sat down on a cot and began pulling on a pair of old army boots when suddenly one of the officers started ludicrously screaming at him: "Not my boots! Not my boots!" "Fine, *señor,* keep your boots," Fidel shouted back, almost merrily. Then he rejoined the crowd, which struck him as being like some gigantic amoeba that formed, flowed, and reformed, "as if set in motion by a spring."

The sense of humor that Fidel occasionally had in his life was shown by the fact that, years later, after he had taken power, it was the "boots" story that he recalled to Gloria Gaitán when he reminisced with her in Cuba over the *Bogotazo.* "The only story that Fidel told me was that the police wouldn't let him take those boots," Gloria told me, smiling suddenly at the curious memory.

Out on the streets again, Fidel watched as wild-eyed students carried the bodies of their dead comrades atop their cars like revolutionary banners. But, despite his excitement, as he wandered the city, he became increasingly disturbed by the rampant looting. When night fell, he got into a jeep with some police officers who seemed sympathetic to the revolutionary forces, and they started downtown, the chief in the first jeep and Fidel in the second. Fidel, always acutely sensitive to positioning, considered himself "practically his deputy now." But when the first jeep broke down, Fidel, who was becoming more and more enraged by the incomprehensible lack of organization in the country, was nearly beyond himself with fury. He got out of his jeep and yelled at the police he had been riding with, "You are all a bunch of damned irresponsibles." Then he stalked off.

Finally he joined a company forming in the central courtyard of a building. He immediately began a discussion with the police chief there on the tactical errors they were making. "I explained that I was from Cuba," Fidel reminisced later, "and knew, from what had happened there, that forces garrisoned like ours in a fortress were always crushed. Why not take the offensive, lead the men out in columns, and set up positions at strategic points? My advice or my attempts to convince him were useless. He heard me out in a friendly, appreciative way, but couldn't make up his mind. . . ."

By morning, Fidel began wondering precisely what it was that he was doing in Bogotá. Should he stay? He began to think of the adventure as a "futile mission." Cut off from the other Cubans, he wondered what it was that tied him to the Colombian people. Finally he resolved his questioning by telling himself, "Okay, the people here are just like those in Cuba or anywhere else: they are the victims of crimes, abuses, injustices; and these people are absolutely in the right, so I'll stay."

It was Sunday morning now, April 11, but no church bells tolled over the darkened city. At least five thousand lay dead and a third of the city was in ashes, burned to the ground.

That Sunday, Fidel and his group flew humbly home to Cuba in a plane that had arrived in Bogotá to pick up some prize bulls for a bullfight in Havana. In the ashes of the city they left behind, the Pan American Conference doggedly dragged on. The delegates met in the garage of a private home because they couldn't meet downtown. They put up twenty to twenty-five folding chairs, and that was where the Organization of American States, to become Fidel's nemesis, was founded. Fidel's part in the *Bogotazo* almost immediately became the stuff of legend—and endless conjecture. Rightists accused him of being an agent of the Comintern; they accused the Colombian Communist party of planning the *Bogotazo;* they brought forth an amorous letter from Mirta, then Fidel's fiancée, which said in part, "Remember that you told me that you were going to Bogotá in order to provoke the outbreak of a revolution." The missive was dated April 3, 1948, six days before the *Bogotazo.*

No one less than the U.S. ambassador to the United Nations, founder of Cubana Airlines, William D. Pawley, testified that after Gaitán's death, he had heard a voice on the radio saying, "This is Fidel Castro from Cuba. This is a Communist revolution. The president has been killed, all the military establishments in Colombia are now in our hands, the navy has capitulated to us and this revolution has been a success."

Yet, none of this makes any real sense, and every serious student of the times dismisses such allegations. The Colombian government brought in a Scotland Yard investigator, who could find no evidence of Communist leadership in the tragedy. Logically, too, had the Communists been involved, with their organization and with their proven ability to use mobs, they would have had the cadres ready to overthrow Colombia's tottering and unpopular Conservative government. They did not. Nor is there any evidence that Fidel was anything but the fervent nationalist and anti-American agitator that he seemed.

Who, then, was behind the murder of Jorge Eliecer Gaitán? Gloria Gaitán and most historians are convinced that, logically and in terms of the evidence, Gaitán was killed by the Colombian far Right, by some conspiracy of oligarchic conservatives. But for Fidel, the *Bogotazo* was another dress rehearsal in internationalism, more violent and defining this time than Cayo Confites. For Fidel, the *Bogotazo* was a vein of gold of revolutionary lessons. In Bogotá, for the first time, he saw mass violence, analyzed it, and began to try to control it. For the first time, he realized the importance of defeating the traditional army; over and over afterward, he stressed to his people, "All of history demonstrates that a force that remains in its barracks is lost." Genuinely shocked by the looting, not surely because capitalists were being robbed but because it demeaned the "masses" in his terms of that Hispanic honor which preceded glory, he would later constantly remind Cubans never to do anything like that.

But he learned something even more important from the *Bogotazo*. In his memoirs, Fidel repeats again and again his apparently genuine wonderment over the terrible lack of organization. "I can assure you that what happened on the 9th of April was nothing organized by anybody," he told Colombian Communist journalist Arturo Alape. "The only thing was that those who organized the assassination of Gaitán could have imagined that this could occur."

"The Gaitanista movement was Gaitán," the accurate Cuban Communist historian Mario Mencía wrote. When Gaitán was killed, "the masses remained without direction." It was Gaitán, after all, who had said repeatedly, "I am not a man, I am a people." When the "man" was gone, the "people" were helpless. Fidel understood that, too.

8

SUICIDE BY MICROPHONE

Miguelito, do you think still that Chibás was greater than I?
—Fidel Castro to *Bohemia* magazine editor
Miguel Angel Quevedo, 1959

NOT EVEN THE CLOSE friends and political intimates who were with Eduardo "Eddy" Chibás that terrible Sunday in 1951 noticed anything very unusual about the great leader and singular hope of Cuba as he walked purposefully into Radio Station CMQ in downtown Havana. Eddy Chibás, although he was a dynamic political figure, wore prim glasses and had thinning mousy hair instead of the usual vibrant black hair of most Cubans. He was tense, emotional, and eccentric. He always wore white and he was a man who would impress his followers by suddenly fasting for days or even weeks or frighten them by remaining submerged in his bathwater for long periods of time. As his political genius developed in the turbulent and increasingly fanaticized years of the 1940s, some of his followers as well as many observers became more and more concerned that his hortatory speeches were passing from hysteria to incipient madness.

But Chibás was also, in the words of the poetic Cuban writer Guillermo Cabrera Infante, "a genuinely honorable man, the heir to a huge fortune but utterly uninterested in money; a political leader controlled and driven by a single obsession—the need for total honesty in public dealings. He knew that Cuba's Augean stables were sorely in need of cleaning. His great error was to designate as his Hercules a man emotionally incapable of the role—himself."

Still, in the late 1940s, Chibás seemed to remain generally in control of himself and was increasingly seen as the man surely to succeed President Carlos Prío Socarrás. Chibás had been an early supporter of President Ramón Grau, but, like so many, he became disillusioned with the Grau presidency in the years between 1944 and 1948. Despite his bourgeois looks, Chibás was a passionate man, and he employed that passion in believing that Cuba must rid itself of all corruption. So, in opposition to the Grau government, he created his own party, the Ortodoxos or Orthodox party. When Prío Socarrás was elected president in 1948, there was renewed hope that his administration would be an honest one. It was a false hope. Within a short time of taking office, the Prío men were robbing the treasury at every turn and living openly in offensive splendor in a land of many poor. The handsome, mustachioed, debonair Prío even hosted "white parties" with the new and fashionable cocaine; he "lasciviously" surrounded himself with women wearing shorts, even in the palace; and his brother appeared unashamedly on television with his mistress. The worst thing for many decent Cubans was that it was Cuban history wearily repeating itself all over again, and the hopelessness and angry alienation of the young rebounded now with even more force.

Chibás, who was recognized by many (including Fidel Castro) as the political genius of the time, came (not unexpectedly) to blows with the Prío government. It began when Aureliano Sánchez Arango, Prío's minister of education, called Chibás a "master of defamation, dictator, irresponsible, lacking in patriotism, ambitious, lying, useless, mediocre, mendacious, feudal, exploiter, miserable, a man of no honor and a false apostle of the lie, the demagoguery and the calumny." And all this in only one speech!

Chibás responded by accusing Aureliano of "robbing the funds of the public schools to buy a ranch in Guatemala. . . ." The fact was that Chibás had no proof of this—the farm in Guatemala was pure rumor—and the falsehood soon began eating away at Chibás, whose very theme among the honor-hungry Cubans was "honesty." The Eddy-Aureliano "debate" became every day more scandalous; finally it grew into a sordid national pastime, with Chibás using his mastery of the new power medium of the radio to attack his opponent. Chibás seemed to grasp from the start that radio broadcasts could be as deadly in the political sphere as weapons. He began speaking on the radio every Sunday at 8:00 P.M. on CMQ, Havana, and few times in history has a leader so spellbound his people. Cubans everywhere literally stopped whatever they were doing when Chibás spoke. On the streets of Havana, his fiery words bounded from every window, tearing at corruption and reiterating "honor, honor, honor." In cafés, conversation stopped at the first words from this man who both drew on and gave voice to the inner hysteria of the country. His speeches were not political harangues, they were cries of moral outrage and an invitation not to the revolution but to salvation. It was Chibás who would teach Fidel the many uses of radio. For Chibás himself, radio was perfect, for its amorphous and disembodied quality protected him from his own lack of physical machismo.

That Sunday, August 15, 1951, seemed no different from other Sundays, but early listeners were surprised that this time Chibás did not immediately address the corruption issue. Instead, as he began to talk, to exhort, to compel, the masterful manipulator of emotions fell into a theme that eerily preceded Fidel's later power hubris about a small country: the potential and thwarted greatness of Cuba. "Because of her geographical position, the richness of her land and the natural intelligence of her inhabitants, Cuba has reserved for her in history a great destiny, and she must realize it," he was saying.

At the very end—of his life as well as his speech—Chibás gave a particularly rousing cry. "Comrades of the Orthodoxy, forward! To economic independence, to political liberty, to social justice! Take a broom and sweep away the thieves in the government! People of Cuba, rise up and move! People of Cuba, awaken!"

The broom had been Chibás's symbol for sweeping away corruption, and the word *aldabonazo,* which means literally a sharp knock on the door with a door knocker, was his favored word—his mission and his destiny were to knock on the slumbering or decimated consciences of the Cuban people. Now he was to give his last *aldabonazo.*

"Este," cried the great Eddy Chibás in his final semihysterical words, *"es mi último aldabonazo para despertar la conciencia cívica del pueblo cubano. . . ."* "This is my last knock to awaken the civic conscience of the Cuban people. . . ." And then he shot himself in the stomach with his revolver. He was forty-three years old.

One of his leading aides, Fidel's old friend, the handsome and vigorous twenty-five-year-old José Pardo Llada, was standing next to him, but he did not see him take out his gun. "All my life, I have reprimanded myself," Pardo told me, "believing I could have stopped him. . . ."

It was too much to expect in the thwarted Cuba of the time that anything would go quite right, that even a suicide would be accomplished unflawed. For when he did pull the trigger, Chibás was already off the air. Probably because of his nervous temperament and his intent of that day, he had forgotten that he had paid for twenty minutes of air time, no more. Two or three minutes before the shot rang out, the engineer had broken him off to run a series of commercials, one of them being for coffee advertised as "tasty to the last stomachful."

In the panic that ensued, José Pardo Llada and four other supporters were the only ones to remain with the bloody body. These five stunned and dazed men carried the still-alive Eddy Chibás to the street. There, amazingly, Fidel Castro was already waiting for them. Fidel motioned them into a Chevrolet sedan, and drove off smartly to the Centro Médico, or Medical Center. "Fidel was the one who got the auto," Pardo Llada related. "And when Chibás died, Fidel had seven speeches ready because there were seven radio stations. He also organized the hundred old ladies who cried and wailed outside of Chibás's room for all those days."

Chibás lingered for eleven long days, and during that time it was almost as if the very country itself had stopped breathing. No one spoke of anything but the beloved orator who was now suffering, almost Christ-like, for his people. Except that, in the words of Cabrera Infante, Chibás's "crucifixion took the form of suicide by microphone." On August 26, 1951, Eduardo Chibás, the great hope of Cuba, slipped finally into eternity.

All those days, Fidel had maintained an unwavering vigil at the bedside of the man for whom in actuality he felt only an ambivalent and highly self-serving devotion. Now he sprang to the fore. Where should the body of this revered and fated leader lie in state? Orthodox party leaders spent four hours debating the question. Finally, Fidel, who had been only a minor young supporter of Chibás and one whom Chibás did not even like, stepped in and simply took over. It must be at the university, he insisted, and in the Aula Magna, or Great Hall. And there actually were good reasons for this. The police could not enter the university, and so the body would be protected from any "foul play" on the part of the Prío government. It was not irrelevant that the decision also gave Fidel and a few other student leaders control over Chibás's funeral. So it was that Fidel stood for twenty-four hours in the dignified Aula Magna of the university, by the bier, as part of the honor guard. Pictures in the Havana newspapers show him in the first row, fourth from the casket, and staring at the floor. The man who had once been called "Greaseball" by his classmates now wore an excessively formal gray suit and tie, while most of the others were dressed in the more informal white *guayabera* shirt. Fidel appeared by far the greatest and most profound mourner, and perhaps he even was.

When it came time to move Chibás's body to the cemetery—with between two hundred and three hundred thousand Cubans waiting outside the university—Fidel came up to his friend Josá Pardo Llada, demanding to speak with him alone. Fidel took Pardo to a corner of the Aula Magna and there revealed that they were not going to take Chibás's body to the cemetery. "We're going to make use of this enormous manifestation of grief," Fidel explained, "when we have so many people here, and we're going to carry the body to the palace."

Pardo was stunned. "To the palace, what for?"

"To take power," Fidel answered. "You will proclaim yourself president, and I will be chief of the army. We are going to give to Chibás after his death the satisfaction of sweeping away the government of Prío. I assure you, if we carry him to the palace, Prío will flee Cuba. The coward must be terribly frightened."

As Pardo recalled it, he told Fidel: "Listen, Fidel, forget this madness. Remember that with the burial there will march a battalion of the army for the military honors and that all the police are confined to quarters. They are capable of killing thousands of people, if we decide to assault the palace. I will not take responsibility for such a slaughter. . . ."

Fidel, standing there bullishly in his fine suit and sporting a slim pencil mustache, still insisted, "I tell you that they won't do anything. They are not capable of shooting even one shot. They are all cowards. The president, the army, the police, the government, all of them. Let's take Chibás to the palace and seat the dead in the presidential chair."

It was the "seat the dead in the presidential chair" that made Pardo decide to "cut off the dialogue." He said, with finality, "There's nothing more to say, Fidel. I am taking Chibás to the cemetery."

And so the silent multitudes accompanied the great hope of Cuba to still another cemetery of their nightmares, to be buried in the ground instead of seated in the palace to start a revolution. But Fidel's idea of carrying bodies to the palace to take over swiftly and forever was not buried with Eddy Chibás and it is a tactic that tells a great deal about his perception of the grasping of power. He always disdained direct military coups. His brilliance, instead, was his ability to seize control not by traditional coup but by hypnosis of the masses—a coup of the masses—through brilliant tactical insurrectional and inspirational acts.

Years later, in 1955, Pardo Llada spoke to ex-president Carlos Prío in Montreal. Pardo told him the story and asked him if he would indeed have given the order to shoot if they had tried to carry the "wave of the people" to the palace "with the body as a flag." Then Prío slowly replied: "If I had known about it, you can be sure that I would never have ordered anyone to shoot against my people. Nobody could say that my government would kill anybody."

Pardo further discovered that Captain Máximo Rabelo, who accompanied the troops to the burial of Chibás, carried only blanks and had precise instructions from the president not to intervene in case of any disorder, in part because Prío was cowardly and in part because he had a horror of civil war. Additionally, Pardo found out that a pilot of the Military Aviation, Roberto Verdaguer, had revealed five years after the death of Chibás that that very afternoon President Prío had packed his bags and ordered a plane readied to carry him from the country in case the burial resulted in a popular insurrection. It was not the first time, nor would it be the last, that Fidel's incredible vision of the tactically possible, which to everyone else was impossible, turned out to be uncannily precise.

Many years later, José Pardo Llada commented on the crucially important world of political power that Chibás and Castro shared in those years. "Manipulation of images?" he told me. "Fidel is a master in this. And, remember, he had a master teacher: Chibás. Remember, in Cuba we had a press very similar to the American. We watched Drew Pearson. This we learned from the North Americans and not from the Spanish, from whom we learned philosophy. Juan Perón had much the same skill." He paused, then added, "I learned from Perón and Castro—I was a student of two monsters."

Fidel's personal life was now becoming as chaotic as his political life. There were occasional peaceful scenes with Fidel, Mirta, and Fidelito apparently happy at home. But those were growing fewer and fewer. Chino Esquivel remembered stopping by one of their shabby apartments, this one on Calle 3, about 8:00 P.M. one evening. Mirta was there, looking pretty and cooking dutifully, and Chino began playing with Fidelito, then a toddler. Fidel was in his robe, with black shoes and brown socks on. Chino wanted him to go to a political meeting with him. At first, Fidel refused, trying to look and perhaps even trying to be some semblance of devoted husband and father. But at the moment, there was a news flash on the radio—there had been an attempt on the life of the hated Rolando Masferrer. Fidel quickly dressed and he and Chino quickly departed, leaving, as always, Mirta with uneaten dinner and the baby.

One of the many persons who financially helped *los Castros* during this period, and in particular the increasingly long-suffering Mirta, was a lovely and intellectual woman, Blanca del Valle, who, with her husband, Fernando, was active in Orthodox party politics. Fidel would buy things from one special store, for instance, and Blanca would pay the bill. But it was Blanca who also introduced Fidel on the most profound level to what would become still another "key" in his rise to power—the native Indian and black African Cuban mysticism and legends, which he would later use so uncannily well in dealing with tribal religions in his areas of international expansion.

One day, Blanca took Fidel to the Cave of the Indian in Pinar del Río, a place of the magic and mystery of the ancient and long-extinct Arawaks and Caribes who first graced this island of Cuba. The cave of *El Indio* harkened back to the beliefs of these early island dwellers, but it also reflected artifacts from the highly prevalent Afro-Cuban Santería. The variety of myths and legends to be found among the Cuban people appealed to Fidel as a means of manipulating the Cuban people; but it must have appealed to Fidel on another level as well, for he was always searching for an ideology to grasp hold of; in particular, he was searching for the reason and form that would give substance to his desire for power.

At the time of Chibás's death, Raúl was living with Mirta and Fidel in a tall building in Havana, where Mirta's younger and closest brother, Waldo, and another brother, Frank, also lived. Waldo even then found striking differences between the two Castro brothers, ones that would explain a great deal in later years. "Before 1952, for three or four years, I lived in a house with Mirta and Frank and Fidel," Waldo, the artist of the family, related. "It was a three- or four-story house, a brick house, plastered over. I am a very good friend of Raúl." Then he paused, for this was many years later, in Madrid, and he had used the present tense, illustrating once again the strange eternal hold these brothers had on everyone. Then he added, sadly, "I haven't seen him for twenty-five years."

"Everybody had his own bedroom," he went on, recovering his theme, "and Raúl and I lived on top, on the roof. You must realize that there were great differences between Fidel and Raúl. Fidel was very authoritarian and very organized and had followers. I always saw him as authoritarian — you were either pro-Fidel, or forget it! He was always pursuing what he wanted and he didn't care about anything else. So I never talked to him. But Raúl was more idealistic. When he arrived in Havana, he was about eighteen years old. Raúl was curious, very interested in sociology, curious about Communism, concerned about justice. Raúl had a hunger for knowledge, a hunger for resolving the whole situation, and the Communists gave him everything. . . . For Raúl, Fidel was the vehicle to achieve Communism."

Many political analysts like to toy with the idea that, had circumstances turned out differently, Fidel Castro might well have become a democrat or even some kind of capitalist, and, as such, more of a neutral factor toward the United States, if not exactly an enthusiastic ally. Then, too, he did receive his law degree and could have used it to make a good deal of money. Instead, what did he do?

Much has been made of the fact that Fidel practiced law in his little law firm of Azpiazu, Castro y Rosende, on Tejadillo 57 in the picturesque old section of Havana near the docks. But the truth is that he tried only a couple of obscure cases and showed an astounding lack of interest in "law" per se. (One of his clients, a sculptor, "paid" him for settling a minor legal problem with a statue of José Martí, which Fidel guarded for a long time in his library.) Even more incongruous than his attempts at law was the fact that his law firm, Azpiazu, Castro y Rosende, had a second little company, an American-style insurance company whose sign in the law office window announced the future "Communist" dictator of Cuba as the respectable proprietor of the "Protect Home" Insurance Co. There is no evidence that Fidel, who would like to destroy the traditional Cuban state, spent any time at all trying to sell anyone insurance to preserve that state.

It is true, however, that after the death of Chibás in 1951, Fidel had a brief fling at deciding to run for congressman (*representante*) on the Ortho-dox ticket: his sister Juanita, ever critical, recalled that "It was father who helped finance his campaign." As always! The leadership of the Orthodox party, however, did not support him or put him forward as a candidate, for he was already dubbed too radical and too renegade; so Fidel once again just reached out with his inexhaustible animal energy and created his own political world.

"I had worked out certain methods of political labor that proved to be very effective," Fidel related later on. "There were many members of the . . . party who were not controlled by the machinery, especially in Havana Province. I concentrated my efforts on capturing these voters. . . ."

José Pardo Llada was amazed by the persistence with which Fidel waged this new battle. Immediately after Chibás's death, nearly a full year before the spring of 1952 elections, Fidel appeared in Pardo Llada's office accompanied by his "inseparable brother," Raúl, and demanded to see the archive of the party affiliates in the province of Havana.

"And what are you going to do with this archive?" Pardo asked.

"I am going to write a personal letter to each one and then visit them."

"And you know how many members there are of the party in this province?"

"I don't know, but even if there were a hundred thousand, I would visit all of them."

"There aren't a hundred thousand but probably seventy thousand. How are you going to know all of them?"

"I don't know, but I assure you that I will write to all of them and that I will visit all of them."

"He made a fabulous campaign," his friend Max Lesnick recalled later. "He sent out some hundred thousand envelopes. One hundred thousand! He made a stencil and sent his messages out to be printed on the letters in blue ink as though he had written a personal card, greeting every one of the affili-ated of the party. Think of what a bright idea! When they opened the enve-lope, they saw this card in blue ink, signed by Fidel Castro, like a personal card. This had never occurred with anyone in Cuba. . . ." Lesnick brimmed over with enthusiasm and admiration for his friend's tactics of this period. Fidel even went so far as to buy a car just like Pardo Llada's—Pardo was very popular—to make people believe Pardo was supporting him.

Indeed, Fidel was indefatigable. He spoke at two, three, four meetings a night. He was up at five in the morning, traveling all over the province. Women were powerfully attracted to him, as interestingly enough were older people, and not only the marginalized or the "outs" that he would later so depend upon. "Why?" Lesnick asked rhetorically. "Because he was young and he appeared in his manner of speaking to be a man of convictions, of audacity."

Did he really believe in democracy, in the system, or what was left of it? Did he believe the system, or Cuba, was redeemable? It is clear that he was far more interested in the democratic electoral process in terms of gaining personal power than in terms of serving it, which is not surprising given the disappointments and disillusionments of the time. Fidel later spoke rather candidly about this period to photographer Lee Lockwood. "Already," he told the American photojournalist, "I was working with the fervent passion of a revolutionary. For the first time, I conceived a strategy for the revolutionary seizure of power. Once in the Parliament, I would break party discipline and present a program. . . . I hoped, by proposing a program that recognized the most deeply felt aspirations of the majority of the population, to establish a revolutionary platform around which to mobilize the great masses of farmers, workers, unemployed, teachers, intellectual workers and other progressive sectors of the country. . . ."

Fidel, of course, lies. He has lied all his life, although he does not see his "lies" as lies. Since everything revolves around him and his perception of reality, whatever he sees or says at any one moment is indeed "truth." And there are other times, when his "version of events," now or in the past, simply suits either his political purposes or his inner security needs, so one does not need to believe this interpretation of his campaign. But, as a matter of fact, it seems to be true. Presidential elections would be held again in four years' time, and it is logical to assume that Fidel was laying the groundwork for that political future.

It was at this moment that Fidel also illustrated another part of his tactical brilliance—the manner in which, at each crossroad, he cleared his past, almost like a computer screen being "reset" for future use. Now it was time definitively to erase the major bloody blot on his "political" record: to purge his damaging reputation as a gangster. In the fertile period before the planned elections—from the fall of 1951 to the spring of 1952—Fidel moved on two levels. First, he came out publicly and attacked the *pistoleros* in the gangs, naming names and deeds, even in his own UIR. Second, Fidel attacked Carlos Prío. In one of the most audacious investigations and exposés in all Cuban history, Fidel set out to show the links between the Prío administration and the *pistolero* groups. As well, he wanted to show the extraordinarily sumptuous elegance in which Prío lived in his notorious villa, "La Chata," described by the writers Warren Hinckle and William W. Turner as "a mini–Garden of Eden done with the understatement of a Busby Berkeley production."

In this tropical paradise twenty kilometers from Havana, Fidel, dressed as a gardener, took pictures of the fountains, the shooting range, the water-fall roaring into the huge swimming pool, and of the debonair Prío himself, chatting with his guests. The following week, in mid-February 1952, the daily *Alerta* published the pictures with the notably provocative headline, "This is the way the President lives with the money he has robbed from the people."

Fidel accused Prío of distributing eighteen thousand dollars a month to the gangs, and of having "bought and sold assassinations." And so, "Fidel, the accomplice of all the gangsters, now was accusing those gang-sters, including his colleagues of the UIR . . . ," Pardo Llada later wrote. "In this moment, nobody would have given a cent for the life of the young lawyer. Castro was automatically condemned to death by his own com-rades, now indignant before a denunciation that they considered 'high trea-son.' . . . But enormous audacity carries with it its own security, as Fidel always knew. Such was the size of Castro's audacity that the very dispro-portion of the challenge served as a kind of personal guarantee. Nobody dared to do anything. . . ."

This period from the fall of 1951 to the aborted elections of the spring of 1952 marked a major turning point in Fidel's life. At this juncture, he was not only rhetorically but also palpably filling the empty shoes of Chibás. Almost imperceptibly, Cubans began to transfer their hopes to the young, brilliant, honest fighter. A gangster? That was obviously impossible. He himself had denounced the gangs. Conchita Fernández, first the personal secretary of Eddy Chibás and in later years Fidel's personal secretary, recalled that when Fidel would appear at a rally in those days he would wave a copy of *Alerta* with the exposé and the photographs of Prío's *finca* "and within five or ten minutes, that park was full because he had such magnetism that all people needed was to hear him. . . ."

While all of this was happening, nobody except Fidel himself was watching the machinations of Fulgencio Batista. In the end, it was not Chibás's untimely death in 1951 that tolled the last *aldabonazo* for democracy in Cuba, it was Batista's coup against the promised elections the next year. Before that March day of 1952, democracy could still have worked in Cuba had a decent man assumed the presidency and been able to deal with the corruption and the floating but angry anomie. After that day, Cuban democracy was as doomed as a Shakespearean tragic hero; from that moment on, all those years and "generations" of heroic struggle were only historic prologue. And although no one, of course, could then know it, "1952" in Cuba would echo around the world in the 1970s. Far after 1952, a radical answer became the inevitable in Cuba. It would become the sister moment of frustration and desperation of 1972 in Vietnam and El Salvador; of 1977 in Iran; of 1978 in Nicaragua—all moments before the political finale, when hope was lost, and all moments that Fidel Castro would by then either orchestrate or support.

After Castro came to power, he almost never publicly mentioned Eddy Chibás, and in Cuba today the name is totally forgotten; it is not in most of the history books. However, there was one revealing lapse in Fidel's unremitting silence about Chibás. After he had marched on Havana in 1959, and after he finally had total power, he had the habit of going every day to the offices of the popular *Bohemia* magazine, where he would personally check the news and correct anything he did not like.

One day, while he was talking with the editor, Miguel Angel Quevedo, those hooded hawk's eyes of his suddenly fixed intently on the other man. Out of nowhere, he asked, "Miguelito, do you think still that Chibás was greater than I?"

9

THE MOVEMENT

We were born with him.

—Melba Hernández, early *Fidelista*

IDEL WAS AT HOME asleep in Havana that early morning of March 10, 1952, when a friend rushed into his apartment with news of Batista's unexpected coup. Fearing arrest, Fidel fled five blocks in the tense dawn hours to the apartment of his older half sister, Lidia, a calmly dedicated woman who would always remain the sister closest to him. As usual, his feral instincts were impeccable. Only a few hours later, midmorning, with the coup barely consolidated, secret policemen appeared at the Castros' apartment looking for Fidel and Raúl. Both were already gone.

For several days then, Fidel moved, and moved, and moved again: first to the Hotel Andino and finally to the home of Eva Jiménez, an Orthodox party youth militant. The swiftness of his "relocations" certainly saved him from prison, and may well have saved his life; but the overwhelmingly important aspect was that from the moment he heard there had been a coup, he knew that a "new revolutionary cycle" had begun in Cuba.

In some of his conscious or unconscious rewritings of history, Fidel in later years would picture himself at this moment as only a simple soldier fighting the dictatorship shoulder-to-shoulder with other simple soldiers. Nothing, of course, could be further from the truth. Actually, the coup came as a great relief to Fidel, who was by now exhausted and frustrated by attempts to run for elective office. The coup catapulted him into the world of conspiracy that he loved and of clandestine organization at which he so brilliantly excelled. Now he could thrust aside even the pretense of democratic change, even the idea that he would or could submit himself to some other "authority." March 10, 1952, marked the beginning of the Fidel Castro the world would come to know. From that day, he would begin the organization of his own first "movement."

The coup d'état that changed Cuban history took place at 2:43 A.M. that Monday, March 10, when General Fulgencio Batista, wearing a leather jacket and packing a .45 caliber pistol, strode into Camp Columbia and took command of the army. In a mere seventy-seven minutes, it was all over. The *Batistianos* held control of the army, the navy, and the air force, and that was all it took to destroy "democracy" in Cuba. By midday, Batista was in power, and Carlos Prío had fled the palace and, soon, the country, to settle in Mexico. The coup d'état in Cuba did not seem very serious to a world occupied by larger questions. Only two men died that day, and not even the movie theaters closed to mark the moment. The exultant Batista crowed, "My destiny is to carry out revolutions without bloodshed." If the Americans had listened more carefully, they would have heard Batista say after the coup, "The people and I are the dictators." The similarity to words spoken by strongmen Juan Perón and Jorge Eliecer Gaitán was stunning!

Why did Batista choose this moment to retake the formal power he had held from 1940 to 1944? The truth was that, by the winter of 1952, polls showed that Batista had a bare 10 percent of the vote. Chibás, before his death, was the clear front-runner. Even after Chibás's death, if elections were held, not only would Batista have lost ignominiously, he would have looked so unbearably foolish that both his military and his political careers would have been finished. Now confident and stubborn and appearing to be backed by the United States, Batista had become lazy and he spent an inordinate amount of time in little obsessions like worrying over the punctuation of a letter, the correct tying of a tie, the changing of his clothes. Fascinated by the private lives of his opponents, he spent hours listening to their taped telephone conversations and was deeply concerned about his debts incurred with his divorce in order to marry his young second wife, Marta.

Most observers accept as the most simple of "givens" that Fidel Castro abhorred Fulgencio Batista—and perhaps he came to; but the relationships between the young (still only implicitly and secretively military) revolutionaries of the Left and the older (overtly military) caudillos of the Right, like Batista (and later like Franco), were often complicated and contradictory.

In 1951, for instance, when Fidel was still scouting about for and experimenting with techniques and mechanisms to revolution, he asked Rafael Díaz-Balart, who by then had joined the *Batistiano* youth organization, to introduce him to Batista. As far as can be known, it was the only time the two met before Batista's coup. The meeting occurred in Batista's *finca,* "Kuquine," with only Rafael and another Batista loyalist, Andrés Rivero Agüero, present. "Fidel wanted Batista to prepare a coup," Rafael related to me. "Batista would not allow him actually to say it. Finally, Fidel walked up and down in the library, looking at the books. 'I don't see a very important book here,' he said to Batista. Batista asked, 'Which one?' Fidel answered, 'Curzio Malaparte's *The Technique of the Coup d'État.*' "But the veiled invitation to discuss a coup evoked nothing in the cynical Batista and Fidel did not pursue it further. Besides, he was never more than cursorily interested in the coup as a mechanism for revolution, believing its roots to be too shallow to mobilize and transform the people in the ways he already had in mind.

Many years later, sitting in his luxurious exile in Madrid, Rafael recalled that Batista had told him after Fidel had left, "Your young friend is very intelligent, but dangerous." Rafael then told me, relating this for the first time to anyone, "The two made a good study of each other, and Fidel realized that Batista was not a revolutionary leader anymore. Still, they looked at each other with admiration."

A close observer of the time, Fidel's friend Max Lesnick, said that Batista was convinced then that "Fidel was an agent provocateur." Lesnick believes that it is possible that Fidel set up the meeting knowing it would fail and that the failure would in effect convince the Cuban people that "he had nothing to do with Batista." Lesnick added sagely that, "In Fidel Castro, everything is logical. What people do not understand is that there are things in the life of Castro that seem absurd but that everything has an explanation. The mind of Castro is a logical mind."

Once the coup had come, however, the two men were from that moment onward total and irreconcilable enemies; it was a fight to the death in which a complacent and compulsively upward-striving "pretty mulatto" would enormously—and fatally—underestimate his opponent. As for Fidel, he did what he always did: he looked around him with those cannily hooded hawk's eyes and pushed every lever of opposition to the Batista dictatorship that he could find or create.

Within days, Fidel had filed a brief in the Court of Constitutional Guarantees to try to force what was left of the Cuban legal system to declare Batista's seizure of power to be unconstitutional. He asked "modestly" that the man who in effect held total power in the country be sentenced to one hundred years in prison. And again, he tried to transform and demean the concepts of his enemies. In his writings, he claimed over and over that Batista's "revolution," as Batista persisted in calling it, was only a lowly *zarpazo,* or a blow with a paw.

Meanwhile, at home Mirta waited, and waited, and waited. One night during this time of endless hiding from the police, reappearing and hiding again, Fidel and a friend stopped at the Castros' apartment on 23rd Street to find it in total darkness and three-year-old Fidelito crying piteously with a throat infection and high fever. The electricity had been cut off since once again Mirta had had no money to pay the utilities. Typically, Fidel on the spot borrowed five pesos from a friend to give to Mirta, while he himself was carrying a hundred pesos in his pocket. And typically also, he justified such strange and cold parsimoniousness by telling others—and probably himself—self-righteously that those hundred pesos had been collected for the purchase of weapons—and nothing else!

But now Mirta was confronted with a much more serious and threatening problem. Her name was Natalia, and she was very beautiful.

Everything in Fidel's life and behavior shows the extent to which he desperately needed to live always on the edge: of danger, of change, of promised control. He still loved Mirta, as much as a man like him could love a woman, but her patient ways, once comforting and consoling, now were becoming trying and tiresome. The dingy apartment, in its darkness and in its silent pleading for his help and presence, had become increasingly unattractive to him. It was at this period, in November of 1952, that he met Natalia "Naty" Revuelta, one of the most exquisitely beautiful women in Cuba and a woman with an abnormally sensuous appetite for revolution and adventure (and just about everything else).

Naty lived at 15th Calle and 4th Avenida with her wealthy doctor husband in a modern house that was as glorious and luxuriant as she was. Mirta was virginity and home, Naty was pure sensuality and temptation: she brought out the other, sexual side of the boy from Birán, the flip side of the Fidel who had been so physically repulsed as he walked down the street of prostitutes with his priests. Blond, green-eyed, buxom, and always in exuberant spirits, Naty was the kind of woman who stopped eyes and tongues when she entered a room. To make the affair even more delicious to Fidel, she was not only from the Cuban bourgeoisie, she was *haute bourgeoisie,* a well-educated and ambitious young woman who proudly belonged to the Havana Yacht Club and the Havana Country Club.

Naty was the pride and joy of her upper-middle-class family, a girl who attended the distinguished American-run Ruston Academy in Havana and studied at a Catholic girls' high school in Philadelphia, a young woman who held responsible positions in the U.S. embassy in Havana and later with Standard Oil (Esso). When she "married well," to a respected doctor, Dr. Orlando Fernández Ferrer, it seemed that her life was on a straight and flawlessly unmarred track. But after she met Fidel at a political meeting of the Orthodox party, she seemed to be blinded by the political and sexual pull of the young leader. Her family warned her over and over again, but she paid no heed until "Her actions literally destroyed the family," as one uncle put it.

This type of affair between a society girl and a revolutionary was far from rare. Hitler, for example, made use of the German society ladies, who were, in Eric Hoffer's words, "thirsting for adventure, sick of their empty lives, no longer getting a 'kick' out of love affairs. . . ." So Naty fell into a long and "time-honored" revolutionary tradition. The very day of the Batista coup, for instance, before she had ever met Fidel, she gave three sets of keys to her apartment to Ortodoxo leaders, with the specific request that one set be given to Fidel.

Fidel, relieved of the humiliating tensions and restraints of having to run for office, now began exercising his leadership on two distinct levels. To confuse the government, he appeared to be only publicly engaged—a lawyer practicing amateur politics on the side—whereas in truth, underneath that superficial respectability, he was also privately engaged as a conspirator, compulsively and tirelessly organizing secret cells. The rehearsals were over now; the years of experimenting and observing had ended. Keys to his approach as he strode through this antechamber of revolution were absolute secrecy, total control of everything and everyone by him, and the constant evoking of valiant old Cuban images.

Never did Fidel depart in even a minor way from the most heroic Cuban patriotic images that he now began mobilizing against the enemy. Batista was made to look "unauthentic" in the face of the new "authenticity" of Fidel Castro which claimed ideological continuity not only with the ideas of Martí but also with those of earlier Cuban heroes. Fidel was always at his most brilliant when using the heroic but tragically thwarted acts of the Cuban past. Such a political alchemist might be looked upon more as a man of magic and of resurrection than as a mere revolutionary, for as he reopened old wounds, causing new pain, he also began through such revelation a process that some might think would lead to a national healing.

And so the "movement" started, a collection of marginalized Cubans, who, as if sleepwalking, obeyed unquestioningly everything Fidel commanded. Rules were stringent, and any indiscretion meant automatic and often traumatizing separation from the group and from its dreams. Drinking alcohol was forbidden, and weekly meetings were held to analyze the conduct of each member of the group. This collective form of "self-criticism" would foreshadow the later, Marxist structures. Strict sexual morality was the rule (except for Fidel, with Naty). The organization, the secrecy, the impassioned camaraderie of this new underground, gave the movement's members a true sense of potency that none of them had ever experienced before. "When we were barely a small group that didn't even number ten, or barely ten, very small, already Fidel was the leader," Melba Hernández, an early recruit, recalled. "And we didn't feel as though we were ten, we felt like a movement of a tremendous force." Then she added chilling words about the spell that Fidel was beginning to weave over them: "He had been born. We were born with him."

But despite the omnipresent secrecy and strictness of the movement, there were always distinctly odd and human little things that went on. Carlos Bustillo, another early member, recalled that the group would "train on the roof of the science building of the university. . . ." (Right above the heads of anyone who had cared to look!) But Fidel never himself appeared on the roof of the university for the weapons training. He selected several trusted men, like Pedro Miret, to train the new recruits while from the protected shadows he controlled everything with gestures and commands. "It was done in such a manner that nobody was aware of the fact that these people were Fidel's," Miret recalled. "Fidel never went there for anything, absolutely. That way, no one was ever able to link us with Fidel. . . ."

But this was nothing compared to what Fidel and his movement would do on January 27, 1953, the eve of the centennial of José Martí's birth. Now he revealed himself—and the totally militarized character of his movement—in a manner that would seem at first almost stunningly foolish. That day, thousands of all kinds of youths paraded in the name of Martí from the school to downtown Havana. But the hundreds of *Fidelistas* did more; they created a breathtaking torchlight spectacle as they marched shoulder to shoulder with such discipline that anyone who was really observant would have recognized the beginnings of a proto-Fascist movement. And they were prepared for anything. "Our torches had large nails with which to reply to the police if they attacked us," Melba Hernández recalled. "The people were very impressed when they saw us go by. I heard some of them say, 'Those who go there are the Communists!'"

This confusing of Fidel's new-style commandos, who by now had started calling themselves *Fidelistas,* with the Communists was most telling in revealing the Cubans' own lack of understanding of their country at that time; for the Cuban Communist party, like all of the Moscow-line parties then organized in Latin America, was squeamishly antiviolence and believed in patient organizing for the long, long run. The important thing about that daring day, however, was that from then on Fidel's movement began to be known among first the few and later the many as a new generation among Cuban generations: the "Generation of the Centennial," in effect the authentic heirs of Martí! Personally, Fidel preferred to call it only "The Movement," in much the same spirit of one, total belief that the Cambodian Khmer Rouge would employ when they came to power in Cambodia in 1975 and called themselves *Angka,* or "The Center."

Fidel hoped to create a mass movement that would be vastly different from any political party. And, as the great longshoreman/philosopher Eric Hoffer put it, "The practical organization offers opportunities for self-advancement, and its appeal is mainly to self-interest. A mass movement, particularly in its active, revivalist phase, appeals not to those intent on bolstering and advancing a cherished self, but to those who crave to be rid of an unwanted self. A mass movement attracts and holds a following not because it can satisfy the desire for self-advancement, but because it can satisfy the passion for self-renunciation."

Why Fidel showed his hand at this moment is open to question, but his acts did fit in with his enjoyment of balancing the compulsively and obsessively secret with the daringly and insultingly public. He wanted people to sense that some movement of his was around, hanging like a mood or a cloud over a deteriorating situation. What is more remarkable is that Batista and his men did not take more notice of his parade. They suffered from the fatal sins of dictators: arrogance and greed. Pedro Miret revealed much of the *Fidelistas'* own feelings about their society—and about themselves—when he said, "We were certain that nobody would know who we were." Because the government, with its unimaginative tunnel vision, saw only the traditional political parties as enemies, "We were nothing to them, we did not exist."

Artemisa was a town founded in 1803 on the main highway to the west of Havana, en route to the glorious and dramatic province of Pinar del Río, with its weirdly beautiful giant rock formations looming over dreamy green and fertile valleys. It was here, among the young men of the middle and working classes, that Fidel found many of his first followers. "The traditionally rebellious Artemisa region was an excellent training ground," the chronicler and historian of Cuba, Rolando Bonachea, wrote. "It was sufficiently rural to permit military maneuvers. Moreover, it was removed from the prying eyes of Batista's urban secret service, yet close enough to the capital to allow rapid mobilization if necessary."

In addition to Artemisa, the other major meeting place of the budding movement was in Havana at the little house of Haydée Santamaría, who was devoted to Fidel, and her brother Abel, a sandy-haired, calm, and committed young man, who acted as a second kind of magnet for the alienated youth of Cuba. Soon, Fidel and Abel were organizing meetings at the little house at O and 25th, and soon the planning boiled over into plotting.

As Fidel molded and shaped his new movement, dramatic event after dramatic event was shaking the world outside. In 1953, Stalin died of a stroke, France saw mounting criticism of the war in Indochina, and the American secretary of state John Foster Dulles warned that if the Communist Viet Minh were successful in Vietnam, the rest of Southeast Asia would fall like "dominoes" under Soviet domination. The Rosenbergs were executed, Soviet tanks crushed a surprise East Berlin uprising, and the Korean armistice marked the end of the Korean war. In Iran, Mohammed

Mossadegh was overthrown and the young Shah returned under CIA auspices after a fierce battle with Mossadegh's household guards. French paratroopers landed ominously at Dien Bien Phu, an event that presaged the final American involvement in the Vietnam quagmire.

Ideological wars, not only between Russian Communism and American democracy, but also between underdeveloped countries and developed ones, between vertical power (totalitarianism) and horizontal power (democracy) were beginning to rend the world. Meanwhile, in Artemisa and in Havana, Fidel's perfervid followers were scouring the world for their own ideology, for tactics, for belief. They read books by Marx, Engels, and Lenin; Abel Santamaría in particular seemed to be fascinated by Lenin, but there is still no evidence of any serious Marxist indoctrination. Rather, Fidel was teaching them Cuban patriotic history, an amorphous ideology of Cuban "independence" and "autonomy," and above all his own, new kind of perpetual "rebellion." There was nothing really unusual going on in Artemisa or at the Santamaría home in Havana—only the same kind of revolutionary talk about "change" that was catapulting and echoing across the underdeveloped world.

By early summer of 1953, Fidel was almost ready for his first debut into that revolution he had hitherto only talked about. Just twenty-six years old, he had formed a movement of some twelve hundred men and women. He had been tireless in his efforts, showing the same inexhaustible energy he had exhibited when he was rounding up votes for his election campaign in 1951. In the months following Batista's coup, he traveled some thirty thousand miles in his car (more than forty times the length of Cuba itself), searching for money, arms, and men. With his strangely confiding voice and his oddly childlike beseeching quality, he appealed to people by expressing what they themselves had only groped for, in ambiguous and hitherto unfulfilled ramblings. Many repeated over and over that it was little short of wondrous the way Fidel would suddenly be saying what they had been thinking.

"Fidel could convince any person to do anything," Carlos Bustillo, who would be in the car behind Fidel at Moncada, remembered. And another *Moncadista,* Gerardo Pérez Puelles, recalled that "Fidel had this way of captivating people. Maybe it is the warmness of his speech. He could get together with ten guys and he would have ten more recruits. He was very, very good at this, and I think he still is."

But his methods of winning people over depended as much on his example as his evocative words. One afternoon during weapons training on a farm near Los Palos in Pinar del Río, a rifle had been damaged. Fidel immediately began to look for a small spring that had fallen from it into the high grass. Everyone else soon gave up, but Fidel persisted, searching in the rain until he finally found the lost part. He turned then to his weary men and said triumphantly, "See, this shows that perseverance will bring about our victory." That afternoon could have stood as a metaphor for his whole life.

In his search for followers, Fidel looked for people he could mold, souls that had been alienated by the Old Cuba—men and women who, as Max Lesnick put it, "the street does not know." And he found them in the margins of Cuban society. They were young, angry, lost, alienated, deracinated, and left behind, both by their governments and by the great but impersonal American companies where a good number of them worked. Indeed, many of their revolutionary tracts were printed on the mimeograph machine of General Motors in Havana! They were like Fidel himself, the outsider, the Gallego from Birán who didn't clean his fingernails and who carried a gun. But the single most crucially important factor was that each of the men and women in Fidel's movement had to be totally and unequivocally committed to it, and, thus, totally obedient to him, and to him alone. And they were.

In their desperate seeking, they were willing to give themselves over heart and soul to one leader, to one government, to one total and fulfilling truth. This eerily resembled the kind of unquestioning loyalty that would be given by the Iranian people to the Ayatollah Khomeini, not to speak of myriad other "modern" movements led by charismatic leaders. Already, from his words and from the structures he created—but most important from his actions—one could clearly see his latent forming of not only the new Cuban revolutionary man but, most crucial and breathtaking, the new Cuba: his Cuba. The men and women he chose and trained for Moncada were also the nucleus of *las masas* to come, his "masses" devoid of the past and formed by and impassionedly loyal to the person and to the spell of Fidel Castro.

These charismatic leader–charismatic follower relationships arise "in times of psychic, physical, economic, ethical, religious, political distress," as the supreme thinker on the subject, Max Weber, put it. "Thus it may seem that it is mainly the disturbed, the disoriented, the alienated that tend to respond to such appeals—and they necessarily will become most prominent in extreme situations of social change and disturbances. It is in situations . . . of anomie, that more and more people tend to feel helpless, alienated, and disoriented and feel that the society in which they live is meaningless and normless; thus their own pathogenic tendencies become strengthened and the more pathological personalities may become prominent and find a wider scope for their activities." The Israeli psychoanalyst Rafael Moses writes, "We do not need Freud to tell us that the charismatic effect of a leader is related to the primary emotional ties of the child to his parents. . . . In times of crisis the wish for fulfillment of a variety of needs from a leader increases dramatically. At such times, the critical faculties of the members of the large group weaken and the expectation for a leader who can be seen to be strong, knowledgeable, and decisive becomes dominant."

The danger in this exchange is not, however, only to the follower. The pact implicitly involves an intense danger to the leader because, again in the words of Max Weber, "there is a quality of mutual intoxication in the leader's reassuring his followers who in turn reassure him. . . . The leader's charismatic claim breaks down if his mission is not recognized by those to whom he feels he has been sent."

On less metaphysical levels, the other, democratic movements were predictably proving themselves as hapless and hopeless as Fidel knew them to be. When an anti-Batista faction, the MNR, or Nationalist Revolutionary Movement, organized by the liberal university professor Rafael García Bárcenas, planned a coup against Batista, they contacted Fidel, who dismissed their idea with a gesture of his hand. "It was the most advertised action in the history of Cuba," he said. Once again, he was right. The coup failed miserably, betrayed from inside its ranks, which only cemented Fidel's belief in more, and more, and more secrecy.

A second attempt to oust Batista was formally put in writing on June 2 in a Canadian hotel by leaders of some of the old traditional political parties. But this "Montreal Pact" frittered itself away in still another flurry of rhetoric. The whole exercise was soon forgotten and Fidel was left seeming to be the "only one."

In those pregnant days of the high and hot summer, Fidel was, quietly, everywhere. As he traveled across Cuba, raising approximately forty thousand dollars' worth of shotguns, .22-caliber semiautomatic rifles, Browning submachine guns, M-I carbines, and Winchester rifles, he decided to give his father, Don Angel Castro, the opportunity to (again) support him. He went to Birán with one of his followers, Raúl Martínez, to ask Angel for three thousand dollars. Don Angel was not amused. "You have to be perfect dolts," he said angrily, "with a group of wretches and outcasts dying of hunger, to think you would be capable of overthrowing a government like Batista's with all its tanks, cannons and planes." Angel huffed and puffed and finally gave them one hundred forty dollars, which Fidel accepted with minimal good grace. When they were leaving, the old man said with gruff feeling, "Good trip, Loco, and hopefully nothing bad will happen to you."

In the weeks preceding Moncada, Fidel made a number of stops that seem strange in their exposition but in reality were very shrewdly typical of Fidel's tactics. Returning from Oriente, he stopped by his old friend Pardo Llada's house to talk with him about his plans. "I was in bed, with a fever, suffering from a terrible grippe," Pardo remembered, "and I had to listen patiently for hours to Fidel's arguments. Never did I see him with such overflowing confidence and with such security in himself."

At about this time, Fidel also made a clear effort to talk to his old professor, the respected Herminio Portell Vilá. He went to the house of the great Cuban historian and, when told the professor had gone to a nearby restaurant with a friend, doggedly followed them there. Portell Vilá recalled his friend saying, "Castro is behind you on the sidewalk, it seems he wants to talk to you."

Fidel immediately asked, "I understand you used to teach the military history of war?"

The professor said, "Yes, until Batista."

"Did you ever visit the Moncada fortress and barracks?"

"Yes," the professor responded. "When there are special events, they have invited me to visit the barracks."

Then Fidel asked him with a pointedness that was not lost on the man, "You were in the Moncada?"

"Yes, twice."

"Do you think it could be taken by direct assault?"

"You would have the garrison with you?" the professor asked, narrowing his eyes.

"No," Fidel answered, "but young men . . ."

"What weapons?"

When Fidel told him what they had—all they had—the professor was suddenly sick at heart. "You don't have a chance in the world," he told the foolish young man. "You don't know the life in the barracks. It would be a slaughter."

"Yes," Fidel said, strangely calm, "but I'm going to do it."

By July 22, everything was in place. Fidel's followers began closing in on Santiago de Cuba, and thus on the Moncada barracks. They came in ones and twos, from all over the island, like bits of metal drawn to a magnet. It was Carnival time in Santiago, and the gala music and dancing set a grotesque stage for Portell Vilá's "slaughter" that was so soon to come.

10

MONCADA

Man will never risk his life for the lesser of two evils, but he may willingly die for an illusion.

—Old Vietnamese proverb

OF ALL THE GRACEFUL and sensuous cities of Cuba, the most aching with memories is Santiago de Cuba, the capital of Fidel's own Oriente. The historic city lies on a wide and mirrored bay, its horizons marked by arched palm trees and its gentle hills webbed by cobblestoned streets that meander artistically only a few miles from the foothills of the great Sierra Maestra mountains. Founded in 1542, Santiago is filled with lovely Spanish houses and villas that seem to embody the very inner spirit of Old Spain with their protective black grates, stained-glass windows, and stark white façades. But Santiago is also known as the most rebellious city of Cuba, most of Cuba's revolts having started or grown to maturity there. To complete the historic circle, Teddy Roosevelt's pet San Juan Hill, *the* symbol of the great victory of the *americanos* in the Spanish-American War, lies on the outskirts of the city.

Santiago seems never more itself than at Carnival time, that festival in Cuba that nominally honors the African deities with which the Cubans themselves seem always to be on ambiguous but voluptuous terms. On the two nights of Carnival, Cubans of every class and color drink and dance until morning to the sounds of tribal instruments venerating the African Santería religious rites.

The Carnival of July 1953 occurred in oppressive heat, but it was a happy one, for in truth Cuba felt itself then a happy country. Economic prosperity lulled the people into a deeply flawed sense of well-being; and though politically the country was arriving at the point of revolution and schism, most Cubans did not realize it. One of the most middle-class countries in Latin America, semi-industrialized, with half the labor force organized into effective unions, with exports matching imports, with huge gold reserves and with sugar mills rapidly passing from foreign to Cuban hands, the island was at an economic takeoff point. But at the same time, there was a "Third World" within Cuba, and it could be seen clearly in the city of Santiago. Obsessed by injustice and neglect, *Santiagueros* tended to think they existed only to provide minerals and agricultural products to the more educated people in the capital. In a sense, Santiago represented an early miniature, within Cuba, of what would become Fidel's fight of the Third World against the metropole of the United States.

But at Carnival time, the people of Santiago found release from their problems and forgot the threat of revolution that lurked behind the costumes and masquerades, not knowing, as in so many masquerades, that a gruesome reality was already there among them, present in the flesh and even more grotesquely costumed than they. As Fidel was to write later in a letter to his friend Luis Conte Agüero of that fateful early morning of July 26, 1953: "History has never seen such a massacre!" He wrote it with relish and with pride.

For months the *Fidelistas* had been obediently planning for "Moncada" without knowing in the slightest what it was. They simply gathered and talked and practiced shooting and the women busily sewed *Batistiano* uniforms for the group. The uniforms were of tremendous importance. They would not only disguise the *Fidelistas* but also properly dress them for their battle. Fidel loved uniforms; long after the revolution triumphed, thirty years later, his men would still be wearing uniforms, totally unlike all the leaders of the other "Communist" regimes. Even the aristocratic Naty sewed uniforms. Indeed, Naty's closeness to Fidel, by now as lover and confidante, was shown by the fact that it was she who was chosen by him to type his Manifesto and also to select and purchase the records for the music they would play over Santiago radio at the moment of their victory.

Naty wisely and tastefully chose independence war hymns, the Cuban national anthem, Chopin's A Major Polonaise, and Beethoven's Eroica Symphony. Meanwhile, Mirta as usual waited patiently at home, having no idea whatsoever of the imminent attack.

Suddenly, just before the Havana group set out for Oriente, Fidel realized that one of his followers, Gildo Fleitas López, had been engaged to a girl for years and that Gildo might well die at Moncada. Immediately, he organized a wedding, which Melba Hernández described later as having "all the requirements of the law, a wedding with a veil and with everything that goes through a girl's head, with everything a girl dreams about—the wedding of Gildo with Paquita. Gildo had his honeymoon with Paquita. Gildo fell, he did not return."

Actually, it was the beginning of a pattern. Again and again, Fidel would dictate his followers' personal lives as well as their political lives.

Then the group took off for Santiago, many for their deaths, singing as they went along a couplet of the Spanish poet Federico García Lorca, "*Iré a Santiago en coche de aguas negras*"—"I am off to Santiago in a coach decked with mourning waters."

As Haydée Santamaría, the homely but noble-hearted sister of Abel, prepared to leave her home, she thought about the uniquely intimate days and nights of tireless talking and planning with the comrades of the movement. In her mind, she pictured Fidel again pacing back and forth in his own footsteps every night in the small living room as he taught and formed his followers. "Seldom in our lives have we been happier than when our small group was getting ready for Moncada," Haydée, who was affectionately called "Yeyé" by her friends, recalled later. "We had no idea what 'Moncada' would be, but it didn't matter, because in any case it would be 'Moncada.'"

As the *Fidelistas* gathered from all over Cuba for a revolutionary last supper, some stopped overnight in Havana, where they were somberly given train tickets to Santiago, arriving there at dawn and checking into the Hotel Rex or into an apartment rented to them as "Carnival tourists." Abel and Haydée traveled together, a "married couple." Melba Hernández arrived by train, carrying a flower box full of shotguns.

As an omen, perhaps, of things to come, Fidel left his glasses on an ornamental cabinet in his house, and even though he could barely drive without them, he was afraid to return for them because such a move might arouse suspicions of the movements of the conspirators. As a result, the man who was to become Cuba's great revolutionary hero could not see well during his entire first "heroic" episode.

Fidel and Abel had begun planning the attack in February. Leasing an old and roomy farmhouse on a two-acre farm, Fidel played one of his delicious little jokes on authority. The farm, which they called "El Siboney," was located on the road to the famous Siboney Beach, where the crude and brutal commander of the Moncada army barracks, Colonel Alberto "The Jackal" del Río Chaviano, now owned a house. That meant that, several times a day, Chaviano would drive by Fidel's "chicken farm," soon to be brimming with guns gathered precisely for the purpose of killing Chaviano and his men. Fidel, with his cunning sense of where real security lay, realized that this "accident" of planning offered genuine protection. "Every day they were thus reassured that they were far from any suspicion," Marta Rojas, a journalist who prominently covered the Moncada trial, wrote.

The target of the attack, the thousand-man Moncada barracks, incongruously resembled a Rif fortress out of *The Desert Song* with its white-plastered walls and its crenellated moldings. The idea—the ostensible idea, for Fidel's mind was always made up of layer upon layer of interwoven and contradictory thoughts and intentions—was to assault this fortress in the dawn hours after Carnival, when most good *Santiagueros* would be sleeping. Fidel would broadcast "The Revolution" over the new medium of radio he appreciated so well and "the people" would rise as one in revolt. Meanwhile, there would be a second diversionary attack on the nearby barracks at Bayamo, where the war for independence had actually started.

Melba and Haydée, the only two women, arrived at "the ranch" at Siboney (*la granjita*) on Saturday, July 25, and they immediately and devotedly set out to clean it up. They lovingly prepared a fricassee of chicken that would go down in Cuban revolutionary history, on a night of revolution as strange as any in history. When the men arrived, Melba and Haydée walked among them passing out glasses of milk. Fidel stood towering above them all, a figure now more compelling than ever. And now he told them somberly, for the first time, what exactly it was that was about to happen to them.

"When I asked you to come to Santiago de Cuba and then to this farm, I could not tell you, for security reasons, what our mission would be," he began. "Now I can tell you that our target is the Moncada barracks." The group was astounded, gasping with the audacity of it. "We will attack at dawn," he went on, "when the guards are only half awake and the officers are still sleeping off their drunkenness from last night's Carnival parties. It will be a surprise attack and should not last more than ten minutes."

The plan?

"We will go by car. The squad in the first car will take advantage of the confusion caused by our uniforms to take prisoner the guards at Post 3. We will remove the chain between the two stanchions at the entrance. We will drive in, leave the cars, and enter the buildings to our left, taking prisoner those in the dormitory there who surrender. A second force of twenty will seize the hospital, whose back windows open on the fort. They will then provide harassing fire through the windows against the rear of the barracks. A third group of six will take the Palace of Justice and from the roof neutralize the machine guns on top of the barracks inside the fort." There was a pause, then Fidel went on, eyeing each man for signs of restlessness. "You joined the movement voluntarily, and the same is true of this attack," he finished up.

The room seemed caught and held in a taut silence that no one dared break. Most were stunned, but most would nevertheless follow him. At this point, only one *Fidelista*, Gustavo Arcos, in later years to become his most ardent "human rights" opponent, protested. He said the plan was suicidal. Fidel, his eyes now coldly focused, demanded, "You are afraid? You are not with me?"

"I will go to Moncada even if I die," Arcos retorted, then paused and added, "I hope that you are willing to die, too." This compulsive talk of death was their romance and their resurrection, just as it had been with the legendary José Martí. Only a few, like Arcos, seemed to realize what it was really about.

After this initial contretemps, the amazing scene at "El Siboney" settled into the hours of a final night that ranged between the deepest kind of religious experience and sexual ecstasy. It was as though one could plan and will one's last night of life and present it to one's God, instead of having Him present it to you. "The stars were bigger and brighter," Haydée, always the most lyrical of spirits, rhapsodized. "The palms, taller and greener. The faces of our friends were faces we might never see again but would have with us always. Everything was more beautiful, everything was larger, lovelier, finer; we felt ourselves to be better, kinder . . . I looked at my brother Abel and it comforted me to think that if I never saw him again, it would be because I, too, no longer lived. We looked at Fidel, and it was as though something told us that he would surely live . . . because he had to live."

For his part, Abel, tall, blond, and boyishly handsome, shared some if not all of his sister's flowing romanticism. Abel, Fidel's second in command and the man Fidel would call "the best," spent a strangely lighthearted evening, existing in a kind of rare netherworld somewhere between memory and imagination. "Abel was as happy as if nothing were happening," Haydée told me many years later of that night before the fall, when the world gleamed and glittered for a few immensely innocent and idealistic young people. "I couldn't understand it. He laughed and said, 'How surprised they would be if they knew what was going to happen!' He didn't mean just the next day—he meant everything."

In the dark early morning, the men spent a lot of time trying on the *Batistiano* uniforms. Amazingly, Fidel's, which was the largest, did not fit. He stood there, a huge hulk of a man, clean-shaven, without even a mustache, with sleeves too short and pants up around his ankles. "Looking at himself in the mirror," one of the group, Tomás Toledo, recalled, "he worried that he would not look—for the glorious assault on the Moncada—like a soldier of the regime, the role we were to play in attacking the garrison. He had the same worry when Abel tried on his uniform. 'Look, Abel,' Fidel said. 'You will at least have to *act* like a military man.'"

Fidel was not the only warrior of that night to illustrate vanity in battle. Boris Luis Santa Coloma, Haydée's fiancé, had bought special two-tone shoes to wear into battle. "They were his new shoes," Melba recalled later, "and he was like a child. He went with his new shoes into action."

By 3:00 A.M., they were readied and Fidel gave his last speech. "In a few hours," he told them, "you will be victorious or defeated, but regardless of the outcome—listen well, *compañeros!*—this movement will triumph. If you win today, the aspirations of Martí will be fulfilled sooner. If the contrary occurs, our action will set an example for the Cuban people and from the people will arise young men willing to die for Cuba. . . ."

Only one voice came forward to voice what most "rational" people would have said many hours before. Mario Muñoz was the doctor and radio operator they had brought along to go behind the caravan, with Melba and Haydée, in civilian clothes to show, if they were captured, that they were not combatants. "Fidel," Dr. Muñoz said then, "I am ready to die for Cuba, but to think that we can take the Moncada barracks with a few more than one hundred men, when they have a garrison of more than a thousand soldiers, is to send these boys to a sure suicide."

Fidel was enraged, as he always was when anybody challenged him. Coldly, he stood there, not looking at Muñoz, not responding. Finally Abel said, "Those who are afraid can stay behind . . ." Muñoz did not allow him to finish. "I will be in the vanguard," he interrupted, "but I repeat that this plan seems to me to be madness, even a crime." Fidel remained in petulant silence.

Ten of the *Fidelistas* did then separate themselves from the group and decided not to join in on the attack. Fidel, treating them with the scorn such fecklessness deserved, told them to stay in the bathroom at "El Siboney" until the others had left. Then the "poet" of the group, a sensitive youngster of eighteen years, Raúl Gómez García, recited in a tremulous voice some of the verses of the hymn he had composed for the Moncada uprising. He had incorporated part of the Cuban national anthem into it and now he repeated the familiar words: *"Morir por la Patria es Vivir"* — "To die for the Fatherland is to Live." The group, so abnormally happy only a few hours ago, now was silent, standing in a circle of pathos in their ill-fitting uniforms in the darkness before the dawn.

At 5:00 A.M., their convoy of twenty-six cars left "El Siboney" to attack the Moncada barracks. It was the beginning of the Cuban Revolution.

The attack on Moncada that early morning of July 26, 1953, remains one of the great "military disasters" of history. It is too much, as Fidel has tried to do at times, to blame the sanguinary failure all on accidents, for grotesque mistakes were made.

To this day, the exact number of men who took part, the number of cars, and even the exact length of time that the attack involved vary so much that it is impossible to clarify those details. Studying all the accounts, the number of *Fidelistas* ranges from 87 to 115 to 134 to 135 to 147 to 165 men and two women. The number of Batista soldiers on the other side ranges from 262 to 402 to 500 to 1,000. Yet, these are really only minor details; the picture of the attack and the sense and mood of it are very clear indeed.

When the line of cars moved out of "El Siboney," the uniformed attackers sat silently inside them. Renato Guitart, the young *Santiaguero* who was to lead the assault, was in the first car, Fidel drove the second, which also carried two others. The attack began within fifteen minutes of leaving "El Siboney," when Guitart jumped out of his car in front of the Post 3 gate and shouted imperiously at the soldiers on guard, "*Atencíon, atencíon, ya viene el generaľ*"—"Attention, attention, the general is coming." In the deceptiveness of dawn, the guards thought that this new group was a military band that had been brought in from Havana to perform during the several days and nights of Carnival, and so in that confusion the insurgents were able to take their arms away from them. The plan had been to rush Post 3 after disarming the guards; then the others would enter the courtyard, disarm the sleeping soldiers inside, take over the radio transmitter, and fan out through the Moncada with their newly captured weapons. But all of this plan was aborted almost immediately when suddenly there appeared a special patrol that was as unexpected as it was unknown to the *Fidelistas*.

Renato Guitart had observed and studied the fort's defenses for weeks, but he had never seen this roving guard called, curiously, the "Cossack Patrol," because it had been instituted only for the Carnival period. Furthermore, far from the great majority of the soldiers being safely asleep as Fidel had expected, most of them had been at the Carnival all night and were just "coming home" as the insurgents approached; in addition, there were larger numbers of soldiers than usual because many had been brought in to enjoy Carnival leave.

As Fidel jumped from the car, carrying his submachine gun, wild firing began in all directions. The key element of surprise was lost from the very start.

Now everything seemed to go wrong. Fidel jumped back into the car to move forward, but the car wouldn't start. Gustavo Arcos, half out of his car and about to level his rifle at an army officer, was ludicrously knocked over when a swinging car door hit him.

Héctor de Armas was one of the participants in the ill-fated attack. Years later, he talked with me about it. "At the very least, when you are going to make such an attack," he said, "you ought to know where you are going to attack, the access routes, the roads. . . . Nobody gave any orders. So I got out of the car and went behind a tree. I stayed there for about half an hour, throughout most of the shooting. Then Carlos Bustillo came by and we walked away together back into Santiago. . . . The army was looking for people, but luckily I was one of those who had civilian clothes underneath my military uniform."

As Fidel crouched behind his car, several *Fidelistas* led by Guitart actually did get inside the barracks. Here the Cuban Revolution won its first martyrs. As the rebels fired their pathetically small arms—.22-caliber rifles and old shotguns—Batista's soldiers shot back. Within seconds, Renato Guitart lay dead at the door of the radio station, alongside the still bodies of his comrades, Pedro Marrero, Carmelo Noa, and Flores Betancourt.

Where were the reserves? Fidel wondered, as the wild shooting continued. Later, he would learn the unbelievable truth. It seems that the ten men who had refused to go to the fight did not stay in the bathroom at the ranch as they had been instructed. Instead, they left the house, and in driving away they inadvertently drifted into the line of cars heading for Moncada. Making a wrong turn, they led those fighters behind them, who did not know Santiago, into the city. So, as the real battle began, the men who were to back up Fidel and his group in the crucial attack on Post 3 were haplessly wandering the streets trying to find the second largest military garrison in Cuba!

When Raúl and his group realized that the attack had failed and that Fidel had given the order to retreat, he and his men simply took off their outer uniforms, walked casually into the streets of Santiago in their civilian clothes, and disappeared.

The group at the hospital, which included Haydée and Abel Santamaría, did not fare so well. Ironically, Abel had not wanted to be the one to occupy the local civilian hospital, the Saturnino Lora, which was in such a strategic location that it would enable the insurgents to operate as snipers and cover the men in the Moncada courtyard. "I'm not going to the hospital," Abel had argued with Fidel, "that's where the women and the doctor are going. If there is a fight, I must be there. Let the others do the disc-jockeying and distribute the leaflets."

"You are second in command," Fidel replied, ordering. "I have to lead the men and may not come out of this alive."

In the end, Abel obeyed. And so the little group of twenty *Fidelistas* "occupied" the hospital and immediately began to distract the soldiers with diversionary fire, as was the plan.

By the time they realized no one else was firing, it was too late. Runners had been sent to tell them that Fidel had given the order to retreat, and, had the runners arrived in time, they might have saved them, but they never arrived at all.

At about 8:00 A.M., Abel took Melba and Haydée aside. "We've had it," he said. "You know what is going to happen to me, and perhaps to everybody; but it's more important not to risk you two. Hide in the hospital and just wait. You have a much better chance than anybody else of staying alive—do that at all costs. Somebody has to survive to tell what really happened here."

An intern helped all of them quickly to put on hospital gowns and bandages. Many of the rebels got into beds, where they lay terrified, pretending to be patients. Haydée and Melba ran into the children's ward, where they tried to impersonate nurses.

When the *Batistiano* soldiers poured into the hospital, roving like the Khan's horsemen through the wards, the masquerade came extraordinarily close to working. Indeed, the soldiers were just about to leave when a man in a checkered shirt who was the military's public relations man to the hospital and just happened to be there at the moment, whispered to the soldiers what had occurred. Brutally, the soldiers grabbed the insurgents from their beds and literally threw them outside.

The last time Melba and Haydée saw Abel alive was in the hospital courtyard, where he was being beaten mercilessly by the rifle butts of the soldiers' guns. Dr. Muñoz, who had argued with Fidel in those last moments at "El Siboney" about the "suicidal" nature of the attack, was shot in the back at point-blank range. He lay for hours in a darkening pool of his own blood.

After giving the order to retreat, Fidel and eighteen others took to the Sierra. Brokenhearted and physically exhausted, the little group started out by foot for the rough, heavily forested mountains. Peasants along the way helped them, in particular one man who guilefully turned the army in a contrary direction, and in the community of Sevilla Arriba a *guajiro* killed a pig and they all feasted on it. When the peasant spoke of the oppression of the landowners, Fidel gave him his treasured nickelplated .45 pistol (or so the legend would have it) and told him sternly, "When they come to bother you, open fire with this pistol. Don't believe in anyone. Defend what is yours." The blood of Moncada had not even dried on the cobblestoned streets of Santiago, and Fidel already was moving into the next stage of politicizing the peasants of the Sierra Maestra. This "classroom" in the Sierra would end abruptly when Fidel was caught a few days later and imprisoned. But only temporarily.

Meanwhile, Raúl began walking across the country, away from Santiago. He slept in a canefield that night and the next day began walking again. "I went into a town, where I purchased bread and drank some water," he said later in jail. "As I continued walking, I was arrested. They ordered me to halt and asked for my identification. I told them I was from Marcané, that I had come to the Carnival and had run out of money so I had to return home on foot. Since I couldn't prove identification, they took me to the San Luis Garrison. . . ." Raúl was by then a captive; but at least he would survive.

Fidel was right when, during his famous trial and in later times, he correctly estimated that the attack "worked" in the long run for one reason and for one reason alone: the barbarities of the *Batistiano* military. Batista immediately censored the press, allowing only certain "information" to get out—that these were a "group of assassins" who killed patients in the hospital and were infiltrated by foreign mercenaries "from Korea." Yet, what happened in the horrible aftermath of Moncada was that the true nature of Batista's regime was revealed for the first time. Orders came from Havana to kill ten insurgents for every soldier killed, and the officers went about it with such relish that the second in command of Moncada, Captain Andrés Pérez Chaumont, a specialist in taking out the eyes of his prisoners, was surrealistically nicknamed *Ojos Bellos,* or "Beautiful Eyes."

The two women—the only ones to survive the horrors of the hospital, which Abel had scorned as too easy a post—were captured and then taken to prison, where they were subjected to unspeakable terrors. From their cell, they were made to hear the screams of their comrades as they were tortured to death. Melba and Haydée could do nothing but stare at the walls and listen to the terrible final cries of the ones they loved. At one point, they heard the soldiers talking about "that one with the two-toned shoes," and Haydée's hopes rose. But Boris did not survive the torture. And Haydée was to suffer still more.

A sergeant nicknamed *El Tigre,* "The Tiger," came to her in prison and, opening his bloodstained hands, showed her the eye of her brother and demanded that she tell everything or else his other eye would be torn out. Haydée's reply, which every Cuban schoolchild came to know by heart, was: "If he did not tell you under torture, far less will I tell you."

Gómez García, the young poet who had recited the revolutionary hymn in the last minutes before the rebels had left "El Siboney," was so badly beaten in the face that, when the women saw him, they could recognize him only by his sensitive eyes. Eventually Gómez died, slowly, of the tortures. In the end, everyone who gave himself up to the police died. Ten for one, as Batista had demanded.

Melba and Haydée waited in the hell of the VIVAC prison. Always their worst fear was that Fidel, too, had died. "Waiting for Fidel, we had lost hope that anyone else would come," Haydée remembered of those bleak hours. "And days and days went by and no one came. . . . We were convinced that they would not appear. . . . Neither of us breathed a word. . . . Then one day we heard footsteps, and voices louder and more excited than usual. Something big was happening. But if something big—what could it be? Then in a moment I saw some hands in motion, some fingers. I don't know how I knew, but—they were Fidel's. . . . We had been neither dead nor alive. Now we broke free of that thing—you must experience it to know it—that is neither life nor death. And from that moment the question whether we lived or died no longer mattered. Fidel was alive. Moncada lived!"

Batista immediately blamed the Moncada attack on those enemies he was capable of recognizing: the old traditional politicians who had so openly signed the hapless "Montreal Pact" against him plus the Communist party leaders. Blinded by the surface political "facts" of a Cuba that still appeared to be what it had always been, the caudillo within hours had rounded up old-style politicians like Emilio Ochoa and José Pardo Llada, along with various Communists. But rather than finding its roots in any foreign-inspired Communist party ideas, the attack on Moncada—its style, its militancy, its fanatic air—was rooted deep in Cuban history. In fact, exactly such an attack had been planned years before, by Antonio Guiteras, an attractive young social democrat of the 1930s (Hollywood even made a movie about him). Guiteras, who was so honest he was known as the "man with one suit," was the founder of the popular organization Joven Cuba, or "Young Cuba." He had drawn up several daring plans to attack the Moncada in 1931. One was a direct attack, the exact precursor of Fidel's plan; a second was to attack the *cuartel* with bombs thrown from a hijacked civilian airplane. None of the planned attacks was ever carried through, and Guiteras was killed in 1935 in a bloody shoot-out with the military.

So Fidel's idea was not really so new or unusual. Nor was it as implausible as it might seem from afar. "The strategy was good," the historian

Ramón Bonachea concluded, for Moncada was on the opposite end of the island and "victory would give him control over the entire movement. By being far from Havana, the center of conspiracies, and the area of operation for the old politicians, Castro need fear no immediate challenge, and those who eventually joined him would have to go to Oriente." Had the attack been successful, once Moncada and Bayamo were taken, Fidel's idea was to blow up the bridges over the Cauto River, cutting the highway to Havana and the rest of the country; at this moment, he would pronounce the rebellious and complex-ridden southern part of Oriente as Cuba's "first liberated zone." This would have marked an astonishing precedent, and if it had come about, might have stood as a warning of his later attempts, through his guerrilla movements, to create "liberated zones" all over Latin America.

Fidel's attack on Moncada, then, was a miniature model of his bigger and grander battles to come—of the "oppressed" and "exploited" of the earth against the rich. It was never meant to be a single assault for political power; it was to stand as the beginning of his revolution against the right-wing militarism of Batista, against the United States, against the traditional politicians, not to mention the old-fogey Communist party, against the upper classes, and finally against the Catholic and capitalist formation of the Cuban state.

But Moncada was also the most importantly revealing event of his life to that time. In Cayo Confites and Bogotá, the impulses to change flowed toward him from those around him. In Moncada, for the first time, he had directed his own action; he had also transparently revealed the structures inside himself in forms he created outside himself. All were vertical, under the total and unquestioning control of one man.

In rare reflective moods, long after he had taken power, Fidel mused about how lucky he was, not only to have survived Moncada but also not to have somehow taken power through the Moncada attack. "I think," he said, "that if we had liquidated Batista in 1953, imperialism would have crushed us; because between 1953 and 1959, the world witnessed a change in the 'correlation of forces' that was very important. The Soviet state was still relatively weak in this epoch. For us, the Soviet state that helped us so decisively later, in 1953 could not have done it."

What Moncada did do was to catapult Fidel Castro into the leadership role of a Cuba in which every other political possibility had failed—or was failing. "The Moncada attack . . . was a failure from the military point of view," the sensitive Cuban writer Guillermo Cabrera Infante wrote. "But it was a resounding political success. After July 26, 1953, everything in Cuba became of vast historical moment—brutal, bloody, and inevitable."

11

THE ISLE OF PINES, PRISON
AS CLASSROOM

Deal with the people artfully and with a smile....There will be
enough time later to crush all the cockroaches together.

—Fidel Castro to his followers

WHEN THE TRIAL of Fidel Castro and his comrades opened
in the Santiago Palace of Justice on Monday, September 21,
1953, almost two months to the day after the Moncada attack,
Fidel's first act was to grasp domination of the ceremonies. He entered the
courtroom wearing his favorite old dark blue striped suit, a white shirt, and
a red print necktie. His hair was combed with unusual care, and his new
mustache was meticulously trimmed. His physical stature and his defiant
demeanor soon had the onlookers whispering in excitement, "This is
Fidel! There he is!" It was his first leap onto the public stage of Cuban
mass consciousness, and he took full advantage of it in that shimmering
heat of summer.

Holding his manacled hands up toward the judges and offering himself
as a metaphor for Cuba, he said in a loud and resonant voice: "Mr. President, I want to call your attention to this incredible fact. . . . What guarantees can there be in this trial? Not even the worst criminals are held this way
in a hall that calls itself a hall of justice. . . . You cannot judge people who
are handcuffed. . . ."

The chief judge, Nieto Pineito-Osorio, who like all the judges was to show himself vastly sympathetic to the insurgents, agreed and immediately ordered the handcuffs removed not only from Fidel but from all the prisoners. From that moment on, it was not the state's trial against Fidel Castro, it was Fidel Castro's trial against the state.

As a young reporter from *Bohemia,* Marta Rojas, sat ready to take her notes for history, Fidel began in his clear and resonant voice, "I want to express to this tribunal my desire to make use of my right, as lawyer, to assume my own defense."

The tribunal agreed, not understanding in the slightest the use Fidel would put it to, and Fidel immediately donned the lawyer's imposing black robes.

The state, in the person of Colonel Chaviano, then read the list of accused, which included the old politicians (Carlos Prío, Aureliano Sánchez) and also the Communist party leaders (Blas Roca, Juan Marinello) as well as Fidel's group. Focusing on the "Montreal Pact," whose members could barely have used guns if they were set upon by a regiment, the court announced that the arms for Moncada had come from Montreal! Fidel was in a revolutionary tactician's own heaven; he was not only wonderfully amused by his enemies' total incomprehension of reality (once again), but he was now prepared totally to take over the trial and in so doing to create undreamed-of new realities.

When he was finally asked if he had participated in the assault on Moncada and Bayamo, he said simply:

"*Sí, participé.*" "Yes, I participated."

"And these youths?"

"These youths, like me, love the liberty of their country. They have not committed any crime unless you esteem that it is a crime to yearn for the best for one's country. Is that not in fact what they teach in the schools?"

The public prosecutor then asked Fidel how he explained to his followers what was going to happen and instructed him pointedly not to go into a political *arenga,* or harangue.

"I have no interest in making politics," Fidel responded, his voice self-righteously and theatrically chilly. "I only aspire to open the path to truth."

"But tell the court how you convinced them," the man persisted.

"The truth is that I did not have to persuade them," Fidel answered. "They showed me the way, convinced that the road that we ought to take was the one of armed struggle, once we had exhausted all the other possible roads, so that this generation would not face the danger of losing itself. . . ." He had set the scene perfectly.

Fidel then produced one of the greatest theatrical dramas in a lifetime filled with them. One minute, he was defending himself. The next, he was cross-examining his accusers, which was his "right" since he was in effect also a regular attorney of the court. Throughout the trial, he constantly and shrewdly used what were in effect costumes to confuse, amuse, and mesmerize the courtroom. He would put on the black lawyer's robe (when he was acting as lawyer) and then take it off (when he went back to being the prisoner and defendant).

These gestures provided a masterful stroke for showing people how a person can be of "the state" at one moment and outside it the next, and how one can go from legitimacy to illegitimacy and back again from moment to moment. Indeed, it was his first public lesson to his people of how legitimacies can change even before your eyes, and the Cuban leaders would have done well to observe him rather more carefully than they did.

As Fidel built his powerful case, he also very deliberately showed the Cuban people the brutality of the Batista regime. But of even more importance, Fidel used the trial to educate the people of Cuba in a very specific idea that was crucial to the final success of the Revolution. This was the belief that revolutions such as his were themselves supralegal, that he and his men had not only the right, but the duty, to take supposedly "extra-constitutional" means to overthrow a dictator who was himself the usurper, having taken power in an illegitimate way.

The top leadership group, including Raúl Castro and Pedro Miret, were sentenced to thirteen years in prison. Twenty others received ten years, and three men got three years in jail. Fidel was not yet sentenced. Instead, it was decided that he would be tried separately, in extraordinary secrecy, and (as was only aesthetically appropriate for him) in an extraordinary place, the small nurses' lounge, which measured a mere twelve feet by twelve feet, in the Saturnino Lora civilian hospital, the same hospital where Abel and his small contingent had suffered so. Once again he asked for and was granted permission to defend himself.

Fidel's own trial probably began about nine o'clock on a morning in early October. Fidel was again wearing his blue striped suit. As many writers as there have been on Cuba and Castro, so there are as many interpretations of Fidel's pronouncement that day. It came to be known as the "History Will Absolve Me" speech and even now, despite the fame of both the speech and the man who made it, no one really knows how many times it was written and rewritten, how many times its intent changed or altered as Castro himself over the months changed and altered. Even the amount of time the speech took that day in 1953, when dozens of people were present and listening, is uncertain.

We know the speech had its beginning in Fidel's "Manifesto," the one that Naty Revuelta typed. And we know this first document was written by the doomed young poet Raúl Gómez García, at Fidel's request. This "Manifesto" begins with heroic calls to a modern-day Cuban revolution and ends with nine "revolutionary laws," which include a plan for economic prosperity and for the recognition of the workers and students as the vanguard in the defense of the legitimate rights of the people. But Fidel was not satisfied with it as a program for revolution, so as soon as he came to prison, he began working assiduously on a more comprehensive version of his thinking.

The best historic proof one can muster tells us that on that October morning, in that unlikely nurses' room, Fidel began his historic speech with "Honorable Judges, never has a lawyer had to practice his profession under such difficult conditions. . . ." He then meticulously reconstructed the attack—its reasons, its rationale, its nobility, and its suffering. He spoke of "sacrifices which had no precedent in the struggles of our Republic" and of the "cruelest and most inhuman oppression in all their history."

Programmatically, this new version of the ideas first promulgated in the "Manifesto" centered around five "revolutionary laws," instead of nine. First there was the restoration of the Constitution of 1940, a confused liberal-radical document theretofore little honored. Second, Fidel called for full ownership of small farms worked by tenants, sharecroppers, and squatters. Third, he spoke for the right of workers and employees "to share thirty percent of the profits of all large industrial, mercantile, and mining enterprises, as well as sugar mills." The fourth law demanded the right of sugar workers on plantations "to share fifty-five percent of the value of the sugarcane produced," and the fifth law called for the confiscation of "all property and wealth secured through politically protected fraud and graft during previous regimes."

In perhaps its most telling section, the speech also clearly rejected any idea of "absolute freedom of enterprise, guarantees to investment capital and the law of supply and demand" as guiding principles for an economic solution. It noted especially "that more than half of the most productive land belongs to foreigners" (which was true in 1953). And he particularly singled out the United Fruit Company.

Whom was Fidel speaking to? "When we speak of the people," the document says clearly, "we do not mean the conservative elements. . . . The people we counted on in our struggle were these: 700,000 Cubans without work . . . 500,000 farm laborers . . . 400,000 industrial workers . . . 100,000 small farmers . . ." So it went.

But in the midst of all of his evoking of blood and carnage and rage, Fidel also offered a bright and shining vision of the future: "Cuba can support splendidly a population three times larger than it now has," he insisted. "There is no reason then for the misery among its inhabitants. The market should be flooded with produce, pantries should be full, all hands should be industriously producing. All this is not inconceivable."

As he approached the end of his speech, he reminded the judges once more of the cruel murders of his men by the army's soldiers. "As for me," he went on, his voice rising, "I know that jail will be as hard as it has ever been for anyone, filled with threats, with vileness, and cowardly brutality; but I do not fear this, as I do not fear the fury of the miserable tyrant who snuffed out the life of these brothers of mine."

Then came forth the noble words that would go down in Cuban revolutionary history—and, indeed, revolutionary history across the world. Using the personal form of "you" (*vos*), as he had throughout his speech, he addressed the courtroom, with all the considerable dramatic power at his disposal: *"¡Condenadme, no importa! ¡La historia me absolvera!"*—"Condemn me, it does not matter! History will absolve me!"

The trial was over. Fidel Castro was sentenced to fifteen years and taken to Boniato Prison on the Isla de Pinos, Isle of Pines, the beautiful "Treasure Island" of Robert Louis Stevenson, south of Cuba.

Just as the Communist Manifesto went virtually unnoticed when it was written in 1848, so Fidel's "History Will Absolve Me" speech began fading from the minds of Cubans once the original passion that the killings and the trial had engendered in Cuba was spent. So Fidel made gargantuan efforts to ensure that it was not forgotten and that it would be passed hand to hand across Cuba until it became nothing less than a reverberating revolutionary refrain from seashore to seashore.

In the long days on Isla de Pinos, he began to reconstruct his speech, expand it, and in many ways to change it. The popular Cuban version has it that Fidel had given his speech from notes, and that Marta Rojas, the *Bohemia* reporter, had scribbled furiously as he spoke to get it all down. As Fidel left the nurses' room, he whispered to Rojas with a distinct urgency, "Did you get it all? Do you have all the notes?" Whether this story is exactly true or not, Fidel now began painstakingly and surreptitiously to coalesce and disseminate his ideas. Between the lines of ordinary and apparently prosaic letters to friends, he inserted passages from his speech, revised, reworked, rethought, written in lime juice so they would not be visible to the prison censor. Fidel later told the American journalist and sympathizer Robert Taber, "You would be surprised how much trouble it was. I could write for only twenty minutes or so each evening at sunset, when the sun slanted across the paper. . . ."

When Melba and Haydée were released from prison in February of 1954, they would receive letters from Fidel, often carried from the prison by Mirta; they would perform the curious and delicate work of ironing the sheets of paper to get the lime juice to show; then they would piece them all together. Ever grandiose, Fidel had wanted one hundred thousand copies of his documents to be printed and distributed across the island ("We thought he had gone out of his mind in prison," Haydée commented in later years). But this was much too ambitious; they only had money and time for twenty thousand copies. Melba recalled that they drove across the island in an old car, so loaded down with its revolutionary "cargo" that the springs almost brushed the ground, and they stopped at every town to leave copies for distribution.

And all the while, from prison, Fidel exhorted them with a continual barrage of letters. "Propaganda must not be abandoned for a minute," he wrote to Melba, "for it is the soul of every struggle." He also urged the women to antagonize as few people as possible—it was not yet time to "exclude." For all the efforts of Haydée and Melba, the speech, or declaration of principles, or propaganda tract of the movement—or whatever "History Will Absolve Me" really was—did not become popular and hallowed until after the Revolution triumphed in 1959. But, what was the program it enshrined? Did it point, as various historians and analysts of Cuba and Castro have disputed and argued over, to Castro as idealist? As clear Communist even then? As a betrayed democrat?

There is no doubt that with "History Will Absolve Me" Castro broke out of the parameters of the traditional political parties in Cuba. Samuel Farber, a Castro analyst, insists, for example, that "Castro's program was far more radical than anything the Ortodoxos had ever proposed." But Communist? Not at all. *New York Times* journalist Herbert Matthews points out that had Castro "been the devotee of Marx and Lenin that he later claimed to have been, he would not have proposed anything so unsystematic." Interestingly enough, Fidel himself, in one of those moments of lucidity and truth that are scattered throughout his writings and speeches in the midst of his ever-changing dreams and rewritings of history, seemed at key times to agree with this. In the late 1960s, he told Lee Lockwood that "My Moncada speech . . . could be called Marxist if you wish, but probably a true Marxist would have said that it was not."

In truth, it is not really all that complex. He wanted a radical, progressive, populist revolution of the poor, headed by a rather traditional populist Hispanic caudillo, but one ostensibly (and fashionably) of the Left. There would be a new "equality" of the poor, but only under that caudillo.

There is one more important facet to the "History Will Absolve Me" speech. Listen to these words: "For it is not you, gentlemen, who pass judgment on us. That judgment is spoken by the eternal court of history. . . . You may pronounce us guilty a thousand times over, but the goddess of the eternal court of history will smile and tear to tatters the brief of the state prosecutor and the sentence of this court. For she acquits us."

Those words were spoken by Adolf Hitler at the end of his Rathaus Putsch trial in 1924, after his attempt that November 9 to take over the German government by attacking the War Ministry in Munich with three thousand storm troopers. It too was a "mad and crazy" attack, but it made Hitler a national figure and, in the eyes of the many sick, disillusioned, and sadistic in that profoundly troubled land, a redeeming hero. How many had the demented "courage" to stand before the German court and say, as Hitler proudly did, "Yes, that was what we wanted to do; we wanted to destroy the state."

There is no question that Fidel's last words came from his careful reading of Hitler's Rathaus speech and, indeed, the whole strategy of Moncada parallels in many ways Hitler's failed Putsch. While Fidel would never sink to the savage levels of Hitler, as brother charismatic totalist leaders they had much in common. They both aimed to create a regime beyond the law; they both destroyed their suspected enemies long before they could become enemies in fact. But perhaps nowhere are their similarities so evident as in their trial speeches. Historian Ward M. Morton wrote that both charged their accusers with "betraying the true spirit and destiny of the fatherland. Both put the accusers and the regime they represented on trial for cowardice, cruelty, persecution and base betrayal of the national spirit. Both announced a mission: to realize the true destiny of the fatherland by purging it of all its faults. Both speeches contained many references to blood, death and sacrifice and both ended with almost the same identical phrases."

The year of Moncada, 1953, Fidel Castro was selected by *Bohemia* magazine as one of the twelve "most outstanding world figures," along with the Shah of Iran, the pugilist Kid Gavilán, Costa Rican president José "Pepe" Figueres, Queen Elizabeth of England, and Soviet KGB chief Lavrenti Beria.

The "Presidio" prison on the Isle of Pines was composed of four circle-like buildings surrounding a large round dining building in the center. Each circle had six floors with ninety-three cells per floor. There was a tower in the center of the first floor from which a guard could watch everyone in the circle. Built by General Machado in 1931, the prison had room for five thousand inmates. Legend has it that, when Machado built it, someone asked him in amazement, "Why did you make it so big?" And Machado answered, "Some day a crazy man will come and fill it."

If Fidel had turned the state's trial against him into his trial against the state, now he turned the cells in the "Presidio Modelo," model prison, into a school. The prison became both a revolutionary training ground and a utopian learning center, where Fidel consciously and deliberately created a "vanguard" of men to be the core of the movement to come. These were months of rare quiet and of assiduous preparation.

In sharp contrast to the prisons he would later himself create, Fidel's cell was large enough for him to walk back and forth, as he spun his new ideas and ideologies about in his head. Sometimes he would sit and rock in his rocking chair, sometimes he would cook spaghetti on his small hot plate. But the greatest passion in his life at this time, besides his constant plotting and planning for the future, was books. "The prison is a terrific classroom!" he wrote in a letter to his friends outside on December 19, 1953. "I can shape my view of the world in here and figure out the meaning of my life. . . ."

Fidel was treated in typical Spanish style as a "political prisoner," which meant that he was respected and that he suffered none of the penury and punishments of the common criminal. With the Spanish admiration for the educated man, he was often called "Dr. Castro" by the other inmates and the prison workers. The little "school" he began for his men was in memorial called appropriately the "Abel Santamaría Ideological Academy." "We are permitted to go into the courtyard from 10 to 10:30 A.M. and from 1 to 4 P.M.," he wrote in one of his many letters, this one on December 22, 1953. "Every morning from 9:30 to 10:30, I give a talk—philosophy one day, world history the next. Other comrades give lectures on Cuban history, grammar, arithmetic, geography and English. . . ."

Fidel maintained his group's Spartan separateness by encouraging a united feeling of hostility against the guards and against the government. Moreover, in typical Fidel fashion, he immediately established for his men a far more rigorous (elitist) discipline than ever the prison required. "If we were ordered to get up at 6 A.M., we would get up at 5:30 A.M., very well organized," Pedro Miret said in later years. And the reason was pure *Fidelista*. "By being stricter than the prison regulations," Miret explained, "we were able to do whatever we wanted. To the authorities, we seemed like very quiet prisoners, so they left us alone. They were so ignorant that they never realized what we were doing with education." It was also a way of superseding outer discipline by establishing the group's own, private, inner discipline.

Incredibly, Fidel at this time was also "suing" Batista. As a result of the tortures and killings that had followed Moncada, he had filed three lawsuits against the dictator and three of his top commanders. It was quite within Spanish law for a prisoner to sue the very chief of state who imprisoned him. Indeed, depositions in those cases were still being heard, with inconclusive results, almost until the time of Fidel's amnesty in 1955.

At this point, another mystery or partial mystery occurred, this time regarding Castro's personal life. In the Isla de Pinos prison, all letters in and out passed through a censor, a man named José Miguel Rivas, who was not at all sympathetic to Batista and tried to help the *Fidelista* prisoners a good deal. He would beg them to write letters he could let through, saying, "*Señores,* please don't be so hard in your letters, or I'll be in there with you."

"Those who had extramarital affairs knew very well they shouldn't write letters the same day to both their wives and their mistresses," Tomás Regalado, Sr., told me when we met in Miami in 1985. Regalado was in the prison at the same time as Fidel for his participation in yet another aborted attack against the state. And yet, Fidel did just that. One day, he wrote letters to both Mirta and to Naty. To no one's amazement, the two letters got mixed up and Mirta got Naty's letter and Naty, Mirta's. This, of course, stunned and finally enraged the usually patient Mirta. Indeed, it was the last unbearable blow. Before that, she had dutifully visited Fidel at the prison, often bringing a new nightgown, with perfume, and she had dutifully carried out his messages and letters to the movement. (Most of whose members, not incidentally, did not like her. They thought she was too bourgeois and they were suspicious of her family's Batista contacts.) Now, it was all but over. But—accidental? No one in the prison and no one who knew Fidel ever thought so.

Now Mirta was even more personally and financially desperate than ever. So Rafael decided to help her by giving her a *botella,* a government job that earns pay without the person working. By that time, Rafael was the number two man in Batista's Ministry of the Interior under Ramón Hermida, so Mirta's little *botella* of ninety to a hundred dollars a month came directly from the ministry that Fidel hated above all others.

Once Fidel's single most intimate friend, Rafael was now not only bitterly ideologically opposed to Fidel but also deeply embittered about the way Fidel treated and abused Mirta. "When Fidel was in jail after Moncada," Rafael contends, "he started using Mirta; he would give her statements to be put in the paper. No other Cuban leader used his wife in such a manner. Mirta was ordered by Fidel to make statements against the government—through the press—and he even wanted her to attack me. . . ."

But while Rafael could help Mirta out financially with the *botella,* he could not control his sister's relationship with her husband. One day, not long after the *botella* had been arranged, Rafael got word from a friend that Mirta, acting for her husband, had made an attack on Hermida. The minister immediately gave a press conference and revealed that Mirta had a *botella* in the ministry. Mirta was humiliated, horrified, and ultimately doomed.

At first, Fidel made a rare misinterpretation of what was going on around him. Thinking that Rafael, for whom he now harbored an unabiding and smoldering hatred, had made up the story, Fidel wrote to Mirta with unusual warmth. In a letter dated July 17, 1954, he scrawled: "Mirta: I have just heard from the news (eleven at night) that the ministry . . . has announced the dismissal of Mirta Díaz-Balart. As I cannot believe under any conditions that you have ever been an employee of this ministry, immediately file a criminal charge for defamation of character against this man." He ends the letter with, "I understand your sadness, but count on my unconditional trust and love."

But soon he knew the truth and he was coldly unforgiving. Beginning with the letter to Naty and ending with the *botella,* the marriage was finished. A divorce suit was soon filed by Mirta.

Had Fidel really loved his decent, beautiful, and loyal wife? In all of his billions of written and spoken words, he virtually never spoke of "love." He spoke of honor, of valor, of courage, of martyrdom, and—more often—of hatred, of destruction, and of death. In only one letter, that of March 23, 1954, which came down through history (like most of the collections of his letters) lacking the name of the person addressed, did he write of love between two people: "Love is like a diamond, the hardest and purest of all minerals, able to scratch anything, but nothing can scratch it. But you cannot polish just one facet; it is not perfect until all its edges have been cut and shaped. Then it sparkles from all angles with an incomparable radiance. The metaphor would be perfect if the diamond, once buffed and polished, could grow bigger and bigger. A genuine love is based on many feelings, not just one, and they gradually balance each other off, each reflecting the light of the others." There is little question he was writing about the lost Mirta.

At the time of the *botella* incident, at least for a while, he seemed genuinely sunk in personal despair, if only perhaps because his wife (and thus, supposedly, his most intimate follower) had so betrayed him, and if only because his small son was now in the hands of those "Judases," as he now called the Díaz-Balarts. He wrote to his friend, the famous broadcaster Luis Conte Agüero, in July 1954: "I live because I have duties to fulfill. . . . In many terrible moments I had to suffer in one year, I thought how much more pleasant would it be to be dead." And in another letter to Conte Agüero, he mused, "Have you noticed the number of invisible links that a man must break who is determined to be in accord with his ideas?" It was a perfect expression of the charismatic leader's realization of his inability to have "visible" human ties—and of a rare moment of sadness over it. People close to both Fidel and Mirta insisted that neither one had really wanted the divorce, not even after the "*botella* scandal," but that there was no way out by then; they insisted that for many years they continued to love each other.

By 1955, Fidel was well past those unusual emotions and he was feeling confident again. He listened one night to the radio while former President Grau made a speech. In the background he could clearly hear voices in the crowd chanting, "Fidel Castro . . . Fidel . . . Fidel Castro!" As he listened, Fidel became exuberant, his dark and often unexpressive eyes gleamed.

By 1955, Batista was also feeling confident. He had been "reelected" president, with the great enthusiasm of the United States, though everyone knew that the last elections had been fraudulent. But just as he had done the wrong thing after Moncada because he felt weak, so now he did the wrong thing because he felt strong: he gave in to the appeals and threats of the Ortodoxos party and exchanged seats in the Senate with them for an amnesty for the Moncada prisoners.

So on May 15, 1955, Fidel and Raúl and the others marched victoriously out of the Isla de Pinos prison and rode in a small boat back to the mainland. Fidel, wearing a white shirt and dark trousers, raised his arms victoriously over his head as he disembarked. Raúl, small and wiry and confident, stood dutifully right alongside his big and brawny brother.

Within days of his release, Fidel was saying to the press that now he would leave for some place in the Caribbean because "the peaceful struggle is over." Onlookers could be excused if they wondered exactly at which stage the "peaceful" struggle had occurred.

12

THE MEXICO YEARS

As a follower of Martí, I believe the hour has come to take rights and not beg for them, to fight instead of pleading for them. I will reside somewhere in the Caribbean. From trips such as this, one does not return, or else one returns with the tyranny beheaded at one's feet.

—Letter of Fidel Castro's before leaving Cuba
for Mexico, July 7, 1955

BACK IN HAVANA, Fidel was greeted with wild enthusiasm. This man, who had been so totally unable ever to win a student election, was now carried on the shoulders of worshipful supporters to his sister Lidia's apartment, where the small rooms were mobbed with newspapermen, photographers, relatives, and friends. It was mid-May. By June, there were two court warrants against him and he feared for his life. So on July 7, he left Cuba, traveling to the port of Vera Cruz and then up to the glorious highlands of *la Ciudad de México*. His devoted sister Lidia sold her refrigerator so that he would have enough cash to travel, and as always he carried many more books than clothes.

But Fidel had not wasted even one moment of those brief weeks in Havana. During that time, in complete contradiction to earlier words at a press conference, he began immediately to form his new organization. The somewhat nebulous movement that had marched on Moncada now became the much more focused "26th of July Movement" or M-26-7, as it came to be known to the initiated. The name, commemorating the date of the Moncada attack, also had a number of other symbolic connections, for there was always an esoteric side to Fidel, fed naturally by the Afro-Cuban Santería, with its magical belief in colors and numbers. "Well, I was born in 1926," he later told the priest Frei Betto. "I was 26 when I began the armed struggle, and I was born on the thirteenth, which double is 26. Now that I think of it, there may be something mystical about the number 26."

In addition to giving form and substance to his new movement, Fidel used his short time in Havana to cement important contacts. Perhaps none was more important or had more far-reaching consequences than his meeting with Dr. Mariano Sorí Marín, who was at that time a democratic, anti-Batista revolutionary. First, Fidel guilefully asked Dr. Sorí Marín to introduce him to his brother, Humberto. Here Fidel already was building his future cadre, for Humberto Sorí Marín, a lawyer and economist, would play a major role in the Sierra and would design the all-important agrarian reform; eventually he would be shot dozens of times in the head by Fidel's executors.

Second, Fidel wanted Mariano Sorí Marín to get a message to former Cuban president Carlos Prío, the same luxury-loving chap Fidel had once castigated as the "buyer and seller of assassinations," the same Prío who had fled Cuba after Batista's coup in 1952 and who was now plotting his own "countercoup" and return to power. Fidel wanted Sorí Marín to tell Prío to overthrow Batista within six months or else give Fidel the money so he could do it! Here the cunning intelligence of Castro again shows. He told Sorí Marín, "If a coup is made against Batista, then I am going to go down in history without a name, even though I made Moncada."

So, Sorí Marín dutifully went to see Prío and he gave the former president Fidel's message, to which the affable Prío agreeably answered, "*Chico,* this is a young man—we have to help the young men." Now it was just a matter of time. Fidel could wait.

Not long after the meeting with Sorí Marín, Fidel himself went to see Dr. José Miró Cardona, who had been one of his professors at the University of Havana. He told Miró proudly that he was "going to Mexico to make the revolution."

But Miró was a suspicious man. He narrowed gimlet eyes upon Fidel and said, "And, against whom are you making the revolution?"

Fidel did not even hesitate, and he certainly was not being ironic when he answered, "Against Carlos Prío, of course!"

In 1986, I spoke to Jorge Valls, the respected intellectual "author" of the anti-Batista Directorio Revolucionario (DR), or Revolutionary Directorate. Valls told me that Fidel's remark had confused Miró for many years until he finally realized that Fidel's first and most implacable war was not against Batista at all but against any competitive revolutionaries. Under no circumstances was he about to be preempted!

And there did seem to be a sense of urgency about Fidel at this time. Even before he left for Mexico, he was quite clear about his own revolution. He had already decided to land a rebel force in Oriente, the province of his birth and the province of Moncada. He had decided to arrive by boat, in exactly the tradition of Martí. Meanwhile, Fidel prepared about twenty persons to keep the movement alive in Havana. Being Fidel, he left each of the "anointed ones" thinking that he or she was his sole chosen and empowered representative in Cuba.

At about this time, a raven-haired, upper-class young woman from the eastern end of the island traveled to Havana especially to meet Fidel. She failed to find him, then. Disappointed, Celia Sánchez went back home.

The Mexico City to which Fidel and his comrades traveled to exile that summer of 1955 was a glorious place, an elegant city of broad boulevards and liquid dusks and air so clear you could see the historic city's two grand and protective volcanoes etched against the lucid mountain sky in a kind of magic light. But while that civic magnificence had enchanted José Martí when he too had visited the city on his early roamings, to Fidel Mexico was merely political exile and a rock to stand on while he prepared to move the universe.

For his group, now in the formative process of becoming the vanguard of the M-26-7, those first weeks and months in Mexico had about them much of the same magic feeling and strange joy of that last night at "El Siboney" before the Moncada attack. Again, the men and women arrived secretively in Mexico City, one by one and two by two, and again there was the tremulous sense of noble expectation and purpose. "There I had the joy of finding my battle comrades," Juan Almeida exulted later. "Do you know what it is like, meeting fellow countrymen in a foreign country? We began shooting practice, telling ourselves that each cartridge was paid for with the sweat and blood of comrades still in Cuba. . . ."

The group of sixty to seventy soon were lodged in six rented houses scattered all over the city: simple and unassuming stucco houses, or an occasional apartment. Had anyone known what they were doing, they probably would not have believed it, for they presented an odd and unlikely spectacle of revolution, "training" every day by running up and down the broad and busy Insurgentes Boulevard and rowing for hours in the morning on the lake in Chapultepec Park.

Fidel's customary secrecy became ever more obsessive. The various groups were completely divided in these beginning months, with only Fidel knowing everyone and only his spirit—and spell—holding them together. Discipline was rigorous and monastic, with each of the six houses having its own commander and each group forbidden to visit with the others. "We could not leave without permission," Universo Sánchez Durante, one of the house leaders, remembered. "There was a military discipline that was like iron. From the first moment that you arrived there, you could not speak in the street, couldn't have relations with anyone, couldn't receive visits, couldn't visit other houses, couldn't make telephone calls, couldn't give anyone your address. . . . Every house had a tribunal, made up of two or three *compañeros,* who had the right even to condemn someone to death. . . . We shot people there."

Fidel's commanding spell was not limited to his immediate followers. A perfect example of those outside the movement who nevertheless gave crucial support to his cause was Orlando de Cárdenas, a Cuban who had left Cuba at eighteen because of the Batista dictatorship, married an American in New York, and then gone to Mexico where he met Fidel. "He had a power of convincing that was tremendous," de Cárdenas, a perceptive and bright man, told me years later. "I had more experience of life, but he had more experience of politics. He convinced me of the need to help in the liberation of Cuba. I was determined to help him in everything. Eleven of his followers came to live with me, and we never had enough food. We used Avis cars. They couldn't rent them, so I rented them for them."

Even de Cárdenas's American wife was won over. But not his mother. "She hated him," de Cárdenas recalled, "in part because he was putting her son in danger. Then one day, Fidel said, 'I'm going to speak to her.' He spoke with her half an hour. After that, my mother said, 'I'll do anything. If it's dangerous, I'll do it. Nobody suspects a seventy-year-old lady.'"

But as useful as the de Cárdenases of the world were to him, Fidel's real strength came from a core of four men: his brother Raúl, the Spanish Republican general and guerrilla-fighter Alberto Bayo, the brilliant Argentine physician and radical revolutionary Ernesto "Che" Guevara, and the sober, thoughtful Cuban Baptist revolutionary organizer Frank País. Each one would, in his own way, become an historic and revered figure—and each one, except Raúl, would eventually be denied or in one way or another destroyed by Fidel.

When General Bayo first met Fidel, he knew he had finally met his appointed destiny. "This," he told friends of Fidel, "is a real revolutionary." In his own way, Bayo had been looking for Fidel Castro for a long time— and Fidel had been looking for Bayo or at least "a Bayo."

The big, bluff, and heavyset Bayo, with his neatly trimmed Van Dyke beard, had been born in Camagüey, Cuba, in 1892, and like Fidel was of Spanish parentage. He had fought in the Spanish Republican Air Force against Generalísimo Francisco Franco, and he had fought in Africa, where he had been a captain of the Spanish Foreign Legion and an organizer of guerrilla warfare operations. Bayo lost his right eye in Africa, then returned to Cuba, and ended up incongruously in a furniture factory in Mexico City. Little wonder he was searching for a "Castro," for in Mexico Bayo was a warrior without a war.

They met in August of 1955, when a friend brought the young Cuban to Bayo's home at Avenida Country Club 67. They were not alone, however, so after they had talked for some time, Fidel asked Bayo for a glass of water. Then he intercepted the old general alone in the corridor. "Tomorrow at four o'clock, I will come to see you alone," he told him.

The next day, when Fidel returned, he told Bayo forthrightly, "I am a Cuban lawyer. I want to fight with weapons in my hands against Batista. Though I am only twenty-nine years old, I know that you were in Africa and fought in guerrilla warfare against the Moors for eleven years and that you have written several textbooks on the subject. . . . Please help me train my men."

Bayo then asked practically, "How many men do you have?"

And Fidel answered, "Nobody yet. But I am going to the United States to get men and money, and I would like to know if you could be the instructor for my men."

"I will do it," Bayo replied, "but I'm afraid I don't have much faith in your possible success in such an undertaking. A young man only twenty-nine?"

Fidel answered simply, "I will be successful."

Bayo sold his furniture factory and soon was training Fidel's *guerrilleros.*

At first, Bayo moved daily from safehouse to safehouse, disguised as an "English instructor." Then he trained the men at a firing range called Los Gamitos, outside Mexico City. Finally, he and several of Fidel's trusted aides found a perfect training spot near the town of Chalco, a ranch of ninety-six square miles called "Santa Rosa." Not only was the ranch house roomy, it was surrounded by a nine-foot stone wall, had towers for protection, and looked like a fortress, which in a sense it was. A clever man, Bayo managed to assure the owner he had a millionaire Central American colonel hovering in the wings, eager to buy "Santa Rosa" for its asking price of $240,000 but that first the ranch house had to be repaired and painted. Thus, they paid only an interim rent of eight dollars monthly during the repairs. Esther López, the owner of the property, which had been a small dairy, later insisted testily that "Fidel Castro never did pay for the ranch."

At Santa Rosa, Bayo, under Fidel's distant observation, reigned supreme. He trained the men in night fighting, armaments, aviation, explosives, antitank mines. He was as excited as a child again. One day he asked the men if they had toothpaste, soap, shaving cream. Then he took every object of personal cleanliness away from them, saying harshly, "No guerrilla shaves, nor cleans his teeth, so from now on none of you are going to bathe, nor clean your teeth, nor . . ." Another time he told them, truthfully as it turned out, that "Very few of you will survive in Cuba, you are going to win, but from you there will remain few."

"The idea seemed impossible," he was quoted later in *Ejército Rebelde,* the rebel army magazine in Havana. "I had had thousands of similar conversations with utopian idealists who dreamed of organizing guerrillas to overthrow Franco, Somoza, Trujillo, Pérez Jiménez, Perón, Odria, Batista, Stroessner, Rojas Pinilla, and so many others. But all these conversations, once spoken, dissolved in the air like cigarette smoke."

It is probable that Ernesto "Che" Guevara met Fidel in early July of 1955. We know the meeting took place at the house of their mutual friend, a Cuban, María Antonia González, at No. 49 Emparan, one of those simple stucco

Mexico City houses which pretends to edge up to the street in community friendliness but then protects itself with forbidding Spanish grating. It was one of those rare historic meetings of two men whose myriad strengths and weaknesses gripped and fit into one another like the parts of a finely tuned machine; a moment in time when two raging and complementary political passions met and mated. It was Lenin and Trotsky, Hitler and Goebbels, Mao and Chu Teh. Each man came to the union with his own implacable sense of destiny, but each brought to their strange and fertile collaboration very different gifts. Fidel was ruthless, but he had an amorphous sense, necessary to him, of doing what he was doing for *las masas.* Che, the more human on an individual scale, nevertheless was ready to sacrifice everything for *la idea.*

They talked for ten hours, through the warm Mexican summer night. "At dawn," Che would later write proudly, "I was already the physician of the future expedition." As for Fidel, Che thought with admiration that he "faced and resolved the impossible. He had an unshakable faith that once he left, he would arrive in Cuba, that once he arrived he would fight, that once he began fighting he would win . . . I shared his optimism." Che wrote later that he had been "moved by a feeling of romantic adventurous sympathy, and by the conviction that it would be worth dying on an alien beach for such a pure idea."

Ernesto Guevara had been born in the historic Argentine city of Córdoba, just two years after Fidel's birth in Birán, but while Fidel's more common family was rich, Che's aristocratic parents were poor. His mother, Celia, was a beautiful, passionate, wickedly teasing woman who adored her five children; his father, Ernesto senior, a civil engineer, was the more practical of this very impractical and creative—and, for the time and place, extraordinarily democratic—family.

From an early age, like Fidel, Che was incapable of doing anything the ordinary way, and also like Fidel he liked things *his* way. When he was eight, he was told that ink and chalk were poisonous and never to put either in his mouth. "Watch," he told his apprehensive classmates. Then he ceremoniously set up the chalk and his inkwell like a proper worker's breakfast, dipped the chalk into the ink, bit off a big piece, and remarked with the sure sense of specialness about himself that always bordered on contempt for others, "Not bad, not bad!"

At the age of twenty-three, already a doctor, he left home, telling his parents jauntily, "Here goes a soldier of the Americas." With those words, he started out on an odyssey of Latin America, which he, like Fidel, wanted to save from itself. Already considering himself a free, nonparty Marxist, the more he traveled, the more he became convinced that all the problems of his impoverished and benighted continent were the fault of the native aristocracy and (especially) of the United States. As with Fidel, hatred of America was to be the single most abiding passion of his life, only he would die for it while Fidel preferred, as always, to live for it.

Once he and his Peruvian wife, Hilda, had moved to Mexico and met the Castro brothers, Hilda introduced Fidel to her friend, a Venezuelan poetess named Lucila Velásquez. She became Fidel's first romantic interest in Mexico, but it was a brief one, for like many women Lucila soon tired of his incessant talk about politics. At first, though, the romance was a happy one. "He would brighten my loneliness," Lucila recalled much later, "with ardent strolls along the Paseo de la Reforma or to the taco stands of Avenida Bucareli. We were infected by the bittersweet happiness of a shared experience: the separation from our homelands; our homesickness communicated in hands held, thoughts exchanged, anxieties voiced." She recalled, too, how "the Cuban passion of Fidel and the revolutionary ideas of Guevara came together like the flare of a spark, with an intense light. One impulsive, the other reflective. One emotional and optimistic, the other cold and skeptical. One relating only to Cuba; the other to a scheme of social and economic concepts 'that one must support. . . .' Without Ernesto Guevara, Fidel Castro might never have become a Communist. Without Fidel Castro, Ernesto Guevara might never have been more than a Marxist theorist, an intellectual idealist."

Frank País is immeasurably less known today than Che Guevara but in many ways he was the most extraordinary leader of the 26th of July, other than Fidel himself. A tall, handsome, intensely serious young man, Frank was born on December 7, 1934, to a humble Spanish immigrant and the pastor of Santiago's First Baptist Church. Always a gifted young man, Frank wrote poetry and composed music, while he also studied the Bible and José Martí. What everyone remembers most about Frank País was his utter and uncompromising seriousness and honesty. His common sense and modesty stood in stark juxtaposition—and may have cost him his life—to Fidel's impulsive willfulness. Still, it was to the ANR, or Acción Nacional Revolucionaria group of Frank's that Fidel turned in the summer of 1955 to be the "in-Cuba" wing of the 26th of July. Frank's group began to prepare for the deadly dangerous work of readying Oriente province for the defiance of the Batista regime. So Frank came to Mexico to confer with Fidel at least twice in those two years, once probably in August of 1955 and once again probably in September of 1956. But the big question, which began to develop in that summer of 1955, was the timing of the "in-Cuba" resistance. Fidel insisted that Frank's group must be ready to stage a diversionary uprising in Santiago before the end of 1956. Frank insisted to the very end that his men would not be ready, but his objections did him no more good with Fidel than they had ever done anyone with such a stubborn leader.

In the fall of 1955, Fidel began reaching out for support and for funds among the Cubans in exile in the United States. That he had ready-made allies among those disaffected, often poor, and always homesick Cubans was obvious. That he was deliberately walking in the shoes of José Martí, who after all pursued his work of revolution almost entirely, and tirelessly, on North American soil, was unmistakable. His words and actions would have been plagiaristic, were they not instead patriotic!

Fidel made his first explicit and unwavering public commitment before an audience of eight hundred Cubans in what was then the "Palm Garden" at 52nd Street and Eighth Avenue in New York on October 30, 1955. "I can inform you with complete reliability that in 1956, we will be free or we will be martyrs!" he shouted. Now there was no turning back. Now Fidel walked publicly, as well as in his own soul, in the footsteps of "The Apostle." From New York, where José Martí had written his articles and proclaimed his beliefs, Fidel, like Martí, moved to woo the cigarmakers in Tampa, Florida. From Tampa to Philadelphia, to Union City, New Jersey, to Bridgeport, Connecticut—it was like a moving vaudeville show. And at the end of every performance, cowboy hats were jammed full with dollar bills.

Meanwhile, back in Cuba, as all the other alternatives to an increasingly despised Batista began to fall by the wayside, Fidel was, in general, getting an excellent press. Once in a while there was someone who feared—or understood.

That fall of 1955, political commentator Miguel Hernández Bauzá wrote an article in *Bohemia* headlined "Motherland Does Not Belong to Fidel." In it, he warned urgently, and uniquely at that time, that a triumphant Castro would become "the only dispenser of civic, moral and spiritual grace . . . God and Caesar in one piece of flesh and bones. . . ." All those not with Fidel, the author predicted, would be "executed as immoral." But even this most bitter of critics admitted that Fidel had not absconded with any funds. It would be a long time before the Cuban people would find corruptions deeper and more terrifyingly dangerous than the crass misuse of government funds.

On Christmas Eve, Fidel's inner group gathered for a traditional Cuban Christmas feast: rice and black beans (the Cubans called it "Moors and Christians"), roast pork, and cassava, with the classic Spanish almond dessert. That night Fidel expressed with a startling new clarity his plans for Cuba's future. "He spoke with such certainty and naturalness that one had the feeling we were already in Cuba carrying out the process of construction," Che's Hilda, then seven months pregnant with Hildita, recalled.

Then, suddenly, the uniquely motivated little group seemed collectively and with one will to grow silent. Even Fidel was silent, as he exchanged telling glances with Che and Hilda. Hilda finally broke the silence, saying quietly, "Yes, but first of all we must get to Cuba."

"It is true," Fidel responded gravely.

In January 1956, the real planning for the landing on the Oriente coast—the landing that would follow exactly in the tragic footsteps of Martí—began.

In March, Fidel began to tidy up his own political house, a house that heretofore had always had the door open to avoid excluding any group or person who could be of potential use to him. Now he broke openly with the Orthodox party under the ruse of a procedural quarrel, and he proclaimed the 26th of July Movement as the only "real opposition" to Batista, calling it "the revolutionary organization of the humble, by the humble and for the humble."

On March 18, a baby girl was born to Naty Revuelta in Cuba. The baby was not her husband's, it was Fidel's. Actually, Naty had had her chance and had made her choice. Before leaving for Mexico, Fidel had asked her to go with him, but her upward-striving mother had insisted that she remain in Cuba with her prominent doctor husband, and Naty had dutifully obeyed. Everyone who knew her pitied her, for they knew she was in love with Fidel—it was the talk of the country club.

In April, Fidel watched, first with apprehension and then with relief, from his Mexican redoubt while two attempts were made to overthrow

Batista. Both failed dismally. The first, which would come to be known as the "Conspiracy of the Pure" because it consisted largely of the most honest and liberal military officers, was aborted when the secret police uncovered the plans. It was an important loss, because the conspirators, who constituted the most competent Cuban officers, were lost to the army six months before Castro landed. (Ironically, many of them had received their military training in the United States, and their ideas reflected this.) What now was left of the Cuban army could be described as coming very close to a mercenary unit and this would immensely aid and abet Fidel's long-range plans. The second attempt was waged by none other than former President Carlos Prío, who this time sent a group of his militants to assault the Goicuría army barracks in Matanzas. It was not unlike Fidel's own attack on Moncada, and just as fatal.

Meanwhile, Fidel's visceral dislike for men of democratic action did not stop him from forging some loose links with the democratic labor organizations, particularly the ORIT, which was the international umbrella for all of the national democratic labor movements in Latin America. Fidel made a point of stopping by ORIT headquarters in Mexico City, and he became particularly friendly with the brilliant and honorable Luis Alberto Monge, who would become president of Costa Rica in 1982. The two men would argue and talk animatedly at Monge's unassuming house until the early morning hours. "He spoke of democracy, he spoke of liberating the press," Monge told me in 1990 in San José. "And before he left on the *Granma* he came to say good-bye and gave me a statue of Martí." He paused. "He is an actor, a great actor, an extraordinarily great simulator of sentiments and phrases. He knows to whom he speaks." Fidel knew or at least suspected that ORIT, through the American trade union movement, was getting some money from hidden or disguised CIA sources, and at one point, according to other sources, he quietly asked Monge if he himself could get similar funding!

Despite Fidel's strict insistence on secrecy, Batista knew every single thing that was going on in Mexico, and he basked in his knowledge, supposing himself not only safe but invulnerable. Soon, not surprisingly, he was plotting to get rid of Fidel Castro. Batista's first move occurred in the winter of 1955 when the SIM, or Military Intelligence Service, in Havana announced that they had discovered "a subversive plot to overthrow the government . . . by Fidel Castro," but nothing serious happened until late June 1956, when Fidel and Ramiro Valdés, who would later become his minister of the interior, were suddenly swept up off a street of Mexico City and hustled to prison. In all, more than fifty members of Fidel's group were arrested.

Fidel, of course, made the best—the very best—of this new "prison opportunity." He wrote letters, he exhorted his fellow prisoners, and he appealed to the nobility of the Mexican soul (not to speak of the legal system), saying to the press, "I trust that Mexico will continue to be loyal to its noble tradition toward the politically persecuted. . . ."

It was in prison that Fidel also met Teresa "Teté" Casuso, the voluptuously beautiful blond Cuban woman of intelligence and artistic sensibilities who would now play a key role in his life. The revolutionaries immediately knew her and respected her because her husband, the famous poet and writer Pablo de la Torriente, had been killed fighting in Spain on the Republican side. Thus, for the charming and warmly passionate Teté, there began an odyssey that would alternate between the old desperation and a new redemption. At least she would be "alive again," awakened from her long sleepwalking passivity by the dreams and hopes of Fidel.

Teté had smiled bitterly that Saturday morning when she had seen an editorial referring to some "young Cubans," now in prison, who had been training for an expedition to "liberate" her Cuba. Nevertheless, she decided she would like to meet these romantic renegades, and the next day she appeared at the prison—along with a quite gloriously beautiful and blooming sixteen-year-old Spanish woman, her friend Isabel Custodio. Isabel, Teté recalled later, "looked like an elegant model, with the rims of her enormous, innocent, greenish-brown eyes darkly accented in what she called the Italian fashion. On that day, her hair was its natural color of dark gold."

A large group of Cubans was gathered in the central courtyard of the prison when Teté and Isabel arrived and, in the middle, standing out, as always, like a tall beacon or lighthouse, was Fidel. "He gave one the impression of being noble, sure, deliberate," Teté recalled, "like a big Newfoundland dog. . . ." Fidel told Teté, while watching the beauteous and aristocratic Isabel from the corner of his eye, how honored he was that the widow of the great Pablo should come to see him. Before she left that day, Teté gave Fidel her card and told him to "consider my house your own." (She would quickly come to be astonished by the literalness with which he would graciously accept that "small" suggestion.) Before she and Isabel left that day, they all stood together, in fine dramatic and serried ranks, and sang the Cuban national anthem.

By the end of July, all of the Cubans had been released, largely through the help of the Leftist ex-president of Mexico, Lázaro Cárdenas. But now Fidel felt a sense of urgency even more intense than before; it was clear that his freedom in Mexico was a very temporary thing; it was nearing time for him to leave.

Two days after his release, Fidel was asking Teté if she could keep "a few things" for him. The "few things" turned out to be seven carloads of munitions, which filled her house and kept her distracted and sleepless for days. From then on, Fidel and his group dropped in whenever it pleased them, cleaned their guns in her bedroom, carried away their rifles wrapped in quilts from her beds. When the house next door became vacant, Fidel and Teté took it over to store still more munitions. But although Teté Casuso, like so many, came to have a deep and even masochistic attachment to Fidel, it never was romantic in a love sense; that relationship began to bloom between Fidel and Isabel Custodio, who like Mirta and Naty fulfilled exactly the physical, psychological, and historical qualifications of the women Fidel wanted in his serious moments. "He sought her out with a youthful effusiveness and impetuosity that both startled and amused her," Teté recalled.

But Isabel was not easily won—or even seen. She studied in the mornings, worked in the afternoons, and attended political party meetings at night, so she had little time for this buddingly famous and persistent Fidel Castro. But Fidel seemed obsessed with her, and every time he came to Teté's, he would ask, piqued, "Where is Isabel, where is she?" It became a game, with Isabel avoiding Teté's house when she knew he would be there, until one day he tricked her by arriving by surprise before she had left. "When I started to leave the house, he was there waiting," she recalled later. "We looked at each other and laughed, because his trick was just as evident as mine. It was a very funny encounter, and he offered to drive me to the university. . . ."

From nearly that very moment on, the two were seldom apart. He lectured her on how it made him "vulnerable," caring about a woman like her, and that a "true revolutionary" had to dedicate himself "in body and mind" to the Revolution. But he "treated me like a princess," Isabel related, "with a fine and delicate love, just as a man should. . . . I was like a doll, or porcelain. And he was very preoccupied with the image that I projected." It was clear that Fidel wanted Isabel to mirror him. "He told me that it was very important that I maintain an image equal to his."

The relationship between Fidel and young Isabel moved so rapidly that within two months he had done the extraordinarily bourgeois thing of proposing marriage to her. At first, she accepted and went to live at home with her parents, who were prominent in the Spanish theater, while she prepared for the wedding. Fidel went so far as to obtain their consent, and even bought her a trousseau: new clothes, shoes, a large bottle of French perfume, and a conservative bathing suit to replace her French bikini, which infuriated him. But the engagement passed quickly, the breaking point of the relationship being his unique "invitation" to her to come along on the boat for the invasion of Cuba.

Isabel remembered her refusal a little wistfully. "That idea of going on the boat with him was a subject of discussion because I would be the only woman," she recalled in later years. "It was very difficult. But history decided. I left three or four months before. It was a very difficult break. I left. I can't say why. . . ." Almost immediately, she married a Mexican businessman and faded out of history as rapidly as she had entered it.

In August, Fidel turned thirty.

In September, he began a frantic series of important meetings with leaders and adherents of other groups, both in order to neutralize them and to gain money from them. He traveled to Mexico's Yucatán Peninsula, with its glorious Mayan ruins, to meet secretly with Justo Carrillo, the ex-president of the Development Bank under President Prío and a quintessentially honorable and intelligent man who was then working with a group of reformist officers to overthrow Batista through a coup. Their meeting consisted of three days of nearly nonstop talk about the future of Cuba. But they talked of personal things, too. Carrillo, who knew the Castro family, told Fidel that his father had had to mortgage the farm because of a bad harvest that year. Even thirty years later, when I spoke with him in Miami, Carrillo was surprised by Fidel's extreme reaction. Fidel stood up and paced an angry cadence, Carrillo remembered. "What do you want of me?" he demanded. "What blame do I have to accept for his bad administration, for his production errors, for whatever . . . ? I have no relation to this man anymore."

For five or six minutes, Carrillo recalled, Fidel was in a rage, saying nothing but *barbaridades,* or barbarous things about his father. When the explosion was over, Carrillo eyed Fidel and added, "But he is still sending you one hundred dollars every month, no?" And Fidel answered, "Ah, yes, yes. . . ."

When the talk turned to Naty Revuelta, about her "scandal," about her and Fidel's baby, about his offer to her to bring her to Mexico with him and eventually make her the "first lady" of Cuba, Fidel spoke to Carrillo with unusual frankness. He kept repeating over and over, in a stubborn, angry, and conclusive refrain: "Naty missed the boat . . . Naty missed the boat. . . ."

That same late summer, Fidel also met with the immensely attractive young leader of the important anti-Batista Revolutionary Directorate, José Antonio Echeverría. Fidel theatrically embraced his young competitor, as tears flowed into his eyes. They spoke all through the night of August 30, much of the conversation hushed and conspiratorial. Fidel went into great detail with the ardent and intensely serious young Catholic revolutionary about the strength of the 26th of July Movement within Cuba. In effect, Fidel also "instructed" him on the part he and his quite different group were to play in Fidel's landing. "In order to start the fight and to begin a landing in Cuba, you, Echeverría, you have to do the sabotage, throw the bombs." Echeverría respected him greatly—and, when the time came, he would throw the bombs, bombs he would get from Fidel.

Echeverría's Directorate was so much the antithesis of Fidel's evolving movement that, had it come to power, Cuba would have been structurally and systematically a totally different country. And until a certain point, it could have been. Born in 1955, the Directorate was made up largely of middle-class and upper-middle-class youths who wanted to establish a true Cuban democracy. The Directorate sought unity (it believed in organizing from the bottom up instead of, as with Fidel and his early hero, Primo de Rivera, from the top down) and it believed in direct and violent concerted action against the dictatorship (in place of the long process of mobilizing and ideologizing that was the policy of Fidel). But in that summer of 1956, it was probably already too late for Echeverría and his Student Directorate. History had evolved other plans. Still, this group's presence and popularity showed the extent to which Cuba could have gone many ways.

But those visits—and those men—were mere political feints, flickering shadows on the walls. Now it was time for the meeting with the one man, outside of Batista, whom Fidel most abhorred, former President Carlos Prío. So these two unlike men with two very unlike intentions for their *patria* decided to have their meeting on the Mexican–United States border. They chose the unlikely little town of McAllen, near the southernmost tip of Texas, separated from its neighboring town of Reynosa by the muddy meandering waters of the Rio Grande. With his strong shoulders and long experience at swimming, Fidel easily swam across the river, emerging on the other side dressed as a Mexican laborer—just "another wetback." But they had arranged for him to change clothes in a house in McAllen, so that by the time Fidel walked into the lobby of the Hotel Casa de Palmas, he looked all the picture of the country-club golfer.

"The door to Casa de Palmas' finest suite was opened by a distinguished Cuban gentleman of middle age and imperial bearing," writers Warren Hinckle and William M. Turner wrote evocatively of this rarely described meeting. "His eyes met those of his visitor with an instant's flash of fire. Then the fire was gone, smothered in the practiced warmth of eyes which had smiled through a thousand state receptions. Dr. Carlos Prío Socarrás, the third president of the Republic of Cuba, a millionaire many times over, a veteran 'aficionado' of the good life, graciously waved his young guest toward an unmacho flowered sofa. . . ." As each man took the measure of the other, "they did all but sniff at one another's pants legs. For the first time in their lives, they had something in common. They shared a hatred."

The two men talked for hours. Fidel paced up and down and revealed to Prío what he certainly already knew: that he was about to begin his final attack against the dictatorship, but that he needed money. Finally, Fidel sat down on the couch next to Prío and, as he talked, jabbed the former president's chest with his finger. "The words came in deluges, like tropical rain," Hinckle and Turner wrote. "He talked at full speed, all energy and enthusiasm and concentration. When he finished, it was dark, and Prío had agreed to give him a hundred thousand dollars. Castro could hardly conceal his excitement. With the money, he could buy still more arms, he could bribe the Mexicans to leave him alone while he readied his invasion force, and he could buy a boat to float his revolution."

Prío's only condition was that he and Fidel present a "united" front against Batista. He demanded that Fidel let him know the moment he was leaving for Cuba. Fidel promised; but when the time came, he left without informing Prío of anything. In measured time, Fidel would use Prío's money to destroy both the man and his abhorrent class.

Ever since the *botella* incident and his break with Mirta, and particularly since Fidelito had come under the influence of the hated Díaz-Balarts, Fidel had brooded about losing control of the chubby, dark-haired, playful little boy. Then, when he heard that Mirta was going to be remarried to a conservative Cuban, he was incensed even further. So he carried out still one more bizarre "coup," this time against his former wife. He arranged for Fidelito to be "kidnapped" and brought to him in Mexico.

"Fidel called Mirta that summer before she remarried," Rafael Díaz-Balart told me many years later. "Fidel said he would like her to send Fidelito to Mexico for two weeks to visit him. Mirta said, 'Fine.' The only thing she asked was that he give his word of honor that after two weeks he would return her boy to her. Fidel said he would send him back with his sister Lidia, who had good relations with Mirta. Five weeks passed. There was no word of the child. Mirta was crazy. Finally she was able to reach Lidia—what had happened to the child? Lidia said she was very sorry, but Fidel said that the boy can no longer live in a family of *esbirros*. This is a Cuban word that means 'thugs'; and it was used widely against the Machado people."

What had happened was that Fidelito had been brought to Mexico on September 17, 1956, just at the time when Mirta was marrying Emilio Núñez Portuondo, the son of the Cuban ambassador to the United Nations. Fidel placed Fidelito with two of his patrons, Alfonso "Fofo" Gutiérrez, a Mexican civil engineer, and a beautiful Cuban former nightclub singer, Orquídea Pino, an ardent admirer of Castro. The boy got a new name, Juan Ramírez, and incongruously joined the Boy Scouts. Fidelito lived now in the Gutiérrez's gorgeous modern villa complete with swimming pool and surrounded by a high protective wall. Whenever Fidel came to visit the boy, he would blow the car horn in a special signal and soon the heavy wooden gate would swing open.

As he prepared to leave for Cuba, Fidel wrote an historic letter to the Gutiérrez family. Dated November 24, 1956, the letter stated that, "I leave my son in the custody of Engineer Alfonso Gutiérrez and his wife, Orquídea Pino." The reason? He refused to see his son "in the hands of those who have been my most ferocious enemies and detractors." And finally he wrote: "I leave my son to them and to Mexico, so that he can grow and learn in this friendly and free country where children have turned into heroes. He should not return to Cuba until it is free or he can fight for its freedom."

But Mirta and her family had no intention of allowing the six-year-old boy to stay in Mexico. On December 8, with the help of the Mexican police and security forces, Fidelito was "rekidnapped" and taken to the Cuban embassy, whence he was duly returned to his mother and to Cuba.

Meanwhile, on October 21, Angel Castro, the Gallego patriarch of the Castro family and the ambivalent father figure of Fidel's life, died suddenly in Birán, leaving an estate worth one million dollars. The Castro family patriarch, who had crept away from the "place where the world ends," from Galicia, a humiliated boy, now was recognized in death by all of Cuba as a wealthy and respected man. The funeral was held in Ramón's house, and while no one really expected Fidel to be there (and he wasn't), Batista took no chances. The entire town was surrounded by his soldiers. But around midnight, something extraordinary happened—out of the darkness crept several men of the 26th of July Movement. Padding quietly like cats, they emerged from the shadows of Oriente to pay their respects to the *padre* of their *líder máximo*. Respectfully, they put roses on the bier and then they left, fading away again into the steamy, hot tropical night.

The day his father died, Fidel was expected at the home of Orlando de Cárdenas on La Quemada Avenue. It was de Cárdenas's wife's birthday, and after the celebration there was to be yet another meeting to "discuss" the revolution. But, as always, the discussions devolved always in one direction. Fidel had already phoned that day and ordered de Cárdenas to get rid of the guests by 1:00 A.M. because he wanted to have a meeting. For the birthday, Fidel sent a gift box of chocolate candy, but he, himself, did not arrive until long after the birthday celebration. It was around one in the morning that "Alejandro"—which was Fidel's nom de guerre in the resistance, as well as his middle name—finally appeared at the de Cárdenas home. A cable had arrived, de Cárdenas told him, and he read it: "Tell Alejandro that Papa died this morning, Ramón."

When de Cárdenas read the cable to Fidel, he expected some emotion. Instead, Fidel's face did not change in the slightest. All he said was, "Don't tell my sisters yet." The de Cárdenases did not like Fidel's reaction, or rather lack of reaction, to the news of his father's death. For one thing, it was very un-Cuban. But in those days, wanting desperately to believe and to have hope in the possibility of a "new Cuba," they explained it to themselves by saying that this man was so obsessed with the Revolution that he could not even be emotionally sidetracked by the death of his own father.

At one point during these endlessly turbulent months and years, Mirta escaped Cuba—and Fidel's endless machinations—for at least six months after the Mexico kidnapping to bury herself, with the boy, in desperate anonymity in Fort Lauderdale, where she worked quietly as a hostess and cashier at the popular Creighton's Restaurant. In those months, she kept to herself, roomed with another waitress, and was lovingly tender to her little boy. The two were very close in those days, and the other waitresses recall that Mirta said very little. "When she came, she was afraid, very much to herself," Pat Keegan, one of the Creighton's waitresses, remembered of Mirta and the time. "Most of the time, she was in a shadow, afraid something would happen. She was a serious girl, and she acted as if she always had something on her mind. Then one day, she made up her mind suddenly to go back to Cuba—it was here today and gone tomorrow."

By November, Fidel was bursting with a sense of urgency; he was as determined as ever to leave Mexico and land in Cuba before the end of 1956. Now it was good-bye to the Bar Reforma and La Mundial, the little cafés where Fidel went with the others to eat tortas and tacos; farewell to the Café La Habana and (less sentimental) to the prison where they were held. . . .

On the advice of Orlando de Cárdenas, Fidel decided that his group of rebels would depart from Tuxpan, a small port on the Gulf of Mexico. Orlando de Cárdenas told me when I spoke with him in 1985: "It had three advantages: it had never been used before as a launching point against Batista, there was no customs house inspection on the road, and there was no immigration inspection so you could travel freely."

In Tuxpan, Fidel found his boat, an American-owned little yacht named the *Granma*. It could hardly have been more inappropriate. A shabby thirty-eight-foot wooden boat, it could carry no more than twenty-five persons safely and was propelled by two small diesel engines. No matter. Fidel declared confidently, "In this boat, I am going to Cuba. . . ." The American owner sold this unlikely revolutionary vehicle to the Cuban "fool" for twenty thousand dollars.

Tuxpan itself was an often foggy, impoverished little port city, humid and misty, perched along the meandering Río Tuxpan. In later years, a crumbling model of the *Granma* would be displayed in a small museum there, and pictures of the "great historic expedition" would garnish the walls. But now, on the rainy night of November 24, 1956, no one in Tuxpan knew of the historic event taking place in their town. As they had before Moncada, Fidel's men began to arrive by ones and twos, staying overnight in different small towns and in those shabby, lightless hotels that have housed revolutionaries from time immemorial.

When it came time to say good-bye, Che held Hilda close and whispered, "I'm your boy forever. I have always been and don't you forget it." She would long remember that last moment together.

Once they were all aboard the little boat, with their pitiful weapons and slim provisions, the *Granma* was so overloaded that the water was almost slopping up over the sides. "My wife lost her shoe," de Cárdenas recalled, with a smile. "Fidel, before getting aboard, put his arm around my wife, me, and Orquídea Pino and said, 'Hide, all of you, hide yourselves and don't go out until you hear we either got there or were arrested.' He didn't want any danger to them from our talking under torture."

As they sailed away from Tuxpan in the dark and moonless early morning of November 25, they passed a ship from the Mexican navy. But the little *Granma* went unnoticed because of the rain. On board, Fidel and his men were so crowded that some were forced to sit with their legs doubled up; others couldn't sit at all. Some got sick and vomited.

Then, as the little, overloaded, unlit boat chugged out into the Gulf, these men, most of them soon to die, bedraggled and already exhausted, without even room to move or to turn in, spontaneously began to sing the Cuban national anthem. The lights were put on briefly and they all stood and looked at one another for long, silent minutes.

Then they hugged one another as best they could, turned out the dim lights, and sailed out into the unrelieved and unknown darkness of the Gulf of Mexico—toward Cuba.

13

THE LANDING

We will be free or we will be martyrs.

—Fidel Castro

RUNNING A BARE 7.2 knots an hour, the *Granma* headed to sea, tossed by huge waves. Che Guevara, always the supreme ironist of the group, described the voyage graphically: "The entire boat had a ridiculously tragic aspect: men with anguish reflected in their faces, grabbing their stomachs; some with their heads inside buckets, and others fallen in the strangest positions, motionless, their clothes filthy from vomit. . . ."

The rewriting of the *Granma*'s near-disaster at sea began within six months, when Fidel's sisters Emma and Lidia pictured Fidel and the men going off in the name of Christ to save the "soul" of the Cuban *masas.* Writing in *El Diario de Nueva York,* the sisters described the scene in Tuxpan: "There, Fidel and his men, surrounded in a hidden beach of Tuxpan, with an improvised cross elevated to our Lady of Charity, prayed that she would help them to carry the flags of victory to her Sanctuary in the province of Oriente." This is the earliest point to which one can trace the beginnings of the myth of Fidel as a Christ-like figure. It was a myth he would carefully cultivate and which would serve him well. "He had the 'Jordan River syndrome,' "the Cuban psychiatrist Dr. Rubén Darío Rumbaut explained to me. "If people came to him, they would be purified. It was the idea that 'I am the measure of all things.'"

In truth, on that dark and awful voyage of the *Granma,* the ship battered by the *El Norte* winds and repeatedly coming near to sinking, there did emerge out of the adversity a strange and eerie faith in Fidel and their purpose. "The *Granma* was invincible," Faustino Pérez decided breathlessly, as the water level lowered in the boat and the seas gradually calmed. "Forces other than purely physical ones had resisted the storm and were driving the ship to her destination."

And Fidel, the invincible leader of the invincible ship of the invincible cause, was not even seasick. Indeed, he seemed to be everywhere, his hyper psychic level of intensity heightened even more than usual. He talked only of plans. "Where are we? When do we arrive? Let me see the map!"

Two days into the voyage, however, both Fidel and the men began to realize that they had a bigger problem than the heavy rain and high winds. Once again, Fidel's organizational abilities, in clear contrast to his inspirational, tactical, and strategical abilities, were seriously flawed. Instead of the trip taking five days and nights, as he had predicted, it was obvious now that it would take at least seven days. This meant that the *Granma* was not going to arrive in time to take advantage of the uprising in Santiago that Frank País was desperately organizing.

On November 30, five days into their voyage, the hapless men on board the *Granma* heard over the scratchy ship radio the tragic news of the failure of the Santiago attack. The serious Frank País, whose sheer organizational abilities far exceeded Fidel's, had obediently and loyally gone ahead and waged his attack on Santiago. While Frank himself still survived, scores of his men lay dead across the silent streets of Santiago, dead in still another of Fidel's wasteful gestures. Now there would be no simultaneous attack within Cuba to divert attention from the Granma landing. For his part, Fidel was angry and bitter, exploding to Faustino Pérez in rage, "I wish I could fly."

Later Fidel and his government would create an "official" version of Frank País's Santiago uprising. In the account of the *Granma* trip, *De Tuxpan a La Plata,* printed in 1979 after deep "investigations" into history, Fidel Castro's regime duly decided that "the popular armed uprising of the 30th of November of 1956 in Santiago de Cuba constituted a political victory." The account speaks correctly of how the revolutionaries were able to gain control of the streets for hours, how they put forward a manifesto of the July 26, how the people fought with them. But there is at least one thing rather strangely missing in this "official account"—Frank País's name is never mentioned. And by then, Frank País was not around to correct Fidel's version of his history.

While their fellow revolutionaries were dying in Santiago, the men of the *Granma* sailed on, adrift in time and tied together only by their *líder máximo,* Fidel. As they neared the Cayman Islands, a small plane ominously approached, a momentarily dangerous reminder of those "others" out there. But then the plane swerved away and left them alone, suspended in those weightless moments in time between the despair of yesterday and the promise of tomorrow, between Mexican exile and ultimate Cuban victory.

On December 1, when they were still 180 miles from their destined disembarkation point at Niquero, Roberto Roque, the navigator and an ex–Cuban navy lieutenant, climbed up to the cabin roof to try to sight land. Suddenly, cries of "Man overboard" were heard throughout the ship. Leaning on the antenna as he came down from the roof, Roque had fallen into the sea. Fidel immediately ordered the ship to stop so they could search for the man. He is supposed to have emoted grandly, "While he has a voice, we will hunt for him."

But it was pitch black in the strange and phantasmagoric "world" of the *Granma.* They were forced to turn on the searchlight. But "nothing helped," Faustino Pérez recalled. "Our comrade was being swallowed by the deep." Never willing to give up, Fidel ordered one more search, and finally the men heard a weak cry, "Here!" Roque was saved, against all odds, giving the men what they gladly perceived as a sign of the hand of godly approval raised over their sacrificial voyage. Amazingly, they had virtually no real idea or even much fear of what was to come next.

Before landing, Fidel checked the rifles, one by one. But the salty seawater had oxidized the steel parts. Then, in that odd ritual of the warrior, the men began to put on their uniforms, just as they had in the dark early morning hours before Moncada. From that moment on, following Bayo's dictums, they did not shave; thus the myth of the *barbudos,* or the "bearded ones," following their Christ-like shaman, was born. At five o'clock on the morning of December 2, 1956, the *Granma* touched Cuban soil.

Che Guevara called the landing a "shipwreck," and for once he was not being unnecessarily ironic. More than a mile from its intended sandy beach landing spot and near a place appropriately called Purgatory Point, the *Granma* literally became stuck in the mud. The odd little band, so gravely uniformed, was soaking wet and grimed with dirt. Worse, the urban wing of the invasion was destroyed, and the Batista regime knew exactly where the landing party was.

Despite all this, Fidel remained bursting with spirit. He later spoke of how he had been "moved by the raw beauty of the coastline, with the craggy green mountains of the Sierra Maestra rising straight out of the water." With his constantly catapulting mind, at that very moment he skipped far ahead and vowed to make the area into a great tourist magnet once he came to power. At this point in time, however, Purgatory Point was simply a very dangerous area. Within an hour of the landing, airplanes were flying over the district, throwing bombs down at the intruders. Nothing could daunt Fidel. After all, he had fulfilled his promise to land in Cuba in 1956—now he was in his own mind already the true son of "The Apostle."

Meanwhile, up in the Sierra, a very clever and powerful old man, Crescencio Pérez, a local *cacique* and producer of marijuana whom the Batista government called "the bandit of the Sierra Maestra" because he controlled fifty thousand peasants in an area of twenty-five hundred square kilometers, wondered what had become of Fidel Castro. He and Celia Sánchez, the gaunt, raven-haired upper-class young woman who was already deeply involved in the urban 26th of July and who had tried to meet Fidel before he went to Mexico, had waited through the entire day of November 30, growing more and more alarmed at the inexplicable absence of the *Granma,* which they were to meet with trucks to carry the men to the Sierra. They went to the appointed rendezvous again on December 1. Still no *Granma*. But they never despaired.

"You'd better get going, *compañero,*" Celia told the old bandit on December 2. And on this day, in an inauspicious beginning, Crescencio finally found some of Fidel's men. They were hiding in the unused freezing room of an ice plant in the little port of Niquero. The others had vanished.

Meanwhile, in Havana, Batista basked in his supposed initial victory over Fidel, but, as always, he made the ultimately fatal mistake of not taking this strange young man seriously enough. "Batista committed errors," Rafael Díaz-Balart recalled. "Batista was in the house of his prime minister playing canasta with several officials. When they urged him to put two naval boats there and push the rebels to the Sierra Maestra, remembering how in an earlier epoch he had been accused of the assassination of Guiteras he said, 'I don't want to be accused of the assassination of Fidel Castro.'" Later, Batista would say bitterly, "When I could have been done with Fidel, I didn't want to—and when I wanted to, I couldn't."

Far from being "done with," a very alive Fidel was in the peasant hut of Angel Pérez Rosabal regaling the humble family with his unmistakable air of prophecy: "Have no fear, I am Fidel Castro." It was not unlike the revelation that Christ had made to His people when He announced His presence on earth—and it was not supposed to be unlike it—for Fidel, forging his spiritual nexus, was beginning the myth of *Los Doce,* or "The Twelve." In Fidel's version, only twelve of his original rebels survived those first fearful days to get to the Sierra. Asked thirty years later how many men there really were, Faustino Pérez answered honestly, "This is very difficult to say, because they had chosen the number twelve. You could say, three, in any moment, eight in another, but the number twelve is a symbolic thing." There were certainly more, probably around eighteen.

After landing on December 2, the men spent the night on a wooded hill. On December 3, they began marching eastward. On the morning of December 5, they reached a small area called Alegría del Pío near the actual Sierra. In three days, they had covered a bare twenty-two miles. Utterly exhausted, they set up their campsite in a dangerously exposed area where a low and totally unprotected hill jutted out into a canefield. Inexplicably, they then posted sentries too close to the campsite, thus cutting down any possible warning time.

At 4:00 P.M., the rebels were accosted by a barrage of bullets, as the Batista soldiers swarmed over them. Che was hit by a bullet in his lower shoulder, but escaped with four other men, wandering for days through the moonscapes and forests of the Sierra. As the military continued to napalm the forests, the men found themselves in the most horrible of situations. They had no water and no food. They were forced to drink their own urine and survive on herbs, raw corn, or crabs. Che actually attempted to draw water from a rock with his asthma apparatus.

The men had been separated into many small groups, and they didn't know where they were, so little did they know of the Sierra. They were not even aware that the great rivers, the Cauto, the Contramaestre, and the Yara, arose there! But, miraculously, among those remaining were most of Fidel's top leadership. As for Fidel, he seemed only to grow in inner confidence and stature, as though defeat were to him spiritually fungible. At one point, as he and two others lay hidden in a canefield, communicating only in whispers, Castro cleared his throat and said with force, "We are winning. . . . Victory will be ours." And, in fact, the "defeat" at Alegría del Pío, crowed over by Batista far away in Havana, was the birth of Fidel's next formative step—the real birth, not in training but in action, of the 26th of July's military arm, the Rebel Army.

After eleven grueling days of marching up and down mountainsides, Fidel and Raúl were finally reunited. The brothers embraced out of sheer joy. Then, "How many rifles did you bring?" Fidel asked Raúl.

"Five. . . ."

Fidel was elated. His eyes gleaming, he shouted, "And with the two I have, this makes seven! Now, yes, we have won the war!"

Whatever the words, or whether they were even spoken, it was this confidence, or the unrelenting appearance of such confidence, that time after time after time would draw Fidel's men back to him and imbue in them the inevitability of victory.

And now this enormous confidence of Fidel's began reaching out to the peasants of the Sierra. Guillermo García, a square-jawed mountain man who was the first peasant to join the Revolution and helped conclusively in rounding up the scattered rebels after the bombing at Alegría del Pío, remembered walking through a field of bananas when Fidel suddenly swerved and asked, "Are we already in the Sierra Maestra?"

García said that, yes, they were.

Fidel was jubilant. "Then the Revolution has triumphed!" he cried.

Many years later, when he was commander in chief of the three western provinces, asked if he believed Fidel at the time, García laughed and said, "You know, Fidel spoke with so much emotion—you had to believe him. Even in that banana field, though it seemed crazy, I believed him. . . . And something else. There we were in the mountains, far away from civilization. We had no troops, no arms, no clothes, no food. Yet even then Fidel was always studying. We hadn't even started to fight the enemy and Fidel was already analyzing international affairs. I remember we would be worrying about where we could find something to eat, and Fidel would be talking about . . . Eisenhower and making plans for the future.

"Another thing," García added, "Fidel had never been in these mountains before. But in six months he knew the whole Sierra better than any *guajiro* who was born here. He never forgot a place that he went. He remembered everything—the soil, the trees, who lived in each house."

Now, indeed, they were in the Sierra, that abysmally impoverished but magically beautiful world one hundred miles long and between twenty and thirty miles wide that was to nourish as mother's milk the savagely reduced but ever more intensely dedicated band of Fidel's. Pico Turquino, the highest peak of Cuba, later to become the geographical symbol of the Revolution, rose above them to a grand 6,561 feet. And the Sierra's sheer poverty and its historic sense of injustice soon bonded many of the peasants, most of them squatters without title or security to their land, to the passionate young revolutionaries. Fidel and his men came to feel a deep kinship with the *muchachos,* and soon they were depending upon them for almost everything. Why should not the peasants have welcomed the romantic young fighters? For the first time they were being recognized and treated as human beings worthy of attention. And there was the crucial fact that young men like Guillermo García did indeed consider themselves a new "peasant generation," one which fit perfectly into Fidel's concept of generational change. The little Rebel Army began to grow.

On Christmas Eve, Fidel and his handful of followers were actually celebrating, eating roast pig with a sympathetic peasant family. By New Year's Eve, they were lying under a freezing rain, Raúl huddled inside a corn-flour sack and Fidel his usual buoyant and unquenchable self. He asked one of the men the name of the mountain they could see in the distance through the rain, and the man answered, "Caracas." "If we can get there," Fidel exulted in the midst of the storm, "neither Batista nor anybody else can defeat us in this war."

But before leading his men into the mountains, Fidel decided to answer Batista's attack with one of his own. He planned to march his men down to the sea and attack the coastal garrison at La Plata. The column marched for eleven days, gathering new recruits as peasants began to join along the way. By the time they reached La Plata, the army numbered thirty-three men. This time, Fidel's "battle" was brief—and even successful.

The rebels attacked the little garrison directly, leaving behind them two dead soldiers and five wounded. They carried off nine Springfield rifles, a Thompson submachine gun, and a wealth of munitions and supplies. It was in this battle that Fidel deliberately ushered in a campaign of military "humanism," a conscious invention of his. He freed the military prisoners being held at the garrison and he even left them with medicine for their wounded. After setting fire to all the buildings, the rebels simply melted back into the devouring jungles of the Sierra.

Attacks from the Batista forces now came fast and furiously. Two weeks after La Plata, the rebels barely survived a terrible surprise air attack that came almost directly upon their camp. By accident or miracle, none of them was killed.

The group also had to deal with their first traitor, an initially ingratiating *campesino* whose name has gone down in Cuban revolutionary history: Eutemio Guerra. This peasant, about thirty years of age, thin and cordial, was a respected guide of the Revolution; and for once Fidel's usually uncanny second sense about people failed him. He liked Eutemio. He even gave him a pass to visit his home away from the Sierra, which was when the peasant made contact with the Batista army. On the cold night of January 27, Fidel actually shared his blanket with Eutemio as they lay down to sleep side-by-side on the hard ground. Eutemio kept asking Fidel questions about the sentries' locations, but Fidel barely answered. It has become a favorite tale of revolutionary lore that, even though Eutemio had his Colt pistol and two hand grenades under the blanket, he did not have the courage to shoot Fidel that night, as he had agreed to do for a ten-thousand-dollar payment from the army. This, too, became legend.

When Fidel discovered the betrayal, he confronted the peasant, who confessed and was duly executed on February 17. A small cross carved in a tree in that remote eyrie of the Sierra still marks the legendary and well-used "treachery of Eutemio."

Once again, Fidel had survived. This, along with the victory at La Plata, inspired more than ever the magical belief that Fidel was invincible, that he was indeed Cuba's true man of destiny, and that he was even the final fleshly incarnation of "The Apostle's" grand and unfinished dreams.

14

GUERRILLA THEATER

A bell tolled in the jungle of the Sierra Maestra.
—Herbert Matthews

O NLY TWO MONTHS after the *Granma* landing, and only three weeks after Fidel and his men had found a spot deep in the forests of the Sierra to settle and regroup, Fidel sent Faustino Pérez to Havana to "bring back a foreign journalist." The *barbudo* intended to show the world that he was indeed alive and well, and invincible—but the confirmer of those facts had to be a foreign journalist for the simple reason that Batista would have censored a Cuban reporter. So it was a bold move, brilliant in its timing and also totally within the memoried parameters of that Cuban history that Fidel would forever evoke to give himself legitimacy and authenticity. In the Cuban war for independence between 1895 and 1898, for instance, General Máximo Gómez had stated, "Without a press, we shall get nowhere." More significantly for Fidel, José Martí had made *New York Herald International* correspondent George E. Bryson his revolutionary muse, deliberately outlining his plans to the journalist for all the world to see.

Faustino Pérez understood well the mission Fidel had entrusted to him. Dressed like a *guajiro* with a straw hat, he simply walked out of the Sierra and made his way to Havana, where he went directly to the home of Felipe Pazos, a small, witty man with a mischievous laugh that seemed to belie the fact that he was the country's leading economist. The first thing Pazos asked Faustino was, "Is Fidel alive?"

"Yes, Dr. Pazos," Faustino assured him, "he is alive."

"Positively, Faustino?" Pazos insisted. "Can you assure me he is alive?" It was the question all Cuba was asking, so Faustino ever more decidedly assured Pazos that Fidel was indeed very much alive. But Pazos, a man with a demandingly vigorous mind, persisted. "Even if Fidel has been killed," he told Faustino, "you would be telling me that he is alive."

Faustino threw up his hands. "Dr. Pazos, with this reasoning, how can I convince you?"

But Pazos's reasonable doubts were playing directly into Faustino's hands, and he now presented the idea he carried with him: the only way it could be proven that Fidel was alive would be for a foreign journalist to go to the Sierra personally to confirm it.

Since Pazos knew the famous and intrepid *New York Times* bureau chief, Ruby Hart Phillips, a big and rawboned woman with an honest and generous spirit, he went immediately to see her in her office. It was not a particularly private place, and that day there were a lot of people laughing and talking and milling around outside the small office. Inside, Pazos spoke in a very low voice, almost whispering. "Mrs. Phillips," he said, "I have received a request from Fidel Castro for a foreign correspondent to go to see him."

Belying her size and stature, Mrs. Phillips had a high and penetrating voice, and she now squeaked at him, dangerously loud for their secrecy, he thought, "Are you telling me that Fidel Castro is alive?"

At this point, Pazos's eyes swept worriedly to the corridor outside. He hoped against hope that no one knew English. Then he asked Mrs. Phillips if she would consent to continuing the conversation in his more private office. Once there, she told Pazos that she, as a resident correspondent, should not be the one to go to the Sierra—it was too compromising. But the highly respected *New York Times* foreign correspondent Herbert Matthews was arriving for vacation on February 9, with his wife. Matthews offered the perfect solution.

A tall, graying man of fifty-seven, Matthews had distinguished himself reporting Chiang Kai-shek's triumph in Peking in 1929, the Italian army's horrors in Ethiopia in 1935, the Spanish Republic's tragedies during the 1930s. But despite his experiences—or perhaps because of them—

Matthews remained a hopeless romantic who sought desperately to find and believe in causes. As so often in his life, Fidel was to stumble onto the consummately right person at the right moment.

Just before dawn on February 16, the Matthews party arrived at the appointed place. Matthews later wrote excitedly that "the dripping leaves and boughs, the dense vegetation, the mud underfoot, the moonlight, all gave the impression of a tropical forest, more like Brazil than Cuba." Fidel was not there to greet them, but it was whispered to Matthews that the guerrilla fighter would soon arrive, after an important meeting with his "general staff." Fidel had ordered his men to make the jungle clearing look as much like a "busy command post" as possible. So the Matthews party actually believed they were in a remote and isolated clearing in the jungle when, in fact, they were a bare twenty-five miles from the city of Manzanillo!

Then, out of the mist, came Fidel, appearing like a legendary hero. The middle-aged American journalist was immediately smitten. "Here was quite a man," he wrote in the fullness of his exuberance, "a powerful six-footer, olive-skinned, full-faced, with a scraggly beard. The personality of the man is overpowering." Haunted still by his unrequited love for Republican Spain, Matthews would then write sadly and reminiscently that, now in place of Hemingway's tragic Spain, "A bell tolled in the jungle of the Sierra Maestra."

For hours, under the dense foliage, the man from the *Times,* with the greatest and most powerful journalistic establishment of the world behind him, and the shrewd young Cuban revolutionary, with neither organization nor real army to his name, sat and talked, Fidel whispering hoarsely in his ear. Matthews thought he was in a jungle, and, in truth, he was: a jungle of obfuscation and deliberate deceit. For at this point, Fidel staged one of the most extraordinary shows of Sierra history, which some have rightly called "guerrilla theater." For his part, Matthews thought he counted approximately forty fighters where there were no more than twenty, and he was convinced that a much larger force hovered hungrily in the high jungles.

Actually, it was all quite simple. Fidel had instructed his men to "adopt martial airs." One by one, then two by two, they marched by Matthews. Then they marched by him again, and again, and again. (One man had no back to his shirt and had to march sideways.) Raúl even brought one exhausted man, Luis Crespo, over to Fidel and Matthews, reporting smartly, "Comandante, the liaison from Column Number 2 has arrived," to which Fidel haughtily replied, "Wait until I'm finished."

When Matthews left, carrying his box camera with pictures of Fidel as well as a paper signed and dated by him, he was clearly enthralled by this new and palpably real and undiscovered revolution. "From the look of things," he wrote, in words that would turn out to be utterly true, "General Batista cannot possibly hope to suppress the Castro revolt."

Matthews's long story, the first of three, appeared in the *New York Times* on February 24, 1957, and the world was never quite the same again.

Matthews had pushed Fidel to describe the kind of society he envisaged for Cuba. "His is a political mind rather than a military one," Matthews summed up. "He has strong ideas of liberty, democracy, social justice, the need to restore the Constitution, to hold elections. . . . The 26th of July Movement talks of nationalism, anti-colonialism, anti-imperialism. I asked Señor Castro about that. He answered, 'You can be sure we have no animosity toward the United States and the American people. Above all, we are fighting for a democratic Cuba and an end to the dictatorship.'"

The articles electrified the world and caused a sensation inside Cuba. But despite the Matthews articles, Batista continued to insist that Castro was dead, until Matthews printed the pictures he had taken of Fidel with his trusty little box camera, as well as the sheet of paper with Fidel's signature and dated "Sierra Maestra."

A bare four days after the Matthews interview was published, the Cuban Communist party publicly rejected Castro, making sterling clear their "radical disagreement with the tactics and plans of Fidel Castro." The old fogies of the Communist party, with their Moscow-line of a gradual approach to change, simply believed armed action to be worthless. Moreover, they hoped still to create their accustomed "popular front" with the bourgeoisie.

As for Fidel, he was already creating his own kind of "popular front." While he was clustering all power in a tiny radius tight around himself, he excluded nobody from the periphery. As the peasants of the Sierra moved to join him, so now did Cuba's educated youth, proving the truth of the maxim that revolution springs to life not out of hopelessness, which man can long endure, but out of aroused and then frustrated hopes and ambitions, which only fuel and feed man's fury. For these young people, though members of a small elite and affluent segment of Cuban society, were, like the *guajiros* in the Sierra, ideologically empty chalices waiting to be filled.

After Matthews's historic visit, other journalists made their way to the Sierra as to the "Third Rome" of revolution. Andrew St. George, the canny and mysterious Hungarian, visited five times for *Coronet* magazine, witnessed six battle actions, and once ended up hiding dramatically from Batista troops in a well covered with leaves. Indeed, the Sierra was becoming so crowded that one big newspaper correspondent on his way up was crestfallen to discover a reporter from *Boy's Life* on his way down.

The day before Fidel met Herbert Matthews, he also met the twenty-nine-year-old Celia Sánchez for the first time. There is no testimony to their meeting in the damp jungles of the Sierra, but from that moment on, the two were first close and they finally came to have one of those historic "romantic friendships" between a great man and an ever-admiring woman, as each one's strengths seemed to balance the other's weaknesses. Where Fidel was disorganized and chaotic, Celia was neatly efficient and calm. Where Fidel dealt expansively in grand schemes and dreams, Celia dealt with the details of life. Where Fidel cared for *las masas,* Celia genuinely cared for individuals, even interestingly enough those who became anti-Castro. Outside of him, she saw the world in relative, ambiguous, more fully human terms, and she was able to some extent to minimize and balance the dangers of Fidel's absolutist side. As she had before she met Fidel, Celia continued to operate as a brilliant and irreplaceable courier, using the code names of "Norma" and "Aly," carrying messages to and from the Sierra and passing in and out of army lines with rare stealth and confidence; but now she moved her "center" to the mountains—to be with Fidel.

Celia soon took over the "business" of the Sierra. She ran things; it was she who tended to guerrilla "headquarters," to Fidel's voluminous correspondence, and to paying bills. (She was sometimes jocularly but accurately called the "patroness of pocket money.") She became a kind of moving office, a floating bureaucracy in her slight person, a gray eminence who husbanded all of Fidel's random notes and thoughts and observations. She was his secretary, his guide, his mother, his protective shadow, that one woman in a man's life who will and must always be there because she is the one woman who has made herself indispensable. She was also, not incidentally, the one woman who would and could tell him when he was wrong, pigheaded, or just damned foolish. And Celia was a kind woman—when they held prisoners in the Sierra, she would send hundred-peso notes down to their families, thus winning over people who would surely otherwise have been against the Revolution. Long after the rebels had "triumphed," it was virtually impossible, even among Cubans who abhorred Fidel, to find anyone who did not like and respect Celia. "She stopped a lot of madness," Rigoberto Milán, one of Fidel's bodyguards, put it simply but truly.

But above all else in the world, Celia took care of Fidel. One day, for instance, he was standing with a map of Cuba from Standard Oil and explaining an attack to the group. Celia had some bad news to tell him, and so she approached him carrying water and a couple of aspirin. "What's that?" he said. "I don't have a headache." "Not now," she replied with her customary cheerfulness, "but you will have one in two minutes when you hear the news." Fidel laughed and took the aspirins.

Born in 1927, Celia came from a well-to-do doctor's family in the provincial city of Manzanillo. The Sánchezes stemmed originally (like Angel Castro) from the north of Spain, and they fulfilled at least part of Fidel's desired political pedigree: Celia's father, who became president of the Cuban Medical Association, as well as other members of the family fought in the underground against Batista.

Many who liked and deeply treasured Celia were disparaging about her looks. Plain, simple, ugly, skinny, long-nosed: those were only a few of the pejorative terms used to describe her. But this is unfair. It comes from comparing her with the sensuous, full-bottomed "ideal" Cuban woman. Celia was more like the Spanish women who can be seen in the old portraits that hang in the Prado Museum in Madrid: gaunt, olive-skinned, tough and sweet at the same time, with very direct and knowing pitch-black eyes that stare haughtily out at you and a pensive and somehow expectantly waiting spirit. Celia was also a very feminine woman and, even in the Sierra, she wore a gold chain around her slim ankle and over her boot.

Were she and Fidel lovers? There are as many interpretations of their relationship as there are people who cared to comment on it. To Robert Taber of CBS, who was with them in the Sierra, "She's the only person for whom Castro shows an unashamed need." To Dr. Alberto Dalmau, a preeminent Cuban doctor who had known Celia well in Havana, "It was a very noble relationship. It was not that she was exactly in love with him, but that she idealized him. And it was mutual." To French journalist Michel Tourguy, who covered Cuba after the Revolution for Agence France-Press, "Her saint was Fidel, and she was his muse. It was one of those historic friendships."

Certainly, Celia's family believed that she and Fidel were having a love affair—and, despite their political involvements, relatives of Celia's have told me that the family was "horrified" when she "ran away" to the Sierra. One family member avers that "Some in the family would say, 'It's so disgusting that she's up there in that terrible life,' but others would say, 'Well, it's because she's with the man she loves.' And in the eyes of the family that made it forgivable. It never occurred to them that she was there for more than love."

As a matter of fact, one has to believe that Fidel and Celia were lovers in the Sierra. They slept in the same room, when there was a room. Both were intensely passionate people—both physically and politically—and it seems impossible to imagine that, with the need and affection they had for each other and at that time and place, so filled with the sensuous enticements of danger and death, they would not make love. Later, when the world was different, she would reminisce romantically about those irreplaceable months in the Sierra. Sitting with Fidel and some American journalists on a farm on the Isle of Pines, she recalled in her husky, throbbing voice, "Ah, but those were the best times, weren't they? We were all so very happy then. *Really*. We will never be so happy again, will we? *Never.*"

In those early months of 1957, Fidel was constantly on the offensive, organizing new groups and recruiting men from the cities to join the rebels in the hills. At all times, Fidel insisted that support for the guerrilla war in the Sierra was the prime priority. In this, he was met with fierce disagreement from Frank País, disagreement that would eventually lead to a crucially important schism in the movement between the *llano,* or lowlands (or urban revolution), and the Sierra.

In fact, the fight in the cities was far more dangerous and brutal than anything that was happening in the relatively "peaceful" Sierra. The rebels in the Sierra were able simply to move away from the enemy without losing psychological advantage, but in the cities Batista launched his most scourging reign of terror. Then, on March 13, 1957, there occurred an event so important, so tragic, and so crucial to the future of the Revolution that it cannot be overmagnified: the revolutionary directorate, under José Antonio Echeverría, attacked Batista's palace in Havana in an all-out attempt to assassinate the hated dictator, but the attack failed and Echeverria—another potential competitor to Fidel—was killed.

Batista was feeling almost dizzily high as he surveyed the broken bodies of the hopeless young revolutionaries around him; one after the other his enemies were being "removed" from the scene. The "pretty mulatto" even laughed gaily when an Associated Press reporter mentioned that his "political opponents" suggested he might be a dictator. "Yes, I've heard that," Batista was quoted, "but I think the only dictatorship around here is that which my beloved wife and four sons exert on me."

Indeed, to look at the surface of the beautiful and languorous country, it was easy to be fooled. Tourism was higher than ever; car sales were up; national income and national output were rising headily. But what could not be "seen" was the extent to which, underneath the superficial power indicators, support for Fulgencio Batista was eroding and often in unexpected ways. Among his followers, Batista had always been able to count on believers of Santería. Before Echeverria's palace attack, hundreds of hand-carved wooden heads depicting Batista had arrived regularly at the palace carrying special "blessings" for the general and special Santería "masses" had been held for him around the island. Now the very nearly successful attack on the caudillo shook the adepts of Santería because Batista, "The Man," was supposed to be infallible. Was it possible that "the saints" no longer were protecting him?

Here again, the shrewd use of the national mind by Fidel is shown in uncanny ways, for now, at his urging, anthropology students began rumors that, after two decades of sturdy protecting, "the saints" were, indeed, abandoning the pretty mulatto. As a result, some of the *santeros,* or spiritual leaders, began subtly to switch their loyalties and now dozens of red, white, and blue beaded collars, blessed by *santeros,* were being sent to the Sierra. It certainly did not hurt that Celia was one of the "initiated ones," an inner member of the cult, herself a *santera.*

While Batista enjoyed the good life in Havana, blindly ignoring the signs around him, life in the Sierra underwent a subtle change. Under the skilled direction of Alberto Bayo, the rebels were beginning to view themselves as "citizens of a guerrilla group" rather than citizens of Cuba. And Fidel himself began using the term "Free Territory," or *Territorio Libre,* to mark his new "nation" of guerrilla "citizens." He was beginning to define this new country as his own.

These were months of restructuring. Food was scarce, and the rebels ate mostly Sierra vegetables, chicken soup on holidays, and an occasional pig. But their spirits never flagged. Such was their camaraderie that two of the men even wrote ballads celebrating life in the Sierra and sang them to the group. One, a man named Calixto Morales, had been on the *Granma* and had nicknamed himself "nightingale of the plains." The other, a peasant named Crucito, called himself, in contrast, an "old Sierra buzzard." Years later, Che Guevara recalled "the old buzzard" Crucito sadly: "This magnificent comrade had written the whole history of the revolution in ballads which he composed at every rest stop as he puffed on his pipe. Since there was very little paper in the Sierra, he composed the ballads in his head, so that none of them remained when a bullet put an end to his life in the battle of Pino del Agua."

There was a continual shortage of money in those early weeks in the Sierra, before funds began pouring in from the cities, and Fidel tried at one point to issue a form of revolutionary "bond" to help finance the Revolution. Another time he proposed creating a new "Sierra Money" in order to pay the workers in the coffee harvest. Actually, in these efforts, he was acting, as always, in a perfectly predictable way and in total psychological accordance with his upbringing and past. "Sierra Money" would have been simply another form of the *vale,* the chits that Angel Castro used to give his men so they could buy in his stores.

For much of 1957, the guerrillas of the Sierra were constantly on the move. Finally Fidel set up a sort of command post at La Plata, the little coastal garrison where the rebels had had their first successful battle. As always, Fidel was everywhere—talking, bellowing, thinking, writing, questioning. He wrote his messages, his manifestos, his appeals—to individuals or to the Cuban people—on little scraps of paper, often while sitting in his hammock, his feet hanging out sideways; Celia then put the scraps together into readable form. He was nearly as voluminous a letter writer as Samuel Johnson, and often his letters had a charm and humanness that his actions did not have, particularly when they were written to Celia, as they so often were.

On May 5, he wrote to Celia with perhaps mock peevishness about an insufferably lost pen, saying, "If my pen was in the other shirt, as you say, it must have gotten lost, because that shirt is in the hands of the boy who travels with me, and the only things that turned up were a couple of pencils, which I've just thrown away because they don't work." He ends the letter with the comically plaintive: "I need a fountain pen; I hate being without one." Another time, when his teeth were bothering him, he wrote to Celia, "When are you going to send me the dentist? If I don't receive weapons from Santiago, Havana, Miami or Mexico, at least send me a dentist so my teeth will let me think in peace. It's the limit; now that we have food, I can't eat. . . ."

He refused to wear his glasses in the Sierra because he said, not without vanity, "A leader does not wear glasses." That Fidel was the leader among the men of the Sierra was never in question; that he was consistently difficult, and contradictory, was equally never in question. *Miami Herald* writer John Dorschner recalls how even in those days, "At times, his face would turn sheepish and humorous, and he could appear as lovable as a teddy bear. But moments later, he might be pacing and bellowing in such a rage that subordinates trembled. At other times, he would withdraw, immersed in reading or thinking, but if he chose, he could talk for hours, hammering home his points again and again with a rhythmic cadence, as if he thought repeating his ideas made them more believable."

These unusual physical and psychological propensities—the frenzied and ceaseless talking, the imposing of his iron will constantly on the other personalities, the manic energy that seemed almost superhuman as he often went days without sleeping—did not, however, turn people away from him or even frighten them. It drew them to him. It was almost as though the more *cóleras,* or rages, that he went into, the stronger was his mythic pull on people. Fidel's hold on his men in the Sierra was a microcosm of what his relationship with the people of Cuba would be, an almost amorous bond. He so captivated them that every action, no matter how bizarre or even how insulting, had all the high intensity of a great love affair.

His enemies called him a coward, a man afraid, the "leader" who almost always disappeared at the moment of danger to the peripheries of the fight. To be sure, Fidel did not lead his men always into battle; he directed from the sidelines. The secret to understanding Fidel, rather, was to understand that he was not lacking in courage—his life was one orgiastic risk after another—but he was also neither suicidal nor a willing candidate for martyrdom. Martí was suicidal. Echeverría, a devout Catholic, found solace in surrendering his soul to God. Che finally, in effect, would commit a kind of revolutionary suicide. For his part, Fidel seemed at times almost a sorcerer in his uncanny ability to determine how to win and how to survive, when to risk and when strategically to withdraw. That he often casually risked others' lives and never mourned them is equally clear, and perhaps never more apparent than in his strategic conflict with Frank País.

From the moment Fidel arrived on Cuban soil, he was dependent on Frank País. The Sierra relied upon Frank for arms, for money, for contacts, and for representation with the outside world. Celia worked closely with Frank and appreciated his talents deeply and Frank won over everyone he met. But, from the beginning, Frank also challenged Fidel, he contradicted him unhesitatingly on strategy and organization, and he criticized him within his own movement. It was only a question of time before the two would clash irrevocably. Meanwhile, Frank lived in a day-to-day and indeed moment-to-moment danger that Fidel and the men in the mountains never even remotely experienced. Once he joked about "going to the Sierra for a rest!" But it was not really a joke.

Frank's title was National Chief of Action of the M-26-7, or 26th of July, and many (probably even Frank) thought that put him on an equal footing with Fidel. After all, under the excoriatingly dangerous eyes of the worst Batista killers, Frank had built up a tight and effective urban movement not only in Santiago but in Manzanillo, Bayamo, Guantánamo, and even remote villages in Oriente. By the spring of 1957, only six months after Fidel had arrived, Frank's most cherished objective was to open a second guerrilla front in the Sierra Cristal. The intent was to ease the pressure on Fidel's guerrillas and, not incidentally, to get himself away from Santiago before the Batista men inevitably closed in on him. This objective of a second guerrilla front clearly presented a profound political and psychological threat to Fidel, as, more and more, did Frank.

Frank was morally impassioned about the Revolution; but he also had a quite remarkable courage that was never tarnished by any of the gnawing questions of character that seemed always to hang uneasily about Fidel. On June 30, for instance, "Daniel" (Frank's code name) not only attacked an army post at the Miranda sugar mill and captured large quantities of arms, he also then daringly used a clandestine radio to break into a speech of the hated Rolando Masferrer and issue a call for revolution! Soon, however, the limited joy evoked by attacks like this were dimmed forever by the death, at the bloodstained hands of Masferrer's terrible "tigers," of Frank's younger brother, Josué. The boy's slim young body can be seen in photographs, lying crumpled and bloody at the feet of steely-eyed men with shotguns. With his customary personal reticence and his deep sense of honor, Frank wrote to "Alejandro," which was Fidel's code name, of Josué: "Among them, the youngest, whose death has left an emptiness in my chest and a very personal sorrow in my soul."

Even while they were joining forces that fateful summer in Mexico, there were always profound differences between Frank and Fidel. A devout Christian and democrat, Frank was also watchfully anti-Communist. He was fully aware of Raúl's and Che's adherence to Communism and their singular influence over Fidel in the theological no-man's land of the Sierra. Soon their personal differences were reflected in their organizations, and the gap between Frank's urban revolution (*llano*) and the Sierra widened.

Frank began a furious exchange of letters with the leader in the Sierra. He rebuked Fidel for failing to send guerrillas to help his men who had been trapped for nearly fifteen days, surrounded by Batista soldiers. No one had ever confronted Fidel like this!

It got worse. In a second letter, dated July 7, Frank told Fidel decisively that he had decided that the entire structure of the M-26-7 in Cuba should be reorganized. He insisted that the movement's leadership should be decentralized and that a homogeneous, disciplined, and tightly controlled urban underground should be built. He informed Fidel that, as of July 7, the leadership of the movement would include six members in a new ruling executive council; and Fidel was to be granted only one delegate to this executive Council of the National Direction.

Fidel responded to this audacious downgrading not with hot, angry emotion but in typically cool Fidelesque tactical terms. He immediately drafted the "Sierra Maestra Manifesto," which was signed without consultation with the "National Direction." The content of the July 12 manifesto, like those of all of Fidel's manifestos or statements, was basically unimportant, calling again for a democratic regime, elections, constitutional government, etc., etc., etc. The manifesto's real intent was to undermine Frank's reforms and to show clearly that it was Fidel, and not the city revolutionaries, who was in charge.

Meanwhile, as the war in the cities became more and more ferocious, the thin and increasingly haunted-looking Frank was forced to move ever more desperately from house to house as the army now searched for him with a cold and icy fervor.

At the end of July, Frank moved into the house of a friend in Santiago, Raúl Pujol. He had been there only a short time when the police suddenly and menacingly surrounded the place. "Peering through a window, País saw several carloads of police and soldiers in the street," Robert Taber, the American journalist who spent much of the spring of 1957 in the Sierra, wrote. "He quickly telephoned Pujol at his shop, thinking to have his friend come and take him out of the district by automobile. Then seeing the searchers coming closer and apparently taking thought of the danger to Pujol's family . . . he suddenly decided to leave, alone and on foot." On the street Frank País died at the hands of a notorious assassin known as *Mano Negra,* or the "Black Hand," who "rushed after the youth and fired a bullet into his back at close range. País fell in the alley. . . ."

Tens of thousands of Cubans, most dressed in white, somberly and angrily jammed the narrow cobblestoned streets of Santiago for the País funeral. Almost the entire "directorate" of the 26th of July was there, undisturbed by the police because in the Spanish tradition, the time of death and mourning is sacrosanct, if life is not.

But only four people had known that Frank was at the Pujol house that day—his fiancée, América Domitro, Raúl Pujol, Pastor Agustín Seisdedos, and Vilma Espín, a Communist who was active in the 26th of July. After evading Batista's men so brilliantly for so long, how did it happen that this day all Frank's meticulous precautions seemed so suddenly and fatally to vanish?

For months, Frank had been working closely not only with Celia, whom he liked, but also with Vilma Espín, whom he did not like. One of those delicately pretty but coldly self-righteous Communist "girls," Vilma had always taken a rigidly far-Left line within the movement, exactly the line that Frank most hated. At this point in the struggle, according to many unrelated and responsible accounts, Frank no longer informed Vilma of the important facts, like where he was hiding out.

"Vilma was a power grabber," Frank's brother, Agustín País, contends. "She had tried to become Frank's girlfriend or mistress, always with the thought of being a power behind the throne. Frank put her off, and in effect named others to be his eyes and ears. This bothered her very much. Vilma didn't know where Frank was the last week of his life. But she found out. The morning of his death she called him. Frank was angry that she had found out where he was. That afternoon he was killed."

There are too many mysteries still swirling around Frank País's death, and particularly Vilma's possible role in it, to dismiss or forget it. Historians like Rolando Bonachea and Marta San Martín have documented how "Santiago de Cuba intelligence section of the M-26-7 was most powerful at the Central Telephone Company, where M-26-7 telephone operators, under Vilma Espín, gathered data on Santiago's police and army movements by monitoring telephone or microwave transmittals. It is strange that Vilma would have risked telephoning Frank that day." She herself has admitted, "I spoke to Frank over the phone eight or ten minutes before he was killed." Since it was common knowledge that an underground fighter did not make calls from private phones or receive them except in an emergency, it is odd that she has testified that she called him only to ask, "Why have you not called me? What has happened?"

At Fidel's campsite the day Frank was killed there was a celebration of the baptism of a peasant child for whom Fidel was to be godfather. When he heard the news of Frank's death, Fidel called him "the most courageous, useful and extraordinary of all our fighters," then went on without observable emotion partaking in the festivities, which included the joyous feast of a roasted pig.

Whether Vilma "informed" on Frank, or led the police to his hiding place, whether she did it for Fidel or for Raúl or for the far Left, or whether Fidel simply again exercised his uncanny instinct for leaving people in places long enough so "inevitable" things just happened to them will never be fully known but can be surmised. Fidel's rage at the insolence of Frank País, whom in death he would then extravagantly praise, was obvious. The outcome we know, and we know that after that any idea of the dividing up of power within the movement was never revived, ever, by anyone. When, in September of 1957, another uprising, in the city of Cienfuegos, failed, Fidel's way was totally cleared. Now, from his mountain hideout, Fidel could peremptorily order without any fear of competition: "All guns, all bullets, and all supplies to the Sierra."

15

A NATION IS DYING

Los caminos de mi Cuba,
Nunca van a donde deben.

The roads of my Cuba
Never lead where they should.

—Carlos Puebla

HAVANA WAS as enticingly beautiful as ever that Christmas of 1957. Sparkling white Christmas trees stood on the palace grounds where nine months before the gallant, foolish boys of the directorate had left their pools of martyred blood. The stores were crowded with last-minute Christmas shoppers and the mood was festive and gay. "But the prisons were full and the armed forces prowled the streets like big cats. . . ." wrote *New York Times* correspondent Ruby Hart Phillips.

For his part, Fidel did his own kind of "Christmas shopping." He visited the village of Veguitas, disarmed the soldiers there, and swiftly returned to the hills with four truckloads of provisions and arms paid for in cash! His rebel guerrilla army was now roaming the Sierra almost at will.

The fall following Frank País's death had been a turning point, for on September 10, at Pino del Agua, Fidel, for the first time, deliberately lured government troops into an ambush. The hamlet of Pino del Agua was built around a sawmill in the deep forest; Fidel paused there briefly to tell the local inhabitants that he was moving on, knowing that one of them would surely pass this information on to the army. One of them did. When Batista's soldiers arrived, the rebels attacked them. It was a great victory for the Sierra guerrillas, despite the loss of the well-loved writer of ballads, the "old Sierra buzzard," Crucito.

That November, a group of moderate politicians in seven opposition groups signed a pact in Miami to create a "Cuban Liberation Junta," which came to be known simply as the "Miami Pact." (Fidel had obliquely encouraged this earlier but, when it occurred, the fact that Fidel received news of the pact through the *New York Times* did nothing to assuage his poor temper!) But the efforts of these moderates were futile; by the time the pact came, Fidel was so strong, he simply rejected all attempts at equity of leadership. He was not on an equal footing with the rest, and he never would be.

In November, the *Fidelistas* began sowing terror across the island by burning the sugarcane. Fearful fires raged from one end of Cuba to the other, killing scores of people. One of the very first plantations to be burned was Lina Castro's, an event that marked the beginning of a lasting estrangement between mother and son.

In the Sierra itself, Fidel was setting up for Cuba and the world to see an almost idyllic guerrilla universe, a utopian model of the Cuba to come and of the other worlds "out there" that he would form. Fidel reminded some visitors to the Sierra of a man "playing the part of the don," others found him kingly. Grandly, he ordered medical treatment given to the enemy, and his men were utterly forbidden to kill, torture, or mistreat prisoners; rather, they were to explain the Revolution to them. Rank barely existed, and the men reveled in being a kind of revolutionary "family."

Then, in the cold early months of 1958, something amazing happened. The once-despised and remote vastnesses of the Sierra, where Cuba's dispossessed "precarious ones" had lived silently in the dense forests, alone and forgotten, began "filling up." Guerrilla warfare was becoming popular, fashionable, safe even, as "Fidel Castro" was becoming a household name from Pittsburgh to Pinar del Río. Fidel's guerrillas did begin to receive some unwelcome competition as the remains of the directorate developed their own guerrilla forces in the Escambray Mountains in central Cuba. There, they too began to fight a courageous guerrilla fight against the Batista troops.

While their numbers would eventually reach some eight hundred men, the Escambray guerrillas lacked cohesiveness; in truth, they lacked a Fidel Castro. Fidel deliberately kept his numbers small and his people united under his command. The last thing he wanted was to have large, uncontrolled numbers roaming the Sierra far from his watchful eye. The Escambray guerrillas finally broke up into two fronts and, within a year, in an almost implausible final lack of will, simply handed the Revolution to Fidel.

Of far more immediate importance than the Escambray guerrillas was the formation, in March 1958, of Raúl's Second Front in Oriente. Although he was certainly still under Fidel's command, Raúl was authorized to do most everything in his area, and his performance was to prove little less than brilliant. With organization and persistence, he in effect lay the groundwork for his later control of the powerful, Soviet-backed Cuban military machine. From March 1 to December 31, 1958, his six guerrilla columns encountered the regular army 247 times, captured six airplanes, intercepted five ships, captured twelve trains, and shot down three air force fighter planes. With 160 casualties of their own, they probably killed 1,979 men in Batista's army—or so at least the Castro brothers claimed.

It was during this time of warfare that the personality differences between the two brothers was especially evident, as were the complementary nature of their characters. Fidel existed somewhere "out there" in political and psychic glory space much of the time, dreaming Napoleonic dreams, pushing his men forward with bold severity and his undimmable faith. And Fidel possessed one of history's most incredible psychic barometers. In the Sierra fighting, he would suddenly stop and say, "No—not through there," and later they would find that Batista troops had lurked in just that spot. Fidel had an extraordinary antenna for the slightest thing that seemed not right. Raúl did not.

Raúl was the organizer, the executor, the far more traditional military man who depended not upon his psychic perceptions and instincts but upon pure military strategy.

As the "brothers show" developed, Fidel carefully and deliberately nurtured the myth of "good brother, bad brother." Whenever he wanted to threaten people with the results of his possible demise, he pointed to Raúl— "He will be much worse than I," he warned repeatedly. And he may have been right. Sierra fighters like Lucas Morán called Raúl's front a "small totalitarian state in which discipline was rooted in the terrible drama of death by execution."

The importance of Raúl's command and success in the Sierra cannot be overstated, for it was at this point, just after his Second Front had been solidly established, that Raúl began to introduce—to Cuba, but also to the world—new guerrilla tactics that would later be carried around the entire globe. One of these new tactics, international kidnapping, proved particularly successful for the rebels.

The first kidnapping by the *Fidelistas* occurred in February of 1958, when the movement in Havana kidnapped the world champion auto racer, Juan Manuel Fangio, in order to get world attention. Fangio was actually quite nice about it; taken at pistol point in the downtown Hotel Lincoln, he said, after he had been safely released, that he understood it was "for the Revolution." But now Raúl launched into these new tactics with relish as he decreed the detention of all U.S. citizens in his front's zone, ostensibly to guard against Batista bombings. Then, in retaliation for the delivery of two hundred training rockets to the Batista army from the United States via Guantánamo (a "mistaken" delivery according to U.S. officials, as it occurred after the American arms embargo of March 1958), Raúl kidnapped a busload of forty-seven American sailors who were returning to Guantánamo naval base from special leave. With his strict military mind, Raúl formally issued Military Order No. 30 to "legitimize" the kidnapping.

When Raúl was ready to negotiate the return of the sailors, he and Vilma "Deborah" Espín (who was to become first his lover and later his wife) swept down in one of the "borrowed" jeeps to the tiny rebel-held town of Calabazas, where they met with Park Wollam, the American consul in Santiago, and his assistant, Robert Wiecha, who was actually a CIA man. When they arrived, Raúl jumped out of the jeep, took off his hat, and bowed deeply, saying grandly, *"Buenos días, señores."* It was indeed a scene worthy of Don Quixote.

The Cubans had two demands: the United States must stop shipping arms to Batista and stop refueling government planes at the Guantánamo naval base. But the larger purpose by far was to intimidate Washington.

While the U.S. government deliberated, there ensued a semicomical scene in the Sierra. Each day Raúl produced two prisoners. They would arrive by helicopter, and an "honor guard" of Raúl's men would form beside the airstrip. Then Wollam and Wiecha would carefully sign receipts for custody of the prisoners. Eventually they would all be released. And while the United States never actually succumbed, the outcome of the kidnappings to the Sierra fighters was much more positive than Raúl could have even imagined. Fidel had again caught the attention of the world; the American public became more aware of the United States' role in the increasingly threatening Cuban Revolution; Batista realized he could no longer extend guarantees of personal safety to foreign investors and technicians; and Batista was obliged to permit the representatives of a foreign government to conduct negotiations within the republic's territory with the enemies of his own government!

With the kidnapping, Fidel honed the tactics of his struggle—the fight of the "weak" against the "strong," with the weak successfully using the vulnerabilities of the strong against them. In later years, such tactical kidnappings—in Lebanon, in El Salvador, in Iran—would, in turn, dictate the foreign policies of the most powerful nations on earth. But Fidel did it first.

The Castro brothers also organized one of the first international hijackings, in 1958, one that resulted in the wreck of the aircraft. Another "first" for Fidel!

Meanwhile, moderate Cubans were growing more and more desperate. On March 15, a broad-based coalition of the most respectable Cuban civil, cultural, fraternal, professional, religious, and sports organizations issued an extraordinary proclamation about their beloved land, which said among other things that they were "now aware that the nation is in the process of dying."

On April 9, 1958, a *Llamamiento a la Huelga,* or "Call to Strike" was broadcast over several radio stations. It began with the rousing words: "Attention, Cubans! Attention, Cubans! This is the 26th of July calling a general revolutionary strike. Today is the day of liberation. . . ." Citizens were urged to throw stones and Molotov cocktails at patrol cars. But, inexplicably, the "call" was made at eleven in the morning, a time when only housewives listened to the radio. In retaliation, Batista passed a law authorizing anyone to kill anyone associated with the strike. It was in fact a license to kill with absolute impunity, and that is exactly what happened. At least one hundred forty youths died, most of them gunned down on the streets by the followers of the hated police chief, Pilar García.

What really happened that sobering morning of April 9? Basically, the whole country was to have gone on a "general revolutionary strike" that

179

was to be carried out by the 26th of July in the cities, backed by guerrilla action in the countryside. Despite the doubts that have been expressed repeatedly over the years, there is every reason to conclude that Fidel himself believed the whole country would go on a massive strike and that such an effort might just mark the end of the Batista regime. Indeed, when Fidel heard the news that the strike had begun, he embraced the Argentine journalist Jorge Masetti, who was with him at that time in the Sierra, and literally danced about, shouting to Masetti, "The general strike has exploded! The hour of liberation has arrived! You are going to Havana with us!"

Instead, a few shops closed, the banks closed, bombs went off sporadically, electric power was cut off in the old part of Havana and in Vedado, forcing people to use kerosene lamps (Ruby Hart Phillips's electric typewriter was useless), and everything seemed to go wrong.

Had Fidel wanted the strike to succeed? He was always ready to try almost any tactic that would work, as long as he maintained control. But he also always carefully hedged his bets. The strike offered a possible opportunity for him without much real risk. Its failure was the privilege of the city organization.

In the bloody aftermath of the strike's dismal miscarriage there were two significant repercussions: the first real meeting of minds between Fidel and the Communists and the unequivocal end of the *llano,* or city, movement of M-26-7. On May 3, a sober postmortem meeting was held in the Sierra to discuss the strike, with Che announcing, correctly, that its failure marked the definitive end of the *llano* leadership. Total revolutionary power now gravitated swiftly to the Sierra and (Fidel's favored term) "revolutionary contradictions" vanished. Fidel had always hated "the city" and its snobbish people anyway; now he had overwhelming reasons finally to read it out of the Revolution.

The first Communist to actually move to the Sierra was a man named José Ramírez Cruz, who was sent that spring to Raúl, who began to use him to organize the peasants politically in the Second Front. Their school became a model for postrevolutionary indoctrination and the first Communist history text was introduced there. Raúl also now organized a peasant intelligence unit, which can be seen as the clear forerunner of Castro's Soviet-trained G-2. In September, he would organize his first Peasant Congress. With his methodic brilliance, Raúl clearly was running on a parallel organizational line to Fidel's rhetorical and charismatic line; but, loyal (and realistic) brother that he was, he waited until Fidel was ready to accept his "line" before offering it to him.

There is no question that Fidel had intended a far more radical revolution than he, at first, expounded. "Naturally, if we had said that we were Marxist-Leninists in the heights of Pico Turquino when we were only a handful of men, we never would have arrived in the plains," Fidel said in a speech on December 20, 1961. But he said this after the fact, and there is no evidence that Fidel planned for even his "radical" revolution to be a "Communist" one. That it worked out that way was more because of Fidel's obsessive need for total power, forever, than his beliefs.

It was actually in February 1958 that the Communist party began, at first hesitantly and then more purposefully, in part because the Batista police had begun killing some of their own, to adopt Fidel's "armed struggle" tactics. But the real moment of change, unnoticed at the time, occurred when the Cuban Communist thinker Carlos Rafael Rodríguez traveled to the Sierra sometime in late spring or early summer that year. He remained at Fidel's side for months—a fact still today only barely noted in most histories—until the *triunfo* of the Revolution.

Carlos Rafael Rodríguez was the cunning old fox of the Communist party. A tall, well-built man with eyes that looked always amused at the world about him and an extraordinary steel-trap intelligence, Rodríguez was unquestionably the mind behind the old Communist party. It was Carlos Rafael, as he was known to everyone, who brought to Che in the Sierra the writings of Mao Tse-tung on the guerrilla war in China (Che mimeographed the texts and made them obligatory discussion materials among his officers and soldiers). In later years it would be Carlos Rafael, who had a wisdom about men that was unusual in the usually rigid Communist mind, who would preserve the strange alliance of Fidel and Marxism, just as it was Carlos Rafael who ignited it.

On the eve of his departure for the Sierra, another Communist chief, Aníbal Escalante, briefed Carlos Rafael on "the line to take with Castro." Then, with all the old imperious rigidity of the party, he literally thrust upon him a long memorandum to give to Fidel, containing endless "advice" on how to conduct the war, run the country, have a "correct attitude toward the other political forces." When they left, the other Communist with them, a man named Osvaldo Sánchez, was almost in tears. He knew Castro.

"Everything is lost," he cried, literally wringing his hands, "he will never put up with this. We are moving toward a new split." A broad grin appeared on Rodríguez's face. "Don't give it another thought," he said. "I haven't the least intention of bringing any of this up with Fidel; I am going to the Sierra to listen to him, to hear what he expects of us, and not to ram our policy down his throat."

It is certain that Fidel was not looking to be absorbed by the Communist party. Rather, he was pragmatically seeking disciplined cadres to run the country when he came down from the Sierra. He would then form his own party, which he would call—out of convenience, out of understanding and respect for the revolutionary fashion of the times, and as a final way to revenge himself against the *americanos*—"Communist."

As for those *americanos* who so obsessed every moment of Fidel's life, their response to the contradictory Cuba of that time was no more obvious than the inner thoughts of Fidel himself.

It was assumed that the United States still dominated Cuba—that was no longer true. It was assumed that the United States still wholeheartedly supported Batista—that was not true either, despite some appearances. It was assumed that the CIA, in particular, was violently against Fidel—that was particularly untrue. But the entire American response to Fidel in those formative years, as so many of its responses in so many other areas to come, was so ambiguous and so without nuance that the picture that emerges is very contorted and strange indeed!

Roy "Dick" Rubottom was at that time the State Department's leading man in Latin America. When I spoke with him in 1986, the stories he told me were all-too-typical of the way the "Colossus of the North" responded to little, basically "unimportant" Cuba in those years.

One day in December of 1957, Rubottom was in the office of Secretary of State John Foster Dulles. "I've got good news for you," the gray-haired, austere Dulles said. "Ambassador Gardner is going to be replaced." This was good news to Rubottom. Arthur Gardner, the American ambassador to Havana, had been an ultraconservative supporter of Batista, and he had already suggested at least once to Batista that together they have the young upstart, Fidel Castro, assassinated. But Batista had almost indignantly refused, drawing genuinely on traditional Spanish ideas of honor, saying, "Of course, we couldn't approve that; we're Cubans."

"I'd like to make two or three recommendations," Rubottom told Dulles.

But Dulles chimed in with, "There is no need. It's been decided. It's Earl E. T. Smith."

Rubottom was bewildered. He had never heard of the man. "Who's that?" he asked.

"He lives in Palm Beach and goes to Havana often," Dulles answered. "He's a graduate of Yale and a heavyweight boxing champ."

"Well, those are all splendid qualifications," Rubottom replied sardonically. The humor was lost.

Ambassador Smith turned out to be just as thoughtless as Gardner had been. Some Cubans laughed—but more cried inside when his wife gave an elaborate fund-raising ball at the Waldorf-Astoria Hotel in New York for a Cuban dress designer while Cuba was sinking deeper and deeper into sorrow. It was also duly announced in those days that Mrs. Smith would be aiding two charities: Cubans and dogs!

Interestingly, however, outside the immediate ambassadorial and military enclaves, most American diplomats in Cuba openly and enthusiastically supported Fidel and the rebels. The consul in Santiago was close to the 26th of July Movement, and Richard Cushing, the public affairs officer of the American embassy in Havana, actually helped American reporters to get to the Sierra to interview Fidel. The embassy knew about the Directorate attack on the palace on March 13, 1957—and did not tell Batista. The radio station inaugurated on February 24, 1958, in the Sierra, entered Cuba with the help of an American consul. The 26th of July had cells all over the American base at Guantánamo, and the base itself provided a special sanctuary for rebels, who used it to smuggle arms to the mountains.

CIA Agent Robert Wiecha himself (who was using an assumed name and living in Washington when I spoke with him in 1987) totally—and believably—denied to me that he had ever given money to Fidel or his group. But, tellingly, he had been definitely pro-Castro. And he insisted with some passion that everyone in the CIA backed Fidel. "They were all pro-Castro," Wiecha, by then a gray-haired middle-aged man left deeply discouraged by his Cuba experience, said. "All. And so was everybody in State except Earl Smith."

While American attitudes toward Cuba seemed to take many and elusive forms, there were specific, written policies. There was a Pentagon policy, a

State Department policy, a White House policy, and many more. The central policy, agreed upon by the top policymakers, was one most of the world never heard of, but it is immensely revealing of the American diplomatic psyche. It was the policy of the "third force," a policy of dreams of moderation, an illusionary policy that people who live in ordered societies so love to insist upon for those who live in disordered ones. Its main proponent, and its enunciator in the policy paper, was William Wieland, the State Department's director of Caribbean and Mexican affairs. Wieland, who many insisted upon shrouding with mystery, would later be blamed by many for "giving" Cuba to Fidel. But it seems more true that Wieland, who had lived many years in Cuba, sought a middle way, the way that "good" Americans always sought. This "middle way" recommended supporting a "third force," made up of persons known to be pro-American and for getting Batista out peacefully.

But it was all quite simply an exercise in unreality. Here you had a Fidel Castro in the mountains who was an absolute genius at, one by one by one, getting rid of any and all competitors—and you had the distant men of Washington who believed that, from afar, they could replace Fidel with a new and unnoteworthy group of "men of good will." Here you had a Fidel Castro who had captured the most perfervid historic and emotional imagination of his people—and you had the well-meaning men of Washington who believed they could neutralize such a desperate connection with good will alone. It was indeed the "American dream."

In a secret CIA "Special National Intelligence Estimate" of that November on "The Situation in Cuba," the study made by all the highest intelligence men of the administration tellingly contained this stunningly unrealistic analysis:

"Castro has failed to convince the majority of the Cuban people that his personality and program, in preference to Batista's, are worth fighting for. Cuba continues to enjoy relative economic prosperity, and a large part of the population, probably concerned that revolution would jeopardize their well-being, appear to hope that there can be a peaceful transition from authoritarian to constitutional government."

In this first real grappling with a new kind of revolution, the United States made all the same kinds of mistakes that were to mark its relations with all the particularist revolutionary syndromes that would follow and that would give the nagging and poisonous phrase of "Who Lost?" to the American diplomatic and power lexicon.

With its total lack of understanding as to the dynamics of revolution, its abiding hope in the military coup (a technique that Castro tellingly had long and deliberately rejected) long after that military was hopelessly corrupted and disgraced, and finally its unwillingness psychopolitically to understand the appeal of new postcolonial-age leaders like Fidel Castro, American policy toward Cuba in the waning years of the Batista regime set the stage for later policies in Vietnam, Nicaragua, Lebanon, Iran, El Salvador, and Panama.

For his part, although only among his intimates, Fidel was beginning to reveal more openly his profound, implacable, but until then largely disguised hatred for the United States. In a scribbled note of June 5, 1958, to Celia after a rocket attack by United States–built fighters, he raged: "I've sworn that the Americans are going to pay dearly for what they are doing. When this war is over, a much wider and bigger war will begin for me, the war I am going to wage against them. I realize that this is going to be my true destiny."

By this time, the Rebel Army occupied or controlled most of the mountain regions of the Oriente. Fidel's "headquarters" at La Plata consisted of a large, rambling wooden house which was open on the sides and gave the impression of hanging over the edge of the mountain. It was covered by a glorious green blanket of growth, and at dawn it was surrounded by the early morning blue mists of the Sierra. It was rustic but it was most definitely a headquarters. The "guerrilla" slowly was being domesticated.

Celebrities were also being drawn by Fidel to the Sierra—or to an "image" of the Sierra, which was all that was really important. By the end of the year, Errol Flynn was in Cuba making a movie appropriately entitled *Rebel Girl,* and the famous Tarzan, Johnny Weissmuller, took part in a celebrity golf tournament in Havana. Weissmuller showed great aplomb when a group of Fidel's rebel soldiers appeared out of nowhere and surrounded him. With all the confidence of one jungle man meeting a few others, Weissmuller simply pulled himself up to full height, beat his chest with his fists, and let out a resonant Tarzan yell! After a few seconds, the rebels began screaming in delight, "Tarzan! Tarzan! *Bienvenido,* welcome!"

At about this time, the man who was to become one of Fidel's four greatest commanders also entered his life.

Huber Matos was a rugged, small, honestly determined man from a family of teachers and judges. He had been a dedicated teacher and rice farmer before, enraged at the Batista killings, he joined the revolutionary movement and went to Costa Rica, where he picked up a shipment of arms and carried them as a revolutionary offering to the Sierra. When the arms arrived, Fidel tried each one in turn delightedly. He was like a small boy, shooting in all directions and crying, as he had so many times, "Now we will win the war." To Matos, he seemed "delirious, shooting into the night . . . with so few weapons, with so few rifles and machine guns." The first meeting between the two men was a propitious one. "He made a very good impression on me at first as a revolutionary rich in democratic ideas," Matos said later. "For a few months, our relationship was personal and generally very good. He was a man apart, aloof. . . . He was opposed to Communists infiltrating the Sierra. . . . I don't think that Fidel was a Communist philosophically. I believe he saw two alternatives—he could bring about a democratic or a Communist revolution. He opted for the latter because it offered him the opportunity of becoming the undisputed ruler of the country for the rest of his life."

But although Fidel respected Matos's remarkable leadership and military qualities, the two men never really got along well. The reason for this was very simple: like Frank País, Matos was his own man.

By the time the big "summer offensive" was started by the Batista army, it was becoming clear to any objective observer that the rebels were, amazingly, winning the war, if only by default. At this point Fidel was actually getting bored. On June 5, he wrote to Celia from the Sierra, "People bore me so. I'm tired of the role of overseer and going back and forth without a minute's rest, to have to attend to the most insignificant details, just because someone forgot this or overlooked that. I miss those early days when I was really a soldier, and I felt much happier than I do now. This struggle," he summed up peevishly, "has become a miserable, petty bureaucratic task for me."

But then in late July Batista almost won, as most of Fidel's guerrillas were caught dangerously inside a "ring" set by General Eulogio Cantillo. Fidel, quite aware of how serious the situation was, immediately sent a messenger to Cantillo's post—let a cease-fire be declared and "talks be held some place in the area!"

Talks? Well, not quite. When Cantillo's first two lieutenants came to see Fidel, they held "talks" for three days. First, Fidel launched into a bitter speech against the government, pacing back and forth angrily and speaking with his usual didactic assurance, as an amused Celia, Che, and several of the guerrillas sat quietly by. At the second meeting, which began in the early morning, Fidel launched into still another attack on the regime. He went on and on until five in the afternoon, when the exhausted colonel in charge finally walked out of the house to his helicopter, stating he saw no purpose in continuing this "discussion" which was clearly a monologue.

But, as always, Fidel's tactical genius worked. Not only did he thus gain time to get most of his men out of the area safely, but the fact that the army was willing to negotiate with him at all deeply angered those army officers who had so long fought against him. Batista's summer offensive finally failed, and Fidel, despite serious military mistakes, again emerged politically and militarily strengthened.

Rebel attacks now increased on the peripheries of the Sierra, and in September, Camilo Cienfuegos and Che took their men westward on what would become known as the legendary "Westward March of Che and Camilo." Meanwhile, Batista's military machine was melting away, refusing to fight, even going over to the rebels as Fidel's marching men spread like an ink stain over the absorbent blotter that was now Cuba. By mid-November, the Rebel Army controlled rail and bus transportation in all of Oriente. In December, town after town, city after city, and army post after army post fell to Castro's rebels: La Maya, Alto Songo, San Luis, Ermita, Miranda, Alto Cedro, Marcané, Borgitas, Algodonal, Santa Clara . . . The turn of the tide, when it came, was as dizzying as a sudden storm at sea, sweeping away everything before it with its unexpected, relentless force.

As the days of both 1958 and the Batista regime dwindled down, Fidel's old Jesuit mentor, Father Armando Llorente, wove his way up and into the Sierra. "One day, my superiors in Havana called me," Father Llorente told me. "The nuncio was coming. They had received a letter from the Vatican, urging us to do a study of what was happening in the Sierra. They were getting contradictory reports. . . . The superior said, 'I have a fear that, if Fidel Castro wins, he is going to persecute the Church.'" Llorente's voice trailed off. "I decided that I would go to the Sierra," he picked up. "It was a picture so different from what you think. First came a *barbudo,* a peasant who gave a shout as a sign, saying, 'Don't be afraid, Padre, I have a gun but no bullets.' That . . . was the vanguard of Fidel. These men had nothing. They were almost barefoot. Nobody had bullets—and it was only three weeks to the victory.

"It was two days later that Fidel suddenly appeared. Now he was very effusive. For four days, I was always with him. In the evening, we listened by radio to all of the battles being won—and they didn't have bullets. The whole world believed they had an army—and people believed that Fidel Castro was fighting all over—and for four days we were having a picnic."

At one point, the priest asked him flatly if he were Communist. "How am I going to be Communist?" Fidel replied impatiently, as they sat there in the deceptively quiet high jungle. "From where am I going to get Communism?"

But then Father Llorente recalled that "as a child, he was always a terrible liar. In fact, at school, he would call it his 'second nature.' I would say, 'You are telling me lies,' and he would laugh."

In those weeks, Fidel was resting, waiting, thinking. It was a bare two years since he had landed from the *Granma,* fulfilling Martí's promise and his own destiny. In that short time, he had defeated the Batista military, brought the city movements under his control, made impotent the old political parties, fooled and neutralized the United States, and used all the disillusioned classes of Cuba to build a mesmerized following that would be his "new Cuba." It had been quite a two years!

PART II

CASTRO

16

FIDELFIDELFIDELFIDELFIDELFIDELFIDELFIDEL

When I return, I will be millions.

—Evita Perón

MOST OF THE PEOPLE at President Fulgencio Batista's party to celebrate New Year's Eve of 1959 did not realize what was going to happen. True, the party was smaller than usual, for the war was now raging everywhere and the "rebels" were deep into central Cuba. But Batista appeared perfectly normal, displaying complete control over the situation and over his emotions. Then, just before 2:00 A.M., he met with his military commanders in a private room and, within minutes, the "macho" men who until that moment had ruled Cuba ruthlessly and totally for almost seven years began to leave the country.

As the little, plump, pouter-pigeon Batista hurriedly entered the plane with his wife and three of his children, he turned to the small crowd below and still with a smile spoke his last words to the Cuban people: "¡Salud! ¡Salud!" Or, "Health, Good Luck!" They were his traditional greetings, but at this point they were outrageously incongruous, especially as paradoxical benedictions to those thousands of Cubans loyal to him whom he was leaving behind.

He was also leaving behind the largest army he ever had controlled: forty-six thousand soldiers, including fifteen thousand new recruits and large new shipments of arms and equipment. This was the force that had now lost to between two and three thousand in the Rebel Army. The total defeat of so many by so few is extraordinary in modern history, and the experience would mark Castro's mind and ambitions forever, reinforcing his belief that all and any "objective" conditions could be overcome by "subjective" or personally willed strengths.

At the same time Admiral Arleigh Burke, chief of the naval staff, was arguing in late-night meetings at the Pentagon that "Castro was not the right man" for Cuba and that even now some action should be taken by the United States to prevent him from taking power. But what action? As historian Hugh Thomas later remarked, "Nothing could be decided, and indeed what could have been at that late hour, other than an immediate intervention by the Marines?"

Meanwhile, Castro was spending New Year's Eve at the home of Ramón Ruiz, the chief engineer of the "Central America," a sugar mill near Palma Soriano. Celia and a few intimates like José Pardo Llada were with him. They knew that victory now was imminent. Celia was joyful, but she was already thinking with a prescient melancholy of losing Fidel. In many ways, that New Year's Eve resembled the quiet, wistfully happy night before the Moncada attack as the protagonists paused to let history take the course they had set for it. If there is an artistry in revolution, and there is, it is at moments like this when hope hangs like a gleaming object suspended and held fast by the nobility in man—before the fall.

But by morning, everything had changed. For some time, Castro had been having semisecret contacts with one of the more resourceful and moderate Batista generals, Eulogio Cantillo, the same general who had had his men surrounded in the mountains. Basically, the contacts were cosmetic on Castro's part, for he had no intention whatsoever of handing victory to any military junta, even without Batista. Now it seemed as though a military junta might indeed be forming, without Batista but also without Fidel, as news came over the radio detailing irregular "movements" at Camp Columbia.

Fidel was simply furious. José Pardo Llada related that he "fingered the hairs of his beard and exerted a force to contain himself. Finally, losing control, he said in a loud voice: 'This is a betrayal! A cowardly betrayal! They want to steal away our victory. I am going to leave for Santiago now! We have to take Santiago right away.'"

His dentist happened to be in the room at the time—Castro was always having dental problems in the Sierra—and the man now spoke up, saying with a touch of sardonicism, "Pardon me, Commander, but I think you should wait, at least for fifteen minutes." But Castro ignored him and continued to issue orders to get to Santiago immediately.

At this point, a teenager from the nearby sugar-mill town burst into the room, wildly excited. "An American station said that Batista and his family have left Cuba," the boy said. Even at this moment of victory, Castro knew that he could still lose everything if even—particularly if even— some reformist version of the same old military caste remained in power. Indeed, in those last, crucially important days, the idea that his "victory" might be snatched from him had become almost an obsession with Fidel. So, once the sun came up, he set out immediately for Santiago, and shortly before 1:00 A.M., the morning of January 2, without a shot being fired he emotionally entered the historic city, home of the tragic *Desert Song* Moncada barracks. But now he entered Santiago as "liberator," and the 163,237 inhabitants of that lovely colonial city, with its legends of defiance, deliriously welcomed the bearded warrior who had taken half a century of frustrated nationalism onto his person as though he were a saint out of biblical times. As for his *guerrilleros,* those simple and brave men who had fought the Spartan battle in the most vaunted Spanish tradition of *la guerrilla,* many seemed almost to be in shock, as if they could not believe that, after so much suffering and against such terrible odds, they had actually "won."

"Night falls as we, the *barbudos,* come down from mountains looking like the saints of old," Carlos Franqui recalled. "People rush out to meet us. They are wild. . . . This was a real New Year's party, and a charge of collective joy ran through the rebels. One of them, though, felt nostalgic, as if he had left the one thing that mattered most to him back in the Sierra: Fidel Castro. . . ."

Meanwhile, Fidel was meeting incongruously with the Rotarians and the Lions, who had supported the rebels and who now sat on wicker-back chairs in city offices watching their hero. He shook their hands and moved to a small wooden balcony, as women in hairnets and men in pajamas cried with happiness. The crowd roared, like a lion suddenly freed.

Before he left Santiago, Fidel spoke in the old Céspedes Square to a crowd that seemed hovering always close to a kind of delirium in response to its savior. It was a new historic moment on many levels, for it was here that Castro really began his mass assemblies. Standing in full glory before the enraptured crowd, he rhetorically asked them what it was they wanted. "Who wants" (here he would insert the name of one or another military candidate he still feared might take over in Havana) "as president?" And he would mold and remold and mold again the answer—until it was his own.

Then, recalling once again the way the Americans had snatched Santiago away from the Cuban troops in 1898, he declared with deep bitterness: "It is Cuba's good fortune that the Revolution will really take power. It will not be as in '98 when the Americans arrived. . . ."

In conclusion, Fidel Castro—who would always remind people that at the year of his grasping power he was the same age as Christ when he was crucified and rose again—proclaimed with some of the truest words of his life, "Neither crooks, nor traitors, nor interventionists. This time, yes, it is a Revolution!"

With that, deliberately and systematically Fidel began to move across the country, first in a parade of jeeps, then in a helicopter, and finally and theatrically on a tank as he entered Havana. He was a modern-day Hannibal crossing the Cuban "Alps" with his "elephants"; he was the Caesars sweeping home to Rome from the conquered territories; but he was also something new, he was the pure Spanish guerrilla, the virile man of the countryside, marching down onto the "sinful" cities of modern times. One thing he was not: he was not José Martí on a white horse sacrificing himself. And when it came to the consolidation of power, his mastery was, as always, unsurpassed.

Che had already moved into Havana on the night of January 1, and taken over the La Cabaña fortress. Camilo was installed in Camp Columbia. Havana was effectively taken, and so now Castro was in no hurry at all to enter it. He was allowing just the right tension to build up and waiting for just the right moment. Moreover, as he moved magisterially across the island, he paused in every major town and city to be sure the rebel position was fully entrenched, that every fort and city hall was in the hands of one of his most trusted officers.

At Cienfuegos, a beautiful white city that lies along the azure southern coast of the Caribbean, Castro stopped to have dinner with the leaders of the "Second Front of the Escambray" who had taken the city. He ate elegantly, at the La Covadonga Restaurant, a fine fish café overlooking the sea. While they dined on the excellent shrimps of the Covadonga and the famous Cuban Hatuey beer, with more and more of the devoted *pueblo* pushing around him, Castro acted out one of his many strange personal scenes, which can really only be seen as carefully wrought "tests" of others' loyalties—and tests of how far, personally, he could go.

Lázaro Asencio, one of the Escambray leaders, told me years later that they had been discussing the American guerrilla fighter William Morgan, who had fought with the Second Front. Suddenly and without warning, Fidel turned gruffly to Lázaro and said, "Listen, Lázaro, I want you to tell this William Morgan to leave Cuba." Lázaro, who admired Morgan, believed he was genuinely committed to the Revolution and was not just another guerrilla mercenary. He replied, "Fidel, you are mistaken. William is a person who is so well motivated and who loves the Cuban Revolution and who is not going to take a single penny." But Fidel was not convinced.

"Look, Lázaro," he went on, "all of these strangers are just mercenaries. You know what I am going to do with Che Guevara? I am going to send him to Santo Domingo to see if Trujillo will kill him. And my brother Raúl—I am going to send him as a minister or diplomat, or an ambassador to Europe."

Lázaro Asencio, thirty years later, remained still a little bewildered by this surreal talk. "What was important," he insisted, "was that it was not only with me. Others were there." And, indeed, Emilio Caballero, another fighter who was at La Covadonga that night, recalled the scene in exactly the same way.

Why would Castro say such strange things even as Che was holding down La Cabaña for him and Raúl had fought so valiantly? "What I have analyzed," Asencio told me, "is that he said this to us precisely as proof that he did not intend to have a Communist government in Cuba and that we had no valid reasons to think this at this moment." It was also one of his tests.

Fidel visited an orphanage run by nuns in Matanzas to give them cash to buy a television set. At 1:30 one morning, he was interviewed by Ed Sullivan. On January 8, still en route like Alexander marching triumphantly through Persia, he ceremoniously stopped at the home of the parents of José Antonio Echeverría, the directorate hero killed in the palace attack nearly two years before. The mother cried tears of gratitude, convinced that now her son's death had reason and meaning. And now, on the edge of Havana, with great emotion and theatrical planning, Castro was reunited with Fidelito, the son he had not seen since 1956 and who was now a sturdy, robust nine-year-old boy.

The story of Mirta and Fidelito in the intervening years could hardly have been more different from the story of the ex-husband and distant father. While Fidel was in the Sierra, Mirta's life had become a sad and purposeless shuttling back and forth between Cuba and the United States. Everyone who knew Mirta during this period remembers her as sweet, thoughtful—and sad. But she remained mindful of her former husband's wishes and sensitivities. So it was that the little boy, Fidelito, was returned to the "New Cuba" from school in the United States on a turbo-prop plane on January 5. Mirta was in Havana and the new "government" insisted that she be at the airport when Fidelito arrived. The sadness she must have felt—the understandable sadness of memory, the sorrow of loss, the jealousy of watching a husband she had adored and lost and who now was a symbol of heroism to women all over the world—can only be imagined.

That day, she said to her old beau and friend Jack Skelly, "You are the only one I have, you have to be with me." But when her son's plane came in, Mirta was separated from him, forced to drive off with other of Castro's officials to official gatherings, where she watched from a distance as the husband she had loved so much enchanted the entire people of Cuba and now began the process of taking her son away as well.

As the political control of Cuba was changing, so, too, were the lives of many of the revolutionaries. To some, the revolution they had dreamed of brought not glory, but only personal loss and despair. To others, it brought new personal relationships, new partners, new loves.

Castro himself was now inextricably linked to Celia, although Celia had made an extraordinarily difficult but wise decision: seeing the adulation of the beautiful women of Cuba for him, she eschewed a life of passion with him; instead, she would tie him to her in far more intricate ways. Naty Revuelta would remain his lover, and now she wanted also to marry him. . . . "All Havana knew her in January 1959," Fidel's interpreter Juan Arcocha reminisced. "She was sensual, provoking. She dressed dramatically. Fidel had loved her desperately, and on January 1, she was ripe for him. She was the first person he called for. She left her husband, told him her second daughter was Fidel's. She expected to be married to him. She was magnificent, more beautiful than ever. Everybody was saying Fidel would marry her. . . ."

How little they still knew Fidel Castro! Not only would or could he never give in to the woman who had earlier spurned his proposal of marriage, but also he now fully realized that he had moved far beyond the possibility of any marriage; it was impermissible in the charismatic leader. "She became pathetic after that," Arcocha summed up, "but she never lost hope."

Che, who had in earlier years self-righteously praised his own revolutionary restraint and good sense in marrying a homely woman, had met a pretty, blond schoolteacher in Santa Clara, a Bible-reading Presbyterian named Aleida March, and they would soon marry. Meanwhile, his devoted wife Hilda Gadea waited in Peru with their daughter, Hildita, working as a journalist at *La Tribuna* newspaper. Now, at the moment of triumph they had all so worked and suffered for, she was left behind, abandoned by her husband. "She kept waiting and waiting in those days," Cecilia Bustamente, a prominent Peruvian poetess who had worked with Hilda at *La Tribuna*, told me. "There was no word from Che. Planes were coming from Cuba to pick up lots of people and carry them back, but none came for Hilda."

The first day after Batista fled, the city had been eerily quiet, like a desirable but nervously uncertain woman awaiting her lover. But the following day a new Havana awoke to the roar of angry crowds, as the long-pent-up emotions of the Cuban *masas* were released. In a raging frenzy that stunned the more sober Cubans, they attacked the parking meters and literally beat and hacked them to ruin, for the meters had been a symbol of privilege of the "ancien régime." Then the mob rushed the Sevilla Biltmore Hotel and trashed the casino, which was a symbol of the "vice and corruption" of the Batista thugs, not to speak of the "corrupting" American influence. One casino was spared. The famous "tough" American movie actor George Raft operated the casino at the Capri Hotel and, when the irate mob started up the stairs at the hotel's main entrance, Raft snarled at them in his famous movie gangster snarl, "Yer not comin' in my casino." Cubans in their confused and unfinished nationalism/dependency were avid aficionados of American gangster films, and they retreated.

From the distance of the Sierra, the lean, hungry, sacrificial men of the mountains had looked like noble saviors. But when these "new men" of Cuba moved in, everything changed for all time. The 26th of July militia—simple men in dirty, sweaty uniforms who had been straggling along the roads across the breadth of Cuba—took over Havana with the harsh discipline they had learned from their master.

"These peasant soldiers, these soldiers-become-peasants, carried into the cities their warlike austerity and country moralism," the French philosopher Jean-Paul Sartre would write. He reminded that, "Several years earlier, with the same defiance, the rural army of Mao had camped in the streets of Shanghai, the corrupted city, the victim and accomplice of the whites." But in those delirious first days of January 1959, it was far too early for the Cuban people to see or even sense the reality of the "uncorrupted" peasant sweeping down to purify the "sinful" city. That would come.

And then, and then, and then . . . In the midst of this instantaneous transformation of Cuba from dictator to rebel, Fidel moved upon the city he would always characterize in a part of his mind as the consummate city of political and sexual sin. "There were no captives tied to Castro's chariot wheels," Ruby Hart Phillips wrote, as she watched with a sense of unease, "but the people of the island were emotionally his slaves." He came, like most of the charismatic heroes that Max Weber studied, fulfilling the destiny and the routine of "coming out of the wilderness . . . down from the mountain or from some place of isolation and incubation" where the "prophet catches a vision."

The newspaper *Revolución* published under Castro's pictures the ecstatic description "The Hero-Guide of Cuban Reform." The Cuban sugar king, Julio Lobo, compared him to Francisco Pizarro, the conqueror of Peru. And his old friend Luis Conte Agüero, who would soon break with him totally, wrote in his original biography of Castro, "Fidel is much more than a good governor, he is a redeemer." It was this Christ-like image of redeemer or savior that Fidel persistently plucked for his own uses. Just before the Rebel Army entered Havana, at the town of El Cotorro, no less a nonbeliever than Ramiro Valdés systematically handed out rosaries to each fighter so that when they entered Havana most had rosaries hanging piously around their necks.

Nor did Fidel forget or ignore the power of Santería. As he marched into Havana, the *santeros,* or priests, of Santería gathered along the road to place their special "protections" in his path. Many of the guerrillas had, alongside the rosaries and religious medals, Santería bead collars of various bright colors. Castro would also come to be called *El Caballo,* or "The Horse." This animal was number one on the Cuban lottery, so it had importance in that sense, but it also had mysterious Santería dimensions. The priest of Santería is known as the "horse" of the saints, and during the Santería initiation, the saints are believed to take possession of their initiates by literally "mounting" them. A closer description of what Fidel Castro did to Cuba and to the Cuban people could scarcely be found.

Castro, riding in the tank with Fidelito beside him and the comandantes Camilo Cienfuegos and Huber Matos just behind him, entered Havana at the Shrine of the Virgin of the Road and moved through crowds of more than a million people. Along the route, Fidel's message to the people began to emerge. "We had a quieter life in the hills than we are going to have from now on," he told the Cuban people, few of whom caught the ominous nature of his words. "Now, we are going to purify this country."

It was at moments like this that Castro brilliantly manipulated not only the Cuban people's hopes, but their fears and their guilt. "Only vaguely mentioned in studies of Cuba is the collective guilt complex that came out in the people at the same moment of revolutionary triumph," Cuban historian Luis Aguilar noted. Watching the victory parades brought out a "displeasing question: what did I do while this handful of heroes was fighting for the liberty of Cuba? The answer was depressing: nothing." With his extraordinary instinct for how to use the fragile feelings of others, Castro immediately grasped this guilt like a piece of revolutionary bread and used it to instill one message: "Now you too can take part, but only by giving me your absolute obedience." And so, houses in Havana where no one had fought suddenly blossomed with signs of "Fidel, ésta es tu casa" — "*Fidel, this is your house*" — while the houses of combatants almost without exception did not need to boast such signs.

Yet, on the surface, Fidel was talking in political terms. The 26th of July would now become a "political party." He was asking for no spoils for himself, only assuming command of the armed forces, a post which he would relinquish soon. The civilian cabinet, under the new president, Urrutia, would rule the island. He might well "retire." But as always, it was not the words that Castro spoke, it was his uncanny grasp of tactics and strategy, coupled with his charismatic appeal, that especially, on that legendary day, effused his entire figure.

The first thing he would do with words that day was to disempower his old nemesis, the Revolutionary Student Directorate, whose leaders Faure Chomon and Rolando Cubela had taken the National Palace as well as the university. Fortunately for Fidel, there already existed some public resentment against the directorate because members had stolen some weapons from one of the military headquarters, apparently to fend off Fidel's rebels. This raised again the hated specter of political gangsterism in the university, and Fidel brilliantly played upon those fears. He stood in front of the people in the parade ground at Camp Colombia, at the height of their deliriousness over his entry into Havana, and both literally and figuratively disarmed his last adversaries. He began as he had in Santiago, by spinning webs of hope and dreams as he established an electric and messianic link between himself and "the people," later to become *las masas*. His voice took on an ominous and threatening tone as he asked, "The first thing we who have made this Revolution must ask ourselves is, why did we make it?" He fingered the microphone during a long and calculated pause, and then he went on to his point: "If some of us are hiding some ambition, are pushing for command, this is not a noble proposition." Speaking to the "Cuban mothers," he built his devastating attack meticulously. "Cuban mothers . . . of the soldier, the revolutionary, of the citizen . . . feel that their sons, finally, are out of danger." But they must not yet relax. Their common enemy was the Student Directorate, which had just stolen arms from a government arsenal. Then, the famous phrase, "*¿Armas, para qué?*" And as the crowd fell under his spell, "Arms, for what? To fight against whom? Arms, for what? To blackmail the president of the Republic? To threaten the government? To create organizations of gangsters? If we have a government of young and honorable men and if the country has faith in them, if we are going to have elections, why should arms be stored away?"

The masses exploded in tumultuous reaction. "*¿Armas, para qué?*" the crowd shouted back. "Arms, for what?" The angry refrain echoed and catapulted up and down the streets. "He made his whole audience an accomplice," a Cuban psychiatrist, Dr. Rubén Darío Rumbaut, recalled of the day. From that very moment, the directorate lost all chance of political participation in Cuban affairs and basically dissolved.

It did not hurt that, at the very moment he began speaking to the multitudes, several white doves, which had been released as a peace gesture, fluttered about. One even landed on Fidel's shoulder while the other two perched just before him. Now the crowd really was mesmerized, as a kind of spiritual calm fell over the masses. Former Batista soldiers removed their caps, some putting their right hands over their hearts and standing at attention, while others fell to their knees in prayer. The Santería faithful rubbed their Santería beads. Finally the Cuban people had someone who would take care of them—the myth was being born before the people's own wondering eyes.

Castro did not move. He acted as though the dove was not even there on his shoulder as he stared straight ahead, telling the bedazzled crowd, "We cannot become dictators. We shall never need to use force because we have the people, and because the people shall judge, and because the day the people want, I shall leave."

His enemies said the doves were "trained," that this was standard practice in Communist parlance, that they were attracted by smell and had been fed lead pellets in order to make them roost so "magically," but while ornithologists say this is certainly possible, particularly with tame doves, there is no evidence of it, and certainly forcing doves to roost on one man's shoulder in a huge crowd is an inexact science. At any rate, his masses only saw in this sublime event another heavenly affirmation of Fidel Castro's power.

Indeed, that day seemed to bring forth one magical moment after another—and one Castro after one Fidel after another Castro. At times, though already it was becoming rarer, there was the boy-revolutionary with the smile, the youth that so many had trusted and adored. This "Fidel" suddenly turned to the bearded, life-loving Camilo Cienfuegos and asked with that certain look of pleading-to-be-loved that his expressive face sometimes assumed: "¿*Voy bien, Camilo?*"—"Am I doing all right, Camilo?"

Camilo, the young man with the gaunt Spanish face of an El Greco canvas and the scraggly undisciplined beard, who looked, in the words of Carlos Franqui, "like a combination of Christ and a rumba dancer," the "chico" loved by everyone, who was soon to die, smiled his infectious smile. "*Vas bien, Fidel,*" he answered. "You are doing well, my friend." The crowd nearly growled with ecstasy. This was to become one of the few really affectionate revolutionary slogans of the time.

Mostly that day there was the Castro who was the overwhelmingly dominant and prepotent personality: a mystical, magical, disciplining, punishing, guilt-evoking, unscrupulous leader. And he was not yet even remotely beginning to exercise his full powers. At one point in his speech, he suddenly raised his right hand. He lowered his voice, and in a different, hoarse, and dramatic tone, he asked the multitude to open a path for him to walk through, so he could pay his "respects" to the ostensible president, Urrutia, at the Presidential Palace. No one had ever seen anything like this in the undisciplined, fun-loving, individualistic Cuba. "From the balcony of the palace he asked the multitudes to open a path . . . ," Carlos Franqui wrote, in some awe. "And like Moses parting the waters, he crossed the sea of people that ran from Misiones Avenue to the bay, a hero out of Greek mythology in a collective orgasm." And always the crowd cried in orgiastic joy and only occasionally in foreboding and fear, "FIDELFIDELFI-DELFIDELFIDELFIDELFIDEL!"

"That guy knows how to press the button," John Topping, the political officer at the American embassy, put it, more simply.

He even invented some of the "buttons" as he went along. Careful observers could have extrapolated from those few days of "taking" Cuba and foreseen what Fidel Castro would become. He had already easily induced the Cuban people, so long overwhelmed with failure, to "suspend individual judgment and repose one's faith in the leadership of someone who conveys his conviction . . . that he knows the way," as psychiatrist Jerrold Post analyzed. He was saying, "Follow me and I will take care of you."

Just once that day there was a glimpse of Fidel, the old guerrilla fighter. As he was entering Havana, with proud little Fidelito at his side, Fidel suddenly spotted the hulk of the *Granma* moored in the harbor. Deeply moved at seeing his old friend of the seas again, he rushed over almost to embrace the scabrous little ship, a Cuban flag now flying from her bow. Then, not unexpectedly, he gave a little speech.

"That boat," he told the crowd, "is like a piece of my life." Then he told the people somberly that he had "the sensation of a person changing jobs. From the role of a warrior, which was what I had been, to the role of a public man. . . . Something that was very difficult had been accomplished. But there is a feeling that everything you know, everything you have been doing in a certain job, to which you have dedicated many years, is no longer relevant." These words were extraordinarily insightful, for this particular man would indeed have a terrible time passing from the guerrilla fighter to public man; from the often jubilant, sometimes playful, and always plotting and ever-watchful "Fidel" of the mountains to the severe Castro of Cuba.

It had been an apocalyptic day of Cuban genesis; from then on, everyone noticed how little he smiled.

17

THE FIRST MONTHS—THIS TRAIN KNOWS WHERE IT IS GOING

> After his triumph, when I remarked to Fidel that the tasks he was going to take over now were infinitely more difficult than anything he had faced in the Sierra Maestra and that the power he held could do great harm as well as good to Cuba, he stopped, turned to face me, put his hands on my shoulders and in an almost bewildered fashion asked, "But how could I do harm ...?"
>
> —Herbert Matthews

AFTER THE WILD triumph of his entry into Havana, Castro took over the Havana Hilton for his headquarters. He settled in on the top three penthouse floors, where he was guarded night and day by the Rebel Army and, above all, by Celia. Ever his paymaster and confidante, she also became now the caretaking portal to his presence for the tens of thousands who now fought to see him. Yet occasionally he would find a way to escape Celia's vigilance; at those times, he would flee to the hotel kitchen to fry steaks or to the hotel lobby to talk endlessly with the hundreds of journalists who were always staying there and hanging around. Castro frankly enjoyed his mastery over the big, modern, characterless Hilton, so symbolic of everything *americano;* it reminded him of his next war. At the same time, he took over (for a token fee) the elegant beach house of a Cuban family in the picturesque fishing village of Cojímar, just ten miles east of Havana. Here he would hide out when he did not want to see anyone. And he also often stayed at Celia's apartment in Vedado.

It was a magical time. Despite the years of turmoil and the revolutionary economic sabotage of the last year, the Cuba that Fidel Castro took over was a flourishing national enterprise. Far from being an "underdeveloped" country, Cuba's national income in 1957 was $2,311,200,000, topped in Latin America only by that of the much larger countries of Argentina, Mexico, and Venezuela. Cuba's national per capita income in the crucial year of 1952, when Batista took over, was roughly $360, which even then was nearly 30 percent above the average of all the other Latin countries.

But the keys to the changes that would come lay actually in the very prosperity and awakening of the country (poor countries may revolt, but not poor and hopeless ones) and in the important fact that the development was uneven; those in the countryside barely shared in the prosperity, and those were the Cubans Castro sought for his "new Cuba," his "new family," and certainly his own "new legitimacy." In addition, although foreign and, in particular, American investment in Cuba had steadily been going down, there remained still about one billion foreign dollars invested in the island; this was "emotion-ridden" money that Castro would use well for his own purposes.

Beneath Cuba's prosperity lay a particular Cuban structure of vice— prostitution, drug trafficking, and gambling—that was singular in Latin America and whose nationalist resentments against the United States Castro would also exploit. In Havana alone at that time, there were approximately two thousand prostitutes living in "houses" ranging from the most luxuriously Dionysian to the most brutally humble. Each *casa* paid off the local police according to the number of its clients, with the richest, Casa Marina, contributing between three thousand to five thousand dollars a night to uniformed police officers, who arrived regularly sometime between midnight and 5:00 A.M. to pick up their fees. When there was an especially large "call" for girls, as when a U.S. Navy vessel was in port, young *guajiritas,* peasant girls, would be brought to the city and initiated into *la vida.* Yet, prostitution was not the major vice in Cuba that Castro would declare it (he would later say there had been one hundred thousand prostitutes, but that was a ridiculous number). Gambling was. Six big houses, owned by a consortium of Batista officials and referred to usually by such typically colloquial and familiar Cuban nicknames as "Juan" or

"La China" or "La Central," controlled the numbers games and regularly paid off the police. The American Mafia controlled the big casinos.

Castro was to go after this only barely subterranean structure of inter-connected and degrading vice with vengeance, not so much because of moral reasons but because of his abiding class resentment and because such corruption clearly corroded his base and made him look less a revolution-ary leader. "We are going to purify this country," Castro had threatened when he marched into Havana. Few realized how profoundly he meant those words.

Always the master political alchemist, Castro now moved swiftly to become the master legal alchemist as well. To give legality to the execu-tions he had planned for the *Batistiano* war criminals (and, later, many oth-ers), he grafted his "Code of the Sierra Maestra" onto existing Cuban law, now allowing capital punishment. Then Castro moved beyond mere execu-tion by the state. Using his uncanny powers of emotional coercion, he invoked the emotional asset of the masses for the execution of, effectively, whomever he chose. To gain approval from his people, he would deliber-ately gather men and women from various backgrounds, many poor, at the presidential palace, where he would ask them basically rhetorical and lead-ing questions, such as "Should war criminals be shot?" So it was that on that Thursday, January 22, 1959, there echoed for the first time in Cuba the odious, hate-filled shouts of "*Paredón*," or "To the wall . . ." Then a colos-sal "Yes," a resounding "Yes!"

Previously, Castro's emotional control of the people in the plaza had been largely didactic; he had been indoctrinating and transforming their ideas by carrying their "old selves" within himself and then releasing them as "new." Now he carried the process of his "spell" a step further. He pre-sented them with his decision and then through his power over them made it appear as though they had empowered him to act. This ominous exchange of emotional control for political control, this unique empowerment of a leader by a "people," is what he soon came to call with exquisite euphe-mism "direct democracy."

The big "trials" and executions were, at first, of "war criminals" like the hated *Batistiano* torturer Major Jesús Sosa Blanco, a man notorious for his wanton killings. Sosa Blanco's trial was held in the sports palace, where seventeen thousand riotous and angry Cubans watched. But the strident American criticism of the trials stung Castro, for even though (and because) he hated the Americans, he also secretly yearned for their respect. The fact is that much of this criticism was unfair, especially since the same Americans had barely noted Batista's brutality. In addition, the executions were also meant to evoke in the Cuban people the kind of catharsis that would purge them and leave them finally free of *Batistianismo*.

Actually, far more questionable both morally and legally than the trumpeted immediate executions of *Batistianos* was the relatively unknown "Airmen Trial." This group of forty-three pilots, bombardiers, and mechanics, accused of carrying out bombings against the Rebel Army, was tried at the end of February in a military court in Santiago. These men had not tried to flee the island and indeed had expressed a clear desire to serve under Castro. Since there was no real evidence against the airmen, they were soon acquitted. But Castro would not let the affair end with that.

Dramatically declaring them "the worst criminals of the Batista regime," he ordered a retrial. Communists in Santiago organized mobs in the streets to protest the tribunal's "outrageous" verdict. Castro then appeared on television, where once again he "alchemized" the law, declaring with the most curious legalistic logic that the acquittal verdict would be appealed because, just as a war criminal had the right to appeal, "so the Prosecutor's Office, which represents the people and the Revolution, has the same right," when the verdict is "unjust." As in his Moncada trial, Castro turned everything on its head: the law was whatever he made of it at the moment. The presiding judge, a comandante, soon killed himself, one of Castro's first suicides.

It was during the days of the airmen's second trial that moderate and liberal Cuban democrats began to doubt—and to fear. Rufo López Fresquet, the new minister of the treasury and one of the preeminent moderates, shook his head with foreboding at the time and said, "I'm scared of Castro. He's like a madman. He's been destroyed." He kept repeating it over and over.

In explanation of Castro's extraordinary actions, the Cuban poet Armando Valladares explained, "They couldn't be found innocent because they would be free to fight him again. They were young officers, educated in and graduated from schools in the United States, and they were not going to follow him along his Marxist path." The airmen were sentenced to thirty years in prison and ten years of forced labor.

Castro was quite cool about it, as he always was about sentencing and executing people, because such deeds were instrumental to him and not emotional, as they were to Che, who sat in his chair in La Cabaña where, from his own specially created window, he could feast upon the details of every execution. "You know, Fidel was nice to people he was going to shoot," his former friend José Ignacio Rasco recalled of him. And that was true; to Castro, these men were mere abstractions, their deaths no more real than that absurd idea that there was a human soul; and their worth lay only in the use they could be to his cause and to his ambitions. Castro never lost time in insulting people unless it was for a purpose; and it was certainly a waste to insult someone you were just about to shoot.

If the airmen's trial sowed seeds of doubt in the minds of Cuban moderates, the trial of Castro's old companion in arms, Comandante Huber Matos, in the autumn of 1959, became a true watershed. A stalwart man of honor and a democrat, Matos agonized over doubts about where the Revolution was going after the first few months. "From the third month of the Revolution, I realized there was a double game going on," Matos told me in 1985 in Miami. "Fidel continued affirming that he was democratic and that he would respect the liberty of the people, but he also continued transforming the social and political life of Cuba until he only had a functioning democracy within certain institutions that the Communists then effectively took over. At the end of June, I spoke with Fidel about my fears and we were going to meet in my house to discuss it. He was going to bring Raúl and Che. Raúl came, but not Che. We spoke of everything except the reason for the meeting. We spoke six to eight hours and never touched the theme. I was quiet, watching. It was all part of a play."

By that time, Matos was in a position to threaten Castro, or so Castro imagined. Matos was running the economically crucial province of Camaguey, where great cattle ranches dotted the picturesque and fertile landscape. More important, Matos, a brilliant commander who won as much undying respect from his men as Castro did from his, in effect had his own army. Making the "threat" even worse, Matos was an efficient manager, and Camaguey was thriving, whereas the rest of Castro's Cuba was in chaotic disarray.

Finally, "I do not want to become an obstacle to the revolution . . . ," he wrote in a letter to Fidel dated October 19. "I can conceive of the revolution's triumph only with the nation united. It is right, however, to recall to you that great men begin to decline when they cease to be just." He then asked Castro only to agree to his request to "return home." At the end of the letter, he even wished Castro "every kind of success for yourself and in your revolutionary efforts for the country. . . ."

These were passive words, yet Castro was enraged and immediately bent upon vengeance, for with Castro—and, in particular, *from* Castro—there was no resignation. He had said many times and in many different words that "inside the revolution, anything, but outside, nothing." From that moment on, the destruction of Huber Matos was assured, although Matos was at that moment unaware of the inner devils he was stirring in Castro. In fact, he wrote still another Delphic letter, saying, "Very well, Fidel, I await calmly what you decide. You know I have the courage to pass twenty years in prison. . . . I shall not order my soldiers . . . to open a single burst of fire against anyone, not even against the cutthroats you may send."

In the end, Castro sent Camilo Cienfuegos to Camaguey to take command of the province. Cienfuegos found, to Castro's distress, that Matos's forces were loyal to him. So Castro resorted to his old tactic—he would personally mobilize the "masses" of Camaguey against their comandante. Castro went immediately to the province, gathered a mob in the square, and denounced Matos for being in the pay of "foreign embassies" and for having prepared a "barracks revolt." Revealingly, he concluded by saying that he himself therefore had come "to my barracks which is the public square, to my barracks which is the city!"

The next day, back in Havana, a meeting of the Council of Ministers was held, but not everyone present sided with Castro on the matter of Matos.

"I think Comandante Huber Matos is innocent and should be set free instantly," Faustino Pérez, Fidel's go-between in the Sierra and one of the more moderate officers, insisted.

Others, not unexpectedly, supported Fidel.

"Huber Matos is a traitor to the Revolution and should be shot," Raúl Castro insisted, his small body ramrod straight in anger and his eyes cold.

"Fidel soon came to the point in that meeting," another of the moderate ministers, Manuel Ray, told me years later. "He said that those who resign put the Revolution in danger. At one point, Faustino Pérez got up and asked, 'Is this *Batistiano* terror?' And Fidel responded, in words ominously similar to those of Lenin, 'No, this is revolutionary terror.' . . ."

Matos and thirty-eight of his officers were tried in the ominous, gray old rooms of La Cabaña fortress. Castro never looked at the prisoners. He harangued the crowd for three hours. This was no court, it was a psychological lynching. At the end, Castro, in an echo of the Moncada speech, shouted at the courtroom, "If you absolve Comandante Huber Matos, history will condemn you!" As for Matos, he was not permitted to speak, which was Castro's real answer to any and all revolutionary questioning. When it was over, Matos was sentenced to twenty years in prison.

Theodore Draper, perhaps the greatest early analyst of the "what" and "why" of the Cuban Revolution, carefully studied all the Castro testimony as well as ninety pages of the Matos trial record, which was uncannily like the Ochoa trial of 1989. "I suspect that the Matos trial will go down in recent Cuban history as the equivalent of the Moscow trials of the 1930s," he wrote. "Not a semblance of treason, in any meaningful sense of the term, was proved, or even charged, against Matos."

After some visiting American travel agents departed on October 26, Castro finally let go his full fury. Addressing the mobs, "he shook his fist, roared defiance at the northern sky, foamed at the mouth, and in every way comported himself in a manner reminiscent of Hitler at his most hysterical and most odious," Ambassador Philip Bonsal reported.

But the "Matos affair" would not die. Were it not for the Matos question, there would not historically be so many questions about the death of the immensely popular Camilo Cienfuegos.

That Camilo was far more a romantic revolutionary than a Communist is beyond question. In those changing months of the fall of 1959, he had expressed to several people close to him his concerns about the probable fate of Matos, whom he liked. Additionally, close observers at the time say that Cienfuegos originally refused to accept an order from Raúl to arrest Matos and that Castro personally had to order him to do it. It was also known that Camilo and Raúl hated each other, and Matos himself is convinced that his imprisonment and Camilo's strange and unsolved death are related.

"There was only one single week between my arrest and the disappearance of Camilo," Matos told me. "There is no question that they killed Camilo, for my arrest put Camilo in a position of crisis. He had to discuss me with Fidel. When Fidel saw in him an attitude that wasn't one of unconditional support . . ." He shook his head, then continued, "Camilo told me that he was in a very difficult situation. In fact, he sent me a message in jail, warning me that I should not allow it to go to a trial."

Probably the mystery of what happened to Camilo will never be solved. All that is known is that, on October 28, he was returning from Camaguey to Havana in a light plane when he and the plane disappeared totally from the face of the earth with not a single clue, never to be seen or heard of again. The disappearance was not even mentioned in Cuba for three full days, when *Revolución* finally came out with the story. While army planes and peasants searched everywhere, rumors abounded. At one point, Ruby Hart Phillips heard a broadcast on November 5 over Havana Radio saying that Camilo had been found. "People poured into the streets to celebrate," she wrote. "Merchants were forced to close their stores because the clerks deserted. I was surprised to learn that Major Cienfuegos was so popular." Cynics could be forgiven for wondering whether Castro himself might not have announced the finding of Camilo falsely in order to judge the Cuban people's real feeling about him.

What is certain is that many of the "facts" given out by the government were totally false. They said he probably had gone down in a squall, and yet it was a brilliantly clear day. The area where the plane had been flying was crisscrossed with radar. Meanwhile, Castro himself "heroically" and "publicly" searched for Camilo. He even brought Camilo's mother and father on the search and had them pose for pictures in which, hands cupped over their eyes, they all looked together upward into the skies.

But not even Camilo's plane was found; nor any sign of it. Without any real evidence, his death or disappearance had to be considered an "accident." And yet . . . Those who were with Castro at that time remember how, in his maddened flights around Cuba searching for Camilo, he was laughing and happy—and utterly indifferent. "He may not have killed Camilo, but he certainly didn't feel his death," observed José Pardo Llada, who was with him. And people remember others mysteriously gone, like Frank País. It was not, his critics say, that Castro actually killed Camilo, it was that "one of the specialties of Fidel is to send people to be killed."

In sharpest contradistinction to the menacing gravity of the executions and imprisonments and "disappearances" that shook that first year of the Revolution was a strange and surreal lightheartedness in other matters. In those first frenetic months, Fidel was everywhere—and nowhere. On any one day, there would be eight hundred to a thousand decrees lying in his office, piling up endlessly. Like many Latins, he had the idea that proclaiming something was actually the equivalent of doing it, and he hated these bureaucratic claims on him. "I haven't had a minute to myself," he literally shouted at Herbert Matthews one day of his new "life," gesturing broadly. "They won't leave me alone. Thousands of things are brought to me that I do not know about. When I tried to get away from the crowd by going from one place to another in a tank, people climbed into and on the tank with me before I knew it. . . ."

In the excitement of the time, the "revolutionary family" and its adepts began closing in upon the "New Rome" of Revolution, adding still further to the confusion. General Bayo flew in from Mexico, Che's parents arrived from Buenos Aires, Hilda Guevara came from Peru with Hildita to learn, as she had feared, that she was no longer Che's "girl and always would be." North American idealists came; European utopians, fools and charlatans and celebrities of every caste came; democrats hoping the Revolution was not Communist and Communists hoping it was not democratic came: all poured into Havana to touch and feel the magic of the "New Cuba" and the new *Hombre*.

As always, the images of Fidel wavered and trembled, changing constantly like some phantasmagoric dream, like a kaleidoscope of quicksilver pictures that one cannot catch and hold. One day, Teté Casuso, who had returned to Cuba and was handling the foreign press for Castro, was preparing him to appear on an important American TV show, *Person to Person*. The show wanted to picture Castro in "domestic relaxation," which was tricky since it was a mode he had never even contemplated in his entire life. When Castro arrived twenty minutes before the show was to start, none of the newly made civilian suits was large enough for him, and by that time he had none of his own. In desperation, they found a pair of pajamas, and producer John Aaron produced a finely tailored dressing gown for him to wear over them.

"The rage he flew into when he saw that dressing gown (it was too luxurious for him) was of epic quality," Teté recalled, remembering her embarrassment and confusion at the time. "With seven minutes left, Fidel, who had not slept for two days, suddenly shut himself up in a room and furiously threw himself on the bed. Even Celia did not dare go in and speak to him. I went in, closed the door, and sat on the edge of the bed. I talked to him softly but firmly, as one talks to an obstinate child. He was lying face down, in a perfect rage, his head buried in pillows." Finally he agreed to appear in his own striped pajamas, but on the condition that he be shown only from the waist up. However, "as soon as he came under the lights," she said with relief, "the 'dragon' grew tame. He was another person. What a great actor was lost to the stage!"

On the international plane, Castro immediately began reaching out to the world or, in reality, reaching with great deliberateness around the United States. He was already beginning to build the anti-American axis he so dreamed of. Indeed, on the night of January 22, within a bare ten days of taking Havana, he left Cuba for Venezuela. The two countries had something in common in that just the year before a popular revolt had overthrown the dictatorship of General Marcos Pérez Jiménez; his democratic replacement in power, Rómulo Betancourt, had supported Castro's fight, despite some doubts. But on this visit everything went wrong between the Cuban strongman and the Venezuelan democrat.

"Why would Fidel come here so rapidly?" Josefina Ache, one of Betancourt's most intimate confidantes, asked me years later. "It amazed all of us. At the moment, there was no explanation. People thought at first that he had come to thank us. People thought, 'How nice, how wonderful.' But they soon came to realize that was not at all the case."

Actually, Castro wanted two things: he wanted oil from Venezuela and he wanted to unite the two countries in a pact against the United States. Castro was also there to size up the possibilities for the "continental revolution" he was already dreaming of.

"Castro came out of the plane with all his guns on," Josefina Ache recalled, "and that bothered Rómulo a lot. When he gave an interview to Fidel, he made sure that everyone could see them together. He did not want a private interview with him." Josefina confided that Rómulo had told her privately that "a well-intentioned man would not leave a country ten days after taking power and make a visit somewhere else." But Betancourt allowed Castro to enter the Congress armed, and there he spoke all night. "When he spoke," Josefina said, "it was against the United States. It was to 'halt Yankee imperialism.' Rómulo did not like that."

Then, at the very end of the Venezuela visit, just as the Cubans were getting into Castro's Bristol Britannia plane to leave, something horrible occurred that the democratic and humanistic Betancourt really did not like. Castro had told his aide, Major Francisco "Paco" Cabrera, to leave the plane to check once more for security. So Paco went out, but as he was walking around the area, Armando Fleites, a Sierra major who was with Castro at the time, recalled, "the propeller caught him and decapitated him. I talked with Fidel about the accident, and he said, 'What happened? Why is he so stupid? This means a lot of trouble for me.' All he said after that was, 'Take the body back to Cuba for burial.'" So ended the Venezuela trip.

The Cuban public saw little of Castro's personal life, but one night, when Castro was scheduled to give one of his by now hours-long speeches on state-controlled CMQ television, his son Fidelito was involved in a terrible car accident that necessitated his spleen being removed, and the boy was actually in danger of dying. "I was there at the studio that day when the program was about to start," Carlos Castañeda, one of Cuba's great newspaper editors, recalled. "Everybody knew that Fidelito had had the accident. Fidel arrived about five minutes before nine, just before the program started. CMQ television was prepared to cancel the program and to announce the accident. But Fidel said no, that he would go on with the show, that the doctor was preparing the boy for an operation and was going to advise him the moment the operation started and that then they could cancel the program."

The first question from the panel of journalists came, and Castro talked for about half an hour; the second question came, and again a long answer. It was during this second question that Castro received a note that the doctor was waiting for him for the operation. Still he did nothing. At that point, the moderator, the famous writer Jorge Mañach, turned to Castro, on the air, telling him that they knew his son was badly hurt and publicly inviting him to leave the panel and go immediately to his son. Still, he hesitated.

By now, the audience of forty to fifty was itself restive and even increasingly angry, for this was a country where "family" had always been the most hallowed of concepts. A woman in the audience finally yelled out to the *líder máximo*, "Comandante Castro, who is it who rules in Cuba?"

"The people," Castro shouted back, triumphally.

"Then," the woman persisted stubbornly, "the people want you to go and see your son."

At this, but only at this, Castro jumped up, threw back his chair theatrically with sudden determination, and left the TV station. Not only was Mirta (again) enraged with her ex-husband, but also Raúl was enraged with him. Raúl, who would have four children of his own, was always the far stronger man in terms of family.

Castro arrived at the hospital at 2:00 A.M., and in the lobby, while he waited for the doctors to save his son's life, he busied himself receiving political sycophants in the manner of a Spanish bishop or a Moorish sheikh and signing checks for random people who passed by and to whom "the state" owed money. Later, Fidelito would show his cousins the scar that ran from his stomach half the way up his back.

By late spring, Castro would forget about the recalcitrant and stubbornly irresponsible democrats of Latin America and begin reaching out to the postcolonial "developing nations" of the Third World for his anti-American power base and primary mantle of world leadership, and then to the Eastern Bloc, where he would find the material ability to sustain and support his desires in that Third World. What Castro was doing with these tentative new international adventures was all too clearly rejecting the old "geographical fatalism" that had tied Cuba to its "ninety miles from Florida" mentality.

In June 1959, Che Guevara was sent to represent Castro in this "new world," and José Pardo Llada reluctantly accompanied him. When Pardo Llada, who had long been a popular radio announcer, questioned Castro as to why he wanted him to travel with Che—"What use can I have in a commercial mission?" Pardo asked; "What do I know of that?"—Castro focused his most piercing eyes on Pardo and, with that fixated and at the same time pleading smile of his, responded, "And perhaps you believe that I also know how to govern?" Pardo found that he no longer laughed at things like that.

Che and Pardo Llada bounced around the world for weeks like a rather comical duo of inexperienced early caravan traders. In private, the two men laughed together and called themselves "Fidel's exiles," which they pointedly were. One time, Pardo by accident saw a letter from Che to his wife, which was incongruous in its sexual explicitness. "He went over their honeymoon . . . 'what you did with me' . . . ," Pardo recalled. "It was absolutely pornographic." He paused, and wondered. Then he added, "It seemed odd for a person so austere."

Economically, little of worth came from their trip, for the consummately simple reason that the Third World governments' exchanging raw materials with one another instead of trading for manufactured goods with the industrialized world "was the equivalent of taking in each other's washing," in Maurice Halperin's wise words. And yet, the whole odyssey was not quite so haphazard as it seemed because it was the rocky beginning of Castro's leadership of the "nonaligned" world; they were new-age counter-Columbuses, setting out from the old "New World" to find new "new worlds" of incongruous power and influence. And, indeed, guerrilla training camps had been established in Cuba as early as February of 1959.

Tellingly, there was to be no Cuban support, none whatsoever, of any democratic guerrilla movements to overthrow dictatorships. Within days of his coming to power, the great Nicaraguan newspaper editor, Pedro Joaquín Chamorro of *La Prensa*, was in Havana hoping for Castro's help in over-throwing his nemesis, the Nicaraguan dictator Anastasio "Tachito" Somoza. Castro disdainfully refused him.

The first Cuban guerrilla attack was planned directly by Raúl, Che, and Bayo. In April 1959, some eighty men set sail from Cuba to "liberate" Panama. But the Panama plan failed and on May 1, the humiliated group surrendered to the Panama National Guard. Undeterred, other attacks soon followed, and also failed. By far the most interesting—and virtually unknown—Cuba guerrilla attack in this first year, and one approved by Castro, was the *Catorce de Junio,* or "14th of June," attack on the hated Generalísimo Rafael Leónidas Trujillo of the Dominican Republic. Castro had pledged long ago to "get Trujillo," and now it seemed—*seemed*—he would actually do it. A group of two hundred Dominican exiles and ten Cubans, commanded by a Rebel Army officer, left Cuba in a plane and two launches on June 14, 1959, for the northern coast of the Dominican Repub-lic. Important mysteries still swirl endlessly about this doomed expedition: the men were almost all killed or tortured, or both. There is enough evi-dence to wonder whether Castro really wanted the attack to succeed; it was all so incredibly amateurish, and it so flagrantly violated all of his own most fundamental guerrilla rules. Some warned of disaster beforehand. Sacha Volman, the great, Bessarabian-born democratic organizer of the Caribbean democrats, begged Camilo Cienfuegos to call it off. But while Camilo agreed ("Sacha is right, it doesn't have a chance"), Castro inexplicably pushed it ahead. "It was set up to fail," Sacha said afterward.

Set up to fail? Why would Castro have set it up to fail? And yet, why would he have let such a harebrained expedition go off in the first place? The survivors were unforgiving. "Fidel Castro sold us like pigs, he betrayed us, he did not help us when we most needed it," Julián Hernán-dez, a survivor, said. Then he added, "Fidel Castro realized that the movement was not Communist and, from that moment on, he began to give us no help. . . ."

Whether Castro explicitly or implicitly sabotaged the expedition because it was not Communist, or because he intended early on to destroy the idea of the "democratic guerrilla," or because he couldn't totally control it, or whether it all represented only a series of accidents when Castro's attention was diverted elsewhere will probably never be totally known. What is known is that virtually all of the few survivors blamed Castro for sabotaging them. "The guerrillas of the 14th of June of 1959 died alone, without help either internal or external," Leandro Guzmán, another of the survivors, testified in a kind of benediction.

While Castro was setting up his fascinating new international persona and setting in place at home the legal, political, and military machinery that would support these worldwide thrusts at revolution, on another level a river of devoted and devouring women was flowing like quicksilver through his life. They were everywhere, fighting to touch him and even, in a new revolutionary variation on the old seigneurial tradition, eager to be deflowered by him; meanwhile, Celia stood guard as valiantly as she could, shouting haplessly at "pretty" Cubanas like Teté Casuso and shooing them out of Castro's bed and bedroom.

One of the most dramatic "romances," if that is exactly the right word for it, was Castro's strange and long sexual alliance with a young German woman named Marita Lorenz. Castro met Marita, then a rather beautiful girl of seventeen with pitch-black hair and green eyes, that early February of 1959. The M.S. *Berlin,* of which her father, Heinrich Lorenz, was captain, pulled into Havana Harbor just as Castro was out in Havana Bay playing with the *Granma.* Always on the alert for ways to win over foreigners, he sailed by and, to the delight of the tourists, agreed to come onto the boat and even to have dinner with them. At the dinner, seated next to the blooming young Marita, he could hardly take his eyes off her as he regaled the delighted group with stories of heroism from the Sierra Maestra. As they strolled alone together afterward on the deck, Castro and Marita's "friendship blossomed."

In a bizarre story in *Confidential* magazine years later, Marita's mother wrote how "Marita nodded at the panoramic beauty of Havana. Castro then spread his arms like a Messiah, looked at the heavens and said, 'I am Cuba.'"

That very night, Castro suggested that Marita return to Havana to work for him. That she did so is certain—in fact, she lived rather publicly with him in a room just off his suite in the Havana Libre. But exactly what occurred after that remains in question, except for the fact that from all reports Marita later joined the extravagant group of CIA agents, under Watergate burglar Frank Sturgis, who ransacked Castro's rooms in the Havana Libre and tried to kill him. Marita Lorenz herself later claimed that Castro had brutally raped her, and that when she was pregnant he sent men to beat her to abort the child. Marita's testimony, if salaciously interesting, is dubious, for of her own accord, she still was often with him, wearing her little Rebel Army uniform and going back and forth from New York to Havana, still under his spell. Eventually she returned to the States, was apparently strangely and peripherally involved in the Cuban mysteries of John F. Kennedy's death, and finally retired into eccentricity, trying to sell her "memoirs" to all comers.

Amid all these brief liaisons, the exquisitely beautiful Naty Revuelta never hovered far from the picture. By then divorced after "missing the boat," Naty lived in those years in Havana with her two daughters, her doctor-husband's Natalia and Fidel's Alina, and though Castro now utterly refused to think of anything so plebeian as marriage, he visited her often. The American head of New York's Citibank, Frank Aldrich, lived with his wife just below Naty's apartment. He came home one evening and, as he walked up the steps, he thought he heard Castro talking on TV. "I told my wife that I could have sworn I had turned off the television set," Aldrich related. And he had. When Aldrich looked over the balcony, he saw Fidel himself. "He was visiting Naty, and the word had spread like wildfire. He was giving a speech to the maids in the patio below!"

Naty undoubtedly would have been devastated had she known that there was soon to be yet another woman in Fidel's life. On the first anniversary of the Revolution, Castro had instructed his ambassador in Colombia to invite the widow and daughter of the great martyred Jorge Eliecer Gaitán to attend the first 26th of July celebrations in Havana. The daughter, Gloria, a woman of both political and artistic expressiveness, recalled that "Fidel arrived to visit my mother and me at the hotel the same night we arrived. . . . He stayed until dawn, speaking to us and telling us what had happened that 9th of April in Bogotá. . . ." The blooming Gloria was naturally caught up in the contagious new spirit of those new times, and those halcyon days marked the beginning of what she was later to classify as a "romantic friendship." It was more than a friendship; a feeling flowered between the two that apparently was much deeper than most of his female attachments. Gloria seemed to be more special to Castro, at least in those days, more on the scale of Mirta, Naty, and Isabel. (Like them, Gloria also was not only physically lovely, like a dark-haired Spanish icon, but also charming and intelligent.) And she, too, had one of the most appetizing political and social pedigrees in the whole hemisphere, one that sprung enticingly from the tragedy of her father.

Fidel wooed her with all his impresario's brilliance. Was she going to the 26th of July celebration? The streets were not good enough—he sent a helicopter to carry her to the plaza. Would she speak at the celebration? She was struck into terror at the very idea. "I had two types of relations with Fidel," Gloria recalled when I spoke with her years later. "When I was with my husband, a professor, the meetings were very serious and transcendental, but they changed when I traveled alone. Then the conversations were very mixed: frivolous and diverting, speculating, formative. We talked— discussed—all the time, naturally the theme of the Revolution being the one that impassioned us most. But Fidel, for example, also asked me one day, '*Bueno,* what do you do in bed with this Greek philosopher who is your husband?' I said, 'But he is a man who is very intelligent.' And he told me, '*Claro,* but if Karl Marx were a woman, I would not marry her!'

"It is impossible for me to construct entire dialogues," she finally acceded, squinting her eyes as though trying to remember actual words.

"Only sensations and feelings. I don't remember well the opinions of Fidel over one or another theme. What I remember is a man with an impressive vitality! With a great charisma! Being close to him was like being close to a phenomenon of nature, like a volcano. One felt oneself before a person in which there was nothing common." And then she voiced what so many others constantly said: "Besides all of those characteristics of his personality, one felt many times that he said what one was intuitively feeling but that he put into words."

In those first exuberant months of enthusiasm for the Revolution, Cuban companies such as Hatuey Beer, as well as many individual Americans, offered to pay their taxes for the year in advance, all to aid the Revolution. And why not? Sterling Cuban democrats were being named to top positions:

Manuel Urrutia was provisional president; José Miró Cardona became prime minister; Rufo López Fresquet was named finance minister . . .

But it soon became clear that they were often working at cross-purposes—cross-purposes orchestrated and crisscrossed precisely by Fidel—particularly in the area of the economy. Traditional economic thinkers like Justo Carrillo, Felipe Pazos, and Ernesto Betancourt (another brilliant young economist who had been Castro's 26th of July representative in the United States during the Sierra years) were doggedly planning ways to obtain aid from international agencies and from the United States. Castro, on the other hand, was thinking in the utopians' spontaneous-combustion economic terms of the classic political guerrilla. He believed, for example, that only outside factors, like "exploitative" foreign ownership, were holding Cuba back.

While differences between the moderates in Castro's new government and Castro himself became more evident, there was never any question as to who would have the final say. Castro played cat to the moderates' mice, sometimes offering them a playful paw and other times pouncing upon them suddenly, ruthlessly, and finally fatally. The principal ministers and economic officials would often grow discouraged. But until they all disappeared in the autumn of 1959, disgruntled and often destroyed, Castro, with his extraordinary capacity for winning over almost everyone, even with his mere presence, could always reinvigorate even his most skeptical people.

In July, for example, he initiated special Thursday-afternoon meetings at the National Bank with all of his economic group. The meetings would start at 1:00 P.M. and last until nine or ten at night. "Fidel always came," Felipe Pazos recalled. "We would all be depressed, thinking that the whole thing was not going to work—until Fidel would come. Then he would listen so carefully and reassure us so, and seem so interested in moderate solutions, that we would all leave happy."

In early spring of that first year, a group of leading newspaper publishers in the American Society of Newspaper Editors, or ASNE, got the clever public relations idea of inviting the virile young Cuban leader to speak at their annual meeting on April 17 in Washington. Contrary to what the world would later think, Fidel was actually ambivalent about a trip to the United States. "Should I go?" he asked his cabinet ministers at a meeting one day, pacing back and forth magisterially, Napoleonically, as by then he always did.

"Yes, of course," Felipe Pazos answered at once. "Of course."

Fidel paused and his expression changed. The sculptured and still boyish face, with the long, straight Spanish nose and the smooth skin, took on one of those expressions of brooding anger that those around him were seeing more and more. Suddenly he stopped pacing and then posited to Pazos, as though it were the only question that mattered in his decision: "And what if Eisenhower receives me and I look as though I've sold out?"

Pazos tried to assure him that there was little danger of that, but at the same time Pazos well understood the nationalist sensitivity of the problem. "After all," Castro said later, "the shame of every Latin head of state is that he goes to Washington, begs and sells out. And that is so much worse for a rebellious, anti-imperialist leader."

Nor had Fidel, despite what many would say later, wanted, much less sought, an official American invitation. None had come—but only because Fidel assiduously rebuffed the State Department's private probings on the matter. But finally Fidel decided to accept the newspaper editors' invitation, and planning for the trip was begun in earnest. Teté worked night and day, answering hundreds of calls from people all over the United States and Canada who desperately wanted this newest hero of the world to visit them.

The trip, scheduled for mid-April, would change history, although probably no one except the extraordinarily canny and masterfully instinctive Castro suspected that. For Cuba was no longer the Cuba that America had for three centuries known and for half a century been tied to in sickness and in health, in friendship and in enmity, in love and in hate. Cuba had changed. Castro knew it, because it was he who had so singularly willed it. Castro's "new" Cuba would no longer be under the tutelage of the *americanos*.

The trip—an odyssey, really—would be a crucial turning point. It would convince Castro's friends that the United States would never help the Cuban Revolution. It would convince his enemies that he was indeed the "Communist" they sought to make him out, and thus an implacable enemy of *El Norte*. As always with Castro, the trip, its trajectory, and its intent were his alone—and had almost nothing to do with what either his friends, or his enemies, believed.

18

CASTRO MEETS *EL NORTE*

What have met and crossed are not memories.
—Pablo Neruda

THE MORNING OF April 15, 1959, was a warm one in Havana—and one that quietly heralded all the mistaken judgments about Fidel and Washington that were to come. When Castro's economic advisers assembled at the big, ultra-American Havana Hilton before leaving for the airport, they had a sudden and strangely revealing impression of their deliriously popular new leader. There, in the then lush and modern rooms, the man who was "familiarly" still called Fidel by just about all the Cuban nation was pacing back and forth in an oddly evocative attire. He was wearing military boots and trousers but a pajama top hung insouciantly down over his waist, much like an ancient warrior's tunic.

Cuba's top economist, Felipe Pazos, drew his breath in for a moment because "I had the impression of a king or a monarch." The picture was indeed breathtaking. This man, Fidel Castro, was huge, with powerful shoulders and a coldly withering gaze. It was a vivid impression that would stubbornly remain with Pazos. It must be the pajama top, he thought. Somehow that incongruent combination of clothing, along with the luxuriant and unkempt beard, pointed to the disparities that would emerge on the trip just beginning. Pazos, along with the minister of economics, Regino Boti, had come to the Hilton that last morning to discuss the "economic package"

221

they still innocently thought they were to negotiate in the States. But Castro was singularly uninterested in economics; his mind was focused on the potential grandeur of the voyage ahead of him.

The flight between the two worlds that April day was one of those many pauses in Fidel's life linking and defining cycles of history and periods of possibility. For two hours, the two countries, the two ways of life, and what would finally become the modern world's two inimical systems were suspended in the clouds above the gorgeous and glittering mere ninety miles of lapis and emerald blue waters that divided them. On board the aircraft, Teté Casuso fussed and dutifully cleaned Fidel's dirty fingernails. He read a couple of comic books. Then he picked himself up and moved down the crowded aisle to talk very deliberately with José "Pepín" Bosch, the powerful head of Bacardi Rum in Cuba. The disheveled and consummately disorganized guerrilla fighter and the meticulously dressed and quintessentially upper-class Cuban capitalist eyed each other warily but also with that kind of special interest that one social species at critical junctures can have for another.

Castro sat for a time on the floor of the plane, next to the seats where his young economist Ernesto Betancourt and Bosch sat side by side, and assumed that special expression of mock humility he always used so masterfully to toy with others' feelings of dependence and independence.

"Why don't you help me?" Fidel asked Bosch. "You could help me a great deal." He was referring to labor problems.

"With people like Fidel Castro, I can be very frank," Bosch told me years later. "I told him, 'I cannot help you because we capitalists are not afraid of labor but we are afraid of the combination of labor and government. If you want me to help you, you have to give freedom to labor.' When I said the word 'freedom,' he got up and left. It was my only conversation with Fidel Castro."

At least a thousand Cubans waited at the Washington airport to greet the man who had "liberated" their country. They unfurled banners and welcomed him with shouts of "¡Viva Fidel!" But Castro was man of the hour to more than Cuban exiles. Everywhere he went, the Americans he feared and hated lionized him. Men who wore proper three-piece suits to the office and dutifully shaved twice a day now, in their fantasies, imagined themselves a Fidel Castro. Women with spindly-legged husbands who left their bungalows every morning for desk jobs and returned tired and irritable at night, for a moment had the daring to see themselves in Fidel Castro's arms. As for Castro, far from being, as many ideological observers have contended, displeased with America, he was, on this trip, enchanted with it. "We have never met Americans like these," he repeated to his group over and over. "We only knew the colonialists."

In Washington, Castro and his party were installed in the elegant old Cuban embassy, where the FBI immediately moved the young Cuban leader into a back room for safety and put Ernesto Betancourt and Regino Boti in the front room with windows, in case there was an attack (economists, apparently, were expendable). Betancourt was assigned the job of awakening Castro at six every morning. "He slept with a pistol on the night table," Betancourt remembered, "so when he told me he wanted me to wake him up so we could have an hour's briefing, or a discussion while we were getting ready for the day's meetings, I said, 'Well, as long as you keep in mind that you are being awakened by a friendly person, so you don't grab the pistol, I will wake you up.'" And Castro laughed. Then.

The whole group was excited and optimistic about this trip, which all of them believed firmly would finally bring their country freedom and accomplishment. Indeed, there was no more morally and ethically sterling group of men and women in Cuba than this group that Castro brought with him to Washington. There was not one Communist, or old conservative, or radical among them. They were the intellectual créme de la créme of Cuban humanity and the leading economic thinkers and doers. But, curiously enough, right from the very start, even before they arrived in Washington, they began to wonder why they in particular had been brought along.

"Castro's reaction to U.S. aid was very categoric," Betancourt remembered. "He said simply that 'We are not going to have any discussions of economic assistance.'" To economist Rufo López Fresquet, Fidel added, "Besides, the Americans will be surprised. And when we go back to Cuba, they will offer us aid without our asking for it." But that was only part of the dust he was throwing in everyone's eyes: the truth was that the very last thing in the world he wanted was more *americanos* running around Cuba telling him what to do with his country—American aid, he knew well, would bring that.

Indeed—and again this goes against the common "wisdom" that has arisen almost to the level of legend regarding Cuba and the United States over the years—from the first day of the trip to the last, American officials kept trying and trying and trying to engage Fidel's decorative economists in talks. It was impossible.

One American who tried was the State Department's assistant secretary of state for Latin America, the urbane Roy "Dick" Rubottom. "I was talking with Pazos about their economic problems," Rubottom told me, "and they were grave. The banks were already talking about draw-downs, 'tranche' for Cuba, where you draw down your obligation to the International Monetary Fund. The U.S. has a significant role in these institutions. So I set up an appointment to see the Cuban economists after lunch. I had arranged for the assistant secretary of the treasury and an Export-Import Bank member and a senior economist to meet with them. The meeting was to be in my office. They said they had to check it out with Castro. At 2:00 P.M., I got a call from Rufo López Fresquet saying they were sorry they couldn't come, that Fidel would not give his approval."

Why, then, were they there? To find out, some of them began to watch the words and actions of their complicated new leader more carefully. During that trip, Ernesto Betancourt's wife, Raquel, for example, a very sensitive psychologist, observed Castro's habits—and their increasing extravagance. "I can assure you that I have seen people like Fidel in St. Elizabeths, where I did field work on abnormal psychology," she told her husband, with only a half smile.

"As a result of that comment, I started wondering about what personality type fitted Castro," Ernesto Betancourt recalled. "We had a lot of books on psychology, and we were looking for patterns. Through some friends of ours, a neurosurgeon and psychoanalyst, I got a book on manic-depressives. I took the book back from Washington to Havana." Then, in a sublimely mischievous move, Betancourt brought the book to a meeting of the board of directors of the Central Bank. "I just walked in with my book, and I started reading!" Betancourt told me. "I read the description of a hyper-manic. And the people started saying"—here, his voice mimicked a whisper—"'Oh, my God, what are you doing? Suppose they have microphones?'

"And I said, 'What are you talking about? I am just describing to you the characteristics of a type of manic-depressive. You are the ones who are concerned. You are the ones who are saying this is Fidel Castro, I didn't say it was.' . . ." And then he smiled an absolutely devilish smile and laughed his contagious laugh.

In fact, contrary to the way he would later describe the trip, Castro was feted, admired, and celebrated everywhere he went. Acting Secretary of State Christian Herter gave an elegant luncheon for him at the Statler-

Hilton, one of the best hotels in Washington. In all, there were twenty-five high-level national personalities whom Herter, with difficulty, had managed to get together very quickly to meet Castro's schedule. To some, it seemed a rather bizarre lunch, as Castro brought eight of his highly armed guards with him and insisted upon their being seated in the dining room. Sips of brandy sidetracked a potentially difficult moment, when finally his men agreed to leave their guns in a neighboring room. They returned and sat on the floor along the walls while the others ate.

There were several amusing moments during this high-level luncheon. William Wieland, who was in charge of Cuban affairs for the State Department, recalled one in particular. Wieland had been innocently introduced to Castro as the "man in charge of Cuban affairs." Castro only smiled slightly, then he immediately and pointedly added, "I thought that I was in charge of Cuban affairs."

Actually, the Herter lunch, proffered to a revolutionary only three months in office and without constitutional power, was a generous gesture. "The State Department went out of its way to provide a cordial welcome," Betancourt insists to this day. And, in fact, Castro agreed, although there is some evidence that he was miffed that Eisenhower was playing golf in Atlanta during his visit. (Castro regarded Ike as a war hero and it was for this reason, unnoted by history, that he wanted to meet him.)

Far from being slighted in the United States, then, Fidel Castro—*el barbudo,* the new rage in revolutionary chic, macho of machos and caudillo of caudillos—was the darling of the hour.

He spent five days in Washington, testifying before the Senate Foreign Relations Committee, where he stated that the Cuban revolutionary government would maintain membership in the hemispheric Mutual Defense Treaty for the defense of the Western Hemisphere and would protect foreign private industry in Cuba. Castro met with Richard Nixon in the vice-president's office off the Senate floor in the Capitol. The two men sat for more than two hours under the famous "Jefferson Chandelier," which had formerly hung happily tinkling away in the age before air conditioning in the president's Oval Office.

"My first impression of him was that he was simply an idealistic and impractical young man," Richard Nixon told me years later. "He talked about primary government capital, arguing that plants licensed by government would serve Cuban interests better than private plants. He kept criticizing the

American press, while I argued that he should learn from criticism both fair and unfair." Nixon leaned forward with some intensity as he said, "I had the feeling he would curtail press freedom in the future. But Castro told me, 'You Americans are always so afraid—afraid of Communism, afraid of everything. You should be talking more about your own strengths and the reasons why your system is superior to Communism or any other kind of dictatorship.'"

In a memo Nixon wrote immediately afterward, he stated that "I suggested at the outset that while I understood some reasonable time might elapse before it would be feasible to have elections, it would nevertheless be much better from his viewpoint if he were not to state so categorically that it would be as long as four years before elections would be held. . . . He went into considerable detail as he had in public with regard to the reasons for not holding elections, emphasizing particularly that 'the people did not want elections because the elections in the past had produced bad government. . . .' It was also apparent that as far as his visit to the United States was concerned, his primary interest was not to get a change in the sugar quota or to get a government loan but to win support for his policies from American public opinion. . . . My own appraisal of him as a man is somewhat mixed. The one fact we can be sure of is that he has those indefinable qualities which make him a leader of men. Whatever we may think of him, he is going to be a great factor in the development of Cuba and very possibly in Latin American affairs generally. . . . He is either incredibly naive about Communism or under Communist discipline. My guess is the former. . . ."

Later, the former American president mused over the historic visit. "I've met many leaders," he told me. "I've met Nkrumah and Sukarno, and they are all the same: they exude charisma, they exude, incidentally, sex appeal. It was not surprising to me to find they were ladies' men. All three would have been successful on the American scene. All three were demagogues. I could sense in private conversation how Castro could move an audience." He paused. "I felt his perception of the U.S. was distorted and that his anti-Americanism was virtually incurable. . . ." Did he like him? "I seldom get involved in like/dislike," Nixon responded cautiously. "I respected him as a strong personality. I found him worthy of talking to. There aren't so many you find like this on the international scene. One thing worse than being wrong, it's being dull. He was wrong; he was not dull. He was someone I'd like to have on our side. Castro . . . was worth two hours."

For his part, Castro was nervous, both before and after the meeting, perhaps because he was finally up man-to-man against one of the highest leaders of the "Colossus of the North." He also felt hurt and angry afterward, and for reasons that lay deep inside his psyche rather than for what had actually happened. He told *Bohemia* editor Miguel Quevedo, "That son-of-a-bitch Nixon, he treated me badly and he is going to pay for it. . . ." But he never said why. Perhaps he didn't know.

At the American Society for Newspaper Editors lunch, which was the ostensible reason for his trip, Castro showed another side of his contradictory personality by going out of his way to insult Herbert Matthews, boasting how he had fooled Matthews by inflating the numbers of his pathetic little group of rebels that long-ago day in the Sierra. Then he showed still another side when asked whether it was true that Joe Cambria, who had been a scout for big-league baseball teams and used to recruit Cuban baseball players, had ever tried to recruit him for a pro baseball team in the United States.

"Yes," he admitted grandly, "there was some conversation of that. . . . But let me tell you one thing. I always play pitcher, never catcher."

In New York, huge crowds fought to see "Fidel," all the way from Grand Central Station to the Statler Hotel. He toured Columbia University, met with U.N. Secretary General Dag Hammarskjøld; visited Yankee Stadium, where, according to legend, he ate hot dogs and hamburgers; and jumped the first barrier at the zoo to approach the lion cage, thus terrifying the FBI agents protecting him, since they were afraid to make a sound for fear of further disturbing the lions! (As to his purported conversations with the lions, most unfortunately there are no serious recollections of the event.) It was in Central Park, where in simpler days he had walked with Mirta on their honeymoon, that he suddenly proclaimed out of the air his "new" philosophy. "Our Revolution practices this democratic principle and is in favor of a humanist democracy," he said, seizing to everyone's amazement upon the word *humanist.* In that Central Park speech, he also for the first time put forth the phrase *Pan con Libertad,* or "Bread with Liberty." The unscientific "invention" of this catchy phrase had come about the day before when Castro was talking with Enrique de la Oza, the top editor of *Bohemia.* "We have a problem here," Castro told de la Oza. "Wherever we go, people are asking questions about what we are. You know we are socialists, but the Americans are so confused. If I say 'socialist,' they believe you are a 'Communist.'"

While Castro paced back and forth, his arms folded in the accustomed monarchical position behind his back, de la Oza began roaming intellectually over the political thought of Latin America, until he came to the catchy phrase, *Pan con Libertad,* which had been coined and used by the founder of Peru's democratic Left, Victor Raúl Haya de la Torre. Suddenly Castro ceased pacing. *"Pan con Libertad,"* he murmured, *"Pan sin Terror . . ."* "Bread with liberty . . . Bread without terror . . ." He turned the phrases over on his tongue, until they grew ever more succulent—he used them successfully in Central Park, then repeated them over and over daily for several months until they became one with the political air.

No Communists had been included in Castro's American contingent (and they could not have gotten visas), but suddenly a number of prominent Cuban Leftists appeared uninvited on the scene, sent by Vilma Espín, who was by now Raúl Castro's wife. Why would Vilma, the beautiful but cold-spirited wife of brother Raúl, do this? In part, because Vilma had the face of a French gamine and the soul and determination of Madame Lafarge. Moreover, a disturbed Raúl, always the loyal epigone but also the loyal Communist party member, seemed bent upon playing a distinctly disruptive role during the New York trip. With considerable distress, he watched as Castro enjoyed himself in this city, José Martí's "entrails of the beast." He began to call his brother nearly every night, warning him that back in Cuba it was appearing as though he was "selling out to the Americans." At one point, Teté Casuso said, Fidel "almost wept" at his brother's accusations.

But the most incredible story of the little-known and historically crucial "Raúl calls" comes from Luis J. Botifoll, a highly respected Cuban lawyer and former newspaperman who was received by Castro in his hotel in New York at this time. Fidel was staying at the Pennsylvania Hotel, by then, and he had called Roberto "Bobby" Maduro, the principal owner of the Cuban baseball team Sugar Kings, and asked him to travel to New York to see him. Botifoll, who owned a small piece of the team, agreed to go along. Maduro and Botifoll were relaxing in the bedroom of Castro's suite, and Castro was asking what it would take for the Sugar Kings to play in the major leagues, when a clearly agitated Celia walked into the room—it was Raúl, on the phone from Havana again.

"Raúl was complaining to Fidel about the press coverage of Fidel's trip," Botifoll revealed many years later. "He said the press was implying that Fidel was ready to cut a deal with the United States and that this was bad publicity for Fidel and that Fidel should return to Havana by May 1, Cuba's Labor Day, and give a speech on that day in order to disperse these rumors.

"Fidel told Raúl that he was not yet ready to make the kind of speech he was suggesting and that his only alternative was not to be in Cuba on the first of May. Fidel then told Celia to call over the Cuban members of the press. Fidel was visibly upset by his conversation with Raúl. He met the press members in the suite's parlor and told them they were lying, that he was not making a deal with the U.S. The meeting ended, and Fidel, Maduro and I returned to the bedroom. I remember trying to calm Fidel down. . . ."

At this moment, another of Castro's top men, the highly respected Regino Boti, arrived, and Castro suddenly asked him, with his own special kind of ingenuous cunning, about a planned meeting in Buenos Aires. "When are you leaving for the conference in Buenos Aires—and what is the conference about?"

Boti told Castro that it was to be an economics conference and Castro on the spot said that he wanted to attend. Boti pointed out to the rash young leader that Cuba already had a delegation attending and that his sudden decision to go was not at all within the "normal protocol." Fidel seemed to regain his spirits as he brushed these tiresome old concerns aside. "Don't worry," he told Boti, "I am going, and there I will suggest that the United States give five billion dollars to Latin America!" Boti shook his head and shivered inwardly, but he agreed to make the necessary arrangements.

In such insouciance and in such hurried deception was Castro's historic next trip born. And it would be there, in Buenos Aires, that he would give the speech that would provide the challenge to and thus the genesis for John F. Kennedy's "Alliance for Progress."

In those same weeks, Castro visited two prestigious American universities, Princeton and Harvard, where he was enthusiastically received by a cheering multitude. But it was at Princeton that Fidel received his most extraordinary reception in all the United States; and it was here, too, that he gave the single most extraordinary (it can only be called that) performance of the entire phantasmagorical trip.

The Princeton visit came about because of the prodigious efforts of a wealthy liberal professor, Roland T. Ely, a tall and very Yankee-looking man who was writing a definitive history of the Cuban economy and who had high-ranking family in Cuba. Professor Ely had already visited Cuba in the first three frenetic months of the Cuban Revolution and had been deeply impressed by the great mass demonstrations. He was so enamored of Castro's Revolution that he had had a surrealistic portrait of Castro done in black and red, the colors of the Revolution, with symbols of strife and bloodshed around the edges. Castro's head shone in the middle. He had left it as a gift of homage to the Cuban leader.

But Professor Ely could not ask Castro to come to Princeton on an authorized visit all on his own. Princeton needed an excuse. Nineteen fifty-nine paused on the early fringe of the massive politicization of the American university that would blossom in the 1960s and 1970s, and inviting such an unusual political leader was not yet considered quite appropriate. "But Professor Robert Palmer was giving a course just then on modern revolutions," Robert Goheen, who was president of Princeton then, recalled. "It was because of Bob Palmer's interest and this course that I authorized the university to receive Castro."

When the Castro entourage arrived at Princeton Junction, there were students perched in trees who unfurled huge Cuban flags. But the truly generous outpouring of love from these students to Fidel and his group would take place that night at Princeton University's Woodrow Wilson School. "It was a festive, crazy atmosphere, bubbling with enthusiasm and seeming, in retrospect, much like a foretaste of the student demonstrations of later years," the Chilean diplomat/writer Jorge Edwards recalled.

Castro entered the hall that night in his trademark fatigues through a small and carefully guarded rear door; and soon an unlikely row of bearded men in olive green uniforms, their hair tied in braids, were marching up the central aisle, some with ironic smiles and all with the sure swagger of victorious warriors. "There was a standing ovation," Edwards recalled, "a mixture of curiosity and a certain thrill of excitement, when Fidel Castro walked toward the stage from the rear door, calmly acknowledging greetings from all sides." Along the way, he spoke in a personal, soft, almost private tone of voice that could only be called seductive. Tellingly, he also ruled that he would (absolutely) not use an interpreter because it would distract the audience from the person, from the magic of the voice, from the total communication through the face movements.

When he reached the front of the room, his commanding figure turned slowly to face the students—and immediately charmed them. Basically his speech was a long plea for cooperation between the United States and the "new" Cuba. He talked about "revolution today" to this group of students whose ancestors were part of the revolution of yesterday. He lectured them, saying that the Cuban Revolution had not been founded on the Marxist model of class struggle.

He talked and talked and talked, until Professor Palmer, who still foolishly considered himself in charge of the seminar, pulled on the back of his jacket to indicate that time was really up. "I've boasted ever since that I'm the only person who has tried to make Fidel Castro stop talking," Palmer said. He paused, and smiled. "I was unsuccessful," he added.

In this speech, Castro said something extremely significant, had people picked it up. He said that his men had "proved that an army—even a modern army—could be defeated." In his own way, he was laying the groundwork for the guerrillas he would train and send around the world to wage war in his name. At the time, however, it seemed a moderate and liberal speech, and the students loved it.

At the end of the "lecture," Fidel marched away from the security men waiting at the rear entrance and departed like a victorious hero through the main door and into the waiting night. The youth of Princeton, cheering and filled with excitement, lifted him shoulder-high and carried him for several minutes until the frantic security men were able to move in again.

That night, there was a party at the eccentric atrium house of Roland and Sally Ely that, even for Castro, set new records for curiousness. The house was well known in Princeton, being locally referred to as the "Ant House" in part because the Elys had four "little ants" of "children." The problem for Mrs. Ely was the women. "I put his four lady friends in the main house, and he was to be in the guest house," Sally Ely recalled many years later. "There were about sixty *barbudos* hanging around. I went out to turn down his bed and all his lady friends were perfectly furious. They knew that, by turning down his bed, you jumped in with him." She paused. "They were all furious with me," she repeated. "Celia was the one who was so rude to me about the business of the bed. And I was so dense and so tired, I didn't understand it." Finally, the four women ended up sleeping in the children's bedrooms and Mrs. Ely slept in the bathtub, while Castro danced all night with the children. When Pennsylvania senator Joe Clark tried to bring some eggs in the next morning, the police stopped him outside and held him for three hours incommunicado while they tested the eggs.

In what might be called an irony of history, a new phenomenon was revealing itself in America just at the time of the visit of Fidel Castro. Jorge Edwards recalled how, that spring of 1959, "a few scruffy, bearded poets had passed through Princeton, without making much of a mark in a place that still remembered the classic works of Thomas Mann. . . . They came on foot, hitchhiking, or in dilapidated buses from far-off San Francisco and they were called Allen Ginsberg, Gregory Corso, Lawrence Ferlinghetti. . . ." Their visit was prophetic: they were the true harbingers of a new era. For the mental, psychological, and sometimes political coming together in the next years of those original "Hippies" with the Cuban *guerrilleros*—and then the American dissidents of the '60s and early '70s—would prove a fateful meeting that would change relations between the "powerful" and the "powerless" for all time. As for their part, the American radical students of the era saw strength and romance in Castro, in place of the ambiguous power and grandfatherly grayness of an Eisenhower. They saw in him a return to the heroic element in modern life, as if, in Norman Mailer's smitten words, "the ghost of Cortez had appeared in our century riding Zapata's white horse."

But it was not just the radical Americans who came under Castro's spell. Others who were as unlike them as it was possible to be were also taken by him. The CIA's chief expert on Latin American Communism, Frank Bender, had a three-hour interview with Castro and came out averring enthusiastically, "Castro is not only not a Communist; he is a strong anti-Communist fighter." (Things would change; it would be Bender, in just two years, who would direct the Bay of Pigs invasion.)

The trip grew in boisterousness as it hurtled toward its end, and Castro's behavior became ever more problemmatical as his patience for formality wore thin. He was at his worst in Montreal, where he strew ashes over the beautiful carpets of the Queen Elizabeth Hotel, pushed all the silverware aside at the formal banquet held in his honor, and downed the glass of sherry, meant for a toast to the queen, in one gulp. When he himself was toasted as the "president of Cuba," he replied with cynical playfulness and with that ingenuous smile, "But I am not the president of Cuba." Even he was embarrassed afterward about that.

After Fidel had left the United States, the American press scrambled to identify the significance of his visit. The consensus seemed to be, as *Commonweal* magazine put it, that "Fidel Castro is merely the symbol of a force which is welling up all over Latin America and that Cuba's plight is merely part of a widespread Latin American pattern. . . ."

But what really had "happened" on this trip? What Fidel Castro did brilliantly on this first trip, and what he would do again and again, was to go over the official heads of the government. He agreed to the visit in the first place because newspaper editors had invited him, not the United States government. He knew that by addressing the editors he could bring his case directly to the media and, thus, through them, directly to the American people. This was power of the new age, and he was the first to recognize it. He had connived psychologically and politically to set up a myth of a revolution of "humanism," a revolution of "bread and liberty," a revolution the *americanos* could not fear and thus would not try to stop or overthrow—but also not finance. He had reached out to a new generation, and he had catapulted a new "power of the powerless" onto the world stage. It had been a wildly successful trip, but its successes had nothing to do with economic aid or any of the other things that rational analysts so earnestly expound upon.

The two countries, peoples, and ways of life came together for a moment that spring, but they did not meet. They passed like ships in a foggy night, ships that already were moving inexorably in totally different and finally antagonistic sea lanes. They met and they crossed. That was all.

The very day after he returned from his trip, Castro announced his agrarian reform. It was really the key to everything, and it was appropriately signed in the highest and (as it turned out) most rainy recesses of the mystical Sierra Maestra with the kind of symbolism and high drama at which Castro so excelled. Officials and scores of journalists trudged up the savage green mountains to what some of them secretly called "Fidel's Eagle's Nest" at his old headquarters at La Plata. There they were joined by thousands of peasants who had come to see Fidel.

"We flew to Manzanillo and then went by truck," Jack Skelly recalled of the grueling experience. "Then we walked up the mountains to the 'Eagle's Nest.' It took us eighteen hours. When we got up there, Fidel arrived by helicopter with some of the cabinet. It rained like hell. And we were there for about three days. No one could get out." But despite the cold rain and the lack of food (no one had thought to bring enough food), there were moments of transformational beauty. The law was signed by Castro, President Urrutia, and several ministers by the light of a lantern on an old

233

wooden table, and everyone slept on the floor without blankets just like the *guajiros* they were going to "save" with the historic bill. Raúl got lost in the mountains and swore unceasingly for days. "I remember Fidel standing there and all these people in line would put their notes (with requests for something) in his pocket," Jack Skelly said. "I remember that up there at the 'Eagle's Nest,' Fidel gave a check to one peasant for cows, to start a cattle cooperative. The check was for three hundred thousand dollars."

Basically, the agrarian reform sounded moderate, and it *was* moderate in its wording; but it was radical in its intent. This was because, as he did so often, Castro had allowed two people to present contrapuntal bills, which he could then use, point to, employ for different purposes. Two agrarian reform bills had been worked out that winter, one by the moderate minister of agriculture, Humberto Sorí Marín, and the other by Che Guevara's group and the pro-Communist Osvaldo Dorticos. Carlos Franqui, who covered all of this for *Revolución,* reported that: "Sorí Marín's plan helped Castro gain time and to calm down the vested interests; Che's plan, which was more to Fidel's liking, would satisfy even the most impatient and could be used when the right moment came."

Humberto Sorí Marín, the serious, dark-haired lawyer who had been a comandante in the Sierra and had written an early agrarian reform law for Castro, realized almost immediately that there was a "double play" going on. Nevertheless, he attended the big emotional fiesta at La Plata, and had his fleeting but real moment of glory as he sat on a white horse in the middle of three thousand peasants grasping in their eager hands the titles to their land. Soon after that, he too left Cuba, another sad and defeated casualty among the moderates.

Under the Agrarian Reform Bill signed on that rainy spring day in the Sierra, American and Cuban sugar mills were stripped of their canefields; no foreigner could acquire farmland in Cuba or inherit it; upwards of two hundred thousand peasants would receive land. But in fact the peasant was simply exchanging the private owner as boss for the government as boss because (1) the land could never be sold or mortgaged, and (2) the peasants were to grow crops ordered by the National Agrarian Reform Institute (INRA) and they were to deliver their crops at the price set.

One of Castro's lasting and extraordinary talents is his ability to create transformational structures, usually under the very eyes of his "enemies." He would then change these structures, carrying them to an entirely different reality without anyone realizing it until it was far too late. He did this now, in one of the tactics he used all his life, in part by calling things by names which bore no relation to what they were to become. The "agrarian reform" was to institute "cooperatives," whereas what Castro really aimed at was "collectivization"—never mind, "the people," who ruled, did not yet need to know that!

INRA in a real sense now became for a crucial parenthesis of time in his revolutionary transformation the new Cuban state, or at least the form of its future. A strong axis was created between INRA and the Rebel Army, with INRA providing the economic and political decision-making body for the former's military power. INRA created its own armed hundred-thousand-man militia with the aid of Raúl, set up its own department of industrial-ization headed by Che, and formed a department of commercialization. INRA built roads, seized private lands, and created tourist resorts. Soon Castro was literally running Cuba through INRA, while the other, formal, even "presidential" structures floundered in the spotlight, mere pretenses to power. Like a deceptively purposeless honeybee creating its hundreds of secreted little pockets of wax, Fidel Castro was busily constructing the social and political rooms of the new Cuban national home.

But was Fidel already a Communist in this era? If so, when did he become one? Or was he, perhaps, always something else? The answer is buried in political, psychological, and ideological quicksand and is obscured by a number of theories, put forth by foreign correspondents, analysts, and biographer Tad Szulc, including one that would have us believe that from the day Castro marched down upon Havana, there was a carefully and secretively structured "hidden government" plotting behind him. According to Szulc, clandestine meetings, with a deliberate objective, were held in a hilltop house in the fishing village of Cojímar, only ten miles east of Havana. But a careful reading of the original interviews upon which this assuring conspiracy ("Fidel was always a Communist!") was based—interviews with Communists Fabio Grobart, Alfredo Guevara, and Blas Roca—shows no such conspiracy. What it does show is that they, like at least six other groups, were working for their own objectives; and that Fidel, with at least six other groups, was working for his own, which was, quite simply, total power for himself. Fidel Castro simply cannot be jammed into anyone's political straitjacket.

The truth is that Fidel Castro never "became" a Communist as one becomes a Mason, a Catholic, an SS officer, a Hare Krishna, or a Zoroastrian.

He did not adapt himself to an ideology; he found an ideology to adapt itself to him. His "Communism" was not—could not be—an act of faith, because his only faith lay in himself and his "noble" intentions. But he did something historic that would be repeated in the "political religions" (political scientist David Apter's phrase) of so many of the Third World countries: he brought "Communism" to power through his own ego, instead of through an ideology imposed through a movement. This would be the theme he would carry like a new sacred offering to the Third World.

In fact, Castro really never became a "Communist" at all. The new thing in history that Castro did was to destroy the Communist party and create his own *Fidelista* party, which he called Communist in order to stand up against the United States and to gain backing and to borrow power from the Soviet Union. For the first time in history, a national leader converted the Communist party to himself!

By the summer of 1959, Castro had consolidated his power completely. Now he would get rid of the man he personally had "groomed" as president, or, really, president-in-waiting.

Manuel Urrutia Lleó was a quiet, inconspicuous but honorable judge who dotted every "i" and for a time really thought he was president of Cuba. When Castro unleashed his full fury against him, it was a storm all Cuba would remember. "Problems with the president!" Castro irritatedly told Carlos Franqui one late spring day, as he strode back and forth restlessly in his usual manner. And then he did what he always did. "I'm not going to resort to the usual Latin American–style coup," he told Franqui. "I'm going directly to the people, because the people will know what to do. You are the only one who knows anything about this, and I want you to publish a special edition of the newspaper announcing it. Seal the place off and don't leak a word. You might as well print a million copies—you know, with those big headlines you like so much!" Why? "I'll give the reasons when I go on TV."

Revolución came out the next morning with huge red letters in a ten-inch headline, "Fidel Resigns!" There were demonstrations everywhere, the entire nation shook and virtually shut down—and it did not hurt at all that Castro had brought to Havana thousands of country *guajiros* to celebrate the 26th of July and to serve as his "Destroy Urrutia!" interlocutors. "This Fidel really likes to fuck around," the fun-loving Camilo Cienfuegos complained acidly at the time. But this was not the usual "fucking around." Castro was going to get rid of his president, but he was going to do it through a new genre of political action; through what was, in effect, a "coup-de-television," in which a man is not simply politically replaced but destroyed and in which "the people" think they have made the decision.

Castro was not only master of movement and dynamics, he was also master of nonmovement. Just at this time, he disappeared, making the people, who by now were utterly dependent upon him, wait in fear and trepidation. Like Hitler, like Qaddafi, like so many of the charismatic leaders, he knew how to use space and time, to use the people's fear of the absence of the *líder máximo* and their fear of abandonment.

When he finally returned to Havana after several days, he went first to the TV station, CMQ, and talked calmly for about thirty minutes. Then he zeroed in on the point, stating that "the reason for my resignation is . . . my difficulties with the president of the Republic." That was the beginning of the determined and deliberate destruction of the honest country judge who had now served Castro's purposes. He went on to accuse Urrutia of "treason" because he had even mildly spoken out against the Communists. The performance would never be forgotten, for it was Castro's most menacing to date, and many who had been with him up until then were stunned by the ferocity of this attack upon a man who had blindly followed his every wish.

As for Manuel Urrutia, a man who had also suffered to save Cuba, he cowered like a cornered animal before such unexpected and ferocious calumnation where before there had been all friendship and amity. The small and becomingly modest man with the long Spanish nose and the accustomed dark glasses hid in his office in the presidential palace, staring into his television set as though in shock as his loyal secretary shouted at Castro's face on the television screen, "You lie, you lie. . . ." It was then that Urrutia started to weep uncontrollably.

For this was not a simple political maneuver where one man replaces another, often without any rancor because it is all simply part of a political power game; this was an emotional, a psychological, a charismatic coup d'état, a *golpe de estado* in Spanish, in which the usurper uses every psychological vehicle and tactic not only to destroy the efficacy, legitimacy, and reputation of the man but to destroy his group and his class with him. Castro quite simply no longer had any need for Urrutia and his moderate views, and so he got rid of him and, with him, anyone else who held similar views.

The man who thought he was president finally fled, disguised as a milkman, and took asylum in the Venezuelan embassy where eventually hundreds would seek refuge. No evidence of any kind was ever presented against him. On July 26, Fidel Castro emotionally "bowed" to the wishes of his "masses" and "acceded" to the demands of the people to return, as prime minister, while a Communist of little note, Osvaldo Dorticós, a forty-year-old lawyer, was named president. Castro's coup-de-television had, for all intents and purposes, destroyed whatever prestige was left of the moderates and democrats.

Christmas of 1959 dawned to a Cuba of profound political ambivalence. Castro had been busy that December abolishing a new "imperialist," the dangerous Santa Claus, whom he considered an unregenerate figure of capitalist overabundance. He tried to replace him with a *guajiro* figure called *don Feliciano,* or "Mr. Happiness," who properly wore a *guayabera,* a *guajiro* hat, and a beard. The children, however, did not like this pretender to Christmas.

But most Cubans still were enamored of their "Fidel." Teté Casuso was one of many invited to see in the New Year with Castro at a huge celebration dinner at the Hilton. She walked into the hotel and found Fidel signing autographs and speaking to adoring crowds. "As I sat with Fidel into the first hours of 1960, listening to Cubans shout his praises, I was still hopeful," she wrote. "I did not believe it could be so sad a year as it has been for Cuba, and that before it was over so many of us would have had to separate ourselves from him and from the dream to build a nation of liberty and kindness together."

19

AN IRON FILING

If there are two rooms, one comfortable and the other dangerous, and in the "comfortable" one they are beating you and giving you blows, and you see the door to the other room open, you are going to the other door.

—Fidel Castro to Spanish journalist Antonio Orlani, in 1959

" . . . FEBRUARY. A glimmering sun, and a warming one! The verdant green of the palms against the depth of a blue sky! We gathered curiously at the little windows of the plane as it was landing in Havana. An enormous crowd—a tapestry of suits and faces—hid the concrete landing strip between the Ilyushin-18, which had just stopped its motor, and the airport building. Between the rainbow of the flowers, the theme of the green was repeated in the uniforms of the armed *barbudos*." An amazed pause. "But there was no evidence of ceremonies, of protocol, of the usual conventions of the frontier or of the customs. . . ."

So the prominent Russian journalist Sergo Mikoyan described the bemused and puzzled response of the Russians as they landed in Havana on February 4, 1960, for the history-boggling visit of his father, Soviet First Deputy Premier Anastas I. Mikoyan. It was a trip that, unbeknownst to the Russians, much less to most Cubans, would constitute the first step in the realignment of Cuba from West to East.

Castro made certain that the airport was filled with every celebrity of the Cuban Revolution. He himself stood strong and utterly determined, a Napoleonic figure in uniform. Next to him were President Dorticós, Che Guevara, and the others. Far from coming there with some sure purpose, as the United States supposed, the bewildered Russians had no idea at all what they would find in this faraway land. They stepped hesitantly out of the plane to the strangely juxtaposed sounds of the Cuban and Soviet national anthems.

Ostensibly, the reason for this first Russian visit to Cuba was to inaugurate a major Russian exhibition of goods and machinery. But on a more soulful level, it was a meeting of the Soviet oriental East with the Latin Christian West. "My first impression was that of a sense of romanticism," Sergo Mikoyan reminisced with me later. "By that time, it had almost been lost in our country." "Communism" was barely mentioned, or even "socialism," during the Mikoyan visit. "It was only during the nine days that my father was there that he began to realize what was happening," he went on. "No, there was no moment, no hour of day; it was gradual. At the time of the Revolution, no one knew what kind of man Castro was. Even Khrushchev's son-in-law, Alexei Adzubei, who was the editor of *Izvestia,* on the last day before our departure said that he didn't think this would go anywhere. In fact, the Russian leaders were surprised at the important results of that visit."

But there were several revealing moments. As Castro took the first deputy premier on one of his exhausting whirlwind tours of the interior, showing him "cooperative" after "cooperative," the dark and swarthy Mikoyan kept saying words in Russian to his translator, which Castro finally realized were not being translated. He asked the interpreter, "What is Señor Mikoyan saying each time he sees a cooperative?" The answer was: "He is saying, 'If we had this in Russia, we would call it Communism.'"

The Mikoyan visit had come about through the efforts of the resourceful KGB agent Alexander Alexeev, who had arrived at Castro's office on the top floor of the huge INRA building in the fall of 1959. Dressed that day in a proper black suit and gray neck tie, he courteously carried gifts of vodka, black caviar, and an album of photos of Moscow wrapped neatly in a Moscow newspaper. "They were dressed in their olive green uniforms with open collars, wearing high military boots, and I appeared dressed for a gala!" Alexeev wrote with his bright sense of humor. "I felt disturbed for a moment. Fidel noted my discomfort and tried to calm me, making jokes that when they passed forty-two years (in these days, we were approaching the forty-second anniversary of the October Revolution) the Cubans would also begin to observe the norms of protocol."

These men, from two worlds that could not possibly have been more different, sat there atop the Americanized skyscraper that was the INRA building "ninety miles from the United States" and spoke of ideas of revolutionary change that would span the world.

After lengthy discussions over agrarian reform, collectivization, and *latifundios* to be turned into *haciendas del estado,* or "state farms," Castro's secretary, Conchita Fernández, brought out crackers and two glasses so they could try the caviar and the vodka, and the two men sat there eating and drinking for some time. "What good vodka, what good caviar!" Castro, with his great appetite, remarked at one point. Then he narrowed those hawk's eyes of his and said to one of his aides, "Núñez, I think it's worth establishing trade relations with the Soviet Union. What do you think?"

That was the moment when the idea came openly from Castro—they would bring the Soviet industrial exposition, which already had been inaugurated in Mexico and New York, to Cuba and show the Cuban people what the Russians were really like! The idea of Mikoyan himself visiting then came up, as did the idea (from Alexeev) of diplomatic relations.

During this unclear period of the realignment of Cuba from West to East, whatever tentative ties Castro still had to his family grew even weaker. His sister Juanita, soon to become his Medusa-like nemesis, in these months began her terrible fights with Castro. His sister Angelita was arrested on orders from Castro, and Juanita, always the lady of the family, stormed the jail, shouting at the jail comandante over the phone, "I regret you're not here before me so that I could empty a pistol in your belly."

Lina was still living on the land that she and Angel had stolen and carved from the heavy jungle, but still she did not like her son's new "moving of the fences" over the land. One day, Manolin Rodríguez, the Castros' neighbor and the faithful keeper of the tales of the Castro family, was at a gas station, outside of Coeto, a small town near Marcanay, in Oriente province. "A jeep came filled with Fidel's guards," Rodriguez recalled. "Lina was in the back of the gas station and she was disgusted to see the guards. She said to my father, 'Manolo, how are they treating you?' Father turned, took off his Stetson and stretched his arms out, as if shrugging. 'Lina,' he said, 'what do you want me to tell you?'

"Then Lina said"—at this point Rodríguez broke down into fits of laughter at the still-vibrant memory—" 'I'm going to tell you something. One of these days, you are going to find that Lina castrated some of these cuckolds up there in Birán!'"

But of all the public family traumas of the "Castros of Birán," none quite equaled Emma's wedding. All the Castro sisters were pretty, with healthy good looks and a sensuous self-assurance that made them attractive to men, but Emma was the most delicate and cultured and she was a romantic. All her life she had dreamed of being married in the weathered old Cathedral of Havana. Two days before the wedding, Fidel, Raúl, Che, and another more radical comandante had a meeting about Emma's wedding and decided it should be not in the cathedral but in a "humble" parish. This was no haphazard decision; it was exactly in keeping with Castro's new campaign to divide the Catholic Church between rich and poor. But Juanita's blood boiled at that idea; "It's Emma's wedding, not yours," she told her brothers.

And she won—or nearly. The wedding was duly held in the scabrously beautiful old cathedral on the loveliest old square of Havana, but Castro found a way to make his point. He had been in the countryside all that day working with the peasants, and he arrived at the wedding with mud all over him. "Fidel had his small revenge," Juanita noted. "He arrived late for the wedding, and the people crowded around him and caused a great commotion just as Emma was saying her vows at the other end of the cathedral."

By the time Lina Castro died on August 6, 1963, she was totally estranged from her Fidel, but both he and Raúl still rushed to the house with their escorts when Juanita called them. "Their entrance was ironic," Juanita wrote, "for already the house was filled with counter-revolutionaries—anti-Communists, or as Fidel called them, *gusanos,* or worms. When Raúl arrived, he cried like a baby. However, Fidel did not shed a tear while he was in the house."

But even as Castro deliberately broke with members of his own family (except, of course, Raúl), he was beginning to create his own "new Cuban family." He no longer would have a personal family; the Cuban people would be his family. After the Revolution, it was even strongly rumored that he would officially decree that all the children born were now "Children of the Revolution," or "Fidel's Children." The boy who was born illegitimate was creating his own legitimacy. But to do this, he had to destroy the ties, the bonds, the attachments to the past. "Only the new was good," the prominent Cuban psychiatrist Dr. Marcelino Feal told me. "They began to teach in school that children only have to obey the party and its doctrine and not their parents. And they began to take the girls and boys at high school and at pre-university age to the fields to do work that they had never done. . . ."

In the fields alone, without their parents, with only their peers and their ideological mentors, the youngsters felt the old strict Spanish cultural norms, traditions, and taboos fall away. Massively, an entire generation lost its inhibitions in the canefields of Cuba. Many of the girls became pregnant. The authority of the family was replaced by the authority of the government.

Cubans began to notice at this time in their society a kind of collective psychosis, a new temper that was almost sexual in its texture, almost an erotic mood floating over the society. "It preceded the creation of the feminine militias," Castro's interpreter Juan Arcocha recalled, "and the literacy campaign that for months removed all the maternal vigilance from thousands of young girls. Many of them returned home in a noticeable state of pregnancy."

Not everyone, however, was ready to give up the old ways and beliefs. Don Juan de Lojendio, a Spanish marqués, was the ambassador in Havana from the regime of Francisco Franco. He was staying in the beautiful old Spanish residence, a very large, aristocratically formal house with a graceful garden surrounded by several languid pools. Every day in that January of 1960 and with ever-increasing intensity, the Castro government had been accusing his embassy of having contacts with the growing "counterrevolution," whose bombs could be heard nightly in the streets of Havana. Then, on the night of January 20, Castro again went on television and again accused both the United States and Spain of aiding the counterrevolution.

A stout, well-built man with black hair and a passion for the dignity of the Spaniard, Ambassador Lojendio suddenly could control himself no longer. "He got up, enraged, and cried, 'I'm going to the TV,'" María Camella, his secretary, recalled. "He was a silent man, but . . . this was too much. Every day he had been insulted." When the Spanish ambassador reached the television station, Castro was sitting among his bearded men and tight-lipped militiawomen, all of them applauding him enthusiastically as he attacked the "counterrevolutionaries." At this moment, the amazed station manager tapped Castro on the shoulder and whispered in his ear that an insanely angry diplomatic apparition was about to appear and seemed even about to accost him.

Virtually every independent analyst who saw it—and it was seen by just about everyone in the country on television—agreed that it was the only time they ever saw Fidel Castro physically frightened. He raised himself half out of his chair, speechless this one time, as Lojendio stalked into the room like a brother madman. "I have been insulted, I have been insulted," the ambassador, giving way to his most profound sense of Spanish pride and honor, kept shouting, "I demand the right to reply!"

At that the studio fell apart, it became a madhouse. Bodyguards leaped to the stage, President Dorticós froze, Castro clutched at his holster. His reaction should not have been surprising; it was one of the few times in his life when he had not been on the offensive; he never knew how to handle the defensive, it was not his mode. Finally, the ambassador, his gaunt Spanish face white with anger, was physically ejected from the studio and would have been mistreated except for the protective actions of several of Castro's men.

As for Castro, his hands shook for a while, then he sipped some of the cognac that he always kept in his "coffee cup." Pardo Llada, the radio broadcaster and long-time Castro intimate, who still then defended his old friend, insultingly introduced his radio program with the sound of a donkey's heehaw—that was supposed to be the voice of the Spanish ambassador.

The next morning, the entire ambassadorial corps conspicuously merged at the ambassador's house to pay their respects before he was thrown out of the country. Castro had his early *turbas divinas,* or "divine mobs," at the airport to scream at him and threaten him with physical beatings (these *turbas* were the direct ancestors of the armed mobs of the same name later used in Nicaragua by the Sandinistas).

When Lojendio arrived safely in Spain, Generalísimo Franco told him with a wry smile, "As a Spaniard, very good; as a diplomat, very bad!"

As Castro continued to sever ties with the "old," he began consolidating ties with the Eastern Bloc through an irregular—untraditional, guerrilla— diplomacy that was in many ways structurally an extension of the guerrilla war in the Sierra Maestra. From October 1959, Che Guevara began making repeated trips behind the Iron Curtain, signing commercial agreements with the Czechs, the Russians, the Chinese, and even the hermit North Koreans. Castro's intent, at this point at least, was not so much even to "make friends" or "do business with" the Communists, as it was part of his profoundly felt and always-exercised idea that Cuba's position in the world had to be strengthened vis-à-vis the always dangerous United States.

But more important in the long run than these commercial dealings was Che's meeting, on one of these early trips, with Tamara Haydée "Tania" Bunke Bider, who had been born in 1937 in Buenos Aires to a German Communist refugee from Nazism. Tania had a sulky and tremulous beauty, more like that of an exotic Slav, and there is no question that Che and Tania became lovers almost immediately and remained so until they died together in Bolivia in 1966, or that Tania was a Russian/East German agent sent to watch Che, who was always too "free" a Marxist spirit for the austere Eastern Communists. Although the relationship was little known outside of inner Cuban circles until the tragic Bolivian "adventure," when Che virtually committed suicide, they began to be seen together in Havana as early as 1961. Then, interestingly enough, they mingled socially—and politically—with early Sandinista founders like Carlos Fonseca Amador and Tomás Borge, who also tellingly were in Havana, savoring the Cuban Revolution and learning early its lessons.

But even as members of the old order were boarding planes at Havana's airport and flying sadly away from the beauties of the Cuba they had so loved, the new order remained undefined. Unlike Communism, which proudly held that the "social" as well as the "scientific" in human society were subject to immutable laws, Castroism could not have been more unscientific. For Castro, anything and everything was possible through the exercise of human will and through his personal hallucinatory power. His ability for endless improvisation, often at the very moment of need, could not have been further from the austere, drudging Communist methods of onerous central planning and "action" through the inactive bureaucrat-upon-bureaucrat levels of Marxist society.

One typical day, when the agrarian reform had begun, Castro went out with some of his economists to the province of Pinar del Río to start distributing the lands among the farm labor. "We were supposed to be in the area at eight A.M.," Gerardo Canet, one of the early moderate economists related. "Hundreds of people were waiting for us, but Fidel didn't arrive until around six in the afternoon. He started talking, and his speech lasted eight hours!

"Fidel talked and talked, and finally I said to him, 'Those fellows have been here since very early in the morning and they are tired.' Then Fidel said, 'Awake!' and 'Yes, let's be concrete!' and he began to talk about what to do with the land. Fidel wanted to industrialize Cuba and was against sugar."

At this point, as he stood up there in his uniform regaling the peasants with all the "concrete things" he was going to do for them, Castro suddenly realized he had no answers. In an unusual moment of bewilderment, he stopped and turned to the economists next to him, whom he never listened to, and asked suddenly, "What should I tell these fellows to do with the land?" But the economists just whispered helplessly among themselves. Suddenly Castro turned back to the avidly waiting peasants and said, "We will plant African palms, we'll extract oil, or we'll plant peanuts or sorghum." He turned around for a moment, then triumphantly faced the peasants again, saying, "Now we will start a big project of planting vegetables to produce oil, like the African palms!"

But these Cuban *guajiros* were sugarcane cutters, and not only were they used to it, they were proud of it. To Castro's distinct annoyance, they began shouting, "No, no, we want sugarcane." Finally, Castro said he would appoint a commission to work with them, but he added with utter certainty that it would not be sugarcane.

During this period, Che made several economic agreements with the Soviets. Russia was to take one million tons of Cuban sugar for five years and was to pay for 20 percent of it in dollars, the rest in Soviet goods. But even those who studied the kaleidoscopic situation closely and were aware of Cuba's tentative approaches to the Soviet Union were bewildered by how fast relations between the United States and Cuba were deteriorating. Washington had finally sent an ambassador to Havana whom Castro could easily have worked with, but it was simply too late. Castro was responding not to the reality of the moment but to other voices, dim and echoing across some distant chasm that only he perceived as a danger.

The new American ambassador to Cuba, Philip Bonsal, was an intelligent, sensitive man, and his first meeting with the young Cuban leader in March 1959 seemed to go well. "Castro had gone out of his way to express a warm desire for frequent meetings with me," Bonsal recalled. "The next day on television he spoke favorably of our first meeting." And Bonsal was also cheered by what he considered a "heartwarming incident" at a Cuban baseball game between the Sugar Kings and the Minneapolis Millers. Castro was in the bleachers mingling with the spectators when Bonsal arrived. "The crowd rose and gave me a prolonged ovation," Bonsal remembered. "I was truly moved by this tribute to my country." He should not have been so moved, for Castro was enraged that an American ambassador should still so appeal to the "revolutionary" Cuban people. Later, asked by a friend what he thought of the welcome to the American envoy, he said only, "Excessive, excessive." He was not smiling.

For the truth was that when Castro looked out at the world from behind that huge beard and those hooded eyes, he saw everywhere a pervasive sense of threat from the overpowering presence of the *americanos*. One day he was lunching with Felipe Pazos and Jorge Beruff at the Central Bank, when the question of U.S. properties in Cuba came up. Suddenly, Castro turned to Pazos and asked with that special ingenuous look of his, "Look, Felipe, can you give me the amount of U.S. direct investment in the world?"

Pazos said he thought the figure was "about thirty billion dollars."

"And how much is invested in Cuba?" Castro then asked.

"About one billion dollars," Pazos answered.

Castro's moody face broke out in a big, boyish smile, as he countered, "Look, gentlemen, tell the Americans not to be so ridiculous! If they have thirty billion dollars in the world, for only one billion dollars in Cuba, they shouldn't be so preoccupied. Tell them to give us the one billion!" Instead, Castro decided to take it.

"The fact is . . . that until March 1960, contrary to popular thought, the policy followed by the United States toward Castro's Cuba was one of complete adherence to the treaty commitments that forbid the intervention of one American republic in the domestic affairs of another," Ambassador Bonsal declared early on. But the fact also was that, in March 1960, that policy changed. That month, President Dwight D. Eisenhower, who never could understand a Fidel Castro any more than Castro could understand him, signed an order authorizing the training of Cuban counterrevolutionaries in the United States. With that signature, the Bay of Pigs was conceived.

All that was needed now to freeze relations between the two countries completely was a handle. Castro had many, but the one he chose was oil. Cuba owed the American- and European-owned oil companies—Esso, Texaco, and Shell—a little over fifty million dollars in accumulated debts for the crude oil they had been importing. When the Cuban government demanded that the oil companies accept less money (about half of what other suppliers were charging) for crude oil received during the last half of 1960, the oil companies grumbled but acquiesced. At first the U.S. government went along with the deal, but then suddenly the Treasury Department urged the oil companies not to accede to Cuban demands, and they did not. On January 29, the Cuban government "temporarily" took over the management of the three refineries. This gave the Russians the opening they wanted. Almost immediately, Russian technicians and Russian crude oil began arriving in Cuba.

"Life on the island was in danger of coming to a standstill," Nikita Khrushchev explained later. "It was urgent that we organize an oil delivery to Cuba on a massive scale. . . ."

It was the point of no return; within months all American properties, from sugar mills to oil refineries to utility companies, were nationalized. Americans filed a staggering 8,816 "asserted" claims of $3,346,406,271.36 against the Cuban government, an amount more than the expropriations of all Communist governments in history combined!

Now everything escalated. On July 6, Eisenhower announced the United States would not import the remainder of the 1960 Cuban sugar quota and would not buy any Cuban sugar until further notice. Castro called this the "Dagger Law," or, in effect, the dagger in the back of the Revolution. In a fiery speech, he darkly prophesized that the loss of the quota "would cost Americans in Cuba down to the nails in their shoes." Ambassador Bonsal clearly sensed the venom in Castro's words. "Castro's goal was the elimination of the American presence in Cuba," he judged correctly.

Castro was changing the role of Cuba from that of an American "playground" to one of international significance; so as he moved summarily to dismiss American business interests from the island, he also concurrently invited world figures to visit Cuba. That spring, Pablo Neruda, the great Chilean poet and a Stalinist, visited and wrote in praise of the Revolution a *canción de gesta, gesta* being an archaic term for an ancient romantic song poem. (The ever-observant Pardo Llada said Neruda asked Castro for "shopping money" for his wife and that Castro gave him twenty thousand dollars!) The fun-loving President Sukarno of Indonesia visited, as did the Marxist Guyanese prime minister, Cheddi Jagan. In other ways, too, Cuba began playing a new and vertiginous world role. "Sometimes we even thought it was rather pompous to refer to Cuba as if it were in the center of the universe," Che wrote in April of 1960 in the Cuban military magazine, *Verde Olivo*. "Nonetheless, it is true or almost true. If someone doubts the Revolution's importance, he should read the newspaper. 'The U.S. threatens Poland because of the Pact with Cuba.' Man, we're strong and dangerous. . . . Oh, it is so great and comfortable to belong to such a strong world power as dangerous as Cuba!" For once, he was not being sardonic.

The restructuring of the country now speeded up everywhere. In the winter of 1960, a Central Planning Board was formed to consolidate economic power, as in the Eastern Bloc countries. New civilian militias of students, workers, and peasants seemed to pop up everywhere. A Board for Revolutionary Propaganda was formed, which began to refer to Cuba as the first *Territorio Libre de América,* or the first Free Territory of America. In Castro's dramatic May Day speech, Cubans and the world heard for the first time what was to become the famous, "*¡Cuba sí, Yanqui no!*" Finally, the Soviet Union began training and equipping the armed forces of Cuba.

During the summer of 1960, Khrushchev himself acknowledged a Soviet connection with Cuba. On July 9, three days after Eisenhower's sugar quota announcement, Khrushchev proclaimed the stunning words: "The U.S.S.R. is raising its voice and extending a helpful hand to the people of Cuba. . . . Speaking figuratively, in case of necessity, Soviet artillerymen can support the Cuban people with rocket fire."

Interestingly enough, Castro was not at all pleased with this rocket-rattling on his "behalf." Indeed, he was personally and politically incensed by it. He saw it as another attempt to insult and threaten the independence of his country. So he pulled one more psychic "trick" out of his bag.

A huge rally had been scheduled for July 10, but Castro did not attend—he was "sick"—and the crowd drifted away from the immeasurably less interesting President Dorticós. As Castro watched on television, he sensed a lessening of commitment from his *masas* to the Revolution, so he immediately arranged for a television appearance from his "sickbed." His dramatic speech made an almost incidental reference to the little matter of the rockets. He stressed cleverly how wonderfully "spontaneous" the Khrushchev act had been, making it seem to the Cuban people that the Russians, the least spontaneous of peoples, had simply been unable to contain themselves in their concern over Cuba! He also thus divorced himself from any direct ties with them in terms of power within Cuba.

But he also did something that lay the groundwork for the Missile Crisis that was to come in a bare two years: from that moment on, he treated the rocket speech as a commitment made by Russia to defend the Cuban Revolution from any armed attack from the United States.

On October 18, Ambassador Bonsal and his family were "recalled" to Washington. Sailing away on the *City of New Orleans* ferry with all their belongings, down to their pet dog, they knew they would not return, and they did not. On October 19, President Eisenhower forbade the export to Cuba of all nonsubsidized foods, medicines, and medical supplies—the "blockade" had effectively begun. Those two formerly "closest friends" of nations were catapulting toward becoming the closest of enemies. Diplomatic relations still existed between Washington and Havana, but just barely—and not for long.

It was all far more simple than it has seemed down the years. While the Americans with their insistence on constitutional government and democracy offered a man like Fidel Castro absolutely nothing he wanted, the Communists offered him every single thing he wanted. From the start, the Russians made it clear to Castro that they would not impose political "rules" in Cuba. Telling is the fact that they even bypassed their own Cuban Communist party and early on recognized that in Cuba there was not a Communist but a "Castro Revolution." In July 1960, Castro's first Russian friend, the smiling Alexander Alexeev, gave Castro a direct message from Khrushchev which said in unmistakable terms that "the Soviet Government wishes to express to you that it does not consider any party as an intermediary between it and you. Comrade Khrushchev . . . considers you to be the authentic leader of the Revolution."

People have thought that Castro allied Cuba with the Soviet Bloc because it was attractive to him, because he was attracted to it. Hardly. As a matter of fact, Castro knew that the Eastern Bloc would be absolutely unattractive to Cubans—particularly culturally (which was the area in which the Americans so guilefully and dangerously attracted the Cubans). Thus, aligning Cuba with Moscow kept him psychically safe. It was like marrying an ugly woman—it kept your brother from lusting after her. But there were psychological and political similarities between Fidel's vision for Cuba and the government of the Soviets. Both Castro and the Russian Communists were at heart medieval, antitechnological, anti–individual effort, anti–Protestant Reformation, and anticapitalism. Both offered a "political religion," in which a seeking and traumatized people were brought together through an "ideological position put forward by a government that identifies the individual with the state." If it was a regressive return to more primitive political relationships and times—and it was—well, so be it!

Finally, the alliance with the Soviets gave Castro the possibility of arriving in history as a new political creature—the "socialist caudillo," as Cuban historian Luis E. Aguilar calls it. The old caudillos of Spain were all-powerful leaders who ruled without question but according to personal power. But in the twentieth century, as societies began to mature, this was no longer enough. The new strongman needed an ideology, a program, a justification for power. Marxist socialism provided the modern "caudillo" with the possibility of even more total dictatorship than the early caudillos, of power undreamed of on a world scale, and all backed by an ideology accepted by the modern world.

As for the Russians themselves, they came to Castro and Castro to them at an unusually propitious moment. The Soviet Union, in the flush of the postwar period and the end of Stalinism, had only in the decade of the fifties acquired the capability and the willingness to underwrite a revolution eight thousand miles from its border. Only now could they take on such a new but delicious burden.

One day in the fall of 1960, Castro was taking a stroll along Doce y Veintitrés Streets, eating *criollo,* or Creole oysters, when he paused to talk with a black shoeshine boy who was known as the most expansive gossip in all of Havana. Suddenly, with barely restrained drama and a small smile playing on his lips, Castro asked the boy, "What do you say I go up to New York and speak at the U.N.?"

"Caballo," the boy supposedly answered, filled with enthusiasm at this new development. "Get on up there and put it to those damn Yankees!"

And so another trip to the United States was planned. This time Castro had a more specific purpose. In the early morning hours before leaving for New York, he met with Santiago Carrillo, the great Spanish Communist leader. "Our talk started at two A.M. and finished at nine A.M.," Carrillo told me. "He gave me a great impression of his sincerity, of his personal valor, and of his vision of the Cuba of the future." Carrillo paused, and smiled at the remembrance. "He kept repeating what he was going to say. The impression he wanted to give the U.N. was largely that of his will to guarantee the independence of Cuba before any attempt of the U.S. against Cuba. His desire was to explain the reasons for the Cuban Revolution and the necessities for profound changes all over Latin America."

Once again, as in April of 1959, Castro was flying across those legendary and mystical "ninety miles." This time, as they took off, he suddenly turned to Ramiro Valdés, his security chief, and asked if there would be an "escort plane" with them.

When Valdés, nervous and embarrassed at his forgetfulness, stuttered out, "No," Castro shook his head.

"We're in danger," he muttered. "If I were running the CIA, I'd shoot down the plane at sea and report the whole thing as an accident." There was dead silence in the plane. "What a mistake," Castro murmured—and everyone knew by then how graciously he sustained mistakes!

Then, as if on cue, there came a huge roar, and as the Cubans peered out of their small windows they saw an entire squadron of Yankee fighter planes bearing down upon them. But the planes were only an honorary escort. The CIA and the American Pentagon literally ushered the Cuban party into the "Colossus of the North" and into what would be Fidel Castro's "greatest show on earth" at the United Nations!

The curtain rose in the lobby of the Shelburne Hotel at Lexington Avenue and 37th Street, where Fidel was railing against the management's supposedly unacceptable cash demands for room deposits (ten thousand dollars, Castro claimed). Furious at this materialistic outrage, Castro and his *barbudos,* dressed in their epic olive green combat fatigues, dramatically left the hotel. Followed by hundreds of reporters and New York police desperate to protect these unprotectables, they clambered into cars and descended upon the U.N. There, the big and imposing Castro told the amenable Dag Hammarskjøld that the revolutionaries were either going to stay at the U.N. or in Central Park, which would be quite all right because "we are mountain people . . . used to sleeping in the open air!" Instead, the *Fidelistas* took off in a symbolic caravan and with symbolic intent for the seedy Hotel Theresa at Seventh Avenue and 125th Street in Harlem, where, with considerable amusement, Castro was able also to bring the attention of the world.

The script of Castro's "play" was deliberately false. In truth, the Shelburne Hotel had rented the Cubans their rooms at the cheap rate of twenty dollars a day because of pleas from the State Department. Even as the Cubans melodramatically left, they had been offered free accommodations at the respectable Commodore Hotel near the U.N. buildings. Indeed, Teté Casuso was distraught and disillusioned to find that the delegation was paying more at the Theresa than it had paid downtown. "He had intended from the start to complain that he was being overcharged at the first hotel," she said, "to plant himself with his whole retinue and all their baggage at the United Nations and thus present the spectacle that they had no place to stay, then to move to Harlem in order to give the impression that it was only among the humble and despised people of the United States, the Negroes, that the humble and despised Cubans and their leader were able to find shelter."

In those same days, the *Baltika* was plowing steadily along in the rough sea when suddenly her most important passenger slipped on the deck. He might have fallen into the dark and treacherous waters had not Soviet diplomat Arkady Shevchenko caught him. "Right now we aren't too far from Cuba," Nikita Khrushchev joked, "and they'd probably receive me there better than the Americans will in New York."

Then, more seriously, he mused thoughtfully, as he stood with Shevchenko at the ship's railing, "I hope that Cuba will become a beacon of socialism in Latin America. Castro offers that hope, and the Americans are helping us." Then he veritably smacked his lips and in his deep, gruff peasant's voice spoke prophetic words as his fat jowls shook with laughter: "Castro will have to gravitate to us like an iron filing to a magnet."

"Nikita Sergeyevich attaches special importance to a meeting with Fidel Castro," top Soviet aide Valentin Zorin told the group at the Soviet mission on Park Avenue. The stage was set for a new play and the Cuban and the Soviet leaders, both great actors, were dressed, combed, and accoutred for their roles.

Against the advice of all security agents, both Russian and American, Nikita Khrushchev determined to go himself to Harlem to meet Fidel Castro for the first time. Castro, dressed neatly in his ever-present military uniform, waited for Khrushchev at the door of the Theresa, and there, on September 20, 1960, the two worlds met and mated. They did not shake hands in the colorless, unconsummated American and Anglo-Saxon way, they fell into a Siberian bear hug. "He bent down and enveloped me with his whole body," was the way Khrushchev himself described the historic moment. Their meeting upstairs in the Theresa lasted a mere twenty minutes, but Khrushchev (who devilishly took a peasant's relish in "the uproar this episode caused in the American press") made it clear that it was all that was needed for a new axis between the two countries. "When Khrushchev returned from Harlem," Shevchenko recalled, "he was extremely pleased with the way things had gone. He told us he had found that Castro wanted a close friendship with the U.S.S.R. and had asked for military aid. Moreover, he got the impression that Castro would be a good Communist." But he added that they must be cautious because "Castro is like a young horse that hasn't been broken." The *New York Times* wrote that it was the biggest event on 125th Street since the funeral of W. C. Handy.

That same afternoon, the drama was furthered when the stocky figure of new friend Nikita Khrushchev, wearing the all-Russian "uniform" of baggy suit and askew tie, strode like a human tank across the entire elegant General Assembly to embrace Fidel Castro. Picture after picture after picture was snapped. "We'll be on every front page in the world!" Pardo Llada exclaimed—and they were. Indeed, he and Carlos Franqui were even in one of those most-used pictures. But in the years to come, the photograph would be edited, then edited again, and still again, in the Cuban "press," until finally all the other faces were blocked out, even Khrushchev's, and only Fidel's was left.

Castro's speech at the United Nations went on, and on, and on. By the fourth hour, even his admirers were falling asleep. The listeners would have done well to stay alert, for this was not just another hortatory, revolutionary speech. In it, had observers understood his particularist personality and passions better, they would have heard him carefully laying the groundwork for the future of Cuba. He linked Cuba deliberately with the oppressed and recently decolonized countries of the world, he dismissed John F. Kennedy, soon to become president, as "an illiterate and ignorant millionaire," and he disdained American Admiral Arleigh Burke for saying that Russian leader Khrushchev "won't fire his rockets" since "he knows he'll be destroyed if he does." Now in booming voice, Castro joyfully shouted as he banged his fist on the podium, "This is indeed a dangerous calculation, because this gentleman actually reckons that in case of an attack against us we are going to be all alone. . . . But suppose that Mr. Burke, even though he is an admiral, is mistaken?"

At the Hotel Theresa, meanwhile, Celia, slim to the point of starvation, tried to watch over her uncontrollable charge with her usual urgent care, preparing his meals, "protecting" him from the hovering, omnipresent women, and overseeing the money. "There were suitcases and cartons filled with dollars," Pardo Llada told me. "They wanted to pay NBC to go to

Cuba, and I saw Castro himself give twenty thousand dollars to Cartier-Bresson, the famous French photographer who was taking photos of the trip for Castro, and twenty-five thousand dollars to Malcolm X." Meanwhile, the rough *barbudos* cooked their favorite recipes on every floor of the hotel. They would go down in New York memory as the ones who "plucked chickens in the city's hotels." Very probably, the "chicken plucking" was not just related to their meals. At least some of those *barbudos* were practicing the rites of Santería, something that certainly no one in the hotel suspected!

From the "nonaligned" Third World group of nations that Castro was determined to woo, he saw Nehru of India and President Kwame Nkrumah of Ghana. Yugoslavia's Marshal Tito declined to see Castro, never having liked the Cuban. President Gamal Abdel Nasser of Egypt saw him but came away with an undying dislike for him, something the world also never suspected.

"I went with Nasser to see Castro at the Theresa Hotel," Mustapha Amin, one of the famous "Amin brothers" who were great Egyptian editors, related to me, "and as we went up in the elevator, there were terrible smells, terrible! The Negroes were cooking on every floor. Nasser was repulsed. Moreover, he had brought Castro an Egyptian silver tea setting. A beautiful one! But when Castro opened it, he only looked at it and said, 'I'm disappointed, I thought you would bring me a crocodile.' Nasser was really offended. He said, 'Crocodiles! We have no crocodiles in Egypt—only in the zoo!' He kept repeating that in the days to follow. I would hear him muttering, 'Crocodiles, crocodiles . . .' From that time on, he thought Castro was crazy because he talked about our having crocodiles in Egypt."

Despite the few resisters to Castro's "spell," there were quite enough who succumbed. "He strode across the streets of New York like a colossus in his battle dress," Sunil Kumar Roy, the former Indian ambassador to Cuba, remembered.

The minute Castro was back in Cuba that fall of 1960, he announced he was creating Comités para la Defensa de la Revolución, or Committees for the Defense of the Revolution (CDRs) to wage a campaign of "collective vigilance." It was a dramatic moment, and an ominous one. These committees were to become infamous in Cuba, as they developed into neighborhood spy organizations; now, no one could park a strange car in an area without being questioned, no one could come and go without being noted, no one's life was anymore remotely his own. This upset many Cubans, for nothing was considered more degrading in Cuba than to be a *chivato,* or informer. Now, the man who had killed *chivatos* without a second thought in the Sierra turned the entire Cuban people into a *chivato* nation.

One after another, the moderates and the democratic forces continued to leave Cuba. Even as they were patiently giving Cuba the work days and the work hours of their lives, Castro had all along been creating around their efforts another, totally different, Cuba. To them it was an alien Cuba. By the time they left disconsolately for foreign shores, many of them were fractured individuals, without following and largely without mourners. All by now realized, usually with considerable pain, that somewhere along the way they had lost their country, their Cuba. The famous radio announcer Luis Conte Agüero left. The man who had been the booming voice of Fidel Castro's Cuba, José Pardo Llada, left. The editor of the prestigious and beloved *Bohemia,* Miguel Quevedo, left. But it was Teté Casuso's defection that told most about the strange, compelling, even sinister hold that Castro had even on the most independent and strong-minded of his people.

As Teté had watched Castro at the United Nations that fall of 1960, she began to have more and more disturbing doubts about the man she had so long adored. Needing desperately to see him before leaving—before she fully intended to defect—she raced around New York like a driven creature, like a madwoman, trying to find him at the Theresa, trying to get through Celia to him, trying to steal just one more moment with him. She never did. In the end she stood on the icy tarmac in the prematurely cold weather and watched as he flew away—forever—from her, from the days in Mexico, from all her hopes. A bitter neuritis in her leg and hip mirrored her inner despair. "For twelve days I was barely able to get out of bed," she wrote later. "My blood pressure fell so low that I had to live on adrenaline. . . . Painfully, during the next three days, I got out of bed whenever I was able and wrote my long letter of farewell to Fidel. . . . I learned through personal experience what fanaticism is, how it breaks every human bond and ethical feeling and tramples even memories, tramples everything. On the same day that I mailed my letter to Fidel, he ordered the first executions of revolutionaries. . . ."

That Christmas of 1960 was to be Cuba's second "free Christmas." In Havana, the traditional Nativity was barely seen, but Ruby Hart Phillips did recognize a huge representation over the CMQ marquee, called "*Jesus en el Bohio,*" or "Jesus in the peasant's house." The three Wise Men were Fidel

Castro, Che Guevara, and the only black Cuban at the very top, Juan Almeida. They carried new gifts: the Agrarian Reform, the Urban Reform, and the Year of Education. Two angels had the faces of dead heroes of the Revolution, and José Martí posed as the guiding star. In the streets of the city, "Jingle Bells" was being sung with the words:

> With Fidel, with Fidel,
> Always with Fidel,
> Eating Corn or Malange,
> Always with Fidel.

But it was Castro's immense January 2, 1961, rally for the second anniversary of the Revolution that showed everyone clearly the extraordinary realignment that Cuba had undergone in just two years. That day, as the mammoth and compelling figure of the *líder máximo* entered in the Plaza de la Revolución, it began to drizzle. Always one to use every tool at his recourse, Castro said in that manner of open-eyed personalism that is always the predecessor of a seduction, "I hope the rain won't spoil our celebration."

Excited by this confrontation of "Fidel" and the downpour, the crowd shouted back, "We'll stay, we'll get wet . . ."

"In that case, I'll get wet, too," Castro shouted. When he removed his rain cape and tried to continue with his speech, the crowd roared, "Put it back on, put it back on." The crowd would care for him. Finally, as the roar continued, he swung the cape back over his shoulders. At that, it started to pour and soon even his luxuriant beard was soggy with water. Now he moved rapidly to the expository lesson that he had in mind for *las masas* on that day.

"The revolutionary government has decided," he cried, "that within forty-eight hours the embassy of the United States must reduce its personnel to the exact number in our embassy in Washington, which is eleven." It was a measure of how far even the mental realignment had gone that these words were greeted by wild applause and hoots against the Americans. "Get them out of here, throw them out!" came from the crowd. The people had spoken. Castro then presented for the damp assemblage what was to go down in history as the coup de grace for the Americans. "There are more than three hundred of them here and eighty percent are spies," he shouted. "If they want to leave, we won't stop them."

Once again, Castro had turned reality on its head. When Washington heard this, it had to accept his "invitation." The Cuban records thus show that it was not Castro who forced the Americans to leave, but the Americans who broke diplomatic relations on January 3, 1961. It was all over. Cuba was effectively realigned, set, and ready for its role in the Eastern Bloc. Cuba could and little "powerless" Cuba would act as a new imperial power never before seen in history: Cuba's own imperial destiny had finally arrived.

20

THE BAY OF PIGS

Bring me a couple of hairs from Castro's beard.
—Luis Somoza on the afternoon of April 14, 1961

BAHÍA DE COCHINOS (Bay of Pigs) is a sparkling finger of water that juts into a vast swamp known as the Ciénaga de Zapata on the southern coast of the province of Matanzas. Even in the first year of the Revolution, Castro had constructed in the empty middle of the swampy lake a small kind of "house." It was put together with sheets of zinc and aluminum, which floated incongruously upon barrels. The impoverished swamp-dwellers referred to it as "The House of Fidel," since he would often retreat to it in the post-triumph days. Some thought he was so taken by the area because in its seclusion it reminded him of the golden, lost days of the Sierra Maestra. Castro himself said at times that this wilderness, facing the open sea toward South America, appealed to his "guerrilla mentality" and to his international appetite. Nikita Khrushchev, who looked at the swampy island through the unromantic and hungry eyes of the Russian peasant, once mused that it reminded him of a "sausage."

But in fact, Fidel was right. Bahía de Cochinos, with its crocodile-ridden swamps and sinuous coves, was indeed an ideal place for a guerrilla landing. Ironically it would not be Castro's guerrillas who would land there, it would be his enemies'.

Thus, the Bay of Pigs became the United States' first (but certainly not last) attempt to use traditional "regular" military power against a brilliant "irregular" enemy. And this was strange, because in the years just before the invasion, Washington was buzzing with ideas about the "new warfare" and about counterinsurgency as the wave of the future. Ironically, it was President Eisenhower, that gray patriarchal military eminence, who first grasped some of the ambiguous contours of the new age. In Rio de Janeiro, in January 1960, he introduced the idea that traditional concepts of "aggression" must now include "subversion," and he stated to the other presidents of the hemisphere that "We would consider it to be intervention in the internal affairs of an American state if any power . . . whether by invasion, coercion, or subversion, succeeded in denying the freedom of choice of any of our sister republics." His words marked an extraordinary ballooning of the Monroe Doctrine; now "coercion" and "subversion" were as intolerable as direct military meddling. But it was John F. Kennedy, the lithe and vigorous ruling prince of Camelot, his mind boiling over with ideas, to whom history bequeathed the task of dealing creatively with this new period and its new methods of warfare.

Like Castro, the Kennedy brothers, and many of the men around them, had a new vision for their country. While Fidel Castro was creating his own form of Marxist or (better said) *Fidelista* internationalism, John Kennedy was trying to sculpt a new, competitive, and ultimately victorious democratic "internationalism" that would include everything from a Peace Corps to the training of guerrillas at the John F. Kennedy Special Warfare Center at Fort Bragg. "Counterinsurgency," Robert Kennedy wrote once, "might best be described as social reform under pressure." They knew the lingo and the language, but they little understood the reality.

In the White Paper on Cuba presented by President Kennedy on April 10, only one week before the invasion, he repeated the amazingly "unknowing" phrase of Robert McNamara's, "Castroism without Castro," as if there could possibly be such a thing. Bob Amory, the CIA's deputy director for intelligence, even appeared at a costume party in those delicate days dressed up as Castro! The Americans could afford to be playful, for to them these were disposable matters and not life-or-death ones, as they were to the Cubans.

With his uncommon prescience, instinct, and feel, Castro visited the Bay of Pigs only two weeks before the exiles would land, to see how his new Tahitian village resort was coming along. As he was strolling along the bay, he suddenly swirled around to a Cuban companion and exclaimed, "This is a great place for a landing. . . . We should place a fifty-caliber heavy machine gun there, just in case."

The intrusive figure of Fidel Castro seemed to obsess the American electorate that fall of 1960. Even at the moment Kennedy had his famous television debate with Richard Nixon, the two men remained fixated upon Cuba in what turned out to be by far the most famous exchange of the entire election campaign. All the historic indications support the theory that Kennedy had been briefed by CIA chief Allen Dulles that a Cuban exile invasion force had been set in motion by the Eisenhower administration. Yet when he faced Nixon, Kennedy vigorously denied it and indeed even attacked the Eisenhower and Nixon administration.

Years later, Nixon was still enraged at what he considered Kennedy's cynical deception. In 1987, he told me, "Allen Dulles said that Kennedy had been briefed. Therefore, I was in the uncomfortable position of knowing about the invasion and having to cover it. Kennedy, who did know about it, went on the attack." Then he remarked, almost wistfully, "You know, that was the first time I was praised in the *New York Times*—and for my restraint. I remember Walter Lippmann's column. It was the first time they ever praised me—first time—and it was because I was not telling the truth!"

Actually, the general outline of a Bay of Pigs invasion was decided upon shortly after Castro's visit to the United States in the spring of 1959, and it came out of Nixon's "memo" on his visit with Castro at the Capitol, although Nixon did not propose an invasion. By the end of 1959, Cuban exiles were being recruited for training by the CIA in camps in Guatemala and Nicaragua. The purpose of the covert action, approved by Eisenhower in March 1960, was "to bring about the replacement of the Castro regime with one more devoted to the true interests of the Cuban people and more acceptable to the U.S. in such a manner as to avoid any appearance of U.S. intervention." Each element was, of course, contradictory to the other.

John F. Kennedy inherited the plan in almost a casual way, and at first looked on it only as a contingency. Then bureaucratic momentum took over, and the event that was to go down in history as his first major presidential act and premier policy disaster was acted out with the star-crossed inevitability of a Greek tragedy. Once approved, the planning for the invasion soon came to have a life of its own and, as it progressed, the military tactics changed from the much-talked-about new guerrilla or "irregular" warfare to a traditional "Normandy Beach"–style landing in the Bay of Pigs. The Americans believed that the Cuban exiles could land there secretly and work their way inland, fleeing to the Escambray Mountains in an emergency. The young American president, meanwhile, barely paid attention when CIA director Dulles briefed him on the change in military strategy for the Bay of Pigs operation, a change that came about largely because the CIA could not bring itself to trust the new "irregular" type of warfare. The agency's covert activist wing, working on its own, simply fell back on what it knew how to do. Meanwhile, Miami's "Little Havana" was so full of "invasion talk" that at times Ramiro Valdés in Havana actually refused to believe the hordes of confirmations he was getting, thinking instead, with his by-then-Russified intelligence mind-set, that there must be some CIA "disinformation" campaign at work.

On Friday, April 14, 1961, Castro paced back and forth, in full battle dress, at the national military headquarters in suburban Havana known as Punto Uno, or Point One. Knowing that something was coming but not yet what or where, Castro was both anxious and exhilarated, in substantial part because this would be the first time he would stand up directly against the Americans. He was more than ready—his regular army of twenty-five thousand well-trained men now was buttressed by some two hundred thousand militiamen, some of them literally trained overnight once the threat became palpable. On that Friday, an American ship was spotted off the coast of Oriente. But Castro simply went to bed; as he rightly suspected, the ship was simply one of many diversions the CIA had planned. The planes that came the next day were not.

Castro awoke at dawn to the ominous noise of B-26 bombers flying low over Havana. The planes, piloted by Cuban exiles and operating under the "disguise" of being flown by Cuban pilots who were supposed to be defecting to the United States, hit Camp Libertad Airport, San Antonio, and Santiago de Cuba, dropping their bombs on Cuban soil.

Always the avid student of military history, Castro had assumed that the first step of the invasion would be an attack on his air force (he well remembered that Nasser's entire air force had been destroyed on the ground in Egypt in 1956), so he had dispersed the planes in his small air force. This one move would come to mean the difference between victory and defeat.

In the bombing raids that Saturday, Castro lost five planes, but he was left with four British Sea Fury light attack bombers, one B-26, and three T-33s. It would be enough.

But it was, as always, in the realm of the psychological and the symbolic that Castro's ramparts were most unbreachable. "On the night of the bombing, thousands of people filed past the row of the bomb victims' coffins at the university," the American journalist Lionel Martin recalled. "Revolutionary music blared deafeningly through loudspeakers. For an hour I sat on a stone bench near the coffins. . . . The following day, tens of thousands of soldiers, militia-people, and women and men, old and young, followed behind the trucks carrying the coffins in a death-cadence march to the cemetery.

"After the burial, once again an enraged Fidel Castro spoke from a jerry-built wooden platform in front of Colón Cemetery's ornate entrance. Fidel's speech was as angry as the sun was hot that day. The people shouted for vengeance over and over again: '¡Paredón . . . paredón . . . paredón!'" Fidel's defiant words seemed to reach a new crescendo that day, his entire body shook with electric emotion. And then came the new message, one he had long been preparing. "What the imperialists cannot pardon us for," Castro shouted, "is . . . for making a socialist revolution in the very nostrils of the United States!"

These words marked an historic moment: the first time Castro had referred publicly and openly to the Cuban Revolution as "socialist." And this new definition of reality traveled across Cuba like blood through open and receptive veins, lodging immediately and comfortably in the Cuban body politic for the simple reason that Castro was himself the political doctor of that body.

The announcement also came as a strange kind of relief for many inside Cuba. Castro aide Norberto Fuentes recalled thinking: "Well, good, now we know what we are. . . ." But it caught the Russians by surprise. "We had trouble understanding the timing of this statement," a genuinely perplexed Nikita Khrushchev wrote later in his memoirs. "Castro's declaration had the immediate effect of widening the gap between himself and the people who were against socialism, and it narrowed the circle of those he could count on for support against the invasion. As far as Castro's personal courage was concerned, his position was admirable and correct. But from a tactical standpoint, it didn't make much sense." What Castro's statement really showed, again, was his ability to manipulate whole governments to his own advantage. In this case, he used "Communism" at a strategic moment to protect "Castroism."

The fourteen hundred *brigadistas,* the Cuban exiles of Brigade 2506, who left Nicaragua by ship the afternoon of April 14, were in a high state of exaltation. They believed with all their hearts that within days they would succeed in becoming the new rulers of Cuba. Four days earlier, John F. Kennedy had stated that no U.S. forces would be involved in their attack, but they simply did not believe he meant it. They assumed his words were for public relations purposes only. And now their American advisers sent them off with the most extravagant of promises, one of them declaring to the avid group, "You will be so strong, you will put your hands out, turn left, and go straight into Havana."

Adding to the sorrowful *comedia,* the Nicaraguan dictator Luis Somoza himself saw them off at Puerto Cabezas. His face powdered and his person surrounded by his ever-present bodyguard, Somoza cried after them, "Bring me a couple of hairs from Castro's beard!" As their bright battalion scarves waved in the wind and a crimson sun set over the beckoning Caribbean, American destroyers carried them inexorably to a Cuba they still pitifully thought of as "home."

Meanwhile, in Havana, Castro had been wondering what in God's name had happened to them. Why, he kept asking himself, had the invaders not yet attacked? Finally, on Monday, the seventeenth of April, shortly after three in the morning, Carlos Franqui received an urgent phone call from the *New York Times* asking him if he had had any news of an "invasion of the island." Franqui immediately telephoned Fidel at Celia's apartment. But Fidel was already one step ahead. He had just received a report from a militia group in the Bay of Pigs: enemy troops had been seen landing at Playa Larga (Blue Beach) and Playa Girón (Red Beach). As he paced back and forth, his beret clamped down firmly on his head, Castro became ever more certain of what the *americanos* were going to do. His response was direct and uncomplicated: enemy supply ships must be sunk immediately and the beachhead must be made to collapse. He would cut off support to the *brigadistas* just as, from the Sierra Maestra, he had cut off human support for the Batista dictatorship.

Castro's first act was to call the air base, where his pilots had been waiting for hours, strapped inside their cockpits. "Chico," Castro shouted over the phone to one of them, "you must sink those ships for me!" A hyperactive Castro was on the phone constantly, alerting all of his troops, sending nearby battalions rushing to the Bay of Pigs and controlling the entire island from Celia's apartment. But it was his small air force that really won the battle, before the rest of the fighting even began. The American "plan" had been prefaced entirely on the idea that Castro's tiny air force would be destroyed before the invasion force landed. Indeed, the *brigadistas* had been told it had already been destroyed. This was the fatal falsehood of the invasion. Castro's little Sea Furies were sent out from their hiding places to sink the invasion fleet of the United States of America. The amazing and unexpected fact is that they did!

Castro himself arrived in the area that Monday afternoon, and set up a command center in an old sugar mill. It was chosen simply because it had the only phone in the region. Behind him Castro had some twenty thousand troops and twenty tanks.

"Combat did not stop for a single minute," Castro related afterward. "We imagined that they wanted to take over a piece of our territory, set up a government to be recognized by the O.A.S. and the United States. But we did not give them the time. For not even a minute, not even a second, did the battle stop for sixty-eight hours. And at the end . . . I entered with the first group . . . and we had the U.S. vessels in front and we placed the tanks right in front of the U.S. vessels."

The battle was not very old when the surviving American ships began steaming out of the bay, stranding some 1,350 *brigadistas,* who only the day before had been happily sunning themselves at sea. Now, virtually abandoned on the beach, they were forced to rely on whatever ammunition and food they carried with them. The CIA had been so certain that Castro's air force would be destroyed that they had not taken even the basic precaution of placing anti-aircraft weapons aboard the ships. As the last U.S. destroyer sailed away from the Bay of Pigs, one *brigadista* remarked: "In the wake of that ship go two hundred years of infamy."

But in Washington, an oddly unique political and diplomatic minuet was being danced out, in sorrow but also in self-righteousness. The meeting of an increasingly troubled and finally aware President Kennedy and his advisers began that Tuesday night at 11:58 P.M. and lasted until 2:46 the next morning. Almost all were in white tails, having come to the meeting directly from a formal White House party, which John Kennedy had entered to the tune of "Mr. Wonderful." They knew the beachhead at the Bay of Pigs was collapsing, and military men like Admiral Arleigh Burke argued that now, certainly, American air cover must be provided to save the men. "This was the critical moment of the invasion," historian Hugh Thomas judged. "Had Kennedy agreed to let loose the aircraft from the *Essex*, the future might have turned out differently. But he only authorized six unmarked jets on the *Essex* to fly over the Bay of Pigs at dawn the next day. . . ."

President Kennedy finally approved what was again in effect the hope-less American middle ground that would doom American policy in all these "irregular" situations. The American navy would make reconnaissance flights over the Bay of Pigs to evaluate the situation and to determine whether the *brigadistas* had any chance of holding out. The reconnaissance missions were authorized to "return fire if fired on during this humanitar-ian mission." Thus, incredibly, as Schlesinger later wrote, "Kennedy was prepared to run more risks to take the men off the beaches than to put them on."

From the small hell that Bahía de Cochinos had become, the exile *brigadistas* exploded into cries of hope when six unmarked jets from the *Essex* flew over them just after dawn Wednesday morning. But as the men stood cheering on the beach, the planes turned and flew away.

In this particular chess game in this particular war, the powerful nation restrained itself in what resulted in self-imposed humiliation, and the weak nation audaciously attacked, and attacked again, and won. In truth, the weak nation never did attack—at least it never attacked the United States. After sinking the initial ships, which were clearly backups for the *brigadistas,* Castro repeatedly and with total deliberateness always hung back when it came to directly confronting the Americans. The Bay of Pigs, therefore, despite Castro's claims that it was the "First Defeat of Yankee Imperialism" in Latin America, represented the first self-defeat of Yankee "imperialism" in Latin America. But what the Bay of Pigs really illustrates is how difficult, if not impossible, it is for an overlegalized world, with uncommon restraints and with fragmented power, to fight a totally nonle-galized world with a totalist leader with no restraints either on his actions or on his commands.

At the time, it was Robert Kennedy, with his uncanny instinct which alone on the American side matched Castro's, who immediately grasped the next and looming threat. On April 19, as resistance was ending on the beaches, Bobby Kennedy added a prophetic end to a memorandum on the Bay of Pigs failure. "If we don't want Russia to set up missile bases in Cuba," he wrote to his brother, "we had better decide now what we are willing to do to stop it."

In the end, Castro would take 1,189 prisoners, including the entire high command of Brigade 2506. The Cuban exiles were taken to various houses in the area, and that Wednesday, April 19, Castro made the rounds to survey his prisoners.

"Is there an American here?" he demanded. Then he snapped his flashlight probingly into the faces of the wounded men. The front door of the house had blown its hinges during the bombings and now it made eerily crackling noises in the wind as Castro scrutinized his prisoners. "Take them to Covadonga and put them in the hospital," he commanded finally, pacing back and forth as he always did, like an emperor. The battle had been great; but this was a singular disappointment. In the face of such a victory, not to find even one American!

As for Castro himself, he used the humiliating defeat of the Americans to put forward deeper and more thoughtful points about his eternal antagonists than he had ever drawn on before. On television that Thursday he spoke for four hours, positing the "mechanistic" mentality of the Yale planner-intellectual versus the "humanistic" outlook of the men and women of the Sierra Maestra. "Imperialist mentality is the reverse of the revolutionary mentality," he told his people. "The imperialist looks at the geography, analyzes the number of cannons, of planes, of tanks, the positions; the revolutionary goes to the social population and asks, 'Who are these people?' To the imperialist, it doesn't matter at all what the population thinks or feels, this is outside of his concern; the revolutionary thinks first of the people, and the people of the Cienaga de Zapata were entirely ours."

Humberto Sorí Marín had fled to the United States in disgust when Castro had supported the radical agrarian reform plan of Che Guevara. But prior to the Bay of Pigs invasion, Sorí Marín returned to Havana, clandestinely, to help organize inside support for the Cuban exiles. But he made a bad mistake; he called the resistance leaders from the provinces to meet with him in Havana. Not surprisingly, with Castro's intelligence, the police surrounded their meeting house after they had come to the city, and Sorí Marín was shot in the buttocks as he tried to get through a window.

"Humberto was in an attic," his brother Mariano recalled to me, years later, telling the story of Humberto's ordeal for the first time. "He took out the air conditioner and escaped. Two hours later, Fidel called my house, saying, 'I want to talk with you immediately, Humberto has escaped.'" It was clearly Castro's plan to use Mariano to find Humberto. "I went with Fidel looking for him," Mariano went on. "Fidel was crazy. All night he was saying, as if talking to Humberto, "*¿Humberto, qué es esto, qué es esto?* How could you do this to me, how could you do this to me?' We were in the car with his escort for two or three hours," Mariano remembered, shaking his head. "Fidel kept saying, 'I love Humberto,' and I would say, 'Don't look anymore, he's surely in the U.S. by now.'"

Unfortunately, Humberto Sorí Marín was unable to make it out of Cuba. "I was in the house of my mother and father and someone called," Mariano recalled of the time. "They had just operated on Humberto there in Havana. I thought he was in Miami, but no, he was in the military hospital." Immediately, Mariano went to see his brother in the hospital. "From here," Humberto told him, "I go to be shot." And, in fact, when Humberto had recovered enough, he was moved to La Cabaña fortress.

Castro's next move was to call Mariano and tell him that he and Raúl wanted to talk with him. A car would bring him to the CMQ radio station at 2:00 A.M. They would be waiting for him on the fourth floor. Even as the Bay of Pigs invasion was proceeding, Castro paced up and down in the room at the station and told Mariano, "I want to talk with you. I love you both. But I learned more in the mountains to love Humberto. And he is an 'historic comandante,' and he came to kill me. But I promise you he won't be killed. . . ." Mariano interjected how worried his parents were. But Castro reassured him, as only he could. "You must believe me," he said, with that special, pleading smile of sincerity. "I will not kill him." Then Castro told Mariano to "give your father and mother a kiss, both, and tell them that Humberto will be safe."

Mariano then went to La Cabaña to see Humberto and reassure him, but the calmly desperate man sat there in his prison cell and said simply, "I will be shot between two and four A.M. You . . . are blind, I see very far. From here, I go to the *paredón*."

Humberto was shot the next day before dawn. When Mariano went to the cemetery to view the body of his brother, he was sick with shock because "they had shot him twenty to forty times in the head." The memory was still painfully vivid nearly a quarter of a century later.

But Castro, who knew intimately the power of martyrdom, had other ideas for the more than one thousand prisoners he now held captive as a result of his victory at Bahía de Cochinos. He intended to show the world that these traitors were not martyrs, but plain, simple, and ultimately totally irrelevant men.

In order to do this, two days after the end of hostilities, Castro began a televised dialogue with his prisoners. It would last four days and become a kind of revolutionary Roman circus. To the watching world, it looked as if Castro were magnanimous in victory, but the reality was quite different. The captives were kept in *el palacio de los deportes,* the sports palace, whose symbolism was not accidental. For twenty-one hours a day, they sat in serried rows on hard, small chairs and throughout the entire time they were not on television, loudspeakers blared out the names of one after the other, ordering them to come forward. They were permitted neither to move nor to stretch their legs, and they had to beg for permission to use the toilet. From 3:00 to 6:00 A.M., they were allowed to lie down on the floor, but the searing white lights were never put out. "In their fevered, dispirited state, some of the men felt as though they were in a vast operating room," Haynes Johnson, the brigade's sensitive biographer, wrote. But "what plagued them most was their own sense of stupidity, their shame at betrayal and abandonment."

"I thought," Amado Gayol, one of the *brigadistas,* said at one point, "that the Americans wanted a cemetery to pass over with their tanks and one of the graves had to be mine."

Castro began the four days of these marathon "performances" in a professorial mode, standing tall and victorious before the men and the world, telling the whole story of the invasion as if it were already legend, pointing out on maps like an instructor where the *gusanos,* or "worms," had come, and displaying captured documents. In everything he said, he lectured the invaders about the Cuban Revolution, reminding always of the "abusive" past and tying them into it. But, although some of the exiles gave in and cooperated with the Cuban government, 90 percent did not. Almost all, however, gained a begrudging respect for Castro. Once again, with his tireless energy and his painstaking tactical sense, he managed to turn an interrogation around. Soon the prisoners were eagerly asking "Dr. Castro" how he himself would have conducted the invasion. He was happy to oblige; he was now their teacher not only of revolution but also of the war that they had tried so pitifully to wage against him. At one point, in front of a watching world, the prisoners gave the man they had come to kill an ovation. It was just exactly what Castro wanted.

That May 1, 1961, more than a million Cubans gathered in the Plaza de la Revolución to hear the words of the man who had actually defeated the United States. Before he even began to speak, the people honored him with a ten-hour parade. "Night fell, and the powerful floodlights were turned on," journalist Lionel Martin recalled, in a memory of a scene that reminded one eerily of the huge Hitler rallies of the 1930s. Fidel began his speech. "I'm going to be brief," he announced, and went on to speak for more than three hours! In those three hours he never once lost control of the huge crowd. "One felt, in the ethereal magic of the moment," Martin wrote, "that there was absolute communion between Fidel and the people."

The months passed. That New Year's Eve some of the exiles in prison drank shaving lotion for "toasts" to the unknown new year, and one man killed himself. The American people, who never had really known very much about these embarrassing men, now effectively forgot them. It was not Castro's plan, however, to let these prisoners be forgotten. One night, early in 1962, Castro went to the prison gallery, turned on the lights, and announced that he was going to demand a ransom for their lives. "In four months, you'll all be gone." He added, "I'm putting a price on your heads."

"How much?" one prisoner called out.

Castro smiled. "Sixty-two million dollars."

The prisoners' spirits plummeted. It was, quite simply, an outrageous amount. But Castro was completely serious. He knew that he could hardly humiliate the men more in the modern age than to make them exchangeable for "things." Speaking to a group of "small farmers" in the spring of 1962, he declared grandly, "History recounts that on a certain occasion the Spanish people exchanged Napoleon's soldiers against pigs. We, on this occasion, are going to be a little more delicate: we will exchange with imperialism the soldiers against tractors."

For once, the American chosen to deal with Castro had some understanding of the power configurations he was dealing with. When James Britt Donovan, a smart, tough Irishman, was asked if he would "negotiate" with Castro, he immediately said that first he would have to "study Castro's personality intensively," something few other American diplomats had thought of. A stocky man of medium height, his youthfully white hair contrasting with his pale blue eyes and his strong forehead, Harvard graduate Donovan had been involved with everything from the development of the atom bomb to the pre-CIA Office of Strategic Services and the Nuremberg trials. His most recent triumph had been negotiating the trade of Eastern Bloc spy Rudolf Abel for U-2 pilot Francis Gary Powers, in February. Donovan now offered to represent, *pro bono,* the Cuban Families Committee, the group that would try to "liberate" Brigade 2506.

After studying Castro, Donovan wrote: "It is my personal opinion that in his heart Fidel Castro is proud of his fellow Cubans now imprisoned for their participation in the invasion of April 17, 1961. Fidel is a Cuban before he is a Marxist and he must have pride in his fellow Cubans — however misguided or misled he may believe them to be. . . . If reasonable conditions can be brought about, in the interests of the Cuban people, I believe he will carry out his pledge with respect to these fellow Cubans. . . ." Donovan understood, whereas so many others had not.

Their first meeting was on August 31, 1962. Donovan entered the Ministers' Hall of the presidential palace in Havana to find Castro already seated at the long table, all alone. The two negotiated directly for four hours, with only interpreters present. Each side had its own pride; the Kennedy administration would have no part of any deal in which Castro received cash, because that would appear too crass. Castro insisted upon his medieval reparations. The next day they met again, and he gave Donovan a list of goods he would accept in exchange for the prisoners. Donovan returned to the States to see what he could do. He was back in Havana in October.

But now the mood of the negotiations, which had been amiable, suddenly and inexplicably soured. Donovan went again to the presidential palace to meet with Castro on October 10, sure they were about to close the deal. But he found Castro now angry and hostile and demanding ever more — lower prices for the medicines, better shipping costs . . . Finally, an angry Donovan simply said, "That's it!" and stalked out. That was not something that Castro was used to, but it was something that, all his life, inside himself he respected.

Then, another event occurred that totally broke the possibility of ransom for the prisoners: the Missile Crisis. After a two-month hiatus, during which the world hovered on the brink of war, 1,113 exiles finally were nevertheless ransomed for fifty-three million dollars' worth of medicine and equipment, the equivalent of forty-eight thousand dollars a head.

"This will be my Christmas bonus," Castro told Donovan. The men's lives were his Christmas gift. He was the feudal lord, giving life and taking it as it suited his purpose. But Donovan was not taken in. "It was like the slave trade," he said, his lips tight. "All they lacked were the chains." Again, Donovan understood.

And when the last prisoner was safely and quietly aboard the last plane, the little compact Donovan walked up to the huge and husky Castro, already smoking one of his long cigars, and said openly and resonantly, "You know, Premier, I have been thinking of all the good I have been doing for the people of Cuba these past weeks. I have relieved you of almost 1,200 liabilities and also I have been helping the children, the sick, the poor and the elderly among the Cuban people. I think that when the next election is held, I'm coming back to run against you. I think I can win."

Castro smiled; he rather liked this Yankee, who was a very different and much smarter *americano* from the others he had known. "You know, Doctor, I think you may be right," he answered with a half smile, "so there will be no elections."

In the immediate aftermath of the Bay of Pigs, a humbled but still determined President Kennedy responded by kicking off the Alliance for Progress in August 1961, at the meeting of the Organization of American States in the sophisticated Uruguayan beach resort of Punta del Este. The hemisphere had laughed in May 1959, when Fidel Castro had demanded in Buenos Aires that the United States give millions of dollars to Latin America. Now, just two years later, the United States promised no less than twenty billion dollars over a ten-year period. John F. Kennedy, leader of the powerful United States, and Fidel Castro, leader of the small and "powerless" island nation of Cuba, were now competitors for what was, in effect, the soul of the developing world. For the Alliance for Progress was Kennedy's pledge not only to defeat poverty in Latin America, but even more so to defeat his nemesis, Fidel Castro.

President Kennedy was inconsolable about the failure of the invasion, whose prospects in retrospect looked so clearly and criminally absurd that he could not believe he could have made such a mistake. He named General Maxwell Taylor to form a commission to investigate "what lessons were to be learned from the Bay of Pigs." But since the commission was composed largely of the very same people who sculpted the invasion, they (not surprisingly) never came up with very much. While his brother agonized in the Oval Office, Bobby Kennedy grew more and more enraged over the failure and more determined than ever to get rid of Castro, this time in his own way. After all, the Kennedy brothers were supreme competitors, and this was their first—and perfect—failure. It was Bobby's "push-push-push" that would lead the Kennedy administration and the CIA to intensify "Operation Mongoose," a series of bizarre attempts to poison Castro, to assassinate him, even to make his beard fall off—and to do it with the help of the Mafia. The obsession with Castro would drive American policymakers to extremes they would never dream of entertaining in their relations with "real" countries.

Allen Dulles, the CIA director who always seemed so imperiously removed from any second-guessing, took the Bay of Pigs disaster with a rare personalness. On April 19, he arrived at Richard Nixon's home for a meeting, and he was noticeably and unaccustomedly nervous. Did he want a drink? "I certainly would," the spy chief said, "I really need one. This is the worst day of my life." Then, again in totally unaccustomed form, he worried over why he had not warned Kennedy that the air cover was absolutely necessary. "I should have told him that we must not fail," he told Nixon. Then he shook his head. "I came close to doing so but I didn't." Soon after, Dulles was removed from the CIA and even the career of America's intelligence chief ended under the shadow of the victory of Fidel Castro over America in the Bay of Pigs.

But there were more—and even more serious—ramifications. At times, Kennedy tried wisely to learn from the failure. "Thank God the Bay of Pigs happened when it did," he told his friend Theodore Sorensen afterward. "Otherwise, we'd be in Laos by now—and that would be one hundred times worse." But, ironically, Kennedy would directly compensate for his humiliation at the Bay of Pigs by getting into—and stubbornly staying in—Vietnam, not wanting to "back down" or "lose" again.

The failed invasion also marked the first great post–World War II disillusionment with American policies for many of the best young American diplomats, journalists, and intelligence officers, and it laid the bitter basis for disillusionments to come, not only in Vietnam but in Iran, Lebanon,

Nicaragua, Cambodia, El Salvador . . . In short, the Bay of Pigs was the first sterling-clear example of what would be a series of American measures in a post–World War II atmosphere of ambiguity in the uses of power.

Finally, an entire new Cuban cadre now emerged from the Bay of Pigs. The names Howard Hunt, Bernard Baker, Rolando Martínez, Felix Rodriguez, and Eugenio Martínez would, in the next quarter century, pop up, often decisively, over and over again in the most dangerous American foreign policy crises. There were Cubans flying missions for the CIA in the Congo and even for the Portuguese in Africa; Cubans were the burglars of Watergate; Cubans played key roles in Nicaragua, in "Irangate," in the American move into the Persian Gulf. In these ways, too, what Fidel Castro had wrought in Cuba was now governing, through hatred of him, important portions of American foreign policy. And there was one more crucial consequence.

From Moscow, Nikita Khrushchev watched the Bay of Pigs first with delight, and finally with concern. "We were quite certain that the . . . invasion was only the beginning and that the Americans would not let Cuba alone," Khrushchev wrote in his memoirs. "The United States had put its faith in the Cuban émigrés once and it would do so again. . . . One thought kept hammering away at my brain: what will happen if we lose Cuba? We had to think up some way of confronting America with more than words. We had to establish a tangible and effective deterrent to American interference in the Caribbean. But what exactly? The logical answer was missiles."

21

THE MARXIST-LENINIST

You can't teach an old dogma new tricks.

—Dorothy Parker

ON DECEMBER 1, 1961, speaking on the *Popular University* television show, Fidel Castro calmly and deliberatively spoke to the world the most defining words of his entire political life: "I am a Marxist-Leninist and shall remain a Marxist-Leninist until the day I die."

Fully as Castro had intended, those words changed history. Exactly as he had expected, they made of the still-hesitant Russians nervous but now totally responsible "parents" of a young tropical "Communist" state eight thousand miles away. And they confirmed American fears of the beginning of a real and total eventual Russian/Marxist takeover of the Third World. In a long rambling speech which began at 11:00 P.M. and went on into the small hours of the morning, Castro reinvented the boy from the wilds of Birán as a veritable Komsomol youth, and he redirected Cuba from her historically Western, Christian, and sublimely individualistic heritage to an Eastern Cuba, a collectivist Cuba, and finally and threateningly a "Communist" Cuba.

Curiously, it was the Russians who were most suspicious of Castro's words. For a full month after the speech, Havana's newspapers waited expectantly for some praise from Moscow, but there was only silence. And when the customary messages arrived to commemorate the anniversary of the Revolution in the first days of 1962, they were worded with extreme caution and carried not a single mention of Castro's "socialism" and his new (or was it old?) "Marxist-Leninism." The Soviets had reason to be cautious—they realized, if the United States did not, that Castro was deliberately trying to involve them inexorably in the eternal defense of Cuba.

The reverberating effects of Castro's Marxist-Leninist declaration were all the more remarkable since his words were false. He would transform Cuba all right, but in his own image, and this transformation was to begin most thoroughly in the area of culture. Castro took over culture by taking over the budding Cuban film industry, by putting his old Communist friend from the university, Alfredo Guevara, in charge of the Cuban Institute of Cinematic Art and Industry, or ICAIC, and by destroying the independent *Lunes de Revolución,* or Monday of the Revolution, the respected weekly literary supplement of Carlos Franqui's *Revolución.*

When Castro decided to get rid of *Lunes,* his creative mind settled again on the technique of still another kind of "trial," disguised as three Sunday meetings, supposedly to discuss the future of culture in Cuba. He called together the finest intellectuals in the country to meet at the José Martí National Library in Havana. Before each meeting, as he sat down, Castro studiously removed his pistol and carefully laid it on the table. The symbolism was clear. The library was to become still another of his courtrooms, with the intellectuals seated on one side looking up at "the government" that was both judge and jury. The intellectuals lost. They were symbolically "found guilty" and were soon purged from public life.

Lunes soon was closed. True culture was dead in Cuba and a "popular" culture, one which would leave no interpreters between Castro and *las masas,* was born. Interestingly enough, although the Cuban people of course responded frenetically to Castro himself, from the very start they did not respond enthusiastically to his "popular" culture. They applauded little at the "new" films. Castro noticed the change and explained with considerable truth that "enthusiasm was being turned into awareness."

The steps Castro would take to effect Cuba's political transformation were more complicated. First, he announced the formation of the new "vanguard party," the *Organizaciones Revolucionarias Integradas,* or Integrated Revolutionary Organizations, or ORI, which would bring together members of the old 26th of July, the Communists, and what remained of the Student Directorate. In order to "confirm" the ORI, which would be remarkably short-lived, Castro brilliantly employed again his irresistible and controlling tactics of "direct democracy." When he shouted in a kind of ecstasy to the hundreds of thousands sweltering in the plaza, "All in favor, raise your hands," the people shouted and raised their arms, no longer individuals but now only one great and indivisible breathing amoeba.

To support his somewhat masked but nonetheless total control of the island, Castro now solidified the educational honeycomb of ideological schools, the Escuelas de Instrucción Revolucionaria, or Schools of Revolutionary Instruction, or EIR, that he had begun to put together early in 1960. These were mysterious schools, little known to the people of Cuba. Courses included the Cuban revolutionary experience and the type of centralized "planning" Cuba would have in the future. At times Fidel would say jokingly that this offered a "master's degree in Communism," but it was more complicated than that. Emphasis was on the materials of Scientific Communism, Scientific Atheism, the construction of the party, and the ideological fight.

Often, despite the cold orthodoxy of the Old Communist teachers, the training slipped deliciously over into the Fidel-Che utopian ideas of the "pure," uncompromising form of Communism. The importance of "moral incentives" above material incentives was emphasized, for example, and even such wondrous dreams as the destruction of money. In this pure *Fidelista* spirit, the students would be taken to the Sierra Maestra's holy Pico Turquino, where they would be ushered into the mysteries of the magical and sacred world of *Fidelismo*. In those tender days of faith, the person and the persona of "Fidel Castro" was like a hurricane sweeping over the minds of these impressionable and seeking young Cuban cadres, as they gave not only their lives but their very souls into his keeping.

But from the beginning, if these students knew and learned Fidel's magic Marxism, they learned remarkably little about real, organized, disciplined Communism. "We Cubans arrived in the Marxist world in a very confusing moment," Juan Benemelis, later to become one of Castro's leading diplomats in Africa, recalled of his experience at the time in the EIR school for diplomats. "We were not aware of the history of the Marxist countries. For instance, it was a shock to find out about the rift between the Soviet Union and China, it was a shock to find different interpretations of Marxism."

As they fell under the personal spell of the *líder máximo,* however, some began to feel depersonalized, floating in space, without moorings.

"Why did we depersonalize ourselves?" Juan Benemelis asked himself many years later. "It was implicit in the process. Castro was the personality, the only personality. 'I' arrived. Then it became 'we.' In some ways, the way to depersonalize was a way to elude responsibility." He paused, then went on. "Sometimes you didn't know who you were. In Cuba, you were alone, in fear of the state. You didn't have the religion, or the ideology, to confront things. Soon you were in a vacuum. He left you no options."

The year 1962 was called the "Year of Planning," a sobriquet that might seem somewhat surrealistic since even the "planning" that existed was ludicrously chaotic. In January, Cuba was expelled from the Organization of American States at the United States' urging. Castro responded typically to this insult by issuing his deliberately provocative "Second Declaration of Havana," which was no less than a revolutionary call to "armed struggle" throughout the hemisphere. Meanwhile, domestically, food and consumer goods rationing was imposed in one of the most agriculturally rich countries on earth.

During all this time, Castro was above all constantly and endlessly more obsessed with the arming of Cuba. Far from being relieved by his victory at the Bay of Pigs, his profound inner need to build a strong Cuban military increased furiously after the invasion.

So it was that Raúl made frequent trips to Eastern Bloc countries and to Moscow. In July of 1962, during one of Raúl's visits to the pleasant, bucolic countryside dacha of Nikita Khrushchev, Castro finally got what he wanted. By now Raúl and the Russian leader had become cozy with each other, so cozy that Khrushchev would often bring with him his handsome mistress, that "Furtseva woman" whom he had named minister of culture, to enjoy a special afternoon with Raúl, who by now called the Russian leader *abuelo*, or "grandfather."

On one of those afternoons, according to Armando López, chief of the Cuban Intelligence Center in Paris, the two men were engrossed in their usual obsessive talk about weapons and security, when Khrushchev, with a new and special gleam in the slits of his sly Ukrainian peasant's eyes, hit the table suddenly with his tightened fist. His voice had a new pride, and a new arrogance too, as he declared, "What is more, I am going to give you offensive weapons also because if you are attacked, then you have a right to attack and defend yourselves."

Khrushchev piled dare upon dare, and for reasons that were little understood in Washington at the time. Bringing missiles and Russian troops to Cuba would mark a breathtaking challenge to history; it would be the first time since Napoleon III's disastrous expedition to Mexico that a non-American power would attempt to establish itself in the Americas. The very act would symbolically and physically break the back of the arrogant Americans' prided Monroe Doctrine and open up the heretofore arrogantly closed and naively protected Western Hemisphere. The installation of missiles — with ranges of from one thousand to two thousand miles — would double the capacity of Russia to strike the United States, and (perhaps most important) these weapons, approaching from the south, would escape the U.S. early-warning system, thus sabotaging any retaliation. But where did the actual daring idea of establishing missiles in Cuba come from?

Nikita Khrushchev had studied the Bay of Pigs debacle and he had concluded that Kennedy was, as the *New York Times* columnist James Reston put it, "an inexperienced young leader who could be intimidated and blackmailed."

"My thinking went like this," Khrushchev wrote in his autobiography, "if we installed the missiles secretly and then if the United States discovered the missiles were there after they were already poised and ready to strike, the Americans would think twice before trying to liquidate our installations by military means." It was both quite breathtakingly romantic and quite satisfyingly vengeful to the peasant from the Ukraine who saw Cuba as a common village "sausage" and yet who dreamed of expanding Soviet grandeur in the world. And there was one more part of it: like so many leaders of countries who had the rotten historic luck to sit astride eternal barbarian invasion routes, he deeply resented America's unique geographical protections. He felt peevishly that "it was high time America learned what it feels like to have her own land and her own people threatened."

But it is also certain that Castro had been cleverly laying the ground for just such a "possibility." From the Bay of Pigs in the spring of 1961 to the Missile Crisis in the fall of 1962, Cuban diplomats all across the Eastern Bloc in the privacy of diplomatic parlors kept hammering away at one single message — the Americans were going to invade Cuba again, this time with American troops.

The stories that Castro would tell later about the Missile Crisis would change with the whim and the wind, but several times he said what is unquestionably closest to the truth. To Julio Scherer of the Mexican magazine *Proceso,* he said: "We planted the idea of an American invasion of Cuba with the Soviets, and the idea of the measures they should take in order to avoid it, because the invasion of Cuba could provoke a world crisis. The proposition was to persuade Washington that they could light the spark that would inflame the world. That was how the idea of establishing missiles in Cuba came about."

Then he sat back to wait. It was a short wait.

Late in August, the Russian ships carrying their deadly cargo began slipping out of the secret coves of the Black Sea. Between September 18 and 21, reports began arriving in Washington of inexplicable movements in the mountainous and forested San Cristóbal area of Cuba, but no one wanted to believe such a "preposterous" possibility as the installation of missiles. Nevertheless, without the defection of Soviet military man Oleg Penkovsky, who brought with him the plans for these missiles, the Americans would never have recognized them as the new weapons they were. Without the reports from CIA-supported guerrillas in Cuba and from agents, at least one of whom accidentally lived next door to the prime missile site, they would not have believed it. And without the arrogance of the Russians, who thoughtlessly did not even bother to camouflage the missiles from U-2 photography, President Kennedy would never have been fully convinced.

At this point, Castro could be observed in the throes of a military ecstasy of Napoleonic calibrations. The world of the superpowers was at his feet. He was plotting their moves; not they, his. Who was powerless now? In those "high" days, he was even considering "contingency plans" like blowing up a ship. Obviously he "remembered the *Maine,*" and the *Coubre,* too.

Once the Americans did believe that the Russians were wantonly trying to threaten the American homeland directly, a delighted if agitated Castro watched as the mood in Washington approached Armaggedon temperature. It was "the most dangerous crisis the world has ever seen" (Dean Rusk), it was "the Gettysburg of the Cold War" (Theodore Sorensen), and finally it became "the finest hour of the Kennedy presidency" (Arthur Schlesinger, Jr.). Asked the odds of going to war, Kennedy estimated soberly that he believed they were "between one out of three and even." And in Buenos Aires, Billy Graham preached to ten thousand intently listening people on "The End of the World."

But Castro's joy was soon tempered. Suddenly it became clear that something was going very, very wrong with his scenario: Castro—the defiant Spartacus of this potentially world-destroying fight in the antechambers of the superpowers—was not even being mentioned by the men he now chose to see as his puppets. Indeed, once the conflict was enjoined between Washington and Moscow, the name of Fidel Castro almost never entered into the discussions anymore!

That dawning came cruelly for Castro. He had entered the Game of Nations as vainglorious croupier, but once the game became serious, it was played out by the casino owners. He responded angrily by first fueling and then dramatically building up the always volatile levels of fear within Cuba. For months he had been preparing the island for the "final battle" with the Americans. Now he began talking instead in morbid terms of an apocalyptic last stand. Far from appearing triumphant in those troubled days, he began holding cabalistic meetings at the university during which he told the students, in dark and whispered tones, that they must be prepared to tighten their belts and perhaps even to die. Foreign observers were more than a little stunned to see the manner in which "the Cuban young people were prepared to make for Fidel the 'supreme sacrifice' . . ."

At the same time, he was, however, "lucky," as *New York Times* columnist C. L. Sulzberger told him, "to have his historical importance at this time when the really great powers like the U.S.A. and Russia were so strong that they became weak. Their possibilities of action were almost paralyzed by the terrible potential of their weapons and this allowed more freedom of action to smaller countries." Castro, of course, had long understood this.

Then, on Saturday, October 27, 1962, the American U-2, piloted by Major Rudolph Anderson, who had brought back the original pictures of the missile installments, was shot down over Cuba. When that strange "bird," with its tapering glider-like wings eighty feet across, crashed to earth, the Missile Crisis almost crashed with it. In the White House, preparations now began for war, as Bobby Kennedy reported that "the noose was tightening on all of us . . . and the bridges to escape were crumbling."

But, who had fired the missile that brought down the U-2 and almost started World War III? Was it the Russians, as everyone then supposed?

The truth of what really happened remained uncertain for many years, and even today there are conflicting stories. Carlos Franqui was the first to accuse Castro. He insisted Castro had deliberately shot down the U-2 in order to bring the world to the edge of destruction, because he felt he had been removed from the power centers of a world crisis he himself had created.

Indeed, on that Saturday, Franqui insists to this day that "Castro drove his jeep to Pinar del Río, and went to one of the Russian rocket bases, where the Soviet generals took him on a tour of their installation. Just at that moment, an American U-2 appeared on a radar screen. Fidel asked how the Soviets would protect themselves in war if that had been an attack plane instead of a reconnaissance plane. The Russians showed him the ground-to-air missiles and said that all they would have to do would be to push a button and the plane would be blown out of the sky.

"'Which button?' Fidel asked.

"'This one,' one of the Russians indicated.

"Fidel pushed it and the rocket brought down the U-2. . . . The Russians were flabbergasted, but Fidel simply said, 'Well, now we'll see if there's a war or not.'"

Despite Franqui's colorful statements, the most credible theory of what actually happened on October 27 is that a Russian commander of one of the missile batteries, most probably without orders from Khrushchev, nervously or by accident shot down the U-2. This was the conclusion of both the Kennedy administration and of the Russians. The Soviets' long-time ambassador to Cuba, Alexander Alexeev, wrote later in TASS, "In reality, as we now know, the plane was hit by the order of a group . . . of Soviet troops in Cuba. It was hit by the commander of the group." The Harvard report backs this up; in the confusion of those days—a confusion that included the question of orders, standing or otherwise, from Moscow—the Harvard group concluded that the "local commander who actually gave the order to fire was apparently General Georgy A. Voronkov, now retired and living in Odessa."

What was unquestionable was the fact that the shooting down of the U-2 led directly to the real possibility of the United States attacking Cuba as early as that Sunday, October 28, and the Soviets' agreeing to pull the missiles out in exchange for an American promise not to invade Cuba.

The crisis was over. Castro watched from behind those hooded and distrustful eyes as the world applauded the Kennedy administration for not humiliating Khrushchev and yet getting the Russian missiles out. He watched as the same Russian troops who had brought the missiles into Cuba now dismantled them and shipped them home. Castro was left alone, in a rage of rages, having really learned for the first time that despite his brilliance in manipulating the images of the modern world, when it came to the "big decisions," the great powers made great decisions by their great selves.

As the missiles were leaving his island, Castro's tongue exploded with every scatological and cursing word he could grasp for. He railed at Khrushchev to the editors of *Revolución,* screaming, "Son of a bitch! Bastard! Asshole!" Later he would call Khrushchev a *"maricón,"* or homosexual. Then, as Castro swore still more, he swung around and violently kicked the huge mirror that hung on the wall. A veritable shower of glass rained down on the office.

But the scope of Castro's real—and ominously violent—response to the humiliations of the Missile Crisis was not really revealed until after the Harvard University meetings in Cambridge, Moscow, and Havana in the period between 1988 and 1990. Among their many revelations was the beginning clarification of Castro's attempt, in those dangerous waning days of the crisis, to persuade Khrushchev to hit the United States with the nuclear missiles. There remains confusion about a specific telegram sent by Castro to the Russian leader. (Did the acknowledged cable urge outright nuclear strikes or only "communicate the Cuban people's willingness to fight to the last man and the last bullet in the event of an American attack," as Cuban official Emilio Aragonés put it?) But there is little question anymore that Castro was perfectly ready (fulfilling his apocalyptic promise in the Sierra Maestra that his next war would be against the Americans) to launch a nuclear war against the United States. And, indeed, Nikita Khrushchev confirmed this further when the third volume of his memoirs was printed in the fall of 1990—Castro had wanted a "preemptive" strike against the U.S.!

"Talking to Cubans about the Missile Crisis was like talking to my father about Pearl Harbor," James G. Blight, a psychologist at Brown University with historical interests, recalled of the meetings of the Harvard group. "Mentioning a time to them meant they could recall just where they were. In particular, we started conversing about that telegram that Ambassador Alexeev reputedly took to Khrushchev from Castro. Sergei Khrushchev then said to us that his father remembered getting a telegram which urged him to launch a preemptive strike against Florida immediately. Cuban official Aragonés told us that, as they understood it, the deal was that the missiles would be launched if America attacked Cuba and the order came from Moscow." Meanwhile, the final report of the Harvard group, the second edition of *On the Brink,* reported that, since the Cubans had "no atomic culture," the "consequences for Cuba of a full-scale American invasion would not have differed in important respects from the consequences of a nuclear war. In either event, the island faced devastation." This important report concluded that "Castro's apparent willingness to see Soviet nuclear missiles fired from Cuban soil in the event of a full-scale invasion must be understood from this perspective."

The entire crisis, caused by Fidel Castro, then goes down in history as the closest the world had come to nuclear war, and Castro unquestionably sustained such a breathtaking possibility. But the misperceptions and the misjudgments belonged to all sides. The Americans thought there were twelve thousand military personnel in Cuba, whereas in reality, there were forty-two thousand. So, had the invasion Kennedy was considering been carried out, thousands more would have died than was estimated in Washington. But the ripples from the Castro-created missile brink, like those created in the aftermath of the Bay of Pigs, spread like a tidal wave, as "little Cuba" once again affected American relations everywhere.

It would be many years before the two superpower protagonists would truly realize how Castro had set them against each other, and, most disturbing, how easy it had been for a Castro to foment such confrontation because they themselves had so profoundly misunderstood each other. At the Harvard and Moscow meetings between the leading members of the American and the Russian Cuban Missile Crisis "teams" who were still alive, each side was constantly stunned when apprised of their misperceptions of that time—and of Castro's adept puppeteering. John F. Kennedy's aging national security adviser, McGeorge Bundy, shook his head as he considered the great historic misunderstanding that none of them had even begun to grasp at the time. "We had no intention to invade Cuba," he kept insisting, "and so the primary Soviet motivation was something that completely escaped us. Not having the motivation, we did not address it. . . . The only thing we did know was that we did not want a replay of the Bay of Pigs."

Bad feelings pass: they give way, in time, to self-interest. Not since World War II had the Russian people witnessed such a spectacle as Fidel Castro's triumphant 1963 trip. He came, he saw, and he stayed—and stayed and stayed. From April 27 to May 23, he flew like a modern Phoenix, strode like a revolutionary Gulliver, and mystified all of the Soviet Union as had no other foreign visitor of modern times. He walked into the Russian spring wearing a fur hat, and by the time he got to Moscow more than one hundred thousand Russians were waiting to shout his acclaim in Red Square. Khrushchev could not admire or applaud him enough—he went so far as to order that the 26th of July hymn be played in Red Square, the first time in forty-five years that a foreign anthem had been played during a Soviet parade.

On his second night in Moscow, Fidel suddenly decided to go for a "walk in Red Square." It was Sunday, April 28, around 10:00 P.M. Castro and his inner group had just finished dinner, when Castro suddenly decided to leave his Kremlin eyrie. "There was general consternation in the old palace," Juan Arcocha, the sophisticated radical Cuban intellectual who was then *Revolución*'s correspondent in Moscow, recalled. "The servants went crazy and rushed up and down the corridors. Telephones rang in dark-ened offices in various parts of the compound. The sentinels were suddenly jerked out of their boredom, their eyes popping. What was going on? It was not in the program. The worst of it was that nothing like this had ever hap-pened before. As a result, they had no clear idea of what they ought to do." When Castro returned to his hotel, Arcocha noticed a roguish bad-boy's grin on his face. How he enjoyed shaking up the Russian empire!

On this trip, in the beautiful old Ukrainian capital of "Christian" Kiev as they were visiting a factory, Castro suddenly saw a rather voluptuous Russian blond. "Fidel likes her," Castro's aide told Juan Arcocha, motion-ing subtly to the woman. "Get her for him for tonight." "At the risk of being gravely disobedient," Arcocha recalled later of his amused sarcasm at the time, "I asked, 'Since I have this honor because of my linguistic talents, may I please know in which moment of the process I should stop translat-ing?'" He recalled that the aide did not smile. "It's an order," the aide said dryly. The blond turned out to be uniquely prepared for such an adventure, and neither Arcocha nor the aide received the slightest reproach the next morning—nor any new instructions on translations.

But Castro came home from his Russian "triumph" with an astounding new message for the Cuban people: he and the Russians were going to reimpose upon Cuba what he had always called, when it was American, the "humili-ating, unjust, degrading" single-crop sugar economy. He had accepted it because he had had to, and the Soviets had assured him they would pay more for Cuban sugar and that they would design a mechanical harvester in two years. Sugar, yes. Monoculture, yes. But industrialized monoculture?

Before the Cuban people, Castro got up and soberly quoted Khrushchev verbatim: "As Comrade Khrushchev explained, 'We have solved the problems of cosmic travel; how can we fail to construct machines for harvesting sugarcane, which is an incomparably simple problem?'" Watching Castro say these words on television, the sympathetic Canadian professor Maurice Halperin nevertheless shook his head and observed, "It was the classical trap into which amateurs fell when extolling the wonders of the Soviet technology and economy. The fact, of course, was that the development of space technology—a very advanced but also narrow field of specialization—once it was given top priority by the Soviet state . . . was incomparably easier than creating a modern, mass construction industry involving, in addition to other complexities, the training and management of hundreds of thousands of unskilled workers."

Castro's personal life was practically nonexistent to the Cuban people now. The notice of his mother's funeral in August 1963 was the last time Fidel's private life was mentioned in the press (eccentric sister Juanita's melodramatic defection in 1964, for example, went unreported). Castro meticulously and instinctively complied with one of the cardinal rules of all charismatic dictators: no apparent personal life, no individual loves, and above all no public need for others.

Castro's relationship with Naty Revuelta, however, continued in these years, and she often stayed with him at his Varadero beachhouse. Mirta had gone to live in Madrid with her second husband, Emilio Núñez, and two daughters, Mirtica and the ironically and daringly named América, or "Meki." His hatred for his ex-wife—or perhaps some degree of continuing love—had been shown one night in Varadero before she emigrated when Castro found Mirta and Emilio eating steaks in the only steakhouse and, enraged, ordered Oscar Mori to throw out "those people." (Mori refused.)

Fidelito stayed in Havana for a while, and even appeared with his famous father on the American *Person to Person* television show. A saucy boy who often wore a beret tipped sidewise like his father's, Fidelito had at that age some of Lina's piquant looks. His cousins remember him as "very stubborn" and as "a kid who always seemed to be missing something, like a father." But soon Fidelito, too, disappeared from public sight and was secretly placed in school under a false name, until his later years when he would study in Russia under his nom de guerre, Raúl Martínez, and eventually marry an attractive blond Russian woman.

Tellingly, while Castro felt no or almost no attachment to his family, he often returned sentimentally to Birán, to the ranch. There he made good on the favors he promised his people in much the same manner as a medieval grand seigneur would grant favors to his serfs. One night, for instance, he went to nearby Marcané and stopped at the Club Marcané for a bottle of rum. It was late at night and it had rained a lot. While the leader of Cuba was drinking rum, Fillo Alcalde, a little chap who was one of his old neighbors, came up to him eagerly. Fillo was impeccably dressed, with two-tone shoes like those Haydée's fiancé had worn to his slaughter at Moncada. Fillo liked parties and women; they called him "Shorty" or "Millionaire." As they sat there in the quiet night, Fillo said plaintively to the powerful man who had once been his neighbor, "Let me ask you something. What do you think is going to become of my life?"

"What do you want?" Castro asked.

"I want you to take me to Havana," Fillo answered. He then regaled Fidel with his dreams of leaving the countryside for the "high life." Then he patted Fidel's beard and said in the old familial way of Birán, "What a beautiful beard!"

Before Castro's guards could jump on poor Fillo for such an outrageous action, Fidel stopped them. "He can do that," he said, barely hiding an amused smile. "He's my family." Several days later, military trucks arrived at Marcané asking for "Fillo's house." Fillo was duly moved to Havana, where neighbors said he drank himself to death within a year.

Castro roamed about "his" island at will. But never alone. His specially trained guards, who now reported directly to the minister of the interior, Ramiro Valdés, and to the Russian KGB who trained them, traveled everywhere with him. His unpredictable habits (he still rarely slept in the same place two nights in a row), however, made him a deliberately problematic target, and as always he was best protected by his "sorcerer's instinct." In these years following America's humiliation at the Bay of Pigs, Castro needed all the protection he could get, and a little luck as well. For the Bay of Pigs resolved nothing between Castro and the Kennedy brothers; to the contrary, it only more hopelessly envenomed their strange and in many ways ever more dependent relationship.

Castro knew what was happening. He knew that the American government was working with the Mafia to assassinate him; to him, it was simply a replay of the "old days" in Havana, when he had begun his program to purge the city of vice and mob chief Meyer Lansky had placed a million-dollar "bounty" on his head. Now Castro watched as the United States government broke its own laws, not for Berlin, not because of a nuclear threat from Russia, but because of Cuba, always little Cuba.

Actually, the CIA's Mafia attempts against Castro had started in conjunction with the Bay of Pigs invasion. Mobster Johnny Roselli and top mobster Sam Giancana met in March of 1961 in Miami at the Fountainbleau Hotel with Florida Mafia Boss Santos Trafficante. There, heaps of cash were dumped melodramatically into laps, and poison capsules were readied. The plotters duly noted the method's versatility—the capsules could be used in boiling soups or alternate "vehicles." There were two major assassination plots timed to coincide with the invasion; one was with the Mafia and the other was to be in collaboration with the Cuban underground. Because of the swiftness of Castro's victory, neither plot was activated; but that fact only created more of a sense of urgency for the postinvasion plans. And in the anger and embarrassment inside Washington after the invasion, the attempts became more "respectable."

Ironically, one of the few men who had loudly criticized the planning of the Bay of Pigs, General Edward Lansdale, was put in charge of "Operation Mongoose." A tall, gangly Special Forces army officer, Lansdale had successfully employed "irregular" warfare in the Philippines to defeat the Communist-backed Hukbalahps guerrillas. Lansdale, who was without question a brilliant and innovative man, in the mood of the times now seemed to go crazy. He used nonlethal chemicals to incapacitate sugar workers, he hired "gangster elements" to attack police officials. According to one witness, Lansdale went so far as to spread the word that Castro was the Antichrist and that the Second Coming was imminent.

There were numerous attempts on Castro's life, but Minister of the Interior Ramiro Valdés contends that only one came close to succeeding. Castro often stopped for a milk shake at the Havana Libre cafeteria and one time a cafeteria employee, who had been hired by the CIA, was about to slip a cyanide capsule into the milk shake. The capsule, however, was frozen and it broke. The man was too nervous to pick up the pieces and put them in the milk shake.

Soon after the Missile Crisis, "Operation Mongoose" was disbanded, and it would be only of historic curiosity, were it not for the terrible fact that on November 22, 1963, the young American president, John F. Kennedy, was assassinated. For years experts and the public alike have wondered about a connection between Kennedy's death and the attempts on Castro's life. There are so many questions still unanswerable. And yet, there are some clues.

Castro was at Varadero that Friday, talking with the editor of the French journal *L'Express,* Jean Daniel. Ironically, Daniel was ostensibly there to discuss a possible rapprochement between Kennedy and Castro. It was Oscar Mori, the man who managed the Varadero property for Fidel, who first told Castro the astounding news that President Kennedy had been shot. Mori is very precise about exactly what happened. "I have books about what Fidel said and what Fidel did not say, and I know because I was the one who gave him the news. . . . He did nothing. Not a gesture, not the bat of an eye. The only thing he did was not to speak anymore. He went to the living room, he sat down, and he did not say anything. His expression? It was one of sadness."

Jean Daniel recalled that Castro went to the phone. "*¿Cómo?*" he said. "*¿Un atentado?*"—"What's that? An attempted assassination?" "He then turned to us to say that Kennedy had just been struck down in Dallas," Daniel wrote. "Then he went back to the telephone and exclaimed in a loud voice, 'Wounded? Very seriously?' He came back, sat down and repeated three times the words, 'This is bad news.' He remained silent for a moment, awaiting another call with further news."

The small group at Castro's pleasant Varadero ranch house, with its big windows overlooking the glorious azure beach, and its simple furnishings, gathered around the radio. "'Kennedy wounded in the head; pursuit of the assassin; murder of a policeman'; finally the fatal announcement: 'President Kennedy is dead,'" Daniel related. "Then Fidel stood up and said to me, 'Everything is changed. Everything is going to change. . . . I'll tell you one thing: at least Kennedy was an enemy to whom we had become accustomed. This is a serious matter, an extremely serious matter.'"

Then something eerily strange occurred. The American radio station began somberly playing the American national anthem. There, in the very house of Fidel Castro, a strange circle of men, including those who loved John F. Kennedy and those who hated him, rose to their feet and stood quietly for a few seconds listening attentively to the "Star-Spangled Banner."

Castro's first public guess was that the assassin was a Vietnamese come to "take revenge" for the war. But as he listened further to the radio, he heard talk about an American with ties to Cuba through the Fair Play for Cuba Committee. According to Daniel, he blew up!

"'I know them,'" Daniel remembered Castro shouting, "'they will try to put the blame on us for this thing. . . .'" Then he went on about how he had always been repelled by assassination, from the viewpoint of political self-interest as well as everything else.

Was Castro to blame? He heatedly insisted to me in interviews in 1966 that he had had no hand at all in Kennedy's death. And, as always, he vowed his friendship for the young American president. Part of this—at least—was false. The picture he drew of how much he "liked" Kennedy was cynically calculated and far from true. Castro in truth hated John F. Kennedy. In his speeches, Castro made Kennedy into a monster. Billboards all over Havana derided and abused Kennedy, and Castro had even threatened the American president. It was part of the long play of hatred between Cuba and America. As late as September 7, 1963, the Cuban leader had very calculatedly held an impromptu but key three-hour interview at the Brazilian embassy in Havana, where he clearly issued the following warning to any American leader who tried to assassinate Cuban leaders: "We are prepared to fight them and answer in kind. United States leaders should think that if they are aiding terrorist plans to eliminate Cuban leaders, they themselves will not be safe." President Lyndon Johnson believed until the day he died—and said on at least four occasions—that Oswald had been put up to the murder by Castro.

On the other hand, Castro liked and needed to pit himself against worthy adversaries. He would rather be up against a John Kennedy than a Jimmy Carter, if only because it enlivened his own status and heightened the temperature of the game. On that level, Castro not only wanted but needed Kennedy alive, a fact that was most probably the chief source of any sorrow that bleak November day.

But even on that sober and sobering day, the differences that fueled his relationship with the United States suddenly erupted into fury. Jean Daniel was still there when Castro heard on the radio that Jacqueline Kennedy was, in public, having trouble getting rid of her bloodstained stockings. "He began to shout," Daniel wrote later, "'What sort of a mind is this? What sort of a mind? There is a difference in our civilizations after all. Are you like this in Europe? For us Latin Americans, death is a sacred matter; not only does it mark the close of hostilities, but it also imposes decency, dignity, respect. There are even street urchins who behave like kings in the face of death.'"

Nearly three decades after the assassination, there is still no absolute proof that Fidel Castro took part in, connived in, or planned John F. Kennedy's death. But there are simply too many "accidents" not to assume that there could have been some Castro involvement. Lee Harvey Oswald had been in the Soviet Union, and he had lived there in that special manner (barely working, having an apartment, his Russian wife being allowed to leave Russia with him) that only "special guests" were awarded. Once back in the United States, Oswald sought out Cuba and Cuban connections at every turn. In September 1963, this normally reticent and secretive man took the bus from Houston to Mexico City, and it was as if he were transformed on the bus, talking spiritedly to people and even boasting that he was going to Cuba to see the wondrous "accomplishments of the Cuban revolution." The CIA, listening in on the telephone lines between the Soviet and Cuban embassies in Mexico City, made a recording of a dialogue between Oswald and Ob'edkov, a Soviet guard, on October 1. Oswald was seen at private parties conversing with Mexican Communists and with Cuban diplomats. Upon his return to the United States, Oswald made contact with Jack Ruby in Dallas. . . .

The most extraordinary evidence by far—and evidence which has too much of a distinct ring of truth about it—came after the assassination from the well-informed investigative columnist Jack Anderson. Johnny Roselli had chosen Anderson as the person to talk to about the Mafia, Cuba, and the Kennedy assassination. What did he tell Anderson, before Roselli himself was "eliminated" by his old friend Trafficante? "He told me that the JFK assassination was done by the last three sharpshooters who had tried to assassinate Castro from a high building in Havana," Anderson told me many years afterward. "He told me that Fidel Castro was directly involved—this was the deadly secret for which he was killed. He said that Castro used the same ones out of a sense of Latin irony. Later, the Church committee confirmed everything else Roselli told me, and Lyndon Johnson [slipped and] told Howard K. Smith in a TV interview, 'Well, Kennedy tried to get Fidel

Castro, but Fidel Castro got Kennedy first.' It was the biggest secret in history, and he blurts it out." In short, according to these theories, John F. Kennedy was killed when his obsessive plot against Castro was turned against the American president; he was killed when the ever-flexible Mafia, which had substantial interests on both sides of the question, only now swiveled around to serve a Cuban master instead of an American one.

But even if one accepted that Castro had no direct hand in Kennedy's assassination, it was, nonetheless, the existence of Fidel Castro, of his Revolution, and of the ominous realities he introduced to the world that unmistakably led to the death of John Kennedy. Without the humiliating failure at the Bay of Pigs, without the almost crazed assassination attempts against Castro and the Mafia connection to those attempts, without Castro's counterhumiliation over his abandonment by the superpowers during the Missile Crisis, it is hard to believe that John F. Kennedy would have been assassinated that fateful day in Dallas—with all that would come to mean to the world.

22

GUERRILLA TO AN AGE

The revolutionary movement will break out sooner or later in all oppressed and exploited countries, and if "nuclear equilibrium" creates a situation in which thermonuclear war would really be increasingly difficult ... the United States will inevitably lose the fight against the revolutionary movement. . . .

—Fidel Castro to photographer Lee Lockwood

THEY CAME FROM ALL OVER, young men and women alienated from their societies and seeking not so much political revolution as personal redemption in Fidel Castro's new Cuba and through his "inspired" word. Born not out of poverty but out of an insatiable fury over the past and the aroused expectations of the moment, this flow of restless young poured into Havana like nervous quicksilver from 1959 on. Not for them the long, patient, imperfect, Anglo-Saxon business of economic development—that was far too tiresome and unheroic. Not for them the tedious business of political campaigns—their extravagant hope was to forge no less than a new world.

Everywhere in those halcyon and heroic days, legends were for the making. The "heroic guerrilla" would be sung about, rhymed about, and novelized about. Even the conservative Peruvian writer Mario Vargas Llosa would take Fidel Castro's "guerrilla" with the seriousness that the age demanded of this new—or, more accurately, revitalized—political creature.

Vargas Llosa has his guerrilla hero in *The Real Life of Alejandro Mayta,* a nice and seemingly modest chap, whisper to his friend at one point, "We are going to begin another life. Out of the cave, into the air, out of garage and café intrigue to working with the masses. . . . We are going to plunge right into the heart of the people. . . ."

Those breathless words, reflecting what was in effect his "real life," captured the euphoria of the time. In Cuban training camps from the wilds of Pinar del Río to the heights of Minas del Frío to the seclusion of the Isle of Pines, Castro would train men and women to overthrow governments, not by the traditional methods of military defeat or coup d'état, but by figuratively plunging into the gut and soul of the people from Guatemala to Panama, from Zanzibar to Congo-Brazzaville, from Grenada to Surinam.

Certainly there existed an historic predecessor to Castro's "global guerrillas," and to their talents for burrowing into societies and transforming them; the Russian Comintern, formed in 1919 by Lenin, was organized to communize the world by sending agents around the globe to form new Communist parties. But by Castro's standards, even the famous Comintern was modest; amazingly, it never matched in size or in scope Castro's long arm of the guerrilla. By the height of his "military globalism," in the 1960s when the Cuban population grew to about eight million, Castro had deployed across the globe. He had twenty-seven active guerrilla organizations with twenty-five thousand armed and trained members from other countries backed up by an additional twenty thousand individuals from African countries and from Nicaragua who had gone through political indoctrination classes in Cuba. These guerrilla forces were backed up by Castro's regular soldiers, at least four hundred thousand of whom served in Angola alone. Nor was it that Cuba was incidental, or instrumental, or a secondary force; Castro made Cuba into one of the two "polar centers" for guerrilla warfare (the other being the Middle East's Palestinian resistance).

The aim of the Cuban leader was clear, although his deliberately obfuscating and contradictory statements obscured it. Orlando Castro Hidalgo, one of Castro's leading intelligence officers, knew what it was from the beginning. Castro wanted nothing less, Hidalgo said, than the "final storming of the imperialist heights: the United States."

Castro poured all of his tactical, strategic, and psychological brilliance into his "guerrilla international." Palestinians, Italians, Germans, French, Spanish Basques, Vietnamese, Iranians, Africans, American blacks, American whites, American Indians—a minimum of fifteen hundred of them a year came to Cuba for "training." What was so extraordinary about Castro's worldwide guerrilla empire was its machine—precision organization, which was in dramatic contrast to his regime's bleak inability to organize the merest or most modest accomplishment in the economic sphere. Militarize! Mobilize! Demonize!—those were Castro's talents, not bottling beer or selling sewing machines or preparing proposals for the World Bank.

As Castro was creating his worldwide apparatus for revolutionary change, the United States was beginning to implement its long-range economic development program, its Alliance for Progress in Latin America. This led to an epic, although oddly enough, little-known, historic confrontation. Everywhere the United States began a program for economic improvement in Latin America, Castro's tenaciously stuck-together international network opposed it.

Castro also by this time had the incalculable benefit of the Soviet Leninist intelligence system, which perfectly fit his authoritarian mind-set. As early as late 1961, Cuban intelligence agents were being sent to Moscow for training, and some were recruited by the KGB (something that enraged Castro). Cuba's Dirección Generál de Inteligencia, or Directorate General of Intelligence, or DGI, would come to be considered by intelligence professionals everywhere as the fourth most efficient intelligence service in the world, after the CIA, the KGB, and Israel's Mossad.

Two Cuban patterns for expansionism evolved. One was to support a Leftist government already in place (as in Angola, Mozambique, Chile, Nicaragua). The other was to overthrow an antagonistic government through a guerrilla landing (as in Peru, Venezuela, Bolivia, Guatemala, El Salvador, Colombia).

Guerrilla warfare—or the "little war" of the "little fighter" or "*guerrillero*"—was, of course, nothing new. It was as old as Xun Tzu-wu, who employed it to fight in China five centuries before the birth of Christ, and, in fact, guerrilla strategy helped the rebels defeat the British in the American Revolution. But the guerrilla warfare that most inspired Fidel Castro was the Spanish type that had sprung to life in the nineteenth century as tens of thousands of Spaniards fought to rid their homeland of the hated French. Castro took this history, absorbed it, thrashed it around in his psyche, factored in some other related political and metaphysical ideas—and came out with the basis for his own "guerrilla." And he understood instinctively that the men and women he so passionately appealed to were not seeking "freedom" but anonymity, belief, belonging; far from wanting or being willing to tolerate that Western individualism as represented by the United States, they were trying to escape from it and from its incessant—and too often unfulfillable—demands.

Some said what most allowed Castro to be so successful in the revitalizing and internationalizing of guerrilla tactics was that he was actually fulfilling a peculiarly Cuban impulse. Ever since it had been the proud way station for the colonial Spaniards, carrying out *Madre patria*'s noble mission of subduing (and looting) the "New World," Cuba had had a delirious and unrealized ambition for imperialism, Cuban writers like Luis Ortega contended. In earlier years, the bars, coffeehouses, and parlors of Havana were filled with talk about Cuba being another England, another America, and Castro was making this "delirious idea" surrealistically come true. There was a certain perverted reality about this reality. For the Cuban people, in part through the Spanish heritage of dependence upon the powerful leader and his "testimony" and in part because of the dependency upon capricious external forces like the sugar market, finally gained through Castro's "internationalism" a sense of control over that ever-threatening external environment. Before Castro, they had been historic recipients of a collective sense of impotence in the face, particularly, of the United States—guerrillas not only drew the attention of the Americans away from Cuba, they also made Cubans feel finally powerful and free in the world.

Venezuela was to be first, just as that advanced country had been the site of his first political trip. Castro's jealous hatred of the highly effective Venezuelan democratic president, Rómulo Betancourt, led to Cuban support of the Venezuelan guerrillas as early as 1961. Suddenly, in this rich and contradictory land of Andean peaks and jungles so vast they appear from the air to be ocean waves of green, humble policemen were being gunned down on the streets, bombs were exploding in Caracas, and guerrilla *focos* were appearing all over. (*Foco* is a uniquely Spanish word that means a center of guerrilla operations, rather than simply a military base in the usual sense. From the *foco,* revolution is spread in growing waves of concentric politico-human circles.)

"We almost had civil war in Venezuela in the early 1960s," Orlando García, an original Cuban revolutionary who broke with Castro and became the powerful head of the Venezuelan security police, told me in Caracas. How much of the guerrilla fighting was due to the "objective realities" of the time, and how much was actually Castro's influence? García did not hesitate a moment. "Their inspiration was all Fidel," he insisted. "All Fidel, exactly! These groups never won popular support."

Colombia—beckoning ever since the heady days of the *Bogotazo*— was to be second. Its incessant and incipient violence, its chasmic divisions between the classes, its dark and brooding Andean wildernesses, all made it the perfect country for Castro's guerrillas. Soon there appeared in the savage peaks the Colombian Army of National Liberation, the Colombian Revolutionary Armed Forces, and the Workers', Students' and Peasants' Movement (founded in January 1960, as the "first *Fidelista* political movement" outside Cuba). Later would come the M-19, directly Cuban-trained and the first movement to serve as well-paid protectors of the drug cartels. The beautiful but equally tormented little Central American country of Guatemala was next. With its brutish military and landed gentry caste, with its 60 percent pure-blood and passive Mayan Indian population, with its constant American intervention over the years, Guatemala of the volcanoes and the early morning mists was also a perfect guerrilla target.

In October 1966, I lived for a week in the high forests of the Sierra de las Minas with the rebels of Guatemala's Fuerzas Armadas Rebeldes, or FAR. I watched as the movement's slim, intense, hard-eyed young *Fidelista* leader, César Montes, gave the Guatemalan Indian peasants almost exactly the same rhetorical and ideological training that Fidel had given the *guajiros* of the Sierra Maestra.

A peasant would say, haltingly, that he had to pay twenty-five dollars a year to the landlord for his land, and Montes would cut in scornfully, "The landlord you never see."

"We're not allowed to live in our village anymore," the peasant would begin again. And Montes would insert, "For helping us, you were forced to move here. The police burned your houses, burned down your chapel."

"And they destroyed our honeybees, too. . . ."

This echoing, repeating "indoctrination" was a constant in all the movements. In El Salvador many years later, Marxist guerrillas would chant over and over, "Our leader is Farabundo Martí, and he will save us." It was as close to the mystical and hypnotizing repetition of the Hail Marys of Catholicism as it was to Castro's own revolutionary incantations.

Indeed, it seemed, in those heady days, that the reach of Castro's long arm of the guerrilla was everywhere. In Haiti, always so close physically to Cuba, Castro air-dropped little radio receivers to the peasants, who later complained that they could hear only Havana on them. Guerrillas were organized in El Salvador, Honduras, Costa Rica, and on many of the islands in the Caribbean. Most amazing, tight groups were even organized in classically democratic countries like Uruguay (the Tupamaros), Chile (the MIR, or Movement of the Revolutionary Left), and Argentina (the Montoneros). In short, it is no exaggeration to say that, from the earliest days of his regime, Castro shook the traditional and entrenched institutions of the hemisphere like an angry but deliberate Adam shaking a dangerous tree of apples suddenly loosened by a frightful windstorm.

Castro's interest in postcolonial Africa was perfectly in tune with Cuba's black population. As he plotted to expand his guerrilla empire to the African continent, he was calling upon the dreams of the followers of Santería for their mythical "homeland" in Africa called "Guiné."

In 1961, for instance, an office of the revolutionary Zanzibar National Party was opened mysteriously in Havana, and United States intelligence officials were understandably confused by sudden reports of black Africans there at the same time the Soviets were beginning to move over the island. Soon, Cuban agents and guerrillas were meeting with Zanzibaran rebels in the Sea View Hotel in Dar-es-Salaam, Tanzania. Victory came to those renegade Zanzibarans in January of 1964, when the violent, Cuban-trained John Okello, a brutal giant of a man who always carried two guns in his belt, swept into exotic Zanzibar Town with a force of six hundred Cuban-trained guerrillas. They handed out weapons and immediately overthrew the pro-Western Arab government of the hereditary sultan to form the "People's Republic of Zanzibar," which was to be the prototype for other Africa revolutionary states. Observers were amazed and even a little amused to see the African guerrillas on the streets of the city wearing *Fidelista* beards and berets; but as thousands were brutally slaughtered in the aftermath of the coup, the situation proved far from amusing.

Juan Benemelis, the Cuban diplomat who had studied in Castro's EIR for diplomats in Vedado, became the director of the Cubans' "Africa Corp." When I talked with him in Washington, D.C., years later, he told me, "Castro hoped to implement an ambitious, two-pronged plan simultaneously, unleashing a general offensive on the African continent, led by Che Guevara, together with one in Latin America which he himself would guide directly from Havana."

Castro's prime "agent" in Africa, then, was to be the "irreplaceable" Che. What people knew at the time or have realized since is that Castro wanted his most loyal comrade as far away as possible from Cuba. From Castro's point of view, there was no longer any room for Che in Cuba. He had begun to disturb Castro profoundly with his constant and vociferous anti-Russian pronouncements, in exactly the years that Castro was growing more and more dependent upon the Russians. This was not the contradiction it seemed. Che was a "Marxist," and indeed he was always ineffably more ideological than was his friend Fidel Castro, but he was also a utopian Marxist. When it came to the nitty-gritty of day-to-day and nation-to-nation commercial relations, with all that meant in terms of cunning and compromise, he was particularly capable of becoming enraged even with that "metropole" of Marxism, the Soviet Union. He believed with all his sardonic heart that a power like Moscow should give preference to a "new" revolution like Cuba's. And so, on February 22, 1965, at the Asia-Africa Economic Meeting in Havana, Che sealed his fate. In a burst of anger, he struck out viciously at the Soviet Union for its commercial relations among the socialist countries, relations that directly favored the Russians. Now it was just a matter of time.

En route to Africa in that winter of 1965 to "foment revolution," Che stopped in Egypt to talk with Gamal Abdel Nasser. In conversation after conversation, he poured out his heart to the Egyptian leader, who liked Che much more than (the "crocodiles") Fidel, and there was always one message. Che talked, and talked, and talked about . . . death.

"The turning point in each man's life," Che said at one point in those long discussions, "is the moment when he decides to face death. If he faces death, then he is a hero whether he becomes a success or not. He can be a good or a bad politician, but if he cannot face death, he will never be anything more than a politician." At their last meeting, Che told Nasser that all he was searching for was "a place to fight for the world revolution and to accept the challenge of death." Nasser was again bewildered by these odd revolutionaries of Cuba—he told him to "live for the revolution," not die for it.

When Che returned temporarily to Cuba from his first foray to Africa that winter of 1965, he was met at the airport by a Kremlinesque line of the top officials of the Cuban Revolution, including Fidel, and President Osvaldo Dorticós. The "reunion" was sepulchral. Castro's expressive, theatrical face was notably grim, and even Che's wife, Aleida, who was pregnant still again and who might have been expected to be joyful at her husband's return, looked depressed, her eyes downcast. By then, she knew well that Che was not returning to her and the family, and really not to Cuba either.

Che and Castro talked steadily for close to forty hours. The single agreement known to have come out of the marathon meeting was that Che would return to Africa, to the explosive Congo, this time for a long stay and with several hundred Cuban troops to support the Leftist uprising in that key African country. Then Che "mysteriously" disappeared. Even his elderly mother in Buenos Aires never spoke with him again, not even on her deathbed.

When Che returned to Congo-Brazzaville, that steaming hot little enclave huddled at the mouth of the Congo River that is Joseph Conrad's "heart of darkness," he led his Cuban troops, along with thousands of Leftist Congolese fighters, into battle in Castro's name against the famous and feared European mercenary "Mad" Mike Hoare. "Mad Mike" immediately noticed the difference in the attacks against him as the guerrillas followed the more rational Cuban tactics. But the Congo was maniacal madness, with "Simba" secret societies designed to wipe out all the whites; and Che, or "Comandante Tatu" as he was called by the two hundred Cubans and their Congo-Brazzaville allies, ended up abhorring it. It was far from the noble place he sought "to accept the challenge of death." He left within six months and returned secretly to Cuba, but the story did not end there. The Cubans kept a military mission in Congo-Brazzaville which, even in the mid-1960s, numbered as many as seven hundred to a thousand men and was busily preparing still another way to bedevil the Americans.

Castro never spoke of Che's failed adventure in the Congo until January 1977, when he introduced it into Cuban history for the first time, and with pride. Why? Because by that time, Castro, in his closed nation, could ignore his failures. But also because there was one positive that did come out of the disastrous Congo "campaign." It laid the base and the long-term connections for Cuban work with the Marxists in Angola and Mozambique, which would blossom in 1974–75.

By the time Che returned from the disastrous Congo adventure at the end of 1965, his pictures were emblazoned all over Cuba. But to some, the display seemed eerily more a memorial than a tribute, for Che himself was nowhere to be seen. The world first knew that Castro's companion in arms, the inimitable and dashing Che Guevara, had left Cuba for good exactly when Castro wanted it to know it. Looking theatrically stricken, posturing dramatically, Castro stood up before a stunned group in Havana on October 3, 1965, and read an astonishing "letter from Che." It had been written, Castro declared elliptically, the April before.

"The date was not inserted," Castro said that day, "because the letter was not to be read until the moment was considered opportune. . . ." Thus, in sharpest contradiction to Che's unconstrained outbursts, Castro now not only controlled Che's most important message but also its date. And the timing was hardly accidental. At this same meeting, Castro also announced that the PURSC, or Partido Unido de la Revolución Socialista Cuba, which had followed the ORI in 1963, was to become the new Communist party of Cuba. Che, with his refined taste for sarcasm, must have loved the irony of the situation; for he, who along with Raúl, had urged Castro to putative "Communism" in exactly those years when Castro was constantly and vehemently denying he was a Marxist, not only was not present at this "birth" but his name was nowhere to be found on the new institutional lists of members.

That day in October 1965, Castro's pungent voice and Che's historic words held the assemblage breathless; they were words of only the most copious praise for Fidel Castro: "My only serious failing was not having trusted more in you from the first moments in the Sierra Maestra, and not having understood quickly enough your qualities as a leader and a revolutionary. . . ."

Then came the key words: "Other nations of the world call for my modest efforts. I can do that which is denied you because of your responsibility as the head of Cuba and the time has come for us to part."

There were tears in many eyes as Castro went on reading what was in fact Che's "farewell" to Fidel and to the Cuban people he had so heroically helped to "liberate." "If my final hour finds me under other skies, my first thought will be of this people and especially of you. . . . I embrace you with all my revolutionary fervor, Che."

The true believers around Castro tended to take the letter at face value; Che, after all, had never masked his belief in world revolution and often expressed his desire to serve it again. But to others, the letter appeared ominously like the "confessions" in Russia in 1936, after which all the confessors dutifully disappeared forever. Also, too many people close to Che were too distraught. The famous Egyptian journalist Hamdi Fouad, of Cairo's *Al Ahram,* recalled seeing Che's wife, Aleida, at that time dressed all in black. "We asked her why she was dressed in black," he said, "and she told us, 'Because he is going to die.'"

In a very real sense Che followed in the shadows of Frank País, Camilo Cienfuegos, Huber Matos, and Humberto Sorí Marín. Like them, he was viewed by Castro as a "competitor" for power and, like them, he had to be moved aside—in one manner or another.

The real story of Che Guevara here is of course Fidel Castro's. But, as usual, Castro tells the world only what he wants it to know. The "facts" are known, but the details leading up to Che's death are far from clear. Thus, once again, in order to find out Castro's involvement in the "mystery" of Che, it is necessary to move in on the deceptively voluble but in reality truly secretive man who is Fidel Castro selectively and from the peripheries. It is necessary to see him through what he wrought for others, clearing away the leaves from the forest until the bare winter trees stand stark and alone.

It is probable that Che Guevara was still in the Congo when Fidel read his "farewell" letter in Havana. We know he was back in Cuba, hidden away, for most of 1966, and it is presumed that during this time he and Castro reached agreement on Bolivia as the next step in Che's "intercontinental revolution." Actually, Bolivia was a reasonable choice for such an adventure only if one looked at a map of Bolivia in exactly the same way the CIA planners had looked at Cuba when they chose the Bay of Pigs as a landing site; that is to say, without deigning to note the "subjective" conditions or the human or cultural quotient. (Do human beings not become what they hate too much?) For Bolivia's revolution in 1952 had already completely transformed the lives of the poor Indian population. They were no longer even remotely "ripe" for any outside guerrilla interference.

No mind, in the wilds of Bolivia, Che would build his guerrilla *foco,* and create the "second Vietnam" he so avidly railed about.

So it was that in September 1966 Ernesto Guevara left Cuba for Prague, Paraguay, and finally for that aridly beautiful *altiplano,* or highland, of Bolivia, where the descendants of the great Inca empire stand upon rude piles of stones and wave palms to keep the rains away. While Castro went on with the "business" and institutionalization of the Cuban Revolution, a "new" Che, cleverly disguised as a balding businessman, traveled by plane into the fourteen-thousand-foot-high Bolivian capital of La Paz. From there, he was whisked away by his few followers to a farm called "Ñancahuazú" on the wild and densely forested eastern slopes of the Andes. With seventeen Cubans, who had entered Bolivia by differing and intricate routes, he began building a small guerrilla movement, one that would remain always more pathetic than threatening and which never reached more than seventy persons.

Che, who should have known better, now put himself and his destiny in the hands of the Bolivian Communist party and thus of the Russians—and he did it in an arrogant manner that was thoroughly antipodal to what Castro would have done. Castro would have "united, united, united," until he had the power to destroy the others. Che effectively gave the Bolivian Communist party ultimate power over him by refusing their temporary suzerainty.

In early December 1966, even Mario Monge, the secretary-general of the Bolivian Communist party, traveled to Havana to talk with Castro. There is good evidence that Castro tried, at least halfheartedly, to obtain Monge's support for Che, but as Che's close and old friend Ricardo Rojo insisted, "What Castro was practically asking Monge to do was to let the political leadership on the continent be transferred from Moscow to Havana." That, the Bolivians, jealous of the little (and very high) turf they had, were never going to permit.

Then, fatedly, on New Year's Eve of 1966, Monge traveled across the black, snow-covered Bolivian Andes and down their eastern side into the dense and suffocating high jungle to meet with Che and to discuss the power structure of his guerrilla operation. Out at "Ñancahuazú," Monge explained his demands: the Communist party would take part if (1) Bolivian Communists, who followed the abhorrent Peking line, were not allowed to participate; (2) the military and political direction was in the hands of the Soviet-line party; and (3) Che solicited the help of all Communist parties of Latin America.

Che was furious. He paced angrily back and forth. Why had Monge come at all? He was particularly enraged by the impudent leadership demands. Che would never give up direction of the movement, never!

Before he left, Monge met privately for two hours with the fifteen Bolivians who had joined Che's group, and he told them that Che had refused his demands. Monge tried to infuse them with an awareness of the fate that awaited them. "I'm sure you will fail," he told the young men, "because [you are] under the direction of a foreigner." He paused. "You are going to die very heroically," he added, "because you have no chance for a victory."

And so the Bolivian Communist leader left, never to speak to Che again.

In the year after Che's death, I traveled to Bolivia and followed in Che's footsteps to reenact his last months. While there, in Camiri, I had the first interviews with the surviving guerrillas who had fought with Che. "Monge," they told me, "would inform the new arrivals that the movement was 'a disaster, a failure,' and that they would not be able even to reach the guerrillas. He would convince them to turn back." All of these events had the deliberate effect of working together further to put Che's "movement," if it can even be called that, directly and singularly under Fidel Castro, who had to have anticipated such an eventuality in his Havana talks with Monge.

And then there was Tania.

Looking at Tania's pictures, one sees a slim, attractive, dark-haired woman, severe, with long legs and a mannish posture. She had a reputation for being clever and a little intense when one wasn't looking, party-loving and gay when one was. Looking at her intelligence dossier, were that possible, one would see the files of one of the most intriguing female intelligence agents of all time. She had been Che's intimate since they met in 1961, and now in the faraway mountains of Bolivia, she would play a key—probably *the* key—role in whether Che lived or died.

Laura Gutiérrez Bauer, Laura Gutiérrez Bauer de Martínez, Lary Aguilera, María Aguilera, Elma, Emma, Nadja, "T"—those were only a few of the aliases of the woman whose real name (insofar as she actually had one) was Tamara Haydée "Tania" Bunke Bider. It was Tania who was commissioned by Che to set up the Bolivian "revolution" and it was Tania who was sent into Bolivia ahead of Che. For months she lived in La Paz, and there she showed an ingenuity and a steely dedication that came close to rivaling Castro's own.

In order to become a citizen and move freely throughout the country, she married a hapless Bolivian and then swiftly shipped him off to the Eastern Bloc on a "scholarship." At one point, Tania was giving advice to the lovelorn over the radio, advice that was sometimes unintelligible because it was in reality a coded message to Havana. It was Tania who chose and set up the remote (and fatal) "Ñancahuazú." It was Tania who was to seal Che's fate.

As she accompanied Régis Debray and the Argentine Leftist artist Roberto Ciro Bustos out to the mountains to meet the guerrilla leader, the three stopped in the dusty little town of Camiri, where, against the protests of the two men, she decided to leave their jeep "locked up." The men's reasonable fears turned out to be well founded. In a throwaway town like Camiri, where nothing had happened since the Spanish Conquest, the most careless spy would know that a jeep standing alone, particularly when locked, would cause attention. It did. And in it, the police found a rich batch of incriminating documents that Tania had left—an astonishing "lapse" on the part of such an infinitely clever woman.

Among the papers were four small notebooks filled with the names and addresses of leaders and members of Che's urban organization, as well as Communist contacts outside Bolivia. There were lists of secret sources of funds reaching from Brazil and Peru all the way to Switzerland.

Who was this woman named Tania, who planned Che's life with the care of a German-Argentine Celia? After her death in Bolivia in the summer of 1967, an East German intelligence master, former "Öberleutnant" Günther Männel, who had defected from the East German Ministry of State Security, or MFS, in 1961, saw her picture in the papers. Stunned, he revealed that she had been under his orders in the MFS to spy on the Castro people and Che not only for the East Germans but for the Russian KGB as well! Stories denying this connection simply do not ring true; even Castro's early friend Régis Debray himself told *New York Times* columnist C. L. Sulzberger and French intellectual André Malraux in 1971 in Paris that "part of the reason for total failure was treason in Guevara's ranks. 'Tania,' an East German girl fighting in the small guerrilla band, had been a Soviet agent."

The only question really is whether Castro knew it. While it would seem that he, with his uncanny feel for the slightest deception, would have at least suspected that she might have been an agent, the question remains unanswered. First of all, if Castro himself did not send Tania, he certainly did send Régis Debray, the aristocratic Frenchman who was then one of the stars in Castro's firmament.

When Debray and Bustos arrived at "Ñancahuazú" in March of 1967, sent directly by Castro, they were only slightly less at ease at being there than Che was at having them. Debray insisted upon being armed, but Che refused to allow him, the "journalist," to join the guerrillas. When the two men left, they got as far as the little town of Muyupampa, where they were captured. Without hesitation Debray and Bustos revealed to Bolivian soldiers and investigators that Che Guevara was indeed in Bolivia.

The commonsensical Bolivians stashed the two strangers safely away in jail, where the gaunt and brooding Frenchman from the sainted "École" postured and fretted much like a peacock set down in a watering hole for buffalo. His trial soon became a cause célèbre in the drawing rooms of Paris. Charles de Gaulle publicly pleaded for his release, and the worldwide Left swung eagerly into action with a veritable din of protest to the Bolivian government for a man none of them had even heard of months before. Eventually he and Bustos were released, and Debray returned to Paris, disillusioned with revolution in general and with Fidel Castro in particular.

Now Che's situation grew steadily worse, and one of the reasons was Castro himself. It is a little-known fact that toward the end of March 1967 Castro simply stopped resupplying Che. According to Che's diary, according to the diaries of Bolivian guerrillas who fought with Che, and according to all the interviews with participants afterward, nothing ever seemed to arrive. There was almost no contact with Havana after the initial "battles" of March, and Che complained of his "isolation" for the first time in his April 1967 summary. By May, he spoke of "total lack of contact with Manila" (Manila being the code name for Havana). In July, Che finally received a long message from Havana, but after that, nothing.

In his despair, Che reverted more and more to his earlier hyperintellectualized "priest of violence" self. In the final days of his life, his diary would describe an embittered world of "paroxysms" of terror and of forcing responses from the peasants, who were only "little animals . . . impenetrable as rocks. . . ." Finally Che dropped all pretense of inspiring or liberating the Bolivians, saying that "through planned terror we can neutralize some of them."

On August 11, Castro hailed Che as an "Honorary Citizen of Latin America." On August 14, after the guerrillas lost the important and revealing contents of one of their caves, Che wrote, "A black day. . . . It is the hardest blow they have ever given us; somebody talked. Who?"

It would only get worse. By September 28, he was writing, "A day of anguish. At times it seemed as if it would be our last. . . ." The men were hallucinating; Che was so sick he soiled himself; and the peasants, instead of welcoming them as liberators, fled at the very sight of those terrifying bearded strangers.

By October, the days had dwindled down to the few and the last.

It was an apparently distraught Castro who late in October announced to the world the death of his comrade in arms Che Guevara. As reported on October 19 in *Granma,* Castro sat that night at a wooden desk in front of a red velvet backdrop in the television studio. Members of the government leadership gathered in small groups, speaking quietly. For two full hours, Castro spoke to the country. Now it was his turn to bid farewell to his friend, fallen in that mysterious highland of the Andes. But Castro also reminded the Cuban people subtly (again) of "El Che's" weaknesses. "All the time we knew him," Castro said that night, "he was always characterized by an extraordinary impetuousness, by the absolute scorn for danger. . . . We tried to protect him from the risks of falling in some battle of not-too-great strategic importance, and we ought to say that we were always worried about the possibility that his temperament, this behavior of his in any moment of danger, could lead him to death in any battle. . . ."

Immediately the "Cult of Che" was launched in Cuba—and around the world. Posters of "El Che" soon became the staple of young revolutionaries and New Leftists from Berkeley to Berlin to Baghdad. In Havana's Plaza de la Revolución, portraits of Che and Lenin soared four stories high. His body had been burned in the high jungles of Vallegrande, but the hands had been cut off to await identification by forensic specialists brought in from Argentina. So it was in the "legend of Che" that his hands ended up in Havana, in a sober room in the monument to Martí in the Plaza de la Revolución, framed by the sleeves of his uniform and his major's stars.

The story of Che's hapless capture and death is now well documented. Captured on October 7, 1967, Che was soon face-to-face with the Bolivian officer in charge, Captain Gary Prado Salmón, a hawk-nosed, American-trained officer. "When I captured him, I had to ask him, 'Who are you?'" Prado, by then a general, told me many years later. "He said, 'I am El Che.' That was when I started to tell my men to cover the hills. But he said, 'Don't worry, we have failed.' Then after we talked for a while, his spirits seemed to get better. I asked him why he had come to Bolivia. He talked about the international revolution, about people prepared to fight. But I told him he had missed something, that he had misunderstood Bolivia. He said then, 'The decision was not completely mine. . . .' Finally, he told me, 'It was Castro. . . .'

"Right up to the end, he still had hope. In mid-September, he had received a message from Castro that he was getting a group of Bolivian students together in Havana and organizing another group in Czechoslovakia to send to the guerrilla. . . ." Prado paused and shook his head. "But if you think about what happened," he went on, "the guerrillas were down to a few men. They could only receive messages through the radio, not send them, but they still had the hope that Castro would not abandon them. Where would Castro even find them? Guevara had no support once he left Havana. No support at all. He was completely isolated."

The order to kill the famous Che Guevara came from La Paz by radio, and it was agreed to and given by the entire top Bolivian army command. So Che was killed in a small hut by an officer named Mario Tenán, who shot the revolutionary nine times and who lived peacefully ever after in Santa Cruz. Che lay "in state" on a crude operating table in the very austerely Spanish Bolivian town of Vallegrande, where the superstitious Bolivians who saw him there imagined in his face the same frightening likeness to Christ that Castro had always inspired.

People wondered why Castro was so generous with the memory of Che, launching it as he did into a cult that would invade the universities of mankind like an intellectual guerrilla campaign. There was really little to wonder at. What did Castro have to fear from a dead man who could only complement him in the fullness of his life?

Che's death did mark a moment of change for Castro, who now took a more accommodating stance toward the Soviets and pulled back (at least temporarily) from his huge guerrilla network. "That whole period during the 1960s, the Cubans were a problem," Arkady Shevchenko, the second man in the Soviet U.N. mission in those years, told me. "They did not want to share with us. We knew they were doing things in the Third World, but they weren't telling us what they were doing. We would know of it from others. We made maximum efforts to get their help, we tried to please them as much as possible, we never made such personal efforts for anyone else." He paused a moment, then shook his head in wonderment. "Of course—they were more influential in the Third World than the Soviets were."

Castro did not actually "kill" Che, any more than the biblical David "killed" Uriah when he ordered him into the thick of battle, "hoping" he would die, so that David could have Bathsheba, Uriah's wife. Most stories of love and treachery are very ancient. But, after hearing Che's last words, Captain Gary Prado Salmón, the officer who had captured him, came to feel that Castro had had basically two ideas regarding the Bolivian operation. "If the thing was a success, the owner of it would be Castro," Prado told me. "If the thing went wrong, as it did, he got rid of Che. Castro wasn't going to lose anything." Prado put forward this theory in his own book on capturing Che, and, having read the book, Castro told a European journalist that Prado had the right interpretation.

Now that Che was dead, Castro could make him "live" exactly as he wanted him. In this new resurrected life, under Castro's transforming fingers, Ernesto Guevara became "Che, of the heroic poster." But it was a distorted image. "That poster that was in the dormitory of every young man in the 1960s and 1970s," Ambassador Eugenio Soler, a friend of Che's, mused many years later in Venezuela, "that is not Guevara, that is a myth."

And that is exactly what it was meant to be.

On January 3, 1966, just shortly after Che returned to Cuba from his misadventures in the Congo, Castro opened the First Conference of Solidarity of the People of Africa, Asia and Latin America, or more simply the "Tricontinental." Che, of course, was not there, and his name was not even mentioned.

No fewer than five hundred twelve delegates, sixty-four observers, and seventy-seven invited guests, representing eighty-two countries and territories, gathered in the once-luxurious Havana Hilton. Russian-backed and Russian-sponsored, Castro's Tricontinental was to be, in the words of the scholar of terrorism Claire Sterling, "the beginning of a massive thrust against Western capitalism generally and the United States in particular, through the formation of a Guerrilla International." Everybody was there: the Vietcong, Guatemala's Rebel Armed Forces, Stokely Carmichael, even the new and relatively unknown Palestine Liberation Organization. It was a veritable carnival of the world's atomized, deracinated, angry outcasts searching for ways to take power through violence. The Tricontinental also witnessed the revolutionary birthing of the Venezuelan who would become the world's most feared and formidable terrorist, the man called "Carlos," originally named Ilyich Ramirez. It was at Castro's own Camp Matanzas just outside Havana that he had studied terrorism under the KGB's Colonel Viktor Simenov. From Cuba, from Camp Matanzas, from Castro, "Carlos" went on to work with the Palestinian terrorist Wadi Haddad, to introduce diplomatic hostage-taking to Europe, and to lead such heinous terrorist attacks of the next fifteen years as the Munich Massacre.

The first Palestinians came to "study" in Cuba as early as 1966. They came secretly, and they came several hundred at a time. Both Yasser Arafat and the far more radical George Habbash paid state visits to Havana, and, reciprocally, the Palestinians opened up the Middle East to Castro. Soon there were Cubans teaching Spanish Basques in Libya, Cuban fighters training the anti-Morocco Polisario guerrillas in Algeria, Cubans fighting in tank battles in Syria, Cuban guerrilla instructors in South Yemen and indeed across the entire troubled Near East. Later Castro would pay back these favors by helping to bring the PLO into Angola in 1975 and into El Salvador and Nicaragua four years later.

This turn toward the radical Arab world meant that Castro had finally to give up his admiration for (and even preferential treatment of) the highly organized and dynamically creative Cuban Jewish community, which numbered some twelve thousand when the Revolution came to power. Some observers are convinced that Castro had originally liked the Cuban Jews because he thought that some of his ancestors were *Marranos,* Spanish Jews who had converted to Christianity at the time of the Inquisition. (In Galicia, the name "Castro" was occasionally a *Marrano* name.) Whatever his personal feelings may have been, Castro easily put them aside in his pursuit of the Third World, particularly the Arabs. In 1973, after the Yom Kippur War, he broke relations with the state of Israel. From that moment on Castro was ferociously, if theatrically, anti-Israel. In truth, both his earlier lack of anti-Jewish feeling and his subsequent anti-Israel postures probably reflect only how little ideological, religious, or even politically committed feeling he had about anything, unless or until it suited his own power purposes.

Out of the Tricontinental, as well, grew Castro's first really serious attempts to subvert black America and to influence the young in America who had become so alienated by the Vietnam war. Before it was over, twenty-five hundred young Americans would be selected to visit Cuba in the "Venceremos Brigades" between 1969 and 1977, and black America would be infiltrated at every most vulnerable level. The primary intent again was to destabilize the United States, to use the hatred for the war in Vietnam, to "bring the war home," and gradually to neutralize the very potency and inner will to action of the United States itself.

Castro's tactics, as usual, were flawless. His men would take the young Americans for sessions on the beach at Jibacoa, a white pearl of a beach near Havana; when the moon came up over the Caribbean and a gentle breeze blew, it was a romantic and sensuous place, even for the humorless Eldridge Cleavers, Jerry Rubins, and Bernardine Dohrns of the America of that era. The young *americanos* listened intently as the guerrillas of the Sierra Maestra regaled them with wondrous tales of "the Revolution." And, in the hypnotic moonlight, the Americans would sit, enthralled, next to a revolutionary comandante, insouciantly dressed in the rumpled, informal olive greens that symbolized these commanding "new men" of Cuba, so different from their gray "organization man" fathers back home.

"When we wanted to demoralize the Batista regime," a guerrilla would say, "we threw bombs at guardhouses and in public places, and eventually the whole society stopped."

"Show them how you did it," the comandante would interject.

And soon the Americans were being shown how to make Molotov cocktails. They were never exactly told to use them, they were just constantly told how the Cubans had done it.

Thus, Cuba became a haven for the radical young, with the sparkling water, the moon, the fires in the evening, and the romantic appeal of the guerrillas and comandantes. And Cuba welcomed them; Castro knew well how to make radicals feel important. He flattered them, and gave them a heroic alternative. In place of the country they hated, he offered them his country, his creed, and above all himself.

One of Castro's early American targets was Eldridge Cleaver's radical Black Panther party. Cleaver, a big, handsome, consummately angry black man, already had decided that "Fidel Castro was a great hero" when the Cubans first made contact with him through their U.N. mission in New York, in 1967. The Cuban mission, which fell directly under Castro's Directorate General of Intelligence, was a very active, sophisticated organization. "They had people there assigned to certain regions, and cities," Cleaver told me in 1984. "They had some for the blacks, some for the whites, some for the women. . . . This was a professional operation, with a military hierarchy."

Cleaver went to Cuba with a delegation of black and white radicals. Then wanted by the police for an alleged rape, Cleaver was enticed by the idea of being close to America, in a safe sanctuary, and being able to broadcast his

radical message from there to the States. In Cuba he was given a military uniform, his own pistol, a car, and a penthouse apartment. He had some interesting times, and even befriended an American girl named "Bunny" Hearn
who, like so many, had become enamored of Castro and apparently had even
been another of his romantic involvements.

Bunny, a pretty, brown-haired girl from the South, had begun writing
letters to Castro through Herbert Matthews at the *New York Times;* amazingly, Castro wrote back. They finally met when Castro spoke at the U.N.
in the fall of 1960. After that, Bunny moved to Havana, where every day
Castro sent her special lettuce for her pet rabbit.

It was with these radical young Americans that Castro was most successful in helping the North Vietnamese. Castro never had more than some
hundreds of troops in Vietnam, although in the 1970s he had up to a thousand workers and technicians there and he himself visited Vietnam in 1973;
his aid to North Vietnam was other than combat fighting. He made Havana
a meeting place (the *only* meeting place) where groups like the American
radical Weathermen could meet directly with the North Vietnamese. As
early as 1963, he had established the Cuban Committee of Solidarity with
South Vietnam, the first of its kind in the world. Throughout the 1960s, he
organized constant meetings between the young Americans and Huynh Van
Ba, the Vietcong's chief representative in Havana, who instructed the
Americans how to organize more antiwar demonstrations at home, to
emphasize the number of American casualties and the number of planes
being shot down, and to encourage draft resistance. Van Ba was very insis-
tent on one point that Castro understood better than anyone in the world:
the Americans should be careful not to use the word "Communism," just as
the revolutionary movements in Cuba and Vietnam had avoided it during
the first stages of their revolutions. It was far better, he said, to talk about
the "new life" after victory and in terms that everybody could understand
and agree with—free medical care and better living conditions; you never
got into trouble with those.

These encounters between the young Americans and the North Vietnamese had profound consequences. No one would say that the meeting
between U.S. Weathermen like sober Bernardine Dohrn and Peter Clapp
with a delegation from North Vietnam and the Vietcong in Havana in mid-
1969 was the only inspiration for Chicago's "Days of Rage" that followed
within weeks of the Americans' return to their putative "home." But such

meetings, with their inspiration—and their instruction—to "bring the war home" had a profound effect on the young American radicals, and, as the war continued without resolution, on nonradical Americans as well.

More and more, Castro saw "winning" in terms of plugging into and interrupting the American political process, rather than victory on the "battlefields" of the Third World. He was right. From 1963 to 1966, seeing the anti-Vietnam chaos in the States, Castro actually began to grasp the idea that "revolution" was a possibility there. From 1966 on, he began taking the most active, most deadly serious hand in promoting revolution in America.

Castro's tactics at this time did have some solid historical precedent. Many of the original colonial wars of the 1940s and 1950s had been "won" not in the country in question, but in the world power centers or metropoles of the old colonial power. What was crucially new and important with Castro's tactics, however, was that for the first time rebel, guerrilla, or terrorist/revolutionary organizations of the Third World were being deliberately mated with the radical movement within the United States. Some even thought that the anti-imperialistic struggle and the race war would now march down the road to revolution hand-in-hand.

But as with so many of the Latin and African guerrillas trained in Cuba, the initially euphoric attitudes of the young Americans soon wilted under the force of the sheer unreality and surrealism they found in Cuba. Even Eldridge Cleaver finally tired of Cuba, despite the fact that Castro proudly showed him military installations where Cleaver's Black Panthers were to be trained. Cleaver more and more felt that "you were kind of out there on a little piece of land." The training he had been promised never seemed to happen, and finally the Cubans accused him of attending secret Cuban "black power" movement meetings against the government.

But if Eldridge Cleaver and many others grew weary of Cuba, it was not before Castro had had an extraordinary historic effect on the United States, an effect that burrowed into the American psyche, into American patriotism, and into American self-confidence, in a manner never before seen. Since the Puritans landed in America, carrying with them an ideal of creating the beautiful "City on a Hill" that would shine as an example to all mankind, virtually all ideological and reformational ideas flowed from north to south in the Western hemisphere. Fidel Castro changed all of this. Suddenly, amazingly, there stood a Latin leader who not only dreamed of but was implementing a total change in the currents of influence. If Americans deigned to think about it at all, it frightened them. And it should have. For Fidel Castro was changing the very nature of war in our times.

In those pregnant, watershed years of the 1960s, NATO and its behemothic force of nuclear arms were holding off and even gradually diminishing the freezing powers of the Cold War, the United States was fighting a traditional war in Vietnam that it would lose against the age's consummate guerrillas, and the Pentagon's strategists talked about "low-intensity warfare" without in the least understanding it. Meanwhile, of the eighty wars that began after 1946, only twenty-eight took the traditional form of fighting between the regular armed forces of two or more states. Fully forty-six were civil wars, insurgencies, or guerrilla contests, with the remaining six being riots and coups d'état. By 1984, there were no fewer than forty wars raging across the globe, involving forty-five different nations, and, more important, numerous entities or movements. It was a new age: the age of "the movement," the age of the street gang, the age of the vigilante, of the guerrilla, of the terrorist. It was, in short, the age of Fidel Castro.

23

THE DICTATOR OF THE COWS

I would have preferred an attempt to study nature and see how, by *adapting to it*, one could make maximum use of its resources and potentialities. No, in this military society, man commands, dominates, *violates* nature.

—René Dumont

THE YEARS FOLLOWING Che's death and Castro's rapprochement with the Russians should have been a period of new succor and security for the Cuban leader. Castro's friend, the Soviet Union, was to an extent re-Stalinizing under Leonid Brezhnev, after the heady years of liberalization under the now-deposed Khrushchev. Castro's eternal enemy, the United States, was daily sinking deeper and deeper into the worst period of its modern history, with the Vietnam war growing in horrors and providing a national alienation that was gloriously manipulatable by Castro. But nonetheless, these years were not good for Fidel.

At home, the once-tempestuous Cuba was beginning to look more and more like her dour and doughty cousins in the Eastern Bloc. Beautiful and expressive Havana perhaps best reflected the growing shabbiness of Cuba; her sensuously lovely buildings molted like snakes in season, her paint peeled away from lack of care, and her gardens, like her spirits, fell to weeds. For Cubans, historically accustomed to at least the expectation of the American way of life, there remained now nothing but shortage. A well-known chef, Nitza Villapol, who gave recipes on television, would tell her viewers to get the best meat. Then she would go on to say that if one didn't have that specific cut, well, one could use this, or that, or even wheat flour. How to present a major Cuban meat dish without meat, that was the challenge of the magical Cuba that Castro was constructing! But the most dramatic metaphor for Cuba's move behind the Iron Curtain was to be found in the omnipresent oil slick that covered the streets of the cities like a coat of oozing paint. The Russian oil was of such poor quality that it leaked all over in the heat. More and more Cubans were asking themselves how the Cuban Revolution could have been so endlessly fascinating and the Cuban revolutionary state so stultifyingly dull?

As the look and feel of the Eastern Bloc moved into and over Cuba, Castro very deliberately and systematically destroyed every remnant of the wicked past. Statues of former presidents were hammered to bits, books destroyed. When Castro's childhood friend Rolando Amador departed from his homeland in disillusionment, he left behind a library of twenty thousand books. The Revolution took them and made pulp of them. The bewilderment of men like Amador increased when the entire contents of an exceptional museum in Cárdenas, which included a world-class collection of shells, butterflies, and Roman coins, was either destroyed or sent to Russia. Learning about this "new Fidel," Amador explained to me years later, was "like hearing about a man I'd never known surrounded by people who have nothing to do with the Cuban people."

At one point the angry Russians warningly slowed the crucial Cuban oil deliveries to a virtual standstill. The situation got so bad that sympathetic European Communists stepped into the chasm, with men such as Spain's Santiago Carrillo telling Castro, "You've broken with the U.S., with China . . . a rupture with the Soviet Union would be catastrophic." Then, suddenly and without warning, on August 20, 1968, Soviet troops crossed Czech frontiers and the world awoke to find two hundred thousand troops and Russian tanks poised in the exquisite old city centers of Prague. Cubans waited for professional "noninterventionist" Castro's explanation. Castro sat at a desk that night—always at a desk as though he were a teacher—facing a television studio. In his two-and-a-half-hour, thirteen-thousand-word "speech," he wove into his complex genuine and tactical message the basic wrongness of invading another country—"the sovereignty of the Czechoslovak State has been violated." But then he accepted fully the

Russian contortion that the invasion was "justified" because of the "beginning of a 'honeymoon' between the Czech liberals and imperialism."

Thus, Castro placed himself inexorably on the side of the "Brezhnev Doctrine," which allowed the Soviet Union to take action if another socialist state was "threatened by capitalism." But Castro would not give away what he could sell; he used the occasion to call for a redefinition of Soviet-Cuban ties, and to demand that the same "protection" the Soviets had given Czechoslovakia be extended to North Vietnam, North Korea, and Cuba, should they be similarly endangered by "human face" invasions from within. It was the diplomatic prologue to the Missile Crisis all over again.

Almost immediately (how amazing!), Soviet assistance to Cuba expanded and oil supplies flowed smoothly again, just in time for what was now becoming Castro's real obsession: his beloved "Ten-Million-Ton Harvest."

Although almost entirely unrecognized by the outside world, Castro's dreams about the economy of Cuba were turning out to be blood brothers of his dreams of world conquest. Building on the ancient Spanish Catholic and Moorish heritage of contempt for money, he talked now of demythologizing money, indeed of abolishing it, and even of creating a wondrous "civilization without money." Ideas like this popped up in Castro's mind like mushrooms after the rain. A Camembert better than that of Normandy's was to be produced in Cuba. A campaign was launched to eradicate all weeds—a "weed-free Cuba" became the call of the day. Another day, Castro got the idea of planting an entire "*cordón*" of coffee in a circle of land around Havana. Immediately workers were dispatched as if to still another displaced Bay of Pigs "battle." But the soil there was no good for the delicate coffee plants; within a year, unrelenting nature had destroyed that particular dream of Cuba's premier dreamer.

Oscar Mori, Castro's "impresario" at the treasured Varadero Beach, has vivid memories of his boss during these years.

One time, they were driving out at the very end of the Varadero peninsula, remote and windswept, where "the people" could not go. They were riding along the road when they came upon a cut pine tree. "At this, Castro went crazy," Mori recalled. "He got out and told his guard to give him a machine gun. He was enraged that anyone should cut a pine tree there. I said, 'Comandante, this pine tree was cut by the man who is about to install telephones here.' He insulted me. Then he took the gun and shot at the cables. He hit one, and it fell. Then he turned to me and said, 'I should kill you.' I said only, 'Comandante, I am not to blame for this.' "That was Castro, too, shooting at telephone cables with a machine gun, like a mad Cuban Don Quixote.

The prominent Cuban biology professor José Roque León recalled that when Castro appeared at a plant, "he would be surrounded by people who were not genuine advisers but executors of his caprices, a choir of resonances. When he would come to the biology laboratory, he would only give orders. He would walk in and look around and say, 'The microcopier should not be by the window, it should be in the shade.' And they would move it, even though that was wrong." What did the professors think? "It was as though they wore masks," León told me. "They did not speak much in private. You see, Castro does not have to be in agreement with science, science has to be in agreement with him."

Castro was becoming the Cuban version of the Bolsheviks' Trofimo Lysenko, inventing new genes; he was Moses parting the Red Sea; he was the Thai king as rainmaker. He was, according to Rafael del Pino, who became one of his leading air force officers, a man who dreamed "like Snow White," a man who got into his head on any one day "to make students into professors, to build a new airport five miles south of the present one, which already had only three or four flights a day. . . ."

But it was cows that truly riveted him, cows that became the fulcrum of his obsession to control every living thing on his island, if not the world; for it was with cattle that his "special plans" were carried to new and truly "undreamed-of" levels of genetic engineering. With his cows, Castro would improve on nature, substituting his planned artificial reproduction for the notably haphazard but still dependable natural process. His intent, as always, was not subsumed in modest dreams; he intended nothing less than to create a new human creature, a new animal that would carry his name to new heights. He had created a revolution against all the odds and beyond any man's dreams; now he would create new life beyond other odds. The whole program became so obsessive that even his close and eerily devoted friend Gabriel García Márquez (whose entire literary life was devoted to writing about the patriarchs and macho caudillos of Latin America) suggested lovingly, making a literary pun on his famous novel, *The Autumn of the Patriarch*, that he would write a new work about his friend Castro and entitle it *El Dictador de las Vacas*, or "The Dictator of the Cows."

Cuba would become a center of genetics and Castro the new "Father of Genetics." How? By crossing the Cebú and the Holstein cow to create a wholly new bovine, the F-1, which would uniquely provide Cuba with more milk and more meat and dazzle the world. When an English scientist told him that, yes, he could cross Cebú and Holstein and it would work for one generation but that "the second generation will have the worst defects of the father and the mother," the man was immediately expelled from Cuba. The scientist was right, of course. One cow worked, Castro's Hollywood "star of cows," Ubre Blanca, or "White Udder." She became so famous that, when she died, a distraught Castro stuffed her and placed her in a museum, where "future generations could admire her magnificent udders."

In many ways, his cows became more real, and more personal to Castro, than human beings. At the farms, he called the animals by name. ("But, is it good or bad to know the cows by name?" amused and bewildered onlookers like Carlos Alberto Montaner wondered.) Not only the cows but all the farm animals (like the restricted people) had "animal passports," or tiny metal plates identifying what the creature was, when it was purchased, and by whom. Some bulls had air-conditioned stables. When an animal died, there fell upon the farm manager the sad task of going to the police station to report the demise so the animal could be taken off the police lists.

In these years, and into this world of science-as-magic, Castro constantly imported a lineup of foreign scientists who were commanded to be magicians. When the elderly, white-haired French farmer, teacher, and agronomist André Voison arrived at the Havana airport, he found the Cuban leader standing at attention. A head of state waiting at the airport "to greet a modest French scientist at two o'clock in the morning!" as the amazed Voison put it. Naty had already visited and charmed the modest Voison in France and had persuaded the specialist in pasture grass to visit Havana. Castro now took over. Voison was cyclonically wooed, glorified, deified; Castro mounted a massive campaign of "grass indoctrination" for the whole Cuban people, and the sixtyish Voison unwittingly became the single, unrivaled hero of all of Cuba's honored cows.

Dr. René Dumont, a highly respected French agronomist and scientist, came to Cuba, looked around, and came again and again, always wanting to believe in Castro's "revolutionary" agriculture, but always and ever disquietedly falling back upon scientific reality. At every turn the unhappy Dumont saw only waste and pseudoscience. Dumont just couldn't figure it out when he was informed that *Fidelista* economic philosophy meant that "a devotion to the community will be the fundamental basis for the creation of wealth." Instead, Dumont saw "mile upon mile of banana plantations where the trees were dying because they had been planted in badly drained soil where the water table was tainted with magnesium salts." But the most telling experiment that Dumont saw was the one in anti–soil erosion in Pinar del Río. Here Castro sought to build large parallel terraces on contour lines all up the mountain. Dumont finally understood: the experiment was meant not to fight soil erosion but to go against nature itself, to "dominate the mountain."

In the end, all the hated scientists who failed to recognize the brilliance of the "new genetics" and the "new agriculture" were thrown out, vilified, and excoriated by Castro. Professor Voison was saved, providentially perhaps, although he might have contested the idea, by the grave. He died of a heart attack on December 21 in the same year he had arrived in Cuba (too much excitement, they said). The father of Cuban pasture grass made the front page of *Revolución* and was given a state funeral. Castro himself gave the funeral oration.

Castro's stubborn fascination with genetic engineering fared only somewhat better in the field of cancer research. Just as he had taken a fancy to cows and pasture grass, Castro suddenly took an insatiable fancy to the drug interferon. A protein made by most cells of the body, interferon belongs to the first line of defense against viral infections and was thought to have properties that could block the transformation of normal cells to cancer cells. He struck out in all directions to make Cuba a center for interferon research.

Professor Karl Cantell, a specialist on interferon in Helsinki, was sitting in his office in the lovely gray old Finnish city when the Cuban embassy called: Would he please visit Cuba? The Cubans had converted a luxurious villa on the outskirts of Havana into a lab and had built a new research institute. They wanted Professor Cantell to come for its inauguration. "Cuba is a poor country," the slim, professorial young doctor recalled one day in Helsinki, "but when a dictator wants something, everything is possible. I went there, spent some days, met Fidel Castro. When I saw Castro, there was always a photographer with us—even when we were drinking, they were always taking pictures. They had a huge cow institute, and I saw Ubre Blanca there. I think they treated her with interferon because she had a malignancy."

In the end, however, although the scientific work performed by Cuban doctors was valid, they got little international attention for the simple reason that Castro would not allow them to publish in the international journals. His paranoid closure of Cuba was at odds with his dreams of glory.

Looming above all these dreams as the true zenith of scientific triumph was Castro's greatest obsession—the "Great Ten-Million-Ton" sugar harvest. Into this effort, which pitted the strength of his own will against the cold rationality of science, he poured those mammoth energies that, only for the moment, had been diverted from military expansionism abroad. As he had once militarized his guerrilla international, so now he militarized the harvest and, indeed, the whole of Cuba.

Revealing his innermost self through his choice of metaphors, he said, prematurely, that the harvest "made a man of our country . . . made it grow up . . . made it into a giant." Had the economic mobilization for the harvest, or *zafra,* been a mobilization for war, it would have been one of the great military mobilizations of all time. The entire country was called by its master illusionist to the grandiose delusion. In 1969, the harvest lasted 344 days (an eighteen-month harvest "year") and everyone participated. Christmas was not celebrated that year because of "activity in the cane fields," and the revolutionary "holy day" of July 26 was proffered by Castro as the "new Christmas." As it happened, Christmas was never again celebrated in Cuba. In place of the old holidays, monster rallies, with hundreds of thousands filling the plaza, were held regularly, but there was an almost desperate passion about them, for in truth there was little to celebrate anymore.

Everyone cut sugarcane. Foreign dignitaries cut cane, Soviet Defense Minister Marshal Andrei Grechko cut cane, wives of ambassadors cut cane. And then, it failed. Not only was nine million tons the maximum to be expected, but even that figure was misleading because much of the cane was in actuality left over from the previous harvest or prematurely cut from the next one. How would the proud figure of Fidel Castro get out of this one?

On July 26, 1970, the seventeenth anniversary of the Moncada attack, Castro stood before the Cuban people as much the master of dissimulation and manipulation as ever he had been. In the past he had emotionally and psychologically changed places with his *masas,* making them one with him. Now he made himself one with them, transferring dependencies just as he had transmogrified legitimacies. The all-knowing "macho" caudillo transformed himself for the moment into a contrite and humble human being, a man who could no longer perform "miracles." They were all responsible for the failure, he told his people, but he more than anyone. He was in the end one of the "illiterates." He recognized his mistakes and then, brilliantly, he offered to resign. This was a delicate and dangerous tactic, to be used, as he well knew, only in moments of special danger and pregnancy, as with Urrutia. Now, once again, he set himself up for rejection. This was a risk because, as Max Weber knew intellectually and Fidel Castro knew instinctively, the leader's "charismatic claim breaks down if his mission is not recognized by those to whom he feels he has been sent." But Castro's judgment that *las masas* would not (could not) reject him was, as usual, unfailingly accurate.

"No, no, no," the crowd shouted, in its utter dependency upon the *líder máximo*. "No, no, no!"

In the end the master political alchemist actually gained by his mammoth failure. He was not only anointed once again but he emerged stronger than ever. "The Cubans were well manipulated by Fidel," the high-level defector José Luis Llovio explained. "He told them he had known since April but did not want to say anything to the people." So, in addition, then, Castro in his "concern" for his people had tried to spare them the knowledge of failure. They were again bound forever together, defenseless against an outer world that would now criticize them and mock them more than ever before. He had protected them, and he had made them want to protect him, for he appeared suddenly vulnerable.

But it was hardly for naught. When the *zafra* was over, Castro's island had been transformed into an economic military camp run on more purely and extensively military lines than any "Communist" country in the world. The economy was now organized as an exact national equivalent of the Rebel Army in the Sierra Maestra. Personally terrified of the slightest disorganization, Castro found both sense and security in the total militarization of everything.

Analysts and visitors fretted in these years over what to call Castro's system. They came up with terms like "protosocialism with national bureaucracies" . . . "romantic paternalism" . . . "a Moncada assault mentality and a Sierra Maestra complex" . . . "revolutionary maximalism, in which he seeks strategic breakthroughs" . . . "charismatic hardship Communism" . . . Whatever the social scientists thought, as they searched for words to describe the phenomenon of political nature that was Fidel Castro, in the end it all came down to "will, will, will." And when he linked his stalwart, incredible will to economics, he fully believed that the results would be "scientific," or, playing on the Soviets' sacred "Scientific Socialism," a kind of "Scientific Caudilloism."

Even in failure, Castro seemed triumphant. He came out of the 1960s as the single and only chief, with a personal power unsurpassed even in the other Communist countries. He was first secretary of the Communist party, commander in chief of the armed forces, president of both the Council of State and the Council of Ministers; he held the top leadership post in the party, state, and armed forces. His power *seemed* supreme.

Castro himself would spend time at Varadero Beach during this period, and he saw to it that his top men had beautiful villas there. Unpredictable as always, Castro would simply arrive unannounced at Varadero, but the small, witty, adaptable Oscar Mori was always prepared. "There was the garage," Mori told me, describing Castro's hideaway, "and a small kitchen. There was a sofa in the living room where he sat a lot and looked at the sea. It had three bedrooms upstairs. He slept little, very little . . ." Mori paused, and laughed. "He didn't have discipline in this, either. It was the same for him to be sleeping at six in the morning as at three in the afternoon. There were nights when we had parties and we would have some drinks, but I never saw him drinking too much. He liked Courvoisier cognac. There were days when he was happy and went to a cabaret at the hotel. The women of the comandante were always about. There were times when they went to Fidel's house. But only when Fidel sent for them. They never just went. That, nobody could just do."

The women? The dancer at the Tropicana, a favorite of *americano* tourists in the "old days" and a nightclub still booming under Castro, said he read while he made love. The French actress said he smoked. The European woman complained he never took his boots off. The young American woman who went happily and expectantly off to the beach one promising midnight with him complained he sat there for three hours and "only talked" (surprising) "without stopping" (not surprising) about agricultural reform. A "gorgeous" Cubana named Amparo, whom José Pardo Llada had introduced to Castro, had a similar complaint. The two went to the beach, too, where they spent a few hours on a particularly lovely Cuban night. When Pardo Llada asked Amparo about it later, he told me she said that it had been very strange because "I started caressing his hair and he only talked. . . ."

Castro's affairs became quietly known. Flowers would suddenly appear on the woman's birthday, and her mother, on her birthday, would receive the rare paella and lobster—all dispatched, in the strange fullness of her relationship with the same man, by the ever-efficient Celia Sánchez. Occasionally a boy in some school would see a picture of Castro and blurt out, "That is my papa." Since Castro was surely the "father" of the country, this disconcerted few.

During this time, however, Castro did become involved with a woman who was to give him as close to a "real" family as he was to have. Known by certain insiders simply as *"la mujer de Trinidad,"* the "woman from the city of Trinidad," Dalia Soto del Valle Jorge was still another of those beautiful, black-haired, green-eyed "Cubanas" that Fidel liked so well. Dalia came from a well-to-do family, her father, Enrique, having been associated with a large cigar factory. She had worked as a secretary for the sugar workers' union, where she probably met Fidel. In earlier days, she had gone to a fortune-teller, who looked at her strangely and told her, "You will have the love of a great man." When their affair started in 1962 or 1963, Dalia's family, like Naty's, considered her a "prisoner" of Fidel's, and her father told friends that he had "lost a daughter." As the affair achieved some permanence, his neighbors in Trinidad infuriated him by calling him "the father-in-law," and then, on top of that, by expecting him to gain favors for them from Castro.

By the early 1970s, Dalia had five children by Castro, all of them boys and four of them bearing Fidel's middle name of Alejandro somewhere in their own name. Like Fidelito, they would be educated in the Soviet Union, and one in particular was described as having all of Castro's habits, temper tantrums and all—and thus being Castro's favorite child. Despite the fact that it was "known" in certain "in" circles that Dalia's boys were Fidel's children, Dalia herself remained largely unnoticed. It was Raúl's wife, Vilma, who paraded in public as Cuba's reigning first lady—and even long after she was no longer Raúl's wife.

Despite all the accoutrements and trappings of power in his hands, the enormous failure of the "Ten-Million-Ton Harvest" left Castro dangerously vulnerable to attack in the one area he neither understood intrinsically nor grasped as the looming new power in the world—economics. In December of 1970, the husky, sloe-eyed Carlos Rafael Rodríguez left for Moscow as the head of the Cuban commission for trade with the U.S.S.R., with the intent of renewing the five-year economic treaty with the Soviets. It was the intricate dance, the political minuet, the Kabuki over this renewed treaty that showed more clearly than anything else the Soviets' disillusionment with their "tropical" Communist revolutionary, and it gave to the Soviets, for the first time, the definitive decision-making voice in Cuban economic affairs. In effect, the Russians now took over the planning of the Cuban economy through the setting up of a "Cuban-Soviet Commission of Economic, Scientific, and Technical Collaboration," with the ever-patient survivor, Carlos Rafael Rodríguez, as its head.

This was little realized in a Washington now obsessed with antiwar tumult at home and with negotiations in Paris to get the United States out of Vietnam. Furthermore, on the surface, relations between Cuba and Russia looked rather good. In reality they were not. For example, when Alexander Soldatov, the "tough" and "no-nonsense" Russian who had replaced the smiling Alexeev as ambassador to Cuba, was sent home by Castro in late 1970, the Russians were furious. "Relations fell to one of their lowest points," Arkady Shevchenko, the high-ranking Russian official, related after he had defected to the United States. "Soldatov recalled to me afterwards that his mission was 'mission impossible.' He had been sent to them to squeeze them and cut economic aid. . . . What happened was that Castro didn't even receive him for a long time. When he returned from Cuba, there was a whole year when he was unemployed. He was attached to the office of Gromyko, but he had nothing to do. He used to come to me, wanted to chat. It was pathetic. Cuba was the end of his career."

But the world did not see these private intra–Communist world spats, and in particular, the American intellectuals, journalists, radicals, and liberals who continued to flock to Havana in these years chose doggedly not to see them. How assiduously—and how successfully—Castro wooed these people! What "privileges" he was regally willing to grant them in his society without privilege! What fantastic Potemkin Villages of the body and mind he erected for their theoretical minds and spirits! They, in turn, also had their job—they would serve to build sympathy for Cuba in the United States, thus forging still another protective wall against any American action against him, while also serving as a long-term neutralizing factor in America's capacity to act anywhere in the world.

One of the most unbelievable events of Castro's entire courtship of these Americans occurred in 1977, during the days of the Jimmy Carter administration, when talk was in the air in Washington about a new opening to Cuba. Castro caught the spirit of the moment and sent a message to Senator Frank Church, then head of the powerful Senate Foreign Relations Committee, that if he came to Cuba, the U.S. administration would be "pleased with the results of the visit."

After meeting with Secretary of State Cyrus Vance, Senator Church and his team drew up a list of items they wanted from Castro, which included the release of thirty Americans from Cuban jails and assurances that Cuba would withdraw from its African adventures. Then they boarded the backup plane for Air Force One, the same plane that had carried John F. Kennedy's lifeless body and the hopes of the American nation from Dallas to Washington after the assassination, and flew off to Havana. They considered the deliberate choice of this plane as a kind of gift of high respect for Castro.

Once in Cuba, Castro duly submitted the group to the usual evocative spots, like the guilt-provoking Bay of Pigs, and to the usual lengthy harangues about his days in the Sierra Maestra. There was an "almost boyish sense of 'we won'" about him, Mrs. Frank Church recalled. Senator Church had a moment of déjà vu when he swam with a wet-suited Castro at one of Fidel's private islands; it reminded Frank of all the CIA plots to do Castro in in his wet suit. Finally, Castro suggested that he come aboard the American plane—he wanted to see it.

Once on board, they sipped piña coladas, and Church aide Mark Moran took a picture of Castro sitting in the president's chair, because "Fidel specifically wanted his picture taken while he was sitting in the chair." While there, Moran recalled, "Fidel was shown the phone with the red button for war, and the green button used to call the president in the White House directly." Cuba was never more surreal than at the moment when the Cuban leader, whose involvement in the death of John Kennedy has never been seriously dismissed, sat in the American president's chair in the plane that had so mournfully carried John Kennedy's dead body!

Castro's seemingly warm embrace of his visitors, however, could suddenly become lethal, once he knew of his total power over them. Journalist Herbert Matthews, who persisted in thinking and saying that he was the only one Castro ever really talked to, was treated more and more shabbily by Castro, who derided him at every turn. Finally, Matthews's professional career was ended by his involvement with Castro. The *Times* "declined" to publish his articles on Cuba anymore. *Times* editor Turner Catledge finally decided, "Matthews, despite certain obvious changes in judgment, had lost his credibility as a reporter on Castro."

In 1971, Castro launched out on still another and different cycle of revolutionary transformation. On the surface, when he arrived in Santiago de Chile on November 10, he was merely visiting his "good friend," the Chilean president Salvador Allende. But he stayed almost a month and there was much more to the trip beneath the surface. Castro had alluded to its importance in a press interview as he left Havana, when he said clearly that this was a "symbolic visit . . . between two historical processes."

"Two historical processes"—Cuba and Chile. Cuba, with its *barbudos,* had supposedly traveled the, or at least a, Marxist path. Chile was just beginning on another, more traditional Marxist road, with the first elected Marxist president, the dapper and bourgeois Allende, who was offering to the world "the first nation on earth called to fashion a new model of transition to a socialist society." The two "Marxists" and "Marxisms" could hardly have been more unlike each other and the two men did not really even like each other very much, but Castro's trip was a huge success as the Cuban leader roamed about the beautiful country of Chile like a modern Caesar, speaking to enchanted crowds, visiting, and everywhere employing his brilliant, mesmerizing techniques. When he spoke in Santiago, he requested the "permission" of the crowd. "Maybe you'd be interested in hearing the opinion of a visitor who is a tourist?" he whimsically asked. "Do I have your permission to express it?" To exclamations of "Yes, yes," Castro's Cuban "direct democracy" now arrived full blown in Santiago. "Well, in view of the permission granted me in this sort of plebiscite . . . ," he went on, smiling now, to the shouts of "Fidel, Fidel, Fidel!"

Castro had fun in Chile, at times he even relaxed. Agence France-Presse correspondent Michel Tourguy made the astonishing observation that "there were times when he sat back and spoke as a normal person. One night in Santiago, he was tired. That night, he sat talking, at his side a *barbudo* and two priests with beards. I took a photo of them, and when I looked at it, it was as if it were Christ with his disciples."

But Castro was not in Chile for the carefree joyride he seemed to be having. He was there to cement certain relationships that were of crucial long-term importance. One such relationship was with the new "Christians for Socialism," a group of Christian-Marxists who would form the very spine of the "theology of liberation." This group would support the Nicaraguan Sandinistas when they took over in 1979. Thus, part of the future that would bedevil the United States in the 1980s in Nicaragua was being carefully laid in Chile in 1971.

Actually, if Castro's trip had been more closely studied at the time and not covered merely for its "color," it might have been seen that important new markers were being set. Asked, for instance, whether the Marxists and the Christians would form a "tactical alliance" for the future, Castro responded, interestingly, "No, a strategic alliance in order to realize the social changes that would be necessary for the poor." He also wanted to influence Allende, and his advice to the Chilean president presaged the advice he would later give to the Sandinistas. He told Allende to continue to sell copper in the dollar area and to discourage skilled technicians from leaving Chile, and he told him that good relations with the military were essential until he consolidated support. Castro was becoming more practical, more purely tactical, and less "ideological."

But there was an overarching reason for the trip, as there would be and must be for anything in which Castro invested so much energy and time. That reason was no less than his intent to see and use Chile as the next venue for fighting the United States. He was focusing on the peripheries, challenging the United States from there. Fidel Castro and the United States had met again, on another stage, in a drama he fully intended to turn into a series of endless appointments around the globe. In an extraordinary admission, he told Chilean diplomat Jorge Edwards, "With Cuba and now with Chile, whose example is contagious, the periphery of the Yankee empire has been seriously dented for the first time."

Castro would see to it that revolutionaries everywhere poured into Chile. As the imperialists were also wide awake, Chile was doomed to become the setting for a latter-day Spanish Civil War, where international Fascism and revolution would try out their weapons. Jorge Edwards feared the worst for his homeland. Most probably the country would go through a bloodbath. Had Che not said that it was necessary to create "one, two, many Vietnams" in Latin America? Chile, then, would have the enormous "privilege" of becoming "the first Vietnam in South America."

"In Chile, the problem to us was not Allende but Fidel Castro," CIA chief William Colby revealed to me years later. Fidel's visit? "We took it as rather clear evidence of an alliance between the two countries to carry on the revolution." So the United States now involved itself further in Chile, which became the next cause célèbre for the American Left. The CIA aided the truckers' strikes in Chile and aided the Christian Democrats—to the great criticism of the world. But as the Frank Church congressional committee later verified, it did not in truth take any direct part in Allende's overthrow, as so many on the Left alleged.

When Allende was overthrown by the conservative Chilean army in 1973—thus affirming Castro's belief that you cannot make a revolution with the army intact—socialism died in Chile, and tragically, so did democracy. Under attack in the presidential palace, Allende wore a helmet, gas mask, and bulletproof vest as he ran wildly through the emptied rooms; finally, as the soldiers closed in upon him, he shot himself with a submachine gun that had been a gift from Fidel Castro. On it were engraved the words "To my friend and comrade in arms, Salvador." The country was plunged into Rightist military dictatorship; Castro had failed to create socialism in Chile, but he had managed to play a crucial role in the destruction of Chilean democracy.

None of these setbacks, interestingly enough, set back Castro, for the hemispheric Left simply refused obstinately to believe that "utopian socialism" could not work. So, all through the early 1970s, Castro's foreign policy showed a new and more complex sense of elaboration, of proliferation, and of evolution. He was no longer only fighting dictatorships, he was now offering his aid to fight democracies, not only in Chile but in Costa Rica, Argentina, Uruguay, and particularly in Jamaica. He also forged impressive fraternal links with still other "revolutionary" states: the Leftist military dictatorship that had taken over Peru in 1968, and Forbes Burnham in Guyana, when Burnham in the early 1970s declared Guyana a "cooperative republic" and nationalized its foreign-owned enterprises. At the same time, a different revolutionary language began to appear. Panama, for example, was a "progressive" regime, one with a "gradualist" approach that might allow the "progressive forces" gradually to build coalitions that could challenge American influence. Castro's tactics were becoming far more sophisticated than his early, almost exclusively militarized, guerrilla ideas.

The luxuriant neighboring island of Jamaica became an obvious choice of place for Castro to exercise his new, more complex foreign policy when his "friend," Michael Manley, became prime minister in 1972. Tall and handsome, lean as a greyhound and with dark, charismatic eyes that fixed upon the person, Manley started out with all the stars hovering about him. He was the son of the founding father of his country and he was a man who could move people to tears by his every word. Religious Jamaicans called him Joshua after the beloved leader of the Old Testament. But this Joshua soon turned his back on the ineffable dullness of Jamaican economics, to play happy jester at the modern Third World court. Like Castro, he seemed to think that wealth was manna from Heaven, and that his God-sent mission was simply to divide it up. And he began to pop in and out of Cuba, often secretly, like an adoring cork. In one visit, he said ecstatically, in what would become a famous quote, that he would go "all the way to the mountaintop with Fidel."

For his part, Castro soon had an astonishing amount of influence and power in Jamaica. The Cuban embassy became the center of activity for what was to be the transformation of the island from British-style parliamentary democracy to Jamaican socialism. Cuban planes and officers began flying in and out of Jamaica through their own private airports, unknown and unseen by the people of Jamaica. Manley began ignoring the regular police and army and training a twenty-thousand-man "Home Guards." A Financial Intelligence Unit was set up, ostensibly to deal with economic "crimes," but, with its Cuban advisers, the unit began to target "unconvinced" people in the ministries. Poor and ambitious Jamaican boys were sent to Cuba and came back as *brigadistas* to wait for the uprising. A Suppression of Crime Act gave special powers to the security forces, its intent being to take power away from the judiciary, just as Castro had effectively done in Cuba. Parallel structures were being formed for the day when these structures would become the new legitimacy.

When Manley went back and forth to Cuba in the first half of the 1970s, he would attend all of Castro's meetings and behave like a member of the Cuban Politburo who had an external responsibility. "He was just like one of Castro's lieutenants or emissaries," Sir Edgerton Richardson, the Jamaican diplomat who almost always accompanied him, told me. Manley would wait for almost a full day while Castro went on with his fulminations about people, and at the end of the day he'd have a chance to speak. Never, however, did Manley disagree with Castro, and indeed how could he? A paradigm of the other leaders, Manley saw himself as another Castro. To

Richardson, it appeared that Manley was looking for a "transfer of techniques from one to the other." A transfer of psyches also, perhaps? He smiled when I asked him that, then nodded yes.

In those days, "Joshua" and his friend "Fidel" had some good times together. They would fly off to Africa, for example, for one of the big Non-Aligned Movement meetings and stop in Trinidad to have dinner with the Trinidadian prime minister, Eric Williams. Soon Guyana's Forbes Burnham, newly transformed as a Leftist, would join them in fraternal dining. Then Joshua and Fidel would board another plane, talking like two avid schoolboys—about South Africa, about the dynamics of Soviet-U.S. tension, about cows—until suddenly they saw from their strange vehicle in space the green and inviting African coast of Conakry glistening in the early sunlight. Meanwhile, Manley's son was living well in Havana: he had a town house, servants, and a chauffeur, all provided in "Communism."

But Jamaica didn't "work," either. After eight years of Third Worldism, instructed by Cuba, things only grew stranger and stranger on the island. Instead of more independence and more riches, Jamaica just got poorer and poorer. Charismatic Michael Manley, under his Cuban spell, was coming perilously close economically to killing his country. He didn't mean it; he never said, any more than Castro did, that economics was his long suit; it just happened. All this while, other leaders—less dramatic, less lean, less charismatic, less blessed, with degrees in economics—were getting their countries going. But they didn't get anywhere near the notice that Joshua—and Fidel—got in the world. Those others were not so much fun. They didn't go to the mountaintops, they only worked the valley. Dull, dull, dull.

In the end, the violence of the Cuban-trained Jamaicans began to turn into street massacres. The bauxite industry collapsed. Jamaicans became so angry at the widely disliked Cuban embassy, with all of its artifices and all of its dictates, that they perched in trees around the embassy's yard to spy on what was going on. What they didn't know was that, just before it all fell apart and Edward Seaga became the Conservative prime minister in 1980, Castro had planned to move the Americas Section of Cuban Intelligence to Jamaica, an extraordinary move that would have indicated a further and very specific expansion of Cuban influence throughout the Caribbean. It never happened. But even that failure had virtually no effect on Castro's global plans. There was always a "next time" in his socialism.

Castro's charismatic control of the Non-Aligned Movement meeting in 1976, in Algiers, was superlative; he totally rejected the idea, put forward by moderates, that there were "two imperialisms," the Soviets and the Americans, thus endearing himself once again to the Russians. Indeed, that meeting was the beginning of his effort to transform the Non-Aligned Movement into a more radical and anti-imperialist (read anti-Western and anti-American) posture, in preparation in great part for his hosting of the next NAM conference in Havana in 1979. Castro was now trying to establish himself as a clear broker between the Soviet camp and the Third World.

In the year before the Algiers meeting, Generalísimo Francisco Franco died. Had anyone really been studying Castro's reaction to the death of the Spanish dictator, instead of merely listening to what he said, they would have noticed one of those rare moments when the Cuban leader revealed his inner self.

To many people it seemed "natural" that Castro and Franco would have hated each other; one was a Communist, the other was a Fascist Falangist who had defeated the classic Marxist threat in the Spanish Civil War and then ruled his country with the iron hand of the Catholic caudillo. But such neat ideological classifications most often lie. As a matter of fact, the two twentieth-century strongmen with nineteenth-century roots in Galicia had been filled with admiration for each other for many years. They had yearned to meet, and when Franco died, Castro decreed a full week of official mourning in Cuba.

There had been hints of their "odd caudillo" relationship. Franco never participated in the American embargo of Castro, and kept his Iberia Airlines, the only direct air link between Cuba and Western Europe, flying to Cuba. Indeed, Cuban-Spanish trade under the leadership of two men who were supposed to "hate" each other boomed. Even in the very first year of the Revolution, when the Cuban ambassador to Madrid, José Miró Cardona, met with Franco, he reported to friends that the austere little Spanish generalísimo at the end had asked him, "How is Fidel doing?" Then Franco told him, his voice rising, "Tell Fidel to give hell to the Americans!"

Speaking of Castro, Franco repeatedly told the Spanish journalist Antonio Orlani that "your friend is very intelligent," and a "great strategist," and that "everything he did was that of a good military man" and that "Cuba really had needed a change." For his part, Castro told Orlani that "Franco was right because Franco knew the war and the guerrilla perfectly, and that Franco knew at every moment during the Sierra Maestra where the *Fidelistas* were but in all moments refused to give the information to the Batista government."

The two men's mutual fascination with the old Spanish war of the guerrillas was the key to their fascination with each other, as was that mutual hatred for the United States that had been running through Spanish blood since before "the disaster" of 1898. Franco had been the youngest general since Alexander the Great—Castro was the next youngest. Franco was an abysmal conversationalist, with a squeaky voice, who looked straight ahead in a fixed way at his interlocutor and stared coldly—Castro was the world's most endlessly expressive and antic speaker.

But it was *la guerrilla* that forged the link between the two. Franco admired three men in contemporary history: Mao Tse-tung, Ho Chi Minh, and Fidel Castro, and all three were adepts at the war and trade of guerrillas. Finally, when Franco died, Castro was filled with ever more admiration—Franco, the consummate military man, had died in bed.

24

THE BAY OF PIGS, AGAIN AND AGAIN

Our intelligence services must be deteriorating because we
found out that the Cubans were going to Angola after they
were already there.

—American Secretary of State Henry Kissinger

THAT STRANGE AND UNPRECEDENTED September of 1974 in Portugal, the sovereignty of the beautiful city of Lisbon was so tenuous that one could simply walk, in some astonishment, into the empty presidential palaces and see any of the new Leftist ruling "military junta" who were pensively dissolving the Portuguese empire. Historic, authoritarian, imperial Portugal was falling, but as with so many places across the globe, who was it falling to? A curious little event occurred one day in the southeast African country of Mozambique: as the Portuguese *colonos* sat in one of their beloved cafés, they suddenly heard a page calling. "Mr. Fidel Castro, telephone, please . . ." Silence. Then a mirthful voice shouted out jubilantly, "He is not here, but he won't be long."

That voice was all too prophetic. While "Mother Portugal" herself paused in tremulous confusion at this historic turning point, the colonial "liberation movements," which had been plotting for years for just this moment, groaned to life to position themselves for final victory. What the world completely missed at the time was the degree to which Fidel Castro, waiting and watching in Havana as Portugal and its empire collapsed, was

334

uniquely prepared for his long-planned-for role in Africa. The hundreds of military advisers Che had left in Congo-Brazzaville in 1965 had been planning and scheming for nearly ten years. Now it was time to ignite those embers into revolution.

Almost directly opposite Mozambique on Africa's southwest coast, the country of Angola was now emerging from nearly four centuries of Portuguese domination. It was to be a long and costly transition as two pro-Western movements—the FNLA (National Front for the Liberation of Angola) and UNITA (National Union for the Total Independence of Angola)—and one Marxist movement, the Soviet-supported MPLA (Popular Movement for the Liberation of Angola), became inexorably caught in a final fight for the historic mantle of Portuguese power. But it was to be two outside forces that would win—the Portuguese military's Leftist factions and Fidel Castro.

In the murky months of 1974 and 1975, men walked out of the political underground of Europe and Africa into unaccustomed sunlight, as planners and plotters crisscrossed from Lisbon to Havana, from Angola to Congo-Brazzaville to Guinea-Bissau, and back to Havana again. The Portuguese military Left in particular moved with deliberate drama, back and forth to Cuba, making their deals. A shadowy but important ranking officer in the military junta, and a man later to direct the major Portuguese terrorist force, General Otelo Saraiva de Carvalho, was in Cuba from July 21 to July 30, 1975, and it was then that Castro asked him for permission for the Cuban landing in Angola. When Otelo returned from Havana, he actually burst into tears at the Lisbon airport, saying in rather too loud a voice and with rather too loud a yearning, "If I had such political culture, I'd be the Fidel Castro of Portugal!"

But the key man Castro would depend upon in Africa was the man who would come to be called "*O Almirante Vermelho*," or the "Red Admiral."

Admiral Antonio Rosa Coutinho, named by the Portuguese military junta as the all-powerful commissioner of Angola, found that his tactics fit perfectly with Castro's. From his temporary but powerful perch of power in Angola, he immediately decided and decreed that the Marxist MPLA, with its abundance of doctors, teachers, and intellectuals, "was the only real political force." He would recognize only them, and by giving them money and facilitating the entry of the Cuban troops he would preclude any other victory. Years later, this vigorous man, with the bright eyes of a believer and a totally bald pate, told me without the slightest equivocation that "If it were not for the Cubans, the MPLA would have been annihilated."

In the fall of 1975, Castro's own military actions clearly warned of his long-term plans. In late August and early September, the top Cuban general staff began suddenly appearing in Angola. And in Cuba itself, war exercises began to emphasize not only the holding of positions but also "long marches to occupy extensive areas and the simultaneous use of large numbers of troops from several armies and all military services." Cuban troops from every province were brought together, and Castro formed a two-tier military establishment of top officers, one in Cuba and one in Angola.

All this would never have been possible without the Russians. For it was not true that Cuba "acted alone" in Angola, at worst scorning and at best preempting their Russian comrades. From 1961 on, when Moscow began backing the MPLA, the Russian regime wavered only twice in its support, in 1963 and again in 1974, both being brief periods when it appeared that the MPLA was going to lose.

The Cuban "armada" that Fidel Castro personally sent off to Angola in the dawn of November 7, 1975, might have reminded the romantic of the sailing of the Spanish Armada from Angel Castro's Galicia in 1588, nearly four centuries before. It was a thing to behold, a new creature from a Third World that was flexing its muscles in a remarkably new way. First moved a battalion of Castro's own personal "Prime Minister's Reserve Troops" and the "Special Forces of the Commander-in-Chief," about six hundred and fifty men sent by air. Moving in a dangerous frenzy of bravado flights for thirteen full days, these men stopped in Barbados, flew across a hostile ocean to Guinea-Bissau, then proceeded in secrecy to Congo-Brazzaville, where they landed without lights. Tanned and in summer sportswear, with the air of Cuban insouciance that characterized that era, they looked more like tourists than international revolutionaries. (They carried their machine guns in their briefcases.)

After this first flurry of planes, two passenger ships of four thousand tons each were rigged so their normal capacity of two hundred twenty-six was tripled, with cots set up everywhere, latrines in the cabaret, and weapons literally scattered about the drawing rooms. Cargo ships with a normal capacity of eighty crewmen set sail with as many as one thousand soldiers, plus armored cars, armaments, and explosives. Conditions were so bad that one of Castro's bodyguards compared the ships' "inhuman conditions" to those of the "Negroes in the slave trade." But for Castro, there was a certain sadistic pleasure in the picture of such misery. "It was much worse on the *Granma*," he said unsmiling.

As Gabriel García Márquez observed: "He saw off all the ships, and before each departure he gave a pep talk to the soldiers in the La Cabaña Theater. He personally had picked up the commanders of the battalion of special forces that left in the first flight and had driven them himself in his Soviet jeep to the foot of the plane ramp." García Márquez thought that his Cuban friend was repressing a "deep sentiment of envy for those going off to a war that he could not participate in. There was no spot on the map of Angola that he couldn't identify or a physical feature that he hadn't memorized. . . . He could quote any figure on Angola as if it were Cuba, and he spoke of Angolan cities, customs, and people as if he had lived there his entire life."

Castro's strategy was clear: with Soviet logistical support, he would rout the South African troops who had belatedly entered Angola across the southern Namibian border, and at the same time put the blame for his own new kind of "interventionism" on the apartheid government of South Africa. Not following but leading the hapless MPLA, who were typical African urban and Marxist-prone intellectuals, he would assure that Angola's capital city, Luanda, would be taken by the MPLA before the "independence day" the retreating Portuguese had proclaimed for November 11. The MPLA would then "be" the government in fact of Angola, thus sidestepping the promises of elections already agreed to by the three Angolan movements.

For years, Castro would argue vociferously and (to many) convincingly in the world forums of public opinion that his actions in Angola were different from other "interventions" because he had entered Angola in response to a legitimate "call" from the "legitimate government of Angola." Michael Manley trustingly recalled, believing that Castro had preempted the Russians in Angola: "Fidel told me privately that he figured Moscow couldn't do anything after he moved into Angola. . . . Fidel told me that he had called the central committee together at eight P.M. and they had talked it out till the early morning hours. When the Cuban soldiers were set to fly across the Atlantic, Raúl was on a plane to Moscow. He found the Soviets so infuriated at what they had done that it took two days to calm them down."

As with virtually all the other accepted "givens" about Castro, the world believed something that was palpably absurd and even easily disproven. There *was* no government of Angola when Castro sent in his troops. The beautiful colonial city of Luanda was in the throes of anarchy. Castro knew from his own experience that the government was going to be "elected" by those who took Luanda first. So it was that on November 11, 1975, with all the other movements successfully kept out of Luanda by the intervention of Cuban troops, the MPLA entered the city and proclaimed the country independent. With the absolutely essential help of Castro, the master craftsman of new political legitimacies, the MPLA had created still another revolutionary "legitimacy" and one that was again directly and uniquely threatening to the United States.

Writing of the euphoria that Castro felt at the time, García Márquez recalled delightedly how Castro had again pulled the beard of the Americans because on November 24, 1975, there were many more Cuban soldiers, military specialists, and civilian technicians in Angola "than Henry Kissinger knew about."

Cuba emerged triumphant from Angola. By spring of 1977, Castro was making a widely publicized tour of Africa. Algeria, Libya, South Yemen, Somalia, Ethiopia, Tanzania, Mozambique, and Angola: much like a Caesar inspecting the outer provinces of Rome, Castro spoke of the heady day coming when "feelings will go beyond the narrow horizons of a country's boundaries."

But it was Castro's visit to Luanda that spring that marked the true distance he had traveled. He met with some five hundred of his men outside the capital in a former Portuguese base. The sun was blazing, enervating heat waves rippling over the silent green land lying in the wreckage of revolution. Beautiful Luanda's winding cobblestoned streets, lined by multicolored buildings, were as quiet as a grave; even her poor black people had escaped to the outskirts, where they waited like frozen shadows poised on the hilltops that once overlooked a bustling, happy city. But, for all the unhappiness of the country, Castro seemed to his men a Hercules that day, as he paced back and forth before them. Never before had they seen him in such a mood; never before had they seen this intrinsically secretive and consummately self-protecting man so expansive. Indeed, only in such a moment of utter triumph and among his own men could he be so grandly and dangerously candid.

Exactly ten years later, in the spring of 1988, I spoke with the high-ranking Cuban intelligence operative Florentino Aspillaga, who was one of the men with Castro that day. "Castro was very content," Aspillaga recalled. "Cuban troops had triumphed. When he arrived, there was a euphoria—it was like Napoleon coming. He could have been Napoleon arriving at any of his occupied territories. That day he said to us, 'I can speak for the first time really honestly. Here, nobody is working for the CIA. I can talk openly.' Then he spoke about his charisma, about the nature of his mastery of the Cuban people, but also about the prestige he had now in Africa, how he had triumphed in Angola and Mozambique. It was the first time I ever saw him speak so about himself. I remember perfectly that he spoke about his 'charisma' as one of his major virtues. He spoke for about one and a half hours. He spoke about his principal virtue as being 'my psychology over the multitudes. . . .' The audience was euphoric. When you looked at him like this, you also realized that he was much more Gallego, he was not Cuban. He spoke exactly as a conquistador." He also said that his real dream was of "an America united under a common president." He saw himself as president of all of Latin America.

He was indeed a modern-day conquistador. With his move into Angola, using the troops and the influence left behind by Che as his base, Castro made political and military history that was little realized at the time. It was the first military invasion eastward across the south Atlantic; it showed that the Cubans could now be readied for overseas combat; it illustrated the degree to which Cuba, far from being only some poor "surrogate" of the Soviet Union, was actually a partner of the superpower and of inestimable importance and use to that superpower. But most of all, Castro was in Angola because it was one of the three places in the world where United States–supported forces were at war with Soviet-supported forces—Angola was simply one more new and far more extravagant stage on which to fight the United States.

Behind these astonishing new realities, Castro now held a series of geopolitical suppositions fully as extravagant as his dreams. For Castro had concluded that the "correlation of forces" in the world was now against the United States. He calculated that the United States defeat in Vietnam, coming at the time of the increased strategic reach of the U.S.S.R. and the 1973 oil embargo, had tilted the balance of power toward the Third World and the socialist camp. When the United States so quickly washed its hands of

Angola, the Vietnam-exhausted Congress pushing through the Clark Amendment forbidding U.S. aid to Angola, Castro was further convinced, as were the Soviets, that America was in the political throes of impotence and in the historic embrace of inevitable decline. Castro had never expected such largess from his enemy.

How his history repeated, and repeated, and repeated, always woven around that same core of hatred, like the cycles on the Buddhist monk's wheel of life. On the fifteenth anniversary of the Cuban victory at the Bay of Pigs, Castro spoke at Havana's Karl Marx Theater about his triumph at Girón (the Red Beach at Bahía de Cochinos). "The victory in Angola," he cried emotionally, "was the twin sister" of the victory at the Bay of Pigs. "For the Yankee imperialists, Angola represents . . . an African Girón."

Finally, Cuba's onslaught into Angola ended a budding "spring" of new relations that had been started between the Gerald Ford administration and Cuba in 1975. The secret talks with Havana begun by Secretary of State Henry Kissinger were halted and, as American diplomat Wayne Smith put it: "Subsequently, American administrations were to point to the Angolan case as evidence that talking to the Cubans is of little avail." In fact, it was.

Moreover, all the while he was in Angola, Castro was also serving as an invaluable smoke screen to the Soviets' role there. It was a smoke screen that was quite necessary to convince the Americans that the Soviets were not carrying on subversion in Africa, a fact that, if known, would have harmed the tentative détente emerging just then between the superpowers, not to mention the 1975 European Security Conference to freeze the borders of the East European countries Russia had annexed after World War II. Having a Fidel Castro who moved "on his own" certainly served the Russians' purposes; but the fiction equally served Castro's, for it maintained his image of independent invincibility in the sensitive nationalist psyches of the Third World.

For the first time, as well, power began flowing not only from Moscow to Havana but from Havana to Moscow. It would be Havana that would commit the Soviets to a greater role in Africa, Havana who would radicalize Soviet foreign policy; and, though it could not be seen in those years, it would be Havana who would also lead the Russians to the beginning of the overextension of their power and reach that would eventually hobble them.

But as he dug in to stay, and stay, and stay, Castro's conquistadorial involvement in Angola illustrated with rare clarity how uncannily he was able not only to export fighting men but also to export, inspire, and impose the structures he had created in Cuba. "Liberated" Angola was forced structurally and ideologically into the same mold as "revolutionary" Cuba. The Angolan "Popular Armed Forces for the Liberation of Angola" was structured exactly after the Cuban army. Castro coined a new money for Angola, the Cuanza, named in homage to a battle the Cubans (not the Angolans) had fought at that river. "Special stores" with goods from France, England, and other European countries were soon established, only for the gallant directors of the revolution. Hospitals and large buildings were reserved exclusively for Cuban officials, so much so that one Cuban soldier noted that Angolans could not use the hotels "even on the first night of their honeymoons!" The best beaches were for Cubans only and soon had "private" signs: just like those placed by the hated United Fruit Company on Puerto Rico Beach in the Banes of Castro's youth.

Castro surrounded the Angolan president Neto with intelligence and counterintelligence and with a Cuban-trained bodyguard. President Neto had no need to know that this meant that his meetings were overheard by Cuban intelligence, advised and trained in turn by the Soviet KGB and the East German intelligence. Cuba even exported its dismal economics: between 1975 and 1977, Angola's gross domestic production and growth rate decreased by 15 percent.

As always, Castro used the African "experience" on many complex levels, including most definitely the spiritual. At home, he had already to a large degree "dereligionized" Cuba's African Santería cult. No one leader governed Santería. With no solid unity, the cult was no threat to him. So he had moved ahead to "folklorize" Santería, and now he used this new "folklore" to cement Cuban ties to Africa. "Pichardo," a famous *santero,* recalled years later in Miami that "As early as 1963, Fidel began to recruit people from our form of worship into folkloric dances. He wasn't taking Santería as a form of worship, he was really selling folklore as the true spiritual condition of Cuba. We went from slavery to a worse type of oppression. You see, Fidel wanted to find something in common with the African continent. Recently, one of the African kings went to visit Castro. Now he has something even to offer even a king—look at me, this nice man who has helped African religion in Cuba!"

Then Castro gave Angola *its* assignment: it was now to be the African regional center of infiltration and subversion for the Revolution. "Many

African countries and Yemen on the Arabian Peninsula suddenly discovered Cuba which, although thousands of miles away, had the backing of the Soviet Union to enable it to challenge bigger powers," Castro's old professor, Dr. Herminio Portell Vilá, noted. "African dictators and would-be dictators used the name of Fidel Castro as if he were a protective deity, a bearded, white 'Shango.' Using his name as a threat and a shield, they successfully worked their magic against the U.N., Washington, Bonn, London, Paris, Rome, Madrid and others who made no effort to stop the Communist drive."

Finally, Castro had accomplished something else of supreme importance to his own power and to his own revolution. American diplomat Thomas Reston was sent to Havana in the Carter years and his instructions were to tell the Cubans how serious Washington was about their getting out of Africa. "I had a conversation at that time with a high official of the Cuban Film Institute," Reston recalled, "and he told me, 'We won't withdraw troops from Africa.'" Why? "'There have been generations that have moved through the Revolution. The first generation made the Revolution in 1959. In 1962, the literacy campaign was for the next wave of kids. Then there was the Great Ten-Million-Ton *zafra*. The current one is Angola. This is the revolutionary experience of this generation—the way they receive revolutionary fervor.'"

But what the intensely self-absorbed Castro did not see was the emergence against him of the same revolutionary dialectic that he had so masterfully employed against his enemies. Now, suddenly, others were studying him, just as in his early years he had studied Hitler, Mussolini, and Primo de Rivera for roads to power. Even as Castro was at his most triumphant in Angola, the pro-Western UNITA guerrillas, whom he thought he had defeated, embarked upon a Mao Tse-tung–style "Long March" across the savannahs and deserts of Angola. They walked for four months, starting with two thousand men and ending up with sixty-nine men. As they wandered on their odyssean journey, they studied the Cubans and began to see that what the Cubans had relied upon for victory in Angola, the experience in the Sierra Maestra, for instance, was not valid for them.

"The Sierra Maestra experience was very short," UNITA's foreign minister Pedro Ngueve Jonatão Chingunji finally concluded, as one guerrilla studied another for the lessons of war. "It was only a specific situation in historic circumstances. It was successful against a political climate that was favorable and when they moved into Angola, they found a similar syndrome and they saw an easy victory. The Cubans were fighting the illusion of their success in the Sierra Maestra. They were playing the big winners, the conquerers, emphasizing big weapons but not really knowing guerrilla warfare. The Cubans, when they were flying in Angola, were following the rivers. . . . And we—we were beginning to fight the real guerrilla wars."

But for the moment, it was Fidel Castro who was reaping all the fruits of triumph. After Angola, he moved still more of his troops—but this time, with the Russians in charge—into Ethiopia, making it uniquely possible for the bloodthirsty "Marxist" leader Mengistu to remain in power. Only in Ethiopia, the Russians dropped the pretense of Angola that in effect they were only following the Cubans, thus introducing still another revolutionary "model" into the well of peculiar Cuban expansionism in the Third World. Even the General Assembly of the United Nations gave Castro its approval by recognizing the "legitimacy" of the struggles for "national liberation" in Africa and urging other states to provide similar "moral and material assistance." He was at the dizzying height of his powers—a true Third World Caesar. To see his outlying provinces, lands, and tribes he now needed far more than Angel Castro's perch atop the old house at Birán. And there would be still more.

Just as there could have been no success for the MPLA in Angola without Cuba, so, too, the Marxist Sandinista revolution in Nicaragua would never have existed without Fidel Castro. These were the young Nicaraguans he had wooed to Havana immediately after they formed the FSLN, or the Sandinista National Liberation Front, in a poor *barrio* of Tegucigalpa on July 28, 1961. The front was named after the famous Nicaraguan anti-American guerrilla fighter Augusto Sandino, who had fallen in guerrilla war to the American-supported Nicaraguan military in the defining 1930s. Unquestionably, Sandino was one of Castro's paternal inspirations, and now, in turn, Castro became an inspiration to Sandino's namesakes. The FSLN was so emotionally and politically cloned to Cuba that it even adopted the red and black colors of the 26th of July, and Sandinista Tomás Borge hailed Castro as the very "resurrection of Sandino."

But it was in the last year before the Sandinistas' historic *triunfo* in July 1979, a triumph that would become *the* foreign policy issue of Ronald Reagan's administration, that Castro played his most crucial role in Nicaragua.

He called the directorate of the three groups of Sandinistas to Havana for a series of meetings and presented the divided leaders with dire warnings. He told them that he would support them only if they unified. Political unity, economic moderation, and confrontation avoidance: that was the triumvirate of advice he offered this new generation of revolutionaries. One meeting lasted forty-eight hours and, in those long and didactic hours, Castro told the Sandinistas to avoid confrontation with Washington and thus to get its aid, to refrain from breaking with the Catholic Church, and to maintain the private sector so as to avoid such unpopular measures as rationing.

Castro's moves were largely tactical, but he also was uncertain that, with the increasingly high cost of "loving" Cuba, the Soviets would support still another revolutionary state in the area. And he knew he could not send massive numbers of armed soldiers to Nicaragua, as he had to Africa, without inviting confrontation with the United States. So, as the Sandinistas catapulted toward their own revolutionary denouement, it seemed to the world that the Cubans were playing a surprisingly minor role. They weren't. Behind the scenes, Havana was the intermediary and coordinator of virtually every step of the Nicaraguan rebellion. Even during the actual fighting, ever-present in the communications center of his Ministry of the Interior, Castro personally oversaw the fighting, monitored broadcasts of the failing and increasingly brutal Somoza army, and passed information—and precise orders—on to the Sandinistas.

The battle-wearied Sandinistas—those heroic *muchachos* with their red and black bandannas and their insouciantly noble bearing—marched on to, lurched into, and flowed triumphally over Managua on July 19, 1979, thus finally overthrowing the hated American-supported dictator Anastasio Somoza. The inner leadership still wisely hid their Marxist beliefs behind the creation of a broad front led by still another "*Los Doce,*" or another symbolic "The Twelve," all prominent and ideologically "acceptable" citizens.

On Moncada's twenty-sixth anniversary that July 26, Fidel also toasted the Sandinistas, his very own "*muchachos,*" with revealing words, averring that their victory was "not only . . . over forty-five years of Somocismo . . . but over one hundred fifty years of foreign domination." As he once again obliquely attacked the United States, Sandinista Humberto Belli recalled seeing a "kind of very subtle cynical smile on his face."

Although it was not generally known in Cuba or in Nicaragua, Castro also often flew clandestinely that first year to Managua, landing at a special

344

airstrip at Montelimar on what had been one of the large elegant estates of Somoza. (At first the Sandinistas made a big show of opening Somoza's wealthy home on Sundays so "the people" could splash in the pool, but soon it was closed behind a "wall of military secrecy.") By the first anniversary of the Nicaraguan revolution, Castro was no longer keeping his visits to Managua secret. He was now ready quite openly to dare the United States, which was becoming increasingly troubled over the Marxization of the Sandinistas.

In 1980, Castro arrived on a steamy tropical July day to every possible honor at Managua's renamed Augusto César Sandino International Airport, striding confidently down the steps of the plane and embracing everyone in sight with his huge bearlike grasp. The city was decorated with the red and black banners, and when Castro stepped beyond the row of nine Sandinista comandantes who were there to greet him, onlookers could not miss the fact that they were wearing uniforms almost identical to his. He had promised not to dominate the proceedings, and so he spoke for a mere forty minutes, reminiscing about that time long ago when the Bay of Pigs fighters had sailed away from this very country to bring back some "hairs from his beard." His beard was not only intact, he told the roaring crowd, his beard was now, at this very moment, in Managua. America's fight with the Sandinistas, he intoned solemnly, with his special, pointed reminiscence, was still another "ongoing Girón."

By mid-1982, Castro had two thousand security advisers and four thousand civilian professionals working throughout the country in a wide variety of activities. In 1981, he gave Sandinista Nicaragua $64 million; in 1982, $130 million. Meanwhile, he was also bringing twelve hundred Nicaraguans a year to Cuba for training. In both Managua and Havana, the Cubans taught the Sandinistas the techniques of "hospitality" for visitors, as well as how to recognize those societal vacuums in the United States and Europe that could be filled by them. Because of the knowledge that had flowed from Moscow to Peking to Prague to East Berlin to Havana to Managua, the Sandinistas soon understood Castro's sophisticated political techniques and they used them most effectively against the United States. "When they see an area they want to go into," Latin Americanist Douglas Payne analyzed, "they look at all the players—the middle-class, students, clergy—the forces that create U.S. foreign policy."

Meanwhile, the United States not only did not instinctively understand this kind of deliberate deceit and subversion, but all of its principles in the world denied its very existence, putting the country at a terrible disadvantage. From 1979 to 1985, upwards of one hundred thousand Americans alone were brought to Nicaragua under programs of ideological neutralization. Almost to a man and woman, they took their new mind-sets back home to lobby the U.S. Congress on behalf of the Sandinistas and against American foreign policy in Nicaragua.

There even came to be a word in Spanish for such disciplined deception in the name of revolution. It was called the *manto,* or the "mantle," with all that meant in terms of cloaking reality. After studying the Sandinistas' webs of deception, political analyst Douglas Payne noted that the *manto* was "central to the success and survival of any Marxist-Leninist revolutionary group that aims to secure and expand a foothold in close proximity to its perceived and powerful enemy."

Most important, Nicaragua and Cuba met in kindred psychologies. Both Hispanic, their national psyches were based on deductive logic that derived facts from faith-based definitions of reality, not from empirical proof and experience. The Sandinistas, like Castro, believed only in revolutionary transformation, not reform. In Sandinista analyst David Nolan's terms, "They defined imperialism as the external foe over which the Revolution must triumph," saw "bourgeois consciousness as the internal enemy," and believed ultimately that the "essence of the Revolution is spiritual transformation."

The degree to which tactics, strategies, and techniques flowed from Castro and his Cuba to Sandinista Nicaragua was even more amazing than the degree to which they had flowed to Angola. Castro defined the limits of cultural expression with "inside the Revolution, anything, outside, nothing." Sandinista minister of the interior Tomás Borge reflected that idea with almost identical words: "Anything inside the Revolution, nothing outside the Revolution." Both Castro and the Sandinistas used his phrase "direct democracy" to describe what was, effectively, total control from the top, and the Nicaraguans added a slightly new type of gathering called *cara al pueblo,* or "facing the nation," in which the comandantes faced the people in what was most truly a Moorish or feudal manner, the "lord dispensing justice in return for loyalty." In Cuba, *las masas* shouted, "Commander in chief, order us!" In Managua, they shouted, "National Directorate, order us!" Finally, both built nearly identical "military civilizations."

But there was one distinct new element in the Nicaraguan revolution, and both Castro and the Sandinistas grasped it and its importance at once—

in Managua, there were Christians who joined the revolution and gave it a new respectability and force in the United States and in the West. Significantly, the "liberation theology" Christians in Nicaragua were the direct descendants of the "Christians for Socialism" Castro had met and wooed in Chile in 1971. With this conversion of the Christian Left, Castro brilliantly created for himself new and deeper "political space" in the life of the hemisphere at exactly the moment new currents of theological thinking were making the profoundly antagonistic "religions" of Christianity and Marxism seem almost compatible.

It should not be surprising that the Sandinistas tried to emulate Castro's Cuba, for in those "glory" days they saw Cuba as everywhere triumphant over the capitalists. They even interpreted Castro's war in Angola as a Cuban victory over South Africa, believing, as early Sandinista Arturo Cruz, Jr., put it, that "for the first time in history, a Third World power had met a First World power in combat and triumphed." And so "Cuba's image changed from that of a Soviet naval base in the Caribbean to a true global power, and the Sandinistas decided that the United States feared Cuba too much to interfere in Nicaragua."

As for the Soviets, they saw the victory in Nicaragua as another U.S. defeat, this time in the very land mass of the Western Hemisphere. In an important act on October 20, 1980, the Soviet Central Committee formally added the countries of Central America to the list of states of Africa and Asia that could be expected to undergo revolutionary changes of a "socialist orientation." They owed their revolutionary "son," Fidel Castro, a good deal—and he well knew it.

And, of course, Castro had his own plans for Nicaragua. As he had in Angola, Castro gave Nicaragua an assignment. It was to be the new command point for Latin American insurgencies, just as Luanda was for African ones. The little city of Managua, its center totally destroyed by the 1970 earthquake, now hid secret compounds of guerrilla terrorist groups from all over the world—often located incongruously in the American-style shopping centers that had popped up from the rubble of the earthquake.

Like so much of what happens in Latin America, the Sandinista triumph had a ripple effect that extended the tremors of revolution well beyond the borders even of Central America. One of the most significant consequences was that, for the first time, the Palestine Liberation Organization, which

Castro had wooed and aided since the Tricontinental Conference in 1966, found its way into the very body of Central America and the "American" hemisphere. When the Sandinistas came to power in Nicaragua, they took the unprecedented act of giving the PLO not a compound in Managua, like the other "liberation movements," but an actual "embassy," which would in turn expand PLO influence and aid to the other guerrilla movements in Central America. The link between the Sandinistas and the PLO was as strong as iron—it was their mutual hatred of the United States.

The meetings between PLO leaders and Castro in Havana swung typically between that humorous surrealism and that ominous portent that was so typical of the Cuban leader. A PLO spokesman in Washington, the young Hasan Rahman, recalled that when he visited Havana, "Fidel gave me an *abrazo,* or embrace, and I had the distinct feeling that his hands were on my waist, looking for guns." On the day that Anwar Sadat was assassinated in Cairo by Moslem fundamentalists, Rahman recalled Castro's reaction: "He had gotten five, six, seven videos from TVs around the world, all of the shooting, and he sat there obsessively, watching them over, and over, and over." Castro was going to die in bed, like father Franco.

The PLO introduced Castro not only to the Middle East, where three thousand Cubans fought alongside the Syrians against Israel in the 1973 war (Washington at one point asked the Israelis to design an attack especially to destroy the Cuban troops there, but it came to naught), but they also introduced him to the Khomeini revolution in Iran. Castro had great sympathy for both Khomeini and his revolution, and there were dramatic links between the two men and their passions. First, they shared a mutual abhorrence for the United States—for capitalism, for modernization, technology, popular culture, and for the profound loss of identity that all of those modern engines of change entailed. What brought their two revolutions together was that neither was, at heart, one of those typical post–World War II colonial revolutions where Kenya/Congo/Algeria fought England/Belgium/France in good clean political fights, won, drove the colonials out, and then assumed perfectly normal and even cordial relations with them forever after. The two leaders— Castro and Khomeini—also uncannily resembled each other. "When I saw Khomeini on television," Professor Maurice Halperin, who had known Castro so well in Havana in the 1960s, said, "I said that those were Fidel's eyes."

No, both the Cuban and the Iranian revolutions were something else. And both leaders felt the tie. Theirs were totally new-style revolutions, fighting against the United States not to win independence but to save some vestige of authentic identity. And these new "identity revolutions" were incomparably more vicious, neurotic, and frustrated than the old-style political/military revolutions, because, as the Iranian scholar Majid Tehranian put it, "The new identity politics tend to be totalistic in conception, calling for the extermination of the enemy."

Neither of these countries had been in truth directly oppressed by the United States. Instead, the United States, as the first truly modern nation, the first truly universalist nation, had crept into their very souls on the wings of its ceaseless cultural domination. American "cultural imperialism" flew across the airwaves, poisoned them with its "vulgarly relativistic" television and books, and tarnished their very souls with the ambiguity and slipperiness of its influence. The United States stood as the example and the agent for changes which they could hate or aspire to but never reach.

Despite the international importance of opening Central America to the PLO, the Sandinista victory had an even more immediate and long-run consequence as Castro now moved to support the Salvadoran Marxist guerrillas of the Farabundo Martí National Liberation Front, or FMNLF, who were challenging El Salvador's old Rightist alliance of the landed classes and the army. With Salvadoran rebels, it was exactly the same as with the Sandinistas: Castro forced a putative and uncomfortable, but workable, unity on their part in exchange for arms on his. Managua, unlikely city of *gringo* shopping centers, immediately became El Salvador's "metropole." A mere four months after the Sandinistas had triumphed, Castro told the Salvadoran guerrillas that they and Guatemala would be "next," and that Honduras would now be turned into "one huge Ho Chi Minh Trail." As arms poured in from Russia, Europe, and even Ethiopia (but always via Nicaragua), Castro's patronal intercession had literally opened Central America to a Soviet penetration in the Western Hemisphere never before dreamed of.

But the fact that Castro was never only preoccupied with dictatorships was once again shown in his intent to overthrow Costa Rican democracy. The very next year after the Sandinistas' triumph, he formed a group of Costa Rican guerrillas, which began training on the Río San Juan just across the border in Nicaragua. "They were preparing for the Central American revolution," the prominent Sandinista intelligence officer Alvaro José Baldizon realized after visiting these camps. "They were expecting the

'Vietnamization' of Central America." And when Castro actually visited the border regions on one of his visits to Nicaragua, he stood there, looking at the peaceful little land of Costa Rica, and scoffed, "A nurses' strike could bring that down."

"The idea," Castro's old history teacher, Herminio Portell Vilá, concluded of Castro's Panama policy, speaking of "unredeemed lands," was also "to link the Panama Canal and Guantánamo as *terra irredenta* to be rescued from the United States." Indeed, it was the pressures upon Washington, from Castro and fellow Panamanian strongman Omar Torrijos, that finally did force Washington to agree to give up the canal in 1978. Never in the history of man had a great and still-powerful nation turned over to a small and "powerless" nation like Panama such a unique geopolitical and structural treasure!

During these years, American policy constantly wavered, and was always too little and too late and too unmanipulating to prevent Castro's long-planned-for and brilliantly strategized plans from coming to fruition. For some of the Miami Cuban-Americans, there was no more hope. In 1977, former Cuban president Carlos Prío, along with six other prominent Cuban-Americans, met with Carter's secretary of state, Cyrus Vance, and they were again momentarily filled with hope and faith that the United States would finally take strong measures against Cuba. But Vance told them that, despite the provocations, the United States was not ready to do anything. Prío, with his aging-playboy good looks, insisted that "despite this, we are going to go on fighting," but he did not mean it. His ambivalent fight was finally over. Shortly after that meeting, a melancholy Prío, who could have been the savior of the Cuba he had led for so long, picked up his .32 revolver and shot himself fatally in the chest: like Eddy Chibás, like so unfathomably many Cubans. It was, Cuba's dedicated chronicler of suicides, Guillermo Cabrera Infante, wrote, "the only viable route of departure from history, and the only port of entry into eternity . . . which absolves us."

Castro's one maneuver, manipulation, event in these years that turned out to be a mistake went largely unnoted. His real reverse "Bay of Pigs" turned out to be something quite unexpected. This was his sudden agreement, through the auspices of pro-Castro Cubans in Miami like the shadowy Bernardo Benes, to allow Cuban exiles to return. Castro actually believed that these men and women of Mercedes-Benzes and the bustling cafés of Calle Ocho, of skyscraper Miami banks and Elizabeth Arden salons, with their modish clothes and their Argentine-sleek hairdos, would be impressed with revolutionary Cuba. Instead, their presence totally and uniquely unnerved the island.

Responding to the liberal policies of President Jimmy Carter in trying to "resolve the Cuban question," and in particular to the signing of a maritime and fishing agreement between the United States and Cuba and a relaxation of the embargo, Castro decided that the hated *gusanos,* or "worms," he had thrown out of their native land might be allowed to return. They were magically cleansed and transmogrified into *la comunidad,* or "the external community," and they were even to take part in an actual "dialogue" established by Castro.

So it was that in 1979 no fewer than one hundred thousand of this alchemized group returned from exile to gaze and gawk at the "New Cuba," to wander disconsolately and with tearful sentiment among their old friends and their old homes. By the time they left, they had deposited some one hundred million dollars in Castro's Cuba (he had set up special "dollar stores" for them, charging outrageous prices for everything), but Castro was soon to learn that this money came expensive indeed. For it irrevocably changed how the Cubans who had stayed in Cuba saw their country and themselves. "We thought we were going to see discriminated-against poor people," Manuel Antonio Sánchez Pérez, then a high-ranking Cuban official, recalled. "What kind of Cuban from America came? They had houses, university educations. . . . They asked us what did we need? A ventilator? A radio? It was humiliating to us." He paused. "And we felt that someone had lied to us."

For their part, those who returned found their former homeland "dull and ugly." When Virginia Schofield visited her home near Fidel's in Oriente, she found that Cuba was existing "as if time had stopped . . . as if this was some tropical Poland. . . . It was sort of like living in the womb. . . ."

25

FIDEL'S GRENADA—DEATH IN
A SMALL PLACE

> Comandante Gil then read out a quotation from Karl Marx:
> "We have chosen a path in which we can accomplish the most
> for mankind, then nobody can show us because they are only
> sacrifice for everyone. Then we enjoy no poor limited egoistic
> joy for our happiness belongs to thousands. Our deeds will
> live on working eternally [sic]."
>
> —Verbatim minutes from the Extraordinary Meeting
> of the Central Committee of the New Jewel
> Movement, September 25, 1983, taken from the
> Grenada Documents

WHILE THE EYES of the world were focused on the sudden triumph of the Sandinistas in Nicaragua in July 1979, few realized that another Castro-inspired revolution had come to pass in the single most unlikely spot for revolution in the entire Caribbean, Grenada.

That March, a small band of only forty men had overthrown the strange government of the island's very strange leader, Sir Eric Gairy, a dark-spirited man who could often be found out in the dark of night vigilantly searching the skies for UFOs while his brutal "Mongoose Gang" was out terrorizing the gentle Grenadian people.

How different Castro's young revolutionaries seemed from the evil Gairy. "The revo," as the rebels fondly called the change, announced itself over the local radio station when the reggae music suddenly stopped. The rebels then seized the True Blue army headquarters, and it was all over in forty-eight hours—from "true blue" to "revo" in one fantastic night.

The leader of the coup was a lithely handsome young bearded man, Maurice Bishop. A romantic revolutionary, "Brother Maurice" had been trained as a lawyer (and also in British radical politics) in London, where he devotedly absorbed Trinidadian V. S. Naipaul's "London words, London abstractions, capable of supporting any meaning." Some of the more history-oriented people on the gleaming pearl necklace of islands that made up the archipelago known as the Grenadines whispered that, yes, Bishop had accomplished something important on Grenada—this was the first coup in the deeply and properly British parliamentary history of the West Indies—and coups were not British, they were Latin. Indeed, Bishop's "New Jewel Movement" adepts were soon boasting breathlessly that theirs was finally nothing less than the first Marxist revolution in the English-speaking world!

The charming Bishop early viewed Fidel "like a father," Bishop's mother often said, and that October, when Castro spoke at the U.N. for the first time since his spectacular speech there in 1960, Bishop literally leaped from his seat and ran to Castro to give him a Khrushchevian bear hug as applause resonated across the hall.

But the inevitable paranoia of the Cuban Revolution inexorably began to seep into Grenada, an island where interestingly enough there had never been any anti-Americanism. In 1980, barely a year after the coup, I went on May Day to the lovely Grenadian seaside town of Gouyave, whose weath-ered old houses cling like perched birds, precariously, to the corners of cliffs hanging out over the sea. The ideological "mix" of the crowd was quite extraordinary, with Grenadian trade unionists marching out on one side of the field singing "The Battle Hymn of the Republic," and a Catholic priest, not wanting yet to choose, saying to the crowd, "Comrades, a prayer. . . ." When Bishop stood up before them, he told the breathless crowd darkly that he was flying directly to Cuba to sign a "nonaggression" pact with Castro because Cuba was about to be attacked by the United States. Maybe, Bishop said with a certain hysteria in his voice, Cuba and Grenada would even attack the United States.

By chance, the next day I ran into Bishop when his Cubana de Aviación plane swept back into the mountainous Pearl's Airport of Grenada. By this time the threat of the day before had passed like some sudden squall. When I asked him about the "war" with the United States, Bishop looked at me with his eyes narrowed, as though he had almost forgotten. "Oh yes," he said, remembering suddenly, "there was to be a joint communiqué, but we didn't have enough time to get into it." He waved agreeably and strolled away. Some wars pass quickly.

But if the mood of Maurice Bishop was almost always jovial, the potential at this moment for Caribbean revolution was joylessly real. To the south, Guyana had turned to the Left in the early 1970s; Surinam was on the brink; in 1979 St. Lucia also began to move to the Left. Now, in Grenada, Castro lost no time in supporting his revolutionary "leap" into the eastern Caribbean with tactical backup. By November of 1979, he had sent three hundred Cuban construction workers to build the new airport Grenada so badly needed, and he agreed to pay half of the fifty-million-dollar construction cost. Rumors spread throughout the island that there were truckloads of Cuban arms hidden somewhere. The special military zones, off-limits to ordinary Grenadians and run by Cubans, did not need to be rumored—they could be seen, but never entered.

For Grenada, Castro was to serve as an intermediary in Soviet arms transfers, to be delivered at night to hidden depots across the island, usually during power outages conveniently planned by the New Jewel thinkers. In return, Grenada was to provide information on the other "liberation movements" in the Caribbean. These agreements seemed unimportant, but in truth they provided Castro with his first real opening into that netherworld of the English-speaking Caribbean that his Latin self had never understood. For their part, the Cubans provided the Grenadians with a new window on the world, introducing them to the labyrinth of Third World and Soviet international front organizations. Of course, no one could say that all the Cuban help was perfect. At one political bureau meeting, it was duly recorded that, "of the ten boats that were donated to us by Cuba, only two are working" and those two "can collapse any time." But then, Castro could not give to Grenada what he could not give to Cuba.

By 1981, even the Russian press, on behalf of the Soviet government, had placed Grenada in its firm ideological scheme of things—Grenada was in the midst of a "progressive social transformation" and the New Jewel Movement was in the "political vanguard." Cynics in the West could laugh, but the reality was substantive: these categories of Soviet-influenced countries included some twenty states with a combined population of 220 million people. The Soviets were deadly serious about this growing Third World empire of theirs, and their intent could be measured by the extent to which they allowed this "empire" eventually to bankrupt them. By 1982, the Russians were signing deadly serious, top-secret economic and military treaties, agreements, and protocols with the little island nation of Grenada as though it had grown up into a big country overnight. The amount of military weaponry and equipment they provided was enough to outfit a force of ten thousand men. In addition, the practical Grenadians asked for autobuses, loudspeakers, six English typewriters, two thousand folding chairs—and four guillotines.

Soon Vietnam, as well, was moving into the Caribbean, the "American lake." Through their embassy in Havana, Vietnamese began training Grenadians not only in radioactive warfare and in the "reeducation" of antisocial and counterrevolutionary elements, but in "Yankee tactics and the weapons used in Vietnam." And at Pearl's Airport, a special little Russian Antonov II plane waited patiently for the right moment to move. With its cloth wings and metal body (and, curiously enough, fussy curtains on the little wings), the plane came to symbolize for many Grenadians the changes that were happening on their island that they no longer understood. The Soviets, as always, were not very inventive. They said the plane was for crop dusting, on an island where there were no crops to dust. In actuality, it was waiting to drop off small paramilitary units on St. Vincent, St. Lucia, Dominica, and Antigua, units which could easily overthrow those unprotected little democratic governments. "They even had trial landings," Joseph E. Edmunds of St. Lucia, the ambassador to the O.A.S., related, remembering the feeling of helplessness and fear that pervaded the islands at the time. "It seems to some like a small thing; it wasn't."

But as Castro expanded his guerrilla activities into Grenada, he was hobbled by realities at home. For the first time, in December of 1979, he had to tell the Cuban people what was indeed the truth—that there would be no end to the economic hardship. Cuba was "sailing in a sea of difficulties . . . and the shore is far away. . . ." Before, Castro had been able to keep the Cuban people in a continual stage of vertiginous, unresolved, revolutionary fervor that seemed to them in their isolated and remote state a kind of equilibrium. Now, even he could see that they were beginning to grow exhausted by this endless irresolution, which in fact underlay his entire concept of power.

Forced to liberalize, reform, and open up his closed economy, Castro increased the minimum wage, allowed a certain amount of private business on a limited free market basis, and issued licenses to craftsmen and entrepreneurs. As bait, he told would-be investors, in words that again seemed more fitting to a feudal lord than a Communist party chief and more ironic than he would have meant, "Where else can you find as many well-educated workers guaranteed not to strike, and a government guaranteed not to coup?"

At the same time, in those years of the early 1980s, he created other new military structures in still another alternate military force, the Militia of Territorial Troops, which was, in part, another attempt to return the country internally to the old Sierra Maestra idea of the "war of the people" or of *la guerrilla*. With active-duty armed forces of 225,000, plus 190,000 reservists and 1.2 million persons now being equipped and trained in these new militias, Cuba had not only the best-equipped military force in Latin America—capable of mobilizing more troops than Brazil or Mexico—but also a force that was larger than the U.S. National Guard and military reserves combined! The militias also very deliberately protected him from his "friends," the Soviets—he was convinced they were plotting to replace him, and at that tense moment he was right.

But most said his turn of mood—his turn of luck—came in 1980 because of the one possibility he had never really believed possible: the death of Celia. This consummately loyal human being, this irreplaceable companion in arms and in life, died of cancer on January 11. Since virtually the moment they had met that damp, misty early dawn in 1956 in the Sierra, she had been his first and last and at times his only real tie to reality. Now she was suddenly gone. On those rare occasions when he bothered now to attend diplomatic receptions, he appeared strangely remote, preoccupied, even unaware of important things swirling threateningly around him.

In his office, he whiled away melancholy hours looking at designs for statues to be built to honor Celia. He alternated between choosing a properly "revolutionary" one, which depicted her standing under the broad trees of the Sierra, her thin body insouciantly poised like some sweet and smiling young romantic heroine, and one that showed her surrounded by Cuban children gazing up devotedly at her long, austere Spanish face. More and more of the time, he stalked up and down despondently in the big room next to his office, stopping to study, and restudy, the giant mock-up of the Sierra Maestra upon which he had dramatically marked all their "battles" except this one that was his alone. More and more, he was the sole caretaker of the legend that was also singularly Celia's legend as well, for that most beloved and compelling time of his life was the one thing he could share with no other woman, as Celia had so well grasped.

Then, on April 1, 1980, only three months after Celia's slight, wiry body finally wasted away to the death that was the one force he could not control, his fortunes at home turned disastrously even worse, when six Cubans seeking political asylum innocently enough crashed through the gate of the Peruvian embassy in Havana, killing a Cuban policeman who had been guarding it.

Castro was utterly enraged at this new challenge to his rule as he was always utterly enraged when Cubans exercised their own will. Now, in order to show that the masses would not really desert him, he chose a typical Castro maneuver: instead of defensively closing the Peruvian embassy, he went on the offense, withdrawing the embassy's Cuban military guard, and even going so far as to announce the withdrawal publicly. This time his tactic was terribly wrong. A spontaneous explosion of struggling Cuban bodies poured over the walls of the poor Andean embassy like driving rain. For the next seventy-two hours, an astonishing 10,800 human beings jammed desperately into the rooms and single yard of the red thatched-roof building, desperately seeking escape from their homeland. In the palace, Castro paced and exploded in waves of anger. "I am going to turn this shit against the United States," he told his Jamaican friend Michael Manley, who was visiting Cuba at the time. But he was wrong again, for this time the United States was going to turn things against him.

But by now Castro no longer depended solely upon his own instinct of the moment. By now, he had "crisis management." In the late 1970s, he had established work groups comprised of teams of sociologists and psychologists who were to serve as the government's barometer of any rising heat of discontent or malice within the country. When that discontent grew too great, the experts would recommend, "Open the safety valve!" just as in the final year of the next decade the East German regime would relieve pressure by "opening the wall."

Castro's "opening" utilized several variants, including raising the artificial threat of a United States invasion and the mobilization of large parts of the newest, just-formed militias, like the territorial troops. "The barrage of propaganda would then start," explained General Rafael del Pino, who had stood for years in the very center of military power in Cuba. "This time the Americans really are coming . . . air-raid shelters are opened . . . so are atom-bomb shelters. . . ." To finish the circle, Castro then supported these tactics with his own television magic, creating a unique loop of societal and psychotelegenic control.

On April 21, Castro announced his real plan: those wanting to leave would be permitted to go by boats to Florida from the small Cuban port of Mariel, an open and industrial harbor through which the Soviet ships had brought the missiles that led to the Cuban Missile Crisis in 1962. In the end, 120,000 fled desperately to Miami in the historic "boat lift," bringing the number of Cubans who had left Cuba since 1959 to 1.5 million.

Castro's terms were cruel beyond even the expectations of those who hated him. He permitted only one family member to leave on each boat. The others were chosen by the Cuban government, and many were released criminals and known psychopaths. The Florida ships were overcharged at every turn by the Cuban government, and Cuban soldiers brutishly forced the refugees through a "ritual" of brushing the Cuban soil from their shoes before leaving. Meanwhile, Castro again put the conflict squarely where he wanted it, on television: he told the Cuban people that "We've withdrawn the custody over the Florida peninsula. . . . We've had to withdraw the guard from the peninsula of Florida. . . ."

The Mariel boat lift unexpectedly provided illumination on parts of Castro's heretofore closed world. The *Marielito* homosexuals who arrived in Miami invariably called themselves "men with defects," revealing that in their heart of hearts they believed Castro's vicious edicts about them. The released prisoners talked for the first time about Castro's prisons, and the world learned of sadistic beatings, of cells flooded suddenly and so rapidly that the prisoners thought they would surely drown, of *plantados,* or political prisoners, who refused to be "reeducated" into Castroism (it was their only, desperate way to remain independent) and who were then forced to remain for long periods naked, a particularly humiliating punishment for a Cuban male. One brilliant plastic surgeon, Dr. Alberto Dalmau, even performed surreal plastic surgery on prisoners who were about to be released. Why? "So they would look better on the outside," Dr. Dalmau recalled. "Perhaps they were going to see their wives for the first time in twenty years. . . . So we invented local anaesthetic, and I operated with razor blades."

Once the *Marielito* prisoners were released in the United States, American lawmen across the country were almost immediately faced with a crime wave so vicious, so without norms, so desocialized, that even they were stunned. These men of Castro's prisons seemed to believe in nothing, and to be living effectively outside civilization. "The *Marielitos*," explained Cuban-American psychiatrist Dr. Marcelino Feal, "are the real 'new men' of the Castro regime."

Instead of standing supremely and securely on his accustomed offensive, where he had always found safety, Castro began to find himself now constantly fighting to maintain even a reasonable defensive position. In his speeches, he now raged endlessly against the "*incompetentes*" and "*indolentes*" everywhere inside—the incompetents and indolent ones who were in truth his people. He was raging against a dawning, and he did not recognize the new day.

Castro's position was worsened by far by the election, that same watershed year of 1980, of Ronald Reagan to the American presidency. President Jimmy Carter's originally idealistic efforts to make peace with Castro had failed abysmally. The Republicans were far more cynical—some would say realistic—about the possibility of any genuine rapprochement with Castro; they understood his character far better than did the Democrats, who so often saw in his Cuba the potential social welfare utopia they so ceaselessly sought. But it was when President Reagan sent the shrewd General Vernon Walters, his United Nations ambassador, to Cuba in 1982, that the administration definitively made up its mind on whether to try anything "new" with Castro.

Old fox Walters, by then a hulk of a man whose brilliant linguistic abilities and cynical good sense had kept him close to Ike's presidential side, traveled to Cuba "to see." The contents and results of the crucially important meeting were never publicly revealed and indeed remained top secret until now; yet, despite his public silence, it would be Walters's personal judgments—and his advice to President Reagan—that would form the crucial American response to the last years of Castro's unending fight against America.

Reconstructed from several sources, the meeting began when the two dominating and talkative men met with the inimitable Carlos Rafael

Rodríguez and an aide of Walters's in Castro's big comfortable office in the *palacio* (from which, appropriately, you could glimpse the huge mock-up of the Sierra Maestra battles) and later in his conference room. The conversation went like this:

Comandante Castro: "If you come here to threaten me . . . I've been threatened by every American president." (A smile.) "And I know your Congress will not carry anything through. . . ."

General Walters: "I've come to tell you a truth as old as history. When a country's vital interests are at stake, it must consider all options."

Castro: "Sit down."

Carlos Rafael Rodríguez: "We have nothing to negotiate."

Castro: "Everything's negotiable."

They then went to dinner at the mansion of Carlos Rafael, where Walters typically tweaked the bearded old Communist, his bright Rasputinian eyes shining, telling him what a beautiful house he had. "A gift of the bourgeoisie, undoubtedly," Walters said with an ironic smile. "And involuntarily so."

"*Completamente*," Rodríguez responded, his equally bright, equally Rasputinian eyes shining. "*Completamente.*"

Walters soon realized that once Castro realized the American diplomat and general had not come to threaten him, he could relax—and he did. They began to talk Communist philosophy, and Castro told Walters that, having made a careful study of history, sociology, and economics, he had concluded that Communism offered the only logical explanation of human history. Walters dryly responded that that was indeed interesting, particularly in light of the fact that "the Russians needed thirty-two farmers to our two." When they spoke of "liberation movements," Walters told Castro that "What you call liberation movements, we call irreversible dictatorships."

"Everything's reversible," Castro shot back. "I'm reversible."

Walters pondered aloud, "When?"

At one point, Walters joked with him further, telling him at first very seriously that, "We do have something in common." Castro's eyebrows raised at this. "We're both graduates of the Jesuits," Walters went on. Castro relaxed, nodded his head, but without sentiment. "But there is something different between us," Walters went on. Now Castro raised his eyebrows again, this time more in curiosity. The American went on in his Spanish, so excellent that he could be playful in it, saying, "*Me quedé fiel*," a play on Castro's name meaning, "But I remained faithful."

According to inside sources, Walters left Cuba having impressed Castro, but he also left convinced that nothing could be done about the Cuban leader that would serve American interests. He was convinced that the United States, being the historic nemesis that inspired Castro's true animus, had nothing Castro wanted and that, if he were to come to our side, he would be only "like the president of a banana republic."

After Walters had returned, another diplomat close to the Cubans told him that Castro had spoken of him with as much admiration as he could about any American. However, the diplomat went on, Castro nevertheless felt that, despite his command of Spanish and of history, Walters had "one great defect." What was that? the diplomat asked. Castro answered seriously: "He would not let me talk."

The Walters visit was the single most convincing event that caused Ronald Reagan to give up even any thought of trying to "deal" with Castro. It was followed by hostile move after hostile move. But the most threatening of all to Castro was the formation of Radio Martí and the beginnings of broadcasts to Cuba from America in 1985. Under the directorship of Castro's old nemesis, Ernesto Betancourt, broadcasts of fair and objective news were finally made available to the Cuban people—hour after hour after hour, and week after week. It was as if he himself were being invaded this time; this time it was an airwaves Bay of Pigs against which even his armed legions could not protect him.

In these years, Castro began to reveal himself in new and frightening terms, as he passed to the high-paranoid phase of the caudillo. "Cuba is alone. . . . We cannot wait for the help of anyone, we will have to defend ourselves by ourselves. . . . They are threatening us with an invasion right now. . . . Should we be intimidated? No! We should prepare ourselves!"

Those were Castro's "new" words as, once again, he stood in the historic square of Santiago on July 26, 1983, on the thirtieth anniversary of the attack on the Moncada barracks. The emotions, the heat, and his memories that day made a tremendous impression on the crowd. Sympathetic Spanish journalists noted that, as he talked, this graying man, who had looked so tired and even old when he began the speech, suddenly was transformed again into the young, energetic, and sublimely confident Fidel. The change became particularly noticeable when he compared Moncada with Vietnam, and when he compared old Cuba with new Nicaragua. He seemed again to "be himself" only as he contemplated an American invasion, even yearned for it, some might say. He spoke vividly that day in Götterdämmerung terms, of secret mountain redoubts carved into the rock cliffs of his Sierra Maestra, into the very breasts of his Revolution, which could serve as the last bastion of the last stand of his Revolution. Like Mao's faraway caves of Yenan and like Hitler's Walkyrian "Eagle's Nest," Castro was telling the world that he was at the ready, if necessary, to march backward—still another "counterbirth," some called it—to the mythological beginnings of the Revolution and to stand in a classic Masada posture of eternal and sui-cidal confrontation against the Americans.

The invasion scare let down not for a second. All of a sudden, Cubans were telling foreign diplomats seriously and soberly that all they could do was to absorb the first blow; then they would entrap the Americans and wear them down with guerrilla war. Like the Red Guards of Mao's Cultural Revolution, like the Jonestown followers of Jim Jones, like the unnamed but numbered cadres of Pol Pot talking in Cambodia about "Hour Zero," Castro's militias trained for "Red Sundays," when the invasion from out-side would come. Even the children embarked upon a veritable frenzy of digging air-raid trenches.

It was just at this point that a bizarre and ominous scenario unfolded in Grenada that fulfilled all of Castro's worst nightmares and set the stage for the macabre battle of wills that was to drain all the early sunshine out of the New Jewel Movement and destroy Grenada's "revo." The romantic Mau-rice Bishop now came up against the other side of "revolution" in the fig-ure of the rigid, cold-eyed Soviet-backed Marxist Bernard Coard, a kind of "Caribbean Trotsky," who was determined to get rid of Bishop. In the internecine fighting that ensued that dramatic summer and fall of 1983, ideo-logical clouds of difference darkened the once-beautiful island with blood.

Indeed, when Bishop returned to Grenada from a trip to Cuba and the Eastern Bloc, Castro watched with alarm as the Coard elements put Bishop under house arrest, where he refused even to eat for fear of poison. Then, on October 19, the day that would come to be known in Grenada as "Bloody Wednesday," at least ten thousand of Bishop's "beloved" masses broke in, took Bishop, and carried their tragic and hungry hero—never a killer, always the gallant, ever the bon vivant who had forgotten to declare war on the United States—to the picturesque Fort Rupert overlooking the exquisite, azure bay of St. George's. There, Coard coldly gave the order to shoot. Bishop, his lover, five of his closest associates, and a still-unknown number of others were lined up against still another mural of Che Guevara and wantonly shot to bits. Castro, at this crucial moment, had been singularly unable to outplay or outwit the enemies that now snarlingly surrounded him. Still worse, Castro now watched with growing horror as it became clear that the Americans were preparing to invade Grenada!

This time, the Cuban leader moved carefully. He called forth Colonel Pedro Tortoló Comas, a husky, able, black Cuban officer who had putatively "commanded" the Cuban military mission in Grenada from 1981 until May 1983, and sent him back to Grenada to command the Cuban troops there. He sent still another one hundred fifty to two hundred seasoned Cuban soldiers with him. But in the poor Tortoló, Castro had called upon one of his true "new men," an officer whose utter fealty and obedience could never be questioned, but a man who lacked combat experience. Tortoló arrived less than twenty-four hours before the landing of the U.S.-Caribbean Security Forces. They were now "ready" for what was in effect Castro's first really direct confrontation with the *americanos,* the battle he had predicted to Celia in 1958 and that he had awaited all his life.

On October 20, the seven member islands of the Organization of Eastern Caribbean States held a meeting and invoked Article 8 of their Treaty of Association to seek American and other "friendly" aid. President Reagan immediately decided to send troops.

Castro watched with apprehension, but also with a simmering excitement, as on the early morning of October 25, the U.S.-Caribbean Security Forces landed on the beaches of Grenada. He immediately and without hesitation instructed his men that it was their duty to die fighting, "no matter how difficult and disadvantageous the circumstances may be." At his press conference in Havana that same day, he totally lost control over the reality of the moment, as he stated that "Colonel Tortoló, who is in command of the Cuban personnel . . . had written a chapter in our contemporary history worthy of Antonio Maceo." Comparing the poor, hapless Tortoló to the great Cuban military hero of the independence would bear its costs.

On Cuban television days later, a Cuban working man on Grenada was interviewed saying, "I was standing next to Comandante Tortoló. When I looked around, he had run away." The Cubans had not, however, lost their sense of humor: the joke that immediately spun around Havana like a delicious top was, "If you want to get there first, you must have Tortoló shoes."

Despite genuine American attempts to avoid any fighting with the Cubans, there was some halfhearted engagement. In the end, twenty-four Cubans were killed and fifty-nine wounded.

On Grenada, the Americans found thousands of infantry weapons with millions of rounds of ammunition, five secret military assistance agreements not hitherto known—and the extraordinary "Grenada Documents," which were in fact several tons of papers, dog-eared scraps, and handwritten notes, whose pathetic scrawlings detailed the damaging stories of every relationship between Grenada and the Eastern Bloc.

Grenada was a small and seemingly insignificant island. But the fact was that the finding of these papers marked only the second time in history that the inner working of the takeover of a country by a Communist party had been so meticulously laid out. (The first was the capture by German troops of documents in Smolensk in the Soviet Union in World War II.) When the Grenada Documents of the Bishop regime were discovered squirreled insouciantly away in drawers and desks, Castro's pride and Castro's secretiveness were stripped bare, exploded by the compulsively silly writings and ill-spelled ideological gibberish of these careless "island clowns" he had claimed as his children. Grenada was the turning point because, as the brilliant Cuban-American psychiatrist Dr. Facundo Lima put it, "Remember, for Castro to accept defeat was impossible. The image of the invincible cracked right there. It was not a matter that this was a tiny island, it was a matter of being defeated."

The Grenada Documents also revealed what Castro's wooing of the American Left had wrought. The papers showed beyond the shadow of a doubt a pattern of intimate collaboration between the Marxist New Jewel Movement and Washington's Congressional Black Caucus—to such an extent that the flamboyant 1960s California Democratic congressman Ronald V. Dellums had actually submitted a report prepared for the House Armed Services Committee to Bishop's regime for its approval. The fact that polls of black Americans at the same time showed that six of ten American black citizens supported the Reagan policy in Grenada underlined the discrepancy between the ideological top of the American special-interest groups that Castro had for so long so diligently wooed and the "masses" of people, both Grenadians and Americans, those "leaders" were supposed to be representing.

New gulfs were revealing themselves, and Castro's dreams were beginning to tumble into them.

Castro's face was grotesquely contorted the day he stood on the tarmac at Havana airport to greet the men who, fighting in his image, had failed even symbolically to resist the enemy to which he had devoted his life. His eyes rolled and wandered, and the cheeks that had been so youthfully firm and strong for so many years now seemed suddenly deeply lined. As the men moved slowly off the planes, as the wounded were carried off on stretchers, all sent back to him not by victory but by the grace of the American army, Castro stood alone, his strong shoulders wilted, for long and silent minutes that frightened his people far more than did his tirades.

The first man off the plane moved with a severe limp, others hobbled down the stairs on crutches. All were physically dirty, and many were shirtless. The infamous and incorrigible Tortoló, who would become a figure of consummate ridicule, walked gingerly off the plane wearing a casual sports shirt. He saluted Castro and intoned rhythmically, "*Comandante-en-Jefe* . . . Mission Accomplished." An artillery corps band belted out a few appropriate revolutionary hymns, and women militia members duly goose-stepped across the tarmac of the José Martí Airport. But President Fidel Castro said not a single word.

At first Castro tried to pretend that everything was all right. He visited the men in the hospitals, brought them books, and talked with them. Word would get out about how much the *Comandante-en-Jefe* cared about his soldiers. But in the end, the men were all demoted to lowly positions. The unfortunate Tortoló, whose sole crime was only an understandable lacking in the spirit of self-sacrifice, was court-martialed, demoted to common soldier, and banished to Angola. Finally, in the court-martial, the mood was so bitter that Raúl Castro tore the men's epaulets off their jackets in postured rage. The military slogan for 1984 was "Here, Nobody Surrenders!"

"You see," Florentino Aspillaga, the high-level Cuban intelligence defector, told me, "in Cuba they speak constantly of the 'aggression' of the United States and the CIA. It is to stimulate the people, to try to justify the economic losses. But Fidel knew that there was not going to be any American aggression against Cuba and Nicaragua. . . . So he also believed that there would not be any against Grenada. He fell into his own trap. If he had foreseen an invasion, he would have sent thousands of men. But our forces were not prepared for the confrontation, and our people in our embassy did not know what was happening with the military. It was exactly like the Germans dying for Hitler. Castro wanted the Cuban people to die for him, like Hitler, Stalin, Napoleon. . . .

"Some days after Grenada, he finally gave a speech. I remember he was clapping his hands slowly, like a '*chocho*' — like an automaton. . . . In the intelligence circles, they spoke a lot about it, that he was not in control. At first we thought he was doing it to get the sympathy of the people. But he was shocked . . . because nobody died for him. On radio and TV, you see, they had all died. All those announcements about their dying for Fidel were prepared by him. 'These men, who died, were . . . Cubans . . . combatants. . . .' It was all written by him, because he believed they were dying for him. He didn't care about the dying, he cared about them dying for him."

Still little known is the fact that Castro's rage over all these gnawing elements of the Grenada affair, a rage that ranged between a consuming frustration and a corrosive humiliation, once again in his life came dangerously close to driving him physically to attack the United States. As with the Missile Crisis, Castro was prepared even to launch an airstrike against a nuclear power installation in south Florida, particularly if Washington were to blockade Cuba that fall.

General Rafael del Pino, the highest-ranking Cuban defector, reported in later years that he even went so far as to summon his high military command and to order them to have the fighter planes programmed to fly, apparently against the Turkey Point installation twenty-four miles south of Miami. Again, too, there arose the grotesque Armageddon aspect of it all because, as del Pino put it, "Castro doesn't realize that if this plant is destroyed, it would not only annihilate all the Cubans in Miami but . . . radioactivity would fall on Cuba."

An interesting conundrum arose here. During the Missile Crisis, Castro was certain the United States would invade — and it did not. By the time of Grenada, he had become convinced that Washington would never invade either in Central America or the Caribbean — and they did. The two countries — the two temperaments — would never understand each other.

PART III

"E L"

26

EL—HE

We dared to command the sun and moon to bring a new day.
. . . I curse the flux of time.

—Mao Tse-tung

FROM 1983 ON, although again the world did not or could not grasp it, all Castro could do was to fight to hold position. Cuba's economic situation worsened to the point where the island nation was unable to produce enough sugar for its quota to Russia. Castro was forced even to buy cheap sugar on the world market and to resell it to the Soviet Union. In 1985, Castro tried to recoup by cleverly seizing upon the issue of Third World debt to the United States and to the Western banking network to stoke the fires of his guerrilla fight against the imperium of the North. In the spring and summer of that year, no fewer than five international conferences were held in Havana on "the debt," which for the region had reached an astounding $420 billion. Delegates arriving at José Martí Airport were met by Cuban schoolchildren singing the rousing song "The Debt of Latin America and the Third World Must Be Canceled," but the underlying message from Castro was not economic; he was simply once again mobilizing Latin America's classic resentment against the United States, using whatever complaint, complex, or song that was at hand.

That same year, 1985, things grew even worse for Castro, if they could, as an "unknown," the insufferable Mikhail Gorbachev, came to power in

Moscow. So it was that in 1986, Castro's "Year of Rage," he struck back, and back, and back. He threw veritable tantrums—against waste, against mismanagement, against individual entrepreneurs, against both the United States and (the new element) against the Soviet Union alike. At the Third Congress of the Cuban Communist party that year, his mood was bitter, his predictions downbeat, his visage dark and angry. At the central committee meetings, he would talk somberly for hours, as he paced back and forth, canceling a free market here, dismantling experiments with private farmers' markets and the sale of housing there. Before thirty-five hundred party and administrative leaders, he berated a garlic farmer making fifty thousand dollars a year by privately selling garlic, and he literally rained all the fire and brimstone of his volcanic personality down on the heads of certain enterprising local lads in one Cuban town who had bought the whole supply of toothbrushes and melted them down to produce plastic necklaces. That was what the Revolution had come to, screaming at garlic farmers and the producers of illegal plastic necklaces!

Never mind, he would now step in to "rectify" things at home so he could continue his expansionism abroad. The "Campaign of Rectification of Errors" was his first answer to the *glasnost,* or openness, and *perestroika,* or restructuring, reforms that Gorbachev was trying to make within Communism—or perhaps at the expense of Communism. It was to be an "exciting" new program for a people who had already known nothing but a full twenty-seven years of bruising austerity so that one man could fulfill his dreams of grandeur as he worked out his personal complexes. And if they wanted to know their future, they had only to read a little book, published in 1987 by Castro and called *Por el Camino Correcto, Compilación de Textos,* or *By the Right Road, a Collection of Texts.*

Much like Mao's *Little Red Book* and Qaddafi's *Green Book,* Castro's book instructed his people to fight against everything "that is the incorrect," to fight even harder against the "old system." He tediously warned them once again that "This fight is going to be long." And finally, "It is possible that we commit errors in the process of rectification . . . but if we commit errors . . . we ought to have the valor to rectify the errors that we commit in this process too." He then actually added (yes, he actually did), "*Sí, Señor!*"

Just when he would seem to be pulling the reins of power back to himself, something else happened that revealed far too much of him to the outside world. On May 28, General Rafael del Pino, deputy chief of the Cuban Air Force and hero of the Bay of Pigs, defected to the United States he had so avidly fought in 1961. On June 6, 1987, an important Cuban intelligence chief, Major Florentino Aspillaga, escaped from the Cuban embassy in Czechoslovakia to Vienna and proceeded to lay bare the entire Cuban intelligence system for the West. Not only that, but Aspillaga titillated American public opinion with the information that, on Castro's last birthday, one Cuban agent had presented him with $4.2 million, which the agent carried personally to be deposited for Castro in a Swiss bank account to "finance liberation movements," for the bribery of leaders, and for any "personal whim of Castro." Even the secretive ways in which he financed his worldwide movements were now becoming known.

No wonder, then, that even despite his many extraordinary geopolitical accomplishments, as he stood atop the podium in Santiago de Cuba on January 1, 1989, he was strangely disconsolate, and he was angry. He felt his victories slipping away from him. He knew, if the world did not, that despite his extraordinary imperial and martial accomplishments, he had reason to both reflect and to worry—and to plot the next steps with a care he had never before so needed to exercise.

Once, the Malecón Drive that edged the Caribbean like a sinuously reclining woman had been a joy to walk along—now it was empty and crumbling. Once Havana had been the exotic, heavenly blooming plant of the Caribbean—now, sober Havana waited in food lines, waited at restaurants, waited for the minuscule rations of milk, of meat, of shoes. In Fidel's defiantly "socialist" Cuba, a bride still received a bonus ration of a nightgown, and so did pregnant women, causing some irreverent wags to note that these were exactly the two times when a woman least needed one.

But in the plaza that day in 1989, Castro's problems momentarily fell away from his broad shoulders. Again he breathed deeply of the power that the Cuban people granted him. Again he gazed down on the more than two hundred thousand tiny heads bobbing and swaying and listening. Yes, his beloved "masses" were still there. They had not deserted him, for the very simple reason that they could not. Indeed, *la plaza* was the shrine of Fidel's outer and inner world. It was in the plaza, in the response of the "faithful," that he found the only real love he knew. They were the mirror of his needs and of his leadership. It was in the plaza that he drew in the sands of his time the political and spiritual parameters for his people and then sent them out to conquer whole deserts in his name.

The speech started.

It was a special speech, marking as it did his three defining decades of "transformation." Viewed from below, still tall as a palm tree and strong as an oak, he remained mystically capable of grasping *las masas* in his strangely feminine hands and molding them to his whim and will. His harangue was delivered as always in a voice that altered rhythm only occasionally. His right arm swept in great circles, then crashed down, his second finger outstretched for emphasis, to drive his furious words into the waiting, receptive minds. Occasionally, he cajoled, even joked, even flirted with *las masas*. They loved it. He loved it, too, for the masses not only provided him with the only sure human resonance to his powerful will, they were his only real human contact.

Part of his genius was that while he was projecting this very image of strength, he was able in the same breath to make the people afraid for him. This double imagery of strength and vulnerability bonded the crowd to him even more diabolically. The people in the plaza that New Year's Day of 1989 could see that, although he was only sixty-two, he had suddenly started aging very quickly. They worried about him, told visitors he must not leave Cuba because out there "they" (which had become almost anyone "outside") might kill him. They saw that his beard had grayed, and then whitened, as a frighteningly sudden transformation had begun to overtake the Cuban strongman.

A morbid preoccupation with his health had started to grow inside him, although the Cuban people knew nothing about it and the world heard only rumors: a heart attack, lung cancer, rectal cancer. The gynecologist of his former wife, Mirta, whispered to special friends in Madrid that Mirta had whispered to her that Fidel had had a heart attack. An Egyptian doctor who was a specialist on rectal cancer was suddenly flown to Havana. CIA physicians "confirmed" in their masked anonymity that he had lung cancer, a view which gained in credibility and currency when he suddenly gave up smoking his favorite Romeo y Julieta cigars, which, he had joked, "will be my last contribution to the Revolution." Even the Russians threateningly leaked to the American press that they wanted to talk about Castro's "succession."

Those same anonymous CIA analysts noted on the thirtieth anniversary that his oratory was increasing in anger and even in frenzy. In place of wooing *las masas* out there in the hot sun of the plaza, more and more he was actually "denouncing the people." No longer the patient explainer of the world to an innocent, dependent, and absorptive people, he was coming more and more to lecture them, to scold them, to berate them, as though it was they who had failed him. He was becoming a leader preoccupied with Apocalypse, obsessed with his own fading youth, and morbidly concerned that the next generation of Cubans might resist his orders for the final, judgment-day mobilization.

Then, on that crucial moment of the anniversary, there occurred something unusual and even ominous. Since the birth of the Revolution thirty years before, he had always ended his speeches with the grandiose words of "The Apostle" of Cuban salvation, José Martí's classic *¡Patria o Muerte!*—Fatherland or Death! But that day, with his gargantuan capacity for confounding, he paused first for dramatic effect, he wiped away the sweat on his mobile, mottled face and rangy beard, he stared across the square for a moment, then, in a different voice, he shouted:

"*¡Marxismo-Leninismo o Muerte!*" Marxism-Leninism or Death!

What was he doing? Confusion flickered momentarily across the Cubans' faces, then passed. As always, *las masas* accepted Fidel's "logic." Actually, it was all quite simple. For thirty years, Castro's very favorite game had been to toy with the world over the question of when and if he had become a "Communist." First he was, then he wasn't, then he was again. At this moment, as the Russians effectively launched their de-Communization, Castro was mockingly, but also seriously, proclaiming Havana as the new Vatican of true Marxism, deliberately relegating his Russian "patrons" to some shadowy ideological periphery halfway between Social Democracy and the Republican party.

But that same night, there were portents of a different reality drifting and existing threateningly out there beyond his words. His own Cuban TV followed "Marxism-Leninism or Death!" with a show that started with a U.S. rock video called "Get out of My Dreams, Get into My Car."

Castro's problems were not only from the inside. Changes were closing in upon him in historically unexpected directions from the outside. He had never liked the Russians, but he had trusted them cynically to be there for their own interests. They did not need to be "loved" like the Americans, they only needed him to expand their empire into the Third World that loved him and hated them. But now there was Mikhail Gorbachev, the false Dmitri of modern times, democratizing, liberalizing, reforming. Now, dark and fearful Mother Russia was shedding both her paranoia and her revolutionary fervor. Gorbachev had even held elections in the Soviet Union for the first time since Lenin had wisely abolished them in 1917. And in that cold land, where "the masses" were forever supposedly inertial and unmoving, in historic Leningrad itself, "the people" went out and massively wrote "X" on the ballots to negate the Communist party chiefs.

If that sort of treacherous disobedience had been lurking all this time inside the sober and shrouded Russian people, could it not be lurking too inside those very Cubans who were cheering him in the plaza? If Gorbachev could do these unforgivable things—making even the famous question of Castro's "Communism" no longer relevant—what rock did he himself any longer have to stand on to move the world?

Since 1985, when Mikhail Gorbachev took over the Soviet Union, Fidel had watched with horror as that type of Communist experiment failed. Gorbachev had attempted with all of his stolid provincial Stavropol heart to save Communism by liberalizing politically and intellectually, through *perestroika* and *glasnost*. Fidel saw that Gorbachev had been wrong. The Russian president, intending to tinker around the peripheries but to save the heart of Communism, had instead only released his people's political and intellectual energies. He should first have reformed the economic systems while he had authority to do so. This would have provided him with a sound economic base to support a limited, paced democraticization.

His was a terrible—a fatal—mistake that eventually destroyed the Soviet Union.

So it was, then, that when Gorbachev finally arrived in Havana on April 3, 1989, the incredible weave of dramas of that fateful spring began its inexorable unraveling. New master of public relations Gorbachev deliberately delayed his plane an hour in Ireland in order to arrive just in time for the American nightly news—Gorbachev was manipulating the American press, a job that Fidel had long reserved for himself. It was the Russian leader now who was the younger man, the "new" leader with "new" ideas. Still, at first, the meeting appeared friendly.

But as Castro escorted a patient and resigned-looking Gorbachev to the eternal housing projects, to the countryside, around decaying Havana, signs quickly accumulated of unhappy rifts. But it was when the Russian leader addressed the Cuban National Assembly that the yawning chasm of ideology and of the intentions of power opened before the entire watching world. The hall was filled with Cuban officials, but whereas before they would have sat ramrod straight as they listened to their *líder máximo* and to the new Soviet leader, in this new era they lounged, they coughed loudly, they talked among themselves. Castro's "introduction" of the Russian leader took a full fifty minutes, almost as long as Gorbachev's entire speech. In it, he pointedly insulted Gorbachev with nasty little criticisms of Stalinism, the greatest sore point in the world for this Russian leader.

When Gorbachev got up before the assembly, he first praised Castro as a "living legend." (But "living legends" are always dangerously close to becoming dead legends.) Then, Gorbachev spoke against any further aid to the Castroite guerrilla movements, and Castro's cup of rage boiled over. Now they were threatening his very life's blood. But Gorbachev forged right ahead, calling for "an end to military supplies to Central America from any quarter." On a deeper level, the Soviets were warning Cuba that mobilization without development had reached its limits, that nuclear weapons had changed the nature of war to such a degree that support for wars of liberation should be abandoned, and that the Soviet Union was suffering from a severe case of "imperial indigestion."

On the immediate level, Gorbachev for the first time revealed to Cubans the reforms and even elections that were taking place within the Soviet bloc. In effect, he was forcing his *glasnost,* or openness, down Castro's throat—and in Castro's own country. On the more transcendental level, he was informing the Cuban people that Fidel Castro had tied them for thirty years to a failed ideology, and that to survive, they now had even to mimic the *americanos.*

Lenin had ridden across Germany in a closed railway car to begin the Russian Revolution—Gorbachev rode quietly out of Havana on April 6 in a closed car. The Cubans who waited along the streets complained that they could not make out which car he was in. Castro answered that the Soviets had requested a closed car because "they were afraid Gorbachev would get a cold," which was a little like worrying over Napoleon getting sunstroke en route to Moscow. When Gorbachev arrived directly in London from Havana, he was smiling broadly for the first time in three days. Now, here was a country he could understand—a country with elections, free market mechanisms, and the likable Margaret Thatcher, who appreciated Gorbachev as a "man I can do business with."

The aftereffects of Gorbachev's visit flooded over the suddenly beleaguered Castro for months; every week the stream of troubles grew ominously larger. He had depended upon East Germany for intelligence training; upon Czechoslovakia for weaponry. In the fall of 1989, "Communist" Eastern Europe collapsed like a treacherous house of cards before his very eyes. Now, where would he go?

From that moment onward—from Gorbachev's hapless trip and Castro's thoroughgoing realization that he had no longer an ideological homeland, from that watershed spring of the thirtieth anniversary of the Revolution—Cuba descended into a realm of cold brutality that the country, even in its worst days, had never before witnessed.

Like so many dictators in their waning years, as their power falls away from them, Castro sat surrounded by his little court of fulsome—and now ever-changing—courtiers, who could be identified by their Rolex watches and foreign cars (gifts and insignias of Fidel's grace). While the world spoke trustingly of a Cuban Communist apparatus—a politburo, a central committee, a collective leadership—all of that was by then a mirage.

Cuba was now being run by Castro's tight little "Group of Coordination and Support," or simply "the team" of fourteen or fifteen persons who hovered ever around him at his beck and call. Each one had his or her finger on the control of one major unit of power, like the courtiers of a king or lord, and they reported to him privately on what was happening in the factories, in the industries, and in the long and sullen lines on the streets where people whispered incessantly now about the *mayimbes,* or the privileged party classes. And they made very sure never to tell Castro anything that did not please him. To arrive at this point of guarded inner-circle perfection, Castro had to purge, and purge, and purge; and then to replace, and replace, and replace all of his old and most "trusted" comrades in arms.

When Chinese revolutionary leader Mao Tse-tung found his "revolutionary immortality" fading away, he launched the horrendous Cultural Revolution, destroying an entire generation of intellectuals. When Adolf Hitler saw his Third Reich failing, he launched a last Götterdämmerung from his Berlin bunker. When Fidel Castro saw old age and the failure of Communism closing in on him, he turned ruthlessly against his very finest military officers, executing them in the name of "corruption" but in truth for posing an alternative to him.

If Cuba had had one truly exemplary military officer, it was Arnaldo Ochoa Sánchez, a hawk-nosed, handsome, Rommel type who would have stood out for excellence and honor in any army. He had served in the Sierra Maestra with Castro, he had studied at the famous Frunze and Voroshilov military academies in the Soviet Union, he spoke perfect Russian. He had fought at the Bay of Pigs, in Venezuela with Castro's first Marxist guerrillas, in the Congo, in Angola, in Ethiopia, and in Nicaragua, finally becoming the top commander of troops in Fidel's favorite foreign war, Angola. But when the Soviets began forcing Castro to bring home his fifty-seven thousand troops from Angola, Ochoa became not only a threat to Castro but *the* threat. Ochoa's house became a gathering place for war veterans frustrated by the quagmirish bureaucracy and the hopelessness of the Cuba they returned to. That thirtieth-anniversary spring, anyone could see the disaffected soldiers shuffling restlessly about outside Ochoa's house; discontent and disaffection were palpable, and discontent was something that Fidel never countenanced. He lost no time in acting.

The drama began, then speeded up dizzily early in June of 1989, when Raúl Castro delivered a strangely rambling and surreal speech to the armed forces he commanded. As Fidel had started doing with *las masas,* Raúl now railed at his officers, instead of praising or inspiring them. Tense and ill at ease, the caustic Raúl told the officers that they must remember that "Fidel is our papá!" and that, if they were unhappy in Cuba, he could easily arrange for them to get visas "to Hungary or Poland." At one point, he insulted them gratuitously, shouting at them, "Do we have democracy here?" And they all yelled back, mesmerized, "Yes!" He smiled a strange smile. "Did you say that because I forced you?" he demanded, as if the original humiliation were not enough. "No!" they all shouted back. Then he looked at them with an expression of utter disgust and said, "You are behaving like schoolchildren."

The Ochoa "trial" that ensued shocked awake a world that had refused, before, to look with any seriousness at the way Castro used courts, trials, and his own forms of "justice." The handsome, gallant Ochoa, with his black curly hair and his long, aquiline nose, sat impassively in the courtroom in his light gray dress uniform. He looked like a man stunned, or drugged, as he stared vacuously at the floor. When Castro accused him of drug-running,

Ochoa could only say finally that, even if he faced execution, "My last thought will be of Fidel, and the great Revolution he has given our people."

It was the Moscow trials of the early 1930s all over again, when Stalin's closest and most innocent associates had stood up in court and veritably demanded their own deaths. But it was more than that: it was another one of Castro's personally devised "trials," in which he had since Moncada changed, and transformed, and still again redefined legality. In the surrealistic world that Castro had turned Cuba into, the military tribunal that tried Ochoa was actually a legally nonexistent body. (The law on military tribunals, article 5, establishes only three jurisdictional bodies, and this was not one.) But, then, the tribunal was also composed of members ineligible for service—and the testimony that convicted Ochoa, his own, was legally inadmissible. In the end, Arnaldo Ochoa, like the Moscow trial defendants, was more willing to die than to admit that his life had been lived in the services of a false ideal—and, of course, there was the question of whether he wanted his children to live. . . .

Cuban revolutionary hero Arnaldo Ochoa and three other high-ranking officers in key positions were executed by firing squad at dawn on July 13, 1989, after being found guilty not even formally of drug-smuggling but of creating "hostile action against foreign nations" through such smuggling. The major foreign nation was, ironically, the United States. Fidel had made his point—there was going to be no post-Angola rebellion, and in fact no rebellion at all, against him. He had purposely involved his men in the drug trade for his own security in the early 1980s, and he had as well made some money through it. Now the tactic, like all his Machiavellian tactics, served him well.

But it didn't end there. General José Abrahante Fernández, the powerful interior minister who had replaced Valdes and was now the third most influential man in Cuban politics (after Fidel and Raúl), was sent to jail for twenty years. With that, Osmani Cienfuegos, Castro's right-hand man in managing the economy, took refuge in the Venezuelan embassy. The *santeros,* meanwhile, began ominously to move away from Fidel—one of the men executed with Ochoa was a twin, and in Santería it was a sign of evil to divide twins. What Castro had done to Batista through the power of the *santeros* was now being done to him.

Many new details began to creep out of Cuba in the early 1990s, not the least of which were those concerning the trial and execution of Arnaldo Ochoa in the summer of 1989.

Castro, of course, has persisted in saying that the "hero of Angola," the handsome, hawk-nosed Ochoa, had been executed for drug-running—that he had shamed the Revolution and compromised the fatherland. To the contrary, as related in the excellent documentary film *Ochoa*, released only in summer of 1992, by the famous Cuban film producer Orlando Jimenez-Leal, and in the Andres Oppenheimer's *Castro's Final Hour: The Secret Story Behind the Coming Downfall of Communist Cuba*, Castro framed Ochoa by accusing him of being an accomplice in a complex Cuban-Colombian drug-smuggling operation that began in 1982. Four high-ranking Cuban officials attempted to bring drugs into the United States in exchange for smuggling weapons to the M-19, a guerrilla movement in Colombia, which was at that time supported by Castro. The involved case came to include the gross Panamanian dictator Manuel Noriega, con man and swindler Robert Vesco, and a whole passel of Cuban officials, including Colonel Tony de la Guardia, an old and close associate of Fidel's who was the powerful head of Fidel's "special forces" all over the world.

Complications came when one of the related operations was infiltrated by the Drug Enforcement Agency of the United States, and when the videotapes showed one of the suspects alleging that the money they were paying "went straight into Castro's drawers."

Enter Arnaldo Ochoa, disillusioned and disgusted "hero of Angola"!

"I was a very great friend of Arnaldo Ochoa," Cuban General Rafael del Pino, who defected from the Cuban Armed Forces, says about the film. "I knew him since 'the victory.' No doubt, he was the most brilliant of the Cuban generals. But he made the big mistake that I did not commit—to speak openly. Thank God, I measured my words when I was about to leave Cuba! That probably saved me from a show like this.

"Ochoa was not in a conspiracy like that one, but all the conditions were there that could doom him. He had already lost all confidence in the Revolution. . . . That was unforgivable. I was inside that hell and I know how the devil works. Ochoa had to pay for two things: he was too dangerous for Fidel, and he was the only one to have the prestige and the love of the Armed Forces."

Del Pino, a short, sturdy, thoughtful man, paused here. "Fidel in his madness can forsee things very well. Looking into the future, he sees he can send a message to the Armed Forces. If he murdered the best hero of the Revolution, he can murder anyone. It showed there was no limit to his madness."

Ochoa died with all the dignity expected of the general of a country that has given him all of its highest honors. According to Oppenheimer, he asked to be allowed to give the order for his own execution, in exactly the style of the Cuban heroes executed by Spanish firing squads during the colonial wars. "Denied!" was the reply—for one of the acts of punishment of Fidel's Revolution was to strip a man of his will, most poignantly at moments such as death. Ochoa then waved away a black kerchief to cover his eyes. After saying in a trembling voice, "I just wanted to let you know that I'm no traitor," he took a deep breath and shrugged his shoulders slightly in a gesture—of what? Of the terrible irony of it all? Of the ultimate hopelessness of human life? Of this final farce of the Revolution that he had in effect already given his life to?

"Fuego!" And Arnaldo Ochoa, who had bravely led Cuban troops in Angola, Nicaragua, and Ethiopia—the Rommel of his generation and of his small nation—was dead.

Andres Oppenheimer: "Castro, watching the scene in a videotape brought to him by the military doctors hours later, was jolted by the sound. An expression of grief on his face, he stared on at the monitor for a few seconds. 'He died like a man,' he finally commented wistfully."

But Ochoa had ceased to be a man, at least in Fidel Castro's Cuba where identity, too, was under the control of the state.

Hours after the executions were announced, an intelligence officer knocked on the door of Ochoa's stricken wife, Maida. He brought Ochoa's death certificate, which read: "Arnaldo Ochoa Sánchez: Profession? Unemployed; Married? Unknown; Cause of death? Unknown." The hero of Angola was buried in an unmarked grave, just like so many of his soldiers who had fallen in Angola and the other unmarked wars of Fidel Castro.

After the trial and after the executions were over, Iliana de la Guardia, the daughter of Tony, told how a psychiatrist and psychologist from the Ministry of the Interior came to see the family. The men explained soberly to the children "the justice of the judgment" inflicted upon their father.

After asking how old they were, the two visitors asked if they "realized the danger in which their father had placed all the children of Cuba? Because with what your father did, the Americans could have invaded Cuba and killed many children, like you."

Then one asked the boy, Antonio, "Let's see, Antonio, are you in agreement with the penalty of death for your father?" The boy screamed in pain and ran from the room.

The Ochoa trial shocked the world, and even some of Fidel's most devoted friends. The most stellar by far was the great Colombian author Gabriel García Márquez, the famous "Gabo" and the infamously fawning friend of Fidel. Gabo, the most loyal, the least critical, one of those great writers and cultural epigones who needs to be always at the side of the Big Man, the strongman, the force of nature, the source of all political and ideological wisdom! What an odd couple they had made for decades, as Gabo was rewarded for his sycophantic addiction to his friend with a beautiful home in Havana, a swimming pool, unrestricted access to Fidel and to his magic, and just about anything he wanted or needed on the island!

But now García Márquez, Nobel Prize winner, could not have what he wanted—the lives of Ochoa, de la Guardia, and the other two men. Andres Oppenheimer relates how Fidel came to Gabo's house just before the executions, and how the short, swarthy Gabo tried to reason in a way that he thought might move the big, stocky dictator. He applied a little psychology.

"I wouldn't want to be in your shoes," Gabo told Fidel, as they stood at his front door at 2:00 A.M., "because if they are executed, nobody on earth will believe that it wasn't you who gave the order."

"You think so?" Castro responded. "Do you really think that people would see it that way?"

Castro then launched into one of his windy perorations: the trial had been meticulously fair, consummately legal; it had been the "unanimous opinion of the court that Ochoa and Tony de la Guardia deserved to be executed," and he had found an "overwhelming majority" in the state institutions for the executions.

"Don't you think they say that because they think that's what you want?" Gabo asked.

Fidel was a little miffed. He certainly did not think that.

Finally, when Gabo saw there was nothing to be done, he said sadly, "I've known many heads of state, and there is one common denominator among them all: no ruler believes he's being told what he wants to hear."

Soon the worshipful Gabo, too, would disappear from the troubled island. He would return to his home in Colombia, after an absence of many years, and become a television commentator. Perhaps by then he had all that he needed; his passion, illustrated by all of his books, was to know and dissect the Latin patriarch, the father, the caudillo. Probably he knew enough by then, from all those years of sitting adoringly at Fidel's right hand.

In earlier and happier years, he had wondered at the "terrible power of seduction" of Fidel, and the "fragility of his . . . hoarse voice which at times seemed breathless." He had written about Fidel's "devotion to the word that is almost magical. . . ." Now, Gabo, too, disappeared into the increasingly turbulent and devouring wake of the Revolution.

The fall of that crucial year of 1989 burst upon Castro like an even more menacing wind. For at least the last ten years, he had depended upon unscrupulous government after unscrupulous government in Panama to smuggle him technology, drugs, medicines, consumer goods. First, the populist Panamanian General Omar Torrijos had helped him; after Torrijos's death in 1981, the little, clever, pockmarked brute, General Manuel Noriega, had staunchly stood with Castro against the United States. Together, they were sure the *gringos* would never invade Panama, they were certain the United States had been too burnt in Vietnam and was now simply a passive player on the world stage. But to assure Noriega, Castro had worked out for the Panamanian dictator a deadly clever protection plan, which involved both a tapestry of bluff against the Americans and the building of an alternate and parallel military structure within Panama, the *Batallones de la Dignidad,* or "Dignity Battalions."

In a life of creating "irregular" military structures and threats, this one stood out as one of his most beautifully calibrated. It combined every nuance of psychological threat, employing as it did the emotions over the Panama Canal, the historic American presence in Panama, and middle-class anti-Noriega Panamanian reformers. In the spring of 1988, Castro had begun sending instructors to train battalions made up of the most violent thugs from the slums, along with dependent city workers and a smaller group of perpetual Leftists. The Cuban instructors were backed up by good numbers of advisers from Nicaragua, in particular those who had trained the *turbas divinas,* or "divine mobs" who were used to break up opposition rallies in Managua with clubs and blows. Always and ever looking back upon his own ascent to power through his guerrilla movement in the Sierra Maestra from 1956 to 1959, Castro genuinely convinced Manuel Noriega that, even if the *gringos* did invade, the battalions would lead hundreds of thousands of Panamanians to the mountains.

But Noriega began to go quite crazy that fall of 1989, and then, amazingly, on December 20, 1989, it happened—the United States did invade. Fidel knew about it when the circles of American planes leaving North

Carolina flocked around Cuba. For minutes, he was sure he was being invaded and in desperation he put the entire island on sudden alert. But the planes passed to the west.

The invasion, a new and original kind of attack launched in the dark at one in the morning in a style the Americans had never been smart enough to use before, did, in fact, swing Castro's "Dignity Battalions" into action. As Noriega's Panama Defense Forces melted away, and as Noriega himself squirmed through the streets for four days before finally giving himself up, the Castro-trained battalions fought ruthlessly. But in the end, it was not enough. They, too, gave up, and the "massacre" of the middle classes and the democratic leaders that Noriega and Castro had been planning did not come to pass.

At first, no one wanted to believe in the "massacre theory." But when the American troops found sixty-five thousand Cuban weapons, still all wrapped up tightly in their Cuban wrapping, the threat to massacre the middle classes was finally taken seriously. "We were waiting for it," the highly respected Panamanian banker and statesman Gilberto Arias told me that winter. "Noriega had studied Hitler and was fascinated with the Holocaust, and he was going to kill us all." Noriega was not a Castro but he liked Castro's tactics. "He was borrowing from Cuba the control mechanism, not the ideology," Ricardo Arias Calderón, the new vice-president of Panama, added. "He was clearly planning for . . . potential guerrilla warfare in case the U.S. carried out the invasion."

But in the end, Noriega only walked disconsolately into the Vatican embassy wearing red underwear in order to ward off voodoo charms. Within a few days, Castro's "Dignity Battalions" were defeated, and on January 3, 1990, Noriega walked out of the papal nuncio's—and straight into the arms of the waiting American army, leaving Castro ever more alone in the Caribbean, and with the enemy Americans now in full charge.

With the "loss" of Panama, Castro had only Nicaragua left for consolation, but it was nowhere near the economic prize Panama had been, for the Sandinistas were even more inept at running an economy than he was (they had had 33,000 percent inflation in 1988). Most important, there was no assurance in this age of Gorbachev (*Time* magazine that Christmas of 1989 named him not only their "Man of the Year" but their "Man of the Decade") that the Soviets would continue to support or even to suffer these obstreperous colonies that no longer belonged to them even by spurious reason or feigned ideology. It was even worse than that because in the same tumultuous year of 1989, Eastern Europe "freed" itself from Soviet rule and renounced Communism completely. Castro's ideological and material hinterlands were completely gone—his Eastern Europe military lifeline and his personal PX had vanished in a matter of mere months. Where would he go now for the arms that used to come from Czechoslovakia? For the intelligence and its mysterious apparatuses that had come from East Germany? For the help for the Sandinistas and the Angolans of the world that had come from Bulgaria, Romania, the Soviet Union?

And then there came the knock-out blow: the Nicaraguan elections of February 25, 1990. The Sandinistas had been lured into these elections by the long and sinuous machinations of Costa Rican president Oscar Arias and his famous Central American "peace plan." But they only allowed the elections to take place because they were absolutely sure they could control them and win them. This would make them look good among the Europeans, from whom they desperately needed money and investment, and elections would finally legitimize Sandinista rule before the world. In truth, there seemed no danger.

In the weeks before the elections, the opposition—which had squabbled and squabbled and had finally grouped together under a sixty-year-old woman, Violeta Chamorro, who seemed no threat—failed and fumbled at every turn. They had no money, and the Sandinistas controlled the television, the campaign buses, and the streets. Sandinista president Daniel Ortega transformed himself overnight from a military man, with uniforms and militarized mien, to a pop-star presidential candidate in tight blue jeans; rock music dominated his campaign. A few close observers noted that the Nicaraguans went to the Sandinista rallies but didn't really talk much about the whole thing.

But by evening of that Sunday, February 25, it was clear that the Nicaraguan people had simply nursed their rage at the mismanagement and oppression of the Sandinistas and, when the moment came, they declared themselves. Violeta Chamorro won overwhelmingly, and the Sandinistas stood about like dazed creatures who could not understand what possibly could have happened to their dream. As for Castro, his "revolutionary son" was now gone, too, and one American cartoon showed an enraged Castro looking at a bloodied Daniel Ortega after the loss, saying, "You what?"

As Castro's "empire" was falling apart politically, so too was he losing intellectual support. Everywhere he looked, he found criticisms from former admirers and even sycophants. But in those years leading up to 1989, it was the case of Régis Debray that disturbed Castro most deeply. Castro remembered all too well how the young Frenchman from a powerful upper-class Gaullist family, the star student at l'École normale supérieure, had come to Cuba as the most entranced of acolytes that pivotal year of 1965, when Castro was organizationally and ideologically at the height of putting his "guerrilla universe" in place.

Debray had played with Communism in those years, traveled about the world, suffered over "revolution" while wearing English tweed jackets and dancing in St.-Tropez. Soon he was personally chosen—blessed—tapped—to sit at Castro's feet, while Castro shrewdly dictated to him the ideas that were to be no less than a new, indigenous Castro Marxism for Latin America and for the Third World, cutting the Soviets out. *Revolución en la Revolución?*, a treatise on guerrilla warfare, was only a small, slim book, but it had a behemothic effect on the world. At the very height of the romance stage of guerrilladom, the book would stand as the creedification of Castro's own revolutionary faith and experience, and the announcement of his intention to impose its form on the rest of Latin America.

But by 1986, Debray was back in Paris, working for the tame and "respectable" Socialist president, François Mitterrand, and writing coolly with a most supreme ingratitude that periods of "wars of national liberation" had nearly everywhere drawn to a close. "Power today is becoming based less on physical and material parameters (territory, military forces) and more on factors linked to the capability of storing, managing, distributing and creating information," he wrote. "Yet the Soviet Union remains a superpower in the traditional sense, strong only in terms of obsolete forces such as tank divisions and conventional military deployments." The worthless, cursed Frenchman could not leave it even there. "The Third World is bidding its farewell to arms," he summed up. "It is seeking God and computers rather than Kalashnikovs. I say 'God' because traditional cultures are resurfacing—they are better suited than ideologies to fill the void created by technological and economic upheaval. . . ." Fidel could hardly speak for rage.

The ingratitude of foreigners was bad enough, but far worse and far more cruel was that now, after thirty years, the youth of Cuba, the very flower of Castro's revolutionary tree, was beginning to leave him. The new technocrat class was clearly bored with the sheer inefficiency of Cuba and exhausted by a sacrifice that had become bureaucratized into eternity. Their favorite whispered phrase about Castro was: "He is like the sun, from afar he warms, but nearby he burns."

It was even worse with the less-educated youth. Castro had himself seen a long video study of Cuban young people, made by his own National Directorate of Police. The study found 48 percent of the Cuban people under twenty-five were listless and disillusioned, and it pictured them in detail and with a shattering honesty. The police included pictures of Cuban homosexuals, whom Castro had always abhorred and persecuted (for one thing, they uniquely were able to resist the spell and the force of his "machismo"), reveling in pornographic and Dionysian dances; statements from youths who did not even know who was the president of Cuba; photos of "freakie-freakies" with shoulder-length hair and skintight jeans who were as far removed as they could be from what a disciplined, upright, neat "Communist youth" should be.

These young people even went so far as to dare to make fun of the sacred iconography of the Revolution. A Cuban *salsa,* or folk song, group released a catchy song, "That Man Is Crazy," supposedly about Ronald Reagan. Instead, Cuban young people began chanting it whenever Castro's aging image came on to the movie or television screen. They avidly listened to broadcasts from the United States and they insulted Castro's most primal feelings when they called running away to live on the streets "joining the guerrillas." While Fidel walked back and forth in his high-ceilinged office in the palace, stopping often to stare at the huge mockup of the Sierra Maestra on one long table, all his great and memoried battles carefully marked on every hillock and mountaintop, these abhorrent and ungrateful young Cubans were haunting the alleys of Old Havana like wild creatures, tormenting their leader by looking for Western tourists with dollars to sell.

Then there were those others who were "leaving him," the suicides: revolutionary Cuba's first president, Osvaldo Dorticós; the minister of labor, Augusto Martínez Sánchez; Cuban ambassador Alberto Mora . . . Suicides had always been part of the surrealist landscape of Cuba, but now suicide actually became the major cause of death for Cubans between the ages of forty-five and forty-nine.

If there had been one genuine heroine of the Revolution, it was Haydée Santamaría, with her square, plain, honest face and her sad seer's eyes. When she realized Fidel had survived the disastrous Moncada attack of 1953, she could barely speak to cry out her feelings, writing: "Finding him, we could begin to speak of a truth and a reality; we could begin with something—for we had nothing." Then, one day in 1980, she went into the bathroom, put a gun to her head, and blew her brains out. Her death was reported on July 28, but she had actually ritually killed herself on July 26, the sacred anniversary of Moncada. Some said her husband had left her for a younger woman; some said that Fidel, in giving her husband permission to marry again, had derided Haydée where he knew she could hear him, calling her *vieja y chocha* or "old and doddering." . . . Whatever the source of her despair, Haydée Santamaría, fervent believer in Castro and his Revolution, was dead by her own hand.

Soon enough, it would become clear that still another great love affair of Fidel's—his *"amor"* for Mother Spain—was over as well.

In the summer of 1992, Fidel finally traveled to his father's Spain for a major trip, one that had been put off for many years. He fully expected the odyssey to be a magnificent, stirring, triumphal moment in his lifetime. But that was not to be. Instead, Spain's most influential newspaper, *El Pais,* called him a "dying star." Everywhere he went, Cuban exiles and others picketed him, shouting obscenities at him and insulting him. (He could barely understand, much less sustain, this. In Cuba, such expressions of discontent were simply never permitted, and so something that was in truth due to his own repression had become, for him, objective reality.)

Spanish president Felipe Gonzalez was coolly friendly, but what could it mean that he would dare say to Castro, "We don't want either political prisoners or political exiles in our community"? It was all too clear to Castro that the mother country's first socialist president had himself traveled a long voyage—from his early socialism to a comfortable moderation approved by the European Community and the United States.

And when Castro finally went to Galicia to visit his father's little home, still leaning exhaustedly against the hillock, the Gallego newspapers noted snippily that his sentimental trip "can only be understood as part of the magical surrealism of those lands," which wounded like the kind of self-satisfied analysis the *americanos* were always making about Latin culture.

In the end, he left Spain early. He did not even say good-bye to his Gallego hosts, and returned home to Havana amid rumors of a coup, which never quite occurred.

Far from grinding to a halt—to some denouement—the cycles stubbornly continued. And, as so often in the past, in the strange point-counterpoint that characterized his relations with the Cuban exile community in Miami, once again that community blindly stepped in to buy more time for Fidel.

By the fall of 1992, there was a small improvement in the Cuban food supply, which was a result of his mobilization of urban residents to grow their own food. Visitors to the island unanimously found the Cuban population disillusioned with the Revolution and quietly desperate about the food and living conditions. Indeed, Cuba was well on the way to nineteenth-century living conditions. The sugar-crop harvest was late, again, still another bad sign.

Indeed, even Fidel's temperamental and angry daughter, the beauteous Naty's Alina, came out, finally giving interviews in the foreign press and attacking her father. "He deserves a medal for having destroyed Cuba," she said sarcastically in one interview. In another, in the ABC newspaper in Spain, she said clearly: "This man is crazy, and everything is going to end in a bloodbath, because the government is still prepared to last many years. . . . They are always inventing some motive in order to make the Cuban people think about other things that are not reality. It is all like a novel that you read until you suddenly open your eyes unless you die."

When the interviewer noted that she looked a lot like her father, the slim, dark, haunted-looking Alina exclaimed bitterly, "Don't say that, don't say that he is my father."

Enter the far Right of the conservative community in Miami: it was not enough that the "Blue Ribbon Commission" was busy planning to take over Cuba once Fidel was gone. The far Right also pressed in Congress for the adoption of the Torricelli bill, which further tightened the American embargo on Cuba by, among other things, forbidding foreign subsidiaries of American companies from trading with Cuba. This would cut off substantial amounts of trade—and, particularly, it would increase the terrible scarcity of much-needed food products, medicine, and clothing.

It also did something else: it gave Castro exactly the excuse that he so needed to blame all the shortages and all the failures again squarely on the *americanos.* Soon, his rhetoric once again was deep into excusing his own regime. Castro was at his revolutionary-demagagogic best, reawakening the old wrath of American meddling and intervention, explaining to the Cuban people that what they were experiencing was nothing less than another "Platt amendment." What's more, the *americanos* again wanted the Cubans "to live in a concentration camp" (Cuba) like those unspeakable camps that the severe and ruthless Spanish general Valeriano Weyler had so cruelly imposed during the Cuban war for independence in 1898. All of the old images were being deliberately and vividly invoked.

But Fidel Castro was never going to give up. Fidel Castro, the caudillo to end all caudillos, was not ever going to go quietly into the night. With his genius for improvisation and with his gift for making people believe in his capacity for change and transformation, Fidel soon was wooing foreign businessmen to invest in the new Cuba—or so it seemed.

First, in the summer of 1991, he traveled ostentatiously to Cozumel, the lovely, luxuriant isle off Mexico, to meet with the democratically elected presidents of Mexico, Venezuela, and Colombia. (The meeting had about it the romantically redolent aura of the golden days of the past; Mexico, after all, had been where he had plotted the Revolution in 1955 and 1956.) The Latin leaders told the press that they saw hope for a "broad political opening" in Cuba, but Castro was seeking to enter the "Group of Three," and to receive oil, commerce, and tourists from it. Inside Cuba, Radio Rebelde dutifully opined that the meeting showed "how different political systems were not an obstacle to friendship and economic relations."

Suddenly, Spanish businessmen and politicos, even "Gallego" ultra-conservative Manuel Fraga, were seen in Cuba, traveling about the island, talking of investment in the old and failing sugar industry, of buying up Cuban sugar mills, and of course chatting with that other famous "Gallego," the mysterious man who ran Cuba.

Suddenly, even American businessmen were in Cuba, looking around for investments. They were all talking about the new five-star hotels, almost all Spanish-built, along the great beaches of Cuba, where 350,000 European tourists came in 1991 to see the "new/old Cuba." Most often, in truth, they came for sexual holidays, where they could make love on the cheap with the new generation of *jineteras* who were everywhere and available for roughly fifty dollars a night. (*Jinetera* is the Cuban word for "jockey," and it refers to Cuban women who "ride" the tourist trade, in order to get access to foreign currency, as well as to the male money changers on the black market.)

Instead of condemning these "counterrevolutionary" practices, Fidel actually tried to explain away this obvious prostitution by saying, in a July 11, 1992, speech, that these women were, after all, not forced into prostitution, as in the evil past of Batista and the *americanos*. Since the government provided housing, education, health care, and food, the women clearly were "volunteers." And they were also clean.

(Still, he never was quite able to explain why, after his constant early insistence that the Revolution had abolished "capitalist" prostitution, so many Cuban women were again "volunteering" for such sad "duty"! And some foreign diplomats in Havana mused with sadness that, with the fall of Communism and the rise of tourism, the "great experiment" had now sunk to the status of a kind of "Communist theme park," or to a "Museum of the Revolution" for foreigners, or to a "tourism apartheid" by which Cubans were regularly denied access to this glittering five-star world. How, indeed, would Fidel explain to the lurking ghost of Che Guevara that Che's daughter had actually been denied entrance to the Havana Libre Hotel because she was not a foreigner? Or how to explain the Cuban teenager who, when asked what he wanted to be when he grew up, answered, "A foreigner"?)

Fidel himself has his primary house on the western outskirts of Havana, a lovely estate that seems to rise majestically out of that brilliant green of the Cuban tropical foliage. Behind three guard posts, only the anointed can find the house whose code name is "160." As with his other estates on the coast, it has a film projection room, beautiful Cuban modern art, primitive African figures (to remind him of his African dreams of conquest), and Scandinavian furniture of native tropical hardwoods.

Still, it has seemed to many that Fidel actually was willing to change with the times. Anne-Marie O'Connor has described in *Esquire* magazine the night in 1992, for instance, when he was dining out in the Country Club district, where his elite still live in the elegant mansions of the old middle classes. He was with a rich Mexican businessman, Mario Vázquez Raña. Suddenly, the Mexican presented the *líder máximo* (who had always loved diving with sharks, whom he thought of as *americanos*) with an extraordinary gift: a gold diver's watch, studded with tiny diamonds that glittered on Fidel's wrist just as "the Revolution" had shone for him in its early days.

According to the story, which was authoritatively related to foreigners, Castro extended his arm and impassively and skeptically stared at the watch, before saying with that accustomed quizzical, bemused, ironic look of his (which always made him seem the eternal wide-eyed teenager): "This is dangerous. I have a small fortune here on my left hand. I will see in my will who I will leave it to, this watch." And then, "People have given me so many things over the years. I've given away many of those things, but I'm going to keep this watch."

He seemed to look within—a most unusual mode for Castro—and even to reveal himself, which was even more unusual. "I still haven't made up a will with some of the new things, and I still haven't given up my books. I'll keep them until the end. And afterward, if anyone is interested in them, if they have some historic value, I will leave them to you with great pleasure."

Many of the guests were stunned. Fidel never discussed his mortality. Was it possible that he was beginning to be able to face or contemplate the end?

Across those same short "ninety miles" that had always separated those two dissimilar but historically tied societies, Americans too were caught up in the new mood. U.S. investors were already readying themselves to "cash in" on a post-Castro Cuba, and they speculated that cash from exiles and corporations would fuel an instant $2 billion market in Cuba for virtually everything from fast-food franchises to the much-needed fresh paint. More than a dozen American companies had coughed up $25,000 apiece to fund a "Blue Ribbon Commission on the Economic Reconstruction of Cuba," sponsored by the far-Right Cuban American National Foundation, and their 1992 report laid out a massive program of privatization, creation of a stable convertible currency, and rapid incorporation into the North American free-trade area—all for a post-Castro Cuba in which once again Cubans on the island were to have no say in their future.

The Rightist Cubans in Miami were even pressing Wall Street to underwrite a $500 million bond issue, while they talked of a "Californian gold rush," once *el líder máximo* was gone.

Yet nothing ever really was realized; somehow, nothing ever got done.

For what all these officious planners were missing was that, far from embracing some new era, Fidel Castro was not changing at all—and even the Cubans who were the most totally disillusioned were not going to give up the Fidel they knew, with all the havoc he had brought them, for ultra-Rightist Cubans in Miami who had "blue-ribbon programs" to take their land and houses back, to invest their money and system in the island, and to destroy the independence that the Revolution had indeed brought Cuba.

And Fidel was not going to let them do that, either.

Actually, Castro's policy and tactics at this time had devolved secretly to taking what basically was a "Chinese way." Fidel was always a shaman at intuiting danger and a master at divining what possible ways he could turn next. All these efforts were aimed at his one invincible intent, which was to keep himself in power forever.

Little did Fidel care about the massacre in Tiananmen Square! Little did he bother himself about what the West euphemistically called "human rights violations"! What he saw was a Communist regime holding on to political and military power while carefully giving up only some economic power. The Chinese were allowing foreign investment and using it to solidify their own political control.

The model was tailor-made for Fidel, and it was very much on his mind as he met with the Spanish conservative leaders, the Americans, and the love-making tourists of the world: he would use them and their economic potential to keep himself and his Communism in power!

Throughout his life, Castro's political trajectory had never gone straight in any direction—never straight upward, never straight downward, but rather in endless circles and cycles. Indeed, if a palm reader were to study the lines of his hand, she would see his life as a series of circles, in which he would seem to be heading in one direction, and be quite convincing in his transformation, but would soon be found to have arrived at a totally different destination. So it was now.

What Fidel was really up to could finally be read in the political tea leaves of October 1991 at the great Congress of the Cuban Communist Party in Havana. That congress marked a moment of renewed hope for many. Nevertheless, seventeen hundred Communist delegates heard Castro repeat that pluralist democracy was "complete rubbish—to embrace it now would divide Cubans, threaten the country's independence, and risk a return to American domination of the island." Many had expected—had wanted and dreamed of—substantial liberalizing changes at the congress. Instead, they saw so many of the generation that made the 1959 Revolution swept away into the increasingly crowded dustheaps of *Fidelista* history—all, of course, except Fidel and Raúl!

The sole concessions to the new age were that Christians could now join in the government (an attempt to bring some ideology and spirit to the increasingly empty-spirited Cuban people) and that small tradesmen—plumbers, mechanics, but not farmers—could work "on their own account." (This small concession marked a way of creating some minimal economic life in the smitten country, but again without giving away anything politically significant.)

This turnaround—this new cycle of Fidel Castro's ever-gyrating political patterns—was followed within a year by the firing of Carlos Aldana, a powerful Castro intimate who dared to support liberalization and question Fidel's political direction. Aldana had been in charge of ideological affairs, an important post that included control of the media, the training of party cadres, foreign affairs, and education.

It was at the party congress in 1991 that Aldana had questioned Castro's "Marxist isolationism" and his stubborn rejection of the reforms sweeping the Eastern Bloc. Although Aldana got the message and gave the appropriate "mea culpa" to Fidel, his career was finished. It would be a good warning to any of the rest who might have "ideas."

Here was Fidel firmly closing the chapter on those relatively hopeful months that had seemed to many Cubans to offer a real chance for change.

Meanwhile, change swirled with ever-quickening speed around Fidel in his personal life as well. In 1984 his only legitimate child, "Fidelito," had been brought out of the closet. Suddenly his name appeared in the papers, even with his matronymic Díaz-Balart. Fidelito, a paunchy, Russian-trained nuclear scientist with a Russian wife and three children, was suddenly appointed head of the Cuban nuclear facility, and he was soon rumored in Russia to have political ambitions (never proven). In 1992, just as suddenly, like Aldana and all the others, he was out; he disappeared from sight and was dismissed from his position.

Rumors surfaced that he was having an affair with another woman (his Russian wife had long wanted to defect from Cuba) and/or that he had made contacts with dissidents. Those reports probably masked the fact that the great nuclear plant Fidel was building—dependent, of course, upon Soviet aid—marked still another failure. As early as 1976, Cuba had signed an agreement with the Soviets to construct two 440-megawatt nuclear power reactors near Cienfuegos, only 180 miles south of Key West. Even after construction began in 1983, the Cubans plodded ahead—until September of 1992, when Castro announced the suspension of the great nationalistic project because his government "could no longer meet the financial terms set by the Russian government." Other reasons: The entire program suffered from poor construction practices and inadequate training for reactor operators.

Even while the unfortunate Fidelito seemed to be out on the dingy streets of Old Havana—or as some said, under house arrest—looking for work, the Americans breathed a small sigh of relief. The two reactors were to go on-line in 1995 and 1997, and it was clear to objective nuclear analysts that they would create, not far off the American coast, a threat perhaps even greater than that posed by the Chernobyl disaster in Ukraine.

The *Wall Street Journal* listed some of the problems: inadequate fire-protection features; containment systems that were not fully pressurized, increasing the probability of an uncontrolled release of radioactivity into the environment during a nuclear accident; and generally slipshod construction (testified to by a dozen Cuban defectors who had worked on the reactors.) Other experts cited many other Chernobyl-like threats: faulty seals and defective welds; long exposure of sensitive equipment to corrosive salt water–saturated tropical air; substandard materials; incompetently designed safety features; and insufficiently trained operators and technicians.

To synthesize, were an accident to occur—and, given all of these defects, it would be far more likely to occur than not—large quantities of radioactive material would spread at least as far as central and southern Florida, and perhaps farther, depending upon rains and winds over the Caribbean Sea. Yet, despite these seemingly impossible odds, there were still rumblings of a big deal among Cuba, Russia, and France to get the plant completed. It was simply another example of the extent to which Fidel just never gave up on anything that he wanted.

It was not only this Chernobyl threat that stalked the Cuban-American relationship (or, perhaps better said, nonrelationship), but also the matter of Fidel's consuming longtime interest in attacking the American nuclear plant at Turkey Point just south of Miami.

All of this was simply a repetition of his behavior during the Missile Crisis, when he scared even Nikita Khrushchev by wanting to strike at the United States: throughout his life, he would have destroyed this hated "enemy of the Cuban people," could he have.

As Castro's empire closed around him, it became clear that his extravagant claims—that he had done great things in Cuba in the areas of race, of literacy, and of health—were also far from accurate. It was true that he had to a large degree abolished racial segregation and increased areas of equality for the 35 percent of the Cuban population that was mulatto or black. He had overseen substantial improvements in spreading health care to the rural poor, so that infant mortality had fallen and life expectancy and literacy had risen. But the terrible and the unpalatable fact after all the years of sacrifice was that, while the Cuba of 1959 had been not only immeasurably ahead of every other nation in the Caribbean and the Third World but actually at the point of economic "takeoff," the Cuba of 1990 had fallen well behind even relatively primitive Latin American countries. In 1952, Cuba had come in third in the hemisphere after oil-rich Venezuela and land-rich Argentina in relative positions of social indicators. By 1981, in World Bank figures, Cuba rated a mere fifteenth.

The Cuban economy under Castro, with its total dependence upon the Soviet Bloc and its success or failure, had simply failed to develop products and industries capable of competing in Western or world markets and earning convertible currencies. In creating his Stalinist central planning system, in placing it completely under him and forcing it to cater to his every whim for his special plans, for his special cows, and for his special visitors, Castro had smothered every impulse of that very independence of will that modern countries required for their economies. Worst of all, out of a resentment so profound and a fury so consuming it would have burned the calluses off the feet of Lucifer himself, Castro had turned Cuba away from the world's consummate modern partner, the United States, and toward an ancient, totalitarian, fettered country and ideology that in many ways carried Cuba back to Spanish medievalism rather than forward into the modern world. One Cuban writer called it another "counterbirth" of Castro's.

His was a politics not of interests but of complexes. But now it was no longer enough—it was no longer even cute—for Fidel to appear on television with his boyish charm and hold out a jar of his new yogurt made from buffalo milk and tell the Cuban people straight-faced, "It is great. Those who have tasted it say that it is very good. It tastes . . . like coconut."

From the very beginning, it was always difficult for Western or even classic economists of any kind to figure out—to characterize—to quantify in any reasonably measurable matter—exactly what was going on inside the "economy" of Cuba. Indeed, it was well-nigh impossible.

In 1962, two years after the march upon Havana, the Castro regime moved swiftly to the Soviet system of economic measurements; since then, one could not really compare statistics directly with the systems and standards of the West. So the best measure has always been to compare where, at any one time, Cuba stood on the scale of Latin American countries in economic development.

In 1958, for instance, just as Castro was coming to power, Cuba was economically among the top five countries in the hemisphere, sometimes rating higher, with exports totaling $732 million. By 1997, Cuba was among the bottom five—in 1996, it was sixteenth, out of twenty-one nations, near the bottom, down there with Paraguay, with $2.832 million in exports. Another comparison can be made using sugar, Cuba's primary national product. In the late 1950s, when Cuba had about six million people, sugar production was six million tons, or about one ton per person; by the turn of the century, Cuba had eleven million people and produced about four million tons, or about a third of a ton per person.

In the 1950s, Cuba had no foreign debt; by the turn of the century, it had a huge one, which in almost every case it utterly refused to pay. In the pre-Castro era, the Cuban peso had been equal in value to the U.S. dollar; by the turn of the century, the peso was twenty to twenty-five to the dollar. And none of this even took into consideration the enormous growth rates of the world over this nearly fifty-year period.

Castro kept pretending that he was open to "international investment," and from the 1990s onward, European, Canadian, and finally even American tourists (including Cuban-born exiles) were again flocking to Cuba. True, a few investments were indeed made, but they were virtually all in either the big, largely Spanish-funded five-star hotels on the beaches, where no Cubans other than employees now dared step, or in mineral-wealth areas special to Cuba like the rich aluminum mines, where there were largely Canadian investments.

In his accustomed spirals of change—of giving and taking power—of smoking dissidents out by a Cuban form of allowing a "thousand flowers to bloom"—Castro in the 1990s perfected his venerable old tactics. First he would pretend to open up, giving his people access to the dollar economy that now ruled the little island nation. Then, usually within ten or eleven months, in fact with traceable regularity, he would brutally clamp down again.

First, he allowed Cubans to take foreigners into their homes; then Cubans could have small restaurants there, but with no more than twelve seats; then, predictably, he would take some action that would appear innocent but would with ruthless effectiveness quickly cancel out all of his gracious "gifts."

In the late 1990s, for instance, just as many Cuban homes were beginning to earn dollars through their home-hotels and home-restaurants, the *líder máximo* put such heavy "taxes" on them ($200 a month for each room, in a country where most people earned the equivalent of $20 a month) that most of them were wiped out.

Meanwhile, those foreign companies which did locate in Cuba were not permitted to operate in any normal capitalist way. Those companies had to go to the government—to Fidel—to be granted their workers. The companies paid Fidel in dollars. The workers were paid in virtually worthless amounts of pesos.

By 1999, the country that had been the most friendly of all to Cuba and to Castro over the years, Canada, had grown tired (actually, sick and tired) of the Cuban leader and his ways. After years of putting up big investments, particularly but not only in aluminum, Canada dramatically drew back in its idealistic "constructive engagement" with Castro, a policy which supposedly would gradually woo him over and draw him out. They had sought to push institutional reform within Cuba through contacts with the younger generation of Cuban officials under Castro; they brought these men and women to Canada to see how an "institutionalized country" worked; and they sought to develop a better business atmosphere for the time when . . .

But that year instead, big Canadian firms like the Sherritt International Corporation froze their proposed big investments, from $500 million to $100 million. By the time of the Summit of the Americas in Quebec City in 2001, Prime Minister Jean Chrétien was saying frostily that he was putting some "northern ice" on the relationship. It didn't help that, when he had traveled to the island a year before, Chrétien had been submitted to a twenty-minute harangue by Castro about the hated United States before he even left the tarmac—or that Canada was by then being called by Castro "the second enemy to the North." But by then, the Canadians did not really feel especially singled out, because at the European-Latin summit meeting in Rio de

Janeiro that same year, Fidel first insulted another of his fading supporters, the Spanish, by insisting that the respected Spanish secretary-general of NATO, Javier Solana, should be prosecuted for genocide over Kosovo!

Nor did it help that when the final photograph of the assembled leaders was being taken, Castro disappeared, only to return to tell the press that he was not there because "I was urinating."

The simple fact was that what Fidel Castro really loved was The Game. He was the master of it, its eternal Croupier. The world was his Las Vegas. Outsiders always made the mistake of thinking that he actually wanted things to change, to move, to develop. Indeed, that was their eternal mistake, because Castro in truth only wanted things to stay as they were, which meant making only whatever changes were necessary for him to stay in the center of power—and in total power.

In the fall of 1997, I traveled to Rome to spend a week at the Vatican. As a journalist and as an analyst, I wanted to treat the historic home of Roman Catholicism as a country (which in many senses, of course, it is) and I wanted to view it with the same tools—analyzing its structures, perusing its policies, and searching for any new interpretations or ideas—that we correspondents and columnists employ for other nations. In fact, it was intellectually a delicious week, spent interviewing cardinals, archbishops, the head of the Jesuit order, and many others.

I soon found, not really to my surprise, that one of Pope John Paul II's next areas of devout attention was going to be Cuba, that beautiful isle that Fidel Castro, trained by the Jesuits, had made "Communist." Indeed, on one of those fascinating days, I sat for two hours in his gorgeous office in downtown Rome with Professor Rocco Buttiglione, the pontiff's close friend, a philosopher and politician and a man widely described as the "interpreter" of the pope's thinking and intentions.

"On the one hand, you have Fidel Castro, the Communist," the handsome and accomplished professor began. "On the other hand, you have Fidel Castro, the Latin American leader, belonging to the great family of caudillos, who represents the resistance of the Catholic and Spanish elements against the colonization of 'Big Brother.' Now, the Holy Father offers Fidel Castro the opportunity of entering history not as a Communist but as a representative of the Latin American people. If Fidel Castro takes a certain distance from Communism and yet wants to affirm himself against the United States, he must go back to Catholicism."

Then he offered the real focus of the pope's profound intention. "This would pave the way for a democratic transition in Cuba," he said. "It would offer a way for mediation with American policy; and it would open the world to Cuba, and Cuba to the world."

The fight between *Fidelista* socialism and Roman Catholic Christianity (as well, of course, as the Protestant churches) had historic roots. From particularly the 1960s onward, as Marxist ideology grew in Latin America, the Marxists, through their "theology of liberation," had been trying to mix up the Christian "theology of redemption" with their own "theology of liberation" and to take "Christ the Redeemer" to "Christ the Revolutionary," and to substitute for the institutional church the "popular church of the Marxists." Now, the struggle ensued once again, and this time between two historical giants.

American theologian George Weigel further compared the visit, which would take place in the winter of 1998, with the pope's earlier visits to Poland, when, with Communism in bloom there during the 1980s, the pontiff's intention was "to give the country back its history and culture, which had been hijacked for fifty years. That is exactly what is happening in Cuba. . . . If that search has already begun to happen in Cuba, then all we're talking about is the details."

But when the aging, admired, and determined Roman Catholic leader finally set foot on Cuban soil in January of 1998, when he addressed throngs of enthusiastic and obviously spiritually hungry Cubans, men and women, Catholics and Protestants, Communists and atheists, across the entire island, when Castro forbade his adepts from taunting or in any way making fun of the visitor, many observers were certain that a new age had come. Oh yes, when the pope arrived, Castro had lectured him, right there on the tarmac, about the "terrible" Catholic history in Latin America—but then, that was what Castro did with everyone.

By the time the pope left, several days later, Castro had promised that the Vatican could bring in more priests and nuns, that the Church could use radio and television to proselytize, and that religious processions, in particular that of the historic "Virgen de la Caridad," or "Virgin of Charity," in which sometimes ten thousand people participated, would be regularized. The Christmas holiday, which had been abolished since 1970, was reinstated. Many around the world anticipated and predicted a resurgence of faith on the long-starved island.

But the innovatively Machiavellian mind of Fidel Castro, always plotting and planning seemingly without effort about how to use whatever situation for his own benefit, could not have been more different from the dull, dour, stolid minds of the Communists in Warsaw, Moscow, or Beijing. And so, Castro "allowed" the pope to come—to talk—and to go.

Largely, after the first unpleasant scene on the tarmac, the pope was treated respectfully by the government. Fidel could afford to make promises—what were promises? After the pontiff was home in the Vatican with all its treasures, Fidel would still rule on the ground. His ground.

The upshot was that virtually none of Castro's promises were kept. As the prestigious Pax Cristi Netherlands noted in a comprehensive report, "Cuba: A Year After the Pope": "So far it is Fidel Castro who has gained the most from the papal visit. With his visit, the Pope legitimized the dictator's rule. As for the Church, Castro's minimal concessions have made the Church steer a safe course, for fear of losing these 'achievements.' In this way, the regime successfully prevents the Church from speaking out more forcefully in matters of democracy and human rights and from fostering ties with the independent opposition."

Moreover, Italian journalists who spent time in Cuba during the pope's visit and afterward were soon warning that Castro was already "hijacking" the visit. He was in the process of simply making it into part of a "new folklore of the revolution"—now the folklore included Fidel's confrontation with one of the greatest spiritual leaders of mankind. Without the cleverness of the pontiff himself, they wrote, the visit could lead to a kind of "Potemkin Catholicism," with Castro employing it simply as a mechanism for maintaining the external image of the regime.

No one could say, of course, which "faith" would win in the end—but the first direct confrontation of *Fidelismo* against *catolicismo* was hardly a victory for Rome.

Within a year, the *Financial Times* was writing of a "new lurch to hardline authoritarianism" in Cuba, "which has all but swept away the goodwill and hopes for wider reform generated by the visit by Pope John Paul." The paper quoted a European ambassador as remarking, "There seems to be no master plan, except to stay in power."

Just when Castro's fortunes seemed again to be down, in the fall of 1999, just as he seemed to be out of crises to manipulate and "impossible situations" with which to apply his masterful political skills, once again an event presented itself to him. The "Elián González case" was a replay of the visit of Anastas Mikoyan to Cuba—all over again; it was the internal upheaval in Cuba precursing the Mariel boat lift—all over again; it was, to look back on the history that had so inspired him all his life, a kind of replay of the disgusting, but useful, case of the U.S. Marines urinating on the statue of José Martí in Havana when Fidel was just a young man.

The difference between Fidel and other leaders was the fact that, faced with a situation like little Elián González—the charming and photogenic five-year-old Cuban left hanging on a raft on Thanksgiving morning of 1999 while his mother died trying to escape to Florida—the other leaders would not have the faintest idea of how to use such a situation. In fact, even Fidel, the master of manipulation, was late on grasping the incredible potential of the winsome and lost little boy.

For the first week, it appeared that the "story of Elián" was simply another case, tragic but "normal," of disgruntled Cubans trying to flee Cuba and meeting with tragedy. The boy had been left floating for days, in the searing sunlight out on that vast and empty sea, while all the others in the boat except two drowned. But after he was rescued by the U.S. Coast Guard on Thanksgiving morning, the stories soon identified him, to Castro and to others, as a kind of "magic amulet" of a child who would define the rights and even future powers of both sides.

At first, it had seemed that the boy would simply be sent home—that was the usual procedure in cases such as this. But then members of the boy's family in Miami stepped in and took him over. After that first week, Fidel grasped the situation well: he would make little Elián González the newest symbol of his fight against the *americanos* by fueling a vast and public fight to get the child back to Cuba, where he "belonged." He employed his usual methods: mass demonstrations, his brilliant and intuitive understanding of how to use the media, his understanding of the American people's sentiment over such a "family case," his knowledge of American law and of Cuban-American fanaticism as a weakness to use to isolate them from other Americans.

But in order to use the child as a means of reviving his own quivering fortunes, Castro needed to make the beautiful and wistful little boy into more than he was—and that was the sort of thing Fidel was very good at. Thus soon it was being said that the child was found, after two sun-searing days at sea and with sharks hovering everywhere, surrounded by protective dolphins—and not even so much as sunburned! Soon, both the Miami anti-Castro Cubans and Castro himself were making him the symbol they wanted. The sacred "Child Elián" became to many in Miami the magical, mystical symbol of an enchanted world, a symbolic Baby Jesus, if you will, sent to mediate between two Cuban worlds that have shown themselves unable to decide their own fates. Meanwhile, the revolutionary "Child Elián" became to the Cuban island the symbol and symptom of the very strength of Fidel Castro to stay in power.

In the winter of 2000, before Elián was finally returned to his father in Cuba, Guillermo Cabrera Infante, one of Cuba's greatest exiled writers, reported in an in-depth article in the Spanish socialist newspaper *El Pais* how Castro was looking at the case as a test of his standing with the priests, the "Babalao," of Santería, the original African religion of the island. If he were unable to regain control of this essentially magical child, Cabrera Infante wrote, the Cuban leader believed that that would be a notably bad "sign" and could even turn the Babalao against him at a time when he was suffering defeat after defeat on his withering island.

This was particularly important because Fidel remembered all too well, in his rich inner sanctum book of methods and maneuvers, how it was the Babalao who had just gradually withdrawn their support from Batista when he, Castro, was fighting to take Havana. Now Castro himself was vulnerable, just as he had been when he executed Tony de la Guardia, and the Santería community was horrified, for he had executed a twin (Santería teaches that you must never separate twins). Fidel now also needed protection from the Babalao.

Finally, Castro came up with the "perfect formula" to solve the Elián problem, which by the winter of 2000 had developed into an all-out struggle between Miami and Havana, with the American government in between and with more and more non-Cuban Americans turning against the Cuban exile community (a development which Fidel, of course, encouraged).

So now he put forward the idea of flying to New York not only the entire immediate family of the child but also Cuban doctors and psychiatrists, twelve of the boy's schoolmates, several Cuban intelligence agents, and even Elián's school desk. The desk had already been made into a kind of national shrine, and now it was to become a movable shrine.

Most well-meaning Americans, naive or innocent about Cuba, could not know that such men and women in Cuba work in a uniquely *Fidelista* kind of "crisis management" that bears no resemblance to the American or European style. Essentially, they act as the government's barometer for rising disaffection within the country, but they also oversee torture sessions to find out how much a prisoner can bear. In the past, for instance, when these specialists in avoiding internal conflicts would feel that the discontent was growing on the island, they would advise the leader to "open the safety valve." Almost always then, Castro would suddenly—and "inexplicably," to the outside world—let people leave in some manner.

It was thus, during the Mariel boat lift in 1980, that Castro allowed tens of thousands to flee Cuba. Now his tactics served to force a little boy to come "home."

In the end, Elián was sent home—and Fidel, at least for a time, was able to claim a triumph in getting this child and symbol of his power back on Cuban soil. The Miami Cuban family was disconsolate; the rest of America was relieved. Very few recalled that Fidel, "father" of his country, had actually kidnapped his own first child, Fidelito, in the mid-1950s when he was organizing the revolution in Mexico; he had kept Fidelito there, in the elegant home of wealthy friends, until the child's mother, Mirta, kidnapped him in return and brought him back to Cuba and to Florida.

Was Elián really the son of his natural father, Juan Miguel González? Was he perhaps also a son of the Revolution and, thus, of the "Maximum Leader" himself? Or was he the son of the mother who lost her life trying to bring him to America?

Only Father Fidel knew.

Where, by now, were the other dreamers? The sweet and vulnerable Mirta still lived where she had for many years, in an unobtrusive, British-style brick apartment building in Madrid, with her conservative and long-suffering husband. She saw Fidelito occasionally, clandestinely, in European capitals, and she knew that if she ever "talked" about Fidel or her life with him, she would never see her son again. When visitors came to see her in Madrid and her husband, Emilio, went out of the room, she would sneak out pictures of her grandchildren in Cuba—Fidelito's children by his Russian wife. Both of her daughters with her second husband were Leftists, and one had married a member of the Spanish Communist party. The wags in Madrid liked to say, cruelly, that her second husband lived with three women, "all of them in love with Fidel."

As for Fidelito, he lived almost unknown in Cuba, with his blond Russian wife and their three children, until something happened in 1983 and 1984 to cause Castro suddenly to allow his only legitimate son to come to the surface of Cuban society. Suddenly Fidelito's name and picture appeared in the newspapers, sometimes even with his Díaz-Balart matronymic. Suddenly, as the head of the Cuban nuclear organization, he was at a scientific meeting here, a scientific meeting there. One definite school of thought felt Fidel was grooming him, not Raúl, to take over, and this group was terrified of him. They said he had an explosive character, his own private intelligence apparatus, and extraordinary power and ambition. But by the 1990s, it was reliably reported that Fidelito was under house arrest—being a child of Fidel's was no security, either.

Alina Fernández, Naty's daughter, had also wanted to leave the island and was eventually successful in doing so. Before leaving, she amused herself by belonging to a group of elite, useless, gilded youth—children of important people in Cuba like ambassadors and generals. But far from being the "children of the Revolution," Alina's friends were ineffably more the children of American videos, of rock music, of a constant yearning for the world outside. Above all, they searched endlessly—and theatrically— for *emociónes fuertes,* or "strong emotions." Every hour of the day, searching for strong emotions—how difficult it was to be one of the privileged children of Cuba!

Mirta's brother, Rafael Díaz-Balart, lived luxuriously and happily in Madrid, having made a small fortune in many ways; while Fidel's older brother, Ramon, tried several times to defect to the United States—but finally gave up and quietly ran a ranch in Cuba.

Beautiful and at times eccentric Gloria Gaitán still lived quietly in Bogotá with her daughters, nursing her tragic father's museum and more than occasionally thinking about the "old days" in Havana. One day in 1988, she suddenly had her father dug up and reburied, this time standing up, in the style of the Colombian Chibcha Indians, in her backyard, because she said she thought it would bring him luck. By then, she understood, sadly so, why Castro had lost interest in her: "He has lived a thousand years, and I have lived only thirty."

The beautiful Isabel Custodio had grown into a lively middle-aged divorcée who wrote on feminist issues for the Mexican paper *Excelsior.* She too returned, as another moth to an eternal flame, to Cuba in the 1980s and met Fidel again for the first time since 1956. "When I saw him," she reminisced afterward, "we revived very important moments we had lived through in Mexico."

In Cali, Colombia, the big, handsome José Pardo Llada still started out his popular radio show every day with the poignant song of the Cuba he had left behind, "Guantanamera."

The men and (particularly) the women in Fidel's life began popping up again in these years, sometimes giving new revelations about their past with the *líder máximo*. Perhaps it was because they thought the end of his life was nearing and that it was time now to talk. Isabel Custodio in Mexico wrote a book about her love affair with him; so did the mysterious and strange Marita Lorenz, whose book, in German, was called *Lieber Fidel,* or *Dear Fidel.*

In the spring of 2001, Marita, now much heavier than the beautiful, black-haired, slim young German woman who had sailed into Havana—and into big trouble in those early years of the revolution—and her book were feted in Germany. The woman who had then got deeply mixed up with the CIA, with the most rabid anti-Castro exiles, and even in the Kennedy assassination, told the *Sueddeutsche Zeitung, "Diktatoren kommen mir nicht mehr ins Bett,"* or "Dictators no longer take me to bed." But the photograph was of her was smiling broadly as she showed an old picture of her with the young Fidel before they lived together for some months in the old Hilton Hotel in Havana in 1959.

Even some information on his "other children," those by Dalia, the still little-known *"mujer de Trinidad,"* or the "woman from Trinidad," began to come out. Knight Ridder correspondent Juan O. Tamayo wrote in the fall of 2000 that Castro had actually been married to Dalia for thirty years and that their sons were named Angel, Antonio, Alejandro, Alexis, and Alex but that they "never have been identified in the island's media." The boys, pictured as big, lusty, handsome young men in a photo from 1994 or 1995, it was said, were constantly instructed by their father not to live or act in any way ostentatiously or to call attention to themselves—and apparently they did not and had not. The government takes care of their every need, but they do not own their own cars and thus must call the family's central security office when they need rides around Havana.

When Alina Fernández, Fidel's daughter by Naty, defected, she spoke somewhat about the five young men, noting that "There is no yellow press in Cuba to report on their lives, but of course when people see a young guy with lots of bodyguards, they start guessing whose sons they are." Almost nothing is known about a sixth Castro son, apparently named Jorge Angel Castro and identified by Alina as the child of a woman who died years ago. There are many grandchildren, and the five Dalia sons were studying medicine and computer technology.

In a documentary, *Fidel: Forty Years of the Cuban Revolution and Its Leader,* by U.S. filmmaker Estele Bravo, who lives part-time in Havana, Castro acknowledged having a general propensity for "permanent conspiracy" and said that "In this sense, I have reserved for myself a total freedom." But the documentary also noted that Cubans still "know very little about the personal life of Fidel."

These attitudes sprung from beautiful Cuba's being a half-finished, an incomplete, an *atimia* society. A desperate people, an unfinished people, a people needing terribly to be consolidated in a society, a people who came to be consolidated in one person, Fidel Castro. He gave them a feeling of completion, the feeling of the totality of a very great love. He gave them his own culture. That is why he sent the Christian, Westernized, socialized Cuban middle class away; that is why he sent vulnerable young virgins out to work in the fields and thus implement his destruction of the traditional Cuban family; and that is why he smashed the old statues and destroyed Rolando Amador's library. It was the only way he could settle his old scores with the United States.

For just at the moment in history when Cuba had been weak, America had crept into her very soul. That was why he had had to close down Cuba. Not because the Americans turned their backs on him, but in order to avoid the wrenching feelings of inferiority, so as not to have to compete with a culture that was so unbearable exactly because the Cuban people so wanted it.

Castro had also created a new—a substitute—Cuba. He had made a massive "identification with the aggressor" (mainly his father, but also Batista and the Jesuits), as psychiatrist Facundo Lima explained it. His father had owned great amounts of land: Fidel became for all intents and purposes the owner of Cuba. Angel Castro had had a number of illegitimate children: Fidel had more of them. His father had had a "divided family," one legitimate and the other a bastard one: Fidel divided utterly the Cuban family so that on the one hand there were the revolutionaries (the legitimate family) and on the other the counterrevolutionaries, the bastards. Marxism, he turned into the new Jesuitical faith, and that faith's "new man" would undo all the history of his illegitimate background.

He had an enormous effect on the twentieth century. The numbers of people who owed their deaths to Fidel Castro are difficult to establish, his influence and power were so often so amorphous, but at the same time so decisive; but when one simply tallies up the force of his influence in countries like Angola, Mozambique, Nicaragua, El Salvador, and even remote and forgotten places and situations like Zanzibar (not to mention the Cubans themselves killed and the more than one million Cubans exiled because of him), one has to come to the conclusion that he is personally responsible for the deaths of hundreds of thousands of persons.

He is also supremely responsible for drawing out poisoned situations into endless conflicts—without his involvement, these conflicts would have ended far more quickly and far more decisively, with immeasurably far less suffering. In the end, he also killed culture; he killed a Cuba that, left alone and with a real reform, would have evolved into a developed and reasonably just nation in the time that he ruled over the days of its destruction. In the end, he left only silence and emptiness, fear and hatred, obsession and exhaustion.

But something distinctly odd happened. Despite the fact that the United States failed in almost every diplomatic, political, and military confrontation with Fidel, in the end the United States "won" the long fight. It won in the very area that Castro had tried so desperately to dominate, but could not: culture. American culture could not be defeated, because it was the culture of modernity and of the future. Indeed, in the end the final irony and the final indignity was that, in destroying every traditional moral basis for Cuban society, he became himself the oppressor. In wanting not to be free from (thus liberating oneself from) the outside "oppressor" but actually to be the "oppressor" (thus melding oneself to it), he in the end became his vision of Americans.

He thus never became really a founder of his own country, as did his old nemesis Rómulo Betancourt in Venezuela, but only a competing metropole to "America" and to "Americanization" in the world.

As the first year of the 1990s slipped by, Castro became increasingly frantic, his paranoia growing exponentially and in morbid intensity as he became more and more isolated and closed in, his friends falling all around him. Havana was going to "sink" into the sea. The Cuban people would return to the mountains, factories would be stoked with wood, not oil. His speeches grew more and more nihilistic and apocalyptic, as though Armageddon hovered nervously just over the horizon. He had closed in upon himself, like a wolf tracking itself under moons it could no longer gauge. He even had already created "experimental zones," where Cubans expecting the final American attack could return to the countryside to live off the land. In San Cristóbal, he formed an El Mango farm where oxen replaced broken-down tractors, where homemade thread was made to replace sutures, and where the *jutía,* a Cuban rat, was the subject of a food-generating breeding program so that it could be used in place of meat. No more dreaming of cows, now the Revolution's dreams had come down to rats! One thing that Castro had never lost was his ironic sense of symbolism: San Cristóbal was also the same area where the missiles of 1962 had been installed!

He seemed to be ending his days in a defeat too different from the mountaintops he had scaled, and he was not going to disappear quietly into the night. Unless he suddenly died naturally, his would be a Götterdämmerung end. Some kind of terrible striking out lay ahead—an attack on the United States, a mass suicide within, a bitter war within the military between the generations, something rightfully commensurate with the greatness and drama of Fidel Castro. Meanwhile, in Miami, the Cubans in exile had also returned to their past—they were organizing, mobilizing, planning, training, dreaming of returning to Cuba, of getting their land back, of restoring the questionable Cuban "grandeur" of the past. . . .

In the beginning, the Cuban people had called him "Fidel"—in adoration, in salvation, in love, like a Spanish woman with her husband before marriage. After the magnificence of the *triunfo,* as after the marriage, they immediately began calling him "Castro"—in sobriety, in respect, in fear. In the end, they called him only "*El*" or "He," for he had become finally a differentiated creature existing away from them—that sun so hot that it burned to come close.

All of that was true, and much more. And yet—and yet—while all the other charismatic leaders and/or dictators of the twentieth century had fallen or died, only Fidel Castro remained in power. In fact, he remained quite prominent and rather successfully in power. He had virtually no economy: no matter, he could still talk his way out of a GNP any day! He had put into practice no modern political system: no problem, he could still sway a crowd like no one else! His "ideas" about development and world governance had been totally passed by by history: don't worry about it, he is still an icon, with attention lavished upon him everywhere he goes.

Before, he had lived in the light of the supposition that he would never need a successor (who, after all, *could* succeed him?). But in the late 1990s, he even began, amazingly, to talk about his succession—he tended to call it "transition," which in "Fidel thought" meant that he would never die but that his passing would only mean a transition into a new form of *Fidelismo!*

What would happen "after Fidel"? What could happen after Fidel? And, by far the most compelling question: Can you have *Fidelismo* without Fidel?

Historically, no charismatic leader has outlived himself in his ideology or doctrine, for the simple reason that essentially these leaders have no doctrine outside of themselves. Their emotional tie to the people is the doctrine, and that tie necessarily dies with them, usually leaving their people not relieved but empty with despair, as after Perón in Argentina and after Stalin in the Soviet Union. It may not be this way in Cuba, but it will hardly be easy for the Cuban people to suddenly take responsibility after forty years.

Jaime Suchlicki, the respected head of the University of Miami's Institute for Cuban and Cuban-American Studies, probably has the most practical scenario. "Fidel Castro dies, he begins, in bed or of a heart attack. Raúl calls the Politburó and it appoints him as Secretary-General of the Communist Party. Then they appoint someone like Ricardo Alarcon (president of the Cuban parliament) or someone like him as president. The situation will evolve, but slowly. There will be a low probability of people marching into the streets. Initially, there will be martial law and nobody will do much of anything."

Economically, Suchlicki and many others predict that there will be attempts to implement the "Chinese model" in which a strong and autocratic government keeps itself in power by allowing some freedom and foreign involvement in the economic and social sectors. (In fact, that is already being done, although not very effectively, because Fidel will not give up any power to independent economic centers.)

Many in Miami believe that Fidel has so empowered his generals that they will simply take over after his death, protecting the island thusly from the hated American "democracy." After Fidel, the regime will be under intense international pressure. Then anything could happen, including mass violence and upheaval, with an attendant mass migration from the island.

And, of course, there was the question of the 650,000 Cubans, most of them by now Cuban-Americans, living in the United States, many of them still determined to return to their homeland and to "free it." What would *they* do?

Meanwhile, there he still was! Occasionally a fainting fit, probably some other maladies, but still there and, for the most part, even thriving! At the turn of the century, he was still only in his mid-seventies and he could boast that he had survived decades of American enmity, plots from within, economic disasters, the collapse of Communism and his Soviet supporters, and the failure of his liberation movements. And yet now there was this new group on the Left, led by President Hugo Chávez of Venezuela, who had even linked his intelligence systems to Fidel's and who was searching for a "new way" on the Left.

In fact, even as most of the world was basking in the comforting idea that, with the end of the Cold War, leaders like Castro were a thing of the past, his style and his tactics were finding new soil. In 2001, Irish Republican Army terrorists went from their base in Havana to Colombia to teach urban warfare to the Marxist guerrillas there. In Washington, the FBI suddenly arrested the top desk officer in the Pentagon as a Cuban spy—hardly evidence that Castro was pulling back from his perfervid anti-Americanism.

And, of course, when the World Trade Center and the Pentagon were blown up on September 11, 2001, these terrorists were following in many of Castro's own tactical "irregular warfare" techniques, not to speak of his having metaphorically "written the manual" for hatred for the United States—and for its modernity—that was now spreading across the world in new terrifying forms.

So the game wasn't over at all, and he was still its Grand Croupier.

But one thing *was* over: the myth that Fidel Castro had been a Communist. Just about no one believed that anymore. In truth, all that time he had been only holding stubbornly to the old Spanish-style caudillo autocracy, even while all the world was transforming itself in the name of individual liberties. In truth, with his megalomania and proud indiscipline and teeming personal demons, he had always been the last man on earth to be a disciplined member of any "doctrine" except his own.

And so in the end, he did finally turn out to be the only kind of "Communist" he could be—the last Communist, but the first survivor.

Neither with you nor without you
Do my sorrows find relief.
With you, because you kill me,
Without you, because I die.

(Old and classic gypsy ballad, untitled, and
popular in Cuba long before Fidel Castro)

SOURCE NOTES

CHAPTER 1: DREAMER OF THE DAY

Books, brochures, papers, and documents: Jiri Valenta, "Perspectives on Soviet-Cuban Relations," paper, 1/10/89, The Cuban American National Foundation, Washington, D.C.; Maurice Halperin, "Summary Outline of Perspectives on the Cuban Revolution/Post Revolution," paper, 7/29/85; Robert E. Quirk, "Fidel Castro: The Full Story of His Rise to Power, His Regime, His Allies, and His Adversaries"; Max Weber, selected papers, "On Charisma and Institution Building"; T. E. Lawrence; "Revolt in the Desert."

Magazine and newspaper articles: *The Atlantic,* "Havana's Military Machine," by John Hoyt Williams, August 1988; *Strategic Review,* "The Cuban Military Under Castro," reviewed by Douglas W. Payne; *El Alcázar,* Madrid, Spain, "La Habana Tal Como Era," by Emilio García Meras, 12/14/86.

Original interviews and oral histories: Fidel Castro, July and August 1966, Havana, Banao, and Pico Turquino, Cuba; Robert Francis Jordan, 4/13/87, Manila, Philippines; Emilio García Meras, 12/13/86, Madrid, Spain; Gloria Gaitán, 7/11/86, Bogotá, Colombia; Vicente Echerri, 11/25/86, New York; Juan Arcocha, 7/9/86, Paris, France; Ambika Soni, 3/17/86, New Delhi, India; Francisco "Pepe" Hernández, 3/22/86, Miami, Florida; Edmundo Flores, 2/12/86, Mexico City, Mexico; Dr. Damien Fernandez, 9/3/99, Washington D.C.; Dr. Jerrold Post, 8/12/99, Washington D.C.; and Dr. Jaime Suchlicki, by telephone, 11/22/99, from Miami, Florida.

SOURCE NOTES

CHAPTER 2: GNARLED ROOTS

Cuban history was culled from: Hugh Thomas, *Cuba;* Jaime Suchlicki, "The Intellectual Background of the Cuban Revolution," *Annals of the Southeastern Conference on Latin American Studies,* volume III, no. 1 (March 1972); Justo Carrillo, "Vision and Revision: U.S.-Cuban Relations, 1902 to 1959," paper; Carlos Alberto Montaner, "The Roots of Anti-Americanism in Cuba," *Caribbean Review,* vol. XIII, no. 2 (Spring 1984); W. Raymond Duncan, "Nationalism in Cuban Politics," in Suchlicki, *Cuba, Castro and Revolution;* Samuel Farber, *Revolution and Reaction in Cuba, 1933 to 1960;* Hubert Herring, *Latin America;* Rafael Fermoselle, *The Evolution of the Cuban Military: 1492–1986;* and Tad Szulc original interview with Antonio Núñez Jiménez, 4/4/85, Havana, Cuba.

Materials on Jose Martí were taken from: Richard Butler Gray, *José Martí, Cuban Patriot;* Jorge Manach, *Martí: Apostle of Freedom;* Ramon Eduardo Ruiz, *Cuba: The Making of a Revolution;* Robert Freeman Smith, *Background to Revolution;* essay by William Rex Crawford, "The Development of Cuban Thought"; Carlos Ripoll, *José Martí;* and Carlos Alberto Montaner, *Cuba, Castro and the Caribbean.*

Books, brochures, papers, dramatizations, and documents: Rosalía de Castro, *En Las Orillas del Sar;* Carlos Franqui, *Vida, aventuras y desastres de un hombre llamado Castro;* Alvaro Cunqueiro, *Ver Galicia;* V. S. Pritchett, *The Spanish Temper;* Fidel Castro / Frei Betto, *Fidel e a Religião, Conversas com Frei Betto;* Carlos Franqui, *Family Portrait with Fidel;* Guillermo Cabrera Infante, *Suicide in Cuba;* Peter Ustinov, public television series, *Russia,* 1/18/88.

Magazine article: *World & I,* "Castro: El Supremo—in Castro Latin American Virtues are Embodied, and Perverted," by Dolores Mayano Martin, April 1987.

Original interviews and oral histories: Salustiano Castro, 8/25/85, Lugo, Galicia, Spain; Rafael Díaz-Balart, 12/14/84, Madrid, Spain; Enrique Trueba, 12/13/84, Madrid, Spain; Dr. Marcelino Feal, 7/25/84, Miami, Florida; Don Hodgkins, 3/26/86, Daytona Beach, Florida; Waldo Balart, 10/26/85, Madrid, Spain; Sandra Hodgkins Francis, 4/24/86, London, England; Barbara Gordon, 4/8/85, Washington, D.C.; José "Pepe" Figueres, 5/27/85, San José, Costa Rica; Luis Ortega, 3/3/87, Miami, Florida; Raymundo Masferrer, 1/25/90, Washington, D.C.

CHAPTER 3: PRAYING TO WIN

Books, brochures, papers, and documents: Luis E. Aguilar, *Cuba 1933;* José Pardo Llada, *Fidel de los Jesuitas al Moncada;* Carlos Franqui, *Diary of the Cuban Revolution;* Fidel Castro / Frei Betto, *Fidel e a Religião: Conversas com Frei Betto;* Samuel Farber, *Revolution and Reaction in Cuba, 1933–1960;* Justo Carrillo, "Vision and Revision: U.S.-Cuban Relations, 1902 to 1959," paper; Emil Lederer,

State of the Masses; Jeffrey W. Barrett, *Impulse to Revolution in Latin America; C. J. Jung Speaking, Interviews and Encounters,* interview by H. R. Knickerbocker; Emil Ludwig, *Talks with Mussolini;* Raymond Carr, *Spain;* Belén Yearbook, supplied by Father Juan Manuel Dorta-Duque, Miami, Florida.

Magazine articles: *Caribbean Review,* "The Roots of Anti-Americanism in Cuba," vol. XIII, no. 2 (Spring 1984); *Newsweek,* Perspectives column, 11/16/87, from State Department files and originally published in *American Archivist Magazine; World Politics,* "The Dictator and Totalitarianism," by Robert C. Tucker, vol. XVII, no. 4 (July 1965).

Original interviews and oral histories: Pepín and Manolo Rodriguez, 1/22/85, Miami, Florida; Carlos Alberto Montaner, 12/13/84, Madrid, Spain; Dr. Rubén Darío Rumbaut, 2/27/85, Houston, Texas; original Tad Szulc interview with Max Lesnick, University of Miami Archives; Luis E. Aguilar, 2/27/85, Washington, D.C.; Father Armando Llorente, 1/22/85, Miami, Florida; José Ignacio Rasco, 1/11/85, Coral Gables, Florida; Ramón Mestre, Sr., 1/25/85, Miami, Florida; Emilio Caballero, 3/20/86, Miami, Florida; Enrique Trueba, 10/28/85, Madrid, Spain; Otilio "Capi" Campuzano, 3/25/86, Miami, Florida; Jack Skelly, 9/29/84, 10/4/84, and 11/28/84, Washington, D.C.; Dr. Marcelino Feal, 1/24/85, Miami, Florida; Antonio Navarro, 4/25/85, New York.

CHAPTER 4: THE UNIVERSITY YEARS—"YOU AND I"

Books, brochures, papers, and documents: Hugh Thomas, *Cuba;* Jaime Suchlicki, *Cuba, Castro, and Revolution, Cuba from Columbus to Castro,* and *University Students and Revolution in Cuba, 1970–1968;* José Pardo Llada, *Fidel de los Jesuitas al Moncada;* Juan Arcocha, *Fidel Castro;* Herbert Matthews, *Fidel Castro;* Lee Lockwood, *Castro's Cuba, Cuba's Fidel.*

Newspaper article: *Revolución,* Fidel Castro speech of 4/10/61, Havana, Cuba.

Original interviews and oral histories: Luis E. Aguilar, 2/27/85, Washington, D.C.; Bernardo Viera, 7/22/86, Caracas, Venezuela; Rafael Díaz-Balart, 12/14/84, Madrid, Spain; Alfredo "Chino" Esquivel, 4/28/85, New York; Dr. Mariano Sorí Marín, 9/25/85, Lexington, Kentucky; Dr. Herminio Portell Vilá, 3/22/86, Miami, Florida; Tad Szulc original interviews with Alfredo Guevara, 1/26/85, Havana, Cuba, and Max Lesnick, 8/10/84, Miami, Florida; Antonio Varona, 1/21/85, Miami, Florida.

CHAPTER 5: REDEMPTIVE VIOLENCE

Books, brochures, papers, and documents: Samuel Farber, *Revolution and Reaction in Cuba, 1933–1960;* Herbert Matthews, *Fidel Castro;* Gerardo Rodríguez

SOURCE NOTES

Morejón, *Fidel Castro, Biografía;* Lionel Martin, *The Young Fidel;* Rolando Bonachea and Nelson Valdés, *Revolutionary Struggle, 1947–1958;* Jaime Suchlicki, *University Students and Revolution in Cuba, Cuba from Columbus to Castro,* and *The Intellectual Life of Cuba;* Nathaniel Weyl, *Red Star over Cuba;* Theodore Draper, *Castroism: Theory and Practice;* Fidel Castro / Frei Betto, *Fidel e a Religião: Conversas com Frei Betto;* Ramón Bonachea and Marta San Martín, *The Cuban Insurrection 1952–1959;* Luis E. Aguilar, *Cuba 1933;* Guillermo Cabrera Infante, paper, "Suicide in Cuba"; José Pardo Llada, *Fidel de los Jesuitas al Moncada;* Juan Bosch, "Cuba: La isla fascinante"; "La Lucha Contra Trujillo," a seminar organized in the Dominican Republic at the National Library, 6/6/81, among the Cayo Confites survivors, published in *Política: Teoría y Acción,* vol. 4, no. 44 (November 1983); and Teresa Casuso, *Cuba and Castro.*

Original interviews and oral histories: Rafael Díaz-Balart, 12/14/84, Madrid, Spain; José Pardo Llada, 7/12/86, Cali, Colombia; Dr. Santiago Touriño, 1/26/85, Miami, Florida; Juan Bosch, 7/24/86, Santo Domingo, Dominican Republic; Carlos Zayas, 3/4/87, Miami, Florida; Vicente Baez, 5/15/85, San Juan, Puerto Rico; Dr. Richard Ferrer, 1/22/85, Miami, Florida; Alfredo "Chino" Esquivel, 11/23/86, New York; José de Jesus Ginjaume, 7/18/86, Caracas, Venezuela; and original Tad Szulc interviews with Alfredo Guevara, 1/26/85, Havana, Cuba, and Max Lesnick, 8/10/84, Miami, Florida, from the University of Miami Archives.

CHAPTER 6: A PARENTHESIS

Books, brochures, papers, and documents: Carlos Franqui, *Vida, aventuras y desastres de un hombre llamado Castro;* Tad Szulc, *Fidel: A Critical Portrait;* José Pardo Llada, *Fidel de los Jesuitas al Moncada;* Gerardo Rodríguez Morejón, *Fidel Castro, Biografía;* H. R. Knickerbocker, *C. G. Jung Speaking, Interviews and Encounters,* interview of C. G. Jung.

Magazine article: *Human Behavior,* "Analyzing Fidel," by Gene Vier, July 1975.

Original interviews and oral histories: Emilio Caballero, 3/20/86, Miami, Florida; Tad Szulc original interview with Max Lesnick, 8/10/84, Miami, Florida; Waldo Balart, 10/26/85, Madrid, Spain; Rina Garcia, 1/24/85, Miami, Florida; Barbara Gordon, 4/8/85, Washington, D.C.; Jack Skelly, 9/29/84, Arlington, Virginia; Rafael Díaz-Balart, 12/14/84 and 11/9/85, Madrid, Spain; Rolando Amador, 3/20/86, Miami, Florida; Marjorie Lord, 1/9/85, Fort Lauderdale, Florida; Alfredo "Chino" Esquivel, 4/28/85, New York; José Pardo Llada, 7/12/86, Cali, Colombia; Jorge Valls, 7/4/86, Washington, D.C.; Dr. Marcelino Feal, 7/25/84, Miami, Florida.

SOURCE NOTES

CHAPTER 7: THE *BOGOTAZO*

Books, brochures, papers, and documents: General history of Colombia and the *Bogotazo* was taken from: Hugh Thomas, *Cuba;* Hubert Herring, *A History of Latin America;* Jaime Suchlicki, *Cuba from Columbus to Castro;* Carlos Franqui, *Vida, aventuras y desastres de un hombre llamado Castro,* and *Diary of the Cuban Revolution;* Arturo Alape, *El Bogotazo, Memorias del Olvido;* Jules Dubois, *Freedom Is My Beat;* Lionel Martin, *The Early Fidel;* and Robert Alexander, *Communism in Latin America.*

Magazine and newspaper articles: *El Espectador,* Bogotá, Colombia, "¿Que hizo Castro en 1948 en Colombia?" by Carlos Reyes Posada, 12/12/61; *Bohemia,* Havana, Cuba, "Fidel Castro en el Bogotazo (April 1948)," by Mario Mencía, April 1978; *La República,* Bogotá, Colombia, "El primer plan comunista en América," 4/10/61; *El Nuevo Herald,* Miami, Florida, "El Bogotazo, Castro: agente del peronismo," by Santiago Tourino and Enrique Ovares Herrera, 4/9/88.

Original interviews and oral histories: Enrique Santos Calderón, 7/11/86, Bogotá, Colombia; Guillermo B. Belt, 3/2/85, Bethesda, Maryland; Gloria Gaitán, tape prepared for the author, July 1986, and interview, 7/11/86, Bogotá, Colombia; Roy Rubottom, 5/12–13/86, Dallas, Texas; General Alvaro Valencia Tovar, 7/8/86, Bogotá, Colombia; Carlos Lleras Restrepo, 7/11/86, Bogotá, Colombia; Enrique Ovares and Fernando Hurtado, 3/10/87, Miami, Florida.

CHAPTER 8: SUICIDE BY MICROPHONE

Books, brochures, papers, and documents: General information on the life and suicide of Eduardo "Eddy" Chibás and on the period of Fidel's electoral campaign was taken from: Jaime Suchlicki, *The Intellectual Background of the Cuban Revolution;* José Pardo Llada, *Fidel de los Jesuitas al Moncada;* José Duarte Oropesa, *Historiología Cubana;* Lionel Martin, *The Early Fidel;* Guillermo Cabrera Infante, *Suicide in Cuba;* Lee Lockwood, *Castro's Cuba, Cuba's Fidel;* Warren Hinckle and William W. Turner, *The Fish Is Red: The Story of the Secret War Against Castro.*

Original interviews and oral histories: Manuel Marquéz Sterling, 3/14/87, Miami, Florida; José Pardo Llada, 7/12/86, Cali, Colombia; Alfredo "Chino" Esquivel, 11/23/86, New York; Waldo Balart, 10/26/85, Madrid, Spain; Rolando Amador, 3/20/86, Miami, Florida; Tad Szulc original interview with Max Lesnick, 8/10/84, Miami, Florida, and with Conchita Fernández, 4/24/85, Havana, Cuba, from the University of Miami Archives; Salvador Lew, 3/4/87, Miami, Florida.

SOURCE NOTES

CHAPTER 9: THE MOVEMENT

Books, brochures, papers, and documents: Lee Lockwood, *Castro's Cuba, Cuba's Fidel;* Hugh Thomas, *Cuba;* Samuel Farber, *Revolution and Reaction in Cuba, 1933–1960;* Ruby Hart Phillips, *The Cuban Dilemma;* José Pardo Llada, *Fidel de los Jesuitas al Moncada;* Herbert Matthews, *Revolution in Cuba;* Tad Szulc, *Fidel: A Critical Portrait;* Robert Merle, *Moncada, premier combat de Fidel Castro;* Eric Hoffer, *The True Believer;* Ramón Bonachea and Marta San Martín, *The Cuban Insurrection, 1952–1959;* Lionel Martin, *The Early Fidel;* Max Weber, *On Charisma and Institution Building;* Jerrold M. Post, *Narcissism and the Charismatic Leader-Follower Relationship;* Rafael Moses, "The Leader and the Led: A Dyadic Relationship," paper; and Marta Rojas, "La manifestación de las antorchas y el desfile del 28 de Enero de 1953 (Enero, 1953)."

Magazine and newspaper articles: *Verde Olivo,* "Siempre supimos que el asalto al Moncada culminaría en la victoria," by Melba Hernández, 7/28/63, Havana, Cuba.

Original interviews and oral histories: Rafael Díaz-Balart, 12/14/84, Madrid, Spain; María Camella, 7/19/85, Madrid, Spain; Carlos Bustillo, 4/27/85, New York; Ramón Mestre, Sr., 1/25/86, Miami, Florida; Herminio Portell Vilá, 3/22/86, Miami, Florida; and Tad Szulc original interviews with Max Lesnick, 8/10/84, Miami, Florida, Melba Hernández, 5/2/85, Havana, Cuba, Pedro Miret, 4/29/85, Havana, Cuba, Ramiro Valdés Menéndez, 6/5/85, Havana, Cuba, all from the University of Miami Archives; Martha Frayde, 7/20/85, Madrid, Spain.

CHAPTER 10: MONCADA

Reconstruction of the Moncada attack was drawn from: Luis Conte Agüero, *Dos Rostros de Fidel;* Fred Judson, *Cuba and Revolutionary Myth;* Herbert Matthews, *Revolution in Cuba;* Hugh Thomas, *Cuba;* Ramón Bonachea and Marta San Martín, *The Cuban Insurrection, 1952–1959;* Robert Taber, *M-26: Biography of a Revolution;* José Pardo Llada, *Fidel de los Jesuitas al Moncada;* Haydée Santamaría, *Moncada;* Carlos Franqui, *Diary of the Cuban Revolution;* Marta Rojas, *La Generación del Centenario en el Juicio del Moncada;* Enrique Meneses, *Fidel Castro;* Jules Dubois, *Fidel Castro: Rebel-Liberator or Dictator?;* Fidel Castro, "La estrategia del Moncada," Casa de las Américas, Havana, July–August 1978; Robert Merle, *Moncada;* Ernesto Cardenal, *In Cuba;* James H. Billington, *Fire in the Minds of Men: Origins of the Revolutionary Faith;* Guillermo Cabrera Infante, *Suicide in Cuba;* Ward M. Morton, *Castro as Charismatic Hero;* and Edward Gonzalez, *Cuba Under Castro: Limits of Charisma.*

Magazine and newspaper articles: *Granma,* "Background on the Assault on Moncada and Bayamo Garrisons," by Thomas Toledo, 7/18/67; *Latin American*

SOURCE NOTES

Research Review, "The Cuban Revolution: The Road to Power," by Andrés Suárez, vol. VII, no. 3 (Fall 1972).

Original interviews and oral histories: Raúl Martínez Arará, 1/12/85 and 1/19/85, Miami, Florida; Héctor de Armas, 1/26/85, Miami, Florida; Carlos Bustillo, 4/27/85, New York; Gerardo Perez Puelles, 7/15/86, Caracas, Venezuela; Haydée Santamaría, Havana, Cuba, August 1966; Ramón Mestre, 7/25/84, Miami, Florida; Arturo Villar, 1/16/85, Miami, Florida; Rolando Amador, 3/20/86, Miami, Florida; Tad Szulc original interviews with Antonio Núñez Jiménez, 4/4/85, Blas Roca, 6/4/85, José Ramón Fernández, 4/11/85, Melba Hernández, 5/2/85, Pedro Miret, 4/29/85 and 6/5/85, from the University of Miami Archives.

CHAPTER 11: THE ISLE OF PINES, PRISON AS CLASSROOM

Books, brochures, papers, and documents: In addition to the books named in Chapter 10, these sources were also drawn upon for Chapter 11: Samuel Farber, *Revolution and Reaction in Cuba;* José Duarte Oropesa, *Historiología Cubana;* Gerardo Rodríguez Morejón, *Fidel Castro;* Maurice Halperin, *The Rise and Decline of Fidel Castro;* Theodore Draper, *Castro's Revolution;* Lee Lockwood, *Castro's Cuba, Cuba's Fidel;* Lionel Martin, *The Early Fidel;* Rolando Bonachea and Nelson Valdés, *Revolutionary Struggle, 1947–1958;* Haydée Santamaría, *Moncada; El Abogado*, Boletin Oficial del Colegio Nacional de Abogados de Cuba an el Exilio, "La Historia Me Absolvera, la Mentira del Siglo," by Dr. José F. Valls; Luis Conte Agüero, *Cartas del Presidio;* William L. Shirer, *The Rise and Fall of the Third Reich;* Tad Szulc, *Fidel: A Critical Portrait.*

Magazine article: *Latin American Research Review*, "The Cuban Revolution: The Road to Power," by Andrés Suárez, vol. VII, no. 3 (Fall 1972).

Original interviews and oral histories: Haydée Santamaría, August 1966, Havana, Cuba; Jorge Valls, 12/1/86, New York; Dr. Marcelino Feal, 1/21/85, Miami, Florida; Tomas Regalado, Sr. and Jr., 1/17/85, Miami, Florida; Jack Skelly, 9/29/86, Arlington, Virginia; Rafael Díaz-Balart, 10/20/85, Madrid, Spain.

CHAPTER 12: THE MEXICO YEARS

Books, brochures, papers, and documents: Rolando Bonachea and Nelson Valdés, *Revolutionary Struggle, 1947–1958;* Jules Dubois, *Fidel Castro: Rebel-Liberator or Dictator?;* Fidel Castro / Frei Betto, *Fidel e a Religião: Conversas com Frei Betto;* Luis Conte Agüero, *Fidel Castro;* Teresa Casuso, *Cuba and Castro;* Richard Gott, *Guerrilla Movements in Latin America;* Ramón Bonachea and Marta San Martín, *The Cuban Insurrection, 1952–1959;* Herbert Matthews, *Revolution in Cuba;* Samuel Farber, *Revolution and Reaction in Cuba, 1933–1960;* Carlos Franqui,

Diary of the Cuban Revolution; Mario Llerena, *The Unsuspected Revolution;* Warren Hinckle and John W. Turner, *The Fish Is Red: The Story of the Secret War Against Castro;* Hilda Gadea, *Ernesto: A Memoir of Che Guevara.*

Magazine and newspaper articles: *Ejercito Rebelde,* Havana, Cuba, "Mi aporte a la Revolución," by General Alberto Bayo, January 1960; *Granma,* Havana, Cuba, "Che en Guatemala, de una entrevista del periodista argentino Jorge Ricardo Masetti con Che en la Sierra Maestra," 10/29/67; *Vida Universitaria,* "Una revolución que comienza," by Ernesto "Che" Guevara, vol. 20, no. 214 (January–March 1969); *New York Times Magazine,* "The Making of a Revolutionary: A Memoir of the Young Guevara," by Dolores Moyano Martin, 8/18/68; El Nacional, Caracas, Venezuela, article by Lucila Velasquez, 1967; *Diario 66,* Madrid, Spain, "Entrevista Alina Fernandez, Tengo el derecho a decir que soy la hija de Fidel," 1/26/89; *El Diario de Nueva York,* New York, "Secuestran a Fidelito en Mexico," by Emma and Lidia Castro, 4/29/57.

Original interviews and oral histories: Dr. Mariano Sorí Marín, 9/25/85, Lexington, Kentucky; Jorge Valls, 7/4/86, Washington, D.C., and 12/1/86, New York; Orlando de Cárdenas, 1/24/85, 2/22/86, and 3/22/86, Miami, Florida; Dr. Facundo Lima, 5/2/87, Washington, D.C.; Luis Alberto Monge, 2/6/90, San José, Costa Rica; Sacha Volman, 10/15/86, Washington, D.C.; Ben Stephansky, 10/27/86, Washington, D.C.; Isabel Custodio, 1987, Mexico City, Mexico; Alvaro Custodio, 12/11/86, San Lorenzo de Escorial, Spain; Justo Carrillo, 1/16/85 and 3/27/86, Miami, Florida; Rafael Díaz-Balart, 12/14/84; Manolo Rodríguez, 1/22/85, Miami, Florida; César Gómez, 7/8/86, Bogotá, Colombia; Tad Szulc original interview with Universo Sánchez Durante, 7/4–5/85, Havana, Cuba, from the University of Miami Archives; Mario Llerena, 1/18/85, Miami, Florida; Esther López Castro, 2/9/86, Mexico City, Mexico; Manuel Arques, 3/27/86, Miami, Florida; Lomberto Díaz, 1/22/85, Miami, Florida; Pat Kegan, 1/24/85, Fort Lauderdale, Florida.

CHAPTER 13: THE LANDING

Books, brochures, papers, and documents: Tad Szulc, *Fidel: A Critical Portrait; De Tuxpan a la Plata,* the Castro regime official report of the trip of the *Granma,* with research done by the Sección de Historia de las Fuerzas Armadas Revolucionarias de la República de Cuba; Ruby Hart Phillips, *Cuba: Island of Paradox;* Lee Lockwood, *Castro's Cuba, Cuba's Fidel;* Carlos Franqui, *The Twelve;* Ernesto "Che" Guevara, *Reminiscences of the Cuban Revolutionary War.*

Newspaper article: *El Diario de Nueva York,* "Desembarco y Combates en Sierra Maestra, Historia de Fidel Castro," by Emma and Lidia Castro, 5/1/57.

Original interviews and oral histories: Dr. Rubén Darío Rumbaut, 2/27/85, Houston, Texas; Rafael Díaz-Balart, 12/14/84, Madrid, Spain; Dunney Pérez

Alamo, 3/5/87, Miami, Florida; Tad Szulc original interview with Faustino Pérez, 6/1/85, Havana, Cuba, from the University of Miami Archives.

CHAPTER 14: GUERRILLA THEATER

Books, brochures, papers, and documents: Herbert Matthews, *The Cuban Story, Fidel Castro,* and *Revolution in Cuba;* Robert Taber, *M-26: Biography of a Revolution;* Frank Mankiewicz, *With Fidel;* Lee Lockwood, *Castro's Cuba, Cuba's Fidel;* Ramón Bonachea and Marta San Martin, *The Cuban Insurrection, 1952–1959;* Michael S. Radu, "Revolutionary Violence in Latin America," paper; Ernesto "Che" Guevara, *Reminiscences of the Cuban Revolutionary War;* Carlos Franqui, *Diary of the Cuban Revolution;* John Dorschner and Roberto Fabricio, *The Winds of December;* Manuel Rojo Del Río, *La historia cambió en la sierra.*

Magazine article: *Parade* magazine, "The Woman Behind Fidel Castro," by Andrew St. George, 4/11/65.

Original interviews and histories: Felipe Pazos, 7/17/86, Caracas, Venezuela; Dr. Alberto Dalmau, 7/22/85, Madrid, Spain; Michel Tourguy, 12/5/84, Warsaw, Poland; Eugenio Soler, 7/19/86, Caracas, Venezuela; Victor Mora, 3/14/87, Miami, Florida; Agustín País, 3/22/86, Miami, Florida; Raúl Chibás, 5/17/85, San Juan, Puerto Rico; Manuel Ray, 4/13/85, San Juan, Puerto Rico; Javier Pazos, 7/21/86, Caracas, Venezuela; Dunney Pérez Alamo, 3/5/87, Miami, Florida; Rogelio Cisneros, 7/22/86, Caracas, Venezuela.

CHAPTER 15: A NATION IS DYING

Books, brochures, papers, and documents: Ramón Bonachea and Marta San Martín, *The Cuban Insurrection, 1952–1959;* Teresa Casuso, *Cuba and Castro;* Lucas Moran Arce, *La Revolución Cubana (1953–1959), una version rebelde;* Jules Dubois, *Fidel Castro: Rebel-Liberator or Dictator?;* Robert Taber, *M-26: Biography of a Revolution;* Enrique Meneses, *Fidel Castro;* Theodore Draper, *Castroism, Theory and Practice;* K. S. Karol, *Guerrillas in Power;* Lionel Martin, *The Early Fidel;* Carlos Franqui, *Family Portrait with Fidel;* Roger W. Fontaine, *Terrorism: The Cuban Connection;* Edward Gonzalez, *Cuba Under Castro.*

Song: "Los Caminos de mi Cuba," famous melancholic song of these years, sung nightly in the 1950s by its popular composer, Carlos Puebla, at La Bodeguita del Medio, the favorite bohemian restaurant off the Plaza de la Catedral.

Magazine, newspaper, and journal articles: *Reader's Digest,* "The Complete Book of the Olympics," by David Wallechinsky; *National Review,* "Huber Matos, the Undefeated," by Lorrin Philipson; *Review of Politics,* "The Peasantry in the Cuban Revolution," by Gil Carl AlRoy, vol. 29, no. 1 (January 1967).

SOURCE NOTES

Intelligence reports: Special National Intelligence Estimate No. 85-58, "The Situation in Cuba," 24 November 1958, submitted by the Director of Central Intelligence, obtained through the Freedom of Information Act; Special National Intelligence Estimate No. 85-1-58, "Developments in Cuba Since Mid-November," 16 December 1958, submitted by the Director of Central Intelligence, obtained through the Freedom of Information Act.

Original interviews and oral histories: Robert Wiecha, 7/16/87, Washington, D.C.; Carlos Franqui, 7/23/85, Madrid, Spain; Roy Rubottom, 5/12–13/86, Dallas, Texas; José Pardo Llada, 7/12/86, Cali, Colombia; Fr. Armando Llorente, 1/22/85, Miami, Florida; Víctor Mora, 3/13/87, Miami, Florida; José Ramón Gonzalez Regueral, 10/30/85, Madrid, Spain; Carlos Castañeda, 4/17/85, San Juan, Puerto Rico.

CHAPTER 16: FIDELFIDELFIDELFIDELFIDELFIDELFIDELFIDEL

Books, brochures, papers, and documents: Ruby Hart Phillips, *Cuba: Island of Paradox* and *The Cuban Dilemma;* Hugh Thomas, *Cuba;* Ramón Bonachea and Marta San Martín, *The Cuban Insurrection, 1952–1959;* Wayne Smith, *The Closest of Enemies;* José Pardo Llada, *Memorias de la Sierra Maestra;* John Dorschner and Robert Fabricio, *The Winds of December;* Jules Dubois, *Fidel Castro;* Carlos Franqui, *Family Portrait with Fidel;* Maurice Halperin, *The Rise and Decline of Fidel Castro;* Lionel Martin, *The Early Fidel;* Paul Bethel, *The Losers;* Jean Paul Sartre, *Sartre on Cuba;* Ward M. Morton, *Castro as Charismatic Hero;* Lee Lockwood, *Castro's Cuba, Cuba's Fidel;* Luis Conte Agüero, *Fidel Castro: Vida y Obra;* Migene González-Wippler, *Santería: African Magic in Latin America;* Samuel Farber, *Revolution and Reaction in Cuba, 1933–1960;* Max Weber, *On Charisma and Institution Building;* Jerrold M. Post, *Narcissism and the Charismatic Leader-Follower Relationship.*

Magazine and journal articles: *Revista/Review Interamericana,* "Fidel Castro: Apuntes sobre un caudillo socialista," by Luis E. Aguilar, vol. III, no. 3 (Fall 1977); *The Nation,* "Revolution Without Generals," by Carleton Beals, vol. 188 (January 1959).

Original interviews and oral histories: Lázaro Asencio, 3/11/87, Miami, Florida; Emilio C. Caballero, 3/20/86, Miami, Florida; Jack Skelly, 9/29/84, Washington, D.C.; Juan Arcocha, 7/9/85, Paris, France; Cecilia Bustamente, 6/4/87, telephone from Austin, Texas; Armando Fleites, 1/23/85, Miami, Florida; Father Juan Manuel Dorta-Duque, 3/19/86, Miami, Florida; Huber Matos, 1/21/85, Miami, Florida; Rolando Cubela, 10/26/85, Madrid, Spain; Lydia Cabrera, 3/18/86, Coral Gables, Florida; Orlando Jiménez-Leal, 11/24/86, New York.

CHAPTER 17: THE FIRST MONTHS—THIS TRAIN KNOWS WHERE IT IS GOING

Books, brochures, papers, and documents: Herbert Matthews, *Fidel Castro* and *The Cuban Story;* Ruby Hart Phillips, *The Cuban Dilemma;* Ramón Bonachea and Marta San Martín, *The Cuban Insurrection, 1957–1959;* Peter Bourne, *Fidel;* Armando Valladares, *Against All Hope;* Teresa Casuso, *Cuba and Castro;* Charles D. Ameringer, *Don Pepe: A Political Biography of José Figueres of Costa Rica;* Luis Conte Agüero, *Fidel Castro: Vida y Obra;* José Pardo Llada, *The Che I Knew;* Pamela Falk, *Cuban Foreign Policy;* Shirley Christian, *Nicaragua;* Carlos Franqui, *Family Portrait with Fidel;* Theodore Draper, *Castro's Revolution.*

Magazine and newspaper articles: *Life* magazine, 2/22/59; *Time* magazine, 2/23/59; "El 14 de Junio: La Raza Inmortal," by Hugo A. Ysalguez, report published by the survivors of the June 14, 1959, attack to overthrow Generalísimo Rafael L. Trujillo; *Confidential,* "Castro Raped My Teen-Age Daughter," by Alice J. Lorenz, 5/31/60; *New York Sunday News,* "American Mata Hari Who Duped Castro," by Paul Meskil, 4/20/75; *New York Daily News,* "How an Invasion of the Canal Zone Was Foiled, Secrets of the CIA" by Paul Meskil, 4/22/75.

Original interviews and oral histories: José Ignacio Rasco, 1/11/85, Coral Gables, Florida; Eugenio Soler, 7/19/86, Caracas, Venezuela; Josefina Ache, 7/18/86, Caracas, Venezuela; Armando Fleites, 1/23/85, Miami, Florida; José "Pepe" Figueres, 5/27/85, San José, Costa Rica; Gonzalo Facio, 5/2/85, San José, Costa Rica; Carlos Castañeda, 5/17/85, San Juan, Puerto Rico; Agustín Tamargo, 1/8/85, Miami, Florida; José Pardo Llada, 7/12/86, Cali, Colombia; Sacha Volman, 1/17/86, Washington, D.C.; Frank Aldrich, 2/8/87, Washington, D.C.; Gloria Gaitán, 7/11/86, Bogotá, Colombia, and tapes prepared for the author by Gloria Gaitán; Felipe Pazos, 7/17/86, Caracas, Venezuela; Huber Matos, 1/21/85, Miami, Florida; Ernesto Betancourt, 11/29/84, Washington, D.C.; Manuel Ray, 5/15/85, San Juan, Puerto Rico; Guillermo Martínez Marques, 1/17/85, Miami, Florida; Maurice Halperin, 1/16/86, Vancouver, Canada; Gonzalo Facio, 4/28/85, San José, Costa Rica; Clarence Moore, 4/11/85, Washington, D.C.; Ramón Barquín, 4/14/85, San Juan, Puerto Rico; Emilio Guede, 4/15/85, San Juan, Puerto Rico; Marco Falcón Briceño, 7/23/86, Caracas, Venezuela; Hilda Felipe de Escalona, 3/10/87, Miami, Florida.

CHAPTER 18: CASTRO MEETS *EL NORTE*

Books, brochures, papers, and documents: Pablo Neruda, "There Is No Forgetfulness," in *Twenty Poems;* Rufo López Fresquet, *My 14 Months with Castro;* Christian Herter, *American Secretaries of State;* original Richard Nixon confidential

SOURCE NOTES

memo, "Summary of Conversation Between the Vice President and Fidel Castro," 4/19/59, provided by Richard Nixon to the author; Teresa Casuso, *Cuba and Castro;* Carlos Franqui, *Family Portrait with Fidel;* Jorge Edwards, *Persona Non Grata;* Norman Mailer, "The Letter to Castro" in *The Presidential Papers;* Ruby Hart Phillips, *The Cuban Dilemma;* Tad Szulc, *Fidel: A Critical Portrait.*

Newspaper articles: *Daily Princetonian,* Princeton, N.J., "The Story Behind Castro's Visit Here, Ely Makes Trip to Cuban Palace," by José M. Ferrer III, 4/17/59; *Daily Princetonian,* Princeton, N.J., "Castro Schedules Address Here, Cuban Leader to Visit ACP Seminar Monday," by José M. Ferrer III, 4/15/59.

Original interviews and oral histories: José "Pepin" Bosch, 1/17/85, Miami, Florida; Ernesto Betancourt, 9/25/84, Washington, D.C.; Roy Rubottom, 5/12–13/86, Dallas, Texas; William Wieland, 8/4/87, telephone from Maryland; Richard Nixon, 8/11/87, New York; Vernon Walters, 3/13/85, Washington, D.C.; Carlos Castañeda, 5/17/85, San Juan, Puerto Rico; Manolo "Manolín" Rodríguez and Manolo Rodríguez, Sr., 3/18/86, Pompano Beach, Florida; Betty Dukert, 2/24/85, Washington, D.C.; Luis J. Botifoll, 1/25/86, Miami, Florida; Roland Ely, November 1974, Teheran, Iran; Robert Goheen, 2/2/87, telephone from Princeton, New Jersey; John Palmer, 2/2/84, telephone from Princeton, New Jersey; Sally Aall, former Mrs. Roland Ely, 10/21/87, telephone from Colorado; Jack Skelly, 10/4/84, Washington, D.C.; Mariano Sorí Marín, 9/25/85, Lexington, Kentucky; Tad Szulc original interviews with Fabio Grobart, 6/6/85, Pedro Miret Prieto, 6/5/85, Alfredo Guevara, 4/30/85 and 1/26/85, and Blas Roca, 6/4/85, Havana, Cuba, from the University of Miami Archives.

CHAPTER 19: AN IRON FILING

Books, brochures, papers, and documents: Ruby Hart Phillips, *The Cuban Dilemma;* Paul Bethel, *The Losers;* Ricardo Rojo, *My Friend Che;* Hugh Thomas, "Cuba: The United States and Batista, 1952–58," paper prepared for Public Policy Week 1985, American Enterprise Institute; Philip Bonsal, *Cuba, Castro and the United States;* Nikita Khrushchev, *Khrushchev Remembers;* Carla Robbins, *The Cuban Threat;* David E. Apter, "Political Religion in the New Nations," in *Old Societies and New States: the Quest for Modernity in Asia and Africa,* edited by Clifford Geertz; Carlos Franqui, *Family Portrait with Fidel;* Arkady N. Shevchenko, *Breaking with Moscow;* Maurice Halperin, *Rise and Decline of Fidel Castro;* Fred Ward, *Inside Cuba Today;* Tad Szulc, *Fidel: A Critical Portrait.*

Magazine, newspaper and journal articles: TASS, Moscow, Russian-language article on "The Missile Crisis," by Alexander Alexeev, November 1988; *América Latina,* printed by Editorial Progresò, Moscow, "Encuentros con Che Guevara, Notas del Periodista," by Sergo Mikoyan, Spanish-language publication of the Soviet government; *Life* magazine, "My Brother Is a Tyrant and He Must Go," by Juana Castro, 8/28/64; *Casa de las Américas,* Havana, Cuba, "Carlos el amanecer ya no es una tentación," Tomás Borge Martínez (May/June 1979); Inter-American Economic Affairs, "U.S. Claims Against the Cuban Government: An Obstacle to Rapprochement," by Lynn Darrell Bender, vol. XXVII, no. 1 (Summer 1973); *New York Times Magazine,* "Fidel Castro's Years as a Secret Communist," by Tad Szulc, 10/19/86.

Original interviews and oral histories: Antonio Orlani, 10/13/85, Madrid, Spain; Juan Arcocha, 7/13/85, Paris, France; Sergo Mikoyan, 2/5/88, Alexandria, Virginia, and 4/18/89, Washington, D.C.; Manolo "Manolín" Rodríguez and Manolo Rodríguez, Sr., 3/18/86, Pompano Beach, Florida; Dr. Marcelino Feal, 1/21/85, Miami, Florida; María Camella, 7/19/85, Madrid, Spain; Dr. Gerardo Canet, 1/10/85, Bethesda, Maryland; Jorge Beruff, 12/21/84, Washington, D.C.; Santiago Carrillo, 10/23/85, Madrid, Spain; José Pardo Llada, 7/12/86, Cali, Colombia; Jorge Valls, 11/24/86, New York; Mustapha Amin, 2/15/86, Cairo, Egypt; Sunil Kumar Roy, 3/4/86, New Delhi, India; Sara McClendon, 2/21/86, Washington, D.C.

CHAPTER 20: THE BAY OF PIGS

Books, brochures, papers, and documents: Arthur Schlesinger, Jr., *Robert Kennedy and His Times* and *A Thousand Days;* Herbert Matthews, *Fidel Castro;* Peter Wyden, *The Bay of Pigs;* Lionel Martin, *The Early Fidel;* Nikita Khrushchev, *Khrushchev Remembers;* Hugh Thomas, *Cuba;* Haynes Johnson, *The Bay of Pigs;* Warren Hinckle and John W. Turner, *The Fish Is Red: The Story of the Secret War Against Castro;* Playa Girón, *Derrota del Imperialismo, La Habana, 1961, tomo 1;* Fidel Castro, *Historia de la Invasión a Cuba, En Pié de Guerra por La Soberanía,* Lima, Peru, Editorial Libertad, Agencia Noticiosa Peruana; Maurice Halperin, *Rise and Decline of Fidel Castro;* Ruby Hart Phillips, *The Cuban Dilemma;* John Prados, *Presidents' Secret Wars;* Archibald Roosevelt, Jr., *For Lust of Knowing;* Richard E. Neustadt and Ernest R. May, *Thinking in Time, The Uses of History for Decision Makers;* Hans Morgenthau, *A New Foreign Policy for the United States.*

Intelligence documents: "A Program of Covert Action Against the Castro Regime," CIA Documents, approved by the President, 16 March 1960; CIA Document 21, "Cuban Operation," for General Maxwell D. Taylor, Signed C. Cabell, General USAF, Deputy Director, 9 May 1961; "Memorandum for the President," Subject: Cuba, 3/15/61 from Arthur Schlesinger, Jr. to President Kennedy.

Film: *Fidel Castro,* film prepared by Kirby Jones.

Magazine and newspaper articles: *Washington Post,* "Why the CIA Leaves Its Contras Hanging," by David Atlee Phillips, 4/6/86; *Life* magazine, "My Brother Is a Tyrant and He Must Go," by Juana Castro, 8/28/64.

SOURCE NOTES

Original interviews and oral histories: Dr. Andrés Vargas Gómez, 1/16/85, Miami, Florida; Richard Nixon, 8/11/87, New York; Dr. Mariano Sorí Marín, 9/25/85, Lexington, Kentucky; Tad Szulc original interview with Norberto Fuentes, 5/22/85, Havana, Cuba, from the University of Miami Archives; William Colby, 10/8/87, Washington, D.C.

CHAPTER 21: THE MARXIST-LENINIST

Special conferences: Missile Crisis meeting at the Kennedy School of Government, Harvard University, Cambridge, Massachusetts, 10/11–13/87, with Russian and American officials attending; Missile Crisis follow-up meeting at Harvard University, 2/14/89.

Books, brochures, papers, and documents: *The Algonquin Wits;* K. S. Karol, *Guerrillas in Power;* Carlos Franqui, *Family Portrait with Fidel;* Jaime Suchlicki, *University Students and Revolution in Cuba;* Orlando Castro Hidalgo, *Spy for Fidel;* Maurice Halperin, *The Rise and Decline of Fidel Castro;* Nikita Khrushchev, *Khrushchev Remembers;* Carla Robbins, *The Cuban Threat;* Jan Sejna, *We Will Bury You;* C. L. Sulzberger, *An Age of Mediocrity;* Ricardo Rojo, *My Friend Che; El Viaje de Fidel Castro a la Unión Soviética, Discusos de N. S. Krushchev y Fidel Castro, en el Mitin Dedicado a la Amistad Cubano-Soviética, Celebrado en Moscú, el 23 de Mayo de 1963,* Moscow; Juan Arcocha, *Fidel Castro;* John W. Hinckle and Warren Turner, *The Fish Is Red: The Story of the Secret War Against Castro;* Arthur Schlesinger, Jr., *Robert Kennedy and His Times;* Cecil B. Currey, *Edward Lansdale: The Unquiet American;* Igor Yefimov, *Kennedi, Osval'd, Kastro, Khrushchev;* James G. Blight and David Welch, *On the Brink,* first and second editions; Elie Abel, *The Missile Crisis;* Graham Allison, *Essence of Decision;* An Introduction to the ExComm Transcripts, tapes made of the meetings of the Executive Committee of the National Security Council during the Missile Crisis, by David A. Welch and James G. Blight, Harvard University; *Cuban Communism,* edited by Irving Louis Horowitz, chapter, "The Missiles of October: Twenty Years Later."

Magazine and newspaper articles: *The New Republic,* "Lights, Camera, Communism, What Castro Is Doing to the Cuban Cinema," by Nestor Almendros, 2/29/88; *Journal of Interamerican Studies and World Affairs,* "Party Development in Revolutionary Cuba," vol. 21, no. 4 (November 1970); *Proceso,* Mexico City, Mexico, Interview with Fidel Castro by Julio Scherer García, 1/12/81; *Revolución,* Havana, Cuba, articles on Fidel Castro's Moscow trip, 4/30/63; *The New Republic,* "When Castro Heard the News," by Jean Daniel, 12/7/63; *The News American,* "Castro Had JFK Killed?" by Marianne Means, 4/22/75; TASS, Moscow, article on the Missile Crisis, by Alexander Alexeev, November 1988; *Boston Sunday Globe,* "Avoiding Another Missile Crisis," by Graham Allison, 2/5/89; *Washington Post,*

SOURCE NOTES

"Was Castro out of Control in 1962?" by Seymour M. Hersh; *New York Daily News*, "Our Havana Triple Spy Helped & Hurt Castro," by Paul Meskil, 4/21/75; *Chicago Sun-Times*, "A Timely Talk with Castro," by Joseph N. Gomez, 12/11/88; *New York Times*, "Warheads Were Deployed in Cuba in '62, Soviets Say," by Bill Keller, 11/29/89; *Rolling Stone*, "The Hughes-Nixon-Lansky Connection: The Secret Alliances of the CIA from World War II to Watergate," by Howard Kohn, 5/20/76; *New York Daily News*, "How U.S. Made Unholy Alliance with the Mafia," by Paul Meskil, 4/23/75; *New York Times*, "The Day Castro Almost Started World War III," by Daniel Ellsberg, 10/13/87; and *Foreign Policy*, "Kennedy and the Cuban Connection," by Donald E. Schulz, Spring 1977.

Original interviews and oral histories: Juan Benemelis, 6/29/85, Washington, D.C.; Arkady Shevchenko, 10/14/87, Washington, D.C.; Theodore Shackley, 2/23/88, Washington, D.C.; David Atlee Phillips, 10/18/87, Washington, D.C.; Robert MacNamara, 1/11/88, Washington, D.C.; Oscar Mori, 10/28/85, Madrid, Spain; Juan Arcocha, 7/13/85, Paris, France; Fedor Burlatsky, Joseph Nye, Jr., Graham Allison, Sergo Mikoyan, Jim Blight, and Sergei Khrushchev, 2/14/89, Cambridge, Massachusetts; Radio Martí interview with Carlos Franqui, 12/8/87; Jack Anderson, 7/20/89, telephone interview, Washington, D.C.; Tad Szulc original interviews with Fabio Grobart 6/6/85, Havana, Cuba, and Fidel Castro, 1/28/84, Havana, Cuba, from the University of Miami Archives.

CHAPTER 22: GUERRILLA TO AN AGE

This chapter in particular drew upon three major series of articles done by the author for the *Chicago Daily News*. The first involved following in Ernesto "Che" Guevara's footsteps all across Bolivia in March 1968, to trace his last months and his death in October 1967. At that time, I interviewed at length Régis Debray, Ciro Bustos, and all the guerrillas in Che's band. The second was a weeks-long stay in Guatemala in October 1966, which included living for a week in the mountains with the Marxist Fuerzas Armadas Rebeldes, or Rebel Armed Forces, and interviews with its leader César Montes and all of the guerrillas. The third was a series of articles on Cuba's influence on American radicals, "Cuba: School for U.S. Radicals," five parts, in collaboration with Keyes Beech, printed in October 1970, and culled from scores of interviews with American radicals, diplomats, and intelligence officers.

Books, brochures, papers, and documents: Luis Ortega, *El Sueño y La Distancia;* Mario Vargas Llosa, *The Real Life of Alejandro Mayta;* "Castro's Americas Department," booklet, the Cuban American National Foundation; Orlando Castro Hidalgo, *Spy for Fidel;* Lee Lockwood, *Castro's Cuba, Cuba's Fidel;* Enrique Meneses, *Fidel Castro;* Jay Mallin, *Fortress Cuba;* Raymond Carr, *Spain*

1808–1975; The Guerrilla Reader: A Historical Anthology, edited by Walter Laqueur; Eric Hoffer, *The True Believer;* Robert J. Alexander, *Romulo Betancourt and the Transformation of Venezuela;* Carla Robbins, *The Cuban Threat;* K. S. Karol, *Guerrillas in Power;* Mohamed Hassanein Heikal, *The Cairo Documents;* Ricardo Rojo, *My Friend Che;* Daniel James, *Che Guevara* and *The Complete Bolivian Diaries of Che Guevara;* Maurice Halperin, *The Rise and Decline of Fidel Castro* and *The Taming of Fidel Castro;* Leo Sauvage, *Che Guevara: The Failure of a Revolutionary;* Richard Gott, *Guerrilla Movements in Latin America;* Marta Rojas and Mirta Rodríguez Calderón, *Tania, la guerrillera;* C. L. Sulzberger, *An Age of Mediocrity;* Régis Debray, *Revolution in the Revolution?;* Yehoshophat Harkabi, *Israel's Fateful Hour;* David J. Kopilow, *Castro, Israel and the PLO;* Ernest Halperin, "The End of Guevarism?" paper, conference, Revolutionary Violence in Latin America, 12/4/85, Washington, D.C.; Juan Benemelis, *Castro Subversión y Terrorismo en Africa;* and Roger Fontaine, *Terrorism: The Cuban Connection.*

Magazine and newspaper articles: *Studies in Comparative Communism,* "The Cuban Military in Africa and the Middle East, from Algeria to Angola," by William J. Durch, vol. XI, nos. 1 and 2 (Spring/Summer 1978); *Chicago Tribune Magazine,* "The Girl Who Betrayed Che Guevara," by Daniel James, 9/21/69; *Insight* magazine, "Skewering the Sixties' Leftover Left," by Peter Collier and David Horowitz, 4/3/89.

Original interviews and oral histories: David Atlee Phillips, 6/6/86, Washington, D.C.; Fausto Amador, 10/19/87, Washington, D.C.; Victor Meza, 5/4/86, Tegucigalpa, Honduras; Orlando García, 7/24/86, Caracas, Venezuela; Gerardo Canet, 1/1/85, Washington, D.C.; Juan Arcocha, 7/13/85, Paris, France; Hamdi Fouad, 6/12/86, Washington, D.C.; Dolores Moyano Martin, 9/15/87, Washington, D.C.; General Gary Prado Salmón, 12/17/87, Washington, D.C.; Felix Rodríguez, 4/12/89, Washington, D.C.; Arkady Shevchenko, 10/14/87, Washington, D.C.; Eugenio Soler, 7/19/86, Caracas, Venezuela; Eldridge Cleaver, 10/14/84, Berkeley, California; James Pringle, 7/7/86, letter from Beijing, China; Francisco Teira, 1/15/85, Miami, Florida; Lutfi Al Kholi and Ihsan Abdul Kuddous, 2/14/86, Cairo, Egypt; General Alvaro Valencia Tovar, 7/8/86, Bogotá, Colombia; Brian Jenkins, 10/19/84, Santa Monica, California; Edward Gonzalez, 10/19/84, Santa Monica, California; Maurice Halperin, 1/16/86, Vancouver, Canada.

CHAPTER 23: THE DICTATOR OF THE COWS

Books, brochures, papers, and documents: René Dumont, *Is Cuba Socialist?;* Carla Robbins, *The Cuban Threat;* Maurice Halperin, *The Taming of Fidel Castro;* Edward Gonzalez, *Cuba Under Castro: The Limits of Charisma* and *Castro, Cuba and the World;* Jorge Edwards, *Persona Non Grata;* K. S. Karol, *Guerrillas in*

SOURCE NOTES

Power; Carlos Alberto Montaner, *Fidel Castro y La Revolución Cubana;* Theodore Draper, *Castroism: Theory and Practice;* Castro speech, 4/22/86, FIBIS; Hugh Thomas, *Cuba;* Paul Hollander, *Political Pilgrims;* Turner Catledge, *My Life and the Times; Fidel in Chile: A Symbolic Meeting Between Two Historical Processes — Selected Speeches of Major Fidel Castro During His Visit to Chile,* November 1971; Nathaniel Davis, *The Last Two Years of Salvador Allende;* Fidel Castro / Frei Betto, *Fidel e a Religião: Conversas com Frei Betto;* Paul E. Sigmund, *The Overthrow of Allende and the Politics of Chile, 1964–1976;* The Church Report, Senate Foreign Relations Committee report on Chile; Raymond Carr, *Spain, 1808–1975.*

Magazine and newspaper articles: *U.S. News and World Report,* March 1, 1964, and August 31, 1964; *El Miami Herald,* "Otoño del Patriarca," by Thomas Regalado, Jr., 10/7/85; *The American Spectator,* "Revolution's End," by R. Bruce McColm, vol. 13, no. 5 (May 1980); *Washington Post,* "Cuba Researchers Test Interferon," by Edward Cody, 8/4/85; *Current,* "The State of Castro's Cuba," by Edward Gonzalez, December 1970; *Estudios Cubanos/Cuban Studies,* "Continuity and Change in the Cuban Political Elite," vol. 8, no. 2 (July 1978); *The Monthly Review,* "Continuities in Cuban Revolutionary Politics," by Richard Fagen, vol. 23, no. 11 (April 1972); *International Herald Tribune,* "Castro Starts Visit to Russia with Top Official Welcome," 6/2/72; *Time* magazine, "Bienvenido, Brezhnev," 2/11/74.

Original interviews and oral histories: Fidel Castro, four interviews, July and August 1966, Havana, Banes, and Pico Turquino, Cuba; Salvador Allende, four interviews, July 1966, 1968, 1969, Santiago, Chile, and Havana, Cuba; Rolando Amador, 3/20/86, Miami, Florida; Santiago Carrillo, 10/23/85, Madrid, Spain; José Roque León, 7/20/85, Madrid, Spain; General Rafael del Pino, 8/26/87, Washington, D.C.; Ambika Soni, 3/17/86, New Delhi, India; Mickey Leland, 4/2/85, Washington, D.C.; Dr. Karl Cantell, 11/9/88, Helsinki, Finland; José Luis Llóvio, 10/9/87, New York; Oscar Mori, 10/25/85, Madrid, Spain; Eduardo Manet, 7/12/85, Paris, France; José Pardo Llada, 7/12/86, Cali, Colombia; Juan Arcocha, 7/13/85 and 7/16/85, Paris, France; Vicente Echerri, 11/25/86, New York; Vicente Mateev, 12/28/84, Warsaw, Poland, and 11/20/88, Moscow; Dusko Doder, 12/28/84, Warsaw, Poland; Arkady Shevchenko, 10/14/87, Washington, D.C.; George McGovern, 1/7/85, Washington, D.C.; Mark Moran, 4/1/87, Alexandria, Virginia; Michel Tourguy, 11/30/84, Warsaw, Poland; William Colby, 10/8/87, Washington, D.C.; Michael Manley, 3/27/86, Kingston, Jamaica; Winston Spaulding, 3/26/86, Kingston, Jamaica; Sir Edgerton Richardson, 3/25/86, Kingston, Jamaica; Edward Seaga, 3/23/86, Kingston, Jamaica; Eugenio Soler, 7/21/86, Caracas, Venezuela; Antonio Orlani, 10/31/85, Madrid, Spain; Mrs. Frank Church, 5/27/86; Florentino Aspillaga, 4/14/88, Washington, D.C.; Alberto Miguez, 11/5/85, Madrid, Spain; Gerardo Canet, 1/10/85, Washington, D.C.

SOURCE NOTES

CHAPTER 24: THE BAY OF PIGS, AGAIN AND AGAIN

Books, brochures, papers, and documents: Michael Manley, *Jamaica: Struggle in the Periphery;* Gabriel García Márquez, "Operation Carlota," in *Fidel Castro Speeches* and *Operación Carlota, Los Cubanos en Angola, El Che Guevara en Africa, La Batalla Contra El Reich Sudafricano;* Rigoberto Milan, *Farsas y Farsantes;* Carla Anne Robbins, *The Cuban Threat;* H. Michael Erisman, *Cuba's International Relations;* Robert Leiken, *Soviet Strategy in Latin America;* Cole Blasier and Carmelo Mesa-Lago, *Cuba in the World;* General Rafael del Pino, "General del Pino Speaks," booklet; Pamela S. Falk, *Cuban Foreign Policy;* Humberto Belli, *Three Nicaraguans on the Betrayal of Their Revolution* and *Breaking Faith;* Wayne Smith, *The Closest of Enemies;* Shirley Christian, *Nicaragua, Revolution in the Family;* Robert Pastor, *Condemned to Repetition: The United States and Nicaragua;* Ernesto Cardenal, *In Cuba;* David Nolan, *FSLN: The Ideology of the Sandinistas and the Nicaraguan Revolution;* Jiri Valenta, *The Soviet-Cuban Intervention in Angola, 1975* and *The USSR, Cuba and the Crisis in Central America;* Roger W. Fontaine, *Terrorism: The Cuban Connection;* David J. Kopilow, *Castro, Israel, & the PLO;* Gianni Miná, *Un Encuentro con Fidel;* "Inside the Sandinista Regime: A Special Investigator's Perspective," U.S. Department of State; Guillermo Cabrera Infante, *Suicide in Cuba.*

Magazine, newspaper, and journal articles: *Cuban Studies/Estudios Cubanos,* "The Cuban Operation in Angola: Costs and Benefits for the Armed Forces," by Jorge I. Domínguez, vol. 8, no. 1 (January 1978); *Studies in Comparative Communism,* "The Cuban Military in Africa and the Middle East, from Algeria to Angola," by William J. Durch, vol. XI, nos. 1 and 2 (Spring/Summer 1978); *Policy Papers in International Affairs,* "Cuba's Policy in Africa, 1959–1980," by William M. LeoGrande, Institute of International Studies, University of California at Berkeley; *Current Problems of Underdeveloped Countries,* Fidel Castro speech text, "Internationalism and Socialism: A Condition for Humanity's Survival," Oficina de Publicaciones del Consejo de Estado, Havana, 1979; *Problems of Communism,* "Complexities of Cuban Foreign Policy," by Edward Gonzalez, vol. XXVI (November–December 1977); *International Security Review,* "Castro's Adventure in Africa," by Dr. Herminio Portell Vilá, Spring 1979; *Foreign Affairs,* "The Uses of American Power," by Stanley Hoffman, vol. 56, no. 1 (October 1977); "Revolutionary Violence in Latin America," by Douglas Payne, conference of the Foreign Policy Research Institute, 12/4/85, Washington, D.C.; paper, by Arturo Cruz, Jr., "Second Thoughts" conference, 10/17–18/87, Washington, D.C.

Original interviews and oral histories: Luis Da Sousa, 11/13/86, Washington, D.C.; Almirante Antonio Rosa Coutinho, 6/18/88, Lisbon, Portugal, and interview on film, Stornaway Productions television show on Angola, by Rob Roy, Toronto,

Canada; Michael Manley, 3/27/86, Kingston, Jamaica; Florentino Aspillaga, 4/14/88, Washington, D.C.; video interview, Cuban *santero,* Pichardo, from University of West Florida, Program on Cuban Studies, Pensacola, Florida; Blanca del Valle, 3/11/87, Miami, Florida; Tom Reston, 8/28/86, Washington, D.C.; Pedro Ngueve Jonatão Chingunji, 10/29/87, Washington, D.C.; Sergio Ramirez, 5/14/85, Fr. Ernesto Cardenal, 8/4/79, Tomás Borge and Daniel Ortega, 8/5/79, Managua, Nicaragua; Rafael del Pino, 8/26/87, Washington, D.C.; Edén Pastora, 3/6/86, McLean, Virginia; Hasan Rahman, 7/24/87, Washington, D.C.; Napoleón Romero, 3/21/86, Miami, Florida; Zeev Schiff, 9/20/88, Tel Aviv, Israel; Majid Tehranian, 11/19/88, Vyborg, U.S.S.R.; eight interviews with Dr. Heinz Kohut, between 1969 and 1980, Chicago, Illinois; Alejandro Montenegro, 7/10/84, Washington, D.C.; Alvaro José Baldizón Avilés, 9/20/85, Washington, D.C.; Arturo Cruz, Jr., 3/1/89, Washington, D.C.; Jack Vaughan, 6/13/86, Washington, D.C.; Cesar Gómez, 7/9/86, Bogotá, Colombia; Manuel Antonio Sánchez Pérez, 12/10/86, Madrid, Spain; Mayín Correa 5/24/85, Panama City, Panama; Virginia Schofield, 5/28/86, Washington, D.C.; T. N. Kaul, 1/31/86, New Delhi, India; Imr Musa, 1/29/86, New Delhi, India; Tabarak Hussain, 10/15/86, Washington, D.C.; Sumil Kumar Roy, 3/4/86, New Delhi, India; Bernardo Benes, 3/21/86, Miami, Florida; Roger Miranda, 1/15/88, Washington, D.C.; Paul Hollander, 8/7/86, Washington, D.C.; Beatrice Rangel, 11/18/86, Washington, D.C.; Jonas Savimbi, 7/1/88, Washington, D.C.; Holden Roberto, 1/29/86, Washington, D.C.

CHAPTER 25: FIDEL'S GRENADA—DEATH IN A SMALL PLACE

Books, brochures, papers, and documents: Jiri Valenta and Herbert J. Ellison, *Grenada and Soviet-Cuban Policy, Internal Crisis and U.S./OECS Intervention;* Pamela Falk, *Cuban Foreign Policy;* "Grenada Documents: An Overview and Selection," released by the Department of State and the Department of Defense, September 1984, Washington, D.C.; Mark Falcoff and Robert Royal (eds.), *Crisis and Opportunity: U.S. Policy in Central America and the Caribbean;* Vernon V. Aspaturian, *Grenada and Soviet/Cuban Policy;* "Grenada: A Preliminary Report," released by the Department of State and the Department of Defense, December 16, 1983, Washington, D.C.; "Grenada Documents, Report on Meeting of Secret Regional Caucus, Held in Managua from the 6th–7th January, 1983"; "The 1982 Cuban Joint Venture Law: Contents, Assessment and Prospect," monograph by Jorge F. Perez-Lopez; Wayne Smith, *The Closest of Enemies; Cuban Communism,* fifth edition; Fidel Castro, *Fidel Castro Speeches;* Robert Lifton, *Revolutionary Immortality;* "Cuba: The Truth About the U.S. Invasion of Grenada, Statement by the Cuban Party and Government on the Imperialist Intervention in Grenada,"

SOURCE NOTES

Havana, Cuba; H. Michael Erisman, *Cuba's International Relations;* Dr. Shahram Chubin, paper, "Trends in Regional Conflict and Implications for World Strategic Order: Towards the Decline of Super-Power Military Involvement"; General Rafael del Pino, "General del Pino Speaks," booklet.

Magazine and newspaper articles: *Caribbean Review,* "Cuba and the Commonwealth Caribbean Playing the Cuban Card," by Anthony P. Maingot, vol. IX, no. 1 (Winter 1980); *New York Times,* "Cuba Says Its Militia Forces Now Exceed a Million," by Joseph B. Treaster, 5/2/84; El País, Madrid, Spain, "Castro asegura que Cuba es un país en pie de guerra que se defendera solo," by Enrique Muller, 7/28/83; *Washington Post,* interview with Einstein Louison, 11/9/83.

Film: *Improper Conduct,* pictures from Cuban television.

Original interviews and oral histories: Maurice Bishop, 4/5/80, St. George's, Grenada; Joseph E. Edmunds, 5/8/87, Washington, D.C.; Michael Manley, 3/27/86, Kingston, Jamaica; Dr. Alberto Dalmau, 7/22/85, Madrid, Spain; Rolando Cubela, 10/26/85, Madrid, Spain; Dr. Marcelino Feal, 1/21/85, Miami, Florida; Vernon Walters, 3/13/85, Washington, D.C.; Dr. Facundo Lima, 8/27/88, Washington, D.C.; Wolf Grabendorff, 12/15/86, Madrid, Spain; Florentino Aspillaga, 4/14/88, Washington, D.C.; Rafael del Pino, 8/26/87, Washington, D.C.

CHAPTER 26: *EL—HE*

Books, brochures, papers, and documents: Robert Lifton, *Revolutionary Immortality;* background brief, Foreign and Commonwealth Office, London, "Cuba: Party Congress and Rectification," February 1987; Fidel Castro, *Por el Camino Correcto, Compilación de Textos;* Hugh Thomas, Georges Fauriol, and Juan Carlos Weiss, *The Cuban Revolution 25 Years Later;* Fidel Castro speech, 10/3/86, printed in *FIBIS;* Jorge Valls, *Twenty Years and Forty Days: Life in a Cuban Prison;* Rafael Moses, "The Leader and the Led: A Dyadic Relationship," paper; Fidel Castro interview, *60 Minutes,* 3/17/85; Fidel Castro interview with NBC Reporter Maria Shriver, 2/28/88, Havana Television Service in Spanish; James V. Downton, *Rebel Leadership, Commitment and Charisma in the Revolutionary Process;* J. L. Talmon, *The Origins of Totalitarian Democracy;* Fidel Castro speech, 12/13/89, reported by *FIBIS;* Leopoldo Zea, *The Latin American Mind;* Ernesto Betancourt, "Cuban Leadership After Castro," paper, and *Revolutionary Strategy: A Handbook for Practitioners;* Gustavo Perez Cott, "Cuba sin Censura," paper; Régis Debray, *¿Revolución en la Revolución?;* video of interviews of two hundred Cuban youths, prepared by the Directorate Nacional de Policia, para el Comité Central del Partido Comunista de Cuba, 1986; Guillermo Cabrera Infante, "Suicide in Cuba," paper; Rigoberto Milán, *Farsa y Farsantes;* Juan Arcocha, *Fidel Castro;* Luis Conte Agüero, *Fidel Castro: Psiquiatría y Política;* "Chronology of Cuba's Ties to

SOURCE NOTES

Panama's General Manuel Noriega," paper, The Cuban American National Foundation; Rafael del Pino, "General del Pino Speaks," booklet; Ernesto Betancourt, *Revolutionary Strategy: A Handbook for Practitioners.*

Magazine and newspaper articles: *New York Times,* "Castro Recoils at a Hint of Wealth," by Joseph B. Treaster, 2/8/87; *Listín Diario,* Santo Domingo, Dominican Republic, "Imagen de Fidel Sufre," by Noel Lorthiois, 7/26/86; *The World & I,* "Castro: El Supremo," by Dolores Moyano Martín, April 1987; Marita Lorenz, "Ein Leben wie ein Thriller," *Sueddeutsche Zeitung,* 4/20/01; Juan O. Tamayo, "Castro's Family; 'Private' People," *Richmond Times-Dispatch,* 10/29/00; "Fidel! Fidel," by Ann Louise Bardach, *Talk* magazine, August 2001; "Cuba: A Year After the Pope: Return of the Iron Curtain?" Report by Pax Christi Netherlands, February 1999; "The U.S. Embargo of Cuba," Jaime Suchlicki, Occasional Paper Series, School of International Studies, University of Miami, June 2000; "Area Cubans Relieved by Chares in Spy Case; Arrest Proves Castro Is a Threat, Groups Say," by Sylvia Moreno, *Washington Post,* 9/23/01; "As Castro Ages, Brother Raul's Profile Rises," by Vanessa Bauza, *Chicago Tribune,* 7/4/01; "The Collapse Heard 'Round Cuba: People Mull Life without Castro," by Andrew Cawthorne, *Washington Times,* 7/19/01; "Chavez Says Ties Make Venezuela, Cuba 'One team,'" by Reuters, 9/6/01; *New York Times,* "On Castro's Ship of State, Is the Ideology Leaking?" by Joseph B. Treaster, 2/7/89; *Wall Street Journal,* "A Visit with Fidel," by Arthur Schlesinger, Jr., 6/7/85; *Time* magazine, "No Cigar," 1/9/89; *Foreign Affairs,* article on Mikhail Gorbachev, by Richard Nixon, 1/9/89; *Harper's* magazine, "Debray: Beyond the Soviet Threat," vol. 272, no. 1631 (April 1986); *Washington Post,* "Restless Cuban Youth Disdaining Revolution," by Julia Preston, 1/16/89; *The World and I,* "Castro: El Supremo," by Delores Moyano Martin, April 1987.

Original interviews and oral histories: Major Florentino Aspillaga, broadcast by Radio Martí, 8/7–10/87; Gloria Gaitán, 7/11/86, Bogotá, Colombia; Isabel Custodio, 1987, Mexico City, Mexico; José Pardo Llada, 7/12/86, Cali, Colombia; Jorge Valls, 10/23/87, New York; Antonio Valle Vallejo, 7/12/88, Washington, D.C.; Dr. Facundo Lima, 5/2/87, Washington, D.C.; Teddy Cordoba-Claure, 7/18/86, Caracas, Venezuela; Brian Latell, 11/18/87, Washington, D.C.; Miguel Antonio Bernal, 12/25/89, Washington, D.C.; Roberto Eisenmann, 12/25/89, Washington, D.C.; Gilberto Arias, 1/30/90, Panama City, Panama; Ricardo Arias Calderón, 3/1/90, Panama City, Panama; Major Steve Slade, 2/3/90, Vulcan, Panama; Régis Debray, March 1968, Camiri, Bolivia; José Luis Llovio, 8/9/87, New York; Waldo Balart, 10/26/85, Madrid, Spain; Rafael Díaz-Balart, 11/9/85, Madrid, Spain; Isabel Custodio, 1987, Mexico City, Mexico; Antonio Vallejo, 7/12/88, Washington, D.C.; Prof. Rocco Buttiglione, Cardinal Pio Laghi, Jesuit Father-General Peter-Fhans Kolvenbach, and Archbishop J. Francis Stafford, Vatican City, 11/15–20/97.

Information on the trial of General Arnaldo Ochoa was drawn from several interviews with Ernesto Betancourt, spring of 1989; paper, "Behind Castro's Narcogate," by Ernesto Betancourt; *Granma*, "Concluyó sus Sesiones el Tribunal de Honor Militar," 6/27/89, Havana, Cuba; *New York Times*, 6/25, 27, 29/89; *Wall Street Journal*, 6/23/89; *Washington Post*, 6/26,29/89, 7/7,13,26/89 and 8/1, 4/89; two research papers, "Legal Aspects of the Ochoa Trial" and "Castro and the Ochoa Affair," prepared by Freedom House, June 1990; *New York Review of Books*, "The Trial That Shook Cuba," by Julia Preston, vol. xxxvi, no. 9 (12/7/89); "Castro's Final Hour: The Secret Story Behind the Coming Downfall of Communist Cuba," by Andres Oppenheimer; and the film, "OCHOA," by Orlando Jiménez-Leal.

BIBLIOGRAPHY

Abel, Elie. *The Missile Crisis*. Philadelphia: J. B. Lippincott Company, 1966.

Aguilar, Luis E. *Latin America 1933: Prologue to Revolution*. Ithaca: Cornell University Press, 1972.

Allison, Graham. *Essence of Decision*. Boston: Little, Brown, 1971.

Almendros, Néstor, and Jorge Villa. *Nobody Listened*. Film.

Almendros, Néstor, and Orlando Jiménez-Leal. *Conducta Impropia*. Madrid: Editorial Playor, 1984.

Amat Osorio, Victor. *Banes 1513–1958: Estampas de mi tierra y de mi sol*. Miami: New Ideas Printing, 1981.

Aparicio Laurencio, Angel. *La Cuba de Ayer*. Mexico: Tlaquepaque Editorial, S.A., 1984.

Apuleyo Mendoza, Plinio. *La Llama y El Hielo*. Bogotá: Planeta Colombiana Editorial, 1984.

Arciniegas, Germán. *Latin America: A Cultural History*. Translated by Joan MacLean. New York: Alfred A. Knopf, 1967.

Arcocha, Juan. *La Conversación*. Millburn, N.J.: Linden Lane Press, 1983.

— — —. *Fidel Castro en Rompecabezas*. Madrid: Ediciones ERRE, 1973.

Banco, Nacional de Cuba. *Economic Report*. N.p., 1985.

Barba, Antonio. *Cuba el país que fue Unos Recuerdos*. Barcelona: Editorial Maucci, 1964.

Barquín, Ramón M. *El Día Que Fidel Castro Se Apodero de Cuba; 72 horas trágicas para la Libertad en Las Américas*. San Juan: Editorial Rambar, 1978.

— — —. *Las Luchas Guerrilleras en Cuba de La Colonia a La Sierra Maestra*, vols. 1 and 2. Madrid: Editorial Playor, 1975.

435

BIBLIOGRAPHY

Barrett, Jeffrey W. *Impulse to Revolution in Latin America.* New York: Praeger, 1985.

Batista, Fulgencio. *Cuba Betrayed.* New York: Vantage Press, 1962.

Belli, Humberto. *Breaking Faith.* Westchester, Ill.: Crossway Books, 1985.

Ben-Ami, Shlomo. *Fascism from Above: The Dictatorship of Primo de Rivera in Spain 1923–1930.* Oxford: Clarendon Press, 1983.

Benemelis, Juan F. *Castro Subversíon y Terrorismo en Africa.* Madrid: Editorial San Martin, 1988.

Bertot, Francisco Lorié. *Rafael Díaz-Balart Pensamiento y Acción.* N.p., n.d.

Betancourt, Ernesto. *Revolutionary Strategy: A Handbook for Practitioners.* New Brunswick, N.J.: Transaction Books, 1991.

— — —. *Cuban Leadership After Castro.* Miami: Research Institute, University of Miami, 1988.

— — —. *Castro and the Bankers.* Washington, D.C.: Cuban American National Foundation, 1983.

Bethel, Paul D. *The Losers.* New Rochelle: Arlington House, 1969.

Billington, James H. *Fire in the Minds of Men: Origins of the Revolutionary Faith.* New York: Basic Books, 1980.

Blas Roca, Francisco Calderío. *The Cuban Revolution: Report to the Eighth National Congress of the Popular Socialist Party of Cuba.* New York: New Century Publishers, 1961.

Blasier, Cole. *The Hovering Giant: U.S. Response to Revolutionary Change in Latin America.* London: Feffer and Simons, 1976.

Blasier, Cole, and Carmelo Mesa-Lago, eds. *Cuba in the World.* Pittsburgh: University of Pittsburgh Press, 1979.

Blight, James G., and David A. Welch. *On the Brink: Americans and Soviets Reexamine the Cuban Missile Crisis.* New York: Hill and Wang, 1989, editions I and II.

Bonachea, Ramón L., and Marta San Martín. *The Cuban Insurrection 1952–1959.* New Brunswick: Transaction Books, 1974.

Bonachea, Rolando E., and Nelson P. Valdés, eds. *Cuba in Revolution.* Garden City, N.Y.: Doubleday & Company, Anchor Books, 1972.

— — —. *Revolutionary Struggle 1947–1958.* Cambridge: The MIT Press, 1972.

Bonsal, Philip W. *Cuba, Castro, and the United States.* London: Henry M. Snyder & Co., n.d. Reprint: Pittsburgh: University of Pittsburgh Press, 1971.

Borge, Tomás, Carlos Fonseca, Daniel Ortega, Humberto Ortega, and Jaime Wheelock. *Sandinistas Speak.* New York: Pathfinder Press, 1982.

Bosch, Juan. *De Cristóbal Colón a Fidel Castro (II).* Madrid: SARPE, 1985.

Bourne, Peter G. *Fidel.* New York: Dodd, Mead & Company, 1986.

Brinton, Crane. *The Anatomy of Revolution.* New York: Vintage Books, 1965.

Brownfeld, Allan C., and J. Michael Walker. *The Revolution Lobby.* Washington,

BIBLIOGRAPHY

D.C.: Council for Inter-American Security, and the Inter-American Security Educational Institute, 1985.

Cabrera, Lydia. *El Monte*. Miami: Colección del Chicherekú, 1983.

Calzadilla, Miguel A. G. *The Fidel Castro I Knew: Biographical Fragments on the Cuban Revolution*. New York: Vantage Press, 1971.

Calzón, Frank. *Castro's Gulag: The Politics of Terror*. Washington, D.C.: Council for Inter-American Security, 1979.

Carbonell, Néstor T. *And the Russians Stayed: The Sovietization of Cuba*. New York: William Morrow & Company, 1989.

Cardenal, Ernesto. *In Cuba*. Translated by Donald D. Walsh. New York: New Directions, 1974.

Carr, Raymond. *Spain, 1808–1975*. Second edition. Oxford: Clarendon Press, 1982.

Carrillo, Justo. *Cuba 1933: Estudiantes, yanquis y soldados*. Miami: Instituto de Estudios Interamericanos, University of Miami, 1985.

Castro, Fidel. *Fidel Castro on Latin America's Unpayable Debt, Its Unforeseeable Consequences and Other Topics of Political and Historical Interest*. Interview granted to EFE news agency. Havana: Editora Politica, 1985.

— — —. *Fidel e a Religião: Conversas com Frei Betto*. São Paulo, Brazil: Editora Brasiliense S.A., 1985 (Portuguese).

— — —. *History Will Absolve Me*. New York: Lyle Stuart, 1961.

— — —. *Por el Camino Correcto*. Havana: Editora Politica, 1987.

— — —. *13 Documentos de la Insurrección*. Havana: n.p., 1959.

— — —. *The World Crisis: Its Economic and Social Impact on the Underdeveloped Countries*. London: Zed Books, 1984. Morant Bay, Jamaica: Maroon Publishing House, 1984. Haarlem, The Netherlands: In de Knpscheer, 1984.

Castro Hidalgo, Orlando. *Spy for Fidel*. Miami: E. A. Seemann Publishing, 1971.

Casuso, Teresa. *Cuba and Castro*. New York: Random House, 1961.

— — —. *Cuba and Castro*. Translated by Elmer Grossberg. New York: Random House, n.d.

Chase, James, and Caleb Carr. *America Invulnerable: The Quest for Absolute Security from 1812 to Star Wars*. New York: Summit Books, 1988.

Cherson, Samuel B. *José Antonio Echeverría: Guía del pueblo cubano*. Miami: n.p., 1982.

Christian, Shirley. *Nicaragua, Revolution in the Family*. New York: Random House, 1985.

Chubin, Shahram. *Committee 8: Trends in Regional Conflict and Implications for World Strategic Order: Towards the Decline of Super-Power Military Involvement*, "The Super-Powers, Regional Conflicts and World Order." Brighton, England: The International Institute for Strategic Studies Thirteenth Annual Conference, 1988.

BIBLIOGRAPHY

Conte Agüero, Luis. *Fidel Castro: Vida y Obra.* Havana: Editorial Lex, 1959.

— — —. *Los Dos Rostros de Fidel Castro.* Mexico: Editorial Jus., 1960.

— — —. *Fidel Castro—Psiquiatría y Política.* Mexico: Editorial Jus., 1968.

Crassweller, Robert D. *Trujillo: The Life and Times of a Caribbean Dictator.* New York: Macmillan Company, 1966.

Cuba: The Truth About the U.S. Invasion of Grenada. [Havana]: Cuban Party and Government, n.d.

The Cuban American National Foundation. *Cuba's Financial Crisis: The Secret Report from Banco Nacional de Cuba February 1985.* Washington, D.C.: The Cuban American National Foundation, Inc., 1985.

The Cuban Economic Research Project. *A Study on Cuba: The Colonial and Republican Periods; The Socialist Experiment; Economic Structure; Institutional Development; Socialism; and Collectivization.* Coral Gables: University of Miami Press, 1965.

Cuba's Internationalist Foreign Policy 1975–1980: Fidel Castro Speeches. New York: Pathfinder Press, 1981.

Cunqueiro, Alvaro. *Ver Galicia.* Barcelona: Ediciones Destino, S.L., 1981.

Currey, Cecil B. *Edward Lansdale: The Unquiet American.* Boston: Houghton Mifflin Company, 1988.

Davis, Nathaniel. *The Last Two Years of Salvador Allende.* Ithaca: Cornell University Press, 1985.

Dealy, Glen Caudill. *The Public Man: An Interpretation of Latin American and Other Catholic Countries.* Amherst: The University of Massachusetts Press, 1977.

Debray, Régis. *La Guerrilla del Che.* Mexico: Siglo Veintiuno Editores, 1975.

— — —. *Revolution in the Revolution? Armed Struggle and Political Struggle in Latin America.* New York: Grove Press, 1967.

De Castro, Rosalia. *En las Orillas del Sar.* Madrid: Clásicos Castalia, 1983.

De Tuxpán a la Plata. Havana: Editorial Orbe, 1979.

Díaz-Balart, Rafael L. *Derecho Agrario y Política Agraria: El Temor a la Reforma Estructural en Iberoamérica.* Madrid: Ediciones Cultura Hispanica, 1965.

Documentos Secretos de la ITT. Santiago-Chile: Empresa Editora Nacional Quimantu Ltda., 1972.

Domínguez, Jorge I. *Cuba: Order and Revolution.* Cambridge: The Belknap Press of Harvard University Press, 1978.

Dorschner, John, and Robert Fabricio. *The Winds of December.* New York: Coward, McCann & Geoghegan, 1980.

Dorta-Duque, Manuel. *Alejandro (Alias) Fidel.* Hato Rey, Puerto Rico: Ediciones Joyuda, Inc., n.d.

Downton, James V., Jr. *Rebel Leadership: Commitment and Charisma in the Revolutionary Process.* New York: The Free Press, 1973.

Draper, Theodore. *Castro's Revolution: Myths and Realities.* New York: Frederick A. Praeger, 1962.

— — —. *Castroism: Theory and Practice.* New York: Frederick A. Praeger, 1965.

Duarte Oropesa, José. *Historiología Cubana Desde 1944 hasta 1959.* Miami: Ediciones Universal, 1974.

Dubois, Jules. *Fidel Castro: Rebel-Liberator or Dictator?* Indianapolis: Bobbs-Merrill Company, 1959.

— — —. *Freedom Is My Beat.* Indianapolis: Bobbs-Merrill Company, 1959.

Dumont, René. *Is Cuba Socialist?* Translated by Stanley Hochman. London: Andre Deutsch, 1974.

Duncan, W. Raymond, and James Nelson Goodsell, eds. *The Quest for Change in Latin America: Sources for a Twentieth-Century Analysis.* New York: Oxford University Press, 1970.

Echerri, Vicente. *Luz en la Piedra.* Madrid: Gonther, 1986.

Edwards, Jorge. *Persona Non Grata: An Envoy in Castro's Cuba.* Translated by Colin Harding. New York: Pomerica Press, 1976.

Efimov, Igor Markovich. *Kennedi, Osval'd, Kastro, Khrushchev.* Tenafly, N.J.: Hermitage, 1987.

Einaudi, Luigi R., ed. *Beyond Cuba: Latin America Takes Charge of Its Future.* New York: Crane, Russak & Company, 1974.

Eisenhower, Milton S. *The Wine Is Bitter: The United States and Latin America.* Garden City: Doubleday and Company, 1963.

Erikson, Erik H. *Young Man Luther: A Study in Psychoanalysis and History.* New York: W. W. Norton & Company, 1958.

Erisman, H. Michael. *Cuba's International Relations: The Anatomy of a Nationalistic Foreign Policy.* Boulder: Westview Press, 1985.

Fagen, Richard R., Richard A. Brody, and Thomas J. O'Leary. *Cubans in Exile: Disaffection and the Revolution.* Stanford: Stanford University Press, 1968.

Falcoff, Mark. *Small Countries, Large Issues: Studies in U.S.-Latin American Asymmetries.* Washington, D.C.: American Enterprise Institute for Public Research, 1984.

Falcoff, Mark, and Robert Royal, eds. *Crisis and Opportunity: U.S. Policy in Central America and the Caribbean.* Washington, D.C.: Ethics and Public Policy Center, 1984.

Falk, Pamela S. *Cuban Foreign Policy: Caribbean Tempest.* Lexington: Lexington Books, 1986.

Farber, Samuel. *Revolution and Reaction in Cuba, 1933–1960: A Political Sociology from Machado to Castro.* Middletown: Wesleyan University Press, 1976.

BIBLIOGRAPHY

Fauriol, Georges, ed. *Latin American Insurgencies*. Washington, D.C.: The Georgetown University Center for Strategic & International Studies, and the National Defense University, 1985.

First Solidarity Conference of the Peoples of Africa, Asia, and Latin America. Havana: General Secretariat of the O.S.P.A.A.A.L., 1966.

Fontaine, Roger W. *Terrorism: The Cuban Connection*. New York: Crane, Russak & Company, 1988.

Franqui, Carlos. *Diary of the Cuban Revolution*. Translated by Georgette Felix, Elaine Kerrigan, Phyllis Freeman, and Hardie St. Martin. New York: The Viking Press, 1980.

– – –. *Family Portrait with Fidel: A Memoir.* Translated by Alfred MacAdam. New York: Random House, 1984.

– – –. *The Twelve.* Translated by Albert B. Teichner. New York: Lyle Stuart,1968.

– – –. *Vida aventuras y desastres de un hombre llamado Castro.* Barcelona: Editorial Planeta, 1988.

Gadea, Hilda. *Ernesto: A Memoir of Che Guevara.* Translated by Carmen Molina, and Walter I. Bradbury. Garden City, N.Y.: Doubleday & Company, 1972.

Geertz, Clifford, ed. *Old Societies and New States: The Quest for Modernity in Asia and Africa.* New York: The Free Press, 1963.

General Del Pino Speaks: An Insight into Elite Corruption and Military Dissension in Castro's Cuba. Washington, D.C.: The Cuban American National Foundation, 1987.

Gilio, Maria Esther. *The Tupamaro Guerrillas.* Translated by Anne Edmondson. New York: Saturday Review Press, 1970.

Gilmore, William C. *The Grenada Intervention: Analysis and Documentation.* Bronx: Mansell Publishing, 1984.

Golendorf, Pierre. *7 Años en Cuba.* Belfond, Guadalupe: Plaza & Janes, S.A., 1977.

Gonzalez, Edward. *A Strategy for Dealing with Cuba in the 1980's.* Santa Monica: Rand, 1982.

Gonzalez, Edward, Brian Michael Jenkins, David Ronfeldt, and Caesar Sereseres. *U.S. Policy for Central America.* Santa Monica: Rand, 1984.

Gonzalez, Edward, and David Ronfeldt. *Castro, Cuba, and the World.* Santa Monica: Rand, 1986.

Gonzaléz de la Fé, Pedro. *Fidel Castro: Gangster que conmovió la America,* N.p., n.d.

González-Wippler, Migene. *Santería: African Magic in Latin America.* New York: The Julian Press, 1973.

Gott, Richard. *Guerrilla Movements in Latin America.* Garden City: Doubleday & Company, Anchor Books, 1972.

BIBLIOGRAPHY

Griffiths, John, and Peter Griffiths, eds. *Cuba: The Second Decade*. London: Writers and Readers, 1979.

Guerra Aleman, José. *Barro y Cenizas: Dialogos con Fidel Castro y el "Che" Guevara*. N.p., n.d.

Guevara, Ernesto "Che." *Guerrilla Warfare*. Translated by J. P. Morray. New York: Random House, Vintage Books, 1961.

— — —. *Episodes of the Revolutionary War*. New York: International Publishers, 1968.

— — —. *Le Socialisme et L'Homme à Cuba*. Havana: Institut du Libre, ~967.

— — —. *Reminiscences of the Cuban Revolutionary War*. Translated by Victoria Ortiz. New York: Monthly Review Press, 1968.

Gugliotta, Guy, and Jeff Leen. *Kings of Cocaine: Inside the Medellín Cartel—An Astonishing True Story of Murder, Money, and International Corruption*. New York: Simon and Schuster, 1989.

Halperin, Maurice. *The Rise and Decline of Fidel Castro: An Essay in Contemporary History*. Berkeley and Los Angeles: University of California Press, 1972.

— — —. *The Taming of Fidel Castro*. Berkeley and Los Angeles: University of California Press, 1981.

Harkabi, Yehoshafat. *Israel's Fateful Hour*. Translated by Lenn Schramm. New York: Harper & Row, 1986.

Hauberg, Clifford A. *Latin American Revolutions (Mexico, Central America, Panama, and the Islands of the Caribbean)*. Minneapolis: T. S. Denison & Company, 1968.

Heikal, Mohamed Hassanein. *The Cairo Documents: The Inside Story of Nasser and His Relationship with World Leaders, Rebels, and Statesmen*. Garden City, N.Y.: Doubleday & Company, 1973.

Heller, Mikhail, and Aleksandr Nekrich. *Utopia in Power: The History of the Soviet Union from 1917 to the Present*. Translated by Phyllis B. Carlos. New York: Summit Books, 1982.

Hernandez S., Plutarco. *El FSLN por Dentro Relatos de un Combatiente*. N.p., n.d.

Herring, Hubert. *A History of Latin America from the Beginnings to the Present*. New York: Alfred A. Knopf, 1956.

Hinckle, Warren, and William W. Turner. *The Fish Is Red: The Story of the Secret War Against Castro*. New York: Harper & Row, 1981.

Hoffer, Eric. *The True Believer: Thoughts on the Nature of Mass Movements*. New York: Harper & Row, Perennial Library, 1966.

Hollander, Paul. *Political Hospitality and Tourism: Cuba and Nicaragua*. Washington, D.C.: The Cuban American National Foundation, 1986.

— — —. *Political Pilgrims: Travels of Western Intellectuals to the Soviet Union, China, and Cuba 1928–1978*. New York: Harper Colophon Books, 1981.

BIBLIOGRAPHY

Horowitz, Irving Louis. *C. Wright Mills: An American Utopian.* New York: The Free Press, 1983.

―――, ed. *Cuban Communism.* Fifth edition. New Brunswick: Transaction Books, 1984.

―――. *Cuban Communism.* Sixth edition. New Brunswick: Transaction Books, 1987

―――. *Cuban Communism.* Sixth edition. New Brunswick: Transaction Books, 1988. Second printing.

―――. *Cuban Communism.* Seventh edition. New Brunswick: Transaction Publishers, 1989.

How Latin American Insurgents Fight. Panama: 193D Infantry Brigade, 1985.

Howard, Michael. *Clausewitz.* Oxford: Oxford University Press, 1983.

Hudson, Rex A. *Castro's America Department: Coordinating Cuba's Support for Marxist-Leninist Violence in the Americas.* Washington, D.C.: The Cuban American National Foundation, 1988.

James, Daniel. *Ché Guevara.* New York: Stein and Day, 1970.

Johnson, Haynes, with Manuel Artime, José Pérez San Román, Erneido Oliva, and Enrique Ruiq-Williams. *The Bay of Pigs: The Leader's Story of Brigade 2056.* New York: W. W. Norton & Company, 1964.

Johnson, John J. *The Military and Society in Latin America.* Stanford: Stanford University Press, 1964.

Johnson, Paul. *Modern Times: The World from the Twenties to the Eighties.* New York: Harper & Row, 1983.

Judson, C. Fred. *Cuba and the Revolutionary Myth: The Political Education of the Cuban Rebel Army, 1953–1963.* Boulder: Westview Press, 1984.

Karol, K. S. *Guerrillas in Power: The Course of the Cuban Revolution.* Translated by Arnold Pomerans. New York: Hill & Wang, 1970.

Kennedy, Robert F. *Thirteen Days: A Memoir of the Cuban Missile Crisis.* New York: W. W. Norton & Company, 1969.

Kidron, Michael, and Ronald Segal. *The New State of the World Atlas.* London: Heinemann, 1984.

Kissinger, Henry. *White House Years.* Boston: Little, Brown and Company, 1979.

Kopilow, David J. *Castro, Israel & the P.L.O.* Washington, D.C.: The Cuban-American National Foundation, Inc., 1984.

Lacouture, Jean. *The Demigods: Charismatic Leadership in the Third World.* New York: Alfred A. Knopf, 1970.

Laqueur, Walter, ed. *The Guerrilla Reader: A Historical Anthology.* New York: Meridian Books, 1977.

Larzelere, Alex. *The 1980 Cuban Boatlift.* Washington, D.C.: National Defense University Press, 1988.

Lavretsky, I. *Ernesto Che Guevara*. Moscow: Progress Publishers, 1976.

Legum, Colin, and Tony Hodges. *After Angola: The War over Southern Africa*. London: Rex Collins, 1976.

Leiken, Robert S. *Central America: Anatomy of Conflict*. New York: Pergamon Press, 1984.

―――. *Soviet Strategy in Latin America*. The Washington Papers/93 Volume X. New York: Praeger Publishers, and the Center for Strategic and International Studies, 1982.

LeoGrande, William M. *Policy Papers in International Affairs, Cuba's Policy in Africa, 1959–1980*. Berkeley: University of California, Institute of International Studies, 1980.

Levine, Barry B., ed. *The New Cuban Presence in the Caribbean*. Boulder: Westview Press, 1983.

Lifton, Robert Jay. *Revolutionary Immortality: Mao Tse-Tung and the Chinese Cultural Revolution*. New York: Random House, 1968.

Liscano, Juan, and Carlos Gottberg. *Multimagen de Rómulo: Vida y acción de Rómulo Betancourt en gráficas*. Caracas, Venezuela: Editorial Arte, 1978.

Liste, Ana. *Galicia: Brujería, superstición y mística*. Madrid: Penthalon Ediciones, 1981.

Llerena, Mario. *The Unsuspected Revolution: The Birth and Rise of Castroism*. Ithaca: Cornell University Press, 1978.

Lockwood, Lee. *Castro's Cuba, Cuba's Fidel: An American Journalist's Inside Look at Today's Cuba—in Text and Picture*. New York: Macmillan Company, 1967.

López Fresquet, Rufo. *My 14 Months with Castro*. Cleveland: The World Publishing Company, 1966.

Lowenthal, Abraham F. *Partners in Conflict: The United States and Latin America*. Baltimore: The Johns Hopkins University Press, 1987.

Macaulay, Neill. *The Sandino Affair*. Chicago: Quadrangle Books, 1967.

MacGaffey, Wyatt, and Clifford R. Barnett. *Cuba: Its People, Its Society, Its Culture*. New Haven: Araf Press, 1962.

MacGaffey, Wyatt, and Clifford R. Barnett, in collaboration with Jen Haiken, and Mildred Vreeland. *Twentieth-Century Cuba: The Background of the Castro Revolution*. Garden City, N.Y.: Doubleday & Company, Anchor Books, 1965.

Mallin, Jay, Sr. *Cuba in Angola*. Coral Gables: Research Institute for Cuban Studies, Graduate School of International Studies, University of Miami, n.d.

―――. *Fortress Cuba: Russia's America Base*. Chicago: Henry Regnery Company, 1965.

Mañach, Jorge. *Martí: Apostle of Freedom*. Translated by Coley Taylor. New York: Devin-Adair Co., 1950.

BIBLIOGRAPHY

Mankiewicz, Frank, and Kirby Jones. *With Fidel: A Portrait of Castro and Cuba.* New York: Ballantine Books, 1975.

Manley, Michael. *Jamaica: Struggle in the Periphery.* London: Third World Media Limited, 1982.

Marrero, Levi. *Cuba: Economía y Sociedad Azúcar, Illustración y Conciencia (1763–1868)* (IU). Madrid: Editorial Playor, S.A., 1985.

Martí, José. *La Edad de Oro.* Cuba: Editora Juvenil/Editorial Nacional de Cuba, 1964.

— — —. *Paginas Escogidas.* Havana: Editora Universitaria, 1965.

Martin, John Bartlow. *Overtaken by Events: The Dominican Crisis from the Fall of Trujillo to the Civil War.* Garden City, N.Y.: Doubleday & Company, 1966.

Martin, Lionel. *The Early Fidel: Roots of Castro's Communism.* Secaucus, N.J.: Lyle Stuart, 1978.

El más alto ejemplo de heroísmo. Havana: Instituto Cubano del Libro, 1973.

Matthews, Herbert L. *The Cuban Story.* New York: George Braziller, 1961.

— — —. *Fidel Castro.* New York: Simon and Schuster, 1969.

— — —. *Revolution in Cuba: An Essay in Understanding.* New York: Charles Scribner's Sons, 1975.

Mencía, Mario. *Time Was on Our Side.* Havana: Political Publishers, 1982.

Meneses, Enrique. *Fidel Castro.* New York: Taplinger Publishing Co., 1966.

Merino, Adolfo G. *Nacimiento de un Estado Vasallo.* Mexico: B. Costa-Amic, 1966.

Mesa-Lago, Carmelo. *Dialéctica de la Revolución Cubana: Del idealismo carismático al pragmatismo institucionalista.* Madrid: Biblioteca Cubana Contemporanea, Editorial Playor, 1979.

— — —. *La economía en Cuba socialista: Una evaluación de dos décadas.* Madrid: Editorial Playor, 1983.

— — —. *Revolutionary Change in Cuba.* Pittsburgh: University of Pittsburgh Press. London: Henry M. Snyder & Co., 1971.

Mesa-Lago, Carmelo, and June S. Belkin, eds. *Cuba in Africa.* Pittsburgh: Center for Latin American Studies, University Center for International Studies, University of Pittsburgh, 1982.

Meyer, Karl E., and Tad Szulc. *The Cuban Invasion: The Chronicle of a Disaster.* New York: Frederick A. Praeger, 1962.

Mikoyán en Cuba. N.p., 1960.

Mil fotos Cuba Territorio libre de América. N.p., n.d.

Milán, Rigoberto. *Farsa y Farsantes de Cuba Comunista.* Miami: Ahora Printing, 1984.

Mills, C. Wright. *Listen, Yankee: The Revolution in Cuba.* New York: McGraw-Hill, 1960.

BIBLIOGRAPHY

Miná, Gianni. *Un Encuentro con Fidel: Entrevista realizada por Gianni Miná.* Havana: Oficina de Publicaciones del Consejo de Estado, 1987.

Montaner, Carlos Alberto. *Cuba, Castro, and the Caribbean: The Cuban Revolution and the Crisis in Western Conscience.* Translated by Nelson Duran. New Brunswick: Transaction Books, 1985.

————. *Fidel Castro y la revolución cubana.* Madrid: Editorial Playor, 1983.

————. *Secret Report on the Cuban Revolution.* Translated by Eduardo Zayas-Bazan. New Brunswick: Transaction Books, 1981.

Montes de Oca, Alberto Fernández. *El Diario de Pacho: La guerrilla del Che.* Santa Cruz, Bolivia: Editorial Punto y Coma S.R.L., 1987.

Moore, John Norton. *Law and the Grenada Mission.* Charlottesville: Center for Law and National Security University of Virginia Law School, 1984.

Morán Arce, Lucas. *La Revolución Cubana (1953–1959): Una Versión Rebelde.* Ponce, Puerto Rico: Imprenta Universitaria, Inc., 1980.

Mortimer, Robert A. *The Third World Coalition in International Politics.* Second edition. Boulder: Westview Press, 1984.

Navarro, Antonio. *Tocayo.* Westport, Conn.: Sharock Publishing Company, Sandown Books, 1981.

Nelson, Lowry. *Cuba: The Measure of a Revolution.* Minneapolis: University of Minnesota Press, 1972.

Neustadt, Richard E., and Ernest R. May. *Thinking in Time: The Uses of History for Decision-Making.* New York: The Free Press, 1986.

El 9 de Abril en Fotos. Bogotá: El Áncora Editores, 1986.

Nixon, Richard. *The Memoirs of Richard Nixon.* Volume I. New York: Warner Books, 1978.

Nolan, David. *FSLN: The Ideology of the Sandinistas and the Nicaraguan Revolution.* Coral Gables: Institute of Interamerican Studies, University of Miami, 1984.

Office of Research and Policy. *Cuba Quarterly Situation Report Covering Cuba Related Events for the Period: October–December, 1985.* Washington, D.C.: Office of Research and Policy, 1986.

Oppenheimer, Andres. *Castro's Final Hour: The Secret Story Behind the Coming Downfall of Communist Cuba.* New York: Simon and Schuster (A Touchstone Book). 1993.

Ortega, Luis. *El Sueño y la Distancia Apuntes para un ensayo.* Mexico: Ediciones Ganivet, 1968.

————. *¡Yo Soy El Che! (El hombre visto desde adentro).* Mexico: Ediciones Monroy-Padilla, 1970.

Padilla, Heberto. *Poesía y Politica: Poemas escogidos de Heberto Padilla.* Translated by Frank Calzón et al. Madrid: Georgetown University Cuban Series, Playor, S.A., 1975.

BIBLIOGRAPHY

Pardo Llada, José. *El "Che" Que Yo Conocí*. Medellín: Editorial Bedout, 1969.

―――. *Fidel*. Bogotá: Plaza y Janes, 1976.

―――. *Memorias de la Sierra Maestra*. Havana: N.p., 1960.

Pastor, Robert A. *Condemned to Repetition: The United States and Nicaragua*. Princeton: Princeton University Press, 1987.

Pflaum, Irving Peter. *Tragic Island: How Communism Came to Cuba*. Englewood Cliffs, N.J.: Prentice-Hall, 1961.

Phillips, R. Hart. *The Cuban Dilemma*. n.p., 1962.

―――. *Cuba: Island of Paradox*. New York: McDowell, Obolensky, n.d.

Playa Giron/Derrota del Imperialismo. Cuarto Tomo. Havana: Ediciones R, 1962.

Playa Giron/Derrota del Imperialismo. Primer Tomo. Havana: Ediciones R, 1961.

Political, Economic, and Social Thought of Fidel Castro. Havana: Editorial Lex, 1959.

Poppino, Rollie E. *International Communism in Latin America: A History of the Movement 1917–1963*. London: Free Press of Glencoe, Collier-Macmillan Limited, 1964.

Portell Vilá, Herminio. *Los "Otros Extranjeros" en la Revolución norteamericana*. Miami: Ediciones Universal, 1978.

Prado Salmón, Gary. *Como Capturé al Ché*. Barcelona: Ediciones B, 1987.

Prados, John. *Presidents' Secret Wars: CIA and Pentagon Covert Operations Since World War II*. New York: William Morrow and Company, 1986.

Presencia de España en Cuba. Madrid: Revista Geográfica Española, n.d.

Prisons and Concentration Camps in Cuba. Madrid: Comite Pro Derechos Humanos en Cuba.

Pritchett, V. S. *The Spanish Temper*. New York: Harper & Row, 1965.

Quirk, Robert E. *Fidel Castro: The Full Story of His Rise to Power, His Regime, His Allies, and His Adversaries*. New York and London: W. W. Norton & Company, 1993.

Rangel, Carlos. *Del Buen Salvaje al Buen Revolucionario Mitos y Realidades de America Latina*. Caracas, Venezuela: Editorial Arte, 1976.

―――. *The Latin Americans: Their Love-Hate Relationship with the United States*. New York: Harcourt Brace Jovanovich, 1977.

Rangel, Domingo Alberto. *Los héroes no han caído*. Valencia: Vadell Hermanos Editores, 1978.

Ratliff, William E. *Follow the Leader in the Horn: The Soviet Cuban Presence in East Africa*. Washington, D.C.: The Cuban American National Foundation, 1986.

―――, ed. *The Selling of Fidel Castro: The Media and the Cuban Revolution*. New Brunswick: Transaction Books, 1987.

The Report of the President's National Bipartisan Commission on Central America. New York: Macmillan Publishing Company, 1984.

BIBLIOGRAPHY

Resistance International, and the Coalition of Committees for the Rights of Man in Cuba. *Castro's Tropical Gulag: The Tribunal on Cuba: Paris, April, 1986.* New York: The American Foundation for Resistance International, 1986.

Ripoll, Carlos. *Harnessing the Intellectuals: Censoring Writers and Artists in Today's Cuba.* New York: Freedom House, 1985. Reprint. Washington, D.C.: The Cuban American National Foundation, Inc., 1985.

— — —. *Jose Martí: Thoughts on Liberty, Government, Art, and Morality: A Bilingual Anthology.* New York: Eliseo Torres & Sons—Las Americas Publishing Co., 1980.

— — —. *Jose Martí, the United States, and the Marxist Interpretation of Cuban History.* New Brunswick: Transaction Books, 1984.

Rius, Cuba for Beginners: An Illustrated Guide for Americans (and Their Government) to Socialist Cuba. New York: Pathfinder Press, 1970.

Rivero, Nicolás. *Castro's Cuba: An American Dilemma.* Washington, D.C.: Luce, 1962.

Robbins, Carla Anne. *The Cuban Threat.* New York: McGraw-Hill, 1983.

Rodríguez, Carlos Rafael. *Cuba en el Tránsito al Socialismo, 1959–1963.* Mexico: Siglo Veintiuno Editores, 1978.

Rodríguez Morejón, Gerardo. *Fidel Castro, Biografía.* Havana: P. Fernandez y C/a.S enC., 1959.

Rojas, Marta. *La Generación del Centenario en el Juicio del Moncada.* Havana: Editorial de Ciencias Sociales, 1973.

Rojas, Marta, and Mirta Rodríguez Calderon. *Tania: La Guerrillera.* Mexico: Editorial Diógenes, S.A., 1971.

Rojo, Ricardo. *My Friend Che.* Translated by Julian Casart. New York: The Dial Press, 1968.

Rojo del Río, Manuel. *La historia cambió en la sierra.* Second Edition. San José, Costa Rica: Editorial Texto, Ltda., 1981.

Rubin, Barry. *Modern Dictators: Third World Coup Makers, Strongmen, and Populist Tyrants.* New York: McGraw-Hill, 1987.

Ruiz, Ramón Eduardo. *Cuba, the Making of a Revolution.* Cambridge: The University of Massachusetts Press, 1968.

Ryan, Henry Butterfield. *The Fall of Che Guevara: A Story of Soldiers, Spies, and Diplomats.* New York and Oxford: Oxford University Press, 1998.

Santamaría, Haydée. *Moncada.* Secaucus, N.J.: Lyle Stuart, 1980.

Sartre, Jean Paul. *Sartre on Cuba.* Westport, Conn.: Greenwood Press, Publishers, 1961.

Sauvage, Léo. *Che Guevara: The Failure of a Revolutionary.* Englewood Cliffs, N.J.: Prentice-Hall, 1974.

447

BIBLIOGRAPHY

Scheer, Robert, ed. *The Diary of Che Guevara. Bolivia: November 7, 1966–October 7, 1967.* New York: Bantam Books, Inc., 1968.

Schiffer, Irvine, M.D. *Charisma: A Psychoanalytic Look at Mass Society.* Toronto: University of Toronto Press, 1973.

Schlesinger, Arthur M., Jr. *Robert Kennedy and His Times.* Boston: Houghton Mifflin Company, 1980.

———. *A Thousand Days: John F. Kennedy in the White House.* Boston: Houghton Mifflin Company, 1965.

Sejna, Jan. *We Will Bury You.* London: Sidgwick & Jackson, 1982.

Shevchenko, Arkady N. *Breaking with Moscow.* New York: Alfred A. Knopf, 1985.

Smith, Earl, E. T. *The Fourth Floor: An Account of the Castro Communist Revolution.* New York: Random House, 1962.

Smith, Robert Freeman, ed. *Background to Revolution: The Development of Modern Cuba.* New York: Alfred A. Knopf, 1966.

Smith, Wayne E. *The Closest of Enemies: A Personal and Diplomatic Account of U.S.-Cuban Relations Since 1957.* New York: W. W. Norton & Company, 1987.

The Soviet-Cuban Connection in Central America and the Caribbean. Washington, D.C.: Department of State and Department of Defense, 1985.

Soviet/Cuban Strategy in the Third World After Grenada: A Conference Report. Washington, D.C.: Kennan Institute for Advanced Russian Studies, Woodrow Wilson International Center for Scholars, and Soviet and East European Studies Program Department of National Security Affairs Naval Postgraduate School, 1984.

Sterling, Claire. *The Terror Network.* New York: Berkeley Books, 1982.

Suchlicki, Jaime. *Cuba, Castro, and Revolution.* Coral Gables: University of Miami Press, 1972.

———. *Cuba from Columbus to Castro.* Washington: Pergamon-Brassey's, 1986.

———. *The Cuban Military Under Castro.* Miami: Institute of Interamerican Studies, Graduate School of International Studies, University of Miami, 1989.

———. *University Students and Revolution in Cuba, 1920–1968.* Coral Gables: University of Miami Press, 1969.

Suchlicki, Jaime, Antonio Jorge, and Damian Fernandez, eds. *The Cuban Studies Project: Cuba—Continuity and Change.* Miami: University of Miami North-South Center, 1985.

Sulzberger, C. L. *An Age of Mediocrity: Memoirs and Diaries, 1963–1972.* New York: Macmillan Publishing Company, 1973.

Szulc, Tad. *Fidel: A Critical Portrait.* New York: William Morrow and Company, 1986.

Taber, Robert. *M-26: Biography of a Revolution.* New York: Lyle Stuart, 1961.

Talbott, Strobe, ed. and trans. *Khrushchev Remembers: The Last Testament.* Boston: Little, Brown and Company, 1970.

448

BIBLIOGRAPHY

Thomas, Hugh. *Cuba: The Pursuit of Freedom*. New York: Harper & Row, 1971.

— — —. *The Revolution on Balance*. Washington, D.C.: The Cuban American National Foundation, Inc., 1983.

Thomas, Hugh, and the Editors of *Life*. *Spain*. New York: Time Inc., 1962.

Thomas, Hugh S., Georges A. Fauriol, and Juan Carlos Weiss. *The Cuban Revolution 25 Years Later*. Boulder: Westview Press, 1984.

United States Central Intelligence Agency, National Foreign Assessment Center. *Cuban Chronology*. Washington, D.C.: CIA, 1980.

United States Congress. *Hearings Before the Select Committee to Study Governmental Operations with Respect to Intelligence Activities*. Washington, D.C.: U.S. Government Printing Office, 1976.

United States Department of Defense, and Department of State. *Grenada Documents: An Overview and Selection*. Washington, D.C.: Department of Defense and Department of State, 1983.

United States Department of State. *Inside the Sandinista Regime: A Special Investigator's Perspective*. Washington, D.C.: U.S. Government Printing Office, 1986.

— — —. *The Sandinistas and Middle Eastern Radicals*. Washington, D.C.: United States Department of State, 1985.

— — —. *Special Report No. 132, "Revolution Beyond Our Borders": Sandinista Intervention in Central America*. Washington, D.C.: United States Department of State, 1985.

United States Department of State and the Department of Defense. *Grenada: A Preliminary Report*. Washington, D.C.: Department of State and the Department of Defense, 1983.

United States House of Representatives, Committee on Foreign Affairs. *U.S. Response to Cuban Government Involvement in Narcotics Trafficking and Review of Worldwide Illicit Narcotics Situation*. Washington, D.C.: U.S. Government Printing Office, 1984.

United States Senate. *Alleged Assassination Plots Involving Foreign Leaders*. Washington, D.C.: U.S. Government Printing Office, 1975.

Urrutia Lleó, Manuel. *Fidel Castro & Company, Inc.: Communist Tyranny in Cuba*. New York: Frederick A. Praeger, Publisher, n.d.

Valenta, Jiri, and Herbert J. Ellison. *Grenada and Soviet/Cuban Policy: Internal Crisis and U.S./OFCS Intervention*. Boulder: Westview Press, 1986.

Valladares, Armando. *Against All Hope: The Prison Memories of Armando Valladares*. Translated by Andrew Hurley. New York: Alfred A. Knopf, 1986.

Valls, Jorge. *Twenty Years and Forty Days: Life in a Cuban Prison*. New York: Americas Watch, 1986.

Vargas Llosa, Mario. *The Real Life of Alejandro Mayta*. Translated by Alfred MacAdam. New York: Random House, Vintage Books, 1986.

BIBLIOGRAPHY

El Viaje de Fidel Castro a la Union Soviética. Montevideo, Uruguay: Ediciones Pueblos Unidos, 1963.

Vivés, Juan. *Los Amos de Cuba*. Buenos Aires: Emecé Editores, 1982.

Walters, Vernon A. *Silent Missions*. Garden City, N.Y.: Doubleday & Company, 1978.

Ward, Fred. *Inside Cuba Today*. New York: Crown Publishers, Inc., 1978.

Weber, Max. *On Charisma and Institution Building: Selected Papers*. Edited by S. N. Eisenstadt. Chicago: The University of Chicago Press, 1968.

Weyl, Nathaniel. *Red Star over Cuba: The Russian Assault on the Western Hemisphere*. New York: The Devin-Adair Company, 1962.

Wiarda, Howard J. *Rift and Revolution: The Central American Imbroglio*. Washington, D.C.: American Enterprise Institute for Public Policy Research, 1984.

Willner, Ann Ruth. *The Spellbinders: Charismatic Political Leadership*. New Haven: Yale University Press, 1984.

Wyden, Peter. *Bay of Pigs: The Untold Story*. New York: Simon & Schuster, 1979.

Young, Allen. *Gays Under the Cuban Revolution*. San Francisco: Grey Fox Press, 1981.

Ysalguez, Hugo A. *El 14 de Junio: La Raza Immortal (Invasión de Constanza, Maimón y Estero Hondo)*. Santo Domingo: Impresora Corporán, 1980.

Zea, Leopoldo. *The Latin-American Mind*. Translated by James H. Abbott, and Lowell Dunham. Norman: University of Oklahoma Press, 1963.

Zeitlin, Maurice, and Robert Scheer. *Cuba: Tragedy in Our Hemisphere*. New York: Grove Press, n.d.

INDEX

INDEX

Arias, Gilberto (Panamanian states-
man), 383
Arias Calderon, Ricardo (Panamanian
vice president), 383
arms
Cuban, 383
Czechoslovakian, 376
Russian, 8, 354–355
army, Cuban, 8
assassination
attempt on Batista, 167
attempts on Castro, 217, 273, 288
Castro, Manolo, 60
in Colombia, 76
Gaitán, Jorge Eliecer, 77–78
involvement of Castro, 45, 50–51,
54, 60
Kennedy, John F., 289–292
País, Frank, 172–174
Sadat, Anwar, 348
Tro, Emilio, 60
Trujillo, Rafael Leónidas, 58
The Autumn of the Patriarch (García
Márquez, G.), 318

Batista, Fulgencio (Cuban president),
7, 52, 101, 104
assassination attempt, 167
coup against, 93–97
exile, 56, 69
flight from Cuba, 191, 193, 197
and invasion of Cuba, 155–157,
158–160
and Moncada, 113–118
negotiations with Castro, 186–187
overthrow attempts, 142–143
plots against Castro, 143–144
relations with U.S., 132
and "Sergeants Revolution," 53
Bayo, Alberto (Argentine physician),
and Cuban Revolution, 168
in Mexico, 137–138
in Panama, 215
Bay of Pigs, 9, 232, 259–274
and CIA, 261–262, 265, 273
desertion of exile force by U.S.,
265–266

and Eisenhower, Dwight, 247–248,
261
and Kennedy, John F., 260–261,
264–266, 272–274
and Khrushchev, Nikita, 274
Bender, Frank (CIA), on Castro's Communism, 232
Benemelis, Juan (Cuban diplomat)
in Africa, 298–299
and EIR, 277–278
Betancourt, Ernesto (Cuban economist), 219, 222–223, 361
Betancourt, Rómulo (Venezuelan president), 75, 77, 393
and Cayo Confites, 57
dislike of Castro, 212
and guerrillas, 296
Bishop, Maurice (Grenadian leader), 353
execution, 362–363
Black Panthers, 311, 313
Blight, James G. (American psychologist), on Missile Crisis, 283
"Blue Ribbon Commission on Economic Reconstruction of Cuba,"
388, 391
boat lift. *See* Mariel boat lift
Bohemia, 82, 93, 126, 128, 141, 227
and Moncada trial, 122
Bolivia, guerrilla warfare in, 302–307
Bonachea, Rolando (Cuban historian),
174
Bonsal, Philip (American ambassador),
246–247
recall, 250
Borge, Tomás (Sandinista), 245, 343,
346
Bosch, Juan (Dominican patriot),
55–58
Boti, Regino (Cuban minister of eco-
nomics), 221–223, 229
"Bread with Liberty," 228
Brezhnev, Leonid (Russian premier),
315
"Brezhnev Doctrine," 317
Brigade 2506 and Bay of Pigs, 264, 267
Bryson, George E. (American journal-
ist), 24, 161

452

INDEX

453

INDEX

use of mass action, 78–79, 87
use of media, 60–62, 161–165,
  228–229, 232–233, 237,
  249–250, 401–402
and violence, 27, 29–30, 35, 49–52,
  68
Castro, Fidelito (son), 72–73, 88, 97,
  286–287, 403–404
  accident, 213–214
  kidnapping, 149–150
  political career, 393–394
  reunion with Castro, 196, 403
Castro, Juanita (sister), 21
  estrangement from Castro, 241, 286
Castro, Lidia (sister), 20
Castro, Lina (mother), 20, 29
  death, 242
  estrangement from Castro, 176
Castro, Manolo (student leader), 53–55
  assassination, 60
  and Cayo Confites, 56
Castro, Mirta (wife), 5, 88, 97, 196,
  403–404
  courtship and marriage, 63, 64,
  67–74
  divorce, 130–132
  escape from Cuba, 151
  remarriage, 149
Castro, Ramón (brother), 21
Castro, Raúl (brother), 21, 36–37
  Castro's plan for, 195
  childhood, 28
  and Communism, 3, 88–89, 172
  and death of Lina, 242
  and Eastern Bloc, 278
  and Khrushchev, Nikita, 278
  legitimacy, 28–29
  marriage to Espín, Vilma, 228
  and Matos trial, 208–209
  in Mexico, 137
  and Moncada, 115, 117, 123
  in Panama, 215
  relationship with Fidel, 177–178
  Second Front, 177, 180
  as successor, 14, 409
Casuso, Teté (friend), 52, 144–146,
  222, 238

in exile, 256
handling of media, 211
Cayo Confites Expedition, 55–60
Central Intelligence Agency. See CIA
Chamorro, Violeta (Nicaraguan president), 384
Chávez, Hugo (Venezuelan president),
  410
Chibás, Eduardo (Cuban politician),
  82–87
Chile
  Cuban influence, 328–329
  "direct democracy," 327
  guerrilla warfare, 298
Chrétien, Jean (Canadian prime minister), 397
Christmas
  banning of celebrations, 238,
  256–257, 321
  reinstatement of holiday, 399
Church, Frank (American senator),
  negotiations with Castro, 326–327
CIA
  attempt to assassinate Castro, 217,
  273, 288
  and Bay of Pigs, 261, 265
  and Castro, 182
  and Kennedy assassination, 291
  labor union funding, 143
  "Special National Intelligence Estimate," 184
  training of Cuban exiles, 261
  and Trujillo, Rafael Leónidas, 58
Cienfuegos, Camilo (Fidelista), 201
  death, 209–210
  in Dominican Republic, 215
  in Havana, 199
  and Matos trial, 208
  "Westward March," 187
Ciro Bustos, Roberto (Argentine artist),
  305–306
Clapp, Peter (Weatherman), 312
Cleaver, Eldridge (Black Panther),
  311–312, 313
Coard, Bernard (Grenadian Communist), 362
"Code of the Sierra Maestra," 205

INDEX

INDEX

INDEX

Trafficante, Santos (American gangster), attempt to assassinate
Castro, 288
Treaty of Paris, 25
Tricontinental, 309
Tro, Emilio (student leader), 59–60
and UIR, 54
Trujillo, Rafael Leónidas (Dominican
president), 55–58
assassination, 58
attempt to overthrow, 215
Turner, William (American writer), 92,
148
"The Twelve," 157, 344
26th of July movement. *See* M-26-7

Uganda, Cuban troops in, 8
UIR, 53
attacked by Castro, 91–92
Unión Insurreccional Revolucionaria,
53, 91–92
UNITA, 335, 342–343
United Fruit Company, 19, 28, 65, 67
and Cuban Revolution, 125
United Nations, 252–254
creation, 69
recognition of Castro, 343
United States
aid to Cuba, 219, 223–224
attempt to replace Castro, 261
backing of Batista, 95
and Bay of Pigs, 259–274
and Cuban nuclear facility, 394
decline of investment in Cuba, 204
economic blockade of Cuba, 250
expansionism in Cuba, 19, 25–26,
65
invasion of Grenada, 362–364
invasion of Panama, 382–384
involvement in Nicaragua, 343–344
nationalization of property in Cuba,
248
relations with Batista, 132
relations with Cuba, 4, 5, 32, 42–43,
182, 183–184, 246–248
University of Havana, 41–42, 51
closure, 31

funeral of Chibás, 85–87
and politics, 43–44
Urrutia, Manuel (Cuban president),
199, 201, 219
estrangement from Castro, 236–237
Uruguay
Cuban influence, 329
guerrilla warfare, 298
U.S.S. Maine, 25
U.S.S.R. *See* Russia

Valdés, Ramiro (Cuban minister of
interior), 144, 287, 288
Valladares, Armando (Cuban poet), on
"Airmen Trial," 206
Vance, Cyrus (American secretary of
state)
and Cuban exiles, 350
negotiations with Castro, 326
Vargas Llosa, Mario (Peruvian writer),
293–294
Velasquez, Lucila (Venezuelan
poetess), 140
Venezuela, guerrilla warfare in,
296–297
Vesco, Robert (American criminal),
379
Vier, Gene (American writer), 73
Vietnam, North, 312–313
Voison, André (French agronomist), 319
Voronkov, Georgy (Russian general),
and Missile Crisis, 282

Walters, Vernon (American ambassador), negotiations with Castro,
359–361
warfare, guerrilla. *See* guerrilla warfare
weapons. *See also* arms
training, 99–100
Weathermen, 312
and Vietnam, 312–313
Weissmuller, Johnny (American actor),
185
"Westward March of Che and Camilo,"
187
Weyler, Valeriano (Spanish general),
24, 389

INDEX

Wiecha, Robert (CIA), 178–179, 183
Wieland, William (U.S. State Department), 184, 225
Williams, Eric (Trinidadian prime minister), 331
Wollam, Park (American consul), 178–179

yellow fever, 30
youth, disillusionment with Castro, 385–386

Zanzibar, 407
   guerrilla warfare in, 298